Java™ Homework Projects

A NetBeans GUI Swing Programming Tutorial

11ᵗʰ Edition

By Philip Conrod & Lou Tylee

KIDWARE SOFTWARE

PO Box 701
Maple Valley, WA 98038

http://www.kidwaresoftware.com

Kidware Software LLC
PO Box 701
Maple Valley, Washington 98038
1.425.413.1185
www.kidwaresoftware.com

Printed in the United States of America

ISBN-13: 978-1-951077-02-0 (Printed)
ISBN-13: 978-1-951077-03-7 (Electronic)

Cover Design by Stephanie Conrod
Copy Editor: Jessica Conrod
Illustrations: Kevin Brockschmidt
Compositor: Michael Rogers

About The Authors

Philip Conrod has authored, co-authored and edited over two dozen computer programming books over the past thirty years. Philip holds a Bachelor's Degree in Computer Information Systems and a Master's certificate in the Essentials of Business Development from Regis University. Philip has served in various Information Technology leadership roles in companies like Sundstrand Aerospace, Safeco Insurance, FamilyLife, Kenworth Truck Company, and PACCAR. Philip last served as the Chief Information Officer (CIO) for Darigold Inc for over a decade before returning to teaching and writing full-time. Today, Philip serves as the President & Publisher of Kidware Software LLC which is based in Maple V alley, Washington.

Lou Tylee holds BS and MS degrees in Mechanical Engineering and a PhD in Electrical Engineering. Lou has been programming computers since 1969 when he took his first Fortran course in college. He has written software to control suspensions for high speed ground vehicles, monitor nuclear power plants, lower noise levels in commercial jetliners, compute takeoff speeds for jetliners, locate and identify air and ground traffic and to let kids count bunnies, learn how to spell and do math problems. He has written several on-line texts teaching Visual Basic, Visual C# and Java to thousands of people. He taught computer programming courses for over 15 years at the University of Washington and currently teaches math and engineering courses at the Oregon Institute of Technology. Lou also works as a research engineer at a major Seattle aerospace firm. He is the proud father of five children, has six grandchildren and is married to an amazing woman. Lou and his family live in Seattle, Washington.

Acknowledgements

I want to thank my three wonderful daughters - Stephanie, Jessica and Chloe, who helped with various aspects of the book publishing process including software testing, book editing, creative design and many other more tedious tasks like finding errors and typos. I could not have accomplished this without all your hard work, love and support. I want to also thank my best friend Jesus, who has always been there by my side giving me wisdom and guidance. Without you, this book would have never been printed and published.

I also want to thank my multi-talented co-author, Lou Tylee, for doing all the real hard work necessary to develop, test, debug, and keep current all the 'beginner-friendly' applications, games and base tutorial text found in this book. Lou has tirelessly poured his heart and soul into so many previous versions of this tutorial and there are so many beginners who have benefited from his work over the years. Lou is by far one of the best application developers and tutorial writers I have ever worked with. Thank you Lou for collaborating with me on this book project.

Contents

1. Introduction

2.   Dual-Mode Stopwatch Project

3.   Consumer Loan Assistant Project

4. Flash Card Math Quiz Project

5. Multiple Choice Exam Project

6. Blackjack Card Game Project

7. Weight Monitor Project

8. Home Inventory Manager Project

9. Snowball Toss Game Project

Appendix. Distributing a Java Project

Appendix. Installing Java and NetBeans

Course Description

JAVA HOMEWORK PROJECTS teaches Java programming concepts while providing detailed step-by-step instructions in building many fun and useful projects. **JAVA HOMEWORK PROJECTS** explains (in simple, easy-to-follow terms) how to build a Java GUI project. Students learn about project design, the Java Swing controls, many elements of the Java, and how to debug and distribute finished projects. The projects built include:

* **Dual-Mode Stopwatch** - Allows you to time tasks you may be doing.
* **Consumer Loan Assistant** - Helps you see just how much those credit cards are costing you.
* **Flash Card Math Quiz** - Lets you practice basic addition, subtraction, multiplication and division skills.
* **Multiple Choice Exam** - Quizzes a user on matching pairs of items, like countries/capitals, words/meanings, books/authors.
* **Blackjack Card Game** - Play the classic casino card game against the computer.
* **Weight Monitor** - Track your weight each day and monitor your progress toward established goals.
* **Home Inventory Manager** - Helps you keep track of all your belongings - even includes photographs.
* **Snowball Toss Game** - Lets you throw snowballs at another player or against the computer - has varying difficulties.

The product includes over 850 pages of self-study notes, all Java source code and all needed graphics and sound files.

System Requirements
You will need the following software to complete the exercises in this book:

* Oracle Java Standard Edition JDK11
* NetBeans 11.0

Course Prerequisites

To grasp the concepts presented in **JAVA HOMEWORK PROJECTS** you should have experience with Java programming. You should also be familiar with using the Java Swing library. Our product **LEARN JAVA GUI APPLICATIONS** can provide the needed background.

You will also need the ability to view and print documents saved in Acrobat PDF format.

You also need to have the current Java Development Kit (**JDK**) and the current version of **NetBeans**, the Integrated Development Environment (IDE) we use with this course. Complete download and installation instructions for the JDK and NetBeans are found in the Appendix (**Installing Java and NetBeans**) included with these notes.

Installing and Using the Downloadable Solution Files

If you purchased this directly from our website you received an email with a special and individualized internet download link where you could download the compressed Program Solution Files. If you purchased this book through a 3rd Party Book Store like Amazon.com, the solutions files for this tutorial are included in a compressed ZIP file that is available for download directly from our website at:

http://www.kidwaresoftware.com/phpj11-registration.html

Complete the online web form at the webpage above with your name, shipping address, email address, the exact title of this book, date of purchase, online or physical store name, and your order confirmation number from that store. After we receive all this information we will email you a download link for the Source Code Solution Files associated with this book.

Warning: If you purchased this book "used" or "second hand" you are not licensed or entitled to download the Program Solution Files. However, you can purchase the Digital Download Version of this book at a discounted price which allows you access to the digital source code solutions files required for completing this tutorial.

Using Java Homework Projects

The course notes and code for **JAVA HOMEWORK PROJECTS** are included in one or more ZIP file(s). Use your favorite 'unzipping' application to write all files to your computer. (If you've received the course on CD-ROM, the files are not zipped and no unzipping is needed.) The course is included in the folder entitled **HomeJava**. This folder contains two other folders: **HomeJava Notes** and **HomeJava Projects**. There's a chance when you copy the files to your computer, they will be written as '**Read-Only**.' To correct this (in **Windows Explorer** or **My Computer**), right-click the **HomeJava** folder and remove the check next to **Read only**. Make sure to choose the option to apply this change to all sub-folders and files. The **HomeJava Projects** folder includes all projects developed during the course. Work through the notes and projects at your leisure.

Forward by Alan Payne, A Computer Science Teacher

What is "Java Homework Projects" and how it works.

These lessons are a highly organized and well-indexed set of lessons in the Java programming language. NetBeans, a specific IDE (Integrated Development Environment) is used throughout the lessons. Lessons are written for the beginner to initiated programmer: the high school, college or university student seeking to advance their computer science repertoire on their own, or the enlightened professional who wishes to embark on Java coding for the first time. Skilled programmers and beginners alike benefit from the style of presentation.

While full solutions are provided, practical projects are presented in an easy-to-follow set of lessons explaining the rational for the solution - the form layout, coding design and conventions, and specific code related to the problem. The learner may follow the tutorials at their own pace while focusing upon context relevant information.

The finished product is the reward, but the learner is fully engaged and enriched by the process. This kind of learning is often the focus of teacher training at the highest level. Every Computer Science teacher and self-taught learner knows what a great deal of work is required for projects to work in this manner, and with these tutorials, the work is done by an author who understands the adult need for streamlined learning.

Graduated Lessons for Every Project. Graduated Learning. Increasing and appropriate difficulty. Great results.

By presenting Homework Projects in this graduated manner, adult students are fully engaged and appropriately challenged to become independent thinkers who can come up with their own project ideas and design their own forms and do their own coding. Once the problem-solving process is learned, then student engagement is unlimited! Students literally cannot get enough of what is being presented.

These projects encourage accelerated learning - in the sense that they provide an enriched environment to learn Computer Science, but they also encourage accelerating learning because students cannot put the lessons away once they start! Computer Science provides this unique opportunity to challenge students, and it is a great testament to the authors that they are successful in achieving such levels of engagement with consistency.

My history with the Kidware Software products.

As a learner who just wants to get down to business, these lessons match my learning style. I do not waste valuable time ensconced in language reference libraries for programming environments and help screens which can never be fully remembered! With every Home Project, the pathway to learning is clear and immediate, though the topics in Computer Science remain current, relevant and challenging.

Some of the topics covered in these tutorials include:

• Structure of a Java and Java GUI Program
• Swing Controls
• Managing NetBeans Files
• Data Types and Ranges
• Scope of Variables
• Naming Conventions
• Arithmetic, Comparison and Logical Operators
• String Functions, Dates and Times, Random Numbers,
• Decision Making (Selections)
• Looping
• Language Functions - String, Date, Numerical
• Arrays
• Writing Your own Methods and Classes
• Sequential File Access, Error-Handling and Debugging techniques
• Distributing a Java Project (in the Appendices)
    and more... it's all integrated into the Homework Projects.

The specific Homework Projects include:
• Dual-Mode Stopwatch
• Consumer Loan Assistant
• Flash Card Math Quiz
• Multiple Choice Exam Project
• Black Jack Card Game
• Weight Monitor Project
• Home Inventory Manager
• Snowball Toss Game

Quick learning curve by Contextualized Learning - "Java Homework Projects" encourages contextualized, self-guided learning.

With the Java Homework Projects tutorials, sound advice regarding generally accepted coding strategies ("build and test your code in stages", "learn input, output, formatting and data storage strategies for different data types", build graphical components from Java's Swing Control class libraries, etc..) encourage independent thought processes among learners. After mastery, then it is much more likely that students can create their own problems and solutions from scratch. Students are ready to create their own summative projects for their computer science course - or just for fun, and they may think of projects for their other courses as well!

Students may trust the order of presentation in order to have sufficient background information for every project. But the lessons are also highly indexed, so that students may pick and choose projects if limited by time.

Materials already condense what is available from the Java SDK help files (which tends to be written for adults) and in a context and age-appropriate manner, so that students remember what they learn.

The time savings for parents, teachers and students is enormous as they need not sift through pages and pages of on-line help to find what they need.

Meet Different State and Provincial Curriculum Expectations and More

Different states and provinces have their own curriculum requirements for Computer Science. With the Kidware Software products, you may pick and choose from Home Projects which best suit your learning needs. Learners focus upon design stages and sound problem-solving techniques from a Computer Science perspective. In doing so, they become independent problem-solvers, and will exceed the curricular requirements of secondary and post-secondary schools everywhere.

Computer Science topics not explicitly covered in tutorials can be added at the learner's discretion. The language - whether it is Visual Basic, Visual C#, Visual C++, or Console Java, Java GUI, etc... is really up to the individual learner !

Lessons encourage your own programming extensions.

Once Computer Science concepts are learned, it is difficult to NOT know how to extend the learning to your own Home Projects and beyond!

Having my own projects in one language, such as Java, I know that I could easily adapt them to other languages once I have studied the Kidware Software tutorials. I do not believe there is any other reference material out there which would cause me to make the same claim! In fact, I know there is not as I have spent over a decade looking!

Having used Kidware Software tutorials for the past decade, I have been successful at the expansion of my own learning to other platforms such as XNA for the Xbox, or the latest developer suites for tablets and phones. I thank Kidware

Software and its authors for continuing to stand for what is right in the teaching methodologies which not only inspire, but propel the self-guided learner through what can be a highly intelligible landscape of opportunities."

Regards,
Alan Payne, B.A.H. , B.Ed.
Computer Science Teacher
T.A. Blakelock High School
Oakville, Ontario
http://chatt.hdsb.ca/~paynea

1

Introduction

Preview

In this first chapter, we will do an overview of how to build a Java project with a graphical user interface (GUI). You'll get a description of what is needed to complete this course, review the steps of building a Java GUI project and delve into use of an Integrated Development environment (IDE).

Introducing Java Homework Projects

In these notes, we will use Java to build many useful home projects with graphic user interfaces (GUI). The projects you will build are (in increasing complexity):

> - **Dual-Mode Stopwatch** – Measures total and elapsed time.
> - **Consumer Loan Assistant** – Helps you determine just how much those loans cost you.
> - **Flash Card Math Quiz** – Practice basic math skills with timed drills.
> - **Multiple Choice Exam** – Set up exams matching like terms.
> - **Blackjack Card Game** – The classic card game.
> - **Weight Monitor** – Tool to aid in your weight management.
> - **Home Inventory Manager** – Keep track of all the stuff you own for insurance purposes.
> - **Snowball Toss Game** – A little game using sounds and animation.

Each project will be addressed in a single chapter. Complete step-by-step instructions covering every project detail will be provided. Before beginning the projects, however, we will review course requirements, Java project structure and our approach to building a Java GUI project.

Requirements for Home Projects With Java

To complete the projects in this course, you should have a basic understanding of the Java language and its syntax, understand the structure of a Java application, how to write and use Java methods and how to compile, debug and run a Java GUI application. You should be familiar with the Swing control library. We briefly review each of these topics in the course, but it is a cursory review. If you haven't built Java GUI projects before, we suggest you try our Java tutorial **Learn Java (GUI Applications)**. See our website for details.

Regarding software, you need two things: (1) the Java Development Kit (JDK) and (2) a development environment. The JDK is a free download from the Java website. Nearly all programmers develop their Java programs using something called an **Integrated Development Environment** (IDE). There are many IDE's available for Java development purposes, some very elaborate, some very simple. In these notes, we use a free IDE called **NetBeans**. If you are comfortable with another IDE, by all means, use it. Complete download and installation instructions are provided in the Appendix (**Installing Java and NetBeans**) included with these notes.

Testing the Installation

We'll use **NetBeans** to load a Java project and to run a project. This will give us some assurance we have everything installed correctly. This will let us begin our study of the Java programming language.

Once installed, to start **NetBeans**, double-click the icon on your desktop. The NetBeans program should start. Several windows will appear on the screen.

Upon starting (after clearing the **Start Page**), my screen shows:

File View　　　　　　　　　　　**Main Menu**　　　　　**Editor Area**

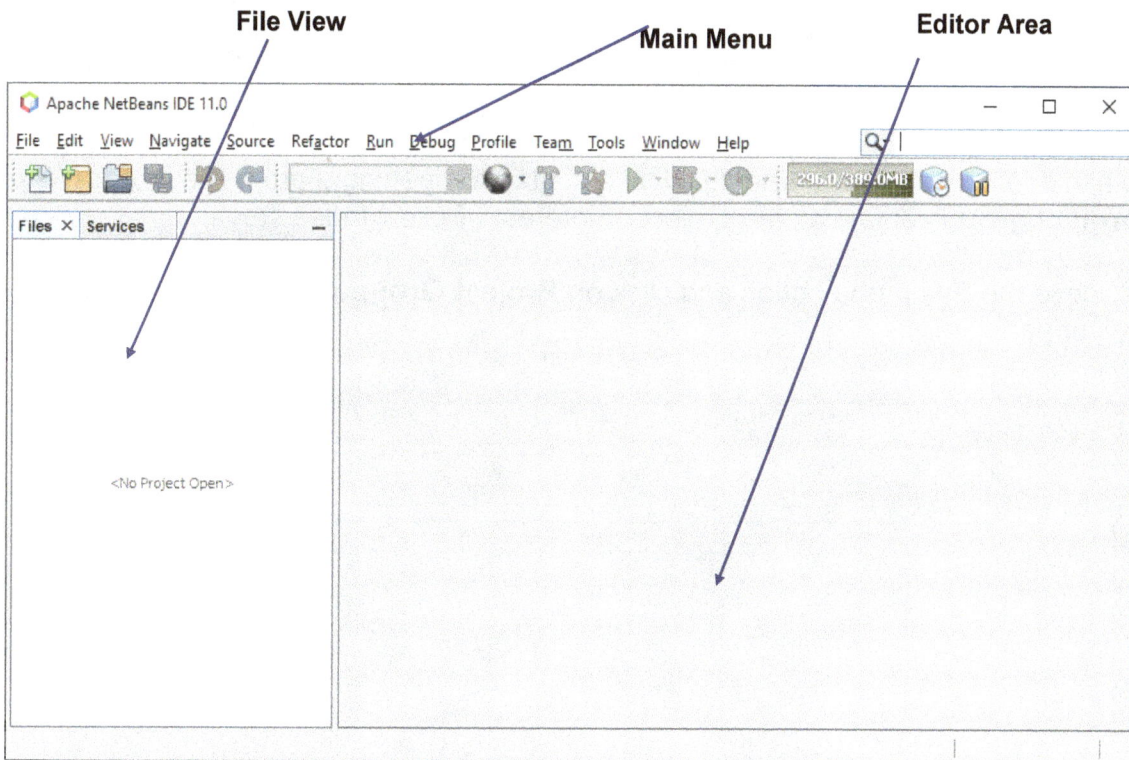

This screen displays the NetBeans **Integrated Development Environment** (**IDE**). We're going to use it to test our Java installation and see if we can get a program up and running. Note the location of the **file view** area, **editor** area and the **main menu**. The file view tells you what Java programs are available, the editor area is used to view the actual code and the main menu is used to control file access and file editing functions. It is also used to run the program.

What we want to do right now is **open a project**. Computer programs (applications) written using Java are referred to as **projects**. Projects include all the information in **files** we need for our computer program. Java projects are in **project groups**. Included with these notes are many Java projects you can open and use. Let's open one now.

Make sure **NetBeans** is running. The first step to opening a project is to **open the project group** containing the project of interest. Follow these steps:

Choose the **File** menu option and click on **Project Groups** option. This window will appear:

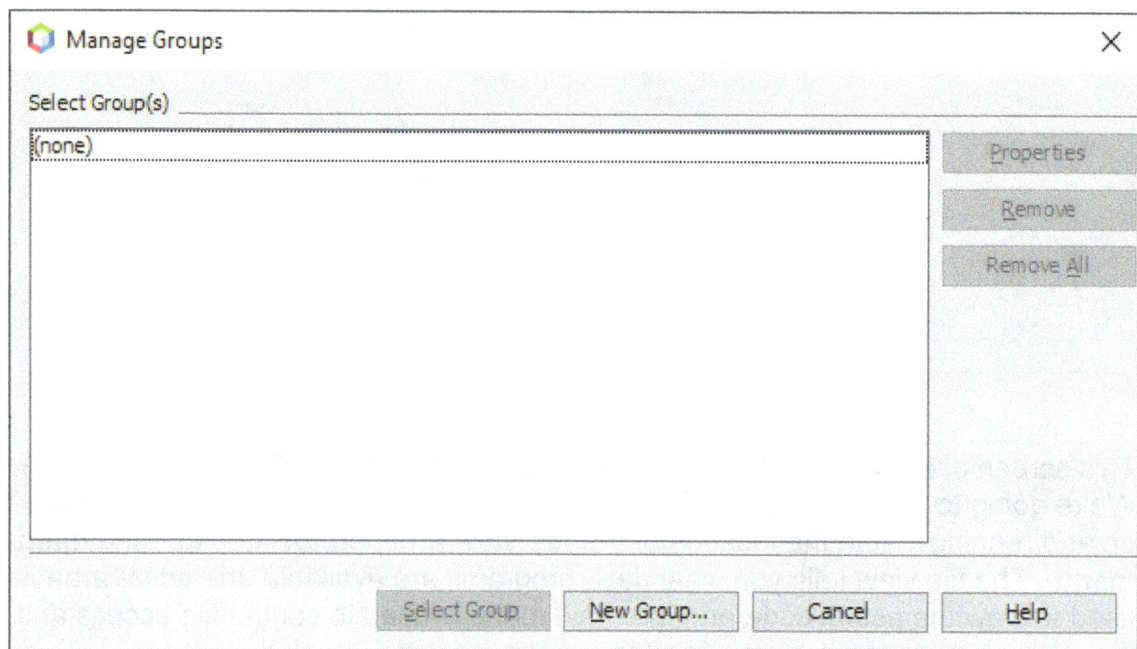

All projects in these notes are saved in a folder named **\HomeJava\HomeJava Projects**. Click **New Group**, select **Folder of Projects**, **Browse** to that folder as shown. Click **Create Group**.

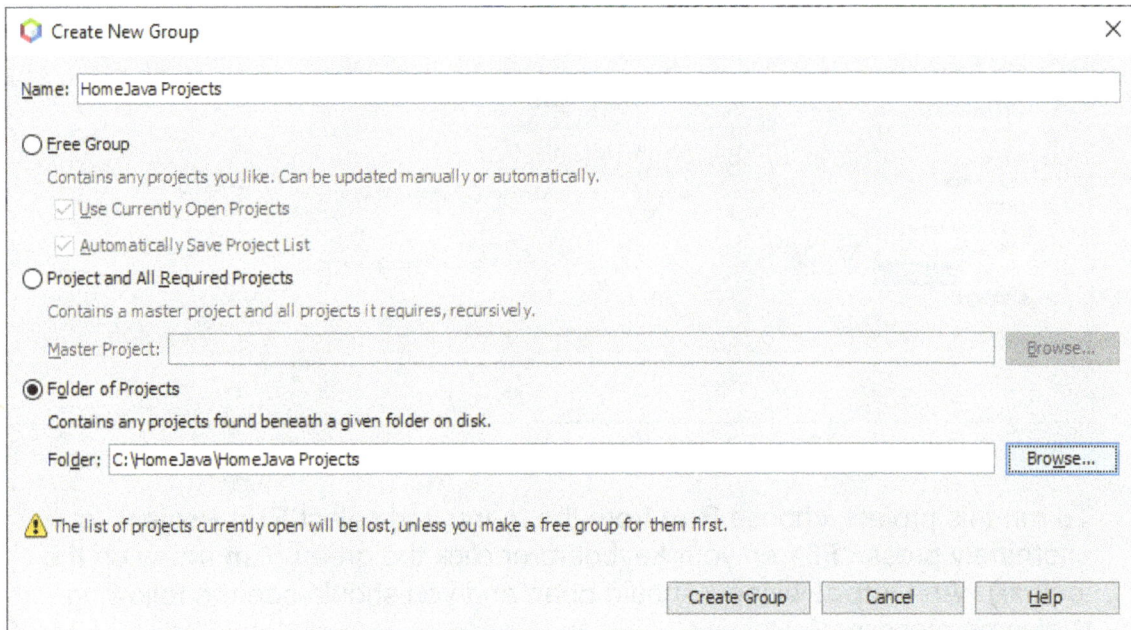

There will be many projects listed in the file view area in NetBeans. Find the project named **Welcome**. Right-click that project name and expand the Welcome project node by clicking the plus sign. Open **Source Packages**, then **welcome**. Note there is one file named **Welcome.java**. If the file contents do not appear in the editor view area, double-click that file to open it.

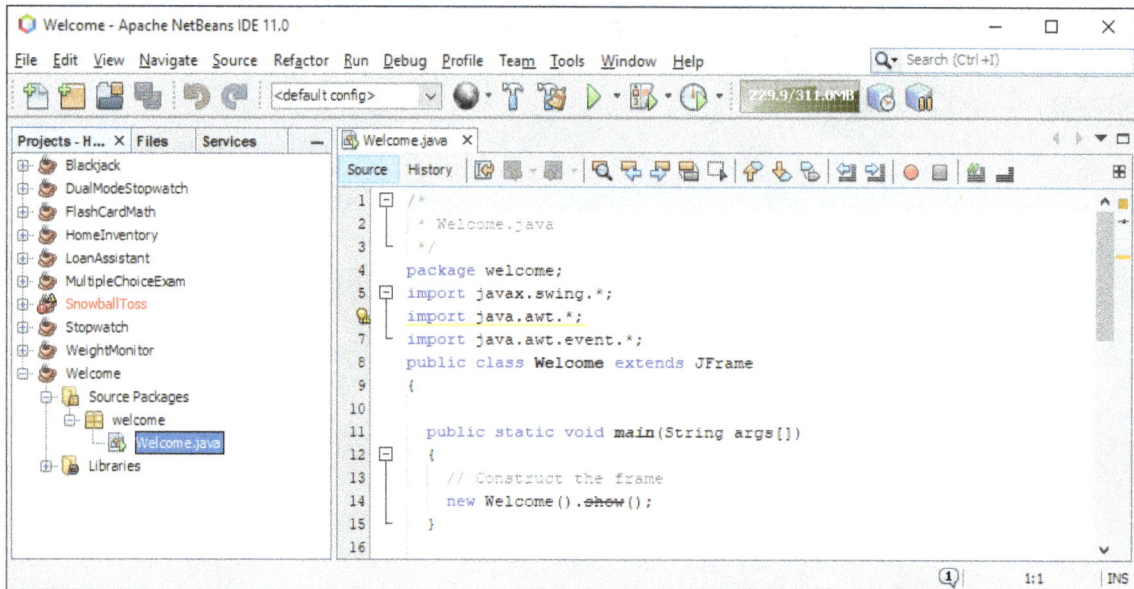

To run this project, choose **Run** from the menu and select **Run Project** (or alternately press <**F6**> on your keyboard or click the green **Run** arrow on the toolbar). An **Output** window should open and you should see the following Welcome message:

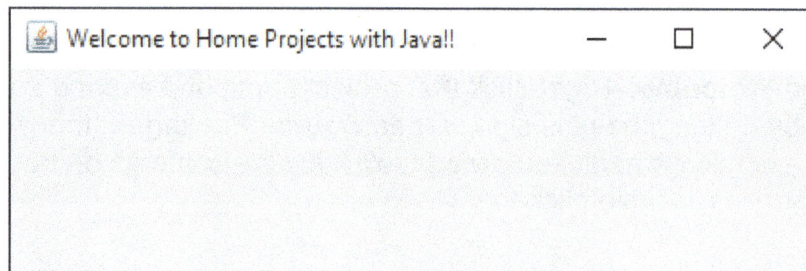

If you've gotten this far, everything has been installed correctly. If you don't see the Welcome message, something has not been installed correctly. You should probably go back and review all the steps involved with installing Java and NetBeans and make sure all steps were followed properly.

To stop this project, you click the boxed **X** in the upper right corner of the window. To stop NetBeans (don't do this right now, though):

- ➢ Select **File** in the main menu.
- ➢ Select **Exit** (at the end of the File menu).

NetBeans will close all open windows and you will be returned to the Windows desktop. Like with stopping a project, an alternate way to stop NetBeans is to click on the close button in the upper right hand corner of the main window.

Getting Help With a Java Program

As you build Java programs, there will be times when you get stuck. You will not know how to do a certain task using Java or you will receive error messages while compiling or running your program that you do not understand. What do you do in these cases? There are several options for getting help.

A highly recommended help method is to ask someone else if they know how to help you. Other Java programmers love to share their skills with people just learning the language. A second option is to look at one of the many Java books out there (you are reading one of them). If you have questions about these notes, just e-mail us (sales@kidwaresoftware.com) and we'll try to help.

The **Java website** (http://www.oracle.com/technetwork/java/index.html) has a wealth of information that could possibly help. The problem with the website is that there is so much information, it can be overwhelming. There are tutorials, example, forums, … The Java **API** (application programming interface) documentation (on-line at the Sun website) is a great place to get help if you can wade through the difficult format. The Java website does offer search facilities. I often type in a few keywords and find topics that help in my pursuit of answers.

There are also hundreds of other Java websites out in WWW-land. Many websites offer forums where you can ask other Java programmers questions and get quick answers. A good way to find them is to use a search utility like **Google** or **Yahoo**. Again, type in a few keywords and many times you'll find the answer you are looking for.

As you progress as a Java programmer, you will develop your own methods of solving problems you encounter. One day, you'll be the person other programmers come to for their answers.

Structure of a Java Program

Java, like any language (computer or spoken), has a terminology all its own. Let's look at the structure of a Java program and learn some of this new terminology. A Java program (or project) is made up of a number of files. These files are called **classes**. Each of these files has Java code that performs some specific task(s). Each class file is saved with the file extension **.java**. The filename used to save a class must match the class name. One class in each project will contain something called the **main method**. Whenever you run a Java program, your computer will search for the **main** method to get things started. Hence, to run a program, you refer directly to the class containing this **main** method.

Let's see how this relates to **Welcome** project. This particular project has a single file named **Welcome.java**. Notice, as required, the name **Welcome** matches the class name seen in the code (public class **Welcome**). If no code is seen, simply double-click on the filename **Welcome.java**. If the project had other classes, they would be listed under the **Welcome** project folder. Notice too in the code area the word **main**. This is the **main** method we need in one of the project's classes.

That's really all we need to know about the structure of a Java program. Just remember a **program** (or project, we'll use both terms) is made up of files called **classes** that contain actual Java code. One class is the **main** class where everything starts. And, one more thing to remember is that projects are in **project groups**.

NetBeans uses a very specific directory structure for saving all of the files for a particular application. When you start a new project, it is placed in a specific folder in a specific project group. That folder will be used to store all files needed by the project. We'll take another look at the NetBeans file structure when we create our first project. You can stop NetBeans now, if you'd like.

Structure of a Java GUI Application

Let's look at the structure of a Java GUI application. In these notes, we tend to use the terms application, program and project synonymously. A GUI application consists of a **frame**, with associated **controls** and **code**. Pictorially, this is:

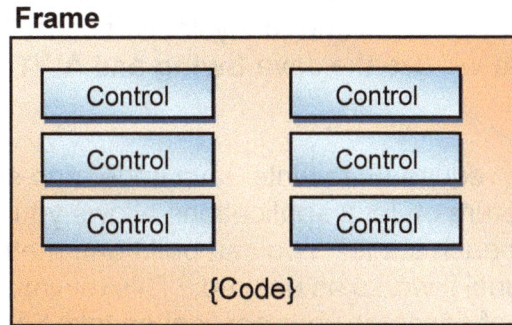

Frame

Control	Control
Control	Control
Control	Control

{Code}

Application (Project) is made up of:

➤ **Frame** - window that you create for user interface (also referred to as a **form**)

➤ **Controls** - Graphical features positioned on frame to allow user interaction (text boxes, labels, scroll bars, buttons, etc.) (frames and controls are **objects**.) Controls are briefly discussed next.

➤ **Properties** - Every characteristic of a frame or control is specified by a property. Example properties include names, captions, size, color, position, and contents. Java applies default properties. You can change properties when designing the application or even when an application is executing.

➤ **Methods** - Built-in procedures that can be invoked to impart some action to or change or determine a property of a particular object.

➤ **Event Methods** - **Code** related to some object or control. This is the code that is executed when a certain event occurs. In our applications, this code will be written in the Java language (covered in detail in Chapter 2 of these notes).

➤ **General Methods** - **Code** not related to objects. This code must be invoked or called in the application.

The application displayed above has a single form, or frame. As we progress in this course, we will build applications with multiple forms. The code for each form will usually be stored in its own file with a **.java** extension.

We will follow three steps in building a Java GUI application:

1. Create the **frame**.
2. Create the user **interface** by placing controls on the frame.
3. **Write code** for control event methods (and perhaps write other methods).

These same steps are followed whether you are building a very simple application or one involving many controls and many lines of code. Recall, the GUI applications we build will use the Java **Swing** and **AWT** (Abstract Windows Toolkit) components.

Each of these steps require us to write Java code, and sometimes lots of code. The event-driven nature of Java applications allows you to build your application in stages and test it at each stage. You can build one method, or part of a method, at a time and try it until it works as desired. This minimizes errors and gives you, the programmer, confidence as your application takes shape.

As you progress in your programming skills, always remember to take this sequential approach to building a Java application. Build a little, test a little, modify a little and test again. You'll quickly have a completed application.

Swing Controls

The controls we use in GUI applications will be **Swing** components. These components are defined in the **javax.swing** package and all have names beginning with **J**. Here, we briefly look at several controls to give you an idea of what they are, what they look like and what they do. You will see more Swing components in several of the projects.

JFrame control:

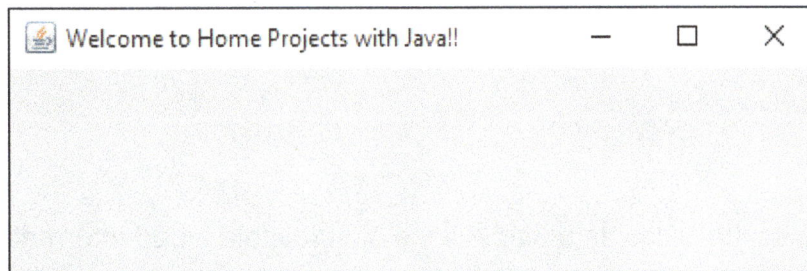

The frame control is the basic 'container' for other controls. It is the framework for a Java project. The **title** property establishes the caption information. Every application we build will start by building a **class** that **extends** the JFrame control.

JButton control:

The button control is used to start some action. The **text** property is used to establish the caption.

JLabel control:

The label control allows placement of formatted text information on a frame (**text** property).

JTextField control:

The text field control accepts a single line of typed information from the user (**text** property).

JTextArea control:

The text area control accepts multiple lines of scrollable typed information (**text** property).

JCheckBox control:

The check box control is used to provide a yes or no answer to a question.

JRadioButton control:

The radio button control is used to select from a mutually exclusive group of options. You always work with a group of radio buttons.

JComboBox control:

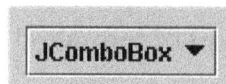

Combo box controls are very common in GUI applications. Users can choose an item from a drop down list (states, countries, product).

JList control:

A list control is like a combo box with the list portion always visible. Multiple selections can be made with a list control.

JScroll control:

A scroll bar control is used to select from a range of values. The scroll bar is always "buddied" with another control related to the scroll bar selection.

JPanel control:

The panel control is a 'workhorse' in GUI applications – we will use many of them. It provides a convenient way of grouping related controls in a Java GUI application. And, the panel can also be used to host graphics.

Now, we'll start NetBeans and look at each step in the application development process, including using Swing controls. We will use a stopwatch application as an example.

Stopwatch - Creating a Java Project with NetBeans

We will now start building our first Java GUI application (a computer stopwatch). It might seem like a slow, long process. But, it has to be in order to cover all the necessary material. The more projects you build, the simpler this process will become. We begin by creating a new project and creating a frame. We will store all created projects in a separate project group named **Home Projects**. Create that folder now. If using Windows, you can use **Windows Explorer** or **My Computer** to that task.

If it's not already running, start **NetBeans**. The program group containing the **Welcome** project should still be there. We are going to remove this program group and create a new one. (You should only use the **HomeJava Projects** program group when you want to refer to the code included with the class notes. For all your projects, you will use your own program group).

Choose **File** from the main menu and select **Project Group** The **Manage Groups** window appears – choose **New Group** to see

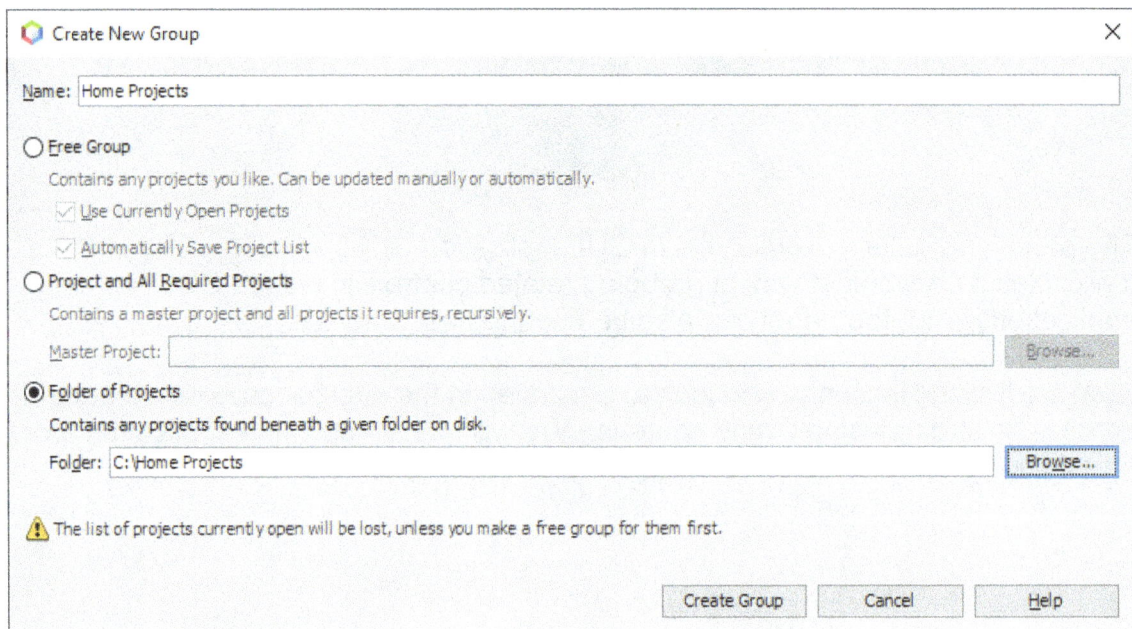

Create New Group   ✕

Name: Home Projects

○ Free Group
   Contains any projects you like. Can be updated manually or automatically.
   ☑ Use Currently Open Projects
   ☑ Automatically Save Project List
○ Project and All Required Projects
   Contains a master project and all projects it requires, recursively.
   Master Project: [   ]   Browse...
◉ Folder of Projects
   Contains any projects found beneath a given folder on disk.
   Folder: C:\Home Projects   Browse...

⚠ The list of projects currently open will be lost, unless you make a free group for them first.

                          Create Group   Cancel   Help

As shown, click **Folder of Projects**, then **Browse** to your **Home Projects** folder.
Click **Create Group**. The project group is displayed in the file view area (it is
empty).

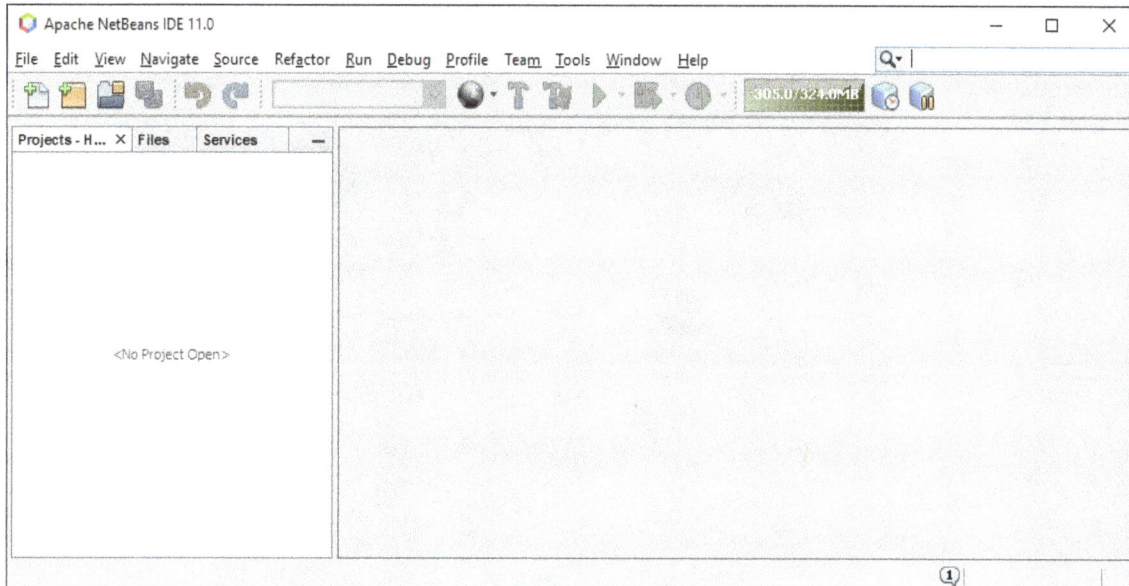

Now, we want to add a project to the project group. Pay close attention to these steps because you will repeat them every time you need to create a new Java project. Right-click the project group area in the file view and choose **New Project** to see:

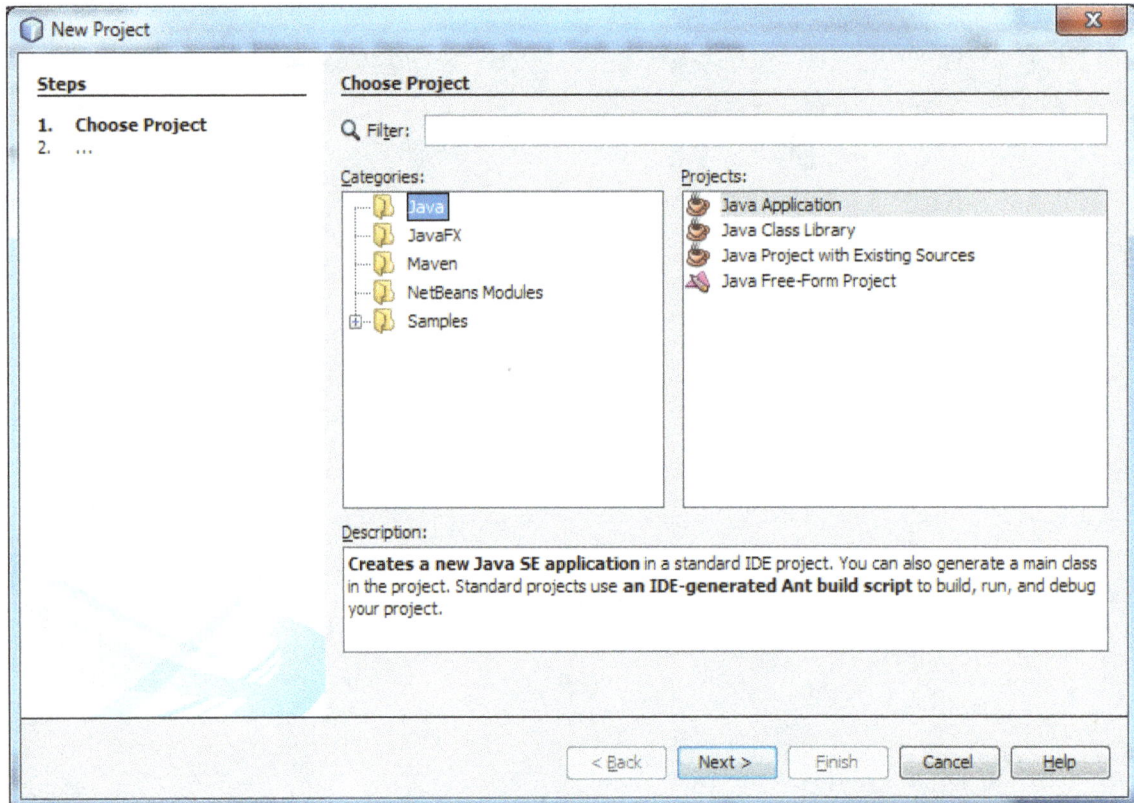

Select **Java with Ant** in **Categories** and **Java Application** in **Projects**. Click **Next**.

This window appears:

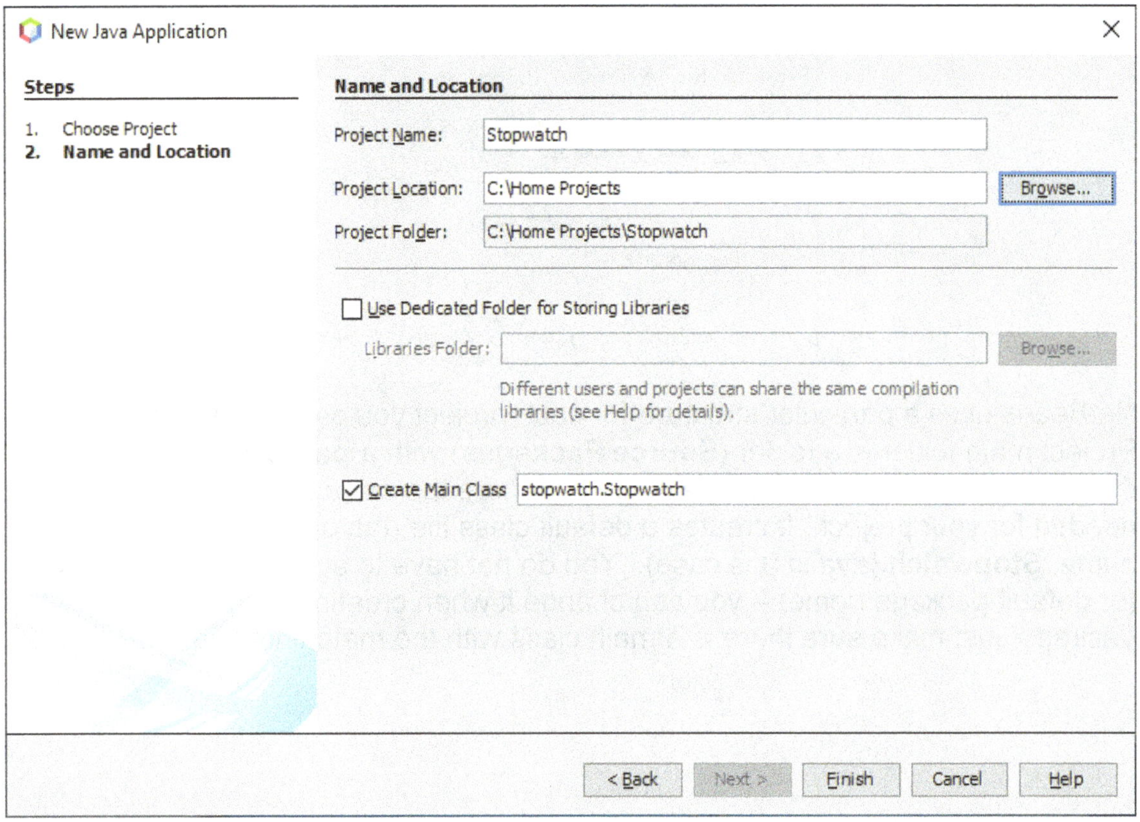

Type **Stopwatch** in the **Project Name** box (as shown above). Browse to the
Home Projects folder for **Project Location**. Click **Finish** to create the project.
Once created, click **Finish** in the resulting window.

The project group view window should now show a project (**Stopwatch**) in the project group (I've expanded all the folders):

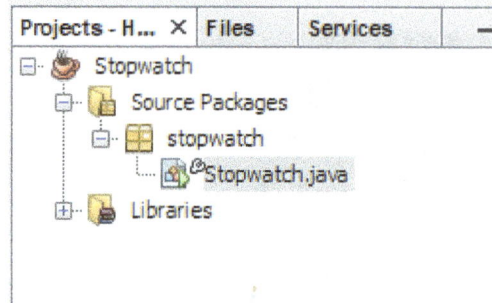

```
Projects - H...  ×  | Files | Services |  ─
☐ ☕ Stopwatch
   ☐ 📁 Source Packages
      ☐ 📒 stopwatch
         📄 Stopwatch.java
   ☐ 📚 Libraries
```

NetBeans uses a particular structure for each project you create. Under the Project main folder is a folder (**Source Packages**) with a **package** it names (in this case, **stopwatch**). In that package folder are the class files (**java** files) needed for your project. It creates a default class file (the one with your project name, **Stopwatch.java** in this case). You do not have to accept the default name (or default package name) – you can change it when creating the project, if desired. Just make sure there is a main class with the matching filename.

Double-click on the **Stopwatch.java** file to see a framework for the file in the editor view area:

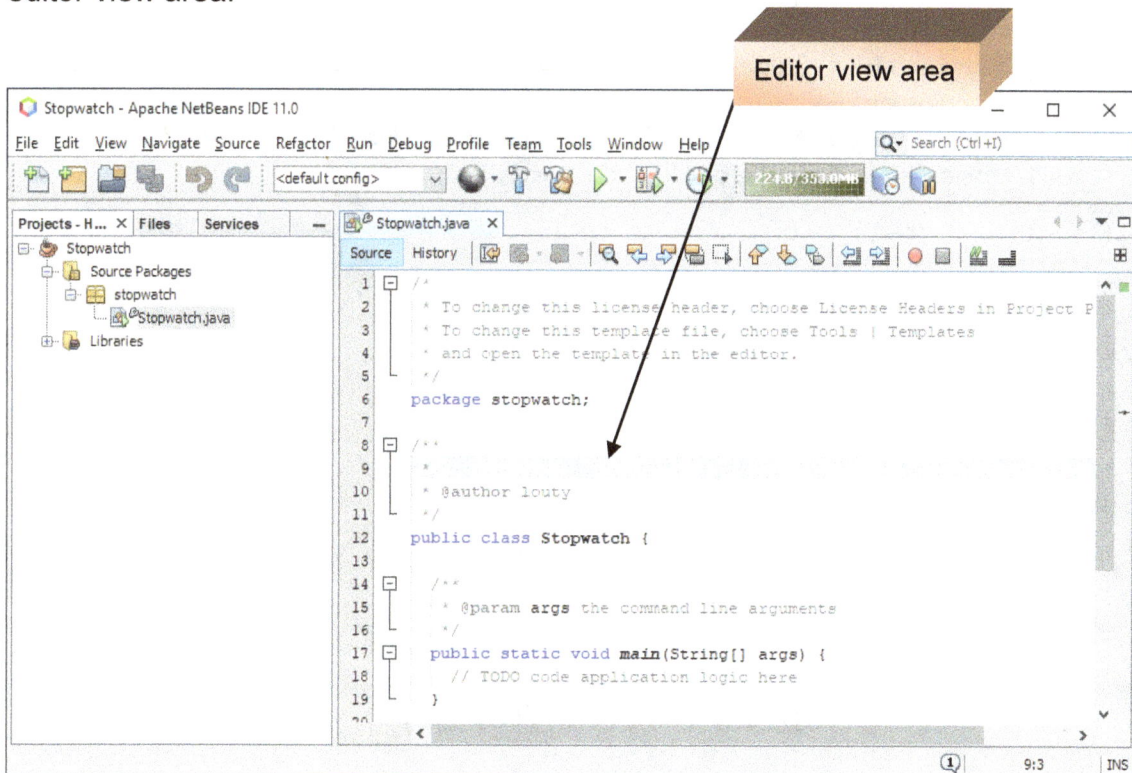

Editor view area

The default code created by NetBeans is:

```
/*
 * To change this license header, choose License Headers in
Project Properties.
 * To change this template file, choose Tools | Templates
 * and open the template in the editor.
 */

package stopwatch;

/**
 *
 * @author tyleel
 */
public class Stopwatch
{

  /**
   * @param args the command line arguments
   */
  public static void main(String[] args)
  {
    // TODO code application logic here
  }

}
```

We will always replace this default code with our own code (or you can modify it if you want to avoid a little typing). Delete the default code.

Recall, there are a few rules to pay attention to as you type Java code (we will go over these rules again in the next class):

> Java code requires perfection. All words must be spelled correctly.
> Java is case-sensitive, meaning upper and lower case letters are considered to be different characters. When typing code, make sure you use upper and lower case letters properly
> Java ignores any "**white space**" such as blanks. We will often use white space to make our code more readable.
> Curly **braces** are used for grouping. They mark the beginning and end of programming sections. Make sure your Java programs have an equal number of left and right braces. We call the section of code between matching braces a **block**.
> It is good coding practice to **indent** code within a block. This makes code easier to follow. NetBeans automatically indents code in blocks for you.

➤ Every Java statement will end with a semicolon. A **statement** is a program expression that generates some result. Note that not all Java expressions are statements (for example, the line defining the main method has no semicolon).

Stopwatch - Create a Frame

The first step in building a Java GUI application is creating a frame. At the same time we create the frame, we establish the basic framework for the entire program. The code (**Stopwatch.java**) that creates a frame within this basic framework is defined by a Java **class** of the same name:

```java
/*
 * Stopwatch
 */
package stopwatch;
import javax.swing.*;
import java.awt.*;
import java.awt.event.*;
public class Stopwatch extends JFrame
{

  public static void main(String args[])
  {
    // Construct the frame
    new Stopwatch().setVisible(true);
  }

  public Stopwatch()
  {
    // Frame constructor
    setTitle("Stopwatch Application");
    setSize(300, 100);
  }
}
```

Type one line at a time, paying close attention that you type everything as shown (use the rules).

As you type, notice after you type each left brace (**{**), the NetBeans editor adds a corresponding right brace (**}**) and automatically indents the next line. This follows the rule of indenting each code block. Like the braces, when you type a left parenthesis, a matching right parenthesis is added. Also, another thing to notice is that the editor uses different colors for different things in the code. Green text represents comments. Code is in black and keywords are in blue. This coloring sometimes helps you identify mistakes you may have made in typing.

When done typing, you should see:

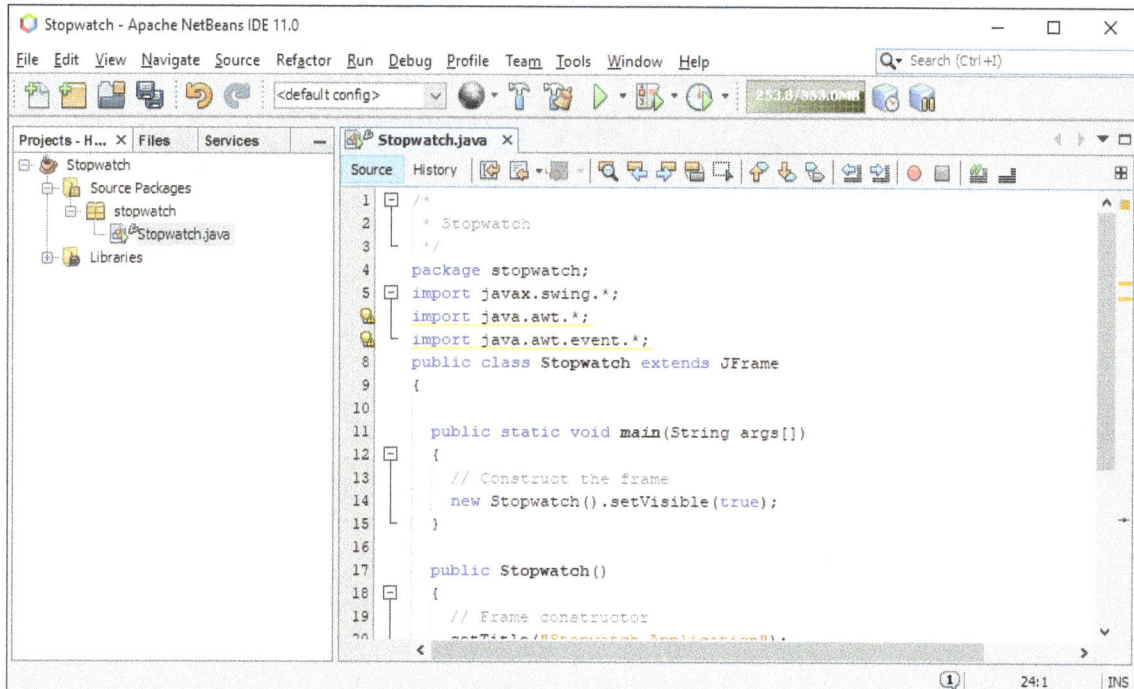

This code creates the frame by **extending** the Swing **JFrame** object, meaning it takes on all characteristics of such a frame. The code has a **constructor** for the **Stopwatch** object. You should see it executes two methods: one to set the title (**setTitle**) and one to set the size (**setSize**). The constructor is called in the **main method** to create the frame. We will use this same basic structure in every project built in this course. A constructor for the frame and all associated controls and control events will be built. The frame will be constructed in the main method.

Run the project (press <F6> or choose **Run**, then **Run Main Project** in the menu).
You will see your first frame:

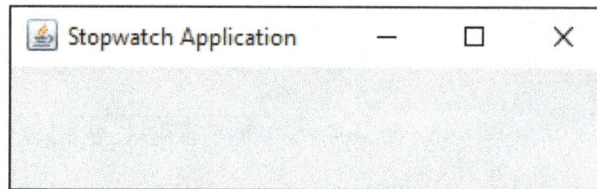

Saving Java Projects with NetBeans

Whenever you run a Java project, NetBeans automatically saves both the source files and the compiled code files for you. So, most of the time, you don't need to worry about saving your projects - it's taken care of for you. If you want to save code you are typing (before running), simply choose **File** from the main menu and click **Save All**. Or, just click the **Save All** button on the toolbar:

You do need to save the project group anytime you make a change, for example, if you add/delete files from a project or add/delete projects. This is also done using the **Save All** option.   If you try to exit NetBeans and have not saved projects, NetBeans will pop up dialog boxes to inform you of such and give you an opportunity to save files before exiting.

NetBeans and Java Files

So, how does all this information about program structure, files, compiling and running fit in with NetBeans, our development environment. We have seen that Java projects are grouped in project groups. And projects are made up of different folders and files.

Using My Computer or Windows Explorer (if using Windows), go to the folder containing the **Stopwatch** project you just built. There are many folders and files. In the **src/stopwatch** folder, you will see

Stopwatch.java

This is the source code that appears in the editor view area of NetBeans. In the **build/classes/stopwatch** folder is **Stopwatch.class**. This the compiled version of Stopwatch.java (this is the file needed by the Java virtual machine). Most of the other files are used by NetBeans used to keep track of what files make up the project.

Be aware that the only true Java files here are the ones with **.java** and **.class** extensions. The other files are created and modified by our particular development environment, NetBeans. If you want to share your Java program with a friend or move your Java program to another development environment, the only files you really need to transfer are the **.java** files. These files can be used by any Java programmer or programming environment to create a running program.

Create the User Interface

Having created a frame, we now create the user interface by "placing" controls in the frame. This placement simply involves several lines of logical Java code per control desired.

An object called a **layout manager** determines how controls are arranged in a frame. Some of the layout managers and their characteristics are:

FlowLayout	Places controls in successive rows, fitting as many as possible in a given row.
BorderLayout	Places controls against any of the four frame borders.
CardLayout	Places controls on top of each other like a deck of cards.
GridLayout	Places controls within a specified rectangular grid.
GridBagLayout	Places controls with a specified very flexible rectangular grid.
BoxLayout	Arranges controls either in a row or column.
SpringLayout	Arranges controls with positions defined by sprints and struts.

In this class, we will use the **GridBagLayout**. In our opinion, it offers the nicest interface appearance. As we work through the course, you will learn more and more capabilities of this manager. Study the other layout managers if you'd like.

A frame is actually made up of several different **panes**. Controls are placed in the **content pane** of the frame. The **GridBagLayout** manager divides the content pane into a grid of rows and columns:

	Column 0	Column 1	Column 2	Column 3	Column 4	Column 5
Row 0						
Row 1						
Row 2						
Row 3						
Row 4						
Row 5						

The top row is Row 0 and row number increases as you go down the grid. The left column is Column 0 and column number increases as you move to the right in the grid.

The **GridBagConstraints** object is used for control placement and positioning within the various grid elements. Controls are placed in this grid by referring to a particular column (**gridx** location) and row (**gridy** location). Rows and columns both start at zero (0). The grid does not have to be (but can be) sized. It automatically grows as controls are added. We will see that the GridBagLayout manager is very flexible. Controls can span more than one column/row and can be spaced (using **insets**) anywhere within a grid element.

A single line of code in our frame constructor is needed to specify we are using the GridBagLayout in the frame content pane:

```
getContentPane().setLayout(new GridBagLayout());
```

To place a control in the GridBagLayout grid, we follow these steps:

> ➢ **Declare** the control.
> ➢ **Create** (construct) the control.
> ➢ Establish desired control **properties**.
> ➢ **Add** the control to the layout content pane at the desired position.

In the projects we build, all controls will be declared with **class level scope**, meaning the controls and associated properties and methods will be available to any method in the class. Hence, all controls will be declared following the left opening brace of the class, before the first method.

We will also give **meaningful names** to controls. Accepted practice is to give the control a name beginning with some description of its purpose, then concatenating the type of control at the end of the name. Such a naming convention makes reading and writing your Java code much easier. Examples of names for button, label and text field controls (the ones we use with our stopwatch example):

```
startButton
stopButton
elapsedLabel
startTextField
```

To declare a control, you type the statement:

```
ControlType controlName;
```

In the Swing library, a button control is of type **JButton**. Hence, to declare our **startButton**, we use:

```
JButton startButton;
```

To create a previously declared control, use:

```
controlName = new ControlType();
```

For our start timing button, the Java code is:

```
startButton = new JButton();
```

The process of **declaring** and **creating** a control can be combined into a single line of code. We will always do this. For our example, the control declaration would be:

```
JButton startButton = new JButton();
```

The next step is to set any desired control properties. The format for such code is:

```
controlName.setPropertyName(PropertyValue);
```

Where **setPropertyName** is a method to set a desired property. When we discuss controls in detail, we will cover many of these methods. For now, we will just give them to you. As an example, to set the text appearing on the start timing button to "**Start Timing**," you would use:

```
startButton.setText("Start Timing");
```

The next step (yes, I know there are lots of steps) is to position the control in the **GridBagLayout** grid. First, we need to declare an object of type **GridBagConstraints** to allow positioning. Assuming this object is named **gridConstraints**, the declaration is:

```
GridBagConstraints gridConstraints = new
GridBagConstraints();
```

This statement is placed near the top of the frame constructor code.

Now, we use a three-step process to place each control in the grid. Decide on an x location (**desiredColumn**) and a y location (**desiredRow**). Then, use this code for a sample control named **controlName**):

```
gridConstraints.gridx = desiredColumn;
gridConstraints.gridy = desiredRow;
getContentPane().add(controlName, gridConstraints);
```

We will place the start timing button in the upper left corner of the grid, so we use:

```
gridConstraints.gridx = 0;
gridConstraints.gridy = 0;
getContentPane().add(startButton, gridConstraints);
```

To finalize placement of controls in the frame, execute a pack method:

```
pack();
```

This "packs" the grid layout onto the frame and makes the controls visible.

In summary, decide what controls you want to place in a frame. For each control, you need:

> - a **declaration** and **creation** statement (class level)
> - three lines of code for **placement** (in constructor method)

Once all controls are in the frame, you must execute a **pack** method to finalize placement. We'll clear this up (hopefully) with an example.

Stopwatch – Adding Controls

Continue with the **Stopwatch** example where we created a frame. We want to build this frame:

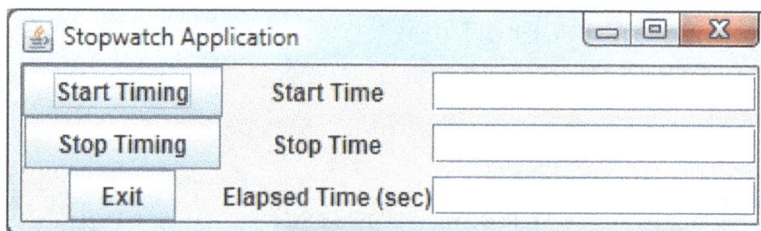

1. We will place nine controls in the frame: three buttons (**JButton** class), three labels (**JLabel** class) and three text fields (**JTextField** class). The buttons will start and stop the timing. The labels and text fields will be used to display the timing results: We will place these controls in a 3 x 3 array:

	gridx = 0	gridx = 1	gridx = 2
gridy = 0	**startButton**	**startLabel**	**startTextField**
gridy = 1	**stopButton**	**stopLabel**	**stopTextField**
gridy = 2	**exitButton**	elapsedLabel	elapsedTextField

Properties we will set in code:

startButton:
text	Start Timing
gridx	0
gridy	0

stopButton:
text	Stop Timing
gridx	0
gridy	1

exitButton:
text	Exit
gridx	0
gridy	2

startLabel:
    text   Start Time
    gridx   1
    gridy   0

stopLabel:
    text   End Time
    gridx   1
    gridy   1

elapsedLabel:
    text   Elapsed Time (sec)
    gridx   1
    gridy   2

startTextField:
    text   [Blank]
    columns   15
    gridx   2
    gridy   0

stopTextField:
    text   [Blank]
    columns   15
    gridx   2
    gridy   1

elapsedTextField:
    text   [Blank]
    columns   15
    gridx   2
    gridy   2

2. First, type the code to declare the nine controls (recall these lines go after the opening left brace for the class definition):

```
JButton startButton = new JButton();
JButton stopButton = new JButton();
JButton exitButton = new JButton();
JLabel startLabel = new JLabel();
JLabel stopLabel = new JLabel();
JLabel elapsedLabel = new JLabel();;
JTextField startTextField = new JTextField();
JTextField stopTextField = new JTextField();
JTextField elapsedTextField = new JTextField();
```

3. Replace the **setSize** line in the constructor code with the line establishing the grid layout:

```
getContentPane().setLayout(new GridBagLayout());
```

4. The code to set properties of and place each of the nine controls (also goes in the constructor method):

```
GridBagConstraints gridConstraints = new
GridBagConstraints();
startButton.setText("Start Timing");
gridConstraints.gridx = 0;
gridConstraints.gridy = 0;
getContentPane().add(startButton, gridConstraints);

stopButton.setText("Stop Timing");
gridConstraints.gridx = 0;
gridConstraints.gridy = 1;
getContentPane().add(stopButton, gridConstraints);

exitButton.setText("Exit");
gridConstraints.gridx = 0;
gridConstraints.gridy = 2;
getContentPane().add(exitButton, gridConstraints);

startLabel.setText("Start Time");
gridConstraints.gridx = 1;
gridConstraints.gridy = 0;
getContentPane().add(startLabel, gridConstraints);

stopLabel.setText("Stop Time");
gridConstraints.gridx = 1;
gridConstraints.gridy = 1;
getContentPane().add(stopLabel, gridConstraints);
```

```
    elapsedLabel.setText("Elapsed Time (sec)");
    gridConstraints.gridx = 1;
    gridConstraints.gridy = 2;
    getContentPane().add(elapsedLabel, gridConstraints);

    startTextField.setText("");
    startTextField.setColumns(15);
    gridConstraints.gridx = 2;
    gridConstraints.gridy = 0;
    getContentPane().add(startTextField, gridConstraints);

    stopTextField.setText("");
    stopTextField.setColumns(15);
    gridConstraints.gridx = 2;
    gridConstraints.gridy = 1;
    getContentPane().add(stopTextField, gridConstraints);

    elapsedTextField.setText("");
    elapsedTextField.setColumns(15);
    gridConstraints.gridx = 2;
    gridConstraints.gridy = 2;
    getContentPane().add(elapsedTextField, gridConstraints);

    pack();
```

Notice how each control is located within the grid. Notice, too, how we set the number of columns for the text field controls. If we didn't do this, you wouldn't see the controls. I know there's lots of code here (and there will always be lots of code for GUI interfaces). You can choose to type the code or copy and paste from these notes into NetBeans. If you choose to type the code, notice much of the code is similar, so copy and paste operations come in very handy.

For reference, here is the complete **Stopwatch.java** code at this point (newly added code is shaded – the line setting the frame size has been deleted):

```
/*
 * Stopwatch.java
 */
package stopwatch;
import javax.swing.*;
import java.awt.*;
import java.awt.event.*;
public class Stopwatch extends JFrame
{
    // declare controls used
    JButton startButton = new JButton();
```

```java
  JButton stopButton = new JButton();
  JButton exitButton = new JButton();
  JLabel startLabel = new JLabel();
  JLabel stopLabel = new JLabel();
  JLabel elapsedLabel = new JLabel();;
  JTextField startTextField = new JTextField();
  JTextField stopTextField = new JTextField();
  JTextField elapsedTextField = new JTextField();
public static void main(String args[])
{
  // Construct frame
  new Stopwatch().setVisible(true);
}
public Stopwatch()
{
  // Frame constructor
  setTitle("Stopwatch Application");
  getContentPane().setLayout(new GridBagLayout());
  // add controls
  GridBagConstraints gridConstraints = new
GridBagConstraints();

  startButton.setText("Start Timing");
  gridConstraints.gridx = 0;
  gridConstraints.gridy = 0;
  getContentPane().add(startButton, gridConstraints);

  stopButton.setText("Stop Timing");
  gridConstraints.gridx = 0;
  gridConstraints.gridy = 1;
  getContentPane().add(stopButton, gridConstraints);

  exitButton.setText("Exit");
  gridConstraints.gridx = 0;
  gridConstraints.gridy = 2;
  getContentPane().add(exitButton, gridConstraints);

  startLabel.setText("Start Time");
  gridConstraints.gridx = 1;
  gridConstraints.gridy = 0;
  getContentPane().add(startLabel, new
GridBagConstraints());

  stopLabel.setText("Stop Time");
  gridConstraints.gridx = 1;
  gridConstraints.gridy = 1;
  getContentPane().add(stopLabel, gridConstraints);
```

```
        elapsedLabel.setText("Elapsed Time (sec)");
        gridConstraints.gridx = 1;
        gridConstraints.gridy = 2;
        getContentPane().add(elapsedLabel, gridConstraints);

        startTextField.setText("");
        startTextField.setColumns(15);
        gridConstraints.gridx = 2;
        gridConstraints.gridy = 0;
        getContentPane().add(startTextField, gridConstraints);

        stopTextField.setText("");
        stopTextField.setColumns(15);
        gridConstraints.gridx = 2;
        gridConstraints.gridy = 1;
        getContentPane().add(stopTextField, gridConstraints);

        elapsedTextField.setText("");
        elapsedTextField.setColumns(15);
        gridConstraints.gridx = 2;
        gridConstraints.gridy = 2;
        getContentPane().add(elapsedTextField, gridConstraints);

        pack();
    }
}
```

Run the project. The interface should look like this:

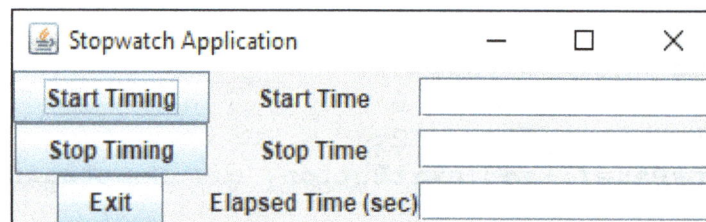

Notice how each control is located and sized in the layout of the frame. Save this project. We have no code to stop this project. To do this, select **Tools** in the NetBeans menu and choose **Stop Tool**.

Adding Event Methods

At this point, our interface has a finished look. What is missing is the code behind the control events. The next step in building a Java GUI application is to add this code. But, to add the code, we need a place to put it. We need to add event methods and their corresponding **listeners** to our application. There are two ways to add listeners, one for **AWT** objects and one for **Swing** objects. Listeners are added in the frame constructor code.

Java **event listeners** for AWT objects (primarily those for mouse and keyboard inputs) are implemented using something called **adapters** (also available from the AWT). The best way to see how to add such a listener is by example. In every project we build, we need to "listen" for the event when the user closes the window. The adapter that implements events for the frame (window) is called the **WindowAdapter** and it works with the **WindowListener**. There are certain window events that can be "listened for." In our case, we want to listen for the **windowClosing** event. The code that adds this event method to our application is:

```
addWindowListener(new WindowAdapter()
{
    public void windowClosing(WindowEvent e)
    {
        [Java code for window closing]
    }
});
```

This is actually one very long Java statement over several lines. It calls the **addWindowListener** method and, as an argument (all in parentheses), includes a **new** instance of a **WindowAdapter** event method (the **windowClosing** event). It's really not that hard to understand when you look at it, just very long!!

In the **windowClosing** method, we would write the code to execute when the window is closing. The **windowClosing** method must have a single argument (**WindowEvent e**). We can use this argument to determine just what event has occurred. In the stopwatch example, we assume a window closing event.

For Swing components, like the button, label and text field used here, event methods (**actionPerformed**) are added using the **ActionListener**. If the component is named controlName, the method is added using:

```
controlName.addActionListener(new ActionListener()
{
  public void actionPerformed(ActionEvent e)
  {
        [Java code to execute]
  }
});
```

Again, note this is just one long line of Java code. The method has a single argument (**ActionEvent e**), which tells us what particular event occurred (each control can respond to a number of events). For our stopwatch example, we will assume click events for the three button controls.

Note when we add a listener, we also need to add code for the event method. We could type the code at the same time we add the listener, but we take a different approach. When a method is added, the method code will be a single line of code invoking an "external" method where the actual code will reside. This separates the coding of method events from the code building the frame and makes for a "cleaner" code. For Swing components, we will name these external methods using a specific convention – the **control name** and **method name** will be concatenated into a new method name. Similar conventions are followed for AWT events. For our example above, the code adding such a method would be:

```
controlName.addActionListener(new ActionListener()
{
  public void actionPerformed(ActionEvent e)
  {
     controlNameActionPerformed(e);
  }
});
```

Once the method is added, the actual code is written in a method defined elsewhere in the program. The form for this method must be:

```
private void controlNameActionPerformed(ActionEvent e)
{
    [Java code to execute]
}
```

By separating the event method code from the code constructing the frame, editing, modifying and testing a Java GUI application is much easier. And, the naming convention selected makes it easier to find the event method associated with a particular control. The control event methods are usually placed after the constructor method.

Let's summarize the many steps to place a control (named **controlName** of type **controlType**) in a frame and add an event method:

➢ Declare and create the control (class level scope):

```
ControlType controlName = new ControlType();
```

➢ Position the control:

```
gridConstraints.gridx = desiredColumn;
gridConstraints.gridy = desiredRow;
getContentPane().add(controlName, gridConstraints);
```

(assumes a **gridConstraints** object has been created).

➢ Add the control listener:

```
controlName.addActionListener(new ActionListener()
{
    public void actionPerformed(ActionEvent e)
    {
        controlNameActionPerformed(e);
    }
});
```

> ➢ Write the control event method:

```
private void controlNameActionPerformed(ActionEvent e)
{
    [Java code to execute]
}
```

The first few times you add controls, this will seem to be a tedious process. As you develop more and more GUI applications, such additions will become second nature (and, you'll get very good at using the copy and paste features of NetBeans).

Stopwatch - Writing Code

All that's left to do is write code for the application. We write code for every event a response is needed for. In this application, there are three such events: clicking on each of the buttons.

1. Under the lines declaring the frame controls, declare three class level variables:

```
long startTime;
long stopTime;
double elapsedTime;
```

This establishes **startTime**, **endTime**, and **elapsedTime** as variables with class level scope.

2. In the frame constructor, add the **windowClosing** event method (every GUI project will need this code - place it after line establishing frame title):

```
addWindowListener(new WindowAdapter()
{
  public void windowClosing(WindowEvent e)
  {
    exitForm(e);
  }
});
```

And, add the corresponding event method code:

```
private void exitForm(WindowEvent e)
{
  System.exit(0);
}
```

This method is placed before the final right closing brace of the Stopwatch class (the normal place for methods). This one line of code tells the application to stop.

3. Let's create an **actionPerformed** event for the **startButton**. Add the listener (I place this after the code placing the control on the frame):

```
startButton.addActionListener(new ActionListener()
{
  public void actionPerformed(ActionEvent e)
  {
    startButtonActionPerformed(e);
  }
});
```

Then, add the event method after the constructor method:

```
private void startButtonActionPerformed(ActionEvent e)
{
  // click of start timing button
  startTime = System.currentTimeMillis();
  startTextField.setText(String.valueOf(startTime));
  stopTextField.setText("");
  elapsedTextField.setText("");
}
```

In this procedure, once the **Start Timing** button is clicked, we read the current time using a system function (in milliseconds, by the way) and put it in a text field using the **setText** method. We also blank out the other text fields. In the code above (and in all code in these notes), any line beginning with two slashes (//) is a comment. You decide whether you want to type these lines or not. They are not needed for proper application operation.

4. Now, add a listener for the **actionPerformed** event method for the **stopButton**:

```
stopButton.addActionListener(new ActionListener()
{
  public void actionPerformed(ActionEvent e)
  {
    stopButtonActionPerformed(e);
  }
});
```

Then, add this event method after the **startButtonActionPerformed** method:

```
private void stopButtonActionPerformed(ActionEvent e)
{
  // click of stop timing button
  stopTime = System.currentTimeMillis();
  stopTextField.setText(String.valueOf(stopTime));
  elapsedTime = (stopTime - startTime) / 1000.0;
  elapsedTextField.setText(String.valueOf(elapsedTime));
}
```

Here, when the **Stop Timing** button is clicked, we read the current time (**stopTime**), compute the elapsed time (in seconds), and put both values in their corresponding text field controls.

5. Finally, we need code in the **actionPerformed** method for the **exitButton** control. Add the listener:

```
exitButton.addActionListener(new ActionListener()
{
  public void actionPerformed(ActionEvent e)
  {
    exitButtonActionPerformed(e);
  }
});
```

Now, add the method:

```
private void exitButtonActionPerformed(ActionEvent e)
{
  System.exit(0);
}
```

This routine simply closes the frame once the **Exit** button is clicked.

For reference, the complete, final **Stopwatch.java** code is (newly added code is shaded):

```java
/*
 * Stopwatch.java
 */
package stopwatch;
import javax.swing.*;
import java.awt.*;
import java.awt.event.*;

public class Stopwatch extends JFrame
{

  // declare controls used
  JButton startButton = new JButton();
  JButton stopButton = new JButton();
  JButton exitButton = new JButton();
  JLabel startLabel = new JLabel();
  JLabel stopLabel = new JLabel();
  JLabel elapsedLabel = new JLabel();;
  JTextField startTextField = new JTextField();
  JTextField stopTextField = new JTextField();
  JTextField elapsedTextField = new JTextField();

  // declare class level variables
  long startTime;
  long stopTime;
  double elapsedTime;

  public static void main(String args[])
  {
    new Stopwatch().setVisible(true);
  }

  public Stopwatch()
  {
    // frame constructor
    setTitle("Stopwatch Application");
    addWindowListener(new WindowAdapter()
    {
      public void windowClosing(WindowEvent e)
      {
        exitForm(e);
      }
    });
    getContentPane().setLayout(new GridBagLayout());
```

```
    // add controls
    GridBagConstraints gridConstraints = new
GridBagConstraints();
    startButton.setText("Start Timing");
    gridConstraints.gridx = 0;
    gridConstraints.gridy = 0;
    getContentPane().add(startButton, gridConstraints);
    startButton.addActionListener(new ActionListener()
    {
      public void actionPerformed(ActionEvent e)
      {
        startButtonActionPerformed(e);
      }
    });

    stopButton.setText("Stop Timing");
    gridConstraints.gridx = 0;
    gridConstraints.gridy = 1;
    getContentPane().add(stopButton, gridConstraints);
    stopButton.addActionListener(new ActionListener()
    {
      public void actionPerformed(ActionEvent e)
      {
        stopButtonActionPerformed(e);
      }
    });

    exitButton.setText("Exit");
    gridConstraints.gridx = 0;
    gridConstraints.gridy = 2;
    getContentPane().add(exitButton, gridConstraints);
    exitButton.addActionListener(new ActionListener()
    {
      public void actionPerformed(ActionEvent e)
      {
        exitButtonActionPerformed(e);
      }
    });

    startLabel.setText("Start Time");
    gridConstraints.gridx = 1;
    gridConstraints.gridy = 0;
    getContentPane().add(startLabel, new
GridBagConstraints());

    stopLabel.setText("Stop Time");
```

```java
      gridConstraints.gridx = 1;
      gridConstraints.gridy = 1;
      getContentPane().add(stopLabel, gridConstraints);

      elapsedLabel.setText("Elapsed Time (sec)");
      gridConstraints.gridx = 1;
      gridConstraints.gridy = 2;
      getContentPane().add(elapsedLabel, gridConstraints);

      startTextField.setText("");
      startTextField.setColumns(15);
      gridConstraints.gridx = 2;
      gridConstraints.gridy = 0;
      getContentPane().add(startTextField, new
GridBagConstraints());

      stopTextField.setText("");
      stopTextField.setColumns(15);
      gridConstraints.gridx = 2;
      gridConstraints.gridy = 1;
      getContentPane().add(stopTextField, gridConstraints);

      elapsedTextField.setText("");
      elapsedTextField.setColumns(15);
      gridConstraints.gridx = 2;
      gridConstraints.gridy = 2;
      getContentPane().add(elapsedTextField, gridConstraints);
      pack();
    }
```

```java
  private void startButtonActionPerformed(ActionEvent e)
  {
    // click of start timing button
    startTime = System.currentTimeMillis();
    startTextField.setText(String.valueOf(startTime));
    stopTextField.setText("");
    elapsedTextField.setText("");
  }
```

```java
  private void stopButtonActionPerformed(ActionEvent e)
  {
     // click of stop timing button
    stopTime = System.currentTimeMillis();
    stopTextField.setText(String.valueOf(stopTime));
    elapsedTime = (stopTime - startTime) / 1000.0;
    elapsedTextField.setText(String.valueOf(elapsedTime));
  }
```

```
private void exitButtonActionPerformed(ActionEvent e)
{
  System.exit(0);
}
```

```
private void exitForm(WindowEvent e)
{
  System.exit(0);
}
```

```
}
```

Study this code to see where all the methods go.

Now, run the application (press **<F6>**). Try it out. If your application doesn't run, recheck to make sure the code is typed properly. Save your application. This is saved as **Stopwatch Project** in the **Projects** program group in **\HomeJava\HomeJava Projects** folder. Here's what I got when I tried:

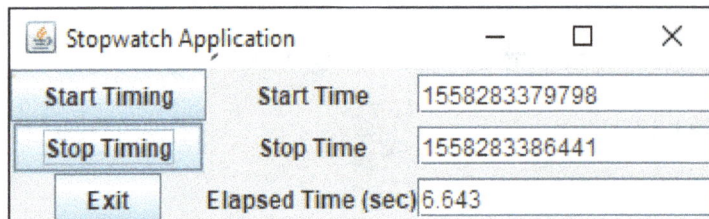

Stopwatch Application		— ☐ ✕
Start Timing	Start Time	1558283379798
Stop Timing	Stop Time	1558283386441
Exit	Elapsed Time (sec)	6.643

If you have the time, here are some other things you may try with the **Stopwatch**. To make these changes will require research on your part (use web sites, other books, other programmers) to find answers. This is an important skill to have – how to improve existing applications by discovering new things. The solutions to the problems and exercises at the end of this class' notes can also shed some light on these challenges:

A. Try changing the frame background color.

B. Notice you can press the 'Stop Timing' button before the 'Start Timing' button. This shouldn't be so. Change the application so you can't do this. And make it such that you can't press the 'Start Timing' until 'Stop Timing' has been pressed. Hint: Look at the button **enabled** property.

C. Can you think of how you can continuously display the 'End Time' and 'Elapsed Time'? This is a little tricky because of the event-driven nature of Java. Look at the **Timer** class (do a little Java research). By setting the **delay** property of this class to **1000**, it will generate its own events every one second. Put code similar to that in the event method for the **stopButton** in the Timer class' actionPerformed method and see what happens. Also, see the exercise at the end of the class for help on this one.

Chapter Review

After completing this chapter, you should understand:

- ➢ The prerequisites for this course
- ➢ How to use NetBeans to build, run an application
- ➢ The structure of a Java GUI application
- ➢ The three steps in building a Java GUI application
- ➢ How to create a frame
- ➢ How to place a control on the frame using the GridBagLayout
- ➢ Proper control naming convention
- ➢ How to add event listeners and event methods
- ➢ How to add code to event methods

2

Dual-Mode Stopwatch Project

Review and Preview

We've completed our review of building Java GUI projects using NetBeans (or any IDE you choose). We now start building some projects. For each project built, we provide step-by-step instructions in designing and building the form's graphic interface and detailed explanations of the code behind the projects.

The first project we build is a **Dual-Mode Stopwatch** that allows you to time tasks you may be doing. It is similar to the simple stopwatch built in the introduction.

Project Design Considerations

Before building this first project, let's look at some of the things that should be considered to make a useful project. A first consideration should be to determine what processes and methods you want your application to perform. What are the inputs and outputs? Develop a framework or flow chart of all your application's processes.

Decide what controls you need. Do the built-in Java controls and methods meet your needs? Do you need to develop some controls or methods of your own? You can design and build your own controls using Java, but that topic is beyond the scope of this course. The skills gained in this course, however, will be invaluable if you want to tackle such a task.

Design your user interface. What do you want your form to look like? Consider appearance and ease of use. Make the interface consistent with other applications. Familiarity is good in program design.

Write your code. Make your code readable and traceable - future code modifiers (including yourself) will thank you. Consider developing reusable code - modules with utility outside your current development. This will save you time in future developments.

Make your code 'user-friendly.' Make operation of your application obvious to the user. Step the user through its use. Try to anticipate all possible ways a user can mess up in using your application. It's fairly easy to write an application that works properly when the user does everything correctly. It's difficult to write an application that can handle all the possible wrong things a user can do and still not bomb out.

Debug your code completely before giving it to others. There's nothing worse than having a user call you to point out flaws in your application. A good way to find all the bugs is to let several people try the code - a mini beta-testing program.

Dual-Mode Stopwatch Project Preview

In this chapter, we will build a **dual-mode stopwatch**. The stopwatch can be started and stopped when desired. Two times are tracked: the time that elapses while the stopwatch is active (the running time) and the total time elapsed between first starting and finally stopping the stopwatch.

The finished project is saved as **DualModeStopwatch** in the **\HomeJava\HomeJava Projects** project group. Start NetBeans (or your IDE). Open the specified project group. Make **DualModeStopwatch** the selected project. Run the project. You will see:

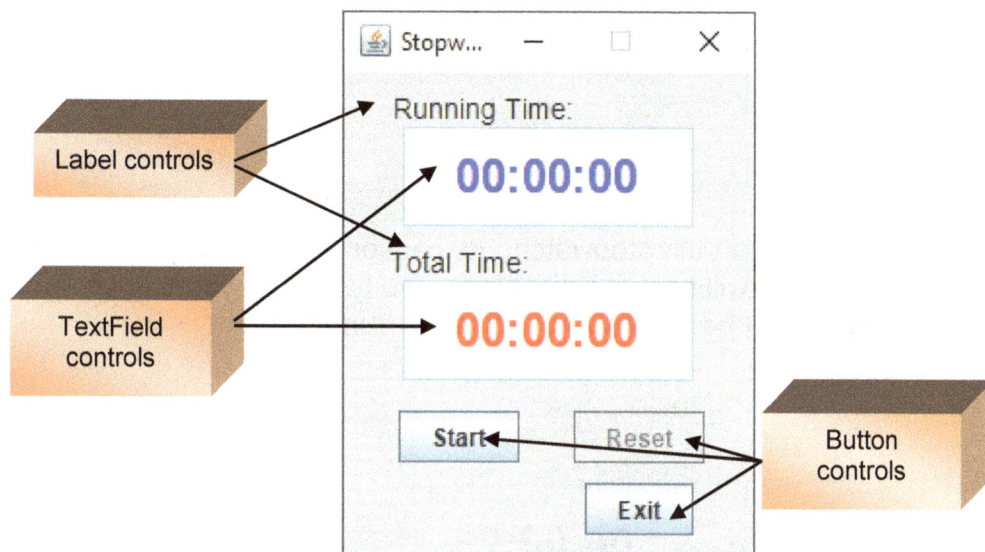

Two text field controls are used for time displays (two labels provide titling information). Three button controls start, stop and reset the stopwatch and one stops the application.

The stopwatch appears in its 'initial' state, with the displayed times set at zero and the **Reset** button disabled:

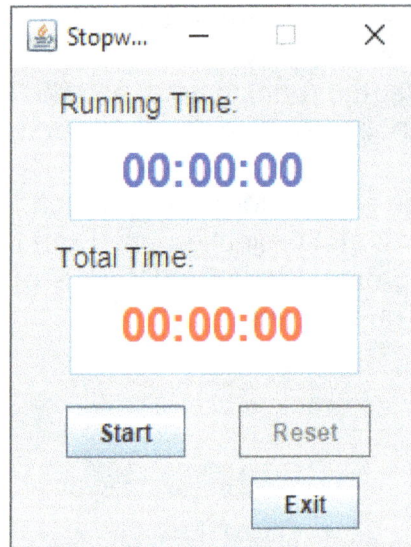

Click the **Start** button to start the stopwatch. Its caption will change (now reading **Stop**) and the **Exit** button will become disabled - the two displayed times will be the same (updating every second). We call this the 'running' state:

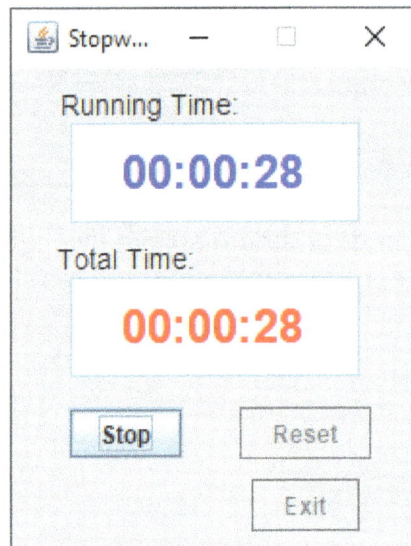

At some point, click **Stop**. When I did, the form appears as:

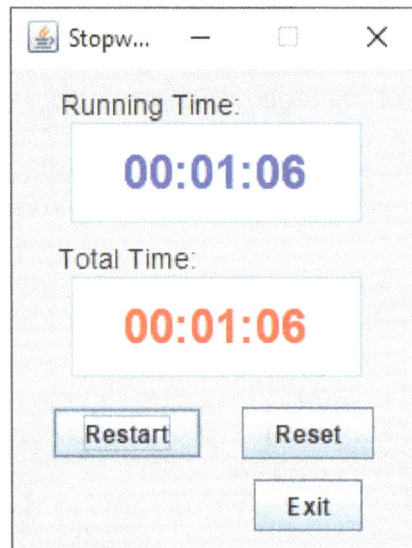

At this point ('stopped' state), all buttons become enabled and you have three options. You can click **Exit** to stop the project. You can click **Reset** to set both times back to zero and return the project to its initial state. Or, you can click the button now labeled **Restart** to restart the timer. When I do this, after a short wait, I get:

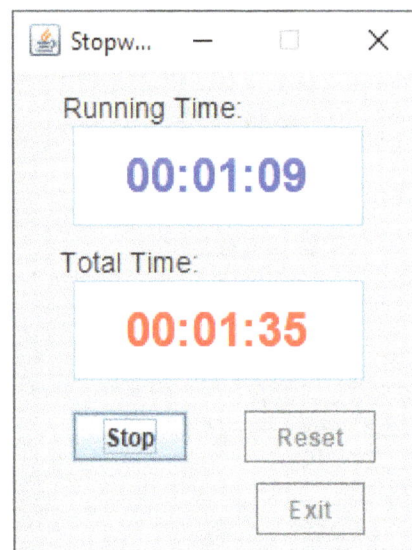

The stopwatch is running again, but the two displayed times are different. The **Total Time** is the amount of time elapsed since we first started the stopwatch. The **Running Time** is the total time less time when the stopwatch is in stopped mode. Based on these values, this stopwatch has spent 0:26 (26 seconds) waiting around.

Continue starting, stopping, restarting and resetting the stopwatch to understand its operation. Click **Exit** when you're done to stop the project. Open the code window and skim over the code, if you like.

You will now build this project in stages. As you build Java projects, we always recommend taking a slow, step-by-step process. It minimizes programming errors and helps build your confidence as things come together in a complete project. This is the approach we will take on all projects in these notes.

We address **frame design**. We present the controls needed to build the frame, establish initial control properties and discuss how to change the state of the controls. And, we address **code design**. We discuss how to do the necessary mathematics to determine the various displayed times. Before diving into this first project, however, we review some of the 'tricks' in using the grid bag layout manager.

Frame Design – GridBagLayout Manager

We use the **GridBagLayout** manager to set up our Java GUI projects (you can, of course, choose to use any layout manager you want). Recall, with this manager, a grid is used to place controls:

	gridx = 0	gridx = 1	gridx = 2	gridx = 3	gridx = 4
gridy = 0					
gridy = 1					
gridy = 2					
gridy = 3					
gridy = 4					
gridy = 5					

The **GridBagConstraints** object is used for control placement and positioning within the various grid elements. Controls are placed in this grid by referring to a particular column (**gridx** location) and row (**gridy** location). We have seen that the grid (and frame) automatically grows as controls are added. Column widths are set by the "widest" control in a particular column. And, row heights are set by the "tallest" control in a particular row.

There are other variables associated with **GridBagConstraints** that can be used to adjust control size and, hence, associated column, row, and frame size. A control can occupy more than one column or row. The number of columns spanned by a control is set with the **gridwidth** variable; the number of rows spanned is set with the **gridheight** variable. By default, a control fills one row and one column. If we have a GridBagConstraints object named **gridConstraints**, a control will occupy two rows and three columns, starting in the second column (gridx = 1) and fourth row (gridy = 3), with this code:

```
gridConstraints.gridx = 1;
gridConstraints.gridy = 3;
gridConstraints.gridheight = 2;
gridConstraints.gridwidth = 3;
```

In our example grid, this control would be placed like this:

	gridx = 0	gridx = 1	gridx = 2	gridx = 3	gridx = 4
gridy = 0					
gridy = 1					
gridy = 2					
gridy = 3					
gridy = 4		**Control goes here**			
gridy = 5					

A particular control may completely fill its region or may not. If the control is smaller than its allocated region, its dimensions may be adjusted to fill the region – use the **fill** variable. There are four values:

GridBagConstraints.NONE	Control is not resized (default value)
GridBagConstraints.HORIZONTAL	Control width fills display area.
GridBagConstraints.VERTICAL	Control height fills display area.
GridBagConstraints.BOTH	Control fills entire display area.

With our example **gridConstraints** object, a control will grow to fill the region width using:

```
gridConstraints.fill = GridBagConstraints.HORIZONTAL;
```

This control would look like this in its grid region:

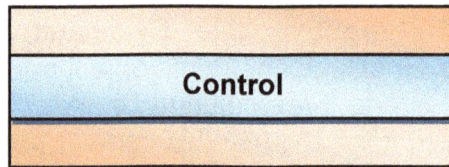

Control

Smaller changes in control size can be made using the **ipadx** and **ipady** variables. These determine how much a control size is to be increased beyond its minimum size (in each direction). To add five pixels to the width and height of a control using our **gridConstraints** example:

```
gridConstraints.ipadx = 5;
gridConstraints.ipady = 5;
```

If you choose not to expand a control to fill its area, its position within its allocated area is set with the **anchor** variable. There are nine possible values:

GridBagConstraints.NORTH	Control is centered at top
GridBagConstraints.NORTHEAST	Control is in upper right corner
GridBagConstraints.EAST	Control is at right, centered vertically
GridBagConstraints.SOUTHEAST	Control is in lower right corner
GridBagConstraints.SOUTH	Control is centered at bottom
GridBagConstraints.SOUTHWEST	Control is in lower left corner
GridBagConstraints.WEST	Control is at left, centered vertically
GridBagConstraints.NORTHWEST	Control is in upper left corner
GridBagConstraints.CENTER vertically	Control is centered horizontally and

To center a control (in both directions) in its display area, use:

```
gridConstraints.anchor = GridBagConstraints.CENTER;
```

This control would look like this in its grid region:

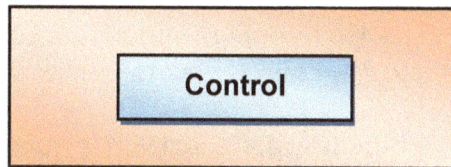

If a control completely fills its allocated display area, a border region (free space) can be established around the control using the **Insets** object. Four values are used to define the **top**, **left**, **bottom** and **right** side margins from the side of the display area. The default is **Insets(0, 0, 0, 0)**. With our example, if we want 10 pixels of space at the top and bottom, 20 on the left and 30 on the right, we would use:

```
gridConstraints.insets = new Insets(10, 20, 10, 30);
```

This control would look something like this in its grid region:

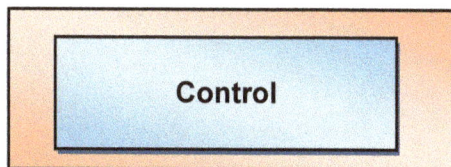

Once the **gridConstraints** are established for a control, it is added to the frame's content pane using the add method. If the control is **myControl**, the code syntax is:

```
getContentPane().add(myControl, gridConstraints);
```

Many times, we add controls to a panel control (with its own **GridBayLayout** manager) within a frame. If the panel is named **myPanel**, the code to add **myControl** is:

```
myPanel.add(myControl, gridConstraints);
```

I think you see the flexibility available with the **GridBagLayout** manager. You are encouraged to learn these ideas and use them to "beautify" your GUI interfaces. Remember to establish all grid constraint values before adding a control to the grid.

Building an interface is an "art," not a science. You will see the process involves lots of trial and error and adjustments. And sometimes, you get results you would never expect – components may not appear as you wish or may not appear at all! The bottom line is – once all adjustments are made, your completed frame size is established. Let's look at one final task - how to center the frame in the screen.

First, to place a frame (**width** by **height** in size) at a horizontal position **left** and vertical position **top**, we use the **setBounds** method:

```
setBounds(left, top, width, height);
```

All the dimensions are **int** types and measured in pixels. To center a frame in the computer screen, we need to know find **left** and **top**.

To find the centering position, we need two things: the dimensions of the frame (use **getWidth** and **getHeight** methods) and the dimensions of the screen. The dimensions of the screen are held in the frame's '**toolkit**'. A **Dimension** object holds the information we need. To retrieve this object, use:

```
Dimension screenSize =
Toolkit.getDefaultToolkit().getScreenSize();
```

With this, **screenSize.width** holds the screen width and **screenSize.height** holds the screen height. So, the code to center the frame using **setBounds** is:

```
setBounds((int) (0.5 * (screenSize.width - getWidth())),
(int) (0.5 * (screenSize.height - getHeight())),
getWidth(), getHeight());
```

This code needs to be after the **pack** method in the code establishing the frame, so that proper frame size is used. We'll use this centering code in every application built in the remainder of this course. Any initializations for a project will be placed after this line in the frame constructor.

Stopwatch Frame Design

We can begin building the **Dual-Mode Stopwatch Project**. Before starting, make sure you have established a project group on your computer for building Java projects. Always save your projects in this project group. Do not save them in the project group used in these notes (**\HomeJava\HomeJava Projects** folder). Leave this project group intact so you can always reference the finished projects, if needed.

Let's build the frame. Start a new project in your Java project group – name it **DualModeStopwatch**. Delete default code in file named **DualModeStopwatch.java**. Once started, we suggest you immediately save the project with the name you chose. This sets up the folder and file structure needed for your project. Build the basic frame with these properties:

DualModeStopwatch Frame:
title	Stopwatch
resizable	false

The code is:

```
/*
 * DualModeStopwatch.java
 */
package dualmodestopwatch;
import javax.swing.*;
import java.awt.*;
import java.awt.event.*;

public class DualModeStopwatch extends JFrame
{
  public static void main(String args[])
  {
    // create frame
    new DualModeStopwatch().setVisible(true);
  }

  public DualModeStopwatch()
  {
    // frame constructor
    setTitle("Stopwatch");
    setResizable(false);
    addWindowListener(new WindowAdapter()
    {
      public void windowClosing(WindowEvent evt)
      {
```

```
        exitForm(evt);
      }
    });
    getContentPane().setLayout(new GridBagLayout());
    GridBagConstraints gridConstraints;

    pack();
    Dimension screenSize =
Toolkit.getDefaultToolkit().getScreenSize();
    setBounds((int) (0.5 * (screenSize.width -
getWidth())), (int) (0.5 * (screenSize.height -
getHeight())), getWidth(), getHeight());
  }

  private void exitForm(WindowEvent evt)
  {
    System.exit(0);
  }
}
```

We use similar code to start each project. It builds the frame, sets up the layout manager and includes code to exit the application. Run the code to make sure the frame (at least, what there is of it at this point) appears and is centered on the screen:

Let's populate our frame with other controls. All code for creating the frame and placing controls (except declarations) goes in the **DualModeStopwatch** constructor.

All controls go directly on the frame. The **GridBagLayout** for the frame is:

	gridx = 0	gridx = 1
gridy = 0	**runningTimeLabel**	
gridy = 1	**runningTimeTextField**	
gridy = 2	**totalimeLabel**	
gridy = 2	**totalTimeTextField**	
gridy = 2	**startStopButton**	**resetButton**
gridy = 2		**exitButton**

The label and text field controls are used to display times and their title information. The buttons (one to start/stop/restart, one to reset and one to exit the project) are used to control operation of the stopwatch. We'll add a few controls at a time to help you get used to the process (you can also use lots of cut and paste for similar controls). Let's add the first label/text field pair.

The control properties are:

runningTimeLabel:

text	Running Time:
font	Arial, Plain, Size 14
gridx	0
gridy	0
insets	10, 25, 0, 0

runningTimeTextField:

size	150, 50
editable	false
background	White
foreground	Blue
text	00:00:00
horizontalAlignment	CENTER
font	Arial, Bold, Size 24
gridx	0
gridy	1
gridwidth	2
insets	0, 10, 0, 10

These controls are declared using:

```
JLabel runningTimeLabel = new JLabel();
JTextField runningTimeTextField = new JTextField();
```

The controls are placed in the frame using:

```
runningTimeLabel.setText("Running Time:");
runningTimeLabel.setFont(new Font("Arial", Font.PLAIN,
14));
gridConstraints = new GridBagConstraints();
gridConstraints.gridx = 0;
gridConstraints.gridy = 0;
gridConstraints.insets = new Insets(10, 25, 0, 0);
getContentPane().add(runningTimeLabel, gridConstraints);

runningTimeTextField.setPreferredSize(new Dimension(150,
50));
runningTimeTextField.setEditable(false);
runningTimeTextField.setBackground(Color.WHITE);
runningTimeTextField.setForeground(Color.BLUE);
runningTimeTextField.setText("00:00:00");
runningTimeTextField.setHorizontalAlignment(SwingConstants
.CENTER);
runningTimeTextField.setFont(new Font("Arial", Font.BOLD,
24));
gridConstraints = new GridBagConstraints();
gridConstraints.gridx = 0;
gridConstraints.gridy = 1;
gridConstraints.gridwidth = 2;
gridConstraints.insets = new Insets(0, 10, 0, 10);
getContentPane().add(runningTimeTextField,
gridConstraints);
```

As a reminder of where particular code segments go, here is the complete code at this point (additions are shaded):

```java
/*
 * DualModeStopwatch.java
 */
package dualmodestopwatch;
import javax.swing.*;
import java.awt.*;
import java.awt.event.*;

public class DualModeStopwatch extends JFrame
{

  JLabel runningTimeLabel = new JLabel();
  JTextField runningTimeTextField = new JTextField();

  public static void main(String args[])
  {
    // create frame
    new DualModeStopwatch().setVisible(true);
  }

  public DualModeStopwatch()
  {
    // frame constructor
    setTitle("Stopwatch");
    setResizable(false);
    addWindowListener(new WindowAdapter()
    {
      public void windowClosing(WindowEvent evt)
      {
        exitForm(evt);
      }
    });
    getContentPane().setLayout(new GridBagLayout());
    GridBagConstraints gridConstraints;

    runningTimeLabel.setText("Running Time:");
    runningTimeLabel.setFont(new Font("Arial", Font.PLAIN,
14));
    gridConstraints = new GridBagConstraints();
    gridConstraints.gridx = 0;
    gridConstraints.gridy = 0;
    gridConstraints.insets = new Insets(10, 25, 0, 0);
    getContentPane().add(runningTimeLabel,
gridConstraints);
```

```
    runningTimeTextField.setPreferredSize(new
Dimension(150, 50));
    runningTimeTextField.setEditable(false);
    runningTimeTextField.setBackground(Color.WHITE);
    runningTimeTextField.setForeground(Color.BLUE);
    runningTimeTextField.setText("00:00:00");

runningTimeTextField.setHorizontalAlignment(SwingConstants
.CENTER);
    runningTimeTextField.setFont(new Font("Arial",
Font.BOLD, 24));
    gridConstraints = new GridBagConstraints();
    gridConstraints.gridx = 0;
    gridConstraints.gridy = 1;
    gridConstraints.gridwidth = 2;
    gridConstraints.insets = new Insets(0, 10, 0, 10);
    getContentPane().add(runningTimeTextField,
gridConstraints);

    pack();
    Dimension screenSize =
Toolkit.getDefaultToolkit().getScreenSize();
    setBounds((int) (0.5 * (screenSize.width -
getWidth())), (int) (0.5 * (screenSize.height -
getHeight())), getWidth(), getHeight());
  }

  private void exitForm(WindowEvent evt)
  {
    System.exit(0);
  }
}
```

Run the project to see the first two controls:

The next two control properties are:

totalTimeLabel:

text	Total Time:
font	Arial, Plain, Size 14
gridx	0
gridy	2
insets	10, 10, 0, 10

totalTimeTextField:

size	150, 50
editable	false
background	White
foreground	Red
text	00:00:00
horizontalAlignment	CENTER
font	Arial, Bold, Size 24
gridx	0
gridy	3
gridwidth	2
insets	0, 10, 15, 10

Notice these are nearly identical to the two previous controls (a good time to try your cut and paste skills). Declare the controls:

```
JLabel totalTimeLabel = new JLabel();
JTextField totalTimeTextField = new JTextField();
```

Add the controls with this code (goes after the code adding the two previous controls):

```
totalTimeLabel.setText("Total Time:");
totalTimeLabel.setFont(new Font("Arial", Font.PLAIN, 14));
gridConstraints = new GridBagConstraints();
gridConstraints.gridx = 0;
gridConstraints.gridy = 2;
gridConstraints.insets = new Insets(10, 10, 0, 10);
getContentPane().add(totalTimeLabel, gridConstraints);
```

```
totalTimeTextField.setPreferredSize(new Dimension(150,
50));
totalTimeTextField.setEditable(false);
totalTimeTextField.setBackground(Color.WHITE);
totalTimeTextField.setForeground(Color.RED);
totalTimeTextField.setText("00:00:00");
totalTimeTextField.setHorizontalAlignment(SwingConstants.C
ENTER);
totalTimeTextField.setFont(new Font("Arial", Font.BOLD,
24));
gridConstraints = new GridBagConstraints();
gridConstraints.gridx = 0;
gridConstraints.gridy = 3;
gridConstraints.gridwidth = 2;
gridConstraints.insets = new Insets(0, 10, 15, 10);
getContentPane().add(totalTimeTextField, gridConstraints);
```

Run to see the newly added controls:

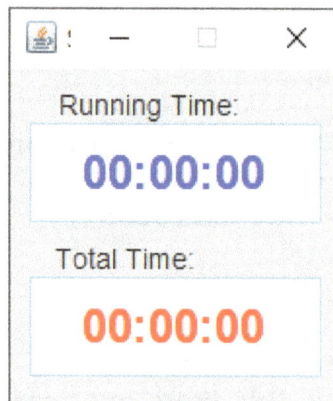

Lastly, let's add the three button controls.

The three button control properties are:

startStopButton:
text	Start
gridx	0
gridy	4

resetButton:
text	Reset
enabled	false
gridx	1
gridy	4
insets	0, 0, 0, 25

exitButton:
text	Exit
gridx	1
gridy	5
insets	10, 0, 10, 25

The controls are declared using:

```
JButton startStopButton = new JButton();
JButton resetButton = new JButton();
JButton exitButton = new JButton();
```

And added to the frame using:

```
startStopButton.setText("Start");
gridConstraints = new GridBagConstraints();
gridConstraints.gridx = 0;
gridConstraints.gridy = 4;
getContentPane().add(startStopButton, gridConstraints);
startStopButton.addActionListener(new ActionListener()
{
  public void actionPerformed(ActionEvent e)
  {
    startStopButtonActionPerformed(e);
  }
});
```

```
resetButton.setText("Reset");
resetButton.setEnabled(false);
gridConstraints = new GridBagConstraints();
gridConstraints.gridx = 1;
gridConstraints.gridy = 4;
gridConstraints.insets = new Insets(0, 0, 0, 25);
getContentPane().add(resetButton, gridConstraints);
resetButton.addActionListener(new ActionListener()
{
  public void actionPerformed(ActionEvent e)
  {
    resetButtonActionPerformed(e);
  }
});

exitButton.setText("Exit");
gridConstraints = new GridBagConstraints();
gridConstraints.gridx = 1;
gridConstraints.gridy = 5;
gridConstraints.insets = new Insets(10, 0, 10, 25);
getContentPane().add(exitButton, gridConstraints);
exitButton.addActionListener(new ActionListener()
{
  public void actionPerformed(ActionEvent e)
  {
    exitButtonActionPerformed(e);
  }
});
```

This code also adds listeners for each button. Add these empty methods:

```
private void startStopButtonActionPerformed(ActionEvent e)
{
}

private void resetButtonActionPerformed(ActionEvent e)
{
}

private void exitButtonActionPerformed(ActionEvent e)
{
}
```

Add code in the proper locations. Run to see:

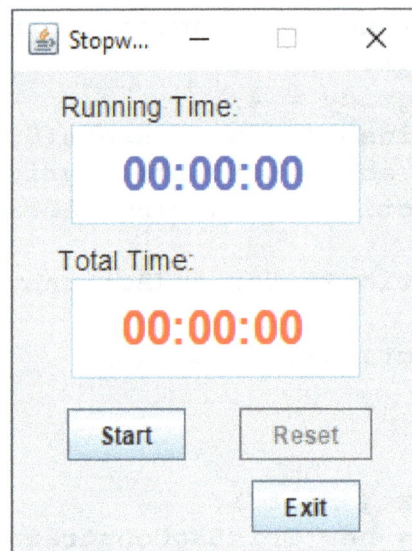

This completes the frame design.

We will begin writing code for the application. We will write the code in several steps. As a first step, we will write the code that takes the stopwatch from this 'initial' state to its 'running' state, following clicking of the **Start** button. During the code development process, recognize you may modify a particular method several times before arriving at the finished product.

Code Design – Initial to Running State

Even though we have yet to write any code, notice you can run the stopwatch project to make sure the form is properly initialized. Initially, we see the stopwatch looks like this:

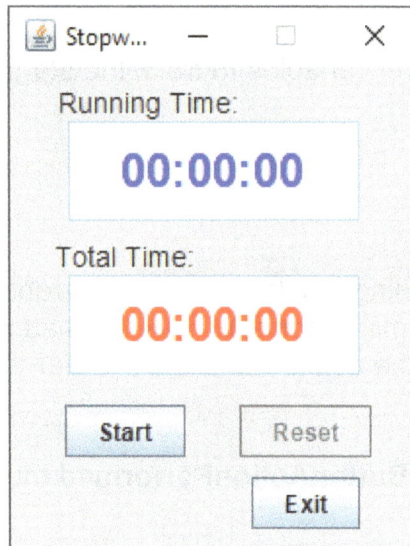

We have two options at this point – either click **startStopButton** (the button with **Start**) or click **exitButton** (the button with **Exit**). (Note the **Reset** button is initially disabled – you can't click this button until the stopwatch has been running.) We write code for both options.

First, the **exitButtonActionPerformed** method is simply:

```
private void exitButtonActionPerformed(ActionEvent e)
{
   System.exit(0);
}
```

This simply says whenever the **Exit** button is clicked, the project ends. Add this code to the code window.

When the user clicks the **Start** button in 'initial' state, several things must happen to switch the stopwatch to 'running' state:

> ➤ Determine the starting time.
> ➤ Initialize the stopped time to zero.
> ➤ Change the **text** property of **startStopButton** to **Stop**.
> ➤ Disable **exitButton**.

We will define two class level variables to track the starting time and the stopped time:

```
long startTime;
long stoppedTime;
```

Times will be established using the Java System.currentTimeMillis() method which returns the current time (in milliseconds). The returned value is a **long** type value. Place these statements in the declarations area under the declarations for the controls

The code for the **startStopButtonActionPerformed** method that implements the listed steps is then:

```
private void startStopButtonActionPerformed(ActionEvent e)
{
// initial to running state
startTime = System.currentTimeMillis();
stoppedTime = 0;
startStopButton.setText("Stop");
exitButton.setEnabled(false);
}
```

Again, note use of the **System.currentTimeMillis()** to obtain the starting time.

Save and run the project. Click the **Start** button and you should see:

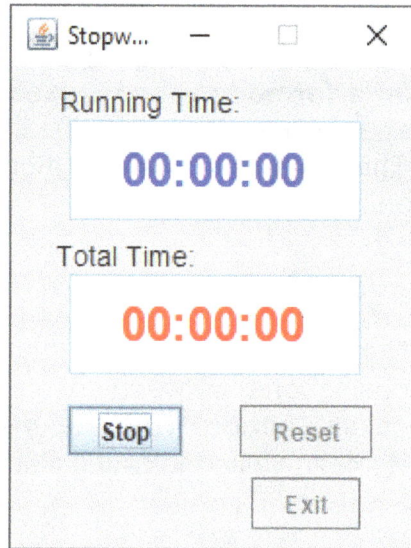

The project is now in 'running' state. However, nothing is seen in the displays. We need to write code to update the displayed times every second. To do this, we use the Java **timer** object. Since this may not be a familiar topic, we'll do a quick review.

Code Design - Timer Object

A **timer object** generates an event every **delay** milliseconds. The code in the timer's corresponding **actionPerformed** method is executed with each such event. Other control events can be detected while the timer object processes events in the background. This multi-tasking allows more than one thing to be happening in your application.

Timer **Properties**:

delay	Number of milliseconds (there are 1000 milliseconds in one second) between each invocation of the timer object's **actionPerformed** method.
running	Boolean value indicating if timer is running.

Timer **Methods**:

start	Used to start timer object.
stop	Used to stop timer.
isRunning	Method that returns boolean value indicating whether timer is running (generating events).

Timer **Events**:

actionPerformed	Event method invoked every **delay** milliseconds while timer object's **running** property is **true**.

To use a timer object, you first declare it using the standard syntax. For a timer named **myTimer**, the code is:

```
Timer myTimer;
```

The constructor for the timer object specifies the **delay** and adds the event (**actionPerformed**) method, using an **ActionListener**, in a single step. The syntax is:

```
myTimer = new Timer(delay, new ActionListener()
{
  public void actionPerformed(ActionEvent e)
  {
    myTimerActionPerformed(e);
  }
});
```

And, the corresponding event code would be placed in a **myTimerActionPerformed** method:

```
private void myTimerActionPerformed(ActionEvent e)
{
    [method code]
}
```

To use the **timer** object, we add it to our application the same as any object. You write code in the timer object's **actionPerformed** method. This is the code you want to repeat every **delay** milliseconds

You 'turn on' a timer in code using the **start** method:

```
myTimer.start();
```

and it is turned off using the **stop** method:

```
myTimer.stop();
```

To check if the timer is on, use the **isRunning** method:

```
myTimer.isRunning();
```

If this method returns a boolean true, the timer is on.

Applications can (and many times do) have multiple timer objects. You need separate timer objects (and event methods) if you have events that occur with different regularity (different **delay** values). Timer objects are used for two primary purposes. First,, you can use a timer object to implement some 'wait time' established by the **delay** property. In this case, you simply start the timer and when the delay is reached, have the **actionPerformed** event turn its corresponding timer off. Second, you use timer objects to periodically repeat some code segment (what we'll do in this project). This is very useful for graphics animation. We will do this in the remaining three projects in these notes.

Typical use of **timer** object:

> Declare timer, assigning an identifiable **name**. For **myTimer**, the statement is:

```
Timer myTimer;
```

> Establish a **delay** value. Create the timer using specified constructor, adding the **actionPerformed** method. Write the method code.
> At some point in your application, start the timer. Also, have capability to turn the timer off, when desired.

Code Design – Update Display

Let's add a timer object (**displayTimer**) to the project to display the time. Use this class level declaration:

```
Timer displayTimer;
```

Add the object with this code:

```
displayTimer = new Timer(1000, new ActionListener()
{
  public void actionPerformed(ActionEvent e)
  {
    displayTimerActionPerformed(e);
  }
});
```

Note we set the timer object's **delay** property to 1000 milliseconds, or 1 second. Hence, every second, the timer object's **ActionPerformed** method is invoked. Each time this happens, we need to:

> Determine the current time.
> Subtract the current time from the start time to obtain the total time.
> Subtract the stopped time from the total time to get the running time.
> Display the total and running times in the appropriate text field controls.

We will use a general method (**HMS**) to display tie values in the desired **hours:minutes:seconds** format:

```
private String HMS(long tms)
{
  int h;
  int m;
  int s;
  double t;
  t = tms / 1000.0;
  // Break time down into hours, minutes, and seconds
  h = (int) (t / 3600);
  m = (int) ((t - h * 3600) / 60);
  s = (int) (t - h * 3600 - m * 60);
  // Format time as string
  return(new DecimalFormat("00").format(h) + ":" + new
DecimalFormat("00").format(m) + ":" + new
DecimalFormat("00").format(s));
}
```

In this method, the time in milliseconds (**tms**) is input as an argument. Integer representations of the hours (**h**), minutes (**m**) and seconds (**s**) are computed. The returned value is a **String** type in the desired **hs:ms:ss** format for display. Work through this method with an example to convince yourself it works. Type the method into the code window. To use the **DecimalFormat** method, this code requires addition of this import statement:

```
import java.text.*;
```

The HMS method is used in the timer object's **ActionPerformed** method, which has the steps outlined earlier. The **displayTimerActionPerformed** code is:

```
private void displayTimerActionPerformed(ActionEvent e)
{
  long currentTime;
  // Determine running and total times
  currentTime = System.currentTimeMillis();
  // Display times
  runningTimeTextField.setText(HMS(currentTime - startTime
- stoppedTime));
  totalTimeTextField.setText(HMS(currentTime -
startTime));
}
```

You should be able to see how this method computes the needed times and displays them using the **HMS** method. Add the method to the stopwatch project code window.

We're almost ready to see times, we just need to get the timer started. Add the single shaded line to the **startStopButtonActionPerformed** method to do the job:

```
private void startStopButtonActionPerformed(ActionEvent e)
{
  // initial to running state
  startTime = System.currentTimeMillis();
  stoppedTime = 0;
  startStopButton.setText("Stop");
  exitButton.setEnabled(false);
  displayTimer.start();
}
```

Code Design – Running to Stopped State

Save and run the project. Click the **Start** button. The times should now be updating every second:

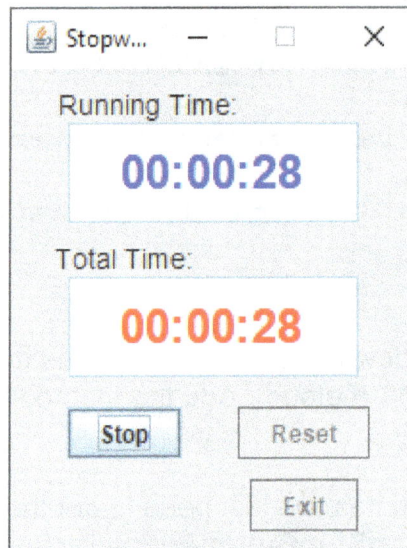

The project is now in the 'running' state. Only one option exists at this point – click **Stop** to put the stopwatch in 'stopped' state.

When a user clicks **Stop** (the **startStopButton** button), the following things need to happen:

> ➢ Determine the stop time (not to be confused with the stopped time).
> ➢ Stop the timer to stop updating the displays.
> ➢ Change the **text** property of **startStopButton** to **Restart**
> ➢ Enable **resetButton**.
> ➢ Enable **exitButton**.

We define another class level variable to store the stop time:

```
long stopTime;
```

Add this statement with the other declarations.

The button now marked **Stop** is the **startStopButton** button. We have already added some code to its **ActionPerformed** method (when the button is used to start the stopwatch). It is common practice to have one button control have multiple purposes - we just need to have some way to distinguish which "mode" the button is in when it is clicked. In this project, we use the **text** property of the button. If the **text** property is **Start**, we switch to 'running' mode. If the **text** property is **Stop**, we switch to 'stopped' mode. The code that does this is (modifications to the current **ActionPerformed** method code are shaded):

```java
private void startStopButtonActionPerformed(ActionEvent e)
{
  if (startStopButton.getText().equals("Start"))
  {
    // initial to running state
    startTime = System.currentTimeMillis();
    stoppedTime = 0;
    startStopButton.setText("Stop");
    exitButton.setEnabled(false);
    displayTimer.start();
  }
  else if (startStopButton.getText().equals("Stop"))
  {
    // running to stopped state
    stopTime = System.currentTimeMillis();
    startStopButton.setText("Restart");
    resetButton.setEnabled(true);
    exitButton.setEnabled(true);
    displayTimer.stop();
  }
}
```

Make the noted modifications to the code.

Code Design – Stopped State

Save and run the project. Click the **Start** button. Let the stopwatch run for a while, then click **Stop**. The stopwatch will go to 'stopped' state:

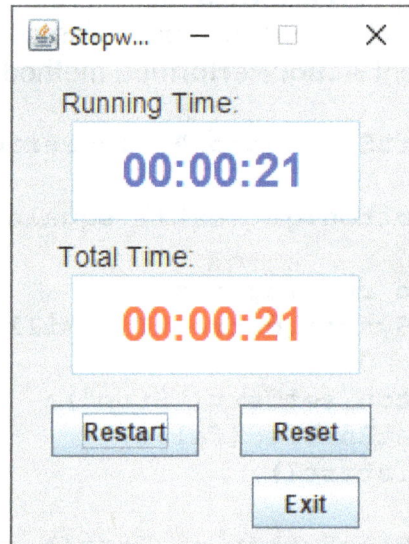

In this state, there are three possible options – clicking **Restart** (**startStopButton**), clicking **Reset** (**resetButton**) or clicking **Exit** (**exitButton**). We'll address each possibility in reverse order.

If **Exit** is clicked, the project ends. We have already coded the **exitButtonActionPerformed** method.

If **Reset** is clicked, we want to return the stopwatch to its 'initial' state. The steps to do this are:

> ➢ Reset the displayed times to **00:00:00**
> ➢ Change the **text** property of **startStopButton** to **Start**
> ➢ Disable **resetButton**.

The **resetButtonActionPerformed** method is thus:

```
private void resetButtonActionPerformed(ActionEvent e)
{
  // return to initial state
  runningTimeTextField.setText("00:00:00");
  totalTimeTextField.setText("00:00:00");
  startStopButton.setText("Start");
  resetButton.setEnabled(false);
}
```

If **Restart** is clicked while in 'stopped' state, the **startStopButtonActionPerformed** method is processed. This is another use for the **startStopButton** button. We need to modify the code already in that method to handle such an event

When a user clicks **Restart** (the **startStopButton** button), the following things need to happen:

> ➢ Update (increment) the stopped time – add in the difference between the current time and the **stopTime**, the time when the **Stop** button was clicked.
> ➢ Start the timer.
> ➢ Change the **text** property of **startStopButton** to **Stop**
> ➢ Disable **resetButton**.
> ➢ Disable **exitButton**.

The modified **startStopButtonActionPerformed** method that implements these new steps (changes are shaded) is:

```java
private void startStopButtonActionPerformed(ActionEvent e)
{
    if (startStopButton.getText().equals("Start"))
    {
      // initial to running state
      startTime = System.currentTimeMillis();
      stoppedTime = 0;
      startStopButton.setText("Stop");
      exitButton.setEnabled(false);
      displayTimer.start();
    }
    else if (startStopButton.getText().equals("Stop"))
    {
      // running to stopped state
      stopTime = System.currentTimeMillis();
      startStopButton.setText("Restart");
      resetButton.setEnabled(true);
      exitButton.setEnabled(true);
      displayTimer.stop();
    }
    else if (startStopButton.getText().equals("Restart"))
    {
      // stopped to running state
      stoppedTime += System.currentTimeMillis() -
stopTime;
      startStopButton.setText("Stop");
      resetButton.setEnabled(false);
      exitButton.setEnabled(false);
      displayTimer.start();
    }
  }
```

Notice how **stoppedTime** is updated. Implement the noted changes.

Save and run the project. At some point, click **Stop**. When I did, the form appears as:

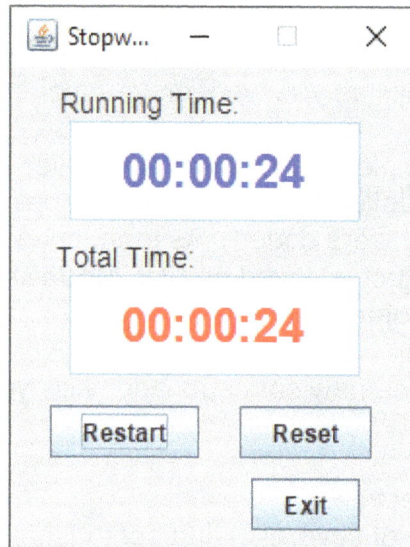

Running Time:

00:00:24

Total Time:

00:00:24

Restart   Reset

Exit

After a wait, click **Restart**. When I do this, I get:

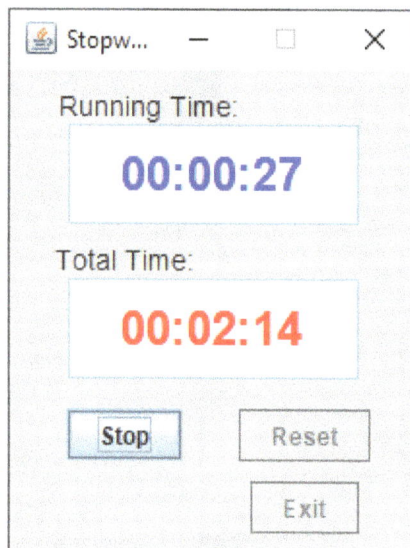

Running Time:

00:00:27

Total Time:

00:02:14

Stop   Reset

Exit

The stopwatch is running again, but the two displayed times are different. The **Total Time** is the amount of time elapsed since we first started the stopwatch. The **Running Time** is the total time less time when the stopwatch is in stopped mode. Based on these values, this stopwatch has spent 1:47 waiting around. Click **Stop** – make sure the **Reset** option works.

Dual-Mode Stopwatch Project Review

The **Dual-Mode Stopwatch** project is now complete. Save and run the project and make sure it works as promised. Check that you can move from state to state correctly. Use it to time tasks as you work on your computer.

If there are errors in your implementation, go back over the steps of frame and code design. Go over the developed code – make sure you understand how different parts of the project were coded. As mentioned in the beginning of this chapter, the completed project is saved as **DualModeStopwatch** in the **\HomeJava\HomeJava Projects** folder.

While completing this project, new concepts and skills you should have gained include:

> ➢ Proper steps in project design.
> ➢ Capabilities and use of several Swing controls.
> ➢ Use of the timer object.
> ➢ How to develop and use general methods.

Dual-Mode Stopwatch Project Enhancements

There are always things you can do to improve a project. At the end of each chapter, we will give you some ideas for the current project. For the dual-mode stopwatch, some possibilities are:

> ➤ Whenever you stop the stopwatch, save that time. Then, when you ultimately stop the watch, provide a review mode. In review, you can see how much time was spent running the stopwatch and how much time was spent stopped.
> ➤ Provide an immediate feedback on each segment of elapsed time – a lap timing feature.

Dual-Mode Stopwatch Project
Java Code Listing

```java
/*
 * DualModeStopwatch.java
 */
package dualmodestopwatch;
import javax.swing.*;
import java.awt.*;
import java.awt.event.*;
import java.text.*;


public class DualModeStopwatch extends JFrame
{

  JLabel runningTimeLabel = new JLabel();
  JTextField runningTimeTextField = new JTextField();
  JLabel totalTimeLabel = new JLabel();
  JTextField totalTimeTextField = new JTextField();
  JButton startStopButton = new JButton();
  JButton resetButton = new JButton();
  JButton exitButton = new JButton();

  Timer displayTimer;

  long startTime;
  long stoppedTime;
  long stopTime;

  public static void main(String args[])
  {
    // create frame
    new DualModeStopwatch().setVisible(true);
  }

  public DualModeStopwatch()
  {
    // frame constructor
    setTitle("Stopwatch");
    setResizable(false);
    addWindowListener(new WindowAdapter()
    {
      public void windowClosing(WindowEvent evt)
      {
```

```
        exitForm(evt);
    }
});
getContentPane().setLayout(new GridBagLayout());
GridBagConstraints gridConstraints;

runningTimeLabel.setText("Running Time:");
runningTimeLabel.setFont(new Font("Arial", Font.PLAIN,
14));
gridConstraints = new GridBagConstraints();
gridConstraints.gridx = 0;
gridConstraints.gridy = 0;
gridConstraints.insets = new Insets(10, 25, 0, 0);
getContentPane().add(runningTimeLabel, gridConstraints);

runningTimeTextField.setPreferredSize(new Dimension(150,
50));
runningTimeTextField.setEditable(false);
runningTimeTextField.setBackground(Color.WHITE);
runningTimeTextField.setForeground(Color.BLUE);
runningTimeTextField.setText("00:00:00");

runningTimeTextField.setHorizontalAlignment(SwingConstants.CE
NTER);
runningTimeTextField.setFont(new Font("Arial", Font.BOLD,
24));
gridConstraints = new GridBagConstraints();
gridConstraints.gridx = 0;
gridConstraints.gridy = 1;
gridConstraints.gridwidth = 2;
gridConstraints.insets = new Insets(0, 10, 0, 10);
getContentPane().add(runningTimeTextField,
gridConstraints);

totalTimeLabel.setText("Total Time:");
totalTimeLabel.setFont(new Font("Arial", Font.PLAIN,
14));
gridConstraints = new GridBagConstraints();
gridConstraints.gridx = 0;
gridConstraints.gridy = 2;
gridConstraints.insets = new Insets(10, 10, 0, 10);
getContentPane().add(totalTimeLabel, gridConstraints);

totalTimeTextField.setPreferredSize(new Dimension(150,
50));
totalTimeTextField.setEditable(false);
totalTimeTextField.setBackground(Color.WHITE);
```

```
    totalTimeTextField.setForeground(Color.RED);
    totalTimeTextField.setText("00:00:00");

totalTimeTextField.setHorizontalAlignment(SwingConstants.CENT
ER);
    totalTimeTextField.setFont(new Font("Arial", Font.BOLD,
24));
    gridConstraints = new GridBagConstraints();
    gridConstraints.gridx = 0;
    gridConstraints.gridy = 3;
    gridConstraints.gridwidth = 2;
    gridConstraints.insets = new Insets(0, 10, 15, 10);
    getContentPane().add(totalTimeTextField,
gridConstraints);

    startStopButton.setText("Start");
    gridConstraints = new GridBagConstraints();
    gridConstraints.gridx = 0;
    gridConstraints.gridy = 4;
    getContentPane().add(startStopButton, gridConstraints);
    startStopButton.addActionListener(new ActionListener()
    {
      public void actionPerformed(ActionEvent e)
      {
        startStopButtonActionPerformed(e);
      }
    });

    resetButton.setText("Reset");
    resetButton.setEnabled(false);
    gridConstraints = new GridBagConstraints();
    gridConstraints.gridx = 1;
    gridConstraints.gridy = 4;
    gridConstraints.insets = new Insets(0, 0, 0, 25);
    getContentPane().add(resetButton, gridConstraints);
    resetButton.addActionListener(new ActionListener()
    {
      public void actionPerformed(ActionEvent e)
      {
        resetButtonActionPerformed(e);
      }
    });

    exitButton.setText("Exit");
    gridConstraints = new GridBagConstraints();
    gridConstraints.gridx = 1;
    gridConstraints.gridy = 5;
```

```java
    gridConstraints.insets = new Insets(10, 0, 10, 25);
    getContentPane().add(exitButton, gridConstraints);
    exitButton.addActionListener(new ActionListener()
    {
      public void actionPerformed(ActionEvent e)
      {
        exitButtonActionPerformed(e);
      }
    });

    displayTimer = new Timer(1000, new ActionListener()
    {
      public void actionPerformed(ActionEvent e)
      {
        displayTimerActionPerformed(e);
      }
    });

    pack();
    Dimension screenSize =
Toolkit.getDefaultToolkit().getScreenSize();
    setBounds((int) (0.5 * (screenSize.width - getWidth())),
(int) (0.5 * (screenSize.height - getHeight())), getWidth(),
getHeight());
  }

  private void exitForm(WindowEvent evt)
  {
    System.exit(0);
  }

  private void startStopButtonActionPerformed(ActionEvent e)
  {
    if (startStopButton.getText().equals("Start"))
    {
      // initial to running state
      startTime = System.currentTimeMillis();
      stoppedTime = 0;
      startStopButton.setText("Stop");
      exitButton.setEnabled(false);
      displayTimer.start();
    }
    else if (startStopButton.getText().equals("Stop"))
    {
      // running to stopped state
      stopTime = System.currentTimeMillis();
      startStopButton.setText("Restart");
```

```
      resetButton.setEnabled(true);
      exitButton.setEnabled(true);
      displayTimer.stop();
    }
    else if (startStopButton.getText().equals("Restart"))
    {
      // stopped to running state
      stoppedTime += System.currentTimeMillis() - stopTime;
      startStopButton.setText("Stop");
      resetButton.setEnabled(false);
      exitButton.setEnabled(false);
      displayTimer.start();
    }
  }

  private void resetButtonActionPerformed(ActionEvent e)
  {
    // return to initial state
    runningTimeTextField.setText("00:00:00");
    totalTimeTextField.setText("00:00:00");
    startStopButton.setText("Start");
    resetButton.setEnabled(false);
  }

  private void exitButtonActionPerformed(ActionEvent e)
  {
    System.exit(0);
  }

  private void displayTimerActionPerformed(ActionEvent e)
  {
    long currentTime;
    // Determine running and total times
    currentTime = System.currentTimeMillis();
    // Display times
    runningTimeTextField.setText(HMS(currentTime - startTime
- stoppedTime));
    totalTimeTextField.setText(HMS(currentTime - startTime));
  }

  private String HMS(long tms)
  {
    int h;
    int m;
    int s;
    double t;
    t = tms / 1000.0;
```

```java
    // Break time down into hours, minutes, and seconds
    h = (int) (t / 3600);
    m = (int) ((t - h * 3600) / 60);
    s = (int) (t - h * 3600 - m * 60);
    // Format time as string
    return(new DecimalFormat("00").format(h) + ":" + new
DecimalFormat("00").format(m) + ":" + new
DecimalFormat("00").format(s));
  }


}
```

3

Consumer Loan Assistant Project

Review and Preview

Ever wonder just how much those credit card accounts are costing you? This project will help you get a handle on consumer debt. The **Consumer Loan Assistant Project** we build computes payments and loan terms given balance and interest information. We look at focus traversal among controls, how to do input validation, and the message box for user feedback.

Consumer Loan Assistant
Project Preview

In this chapter, we will build a **consumer loan assistant**. You input a loan balance and yearly interest rate. You then have two options: (1) enter the desired number of payments and the loan assistant computes the monthly payment, or (2) enter the desired monthly payment and the loan assistant determines the number of payments you will make. An analysis of your loan, including total of payments and interest paid is also provided.

The finished project is saved as **LoanAssistant in** the **\HomeJava\HomeJava Projects** project group. Start NetBeans (or your IDE). Open the specified project group. Make **LoanAssistant** the selected project. Run the project. You will see:

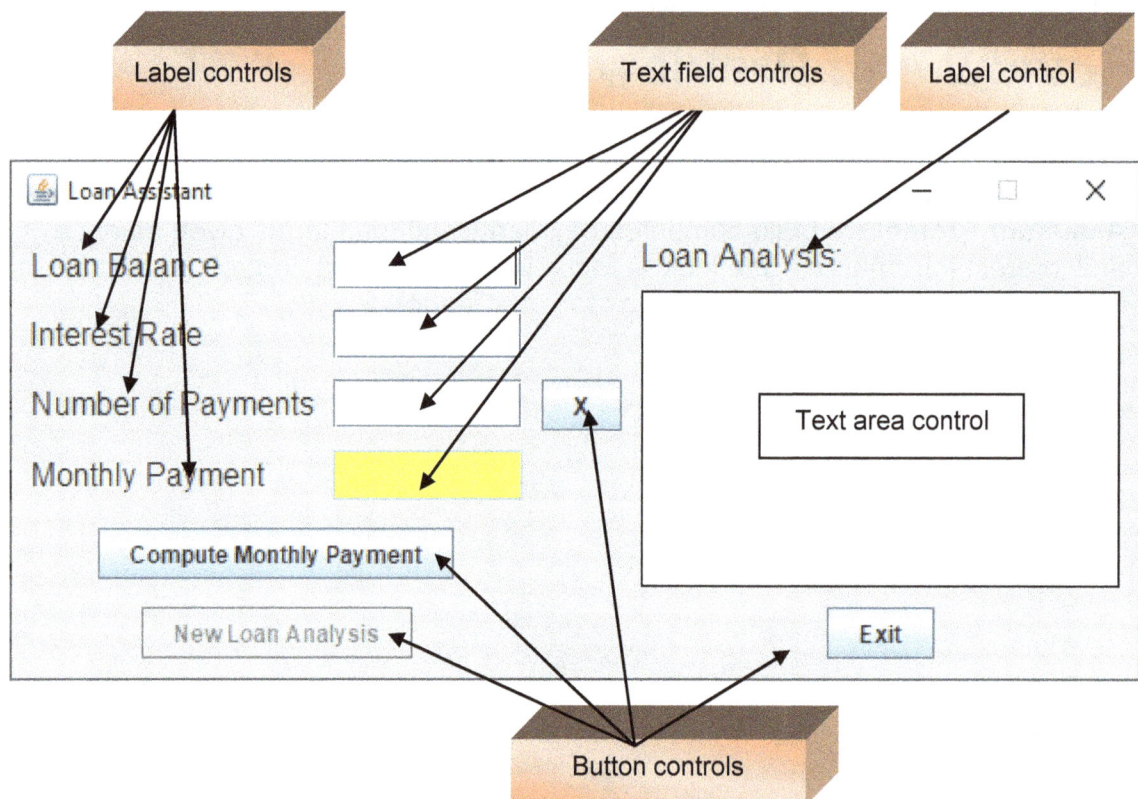

All label controls are used for title information. Two button controls are used to compute results and to start a new analysis. Two small button controls (marked with X; only one is seen at a time) control whether you compute the number of payments or the payment amount. One button exits the project. Four text field controls are used for inputs and a large text area is used to present the loan analysis results.

The loan assistant appears as:

In this initial configuration, you enter a **Loan Balance**, an **Interest Rate** (annual rate as a percentage) and a **Number of Payments** value. Click **Compute Monthly Payment**. The payment will appear in the 'yellow' text field and a complete loan analysis will appear in the large text field. Here are some numbers I tried:

So, if I borrow $10,000 at 5.5% interest, I will pay $301.96 for three years (36 months). More specific details on exact payment amounts, including total interest paid, is shown under **Loan Analysis**.

At this point, you can click **New Loan Analysis** to try some new values:

Loan Assistant	— □ ✕
Loan Balance — 10000	Loan Analysis:
Interest Rate — 5.5	
Number of Payments — 36 [X]	
Monthly Payment	
[Compute Monthly Payment]	
[New Loan Analysis]	[Exit]

Note the **Loan Balance**, **Interest Rate**, and **Number of Payments** entries remain. Only the **Monthly Payment** and the **Loan Analysis** have been cleared. This lets you try different values with minimal typing of new entries. Change any entry you like to see different results – or even change them all. Try as many combinations as you like.

At some point, clear the text fields and click the button with an **X** next to the **Number of Payments** text field. You will see:

```
Loan Assistant                                    —   □   X

Loan Balance      [          ]        Loan Analysis:

Interest Rate     [          ]       ┌──────────────────┐
                                     │                  │
Number of Payments [▓▓▓▓▓▓▓]         │                  │
                                     │                  │
Monthly Payment   [          ] [ X ] │                  │
                                     │                  │
   [ Compute Number of Payments ]    │                  │
                                     └──────────────────┘
      [ New Loan Analysis ]                  [ Exit ]
```

Notice the **Number of Payments** box is now yellow. The button with an **X** has moved to the **Monthly Payment** text field. In this configuration, you enter a **Loan Balance**, an **Interest Rate** and a **Monthly Payment**. The loan assistant will determine how many payments you need to pay off the loan. Here are some numbers I tried:

```
Loan Assistant                                    —   □   X

Loan Balance      [     20000]        Loan Analysis:

Interest Rate     [       6.5]       ┌──────────────────────────┐
                                     │ Loan Balance: $20000.00  │
Number of Payments [▓▓▓▓▓ 59]        │ Interest Rate: 6.50%     │
                                     │                          │
Monthly Payment   [       400] [ X ] │ 58 Payments of $400.00   │
                                     │ Final Payment of: $186.90│
   [ Compute Number of Payments ]    │ Total Payments: $23386.90│
                                     │ Interest Paid $3386.90   │
      [ New Loan Analysis ]          └──────────────────────────┘
                                             [ Exit ]
```

It will take 59 payments (the last one is smaller) to pay off this particular loan. Again, you can click **New Loan Analysis** to try other values and see the results.

That's all you do with the loan assistant project – there's a lot going on behind the scenes though. The loan assistant has two modes of operation. It can compute the monthly payment, given the balance, interest and number of payments. Or, it can compute the number of payments, given the balance, interest, and payment. The text field representing the computed value is yellow. The button marked **X** is used to switch from one mode to the next. To exit the project, click the **Exit** button.

You will now build this project in several stages. We first address **frame design**. We discuss the controls used to build the form, establish initial properties, and discuss switching from one mode to the next. And, we address **code design** in detail. We cover the mathematics behind the financial computations. We also discuss validation of the input values, making sure the user only types valid entries.

Loan Assistant Frame Design

We begin building the **Loan Assistant Project.** Let's build the frame. Start a new project in your Java project group – name it **LoanAssistant**. Delete default code in file named **LoanAssistant.java**. Once started, we suggest you immediately save the project with the name you chose. This sets up the folder and file structure needed for your project. Build the basic frame with these properties:

LoanAssistant Frame:
title	Loan Assistant
resizable	false

The code is:

```java
/*
 * LoanAssistant.java
 */
package loanassistant;
import javax.swing.*;
import java.awt.*;
import java.awt.event.*;

public class LoanAssistant extends JFrame
{
  public static void main(String args[])
  {
    // create frame
    new LoanAssistant().setVisible(true);
  }

  public LoanAssistant()
  {
    // frame constructor
    setTitle("Loan Assistant");
    setResizable(false);
    addWindowListener(new WindowAdapter()
    {
      public void windowClosing(WindowEvent evt)
      {
        exitForm(evt);
      }
    });
    getContentPane().setLayout(new GridBagLayout());
    GridBagConstraints gridConstraints;

    pack();
```

```
      Dimension screenSize =
Toolkit.getDefaultToolkit().getScreenSize();
    setBounds((int) (0.5 * (screenSize.width -
getWidth())), (int) (0.5 * (screenSize.height -
getHeight())), getWidth(), getHeight());
  }

  private void exitForm(WindowEvent evt)
  {
    System.exit(0);
  }
}
```

This code builds the frame, sets up the layout manager and includes code to exit the application. Run the code to make sure the frame (at least, what there is of it at this point) appears and is centered on the screen:

Let's populate our frame with other controls. All code for creating the frame and placing controls (except declarations) goes in the **LoanAssistant** constructor.

All controls go directly on the frame. The **GridBagLayout** for the frame is:

	gridx = 0	gridx = 1	gridx = 2	gridx = 3
gridy = 0	loanBalanceLabel	loanBalanceTextField		analysisLabel
gridy = 1	interestRateLabel	interestRateTextField		analysisTextArea
gridy =2	monthsLabel	monthsTextField	monthsButton	analysisTextArea
gridy = 3	paymentLabel	paymentTextField	paymentButton	analysisTextArea
gridy = 4	computeButton	computeButton		
gridy = 5	newLoanButton	newLoanButton		exitButton

The label controls (**loanBalanceLabel**, **interestRateLabel**, **monthsLabel**, **paymentLabel**, **analysisLabel**) are used for title information. Four text fields (**loanBalanceTextField**, **interestRateTextField**, **monthsTextField**, **paymentTextField**) are for user input. A text area (**analysisTextArea**) will display the loan analysis. Three buttons (**computeButton**, **newLoanButton** and **exitButton**) are used to compute loan results, redo analysis, and/or exit the project. Two other button controls (**monthsButton** and **paymentButton**) are used to switch from one calculation mode to the next. We'll add a few controls at a time. Let's add the four label/text field pairs.

The control properties are:

balanceLabel:

text	Loan Balance
font	Arial, Plain, Size 16
gridx	0
gridy	0
anchor	WEST
insets	10, 10, 0, 0

balanceTextField:

size	100, 25
font	Arial, Plain, Size 16
gridx	1
gridy	0
insets	10, 10, 0, 10

interestLabel:

text	Interest Rate
font	Arial, Plain, Size 16
gridx	0
gridy	1
anchor	WEST
insets	10, 10, 0, 0

interestTextField:

size	100, 25
font	Arial, Plain, Size 16
gridx	1
gridy	1
insets	10, 10, 0, 10

monthsLabel:

text	Number of Payments
font	Arial, Plain, Size 16
gridx	0
gridy	2
anchor	WEST
insets	10, 10, 0, 0

monthsTextField:

size	100, 25
font	Arial, Plain, Size 16
gridx	1
gridy	2
insets	10, 10, 0, 10

paymentLabel:

text	Monthly Payent
font	Arial, Plain, Size 16
gridx	0
gridy	3
anchor	WEST
insets	10, 10, 0, 0

paymentTextField:

size	100, 25
font	Arial, Plain, Size 16
gridx	1
gridy	3
insets	10, 10, 0, 10

Declare these controls using:

```
JLabel balanceLabel = new JLabel();
JTextField balanceTextField = new JTextField();
JLabel interestLabel = new JLabel();
JTextField interestTextField = new JTextField();
JLabel monthsLabel = new JLabel();
JTextField monthsTextField = new JTextField();
JLabel paymentLabel = new JLabel();
JTextField paymentTextField = new JTextField();
```

Note the labels and text fields all use the same font. Let's create a Font object to use in each:

```
Font myFont = new Font("Arial", Font.PLAIN, 16);
```

Now, the controls are added to the frame using (recall code goes in frame constructor):

```
balanceLabel.setText("Loan Balance");
balanceLabel.setFont(myFont);
gridConstraints = new GridBagConstraints();
gridConstraints.gridx = 0;
gridConstraints.gridy = 0;
gridConstraints.anchor = GridBagConstraints.WEST;
gridConstraints.insets = new Insets(10, 10, 0, 0);
getContentPane().add(balanceLabel, gridConstraints);

balanceTextField.setPreferredSize(new Dimension(100, 25));
balanceTextField.setHorizontalAlignment(SwingConstants.RIG
HT);
balanceTextField.setFont(myFont);
gridConstraints = new GridBagConstraints();
gridConstraints.gridx = 1;
gridConstraints.gridy = 0;
gridConstraints.insets = new Insets(10, 10, 0, 10);
getContentPane().add(balanceTextField, gridConstraints);

interestLabel.setText("Interest Rate");
interestLabel.setFont(myFont);
gridConstraints = new GridBagConstraints();
gridConstraints.gridx = 0;
gridConstraints.gridy = 1;
gridConstraints.anchor = GridBagConstraints.WEST;
gridConstraints.insets = new Insets(10, 10, 0, 0);
getContentPane().add(interestLabel, gridConstraints);
```

```
interestTextField.setPreferredSize(new Dimension(100,
25));
interestTextField.setHorizontalAlignment(SwingConstants.RI
GHT);
interestTextField.setFont(myFont);
gridConstraints = new GridBagConstraints();
gridConstraints.gridx = 1;
gridConstraints.gridy = 1;
gridConstraints.insets = new Insets(10, 10, 0, 10);
getContentPane().add(interestTextField, gridConstraints);

monthsLabel.setText("Number of Payments");
monthsLabel.setFont(myFont);
gridConstraints = new GridBagConstraints();
gridConstraints.gridx = 0;
gridConstraints.gridy = 2;
gridConstraints.anchor = GridBagConstraints.WEST;
gridConstraints.insets = new Insets(10, 10, 0, 0);
getContentPane().add(monthsLabel, gridConstraints);

monthsTextField.setPreferredSize(new Dimension(100, 25));
monthsTextField.setHorizontalAlignment(SwingConstants.RIGH
T);
monthsTextField.setFont(myFont);
gridConstraints = new GridBagConstraints();
gridConstraints.gridx = 1;
gridConstraints.gridy = 2;
gridConstraints.insets = new Insets(10, 10, 0, 10);
getContentPane().add(monthsTextField, gridConstraints);

paymentLabel.setText("Monthly Payment");
paymentLabel.setFont(myFont);
gridConstraints = new GridBagConstraints();
gridConstraints.gridx = 0;
gridConstraints.gridy = 3;
gridConstraints.anchor = GridBagConstraints.WEST;
gridConstraints.insets = new Insets(10, 10, 0, 0);
getContentPane().add(paymentLabel, gridConstraints);
```

```
paymentTextField.setPreferredSize(new Dimension(100, 25));
paymentTextField.setHorizontalAlignment(SwingConstants.RIG
HT);
paymentTextField.setFont(myFont);
gridConstraints = new GridBagConstraints();
gridConstraints.gridx = 1;
gridConstraints.gridy = 3;
gridConstraints.insets = new Insets(10, 10, 0, 10);
getContentPane().add(paymentTextField, gridConstraints);
```

Save, run the project. You will see the added controls:

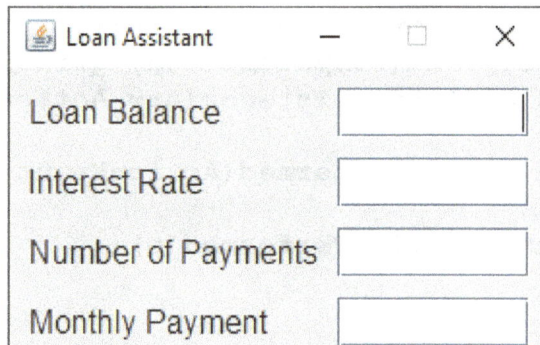

Let's add the two button controls that go under these controls. The properties are:

computeButton:
text	Compute Monthly Payments
gridx	0
gridy	4
gridwidth	2
insets	10, 0, 0, 0

newLoanButton:
text	New Loan Analysis
enabled	false
gridx	0
gridy	5
gridwidth	2
insets	10, 0, 10, 0

Declare the controls using:

```
JButton computeButton = new JButton();
JButton newLoanButton = new JButton();
```

Add the buttons to the frame using:

```
computeButton.setText("Compute Monthly Payment");
gridConstraints = new GridBagConstraints();
gridConstraints.gridx = 0;
gridConstraints.gridy = 4;
gridConstraints.gridwidth = 2;
gridConstraints.insets = new Insets(10, 0, 0, 0);
getContentPane().add(computeButton, gridConstraints);
computeButton.addActionListener(new ActionListener()
{
  public void actionPerformed(ActionEvent e)
  {
    computeButtonActionPerformed(e);
  }
});

newLoanButton.setText("New Loan Analysis");
newLoanButton.setEnabled(false);
gridConstraints = new GridBagConstraints();
gridConstraints.gridx = 0;
gridConstraints.gridy = 5;
gridConstraints.gridwidth = 2;
gridConstraints.insets = new Insets(10, 0, 10, 0);
getContentPane().add(newLoanButton, gridConstraints);
newLoanButton.addActionListener(new ActionListener()
{
  public void actionPerformed(ActionEvent e)
  {
    newLoanButtonActionPerformed(e);
  }
});
```

This code also adds listeners for each button. Add these empty methods:

```
private void computeButtonActionPerformed(ActionEvent e)
{
}

private void newLoanButtonActionPerformed(ActionEvent e)
{
}
```

Run to see the buttons (the **New Loan Analysis** button is disabled):

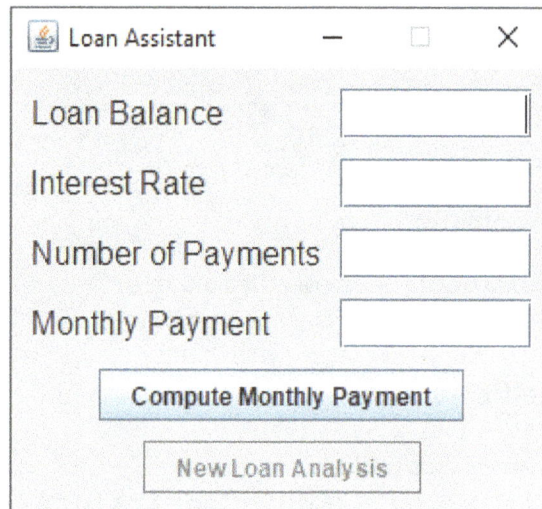

Now we add the two small button controls that go next to two of the text fields. The properties are:

> **monthsButton**:
>
> | | |
> |---|---|
> | text | X |
> | gridx | 2 |
> | gridy | 2 |
> | insets | 10, 0, 0, 0 |
>
> **paymentButton**:
>
> | | |
> |---|---|
> | text | X |
> | enabled | false |
> | gridx | 0 |
> | gridy | 5 |
> | gridwidth | 2 |
> | insets | 10, 0, 10, 0 |

Declare the controls using:

```
JButton monthsButton = new JButton();
JButton paymentButton = new JButton();
```

Add the buttons to the frame using:

```
monthsButton.setText("X");
gridConstraints = new GridBagConstraints();
gridConstraints.gridx = 2;
gridConstraints.gridy = 2;
gridConstraints.insets = new Insets(10, 0, 0, 0);
getContentPane().add(monthsButton, gridConstraints);
monthsButton.addActionListener(new ActionListener()
{
  public void actionPerformed(ActionEvent e)
  {
    monthsButtonActionPerformed(e);
  }
});
```

```
paymentButton.setText("X");
gridConstraints = new GridBagConstraints();
gridConstraints.gridx = 2;
gridConstraints.gridy = 3;
gridConstraints.insets = new Insets(10, 0, 0, 0);
getContentPane().add(paymentButton, gridConstraints);
paymentButton.addActionListener(new ActionListener()
{
  public void actionPerformed(ActionEvent e)
  {
    paymentButtonActionPerformed(e);
  }
});
```

This code also adds listeners for each button. Add these empty methods:

```
private void monthsButtonActionPerformed(ActionEvent e)
{
}

private void paymentButtonActionPerformed(ActionEvent e)
{
}
```

Run to see the buttons:

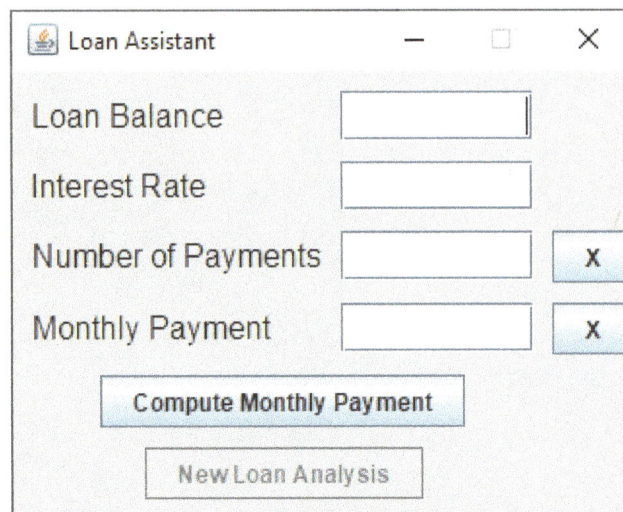

Both X buttons appear now. When we write code, only one of the buttons will display at a time.

Let's finish the frame by adding the three remaining controls (label, text field and button). The properties are:

analysisLabel:

text	Loan Analysis:
font	Arial, Plain, Size 16
gridx	3
gridy	0
anchor	WEST
insets	0, 10, 0, 0

analysisTextArea:

size	250, 150
border	Black line
font	Courier New, Plain, Size 14
editable	false
background	White
gridx	3
gridy	1
gridheight	4
insets	0, 10, 0, 10

exitButton:

text	Exit
gridx	3
gridy	5

Declare the controls using:

```
JLabel analysisLabel = new JLabel();
JTextArea analysisTextArea = new JTextArea();
JButton exitButton = new JButton();
```

Add the controls to the frame using:

```
analysisLabel.setText("Loan Analysis:");
analysisLabel.setFont(myFont);
gridConstraints = new GridBagConstraints();
gridConstraints.gridx = 3;
gridConstraints.gridy = 0;
gridConstraints.anchor = GridBagConstraints.WEST;
gridConstraints.insets = new Insets(0, 10, 0, 0);
getContentPane().add(analysisLabel, gridConstraints);

analysisTextArea.setPreferredSize(new Dimension(250,
150));
analysisTextArea.setBorder(BorderFactory.createLineBorder(
Color.BLACK));
analysisTextArea.setFont(new Font("Courier New",
Font.PLAIN, 14));
analysisTextArea.setEditable(false);
analysisTextArea.setBackground(Color.WHITE);
gridConstraints = new GridBagConstraints();
gridConstraints.gridx = 3;
gridConstraints.gridy = 1;
gridConstraints.gridheight = 4;
gridConstraints.insets = new Insets(0, 10, 0, 10);
getContentPane().add(analysisTextArea, gridConstraints);

exitButton.setText("Exit");
gridConstraints = new GridBagConstraints();
gridConstraints.gridx = 3;
gridConstraints.gridy = 5;
getContentPane().add(exitButton, gridConstraints);
exitButton.addActionListener(new ActionListener()
{
  public void actionPerformed(ActionEvent e)
  {
    exitButtonActionPerformed(e);
  }
});
```

This code also adds listeners for each button. Add these empty methods:

```
private void exitButtonActionPerformed(ActionEvent e)
{
}
```

Run to see the final frame layout:

This completes the initial form. We will begin writing code for the application. We will write the code in several steps. As a first step, we write the code that switches the application between its two possible modes of operation: (1) compute monthly payment, or (2) compute number of payments.

Code Design – Switching Modes

There are two modes the loan assistant can operate in. In the first mode, you enter a loan balance, an interest rate and a number of payments. The assistant then computes the monthly payment. In the second mode, you enter a loan balance, an interest rate and a monthly payment. The assistant computes the number of payments. The buttons with **X** control which mode the assistant operates in. Click the **X** (**paymentButton**) next to the payment text field and you switch to the first mode (compute monthly payment). Click the **X** (**monthsButton**) next to the number of payments text field and you switch to the second mode (compute number of payments). Let's look at the steps for each operation.

When the user clicks the **X** next to the monthly payment text field (**paymentButton** button), we want to make **paymentTextField** available for user input and **monthsTextField** available for output. The steps are taken:

> ➢ Make **paymentButton** disappear.
> ➢ Make **monthsButton** appear.
> ➢ Set **enabled** property of **monthsTextField** to **false**.
> ➢ Set **monthsTextField** background to **White**.
> ➢ Blank out the **paymentTextField** text field.
> ➢ Set **enabled** property of **paymentTextField** to **true**.
> ➢ Set **paymentTextField** background to **Light Yellow**.
> ➢ Set **text** property of **computeButton** to **Compute Monthly Payment**.

When you click the **X** next to the number of payments text field (**monthsButton** button), we essentially 'reverse' the steps just listed:

> ➢ Make **paymentButton** appear.
> ➢ Make **monthsButton** disappear.
> ➢ Set **enabled** property of **monthsTextField** to **true**.
> ➢ Set **monthsTextField** background to **Light Yellow**.
> ➢ Blank out the **monthsTextField** text field.
> ➢ Set **enabled** property of **paymentTextField** to **false**.
> ➢ Set **paymentTextField** background to **White**.
> ➢ Set **text** property of **computeButton** to **Compute Number of Payments**.

Define a class level object to define a 'Light Yellow' color and a variable to keep track of what mode we are working in:

```
Color lightYellow = new Color(255, 255, 128);
boolean computePayment;
```

If **computePayment** is **true**, we are computing the payment, otherwise we are computing the number of payments.

The code for the **paymentButtonActionPerformed** method that implements the listed steps is then:

```
private void paymentButtonActionPerformed(ActionEvent e)
{
  // will compute payment
  computePayment = true;
  paymentButton.setVisible(false);
  monthsButton.setVisible(true);
  monthsTextField.setEditable(true);
  monthsTextField.setBackground(Color.WHITE);
  paymentTextField.setText("");
  paymentTextField.setEditable(false);
  paymentTextField.setBackground(lightYellow);
  computeButton.setText("Compute Monthly Payment");
}
```

The code for the **monthsButton Click** is:

```
private void monthsButtonActionPerformed(ActionEvent e)
{
  // will compute months
  computePayment = false;
  paymentButton.setVisible(true);
  monthsButton.setVisible(false);
  monthsTextField.setText("");
  monthsTextField.setEditable(false);
  monthsTextField.setBackground(lightYellow);
  paymentTextField.setEditable(true);
  paymentTextField.setBackground(Color.WHITE);
  computeButton.setText("Compute Number of Payments");
}
```

We would like the application to begin in the mode where the monthly payment is computed. One way we could do this is by setting properties in design mode that correspond to the properties listed in the **paymentButtonActionPerformed** method. But an easier approach is to have the application 'simulate' clicking on the **paymentButton** button when the application begins. This is done at the end of the frame constructor with

```
paymentButton.doClick();
```

Save and run the project. If the code is entered correctly, the form should appear in the 'compute payment' mode:

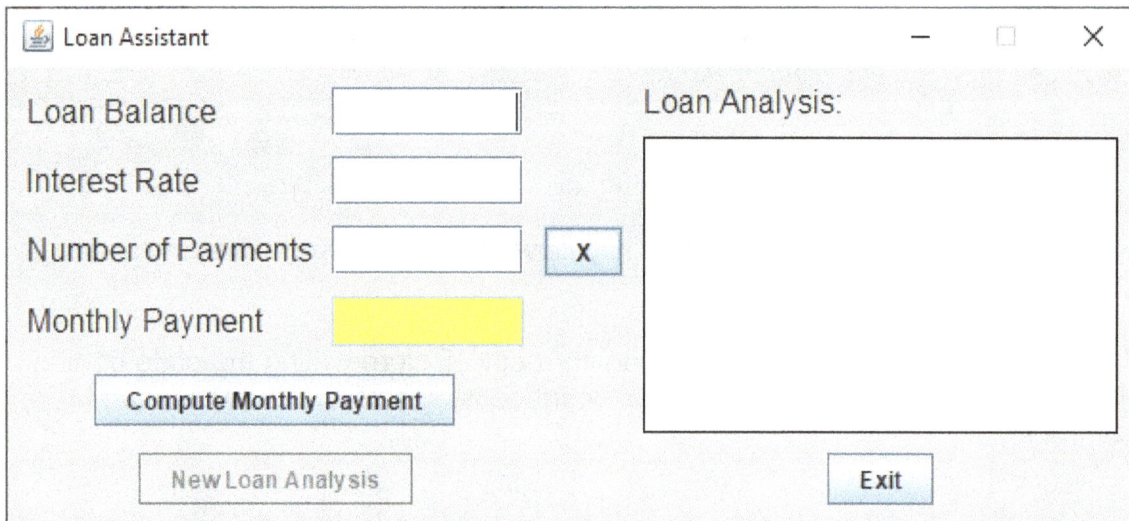

Note the **Monthly Payment** box is yellow, as desired. The **computeButton** caption is **Compute Monthly Payment**.

Click the **X** next to **Number of Payments** and you switch to the 'compute number of payments' mode:

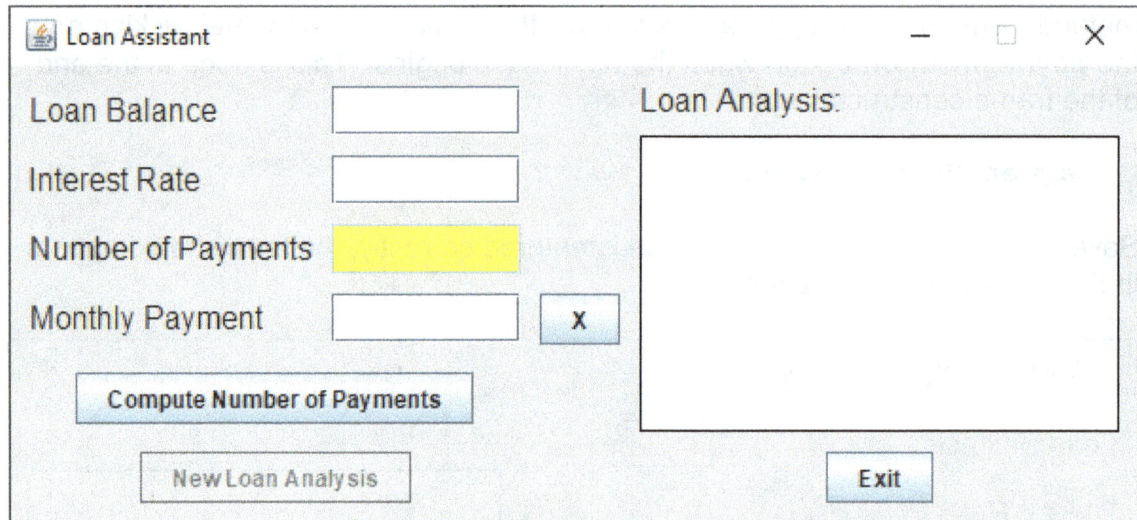

Now, the **Number of Payments** box is yellow and the **computeButton** caption is **Compute Number of Payments**.

The mode switching should be working correctly. Before writing the code behind the actual computations, let's address interface issues of focus traversal and control focus.

Frame Design – Focus Traversal

When you run the loan assistant application, if you try to move from text field to text field using the <**Tab**> key, there may be no predictable order in how the cursor moves. Or, you may move to controls you don't want to move to (for example, a read-only text field). To enter values, you have to make sure you first click in the text field. To make this process more orderly, we need to look at something called **focus traversal**.

When interacting with a Java GUI application, we can work with a single control at a time. That is, we can click on a single button or type in a single text field. We can't be doing two things at once. The control we are working with is known as the **active** control or we say the control has **focus**. In our loan assistant example, when the cursor is in a particular text field, we say that text field has focus. In a properly designed application, focus is shifted from one control to another (in a predictable, orderly fashion) using the <**Tab**> key. Focus can only be given to controls that allow user interaction – buttons and text fields in our example, but not labels.

Java does a good job of defining an orderly tab sequence using something called the **FocusTransversalPolicy**. Essentially, the tab sequence starts in the upper left corner of the **GridBagLayout** and works its way across a row. It then moves down to the next row and continues until it reaches the last column of the last row. At that point, the sequence begins again. The process can be reversed using <**Tab**>in combination with the <**Shift**> key.

There are times you would like to remove a control from the tab sequence (transversal policy). To remove a control (named **myControl**) from the sequence, use:

```
myControl.setFocusable(false);
```

It is also possible to reorder the tab sequence, but that is beyond the scope of this course.

There are several places we'd like to remove focus in the loan assistant project. When computing payment, there is no need for the focus to go to the **paymentTextField** control, since it is not editable. Similarly, when computing number of payments, focus should not go to the **monthsTextField**. We also want to keep focus from three button controls: **monthsButton**, **paymentButton** and **exitButton** to avoid inadvertent option selections or exiting of the program. And, focus never needs to go to **analysisTextArea**, since no editing is possible.

One other modification is needed. Once a user changes the computation mode, it would be nice if focus would be moved to the **Loan Balance** text field so the user can type an entry there. To programmatically assign focus to a control, apply the **requestFocus** method to the control using this dot-notation:

```
myControl.requestFocus();
```

Let's implement the specified changes. Three button controls (**monthsButton**, **paymentButton** and **exitButton**) and the text area (**analysisTextArea**) are permanently removed from the tab sequence, hence modify the code that creates these controls (in the frame constructor) with the three shaded lines:

```
monthsButton.setText("X");
monthsButton.setFocusable(false);
gridConstraints = new GridBagConstraints();
   .

   .


paymentButton.setText("X");
paymentButton.setFocusable(false);
gridConstraints = new GridBagConstraints();
   .

   .


analysisTextArea.setPreferredSize(new Dimension(250,
150));
analysisTextArea.setFocusable(false);
analysisTextArea.setBorder(BorderFactory.createLineBorder(
Color.BLACK));
   .

   .


exitButton.setText("Exit");
exitButton.setFocusable(false);
gridConstraints = new GridBagConstraints();
   .

   .
```

Modifications to the **paymentButton** and **monthsButton ActionPerformed** methods to modify text field traversal and to give focus to the balance text field are shown as shaded lines:

```java
private void paymentButtonActionPerformed(ActionEvent e)
{
  // will compute payment
  computePayment = true;
  paymentButton.setVisible(false);
  monthsButton.setVisible(true);
  monthsTextField.setEditable(true);
  monthsTextField.setBackground(Color.WHITE);
  monthsTextField.setFocusable(true);
  paymentTextField.setText("");
  paymentTextField.setEditable(false);
  paymentTextField.setBackground(lightYellow);
  paymentTextField.setFocusable(false);
  computeButton.setText("Compute Monthly Payment");
  balanceTextField.requestFocus();
}

private void monthsButtonActionPerformed(ActionEvent e)
{
  // will compute months
  computePayment = false;
  paymentButton.setVisible(true);
  monthsButton.setVisible(false);
  monthsTextField.setText("");
  monthsTextField.setEditable(false);
  monthsTextField.setBackground(lightYellow);
  monthsTextField.setFocusable(false);
  paymentTextField.setEditable(true);
  paymentTextField.setBackground(Color.WHITE);
  paymentTextField.setFocusable(true);
  computeButton.setText("Compute Number of Payments");
  balanceTextField.requestFocus();
}
```

Save and run the project. Switch from mode to mode. Notice how in each mode, the tab ordering is now predictable and as desired. Notice how the focus is always on the desired control. Notice how focus ends up on the compute button, where a tap of the space bar can 'click' on that button..

Code Design – Computing Monthly Payment

Let's develop the code to run the loan assistant in its initial 'compute payment' mode. We need an equation that computes the payment, knowing the loan balance, the interest rate and the number of payments. Computer programming is many times mathematical in nature. I recognize different people have different comfort levels with math. For those "math-phobes" out there, I'll just give you the code. For those interested, I'll show you the math behind the code.

Here's the code that does the necessary computations. In these lines, **balance** (**double** type) is the entered loan balance, **interest** (**double** type) is the entered interest rate and **months** (**int** type) is the entered number of payments (each of these values will come from the text field controls):

```
multiplier = Math.pow(1 + monthlyInterest, months);
payment = balance * monthlyInterest * multiplier /
(multiplier - 1);
```

In this code, the input interest (a yearly percentage) is converted to a monthly interest (**monthlyInterest**). This conversion is done by dividing by 12 (the number of months in a year) times 100 (to convert percentage to a decimal number). A **multiplier** term is formed using the mathematical power (exponentiation) method (**pow**). These values are then used to compute **payment** (**double** type).

If you don't want to see mathematics, **stop now**!! Skip ahead to the code steps for the **computeButtonActionPerformed** method. If you're still with me, I'll go over the steps that derive the code above. Let B represent the initial loan balance, i the monthly interest and P the monthly payment (we'll be solving an equation for this value). With this notation, the product of B times i (Bi) represents one month's interest on the existing balance. We add this interest to the balance then subtract the payment to obtain the balance after one payment, B_1:

$$B_1 = B + Bi - P = B(1 + i) - P$$

Using the same approach, the balance after two payments (B_2) would be:

$$B_2 = B_1 + B_1 i - P = B_1(1 + i) - P$$

Substituting the previous equation for B_1 into this equation gets things in terms of the original balance:

$$B_2 = [B(1 + i) - P](1 + i) - P = B(1 + i)^2 - P(1 + i) - P$$

Doing the same for B_3, we can show:

$$B_3 = B(1 + i)^3 - P(1 + i)^2 - P(1 + i) - P$$

Noting the trend in this relation, we can obtain an expression for B_N (the balance after N payments, when the loan is finally paid off):

$$B_N = B(1 + i)^N - P \sum_{k=0}^{N-1} (1 + i)^k$$

The Greek sigma in the above equation simply indicates that you add up all the corresponding elements next to the sigma.

After N payments, we want the balance of the loan to be zero. If we set B_N to zero in the above equation, we obtain a value for P, the payment:

$$P = B(1 + i)^N / \qquad (1 + i)^k$$

This is the desired result and we could easily code it using a for loop to evaluate the summation in the denominator. We can avoid this step by consulting a handbook on "finite series." The denominator term actually has a "closed-form" (one not requiring the summation). It is (trust me on this):

$$(1 + i)^k = [(1 + i)^N - 1]/i$$

Try a few values of i and N to convince yourself this works (if you need convincing). Substituting this into the equation for P and flipping a few terms around gives us the final equation for computing P:

$$P = Bi(1 + i)^N / [(1 + i)^N - 1]$$

Compare this equation to the code we gave you. You should see the code matches this equation (**B** is **balance**, **i** is **monthlyInterest**, **N** is **months** and **P** is **payment**).

When the user clicks **Compute Monthly Payment** (**computeButton**), the following steps are taken:

> ➤ Obtain the **balance** value from user input.
> ➤ Obtain the **interest** value from user input.
> ➤ Determine monthly interest.
> ➤ Obtain the **months** value from user input.
> ➤ Compute **payment** using given code.
> ➤ Display **payment** in **paymentTextField**.

The **computeButtonActionPerformed** method that implements these steps are (note we have declared all variables to have method level scope):

```
private void computeButtonActionPerformed(ActionEvent e)
{
   double balance, interest, payment;
   int months;
   double monthlyInterest, multiplier;
   balance =
Double.valueOf(balanceTextField.getText()).doubleValue();
   interest =
Double.valueOf(interestTextField.getText()).doubleValue();
   monthlyInterest = interest / 1200;
   // Compute loan payment
   months =
Integer.valueOf(monthsTextField.getText()).intValue();
   multiplier = Math.pow(1 + monthlyInterest, months);
   payment = balance * monthlyInterest * multiplier /
(multiplier - 1);
   paymentTextField.setText(new
DecimalFormat("0.00").format(payment));
}
```

This method uses the Java **DecimalFormat** method (to assign to decimal points to the result). To use this, we need to add this import statement:

```
import java.text.*;
```

While we're at it, let's take care of the **Exit** button. Its **ActionPerformed** method is simply:

```java
private void exitButtonActionPerformed(ActionEvent e)
{
  System.exit(0);
}
```

Save and run the project. Enter some numbers for balance, interest and number of payments, then click **Compute Monthly Payment**. Here's a run I made:

A $10,000 loan at 5.5% yearly interest has a monthly payment of $301.96. Try as many possibilities as you'd like. Make sure **Exit** works.

Code Design – Computing Number of Payments

The second mode of operation for the loan assistant is 'compute number of payments' mode. We need an equation the computes the number of payments, knowing the loan balance, the interest rate and the monthly payment. Again, a bit of math is involved. And, again, for those interested, I'll show you the math behind the code.

Here's the code that does the necessary computations. In these lines, **balance** (**double** type) is the entered loan balance, **interest** (**double** type) is the entered interest rate and **payment** (**double** type) is the entered monthly payment (each of these values will come from the text field controls):

```
months = (int)((Math.log(payment) - Math.log(payment -
balance * monthlyInterest)) / Math.log(1 +
monthlyInterest));
```

In this code, we again use the **monthlyInterest** value. The number of payments (**months**, an **int** type) is computed using the **Math.log** function. This is a mathematical logarithm.

All "math-phobes," skip ahead to the code to modify the **computeButtonActionPerformed** method. For those interested, let's see where that logarithm comes from. The equation we derived for the **Payment** (**P**) was:

$$P = Bi(1 + i)^N / [(1 + i)^N - 1]$$

where **B** is **Balance**, **i** is **MonthlyInterest**, and **N** is **Months**. In the current mode, we want to solve for N, given B, i, and P. Multiply both sides of the equation by the denominator on the right side to get:

$$[(1 + i)^N - 1]P = Bi(1 + i)^N$$

Multiply out the left side:

$$(1 + i)^N P - P = Bi(1 + i)^N$$

Then collect terms:

$$(P - Bi)(1 + i)^N = P$$

or

$$(1 + i)^N = P / (P - Bi)$$

Now, take the logarithm (hopefully you remember how these work) of both sides to yield:

$$N\log(1 + i) = \log(P) - \log(P - Bi)$$

Or, solving for N, our desired result:

$$N = [\log(P) - \log(P - Bi)] / \log(1 + i)$$

Look back at the code and you should see this equation. In the code, we cast the result to an **int** type (we can't make a fractional payment).

So when the user clicks **Compute Number of Payments** (**computeButton** when **ComputePayment** is **false**), the following steps are taken:

> ➢ Obtain the **balance** value from user input.
> ➢ Obtain the **interest** value from user input.
> ➢ Determine monthly interest.
> ➢ Obtain the **payment** value from user input.
> ➢ Compute **months** using given code.
> ➢ Display **months** in **monthsTextField**.

The modifed **computeButtonActionPerformed** method that implements these steps are (new code is shaded, notice we now look **ComputePayment** to see what 'mode' we are in):

```java
private void computeButtonActionPerformed(ActionEvent e)
{
  double balance, interest, payment;
  int months;
  double monthlyInterest, multiplier;
  balance =
Double.valueOf(balanceTextField.getText()).doubleValue();
  interest =
Double.valueOf(interestTextField.getText()).doubleValue();
  monthlyInterest = interest / 1200;
  if (computePayment)
  {
    // Compute loan payment
    months =
Integer.valueOf(monthsTextField.getText()).intValue();
    multiplier = Math.pow(1 + monthlyInterest, months);
    payment = balance * monthlyInterest * multiplier /
(multiplier - 1);
    paymentTextField.setText(new
DecimalFormat("0.00").format(payment));
  }
  else
  {
    // Compute number of payments
    payment =
Double.valueOf(paymentTextField.getText()).doubleValue();
    months = (int)((Math.log(payment) - Math.log(payment -
balance * monthlyInterest)) / Math.log(1 +
monthlyInterest));
    monthsTextField.setText(String.valueOf(months));
  }
}
```

Save and run the application. Make sure it still works in the initial mode for computing the monthly payment. When you're sure this is working okay, click the **X** next to the number of payment text field to switch to 'compute number of payments' mode.

Type in some values for balance, interest and payment. Click **Compute Number of Payments**. Here's a run I made:

Loan Assistant	— □ ✕
Loan Balance	20000
Interest Rate	6.5
Number of Payments	58
Monthly Payment	400 X
Compute Number of Payments	
New Loan Analysis	Exit

Loan Analysis:

This tells me if I borrow $20, 000 at 6.5% interest, I would need to make 58 monthly payments of $400 to pay the loan back. If you have a good memory (or look back earlier in this chapter), you'll remember we tried this when demonstrating the loan assistant project. In that earlier run, we obtained a value of 59 monthly payments. Is this a mistake? No – you'll see why next.

Code Design – Loan Analysis

Another desired feature of the consumer loan assistant project is to provide an analysis of the loan, once computations are done. The information this analysis should include is:

> ➢ Loan Balance
> ➢ Interest Rate
> ➢ Number of Payments
> ➢ Amount of Each Payment
> ➢ Total of Payments Made
> ➢ Total Interest Paid

Such information is very useful in analyzing how effective and economical a loan payoff plan is. Our frame has a text area control (**analysisTextArea**) available to provide these results. The analysis is generated after **computeButton** is clicked and the number of payments or payment amount have been computed.

At first, generating a loan analysis seems like a simple task. The balance (**balance**) and interest rate (**interest**) are input numbers. The number of payments (**months**) and monthly payment (**payment**) are either input or computed. So, it seems the total of payments would be given by:

```
totalPayments = months * payment;
```

while the interest paid would be:

```
interestPaid = totalPayments - balance;
```

The second equation is correct (assuming **totalPayments** is correct). But, the first equation (for **totalPayments**) doesn't quite apply. It's not that simple.

The code used for computing the payment amount (**computePayment** is **true**) and the number of payments (**computePayment** is **false**) is not exact. Truncation errors (making sure payments only have two decimal places) can affect the final payment amount. And, forcing the number of payments to be an integer value can result in significant errors in the final payment, perhaps even necessitating a final payment (remember the example we just ran?). We need to develop an analysis that recognizes the possibility of such errors and make necessary adjustments.

Here's the approach we will take. If the loan has N payments of P dollars, we will process all but the last payment and see what the remaining balance is at that point. If that balance is less than P, that will become the final payment. If that balance is greater than P, a payment of P will be applied and an additional payment of the final balance will be created. The displayed loan analysis will then show the final payment and the associated total of payments and interest paid.

For those of you who have avoided all the mathematical derivations up to this point, you need to know how to process a single payment to reduce the loan balance. If B is the current loan balance, i the monthly interest rate and P the payment. The balance (B_{after}) after the payment is:

$$B_{after} = B + Bi - P$$

This equation simply says the new balance is the old balance incremented by interest owed (Bi), then decreased by the payment amount (P). We use this equation to compute the final payment in the loan analysis.

The steps behind generating the loan analysis are:

> ➢ Display **balance**.
> ➢ Display **interest**.
> ➢ Compute **finalPayment** (adding a payment, if necessary).
> ➢ Compute and display total of payments.
> ➢ Compute and display interest paid.
> ➢ Disable **computeButton**.
> ➢ Enable **newLoanButton**.
> ➢ Set focus on **newLoanButton**.

Each of these steps is performed in the **computeButtonActionPerformed** method. The modified method is (changes are shaded):

```java
private void computeButtonActionPerformed(ActionEvent e)
{
  double balance, interest, payment;
  int months;
  double monthlyInterest, multiplier;
  double loanBalance, finalPayment;
  balance =
Double.valueOf(balanceTextField.getText()).doubleValue();
  interest =
Double.valueOf(interestTextField.getText()).doubleValue();
  monthlyInterest = interest / 1200;
  if (computePayment)
  {
    // Compute loan payment
    months =
Integer.valueOf(monthsTextField.getText()).intValue();
    multiplier = Math.pow(1 + monthlyInterest, months);
    payment = balance * monthlyInterest * multiplier /
(multiplier - 1);
    paymentTextField.setText(new
DecimalFormat("0.00").format(payment));
  }
  else
  {
    // Compute number of payments
    payment =
Double.valueOf(paymentTextField.getText()).doubleValue();
    months = (int)((Math.log(payment) - Math.log(payment -
balance * monthlyInterest)) / Math.log(1 +
monthlyInterest));
    monthsTextField.setText(String.valueOf(months));
  }
  // reset payment prior to analysis to fix at two
decimals
  payment =
Double.valueOf(paymentTextField.getText()).doubleValue();
  // show analysis
  analysisTextArea.setText("Loan Balance: $" + new
DecimalFormat("0.00").format(balance));
  analysisTextArea.append("\n" + "Interest Rate: " + new
DecimalFormat("0.00").format(interest) + "%");
  // process all but last payment
  loanBalance = balance;
```

```
   for (int paymentNumber = 1; paymentNumber <= months - 1;
paymentNumber++)
   {
     loanBalance += loanBalance * monthlyInterest -
payment;
   }
   // find final payment
   finalPayment = loanBalance;
   if (finalPayment > payment)
   {
     // apply one more payment
     loanBalance += loanBalance * monthlyInterest -
payment;
     finalPayment = loanBalance;
     months++;
     monthsTextField.setText(String.valueOf(months));
   }
   analysisTextArea.append("\n\n" + String.valueOf(months -
1) + " Payments of $" + new
DecimalFormat("0.00").format(payment));
   analysisTextArea.append("\n" + "Final Payment of: $" +
new DecimalFormat("0.00").format(finalPayment));
   analysisTextArea.append("\n" + "Total Payments: $" + new
DecimalFormat("0.00").format((months - 1) * payment +
finalPayment));
   analysisTextArea.append("\n" + "Interest Paid $" + new
DecimalFormat("0.00").format((months - 1) * payment +
finalPayment - balance));
   computeButton.setEnabled(false);
   newLoanButton.setEnabled(true);
   newLoanButton.requestFocus();
 }
```

You should be able to identify all the steps of the loan analysis, especially the final payment adjustment.

A couple of comments. In the first line of the analysis code, we reassign the **payment** value to the displayed value in the **paymentTextField** text field. The displayed value is formatted to two decimal places. Through this reassignment, we make sure **payment** is just two decimal places. Second, note the analysis in the text field is essentially just one long **text** property. To start a new line, we use the control string **\n**.

Save and run the project. Enter values for balance, interest and number of payments. Click **Compute Monthly Payment** . Here are the results for the example I've been using:

```
┌──────────────────────────────────────────────────────────────────────┐
│ ☕ Loan Assistant                              —      □       X         │
│                                                                        │
│   Loan Balance            [      10000 ]    Loan Analysis:             │
│                                            ┌─────────────────────────┐ │
│   Interest Rate           [        5.5 ]   │Loan Balance: $10000.00  │ │
│                                            │Interest Rate: 5.50%     │ │
│   Number of Payments      [         36 ] [ X ] │35 Payments of $301.96 │ │
│                                            │Final Payment of: $300.54│ │
│   Monthly Payment         [     301.96 ]   │Total Payments: $10869.14│ │
│                                            │Interest Paid $869.14    │ │
│         [ Compute Monthly Payment ]        │                         │ │
│                                            │                         │ │
│      [   New Loan Analysis   ]             └─────────────────────────┘ │
│                                                  [   Exit   ]          │
└──────────────────────────────────────────────────────────────────────┘
```

Note the slight adjustment to the final payment amount. Note the focus on **New Loan Analysis**. You can't do another analysis at this point since **computeButton** is disabled – we'll fix that in the next section. Click **Exit**.

Run the project again, this time clicking the **X** next to the **Number of Payments** text field. Enter values for balance, interest and payment, then click **Compute Number of Payments**. Continuing with the example I've been using (remember we got 58 payments before?) shows:

Loan Assistant	— ☐ ✕

Loan Balance   20000

Interest Rate   6.5

Number of Payments   59

Monthly Payment   400   X

Compute Number of Payments

New Loan Analysis   Exit

Loan Analysis:

```
Loan Balance: $20000.00
Interest Rate: 6.50%

58 Payments of $400.00
Final Payment of: $186.90
Total Payments: $23386.90
Interest Paid $3386.90
```

We now get 59 rather than 58 payments, the same result we saw earlier in the chapter. It was determined that once 58 payments of $400.00 per month were applied, there was still a balance over $400, necessitating a 59th payment of $400.00 plus an additional payment of $186.90. Click **Exit**, since you can't do anything else at this point.

Code Design – New Loan Analysis

Following an analysis, we would like the capability of performing a new analysis. When a user clicks the **New Loan Analysis** button (**newLoanButton**), the following things should happen:

> ➢ If computing payment, clear **paymentTextField**, else clear **monthsTextField**.
> ➢ Clear **analysisTextArea**.
> ➢ Enable **computeButton**.
> ➢ Disable **newLoanButton**.
> ➢ Set focus on **balanceTextField**.

We do not clear the **balanceTextField** or **interestTextField** boxes. If computing the payment, we do not clear the **monthsTextField** box. If computing the number of months, we do not clear the **paymentTextField** box. This allows a user to try different things with a specific loan. Individual boxes can be cleared by the user, if desired.

The **newLoanButtonActionPerformed** method is:

```
private void newLoanButtonActionPerformed(ActionEvent e)
{
  // clear computed value and analysis
  if (computePayment)
  {
    paymentTextField.setText("");
  }
  else
  {
    monthsTextField.setText("");
  }
  analysisTextArea.setText("");
  computeButton.setEnabled(true);
  newLoanButton.setEnabled(false);
  balanceTextField.requestFocus();
}
```

Add this new code. Save and run the project. The project should now have total ability to compute monthly payments or number of payments, providing complete loan analysis results. Play with the project as much as you'd like.

Improving a Java Project

The consumer loan assistant project works fine in its current configuration, but there are some hidden problems. You may have uncovered some of them already. Earlier, we saw the possibility of unpredictable tab ordering and fixed the problem, improving the performance of our project. This is something you, as a programmer, will do a lot. You will build a project and, while running it and testing it, will uncover weaknesses that need to be eliminated. These weaknesses could be actual errors in the application or just things that, if eliminated, make your application easier to use. Some weaknesses are easy to find, some more subtle.

You will find, as you progress as a programmer, that you will spend much of your time improving your projects. You will always find ways to add features to a project and to make it more appealing to your user base. You should never be satisfied with your first solution to a problem. There will always be room for improvement.

If you run the loan assistant project a few more times, you can identify some weaknesses:

> ➢ For example, what happens if you input a zero interest? The program will result in error messages and not compute a payment because the formulas implemented in code will not work with zero interest.
> ➢ As a convenience, it would be nice that when you hit the <**Enter**> key after typing a number, the focus would move to the next control in the tab sequence.
> ➢ Notice you can type any characters you want in the text fields when you should just be limited to numbers and a single decimal point – any other characters will cause the program to work incorrectly.
> ➢ What happens if you forget to input a value (leaving a text field empty)? You could get unpredictable results.
> ➢ A subtle problem arises when using the 'compute number of months' mode. In this configuration, the minimum desired payment must exceed the loan balance times the monthly interest. If it doesn't, you will never get the loan paid off – your balance will just keep growing (!), something called negative amortization.

We can (and will) address each of these points as we improve the loan assistant project. As we do, we'll look at some other Java features.

Code Design – Zero Interest

If you are lucky enough to find a bank or someone to give you a loan at zero percent interest, congratulations!! However, you can't use the current code to compute payment information. Try it if you like – you'll receive error messages in the NetBeans output window and see no computed payment.

The formulas used in the code assume a non-zero interest rate. If **interest** is zero, we can use much simpler formulas. For the 'compute payment' mode, the code is simply:

```
payment = balance / months;
```

While for the 'compute number of payments' mode, the code is:

```
months = (int)(balance / payment);
```

The modified **computeButtonActionPerformed** method (changes are shaded, some unmodified code is not shown for brevity):

```
private void computeButtonActionPerformed(ActionEvent e)
{
  .
  .
  .
  if (computePayment)
  {
    // Compute loan payment
    months =
Integer.valueOf(monthsTextField.getText()).intValue();
    if (interest == 0)
    {
      payment = balance / months;
    }
    else
    {
      multiplier = Math.pow(1 + monthlyInterest, months);
      payment = balance * monthlyInterest * multiplier /
(multiplier - 1);
    }
    paymentTextField.setText(new
DecimalFormat("0.00").format(payment));
  }
  else
  {
    // Compute number of payments
```

```
      payment =
Double.valueOf(paymentTextField.getText()).doubleValue();
      if (interest == 0)
      {
        months = (int)(balance / payment);
      }
      else
      {
        months = (int)((Math.log(payment) - Math.log(payment
- balance * monthlyInterest)) / Math.log(1 +
monthlyInterest));
      }
      monthsTextField.setText(String.valueOf(months));

   }
   .
   .
}
```

Save and run the application, making sure zero interest works under each mode. Notice adjustments to the final payment are only made when the balance is not an exact multiple of the payment. Make sure the non-zero interest options still work, too. Always make sure when you make changes to your code that you haven't disturbed portions that are working satisfactorily.

Code Design – Focus Transfer

We saw that the **<Tab>** key could be used to move from control to control, shifting the focus. Many times, you might like to move focus from one control to another in code, or programmatically. For example, in our savings example, once the user types in a **Deposit Amount**, it would be nice if focus would be moved to the **Interest** text field if the user presses **<Enter>**.

To move from the current control to the next control in the tab sequence, use **transferFocus**:

```
myControl.transferFocus();
```

To move from the current control to the previous control in the tab sequence, use **transerFocusBackward**:

```
myControl.transferFocusBackward();
```

So, where does this code go in our project? When a text field has focus and **<Enter>** is pressed, the **ActionPerformed** method is invoked. Hence, for each text field where we want to move focus based on keyboard input, we add an event method and place the needed code there. Adding event methods for a text field is identical to adding methods for other Swing components. For a text field named **myTextField**, use:

```
myTextField.addActionListener(new ActionListener ()
{
  public void actionPerformed(ActionEvent e)
  {
    myTextFieldActionPerformed(e);
  }
});
```

and the corresponding event method code to move focus would be:

```
private void myTextFieldActionPerformed(ActionEvent e)
{
  myTextField.transferFocus();
}
```

Let's make the modifications to the loan assistant. Each text field will need to have a method to transfer focus to the next control in sequence. In the frame constructor, after each text field is established, add code in the corresponding location to add a listener:

```
balanceTextField.addActionListener(new ActionListener ()
{
  public void actionPerformed(ActionEvent e)
  {
    balanceTextFieldActionPerformed(e);
  }
});

interestTextField.addActionListener(new ActionListener ()
{
  public void actionPerformed(ActionEvent e)
  {
    interestTextFieldActionPerformed(e);
  }
});

monthsTextField.addActionListener(new ActionListener ()
{
  public void actionPerformed(ActionEvent e)
  {
    monthsTextFieldActionPerformed(e);
  }
});

paymentTextField.addActionListener(new ActionListener ()
{
  public void actionPerformed(ActionEvent e)
  {
    paymentTextFieldActionPerformed(e);
  }
});
```

Next, add the four **ActionPerformed** methods that transfer focus:

```
private void balanceTextFieldActionPerformed(ActionEvent
e)
{
  balanceTextField.transferFocus();
}

private void interestTextFieldActionPerformed(ActionEvent
e)
{
  interestTextField.transferFocus();
}

private void monthsTextFieldActionPerformed(ActionEvent e)
{
  monthsTextField.transferFocus();
}

private void paymentTextFieldActionPerformed(ActionEvent
e)
{
  paymentTextField.transferFocus();
}
```

Save, run the project. Try using the **<Enter>** key to move from field to field. Try both the compute payment and compute number of payments modes.

Code Design - Input Validation

In the loan assistant project, there is nothing to prevent the user from typing in meaningless characters (for example, letters) into the text fields expecting numerical data. We want to keep this from happening – if the input is not a valid number, it cannot be converted from a string to a number, resulting in errors. Whenever getting input from a user using a text field control, we need to **validate** the typed information before using it. Validation rules differ depending on what information you want from the user.

In this project, we will perform **input validation** in a general method (named **validateDecimalNumber**) we write. The method will examine the text property of a text field, trimming off leading and trailing spaces and checking that the field contains only numbers and a single decimal point. It will return a **boolean** value indicating if a valid number is found. If the number is valid, the method will return a **true** value. If not valid, the method will return a **false** value. It will give that control focus, indicating the user needs to modify his/her input.

Here's the method that accomplishes that task:

```
public boolean validateDecimalNumber(JTextField tf)
{
  // checks to see if text field contains
  // valid decimal number with only digits and a single
decimal point
  String s = tf.getText().trim();
  boolean hasDecimal = false;
  boolean valid = true;
  if (s.length() == 0)
  {
    valid = false;
  }
  else
  {
    for (int i = 0; i < s.length(); i++)
    {
      char c = s.charAt(i);
      if (c >= '0' && c <= '9')
      {
        continue;
      }
      else if (c == '.' && !hasDecimal)
      {
        hasDecimal = true;
      }
      else
```

```
        {
          // invalid character found
          valid = false;
        }
      }
    }
    tf.setText(s);
    if (!valid)
    {
      tf.requestFocus();
    }
    return (valid);
}
```

You should be able to see how this works. The text field text property is stored in the string **s** (after trimming off leading and trailing spaces). Each character in this string is evaluated to see if it contains only allows number and a single decimal point. If only numbers and a decimal are found, **valid** is **true** and things proceed. If **valid** is **false**, indicating invalid characters or an empty string, the text field is given focus to allow changing the input value. Add this validation method to your project.

Make the shaded changes to the **computeButtonActionPerformed** method to insure we have valid entries before doing a computation:

```
private void computeButtonActionPerformed(ActionEvent e)
{
  double balance, interest, payment;
  int months;
  double monthlyInterest, multiplier;
  double loanBalance, finalPayment;
  if (validateDecimalNumber(balanceTextField))
  {
    balance =
Double.valueOf(balanceTextField.getText()).doubleValue();
  }
  else
  {
    return;
  }
  if (validateDecimalNumber(interestTextField))
  {
    interest =
Double.valueOf(interestTextField.getText()).doubleValue();
  }
  else
  {
```

```
      return;
  }
  monthlyInterest = interest / 1200;
  if (computePayment)
  {
    // Compute loan payment
    if (validateDecimalNumber(monthsTextField))
    {
      months =
Integer.valueOf(monthsTextField.getText()).intValue();
    }
    else
    {
      return;
    }
    if (interest == 0)
    {
      payment = balance / months;
    }
    else
    {
      multiplier = Math.pow(1 + monthlyInterest, months);
      payment = balance * monthlyInterest * multiplier /
(multiplier - 1);
    }
    paymentTextField.setText(new
DecimalFormat("0.00").format(payment));
  }
  else
  {
    // Compute number of payments
    if (validateDecimalNumber(paymentTextField))
    {
      payment =
Double.valueOf(paymentTextField.getText()).doubleValue();
    }
    else
    {
      return;
    }
    if (interest == 0)
    {
      months = (int)(balance / payment);
    }
    else
    {
```

```
        months = (int)((Math.log(payment) - Math.log(payment
    - balance * monthlyInterest)) / Math.log(1 +
    monthlyInterest));
      }
      monthsTextField.setText(String.valueOf(months));
    }
      .
      .
      .
    }
```

In each case where we need a value from a text field, we check to see if it is valid, using the **validateDecimalNumber** method. If valid, computations are as usual. If not valid, the method is exited and the focus is in the text field with the invalid entry.

Run the project again. Try invalid entries. Click the compute button. There should be no error messages, only a blanking out of the offending text field. A user of your program would like some indication of why the program isn't working in these cases (in addition to simply blanking out an invalid entry). Let's see how to add such messages using the **confirm dialog** control.

Confirm Dialog

An often used dialog box in Java GUI applications is a **confirm dialog** (also known as a **message box**). This dialog lets you display messages to your user and receive feedback for further information. It can be used to display error messages, describe potential problems or just to show the result of some computation. A confirm dialog is implemented with the Java Swing **JOptionPane** class. The confirm dialog is versatile, with the ability to display any message, an optional icon, and a selected set of buttons. The user responds by clicking a button in the confirm dialog box.

You've seen confirm dialog boxes if you've ever used a Windows (or other OS) application. Think of all the examples you've seen. For example, confirm dialogs are used to ask you if you wish to save a file before exiting and to warn you if a disk drive is not ready. For example, if while writing these notes in Microsoft Word, I attempt to exit, I see this confirm dialog:

In this confirm dialog box, the different parts that you control have been labeled. You will see how you can format a confirm dialog box any way you desire.

To use the **confirm dialog** method, you decide what the **message** should be, what **title** you desire, and what **icon** and **buttons** are appropriate. To display the confirm dialog box in code, you use the **showConfirmDialog** method.

The **showConfirmDialog** method is **overloaded** with several ways to implement the dialog box. Some of the more common ways are:

```
JOptionPane.showConfirmDialog(null, message);
JOptionPane.showConfirmDialog(null, message, title,
buttons);
JOptionPane.showConfirmDialog(null, message, title,
buttons, icon);
```

In these implementations, if **icon** is omitted, a question mark is displayed. If **buttons** is omitted, **Yes**, **No**, **Cancel** buttons are displayed. And, if **title** is omitted, a title of "**Select an Option**" is displayed. The first argument (**null**) must be there – it indicates the confirm dialog box is associated with the current frame.

As mentioned, you decide what you want for the confirm dialog **message** and **title** information (string data types). Be aware there is no limit to how long the message can be. If you have a long message, use the new line character (**\n**) to break the message into multiple lines.

The other arguments are defined by Java **JOptionPane** predefined constants. The **buttons** constants are defined by:

Member	Description
DEFAULT_OPTION	Displays an OK button
OK_CANCEL_OPTION	Displays OK and Cancel buttons
YES_NO_CANCEL_OPTION	Displays Yes, No and Cancel buttons
YES_NO_OPTION	Displays Yes and No buttons

The syntax for specifying a choice of buttons is the usual dot-notation:

```
JOptionPane.Member
```

So, to display an OK and Cancel button, the constant is:

```
JOptionPane.OK_CANCEL_OPTION
```

The displayed icon is established by another set of constants:

Member	Description
PLAIN_MESSAGE	Display no icon
INFORMATION_MESSAGE	Displays an information icon
ERROR_MESSAGE	Displays an error icon
WARNING_MESSAGE	Displays an exclamation point icon
QUESTION_MESSAGE	Displays a question mark icon

To specify an icon, the syntax is:

```
JOptionPane.Member
```

To display an error icon, use:

```
JOptionPane.ERROR_MESSAGE
```

When you invoke the **showOptionDialog** method, the method returns a JOptionPane constant (an **int** type) indicating the user response. The available members are:

Member	Description
CLOSED_OPTION	Window closed without pressing button
OK_OPTION	The OK button was selected
YES_OPTION	The Yes button was selected
NO_OPTION	The No button was selected
CANCEL_OPTION	The Cancel button was selected

Confirm Dialog **Example**:

This little code snippet (the second line is very long):

```
int response;
response = JOptionPane.showConfirmDialog(null, "This is an
example of an confirm dialog box.", "Example",
JOptionPane.YES_NO_OPTION,
JOptionPane.INFORMATION_MESSAGE);
if (response == JOptionPane.YES_OPTION)
{
  // Pressed Yes
}
else if (response == JOptionPane.NO_OPTION)
{
  // Pressed No
}
else
{
  // Closed window without pressing button
}
```

displays this message box:

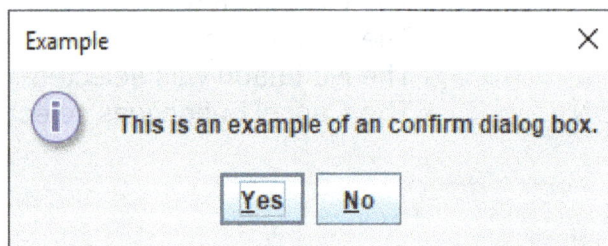

Of course, you would need to add code for the different tasks depending on whether **Yes** or **No** is clicked by the user (or the window is simply closed).

Another Confirm Dialog **Example**:

Many times, you just want to display a quick message to the user with no need for feedback (just an OK button). This code does the job:

```
JOptionPane.showConfirmDialog(null, "Quick message for
you.", "Hey you!!", JOptionPane.DEFAULT_OPTION,
JOptionPane.PLAIN_MESSAGE);
```

The resulting message box:

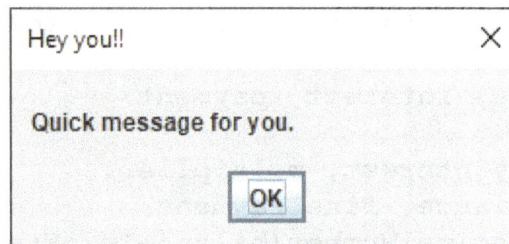

Notice there is no icon and the OK button is shown. Also, notice in the code, there is no need to read the returned value – we know what it is! You will find a lot of uses for this simple form of the message box (with perhaps some kind of icon) as you progress in Java.

Let's use the confirm dialog control to provide our user some feedback when there are invalid entries in the loan assistant project.

Code Design – User Messages

When an invalid entry is encountered (either blank or containing invalid characters), we want to inform our users of the problem. We will use a simple form of the confirm dialog to provide this feedback. It will simply present the message with an **OK** button.

We need four confirm dialogs, one for each text field. The dialogs are added in the **computeButtonActionPerformed** method (changes are shaded):

```
private void computeButtonActionPerformed(ActionEvent e)
{
  double balance, interest, payment;
  int months;
  double monthlyInterest, multiplier;
  double loanBalance, finalPayment;
  if (validateDecimalNumber(balanceTextField))
  {
    balance =
Double.valueOf(balanceTextField.getText()).doubleValue();
  }
  else
  {
    JOptionPane.showConfirmDialog(null, "Invalid or empty
Loan Balance entry.\nPlease correct.", "Balance Input
Error", JOptionPane.DEFAULT_OPTION,
JOptionPane.INFORMATION_MESSAGE);
    return;
  }
  if (validateDecimalNumber(interestTextField))
  {
    interest =
Double.valueOf(interestTextField.getText()).doubleValue();
  }
  else
  {
    JOptionPane.showConfirmDialog(null, "Invalid or empty
Interest Rate entry.\nPlease correct.", "Interest Input
Error", JOptionPane.DEFAULT_OPTION,
JOptionPane.INFORMATION_MESSAGE);
    return;
  }
  monthlyInterest = interest / 1200;
  if (computePayment)
  {
    // Compute loan payment
```

```
    if (validateDecimalNumber(monthsTextField))
    {
      months =
Integer.valueOf(monthsTextField.getText()).intValue();
    }
    else
    {
      JOptionPane.showConfirmDialog(null, "Invalid or
empty Number of Payments entry.\nPlease correct.", "Number
of Payments Input Error", JOptionPane.DEFAULT_OPTION,
JOptionPane.INFORMATION_MESSAGE);
      return;
    }
    if (interest == 0)
    {
      payment = balance / months;
    }
    else
    {
      multiplier = Math.pow(1 + monthlyInterest, months);
      payment = balance * monthlyInterest * multiplier /
(multiplier - 1);
    }
    paymentTextField.setText(new
DecimalFormat("0.00").format(payment));
  }
  else
  {
    // Compute number of payments
    if (validateDecimalNumber(paymentTextField))
    {
      payment =
Double.valueOf(paymentTextField.getText()).doubleValue();
    }
    else
    {
      JOptionPane.showConfirmDialog(null, "Invalid or
empty Monthly Payment entry.\nPlease correct.", "Payment
Input Error", JOptionPane.DEFAULT_OPTION,
JOptionPane.INFORMATION_MESSAGE);
      return;
    }
    if (interest == 0)
    {
      months = (int)(balance / payment);
    }
    else
```

```
    {
        months = (int)((Math.log(payment) - Math.log(payment
    - balance * monthlyInterest)) / Math.log(1 +
    monthlyInterest));
    }
    monthsTextField.setText(String.valueOf(months));
    }
    .
    .
    .

}
```

After making these modifications, save and run the project. Make sure each input validation works correctly. Make sure it works in both computation modes. And, make sure your changes have not affected previously correct calculations.

Each validation is similar. If the text field is not blank and all characters are valid, things proceed as usual. If blank or containing invalid characters, a message box like this appears (this one appears when **balanceTextField** is left blank, other message boxes are similar):

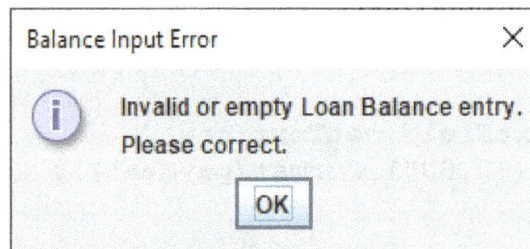

Balance Input Error   ✕

ⓘ   Invalid or empty Loan Balance entry.
        Please correct.

            OK

The user clicks **OK**, the focus is returned to the blank control for another chance at inputting a non-blank value.

We have one last input validation to implement and then the consumer loan assistant project is complete (unless you can think of other improvements). Recall, when computing the number of months, we must enter a minimum payment or the balance will continue to grow. The minimum payment is the loan balance times the monthly interest:

```
minimumPayment = balance * monthlyInterest;
```

If this payment is made each month, it is called an "interest only" loan. This means, we just pay the interest owed each month, never decreasing the balance. Since our goal is to decrease the balance, we will suggest to the user a minimum payment at least $1 greater than the interest only option, or we will use:

```
minimumPayment = balance * monthlyInterest + 1;
```

The steps for minimum payment validation are (only needed when **computePayment** is **false**):

> - If entered **payment** is less than minimum value, display message box informing user of minimum needed and ask if they would like to use that value.
>   - If user responds **Yes**, set **payment**, display in **paymentTextField** and continue.
>   - If user responds **No**, set focus on **paymentTextField** to allow new entry.
> - If entered **payment** is above minimum value, continue as usual.

These modifications go in the **computeButtonActionPerformed** method. While implementing improvements to the loan assistant project, we have made many modifications to this event. For reference purposes, here is the final version of the **computeButton Click** method (with new additions shaded):

```
private void computeButtonActionPerformed(ActionEvent e)
{
  double balance, interest, payment;
  int months;
  double monthlyInterest, multiplier;
  double loanBalance, finalPayment;
  if (validateDecimalNumber(balanceTextField))
  {
    balance =
Double.valueOf(balanceTextField.getText()).doubleValue();
  }
  else
  {
    JOptionPane.showConfirmDialog(null, "Invalid or empty
Loan Balance entry.\nPlease correct.", "Balance Input
Error", JOptionPane.DEFAULT_OPTION,
JOptionPane.INFORMATION_MESSAGE);
    return;
  }
  if (validateDecimalNumber(interestTextField))
  {
    interest =
Double.valueOf(interestTextField.getText()).doubleValue();
  }
  else
  {
    JOptionPane.showConfirmDialog(null, "Invalid or empty
Interest Rate entry.\nPlease correct.", "Interest Input
Error", JOptionPane.DEFAULT_OPTION,
JOptionPane.INFORMATION_MESSAGE);
    return;
  }
  monthlyInterest = interest / 1200;
  if (computePayment)
  {
    // Compute loan payment
    if (validateDecimalNumber(monthsTextField))
    {
      months =
Integer.valueOf(monthsTextField.getText()).intValue();
    }
    else
```

```
    {
        JOptionPane.showConfirmDialog(null, "Invalid or
empty Number of Payments entry.\nPlease correct.", "Number
of Payments Input Error", JOptionPane.DEFAULT_OPTION,
JOptionPane.INFORMATION_MESSAGE);
        return;
    }
    if (interest == 0)
    {
        payment = balance / months;
    }
    else
    {
        multiplier = Math.pow(1 + monthlyInterest, months);
        payment = balance * monthlyInterest * multiplier /
(multiplier - 1);
    }
    paymentTextField.setText(new
DecimalFormat("0.00").format(payment));
    }
    else
    {
        // Compute number of payments
        if (validateDecimalNumber(paymentTextField))
        {
            payment =
Double.valueOf(paymentTextField.getText()).doubleValue();
            if (payment <= (balance * monthlyInterest + 1.0))
            {
                if (JOptionPane.showConfirmDialog(null, "Minimum
payment must be $" + new
DecimalFormat("0.00").format((int)(balance *
monthlyInterest + 1.0)) + "\n" + "Do you want to use the
minimum payment?", "Input Error",
JOptionPane.YES_NO_OPTION, JOptionPane.QUESTION_MESSAGE)
== JOptionPane.YES_OPTION)
                {
                    paymentTextField.setText(new
DecimalFormat("0.00").format((int)(balance *
monthlyInterest + 1.0)));
                    payment =
Double.valueOf(paymentTextField.getText()).doubleValue();
                }
                else
                {
                    paymentTextField.requestFocus();
                    return;
```

```
        }
      }
    }
  else
  {
    JOptionPane.showConfirmDialog(null, "Invalid or
empty Monthly Payment entry.\nPlease correct.", "Payment
Input Error", JOptionPane.DEFAULT_OPTION,
JOptionPane.INFORMATION_MESSAGE);
    return;
  }
  if (interest == 0)
  {
    months = (int)(balance / payment);
  }
  else
  {
    months = (int)((Math.log(payment) - Math.log(payment
- balance * monthlyInterest)) / Math.log(1 +
monthlyInterest));
  }
  monthsTextField.setText(String.valueOf(months));
}
// reset payment prior to analysis to fix at two
decimals
payment =
Double.valueOf(paymentTextField.getText()).doubleValue();
// show analysis
analysisTextArea.setText("Loan Balance: $" + new
DecimalFormat("0.00").format(balance));
analysisTextArea.append("\n" + "Interest Rate: " + new
DecimalFormat("0.00").format(interest) + "%");
// process all but last payment
loanBalance = balance;
for (int paymentNumber = 1; paymentNumber <= months - 1;
paymentNumber++)
{
  loanBalance += loanBalance * monthlyInterest -
payment;
}
// find final payment
finalPayment = loanBalance;
if (finalPayment > payment)
{
  // apply one more payment
  loanBalance += loanBalance * monthlyInterest -
payment;
```

```
        finalPayment = loanBalance;
        months++;
        monthsTextField.setText(String.valueOf(months));
    }
    analysisTextArea.append("\n\n" + String.valueOf(months -
1) + " Payments of $" + new
DecimalFormat("0.00").format(payment));
    analysisTextArea.append("\n" + "Final Payment of: $" +
new DecimalFormat("0.00").format(finalPayment));
    analysisTextArea.append("\n" + "Total Payments: $" + new
DecimalFormat("0.00").format((months - 1) * payment +
finalPayment));
    analysisTextArea.append("\n" + "Interest Paid $" + new
DecimalFormat("0.00").format((months - 1) * payment +
finalPayment - balance));
    computeButton.setEnabled(false);
    newLoanButton.setEnabled(true);
    newLoanButton.requestFocus();
}
```

Make the noted changes.

Save and run the loan assistant project. Switch to 'compute number of payments' mode. Enter a **Loan Balance** and an **Interest Rate**. Enter a "too low" **Monthly Payment** amount. Here's some numbers I used:

Loan Assistant	— □ ✕

Loan Balance   20000   Loan Analysis:

Interest Rate   5.5

Number of Payments

Monthly Payment   10 | X |

| Compute Number of Payments |

| New Loan Analysis | | Exit |

Now, click **Compute Number of Payments**. A message box like this should appear:

Input Error   ✕

? Minimum payment must be $92.00
Do you want to use the minimum payment?

| Yes | | No |

At this point, if you click **No**, you will be returned to the **Monthly Payment** text field for another chance.

Click **Yes** and analysis will proceed using the suggested minimum payment ($92.00 in my example):

```
 ┌─────────────────────────────────────────────────────────────────────┐
 │ ☕ Loan Assistant                                    —   □   ✕       │
 │                                                                       │
 │  Loan Balance          [     20000 ]     Loan Analysis:               │
 │                                         ┌───────────────────────────┐ │
 │  Interest Rate         [       5.5 ]    │ Loan Balance: $20000.00   │ │
 │                                         │ Interest Rate: 5.50%      │ │
 │  Number of Payments    [      1230 ]    │                           │ │
 │                                         │ 1229 Payments of $92.00   │ │
 │  Monthly Payment       [     92.00 ][X] │ Final Payment of: $7.10   │ │
 │                                         │ Total Payments: $113075.10│ │
 │       [ Compute Number of Payments ]    │ Interest Paid $93075.10   │ │
 │                                         │                           │ │
 │       [  New Loan Analysis  ]           └───────────────────────────┘ │
 │                                              [   Exit   ]              │
 └─────────────────────────────────────────────────────────────────────┘
```

With this low minimum payment, it would take over 102 years to pay off the loan!! And, unfortunately, many credit card companies don't let you know how many years it takes to pay off a balance if you just make the minimum payment each month. This new project arms you with the tool you need to make such computations.

Consumer Loan Assistant Project Review

The **Consumer Loan Assistant** project is now complete. Save and run the project and make sure it works as designed. Check that you can move back and forth between computation modes. Use the project to make informed payment decisions regarding any loans or credit cards you may have.

If there are errors in your implementation, go back over the steps of frame and code design. Go over the developed code – make sure you understand how different parts of the project were coded. As mentioned in the beginning of this chapter, the completed project is saved as **LoanAssistant** in the **\HomeJava\HomeJava Projects** folder.

While completing this project, new concepts and skills you should have gained include:

> ➤ Proper use of the text field control.
> ➤ How to use tab order and control focus.
> ➤ Different ways to improve a Java project.
> ➤ How to use message boxes in conjunction with input validation.

This project also showed that once you have built a working project, there is often still a lot of work to do. Much of the code in the loan assistant project was added to improve the application – making it more user friendly and less susceptible to erroneous entries. As mentioned previously in these notes, it is relatively easy to write a project that works properly when the user does everything correctly. It's difficult and takes time to write a project that can handle all the possible wrong things a user can do and still not bomb out. Added improvements separate the good projects from the adequate projects.

Consumer Loan Assistant Project Enhancements

Possible enhancements to the consumer loan assistant project include:

➢ Many times, you know how much you can afford monthly and want to know how much you can borrow. Add a capability to compute balance, given interest, months and payment. Follow similar steps for computing the other parameters.

➢ Add single payment processing capability so you can see how much the balance decreases each month and how much interest you are paying. Show results in the current text field or add other controls.

➢ Add the capability to stop after a certain number of payments have been processed.

➢ Add printing capability to see a complete repayment schedule for any loan you design. Printing is discussed in another project in these notes – **Home Inventory**.

➢ Add an output to the loan analysis that tells you what date your loan will be paid off based on the number of monthly payments.

Consumer Loan Assistant Project Review

```java
/*
 * LoanAssistant.java
 */
package loanassistant;
import javax.swing.*;
import java.awt.*;
import java.awt.event.*;
import java.text.*;

public class LoanAssistant extends JFrame
{

  JLabel balanceLabel = new JLabel();
  JTextField balanceTextField = new JTextField();
  JLabel interestLabel = new JLabel();
  JTextField interestTextField = new JTextField();
  JLabel monthsLabel = new JLabel();
  JTextField monthsTextField = new JTextField();
  JLabel paymentLabel = new JLabel();
  JTextField paymentTextField = new JTextField();
  JButton computeButton = new JButton();
  JButton newLoanButton = new JButton();
  JButton monthsButton = new JButton();
  JButton paymentButton = new JButton();
  JLabel analysisLabel = new JLabel();
  JTextArea analysisTextArea = new JTextArea();
  JButton exitButton = new JButton();

  Font myFont = new Font("Arial", Font.PLAIN, 16);

  Color lightYellow = new Color(255, 255, 128);

  boolean computePayment;


  public static void main(String args[])
  {
    // create frame
    new LoanAssistant().setVisible(true);
  }

  public LoanAssistant()
  {
    // frame constructor
```

```
setTitle("Loan Assistant");
setResizable(false);
addWindowListener(new WindowAdapter()
{
  public void windowClosing(WindowEvent evt)
  {
    exitForm(evt);
  }
});
getContentPane().setLayout(new GridBagLayout());
GridBagConstraints gridConstraints;

balanceLabel.setText("Loan Balance");
balanceLabel.setFont(myFont);
gridConstraints = new GridBagConstraints();
gridConstraints.gridx = 0;
gridConstraints.gridy = 0;
gridConstraints.anchor = GridBagConstraints.WEST;
gridConstraints.insets = new Insets(10, 10, 0, 0);
getContentPane().add(balanceLabel, gridConstraints);

balanceTextField.setPreferredSize(new Dimension(100,
25));

balanceTextField.setHorizontalAlignment(SwingConstants.RIGHT)
;
balanceTextField.setFont(myFont);
gridConstraints = new GridBagConstraints();
gridConstraints.gridx = 1;
gridConstraints.gridy = 0;
gridConstraints.insets = new Insets(10, 10, 0, 10);
getContentPane().add(balanceTextField, gridConstraints);
balanceTextField.addActionListener(new ActionListener ()
{
  public void actionPerformed(ActionEvent e)
  {
    balanceTextFieldActionPerformed(e);
  }
});

interestLabel.setText("Interest Rate");
interestLabel.setFont(myFont);
gridConstraints = new GridBagConstraints();
gridConstraints.gridx = 0;
gridConstraints.gridy = 1;
gridConstraints.anchor = GridBagConstraints.WEST;
gridConstraints.insets = new Insets(10, 10, 0, 0);
```

```java
    getContentPane().add(interestLabel, gridConstraints);

    interestTextField.setPreferredSize(new Dimension(100,
25));

interestTextField.setHorizontalAlignment(SwingConstants.RIGHT
);
    interestTextField.setFont(myFont);
    gridConstraints = new GridBagConstraints();
    gridConstraints.gridx = 1;
    gridConstraints.gridy = 1;
    gridConstraints.insets = new Insets(10, 10, 0, 10);
    getContentPane().add(interestTextField, gridConstraints);
    interestTextField.addActionListener(new ActionListener ()
    {
      public void actionPerformed(ActionEvent e)
      {
        interestTextFieldActionPerformed(e);
      }
    });

    monthsLabel.setText("Number of Payments");
    monthsLabel.setFont(myFont);
    gridConstraints = new GridBagConstraints();
    gridConstraints.gridx = 0;
    gridConstraints.gridy = 2;
    gridConstraints.anchor = GridBagConstraints.WEST;
    gridConstraints.insets = new Insets(10, 10, 0, 0);
    getContentPane().add(monthsLabel, gridConstraints);

    monthsTextField.setPreferredSize(new Dimension(100, 25));

monthsTextField.setHorizontalAlignment(SwingConstants.RIGHT);
    monthsTextField.setFont(myFont);
    gridConstraints = new GridBagConstraints();
    gridConstraints.gridx = 1;
    gridConstraints.gridy = 2;
    gridConstraints.insets = new Insets(10, 10, 0, 10);
    getContentPane().add(monthsTextField, gridConstraints);
    monthsTextField.addActionListener(new ActionListener ()
    {
      public void actionPerformed(ActionEvent e)
      {
        monthsTextFieldActionPerformed(e);
      }
    });
```

```
paymentLabel.setText("Monthly Payment");
paymentLabel.setFont(myFont);
gridConstraints = new GridBagConstraints();
gridConstraints.gridx = 0;
gridConstraints.gridy = 3;
gridConstraints.anchor = GridBagConstraints.WEST;
gridConstraints.insets = new Insets(10, 10, 0, 0);
getContentPane().add(paymentLabel, gridConstraints);

paymentTextField.setPreferredSize(new Dimension(100,
25));

paymentTextField.setHorizontalAlignment(SwingConstants.RIGHT)
;
paymentTextField.setFont(myFont);
gridConstraints = new GridBagConstraints();
gridConstraints.gridx = 1;
gridConstraints.gridy = 3;
gridConstraints.insets = new Insets(10, 10, 0, 10);
getContentPane().add(paymentTextField, gridConstraints);
paymentTextField.addActionListener(new ActionListener ()
{
  public void actionPerformed(ActionEvent e)
  {
    paymentTextFieldActionPerformed(e);
  }
});

computeButton.setText("Compute Monthly Payment");
gridConstraints = new GridBagConstraints();
gridConstraints.gridx = 0;
gridConstraints.gridy = 4;
gridConstraints.gridwidth = 2;
gridConstraints.insets = new Insets(10, 0, 0, 0);
getContentPane().add(computeButton, gridConstraints);
computeButton.addActionListener(new ActionListener()
{
  public void actionPerformed(ActionEvent e)
  {
    computeButtonActionPerformed(e);
  }
});

newLoanButton.setText("New Loan Analysis");
newLoanButton.setEnabled(false);
gridConstraints = new GridBagConstraints();
gridConstraints.gridx = 0;
```

```
gridConstraints.gridy = 5;
gridConstraints.gridwidth = 2;
gridConstraints.insets = new Insets(10, 0, 10, 0);
getContentPane().add(newLoanButton, gridConstraints);
newLoanButton.addActionListener(new ActionListener()
{
  public void actionPerformed(ActionEvent e)
  {
    newLoanButtonActionPerformed(e);
  }
});

monthsButton.setText("X");
monthsButton.setFocusable(false);
gridConstraints = new GridBagConstraints();
gridConstraints.gridx = 2;
gridConstraints.gridy = 2;
gridConstraints.insets = new Insets(10, 0, 0, 0);
getContentPane().add(monthsButton, gridConstraints);
monthsButton.addActionListener(new ActionListener()
{
  public void actionPerformed(ActionEvent e)
  {
    monthsButtonActionPerformed(e);
  }
});

paymentButton.setText("X");
paymentButton.setFocusable(false);
gridConstraints = new GridBagConstraints();
gridConstraints.gridx = 2;
gridConstraints.gridy = 3;
gridConstraints.insets = new Insets(10, 0, 0, 0);
getContentPane().add(paymentButton, gridConstraints);
paymentButton.addActionListener(new ActionListener()
{
  public void actionPerformed(ActionEvent e)
  {
    paymentButtonActionPerformed(e);
  }
});

analysisLabel.setText("Loan Analysis:");
analysisLabel.setFont(myFont);
gridConstraints = new GridBagConstraints();
gridConstraints.gridx = 3;
gridConstraints.gridy = 0;
```

```java
    gridConstraints.anchor = GridBagConstraints.WEST;
    gridConstraints.insets = new Insets(0, 10, 0, 0);
    getContentPane().add(analysisLabel, gridConstraints);

    analysisTextArea.setPreferredSize(new Dimension(250,
150));
    analysisTextArea.setFocusable(false);

analysisTextArea.setBorder(BorderFactory.createLineBorder(Col
or.BLACK));
    analysisTextArea.setFont(new Font("Courier New",
Font.PLAIN, 14));
    analysisTextArea.setEditable(false);
    analysisTextArea.setBackground(Color.WHITE);
    gridConstraints = new GridBagConstraints();
    gridConstraints.gridx = 3;
    gridConstraints.gridy = 1;
    gridConstraints.gridheight = 4;
    gridConstraints.insets = new Insets(0, 10, 0, 10);
    getContentPane().add(analysisTextArea, gridConstraints);

    exitButton.setText("Exit");
    exitButton.setFocusable(false);
    gridConstraints = new GridBagConstraints();
    gridConstraints.gridx = 3;
    gridConstraints.gridy = 5;
    getContentPane().add(exitButton, gridConstraints);
    exitButton.addActionListener(new ActionListener()
    {
      public void actionPerformed(ActionEvent e)
      {
        exitButtonActionPerformed(e);
      }
    });

    pack();
    Dimension screenSize =
Toolkit.getDefaultToolkit().getScreenSize();
    setBounds((int) (0.5 * (screenSize.width - getWidth())),
(int) (0.5 * (screenSize.height - getHeight())), getWidth(),
getHeight());
    paymentButton.doClick();
  }

  private void exitForm(WindowEvent evt)
  {
    System.exit(0);
```

```
   }

  private void computeButtonActionPerformed(ActionEvent e)
  {
    double balance, interest, payment;
    int months;
    double monthlyInterest, multiplier;
    double loanBalance, finalPayment;
    if (validateDecimalNumber(balanceTextField))
    {
      balance =
Double.valueOf(balanceTextField.getText()).doubleValue();
    }
    else
    {
      JOptionPane.showConfirmDialog(null, "Invalid or empty
Loan Balance entry.\nPlease correct.", "Balance Input Error",
JOptionPane.DEFAULT_OPTION, JOptionPane.INFORMATION_MESSAGE);
      return;
    }
    if (validateDecimalNumber(interestTextField))
    {
      interest =
Double.valueOf(interestTextField.getText()).doubleValue();
    }
    else
    {
      JOptionPane.showConfirmDialog(null, "Invalid or empty
Interest Rate entry.\nPlease correct.", "Interest Input
Error", JOptionPane.DEFAULT_OPTION,
JOptionPane.INFORMATION_MESSAGE);
      return;
    }
    monthlyInterest = interest / 1200;
    if (computePayment)
    {
      // Compute loan payment
      if (validateDecimalNumber(monthsTextField))
      {
        months =
Integer.valueOf(monthsTextField.getText()).intValue();
      }
      else
      {
        JOptionPane.showConfirmDialog(null, "Invalid or empty
Number of Payments entry.\nPlease correct.", "Number of
```

```java
Payments Input Error", JOptionPane.DEFAULT_OPTION,
JOptionPane.INFORMATION_MESSAGE);
      return;
    }
    if (interest == 0)
    {
      payment = balance / months;
    }
    else
    {
      multiplier = Math.pow(1 + monthlyInterest, months);
      payment = balance * monthlyInterest * multiplier /
(multiplier - 1);
    }
    paymentTextField.setText(new
DecimalFormat("0.00").format(payment));
  }
  else
  {
    // Compute number of payments
    if (validateDecimalNumber(paymentTextField))
    {
      payment =
Double.valueOf(paymentTextField.getText()).doubleValue();
      if (payment <= (balance * monthlyInterest + 1.0))
      {
        if (JOptionPane.showConfirmDialog(null, "Minimum
payment must be $" + new
DecimalFormat("0.00").format((int)(balance * monthlyInterest
+ 1.0)) + "\n" + "Do you want to use the minimum payment?",
"Input Error", JOptionPane.YES_NO_OPTION,
JOptionPane.QUESTION_MESSAGE) == JOptionPane.YES_OPTION)
        {
          paymentTextField.setText(new
DecimalFormat("0.00").format((int)(balance * monthlyInterest
+ 1.0)));
          payment =
Double.valueOf(paymentTextField.getText()).doubleValue();
        }
        else
        {
          paymentTextField.requestFocus();
          return;
        }
      }
    }
    else
```

```
        {
          JOptionPane.showConfirmDialog(null, "Invalid or empty
Monthly Payment entry.\nPlease correct.", "Payment Input
Error", JOptionPane.DEFAULT_OPTION,
JOptionPane.INFORMATION_MESSAGE);
          return;
        }
        if (interest == 0)
        {
          months = (int)(balance / payment);
        }
        else
        {
          months = (int)((Math.log(payment) - Math.log(payment
- balance * monthlyInterest)) / Math.log(1 +
monthlyInterest));
        }
        monthsTextField.setText(String.valueOf(months));
      }
      // reset payment prior to analysis to fix at two decimals
      payment =
Double.valueOf(paymentTextField.getText()).doubleValue();
      // show analysis
      analysisTextArea.setText("Loan Balance: $" + new
DecimalFormat("0.00").format(balance));
      analysisTextArea.append("\n" + "Interest Rate: " + new
DecimalFormat("0.00").format(interest) + "%");
      // process all but last payment
      loanBalance = balance;
      for (int paymentNumber = 1; paymentNumber <= months - 1;
paymentNumber++)
      {
        loanBalance += loanBalance * monthlyInterest - payment;
      }
      // find final payment
      finalPayment = loanBalance;
      if (finalPayment > payment)
      {
        // apply one more payment
        loanBalance += loanBalance * monthlyInterest - payment;
        finalPayment = loanBalance;
        months++;
        monthsTextField.setText(String.valueOf(months));
      }
      analysisTextArea.append("\n\n" + String.valueOf(months -
1) + " Payments of $" + new
DecimalFormat("0.00").format(payment));
```

```java
    analysisTextArea.append("\n" + "Final Payment of: $" +
new DecimalFormat("0.00").format(finalPayment));
    analysisTextArea.append("\n" + "Total Payments: $" + new
DecimalFormat("0.00").format((months - 1) * payment +
finalPayment));
    analysisTextArea.append("\n" + "Interest Paid $" + new
DecimalFormat("0.00").format((months - 1) * payment +
finalPayment - balance));
    computeButton.setEnabled(false);
    newLoanButton.setEnabled(true);
    newLoanButton.requestFocus();
  }

  private void newLoanButtonActionPerformed(ActionEvent e)
  {
    // clear computed value and analysis
    if (computePayment)
    {
      paymentTextField.setText("");
    }
    else
    {
      monthsTextField.setText("");
    }
    analysisTextArea.setText("");
    computeButton.setEnabled(true);
    newLoanButton.setEnabled(false);
    balanceTextField.requestFocus();
  }

  private void monthsButtonActionPerformed(ActionEvent e)
  {
    // will compute months
    computePayment = false;
    paymentButton.setVisible(true);
    monthsButton.setVisible(false);
    monthsTextField.setText("");
    monthsTextField.setEditable(false);
    monthsTextField.setBackground(lightYellow);
    monthsTextField.setFocusable(false);
    paymentTextField.setEditable(true);
    paymentTextField.setBackground(Color.WHITE);
    paymentTextField.setFocusable(true);
    computeButton.setText("Compute Number of Payments");
    balanceTextField.requestFocus();
  }
```

```java
  private void paymentButtonActionPerformed(ActionEvent e)
  {
    // will compute payment
    computePayment = true;
    paymentButton.setVisible(false);
    monthsButton.setVisible(true);
    monthsTextField.setEditable(true);
    monthsTextField.setBackground(Color.WHITE);
    monthsTextField.setFocusable(true);
    paymentTextField.setText("");
    paymentTextField.setEditable(false);
    paymentTextField.setBackground(lightYellow);
    paymentTextField.setFocusable(false);
    computeButton.setText("Compute Monthly Payment");
    balanceTextField.requestFocus();
  }

  private void exitButtonActionPerformed(ActionEvent e)
  {
    System.exit(0);
  }

  private void balanceTextFieldActionPerformed(ActionEvent e)
  {
    balanceTextField.transferFocus();
  }

  private void interestTextFieldActionPerformed(ActionEvent
e)
  {
    interestTextField.transferFocus();
  }

  private void monthsTextFieldActionPerformed(ActionEvent e)
  {
    monthsTextField.transferFocus();
  }

  private void paymentTextFieldActionPerformed(ActionEvent e)
  {
    paymentTextField.transferFocus();
  }

  private boolean validateDecimalNumber(JTextField tf)
  {
    // checks to see if text field contains
```

```java
    // valid decimal number with only digits and a single
decimal point
    String s = tf.getText().trim();
    boolean hasDecimal = false;
    boolean valid = true;
    if (s.length() == 0)
    {
      valid = false;
    }
    else
    {
      for (int i = 0; i < s.length(); i++)
      {
        char c = s.charAt(i);
        if (c >= '0' && c <= '9')
        {
          continue;
        }
        else if (c == '.' && !hasDecimal)
        {
          hasDecimal = true;
        }
        else
        {
          // invalid character found
          valid = false;
        }
      }
    }
    tf.setText(s);
    if (!valid)
    {
      tf.requestFocus();
    }
    return (valid);
  }
}
```

4

Flash Card Math Quiz Project

Review and Preview

In this chapter, we build a project that lets kids (or adults) practice their basic addition, subtraction, multiplication and division skills. The **Flash Card Math Quiz Project** allows you to select problem type, what numbers you want to use and has three timing options. We look at using random numbers and review the timer object.

Flash Card Math Quiz Project Preview

In this chapter, we will build a **flash card math** program. Random math problems (selectable from addition, subtraction, multiplication, and/or division) using the numbers from 0 to 9 are presented. Timing options are available to help build both accuracy and speed.

The finished project is saved as **FlashCardMath** in the **\HomeJava\HomeJava Projects** project group. Start NetBeans (or your IDE). Open the specified project group. Make **FlashCardMath** the main project. Run the project. You will see:

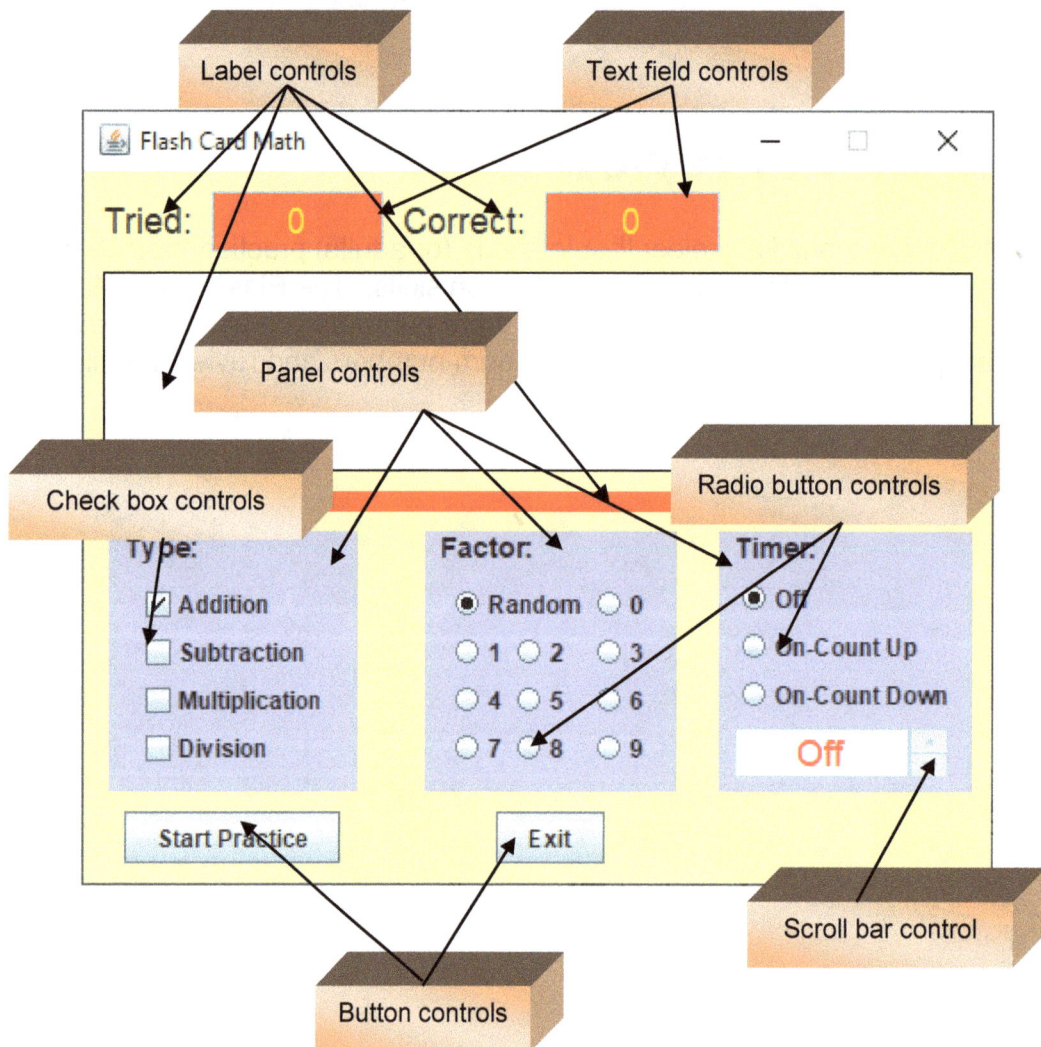

There are lots of controls. Two label controls are used for title information, two text fields for scoring. There's a large label in the middle of the frame (there is nothing in it, so you can't see it) used to display the math problem. And, a final label (the skinny red box) is just used for "decoration." Two button controls are used to start and stop the problems and to exit the project. There are also three panel controls. The first holds four check box controls used to select problem type. The second holds eleven radio button controls used to select numbers used in the problems. The third panel holds three radio button controls used to select the timing option. A vertical scroll bar control (next to a text field) is used to adjust the amount of time used in the flash card drills.

The flash card math program appears as:

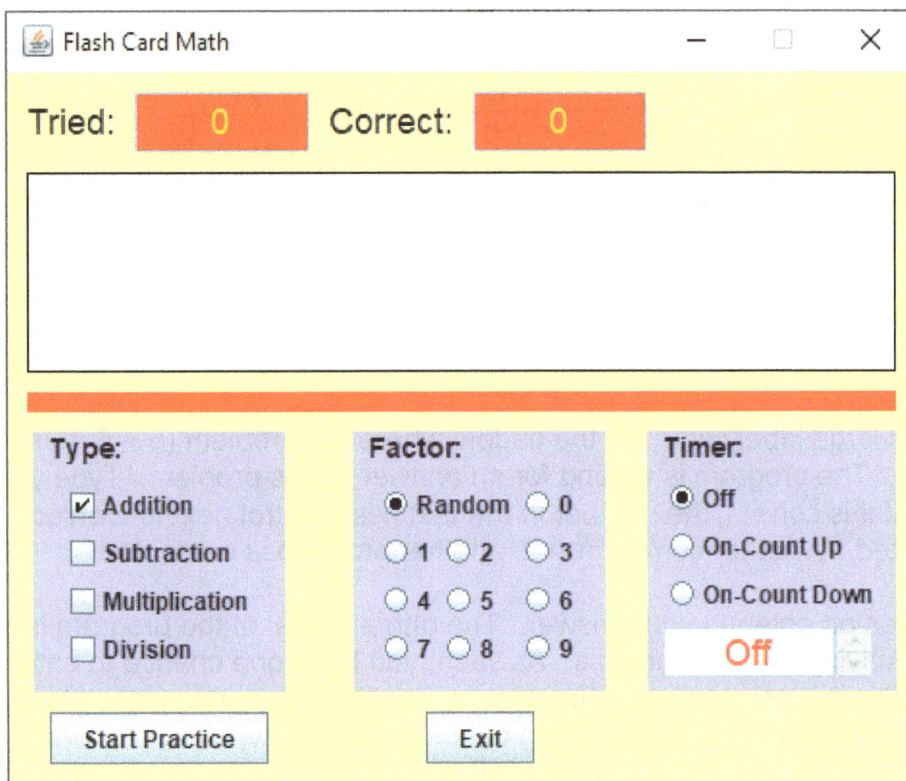

Many options are available. First, choose problem type from the **Type** panel. Choose from **Addition**, **Subtraction**, **Multiplication**, and/or **Division** problems (you may choose more than one problem type). Choose your **Factor**, any number from 0 to 9, or choose **Random** for random factors. These options may be changed at any time. To practice math facts, click on the **Start Practice** button.

When I click **Start Practice** (using the default choices), I see:

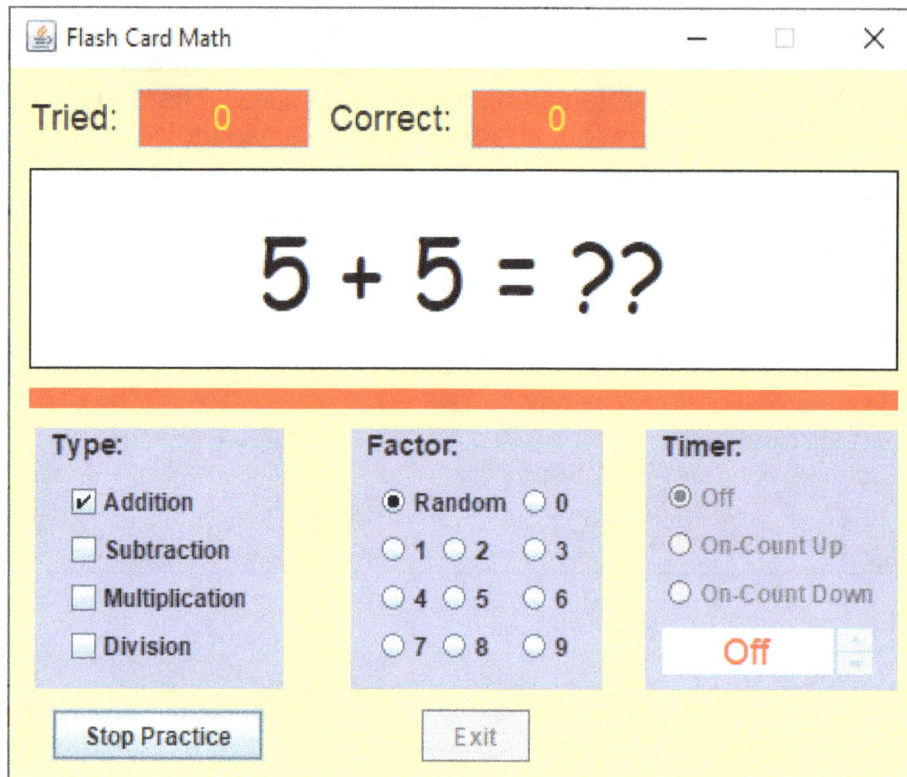

There is a large label control in the middle where the problem (5 + 5 =) is displayed. The program is waiting for an answer to this problem. Type your answer. If it is correct, the number in the text field control next to **Correct:** is incremented. Whether correct or not, another problem is presented.

A few notes on entering your answer. The primary goal of the program is to build speed in solving simple problems. As such, you have one chance to enter an answer - there is no erasing. If the answer has more than two digits (the number of digits in the answer is shown using question marks), type your answer from left to right. For example, if the answer is 10, type a 1 then a 0. Try several addition problems to see how answers are entered. You can stop practicing math problems, at any time, by clicking the **Stop Practice** button.

Other problem types can be selected and a new factor chosen at any time. Each problem is generated randomly, based on problem type and factor value. For **Addition**, you are given problems using your factor as the second addend. If you choose **7** as your factor, an example problem would be:

For **Subtraction**, you are given problems using your factor as the subtrahend (the number being subtracted). Selecting a factor of **5**, an example subtraction problem is:

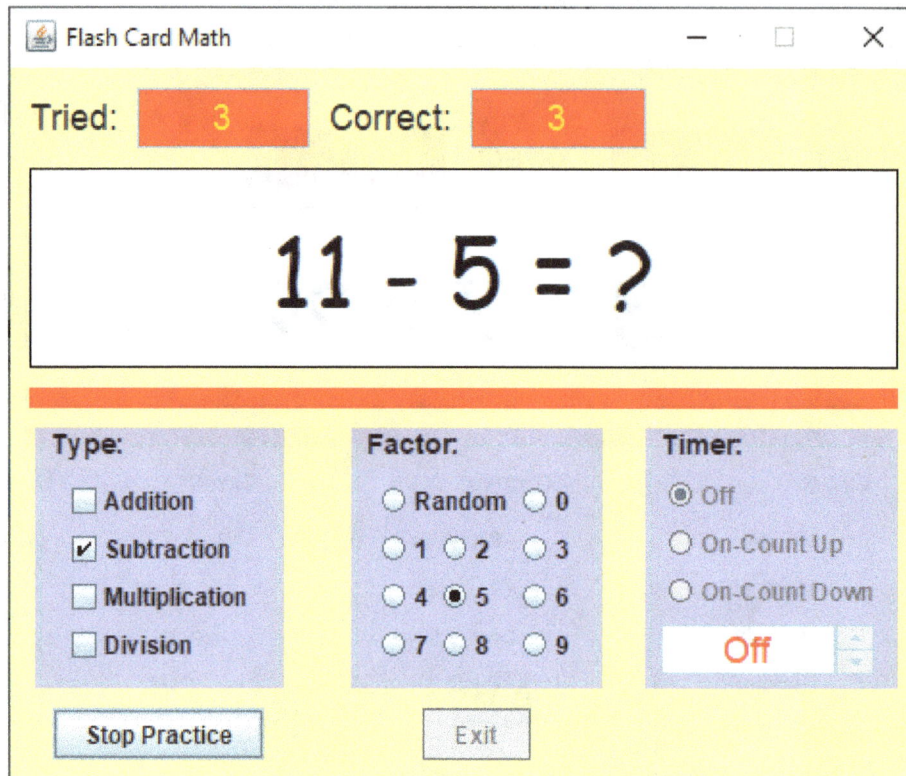

For **Multiplication**, you are given problems using your factor as the multiplier (the number you're multiplying by). If a factor of **9** is selected, an example multiplication problem is:

Lastly, for **Division**, you are given problems using your factor as the divisor (the number you are dividing by). If the selected factor is 4, a typical division problem would be:

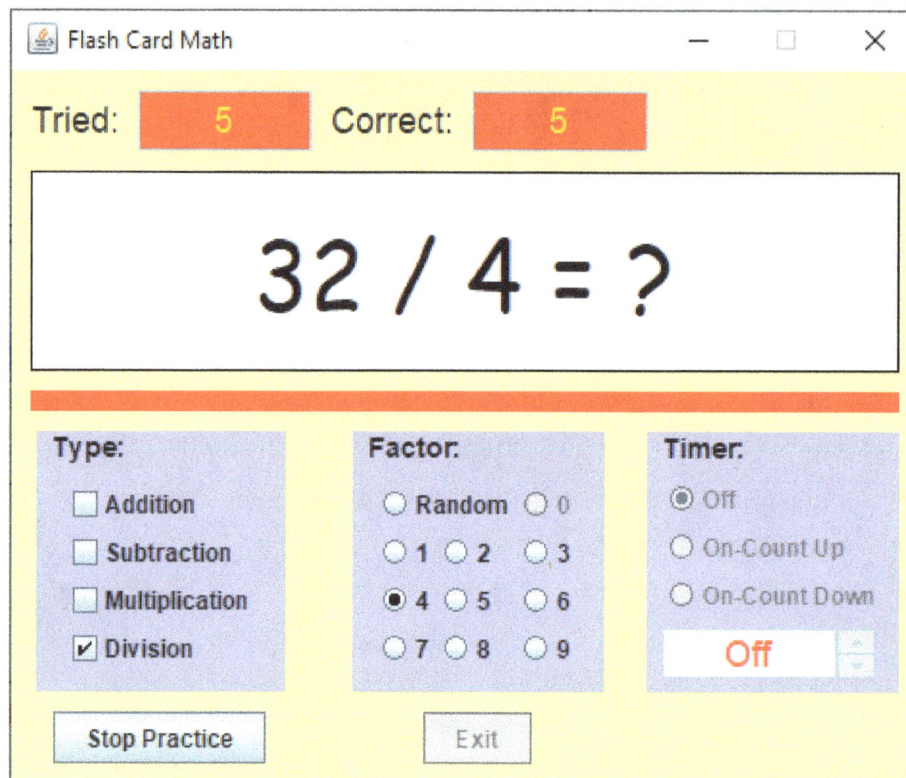

As mentioned, you do not have to choose a specific factor – **Random** factors can be chosen. Try all kinds of factors with all kinds of problem types.

There is another option to consider when using the flash card math project – the corresponding option choices are in the **Timer** panel. These options can only be selected when not solving problems. There are three choices here. If you select **Timer Off**, you solve problems until you click **Stop Practice**. If you select **On-Count Up**, a timer will appear and the computer will keep track of how long you were solving problems (a maximum of 30 minutes is allowed). If you select **On-Count Down**, a timer will appear, along with a scroll bar control. The scroll bar control is used to set how long you want to solve problems (a maximum of 30 minutes is allowed). The timer will then count down, allowing you to solve problems until the allotted time expires.

Try the timer options if you'd like. Here's the beginning of a run I made using the **On-Count Down** option (starting at 1 minute):

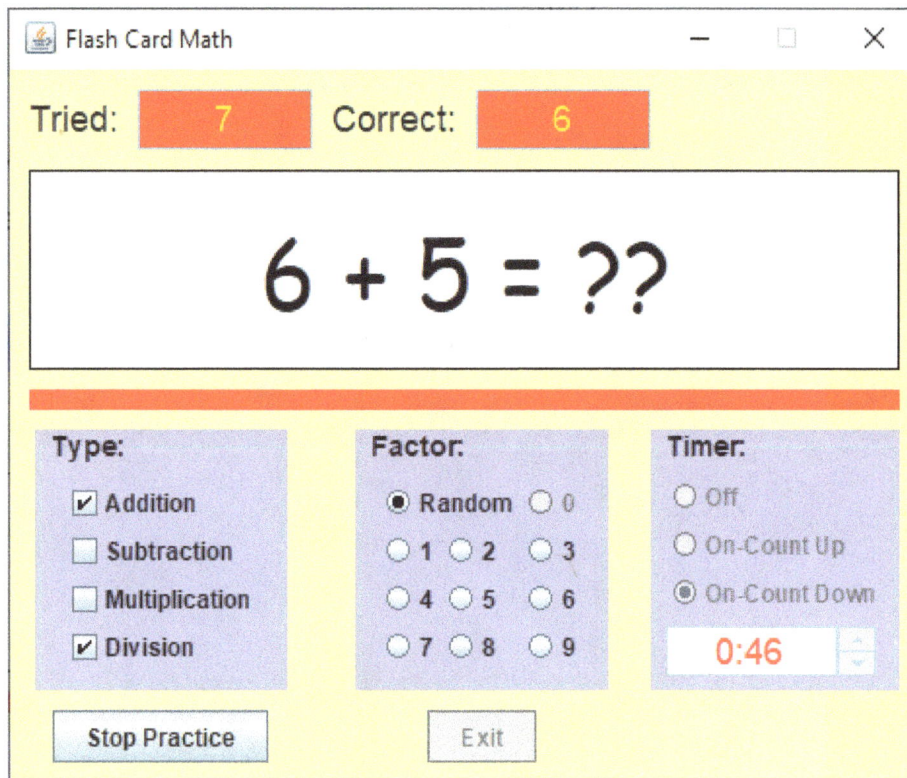

Once you are done practicing math problems (either you clicked **Stop Practice** or time ran out with the **On-Count Down** option), a message box appears giving you the results of your little quiz. This box tells you how many problems you solved and how many you got correct (including a percentage score). If the timer was on, you are also told how long you were solving problems and how much time (on average) you spent on each problem. Here's the message box I saw when I finished the quiz I started above:

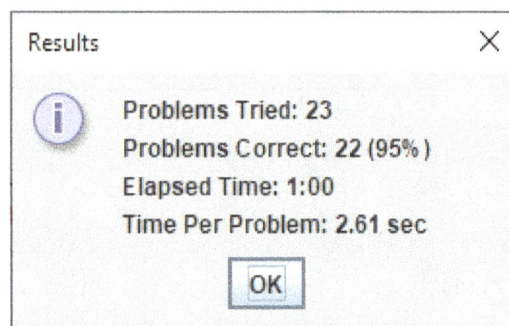

Click **OK** and you can try again. Click the **Exit** button in **Flash Card Math** when you are done solving problems.

You will now build this project in several stages. We first address **frame design**. We add the controls used to build the frame and establish initial properties. And, we address **code design** in detail. We cover random generation of problems, selection of the various program options, and how to use timing.

Flash Card Math Frame Design

We begin building the **Flash Card Math Project.** Let's build the frame. Start a new project in your Java project group – name it **FlashCardMath**. Delete default code in file named **FlashCardMath.java**. Once started, we suggest you immediately save the project with the name you chose. This sets up the folder and file structure needed for your project. Build the basic frame with these properties:

FlashCardMath Frame:
title	Flash Card Math
color	Color(255, 255, 192)
resizable	false

The code is:

```java
/*
 * FlashCardMath.java
 */
package flashcardmath;
import javax.swing.*;
import java.awt.*;
import java.awt.event.*;

public class FlashCardMath extends JFrame
{
  public static void main(String args[])
  {
    // create frame
    new FlashCardMath().setVisible(true);
  }

  public FlashCardMath()
  {
    // frame constructor
    setTitle("Flash Card Math");
    getContentPane().setBackground(new Color(255, 255,
192));
    setResizable(false);

    addWindowListener(new WindowAdapter()
    {
      public void windowClosing(WindowEvent evt)
      {
        exitForm(evt);
      }
```

```
    });

    getContentPane().setLayout(new GridBagLayout());
    GridBagConstraints gridConstraints;

    pack();
    Dimension screenSize =
Toolkit.getDefaultToolkit().getScreenSize();
    setBounds((int) (0.5 * (screenSize.width -
getWidth())), (int) (0.5 * (screenSize.height -
getHeight())), getWidth(), getHeight());
    }

  private void exitForm(WindowEvent evt)
  {
    System.exit(0);
  }
}
```

This code builds the frame, sets up the layout manager and includes code to exit the application. Run the code to make sure the frame (at least, what there is of it at this point) appears and is centered on the screen:

Let's populate our frame with other controls. All code for creating the frame and placing controls (except declarations) goes in the **FlashCardMath** constructor.

The **GridBagLayout** for the project frame is:

	gridx = 0	gridx = 1	gridx = 2	gridx = 3	gridx = 4
gridy = 0	triedLabel	triedTextField	correctLabel	correctTextField	
gridy = 1	problemLabel				
gridy = 2	dividerLabel				
gridy = 3	typePanel		factorPanel		timerPanel
gridy = 4	startButton		exitButton		

The top label controls (**triedLabel** and **correctLabel**) are used for title information. The text fields (**triedTextField** and **correctTextField**) are for scoring. One label (**problemLabel**) will display the math problem while the other (**dividerLabel**) is a dividing line. **typePanel** holds the check boxes used to select problem type, **factorPanel** holds the radio buttons used to select the factor, and **timerPanel** holds controls used to establish timing options. One button (**startButton**) starts and stops the problem solving while the other button (**exitButton**) exits the program. We'll add a few controls at a time. Let's add the controls 'above' the three panel controls.

The control properties are:

> **triedLabel:**
> | | |
> |---|---|
> | text | Tried: |
> | font | Arial, Plain, Size 18 |
> | gridx | 0 |
> | gridy | 0 |
> | anchor | WEST |
> | insets | 10, 10, 0, 10 |
>
> **triedTextField**:
> | | |
> |---|---|
> | text | 0 |
> | size | 90, 30 |
> | editable | false |
> | background | Red |
> | foreground | Yellow |
> | horizontalAlignment | Center |
> | font | Arial, Plain, Size 18 |
> | gridx | 1 |
> | gridy | 0 |
> | insets | 10, 0, 0, 0 |

correctLabel:

text	Correct:
font	Arial, Plain, Size 18
gridx	2
gridy	0
anchor	EAST
insets	10, 10, 0, 10

correctTextField:

text	0
size	90, 30
editable	false
background	Red
foreground	Yellow
horizontalAlignment	Center
font	Arial, Plain, Size 18
gridx	3
gridy	0
insets	10, 0, 0, 0

problemLabel:

border	Black line
size	450, 100
background	White
font	Comic Sans MS, Plain, Size 48
horizontalAlignment	Center
gridx	0
gridy	1
gridwidth	5
insets	10, 10, 0, 10

dividerLabel:

size	450, 10
background	Red
opaque	true
gridx	0
gridy	2
gridwidth	5
insets	10, 10, 10, 10

Declare these controls using:

```
JLabel triedLabel = new JLabel();
JTextField triedTextField = new JTextField();
JLabel correctLabel = new JLabel();
JTextField correctTextField = new JTextField();
JLabel problemLabel = new JLabel();
JLabel dividerLabel = new JLabel();
```

Note the top labels and text fields all use the same font. Let's create a Font object to use in each:

```
Font myFont = new Font("Arial", Font.PLAIN, 18);
```

Now, the controls are added to the frame using (recall code goes in frame constructor):

```
triedLabel.setText("Tried:");
triedLabel.setFont(myFont);
gridConstraints = new GridBagConstraints();
gridConstraints.gridx = 0;
gridConstraints.gridy = 0;
gridConstraints.anchor = GridBagConstraints.WEST;
gridConstraints.insets = new Insets(10, 10, 0, 10);
getContentPane().add(triedLabel, gridConstraints);

triedTextField.setText("0");
triedTextField.setPreferredSize(new Dimension(90,30));
triedTextField.setEditable(false);
triedTextField.setBackground(Color.RED);
triedTextField.setForeground(Color.YELLOW);
triedTextField.setHorizontalAlignment(SwingConstants.CENTE
R);
triedTextField.setFont(myFont);
gridConstraints = new GridBagConstraints();
gridConstraints.gridx = 1;
gridConstraints.gridy = 0;
gridConstraints.insets = new Insets(10, 0, 0, 0);
getContentPane().add(triedTextField, gridConstraints);

correctLabel.setText("Correct:");
correctLabel.setFont(myFont);
gridConstraints = new GridBagConstraints();
gridConstraints.gridx = 2;
gridConstraints.gridy = 0;
gridConstraints.anchor = GridBagConstraints.EAST;
gridConstraints.insets = new Insets(10, 10, 0, 10);
```

```
getContentPane().add(correctLabel, gridConstraints);

correctTextField.setText("0");
correctTextField.setPreferredSize(new Dimension(90,30));
correctTextField.setEditable(false);
correctTextField.setBackground(Color.RED);
correctTextField.setForeground(Color.YELLOW);
correctTextField.setHorizontalAlignment(SwingConstants.CEN
TER);
correctTextField.setFont(myFont);
gridConstraints = new GridBagConstraints();
gridConstraints.gridx = 3;
gridConstraints.gridy = 0;
gridConstraints.insets = new Insets(10, 0, 0, 0);
getContentPane().add(correctTextField, gridConstraints);

problemLabel.setText("");
problemLabel.setBorder(BorderFactory.createLineBorder(Colo
r.BLACK));
problemLabel.setPreferredSize(new Dimension(450, 100));
problemLabel.setBackground(Color.WHITE);
problemLabel.setOpaque(true);
problemLabel.setFont(new Font("Comic Sans MS", Font.PLAIN,
48));
problemLabel.setHorizontalAlignment(SwingConstants.CENTER)
;
gridConstraints = new GridBagConstraints();
gridConstraints.gridx = 0;
gridConstraints.gridy = 1;
gridConstraints.gridwidth = 5;
gridConstraints.insets = new Insets(10, 10, 0, 10);
getContentPane().add(problemLabel, gridConstraints);

dividerLabel.setPreferredSize(new Dimension(450, 10));
dividerLabel.setBackground(Color.RED);
dividerLabel.setOpaque(true);
gridConstraints = new GridBagConstraints();
gridConstraints.gridx = 0;
gridConstraints.gridy = 2;
gridConstraints.gridwidth = 5;
gridConstraints.insets = new Insets(10, 10, 10, 10);
getContentPane().add(dividerLabel, gridConstraints);
```

Save, run the project. You will see the added controls:

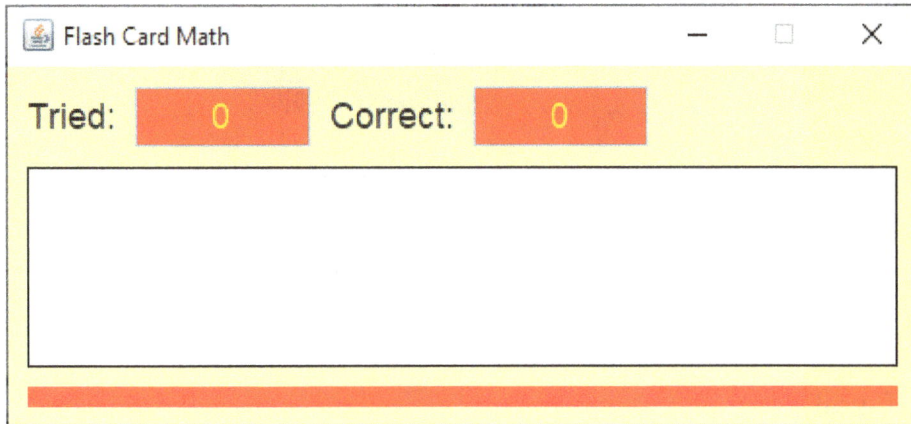

The **typePanel** will hold four check box controls (an array named **typeCheckBox**) used to select problem type. The **GridBagLayout** for typePanel is:

	gridx = 0
gridy = 0	**typeCheckBox[0]**
gridy =1	**typeCheckBox[1]**
gridy = 2	**typeCheckBox[2]**
gridy = 3	**typeCheckBox[3]**

The panel and check box properties:

typePanel::
size	130, 130
title	Type:
font	Arial, Bold, 14
background	Color(192, 192, 255), lightBlue
gridx	0 (on frame)
gridy	3 (on frame)
gridwidth	2
anchor	NORTH

typeCheckBox[0]:
text	Addition
background	lightBlue
selected	true
gridx	0 (on typePanel)
gridy	0 (on typePanel)
anchor	WEST

typeCheckBox[1]:
text	Subtraction
background	lightBlue
selected	true
gridx	0 (on typePanel)
gridy	1 (on typePanel)
anchor	WEST

typeCheckBox[2]:

text	Multiplication
background	lightBlue
selected	true
gridx	0 (on typePanel)
gridy	2 (on typePanel)
anchor	WEST

typeCheckBox[3]:

text	Division
background	lightBlue
selected	true
gridx	0 (on typePanel)
gridy	3 (on typePanel)
anchor	WEST

These controls are declared using (we've added a **Color** object to define the light blue color):

```
JPanel typePanel = new JPanel();
JCheckBox[] typeCheckBox = new JCheckBox[4];

Color lightBlue = new Color(192, 192, 255);
```

The check boxes are placed in the **typePanel** (which is placed in the frame) using:

```
UIManager.put("TitledBorder.font", new Font("Arial",
Font.BOLD, 14));

typePanel.setPreferredSize(new Dimension(130, 130));
typePanel.setBorder(BorderFactory.createTitledBorder("Type
:"));
typePanel.setBackground(lightBlue);
typePanel.setLayout(new GridBagLayout());
gridConstraints = new GridBagConstraints();
gridConstraints.gridx = 0;
gridConstraints.gridy = 3;
gridConstraints.gridwidth = 2;
gridConstraints.anchor = GridBagConstraints.NORTH;
getContentPane().add(typePanel, gridConstraints);

for (int i = 0; i < 4; i++)
{
   typeCheckBox[i] = new JCheckBox();
   typeCheckBox[i].setBackground(lightBlue);
   gridConstraints = new GridBagConstraints();
   gridConstraints.gridx = 0;
```

```
gridConstraints.gridy = i;
gridConstraints.anchor = GridBagConstraints.WEST;
typePanel.add(typeCheckBox[i], gridConstraints);
typeCheckBox[i].addActionListener(new ActionListener()
{
public void actionPerformed(ActionEvent e)
{
  typeCheckBoxActionPerformed(e);
}
});
}
typeCheckBox[0].setText("Addition");
typeCheckBox[1].setText("Subtraction");
typeCheckBox[2].setText("Multiplication");
typeCheckBox[3].setText("Division");
typeCheckBox[0].setSelected(true);
```

The first line here uses the **UIManager** to set the font for the panel borders.
Notice how properties are set and a method is added in the **for** loop.

The code above also adds an **ActionPerformed** method for each check box. Add
this empty method:

```
private void typeCheckBoxActionPerformed(ActionEvent e)
{
}
```

Add this code in the proper locations. Run to see:

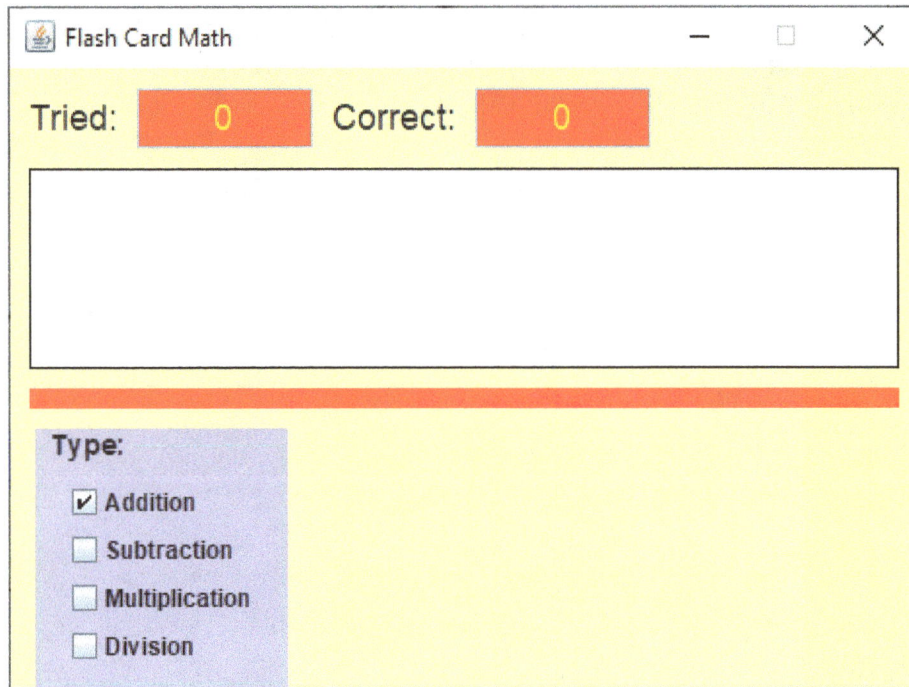

The type panel is displayed with a check mark next to **Addition**.

The **factorPanel** will hold eleven radio button controls (an array named **factorRadioButton**) used to select the factor used in the problems. The first ten buttons (factorRadioButton[0] – factorRadioButton[9]) choose the digits 0 through 9, the final button (factorRadioButton[10]) is for a random factor. The **GridBagLayout** for factorPanel is:

	gridx = 0	gridx = 1	gridx = 2
gridy = 0	factorRadioButton[10]		factorRadioButton[0]
gridy =1	factorRadioButton[1]	factorRadioButton[2]	factorRadioButton[3]
gridy = 2	factorRadioButton[4]	factorRadioButton[5]	factorRadioButton[6]
gridy = 3	factorRadioButton[7]	factorRadioButton[8]	factorRadioButton[9]

The panel and radio button properties:

factorPanel::
size	130, 130
title	Factor:
font	Arial, Bold, 14
background	lightBlue
gridx	2 (on frame)
gridy	3 (on frame)
gridwidth	2
anchor	NORTH

factorRadioButton[10]:
buttonGroup	factorButtonGroup
text	Random
selected	true
background	lightBlue
gridx	0 (on factorPanel)
gridy	0 (on factorPanel)
gridwidth	2
anchor	WEST

factorRadioButton[0]:
buttonGroup	factorButtonGroup
text	0
background	lightBlue
gridx	2 (on factorPanel)
gridy	0 (on factorPanel)
anchor	WEST

factorRadioButton[1]:
buttonGroup	factorButtonGroup
text	1
background	lightBlue
gridx	0 (on factorPanel)
gridy	1 (on factorPanel)
anchor	WEST

factorRadioButton[2]:
buttonGroup	factorButtonGroup
text	2
background	lightBlue
gridx	1 (on factorPanel)
gridy	1 (on factorPanel)
anchor	WEST

factorRadioButton[3]:
buttonGroup	factorButtonGroup
text	3
background	lightBlue
gridx	2 (on factorPanel)
gridy	1 (on factorPanel)
anchor	WEST

factorRadioButton[4]:
buttonGroup	factorButtonGroup
text	4
background	lightBlue
gridx	0 (on factorPanel)
gridy	2 (on factorPanel)
anchor	WEST

factorRadioButton[5]:
buttonGroup	factorButtonGroup
text	5
background	lightBlue
gridx	1 (on factorPanel)
gridy	2 (on factorPanel)
anchor	WEST

factorRadioButton[6]:

buttonGroup	factorButtonGroup
text	6
background	lightBlue
gridx	2 (on factorPanel)
gridy	2 (on factorPanel)
anchor	WEST

factorRadioButton[7]:

buttonGroup	factorButtonGroup
text	7
background	lightBlue
gridx	0 (on factorPanel)
gridy	3 (on factorPanel)
anchor	WEST

factorRadioButton[8]:

buttonGroup	factorButtonGroup
text	8
background	lightBlue
gridx	1 (on factorPanel)
gridy	3 (on factorPanel)
anchor	WEST

factorRadioButton[9]:

buttonGroup	factorButtonGroup
text	9
background	lightBlue
gridx	2 (on factorPanel)
gridy	3 (on factorPanel)
anchor	WEST

These controls are declared:

```
JPanel factorPanel = new JPanel();
ButtonGroup factorButtonGroup = new ButtonGroup();
JRadioButton[] factorRadioButton = new JRadioButton[11];
```

The radio buttons are placed in the **factorPanel** (which is placed in the frame) using:

```
factorPanel.setPreferredSize(new Dimension(130, 130));
factorPanel.setBorder(BorderFactory.createTitledBorder("Fa
ctor:"));
factorPanel.setBackground(lightBlue);
factorPanel.setLayout(new GridBagLayout());
gridConstraints = new GridBagConstraints();
gridConstraints.gridx = 2;
gridConstraints.gridy = 3;
gridConstraints.gridwidth = 2;
gridConstraints.anchor = GridBagConstraints.NORTH;
getContentPane().add(factorPanel, gridConstraints);

int x = 2;
int y = 0;
for (int i = 0; i < 11; i++)
{
  factorRadioButton[i] = new JRadioButton();
  factorRadioButton[i].setText(String.valueOf(i));
  factorRadioButton[i].setBackground(lightBlue);
  factorButtonGroup.add(factorRadioButton[i]);
  gridConstraints = new GridBagConstraints();
  if (i < 10)
  {
gridConstraints.gridx = x;
gridConstraints.gridy = y;
  }
  else
  {
gridConstraints.gridx = 0;
gridConstraints.gridy = 0;
gridConstraints.gridwidth = 2;
  }
  gridConstraints.anchor = GridBagConstraints.WEST;
  factorPanel.add(factorRadioButton[i], gridConstraints);
  factorRadioButton[i].addActionListener(new
ActionListener()
  {
    public void actionPerformed(ActionEvent e)
```

```
      {
         factorRadioButtonActionPerformed(e);
      }
   });
   x++;
   if (x > 2)
   {
x = 0;
y++;
   }
}
factorRadioButton[10].setText("Random");
factorRadioButton[10].setSelected(true);
```

Notice how properties are set and a method is added in the **for** loop.

The code adds an **ActionPerformed** method for each radio button. Add this empty method:

```
private void factorRadioButtonActionPerformed(ActionEvent e)
{
}
```

Add this code in the proper locations. Run to see:

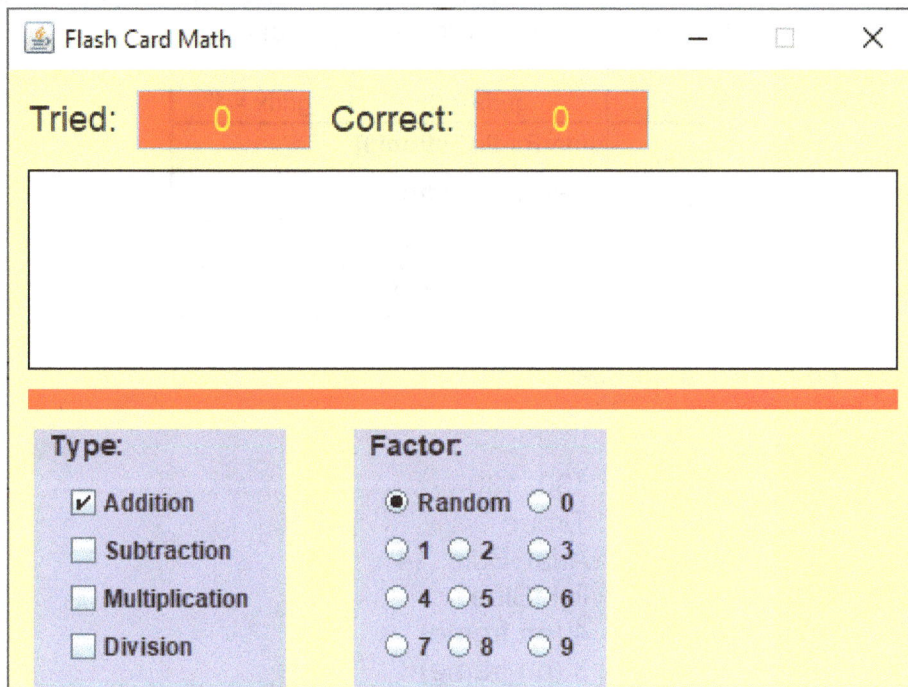

The factor panel is displayed with the **Random** button selected.

The **timerPanel** has three radio buttons to allow selection of timer options (an array named **timerRadioButton**). I also holds a text field and scroll bar used to display/set times. The **GridBagLayout** for timerPanel is:

	gridx = 0	gridx = 1
gridy = 0	timerRadioButton[0]	
gridy =1	timerRadioButton[1]	
gridy = 2	timerRadioButton[2]	
gridy = 3	timerTextField	timerScrollBar

The panel and control properties:

timerPanel::
size	130, 130
title	Timer:
font	Arial, Bold, 14
background	lightBlue
gridx	4 (on frame)
gridy	3 (on frame)
insets	0, 0, 0, 10
anchor	NORTH

timerRadioButton[0]:
buttonGroup	timerButtonGroup
text	Off
selected	true
background	lightBlue
gridx	0 (on factorPanel)
gridy	0 (on factorPanel)
gridwidth	2
anchor	WEST

timerRadioButton[1]:
buttonGroup	timerButtonGroup
text	On-Count Up
background	lightBlue
gridx	0 (on factorPanel)
gridy	1 (on factorPanel)
gridwidth	2
anchor	WEST

timerRadioButton[2]:

buttonGroup	timerButtonGroup
text	On-Count Down
background	lightBlue
gridx	0 (on factorPanel)
gridy	2 (on factorPanel)
gridwidth	2
anchor	WEST

timerTextField:

text	Off
size	90, 25
editable	false
background	White
foreground	red
horizontalAlignment	Center
font	myFont
gridx	0 (on factorPanel)
gridy	3
insets	5, 0, 0, 0
anchor	WEST

timerScrollBar:

size	20, 25
minimum	1
maximum	60
value	1
blockIncrement	1
unitIncrement	1
orientation	Vertical
enabled	false
gridx	1
gridy	3
insets	5, 0, 0, 0
anchor	WEST

The scroll bar is disabled initially since the timer is off by default.

These controls are declared:

```
JPanel timerPanel = new JPanel();
ButtonGroup timerButtonGroup = new ButtonGroup();
JRadioButton[] timerRadioButton = new JRadioButton[3];
JTextField timerTextField = new JTextField();
JScrollBar timerScrollBar = new JScrollBar();
```

The controls are placed in the **timerPanel** (which is placed in the frame) using:

```
timerPanel.setPreferredSize(new Dimension(130, 130));
timerPanel.setBorder(BorderFactory.createTitledBorder("Tim
er:"));
timerPanel.setBackground(lightBlue);
timerPanel.setLayout(new GridBagLayout());
gridConstraints = new GridBagConstraints();
gridConstraints.gridx = 4;
gridConstraints.gridy = 3;
gridConstraints.insets = new Insets(0, 0, 0, 10);
gridConstraints.anchor = GridBagConstraints.NORTH;
getContentPane().add(timerPanel, gridConstraints);

for (int i = 0; i < 3; i++)
{
   timerRadioButton[i] = new JRadioButton();
   timerRadioButton[i].setBackground(lightBlue);
   timerButtonGroup.add(timerRadioButton[i]);
   gridConstraints = new GridBagConstraints();
   gridConstraints.gridx = 0;
   gridConstraints.gridy = i;
   gridConstraints.gridwidth = 2;
   gridConstraints.anchor = GridBagConstraints.WEST;
   timerPanel.add(timerRadioButton[i], gridConstraints);
   timerRadioButton[i].addActionListener(new
ActionListener()
   {
public void actionPerformed(ActionEvent e)
{
   timerRadioButtonActionPerformed(e);
}
   });
}
timerRadioButton[0].setText("Off");
timerRadioButton[1].setText("On-Count Up");
timerRadioButton[2].setText("On-Count Down");
timerRadioButton[0].setSelected(true);
```

```
timerTextField.setText("Off");
timerTextField.setPreferredSize(new Dimension(90,25));
timerTextField.setEditable(false);
timerTextField.setBackground(Color.WHITE);
timerTextField.setForeground(Color.RED);
timerTextField.setHorizontalAlignment(SwingConstants.CENTE
R);
timerTextField.setFont(myFont);
gridConstraints = new GridBagConstraints();
gridConstraints.gridx = 0;
gridConstraints.gridy = 3;
gridConstraints.anchor = GridBagConstraints.WEST;
gridConstraints.insets = new Insets(5, 0, 0, 0);
timerPanel.add(timerTextField, gridConstraints);

timerScrollBar.setPreferredSize(new Dimension(20, 25));
timerScrollBar.setMinimum(1);
timerScrollBar.setMaximum(60);
timerScrollBar.setValue(1);
timerScrollBar.setBlockIncrement(1);
timerScrollBar.setUnitIncrement(1);
timerScrollBar.setOrientation(JScrollBar.VERTICAL);
timerScrollBar.setEnabled(false);
gridConstraints = new GridBagConstraints();
gridConstraints.gridx = 1;
gridConstraints.gridy = 3;
gridConstraints.anchor = GridBagConstraints.WEST;
gridConstraints.insets = new Insets(5, 0, 0, 0);
timerPanel.add(timerScrollBar, gridConstraints);
timerScrollBar.addAdjustmentListener(new
AdjustmentListener()
{
  public void adjustmentValueChanged(AdjustmentEvent e)
  {
timerScrollBarAdjustmentValueChanged(e);
  }
});
```

The code adds an **ActionPerformed** method for each radio button and an **AdjustmentValueChanged** method for the scroll bar. Add these empty method:

```
private void timerRadioButtonActionPerformed(ActionEvent
e)
{
}

private void timerScrollBarAdjustmentValueChanged
(AdjustmentEvent e)
{
}
```

Add this code in the proper locations. Run to see:

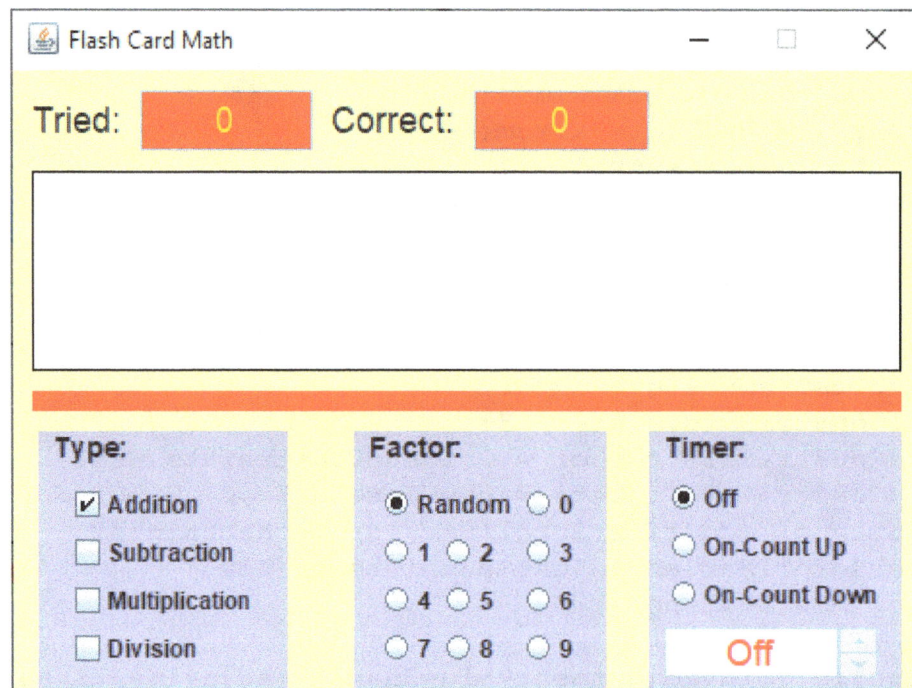

The timer panel is displayed with the **Off** button selected. Let's add a couple of buttons and we're done.

The two button controls (**startButton** and **exitButton**) are placed directly in the frame. The properties are:

startButton:

text	Start Practice
gridx	0
gridy	4
gridwidth	2
insets	10, 0, 10, 0

exitButton:

text	Exit
gridx	2
gridy	4
gridwidth	2
insets	10, 0, 10, 0

Declare the controls using:

```
JButton startButton = new JButton();
JButton exitButton = new JButton();
```

Add the buttons to the frame using:

```
startButton.setText("Start Practice");
gridConstraints = new GridBagConstraints();
gridConstraints.gridx = 0;
gridConstraints.gridy = 4;
gridConstraints.gridwidth = 2;
gridConstraints.insets = new Insets(10, 0, 10, 0);
getContentPane().add(startButton, gridConstraints);
startButton.addActionListener(new ActionListener()
{
  public void actionPerformed(ActionEvent e)
  {
startButtonActionPerformed(e);
  }
});
```

```
exitButton.setText("Exit");
gridConstraints = new GridBagConstraints();
gridConstraints.gridx = 2;
gridConstraints.gridy = 4;
gridConstraints.gridwidth = 2;
gridConstraints.insets = new Insets(10, 0, 10, 0);
getContentPane().add(exitButton, gridConstraints);
exitButton.addActionListener(new ActionListener()
{
   public void actionPerformed(ActionEvent e)
   {
exitButtonActionPerformed(e);
   }
});
```

This code also adds listeners for each button. Add these empty methods:

```
private void startButtonActionPerformed(ActionEvent e)
{
}

private void exitButtonActionPerformed(ActionEvent e)
{
}
```

Save, run the program one more time. You will see the completed frame:

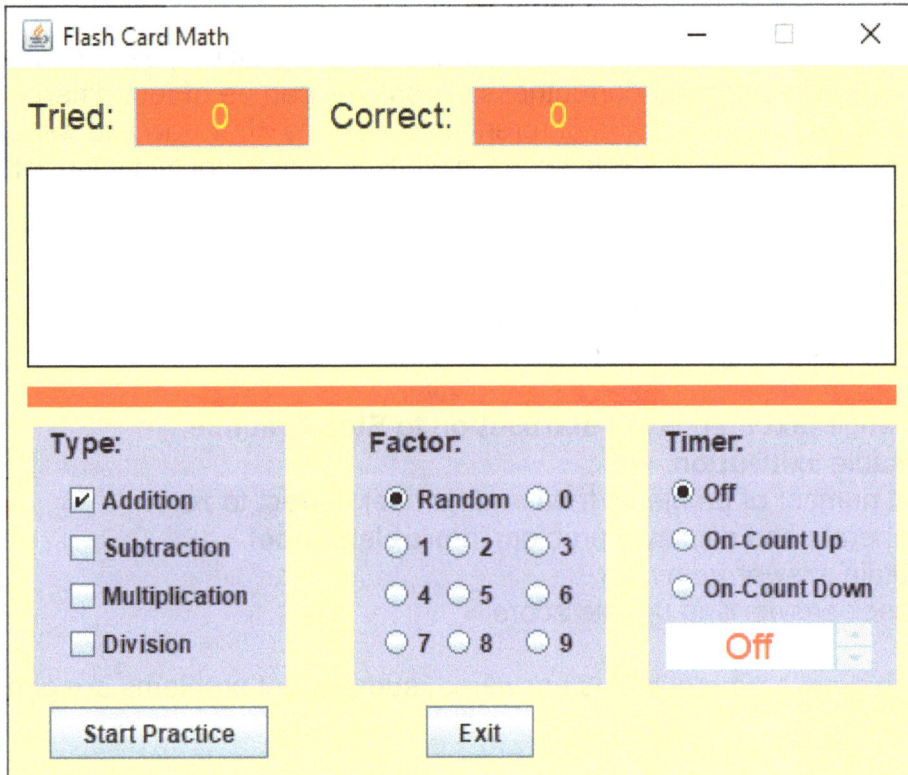

We will begin writing code for the application. We will write the code in several steps. As a first step, we write the code that generates a random problem (using the **Random** object) and gets the answer from the user, updating the score.

Code Design – Start Practice

The idea of the flash card math project is to display a problem, receive an answer from the user and check for correctness. Problems can be of four different types with different factor choices and different timer options. For now, we will ignore the timer options. Once this initial code is working satisfactorily, timing will be considered. Again, this step-by-step approach to building a project is far simpler than trying to build everything at once.

Things begin by clicking the **Start Practice** button (**startButton**). When this happens, the following steps are taken:

> Change **text** property of **startButton** to **Stop Practice**.
> Disable **exitButton**.
> Set number of problems tried and number correct to zero.
> Generate and display a problem in **problemLabel**.
> Obtain answer from user.
> Check answer and update score.

Once each generated problem is answered, subsequent problems are generated and answered.

The user answers problems until he/she clicks **Stop Practice** (or time elapses in timed drills). The steps followed at this point are:

> Change **text** property of **startButton** to **Start Practice**
> Enable **exitButton**.
> Clear **problemLabel**.
> Present results.

This code (for the **startButtonActionPerformed** method) is fairly straightforward. Let's build the framework. First, create a **Random** object and declare two class level variables to keep track of the number of problems tried and the number correct:

```
Random myRandom = new Random();
int numberTried, numberCorrect;
```

The **Random** object requires addition of this import statement:

```
import java.util.Random;
```

Now, use this code in the **startButtonActionPerformed** method (implements the steps above, except for presenting results):

```
private void startButtonActionPerformed(ActionEvent e)
{
  if (startButton.getText().equals("Start Practice"))
  {
    startButton.setText("Stop Practice");
    exitButton.setEnabled(false);
    numberTried = 0;
    numberCorrect = 0;
    triedTextField.setText("0");
    correctTextField.setText("0");
    problemLabel.setText(getProblem());
  }
  else
  {
    startButton.setText( "Start Practice");
    exitButton.setEnabled(true);
    problemLabel.setText("");
  }
}
```

This code uses a general method **getProblem** to generate the random problem and return it as a **String** type. Add this nearly empty method (we'll fill it in soon).

```
private String getProblem()
{
  return ("Problem!");
}
```

And, while we're at it, code the **exitButtonActionPerformed** method.

```
private void exitButtonActionPerformed(ActionEvent e)
{
  System.exit(0);
}
```

Save and run the project. The form should appear as:

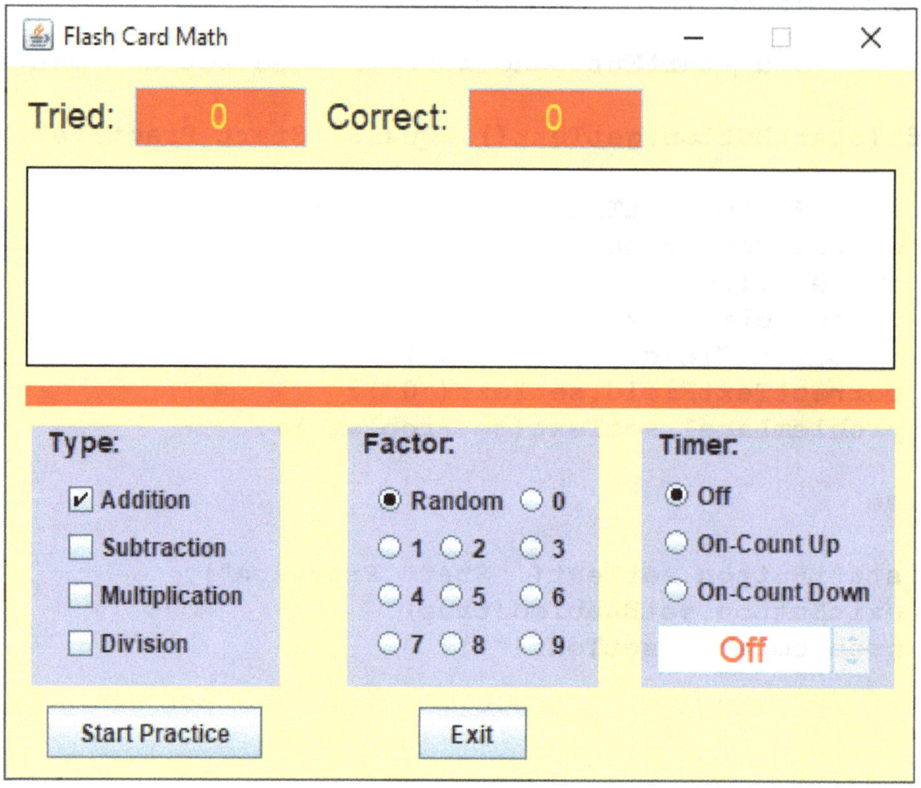

All controls are in their initial configuration. You can change options, but nothing will happen since there is no code behind any of the check boxes or radio buttons.

Click **Start Practice** to make sure buttons change as planned. You will also see the generated "problem":

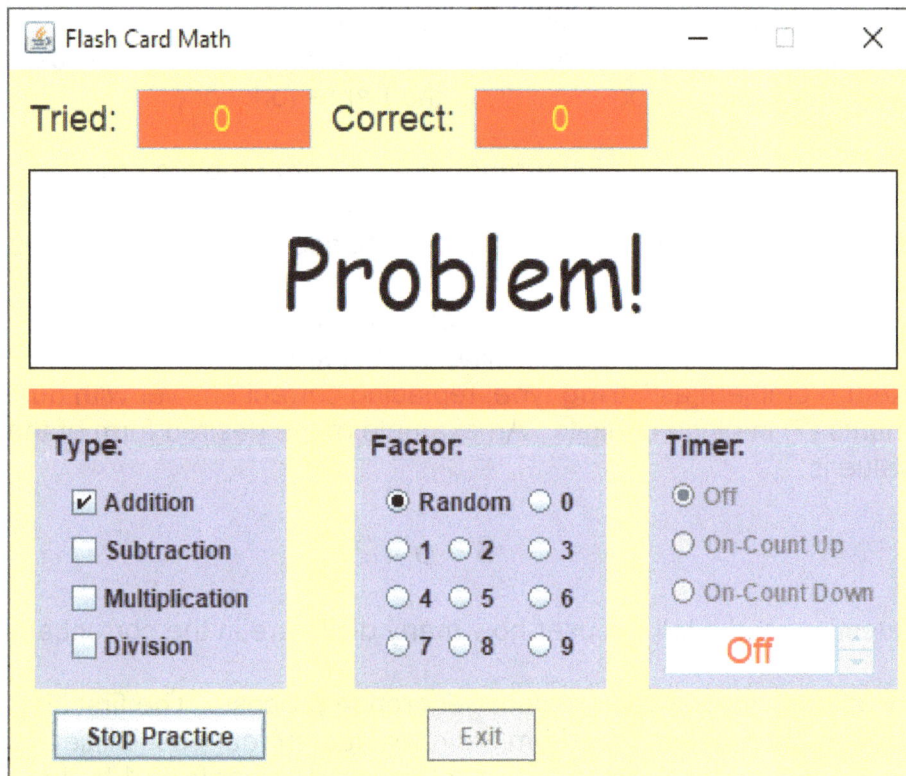

Now, click **Stop Practice**. Make sure **Exit** works.

This framework seems acceptable. We continue code design by discussing **problem generation** and **obtaining an answer** (including **scoring**) from the user. Then, later we discuss **timing** and **presenting the results**.

Code Design – Problem Generation

To generate a problem, we examine the current options selected by the user and produce a random problem based on these selections. All code will be in the **getProblem** general method currently in the framework code.

The steps involved in generating a random flash card problem are:

> ➢ Select problem type (random selection based on checked choices in **Type** panel)
> ➢ Generate factor (based on selection in **Factor** panel)
> ➢ Formulate problem and determine correct answer.
> ➢ Return problem as **String** type, replacing correct answer with question marks (?) in place of digits. An example of the desired form of the returned value is:

$$8 + 6 = ??$$

where question marks tell the user how many digits are in the correct answer.

Let's look at each step of the problem generation process. The first step is to choose a random problem type from the maximum of four possibilities. We will use a simple approach, first generating a random number from 1 to 4 (1 representing addition, 2 representing subtraction, 3 representing multiplication and 4 representing division). If the check box (in the **Type** panel) corresponding to the random number is checked, that will be the problem type. It the check box corresponding to the random number is not checked, we choose another random number. We continue this process until a problem type is selected. Notice this approach assumes at least one check box is always selected. We will make sure this is the case when developing code for the problem type option. There are more efficient ways to choose problem type which don't involve loops, but, for this simple problem, this works quite well.

A snippet of code that performs the choice of problem type (**p**) based on random number **pType** is:

```
p = 0;
do
{
  pType = myRandom.nextInt(4) + 1;
  if (pType == 1 && typeCheckBox[0].isSelected())
  {
    // Addition
    p = pType;
  }
  else if (pType == 2 && typeCheckBox[1].isSelected())
  {
    // Subtraction
    p = pType;
  }
  else if (pType == 3 && typeCheckBox[2].isSelected())
  {
    // Multiplication
    p = pType;
    number = myRandom.nextInt(10);
  }
  else if (pType == 4 && typeCheckBox[3].isSelected())
  {
    // Division
    p = pType;
  }
}
while (p == 0);
```

Once a problem type is selected, we determine the factor used to generate a problem. It can be a selected value from 0 to 9, or a random value from 0 to 9, based on the radio button selected in the **Factor** panel. For now, we assume that value is provided by a general method **getFactor(p)** that returns an **int** value, based on problem type **p**.

Each problem has four variables associated with it: **factor**, representing the value returned by **getFactor**, **number**, the other number used in the math problem, **correctAnswer**, the problem answer, and **problem**, a string representation of the unsolved problem. Once a problem type and factor have been determined, we find values for each of these variables. Each problem type has unique considerations for problem generation. Let's look at each type.

For **Addition** problems, the selected factor is the second **addend** in the problem. The string form of addition problems (**problem**) will be:

number + factor =

where **number** is a random value from 0 to 9, while recall **factor** is the selected factor. A snippet of code to generate an addition problem and determine the **correctAnswer** is:

```
number = myRandom.nextInt(10);
factor = getFactor(1);
correctAnswer = number + factor;
problem = String.valueOf(number) + " + " +
String.valueOf(factor) + " = ";
```

For **Subtraction** problems, the factor is the **subtrahend** (the number being subtracted). The string form of subtraction problems (**problem**) will be:

number - factor =

We want all the possible answers to be positive numbers between 0 and 9. Because of this, we formulate the problem in a backwards sense, generating a random answer (**correctAnswer**), then computing **number** based on that answer and the known factor (**factor**). The code that does this is:

```
factor = getFactor(2);
correctAnswer = myRandom.nextInt(10);
number = correctAnswer + factor;
problem = String.valueOf(number) + " - " +
String.valueOf(factor) + " = ";
```

For **Multiplication** problems, the selected factor is the **multiplier** (the number you're multiplying by) in the problem. The string form of multiplication problems (**problem**) will be:

> number x factor =

where **number** is a random value from 0 to 9, and **factor** is the factor. A snippet of code to generate a multiplication problem and determine the **correctAnswer** is:

```
number = myRandom.nextInt(10);
factor = getFactor(3);
correctAnswer = number * factor;
problem = String.valueOf(number) + " x " +
String.valueOf(factor) + " = ";
```

For **Division** problems, the factor is the **divisor** (the number doing the dividing). The string form of division problems (**problem**) will be:

> number / factor =

Like in subtraction, we want all the possible answers to be positive numbers between 0 and 9. So, we again formulate the problem in a backwards sense, generating a random answer (**correctAnswer**), then computing **number** based on that answer and the known factor (**factor**). The code that does this is:

```
factor = getFactor(4);
correctAnswer = myRandom.nextInt(10);
number = correctAnswer * factor;
problem = String.valueOf(number) + " / " +
String.valueOf(factor) + " = ";
```

Note with division, we must make sure the factor is never zero (can't divide by zero).

The **getFactor** routine provides the factor based on the radio button selection in the **Factor** panel and problem type **p**. For random factors, it will make sure a zero is not returned if a division problem is being generated. The **getFactor** general method is thus:

```
private int getFactor(int p)
{
  if (factorRadioButton[10].isSelected())
  {
    //random
     if (p == 4)
       return (myRandom.nextInt(9) + 1);
     else
       return (myRandom.nextInt(10));
  }
  else
  {
    for (int i = 0; i < 10; i++)
    {
      if (factorRadioButton[i].isSelected())
        return(i);
    }
      return (0);
  }
}
```

If **Random** (**factorRadioButton[10]**) option is selected, 0 to 9 is returned for addition, subtraction and multiplication problems; 1 to 9 is returned for division problems (**p = 4**). If another radio button is selected, the selected factor is returned (we will have to make sure zero is not a choice when doing division).

The **getProblem** method is nearly complete. We want to return the **problem** variable with appended question marks that represent the number of digits (**numberDigits**, another class level variable) in the correct answer. The code snippet that does this is:

```
if (correctAnswer < 10)
{
  numberDigits = 1;
  return (problem + "?");
}
else
{
  numberDigits = 2;
  return (problem + "??");
}
```

We can now assemble all the little code snippets into a final form for **getProblem** method. First, add these declarations for class level variables:

```
int correctAnswer, numberDigits;
String problem;
```

To form the **getProblem** method, start with the snippet that selects problem type. Then, add each problem generation segment (one for each of the four mathematical operations) in its corresponding location. Finally, add the question mark appending code. The finished method is:

```
private String getProblem()
{
  int pType, p, number, factor;
  p = 0;
  do
  {
    pType = myRandom.nextInt(4) + 1;
    if (pType == 1 && typeCheckBox[0].isSelected())
    {
      // Addition
      p = pType;
      number = myRandom.nextInt(10);
      factor = getFactor(1);
      correctAnswer = number + factor;
      problem = String.valueOf(number) + " + " +
String.valueOf(factor) + " = ";
    }
    else if (pType == 2 && typeCheckBox[1].isSelected())
    {
      // Subtraction
```

```
      p = pType;
      factor = getFactor(2);
      correctAnswer = myRandom.nextInt(10);
      number = correctAnswer + factor;
      problem = String.valueOf(number) + " - " +
String.valueOf(factor) + " = ";
    }
    else if (pType == 3 && typeCheckBox[2].isSelected())
    {
      // Multiplication
      p = pType;
      number = myRandom.nextInt(10);
      factor = getFactor(3);
      correctAnswer = number * factor;
      problem = String.valueOf(number) + " x " +
String.valueOf(factor) + " = ";
    }
    else if (pType == 4 && typeCheckBox[3].isSelected())
    {
      // Division
      p = pType;
      factor = getFactor(4);
      correctAnswer = myRandom.nextInt(10);
      number = correctAnswer * factor;
      problem = String.valueOf(number) + " / " +
String.valueOf(factor) + " = ";
    }
  }
  while (p == 0);
  if (correctAnswer < 10)
  {
    numberDigits = 1;
    return (problem + "?");
  }
  else
  {
    numberDigits = 2;
    return (problem + "??");
  }
}
```

Add this to the project along with the code for **getFactor**. Remember to delete the temporary line that just displays **Problem!**

Save and run the project. Click **Start Practice** and you should see a random addition problem:

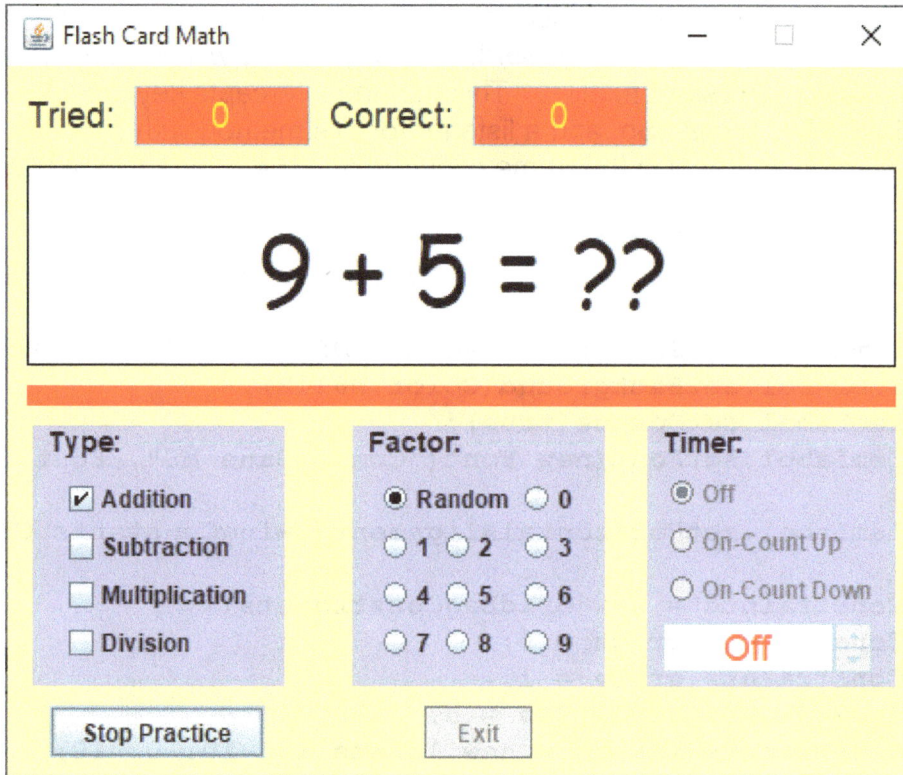

The two question marks tell us there are two digits in the correct answer. We'll see how to get that answer next. At this point, all you can do is click **Stop Practice**. You can then click **Start Practice** to see another addition problem if you'd like. View as many addition problems as you want.

Actually, you can also view other types of problems with other factors. But, you need to be careful. You need to make sure there is always at least one problem type selected. And, if **Division** problems are selected, make sure the selected **Factor** is not zero (**0**). Later, in code, we will make sure this doesn't happen.

Code Design – Obtaining Answer

Once a problem is displayed, the user can enter the digits in the answer. These digits will be entered using the keyboard. The keystrokes will be handled by the **problemLabelKeyPressed** method. This method intercepts keystrokes when **problemLabel** has focus. So, add a listener for this method with the code establishing problemLabel in the frame constructor. The needed code is shaded:

```
problemLabel.setText("");
problemLabel.setBorder(BorderFactory.createLineBorder(Colo
r.BLACK));
problemLabel.setPreferredSize(new Dimension(450, 100));
problemLabel.setBackground(Color.WHITE);
problemLabel.setOpaque(true);
problemLabel.setFont(new Font("Comic Sans MS", Font.PLAIN,
48));
problemLabel.setHorizontalAlignment(SwingConstants.CENTER)
;
gridConstraints = new GridBagConstraints();
gridConstraints.gridx = 0;
gridConstraints.gridy = 1;
gridConstraints.gridwidth = 5;
gridConstraints.insets = new Insets(10, 10, 0, 10);
getContentPane().add(problemLabel, gridConstraints);
problemLabel.addKeyListener(new KeyAdapter()
{
  public void keyPressed(KeyEvent e)
  {
    problemLabelKeyPressed(e);
  }
});
```

Add the empty method **problemLabelKeyPressed** where keystrokes will be examined:

```
private void problemLabelKeyPressed(KeyEvent e)
{
}
```

We will need to insure the label has focus when it needs it. That way, no key strokes will be missed.

The steps for obtaining and checking an answer in the key pressed method are:

> ➢ Make sure keystroke is a number (0 to 9).
> ➢ If number, keep keystroke as part of your answer and replace question mark with number.
> ➢ If a question mark remains, exit waiting for another keystroke.
> ➢ If all question marks are gone, compare your answer with correct answer.
> ➢ Increment the number of problems tried.
> ➢ If your answer is correct, increment the number of correct problems.
> ➢ Update scoring label controls.
> ➢ Generate another problem.

Declare class level variables to hold your answer and the current digit number in your answer:

```
String yourAnswer;
int digitNumber;
```

The **problemLabelKeyPressed** method that incorporates the steps listed above is then:

```java
private void problemLabelKeyPressed(KeyEvent e)
{
  if (startButton.getText().equals("Start Practice"))
    return;
  // only allow number keys
  if (e.getKeyChar() >= '0' && e.getKeyChar() <= '9')
  {
    yourAnswer += e.getKeyChar();
    problemLabel.setText(problem + yourAnswer);
    if (digitNumber != numberDigits)
    {
      digitNumber++;
      problemLabel.setText(problemLabel.getText() + "?");
      return;
    }
    else
    {
      numberTried++;
      // check answer
      if (Integer.valueOf(yourAnswer).intValue() ==
correctAnswer)
      {
        numberCorrect++;
      }
      triedTextField.setText(String.valueOf(numberTried));

correctTextField.setText(String.valueOf(numberCorrect));
      problemLabel.setText(getProblem());
    }
  }
}
```

In the first few lines of code, we make sure we are solving problems before allowing any keystrokes. Notice how all digits in your answer (represented by the typed character in **e.getKeyChar()**) are saved and concatenated into **yourAnswer**. Also, notice how the displayed problem is updated, overwriting a question mark, with each keystroke. As mentioned earlier, the program only gives you one chance to enter an answer - there is no erasing.

You need to add a few lines to the **getProblem** method to initialize **yourAnswer** and **digitNumber**, with each new problem, and also give the problem label focus, so answers can be typed. The modified method is (new lines are coded, most unmodified code is not shown):

```
private String getProblem()
{
  int pType, p, number, factor;
  p = 0;
  do
  {
       .
       .
  {
  while (p == 0);
  yourAnswer = "";
  digitNumber = 1;
  problemLabel.requestFocus();
  if (correctAnswer < 10)
  {
    numberDigits = 1;
    return (problem + "?");
  }
  else
  {
    numberDigits = 2;
    return (problem + "??");
  }
}
```

Save and run the project. You should now be able to answer as many random addition problems as you'd like. Try it. Make sure the score is updating properly. You can stop practicing problems, at any time, by clicking the **Stop Practice** button. As mentioned earlier, you can also solve other types of problems with other factors, if you're careful changing the options. Make sure one problem type is always selected and make sure zero is not used with division problems. And, as programmed, you can only change options when stopped because the problem label loses focus and answers can't be entered. Try it, you'll see what I mean. We'll fix these problems next.

Code Design – Choosing Problem Type and Factor

The selection of problem type seems simple. Choose the check box or check boxes you want and the correct problem will be generated. But there are a couple of problems we've alluded to. Currently, there is nothing to prevent a user from "unchecking" all the boxes, leaving no problem type to select. We must make sure at least one box is always selected. And, if **Division** problems are selected, we cannot allow zero (0) to be used as a factor. We now write code to address these problems.

The code to handle these considerations goes in the **typeCheckBoxActionPerformed** method. In this method, these steps are followed:

> Determine which check box was clicked.
> Determine how many boxes are checked.
> If **Division** (**typeCheckBox[3]**) is checked, make sure zero is not the selected factor; if it is, change the factor to 1. Also, if **Division** is checked, disable **factorRadioButton[0]** (the zero choice).
> If no boxes are checked, "recheck" selected check box.
> Set focus on problem label.

The **typeCheckBoxActionPerformed** method that implements these steps is:

```
private void typeCheckBoxActionPerformed(ActionEvent e)
{
  int numberChecks;
  int clickedBox = 0;
  // determine which box was clicked
  String s = e.getActionCommand();
  if (s.equals("Addition"))
    clickedBox = 0;
  else if (s.equals("Subtraction"))
    clickedBox = 1;
  else if (s.equals("Multiplication"))
    clickedBox = 2;
  else if (s.equals("Division"))
    clickedBox = 3;
  // determine how many boxes are checked
  numberChecks = 0;
  if (typeCheckBox[0].isSelected())
    numberChecks++;
  if (typeCheckBox[1].isSelected())
    numberChecks++;
```

```
if (typeCheckBox[2].isSelected())
  numberChecks++;
if (typeCheckBox[3].isSelected())
{
  numberChecks++;
  // make sure zero not selected factor
  if (factorRadioButton[0].isSelected())
    factorRadioButton[1].doClick();
  factorRadioButton[0].setEnabled(false);
}
else
{
  factorRadioButton[0].setEnabled(true);
}
// if all boxes unchecked, recheck last clicked box
if (numberChecks == 0)
  typeCheckBox[clickedBox].setSelected(true);
problemLabel.requestFocus();
}
```

You should be able to see how the various steps are implemented. Enter this code into your project.

Notice the last step in this method is to return focus to the problem label so answers can be entered. We need similar code if a factor is changed. Add a single line to the factorRadioButtonActionPerformed method:

```
private void factorRadioButtonActionPerformed(ActionEvent e)
{
  problemLabel.requestFocus();
}
```

Save and run the project. Make sure all the newly installed code is doing its job. Try to "uncheck" all the problem type boxes – one box will always remain. Check **Division** problems and notice that the 0 option for **Factor** is disabled. Uncheck **Division** problems. Choose 0 as a factor. Now, check **Division** again. Notice the factor is changed to 1 and the 0 option is disabled. You can now solve any problem type with any factor. If you change options while solving problems, the changes will be seen once you finish solving the current problem. Try solving problems, changing problem type and factors. Notice if you change options while in running mode, you can still enter answers since focus is placed on the problem label control.

Next, we add timing options, using the **Timer** object reviewed in Chapter 2.

Code Design – Timing Options

Having coded problem generation and answer checking, we can now address the use of timing in the flash card math project. Up to now, we've assumed no timer has been used. We have two possibilities for a timer: (1) one where the timer counts up, keeping track of how long you are solving problems, and (2) one where the timer counts down from some preset value. In both cases, a text field control (**timerTextField**) displays the time in **minutes:seconds** form. In the second case, a vertical scroll bar (**timerScrollBar**) is used to set the value. The timing will be controlled with a timer object (**problemsTimer**). There are several steps involved. Let's add the timer object first.

Declare the timer as a class level variable:

```
Timer problemsTimer;
```

Create the timer (using a **delay** of 1000 milliseconds, or 1 second). Place this code in the frame constructor before the **pack()** line:

```
problemsTimer = new Timer(1000, new ActionListener()
{
  public void actionPerformed(ActionEvent e)
  {
    problemsTimerActionPerformed(e);
  }
});
```

And, the corresponding event code would be placed in a **problemsTimerActionPerformed** method:

```
private void problemsTimerActionPerformed(ActionEvent e)
{
}
```

We'll code this next.

We will use a class level variable (**problemTime**) to store the time value (whether counting up or down) in seconds. Add this variable in the general declarations area:

```
int problemTime;
```

When the timer (**problemsTimer**) is running, the time display (**timerTextField**) is updated every second (we use a **delay** property of 1000). The displayed time is incremented if counting up, decremented if counting down. The steps involved for counting up are:

> ➢ Increment **problemTime** by 1.
> ➢ Display **problemTime**.
> ➢ If **problemTime** is 1800 (30 minutes), stop solving problems.

Note we limit the total solving time to 30 minutes.

The steps for counting down are:

> ➢ Decrement **problemTime** by 1.
> ➢ Display **problemTime**.
> ➢ If **problemTime** is 0, stop solving problems.

The code to update the displayed time is placed in the **problemsTimerActionPerformed** method. The code that implements the above steps are:

```
private void problemsTimerActionPerformed(ActionEvent e)
{
  if (timerRadioButton[1].isSelected())
  {
    problemTime++;
    timerTextField.setText(getTime(problemTime));
    if (problemTime >= 1800)
    {
      startButton.doClick();
      return;
    }
  }
  else
  {
    problemTime--;
    timerTextField.setText(getTime(problemTime));
    if (problemTime == 0)
    {
      startButton.doClick();
      return;
    }
  }
}
```

Notice to stop solving problems, we simulate a click on **Stop Practice** (the **startButton** button). Add this method to the project.

This method uses a general method **getTime** that returns the time properly formatted:

```
private String getTime(int s)
{
  int min, sec;
  String ms, ss;
  min = (int) (s / 60);
  sec = s - 60 * min;
  ms = String.valueOf(min);
  ss = String.valueOf(sec);
  if (sec < 10)
    ss = "0" + ss;
  return (ms + ":" + ss);
}
```

This method takes the time (**S**) in seconds and breaks it into minutes and seconds. Add this new code to your project.

Next, we write the code to switch from one timing option to the next. The code goes in the **timerRadioButtonActionPerformed** method. The steps followed in this method:

> If **Off** (**timerRadioButton[0]**) is selected: set **text** property of **timerTextField** to **Off** and disable **timerScrollBar**.
> If **On-Count Up** (**timerRadioButton[1]**) is selected, initialize **timerTextField** and disable **timerScrollBar**. Initialize **problemTime** to 0.
> If **On-Count Down** (**timerRadioButton[2]**) is selectedinitialize **timerTextField** and enable **timerScrollBar**. Initialize **problemTime** to 30 times **timerScrollBar value** property (30 seconds for each increment).

The method (**timerRadioButtonActionPerformed**) that implements the steps is (again, this handles the three radio buttons in the **Timer** panel):

```
private void timerRadioButtonActionPerformed(ActionEvent e)
{
  if (timerRadioButton[0].isSelected())
  {
    timerTextField.setText("Off");
    timerScrollBar.setEnabled(false);
  }
  else if (timerRadioButton[1].isSelected())
  {
    problemTime = 0;
    timerTextField.setText(getTime(problemTime));
    timerScrollBar.setEnabled(false);
  }
  else if (timerRadioButton[2].isSelected())
  {
    problemTime = 30 * timerScrollBar.getValue();
    timerTextField.setText(getTime(problemTime));
    timerScrollBar.setEnabled(true);
  }
}
```

Add this method to the project.

Though not quite finished, we can run our code to make sure all the new changes work. Run the project and click the **Timer-Count Up** button. Notice the text field displays 0:00 and the scroll bar is disabled:

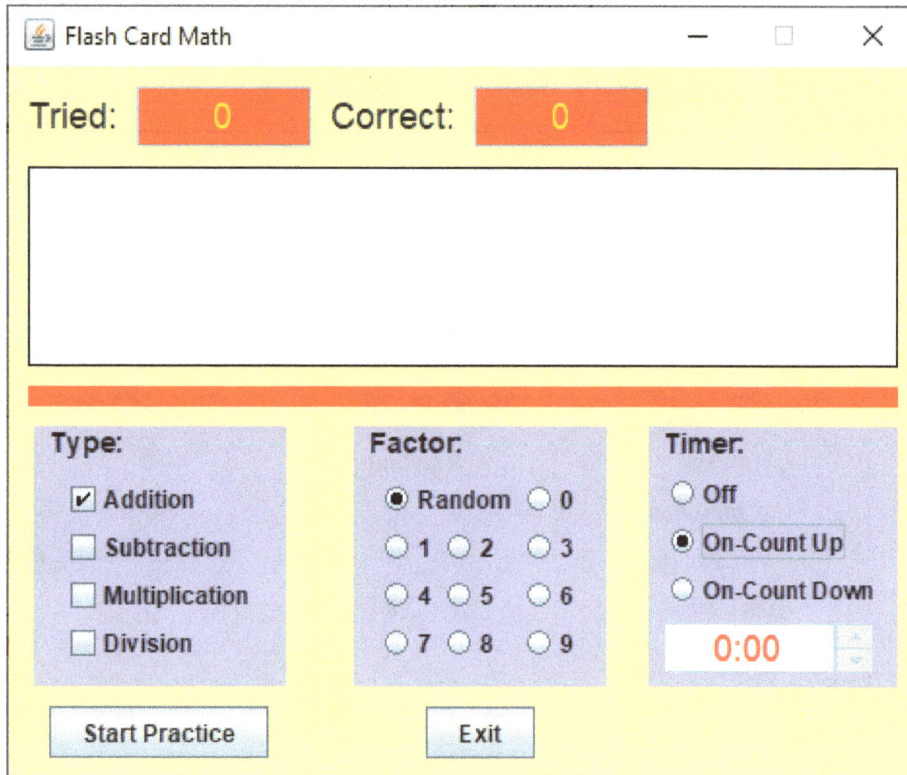

Now, click **On-Count Down**, the display shows **0:30** the scroll bar becomes enabled allowing a user to enter the amount of solution time:

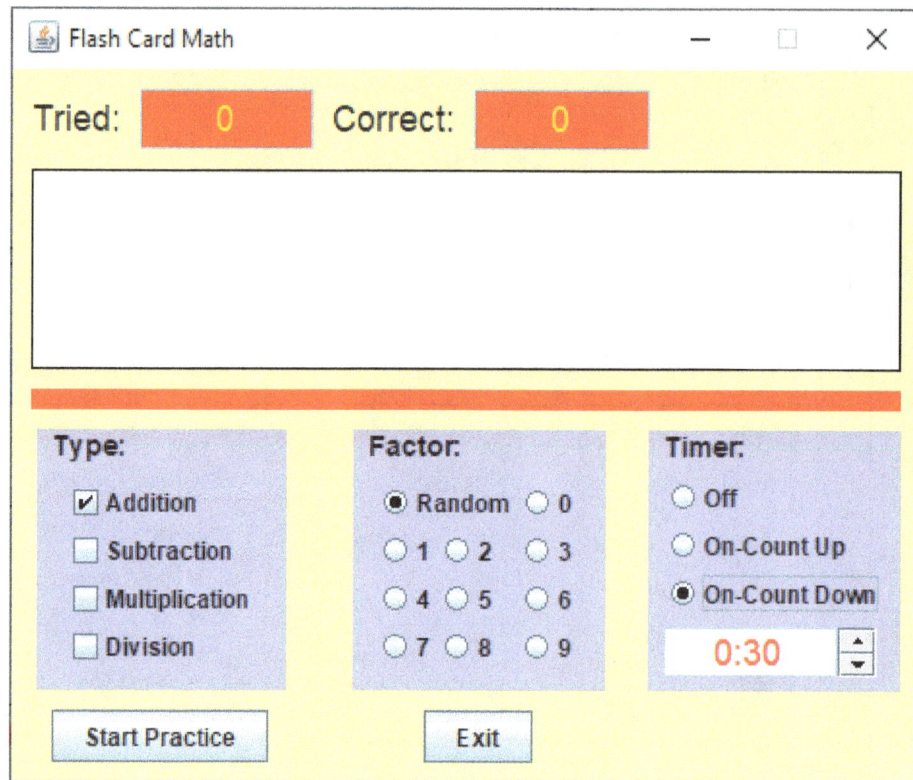

We'll code the scroll bar function now, then finish the timing option by adding code that starts and starts the timer object.

As just seen, when the **On-Count Down** radio button is, the scroll bar (**timerScrollBar**) **value** property is used to initialize the **problemTime** variable. In the code, each increment on the scroll bar adds 30 seconds to the timer. If you look back to where we set control properties, you will see the **maximum** property for this scroll bar was set to 60. This allows a maximum of 30 minutes (1800 seconds) for a timed flash card math session. We need a **timerScrollBarAdjustmentValueChanged** method to changed the displayed time whenever the scroll bar arrows are clicked. That method needs a single line of code:

```
private void timerScrollBarAdjustmentValueChanged
(AdjustmentEvent e)
{
  timerTextField.setText(getTime(30 *
timerScrollBar.getValue()));
}
```

If you like, run the project to try the scroll bar and make sure it works.

We're almost done. We allow changing problem type and factors while solving problems. It wouldn't make sense to be able to change timer options while solving problems – the times would not be correct. We will only allow selection of timer options prior to clicking **Start Practice**. Clicking **Start Practice** will disable the timer panel radio buttons and scroll bar and start the timing process (controlled by **problemsTimer**); the steps are:

- ➤ Disable all controls in **timerPanel**.
- ➤ If **Off** radio button (**timerRadioButton[0]**) is selected, do nothing else.
- ➤ If **On-Count Up** radio button (**timerRadioButton[1]**) is selected:
  - ○ Initialize **problemTime** to zero; display **problemTime**.
  - ○ Start **problemsTimer**.
  - ○ If **On-Count Down** radio button (**timerRadioButton[2]**) is selected:
  - ○ Initialize **problemTime** to 30 times **timerScrollBar.getValue()**; display **problemTime**.
  - ○ Start **problemsTimer**.

Clicking **Stop Practice** will stop the timing process and restore the timer panel controls to allow selection. The corresponding steps:

- ➤ Enable all controls in **timerPanel** (enable **timerScrollBar** only if **On-Count Down** is selected.
- ➤ Stop **problemsTimer**.

Each of these steps is handled in the **startButtonActionPerformed** method. The modified method (changes are shaded) is:

```java
private void startButtonActionPerformed(ActionEvent e)
{
  if (startButton.getText().equals("Start Practice"))
  {
    startButton.setText("Stop Practice");
    exitButton.setEnabled(false);
    numberTried = 0;
    numberCorrect = 0;
    triedTextField.setText("0");
    correctTextField.setText("0");
    timerRadioButton[0].setEnabled(false);
    timerRadioButton[1].setEnabled(false);
    timerRadioButton[2].setEnabled(false);
    timerScrollBar.setEnabled(false);
    if (!timerRadioButton[0].isSelected())
    {
      if (timerRadioButton[1].isSelected())
        problemTime = 0;
      else
        problemTime = 30 * timerScrollBar.getValue();
      timerTextField.setText(getTime(problemTime));
      problemsTimer.start();
    }
    problemLabel.setText(getProblem());
  }
  else
  {
    timerRadioButton[0].setEnabled(true);
    timerRadioButton[1].setEnabled(true);
    timerRadioButton[2].setEnabled(true);
    if (timerRadioButton[2].isSelected())
      timerScrollBar.setEnabled(true);
    problemsTimer.stop();
    startButton.setText( "Start Practice");
    exitButton.setEnabled(true);
    problemLabel.setText("");
  }
}
```

Make the indicated changes

We're done implementing the modifications to add timing in the flash card math project. Save and run the project. You want to make sure all the timer options work correctly. First, check to see that the project still works correctly with no timer.

Once you are convinced the no timer option still works, stop solving problems and choose the **On-Count Up** option. Run the project. Make sure the timer increments properly. Here's a run I just started (note the **Timer** panel controls are properly disabled):

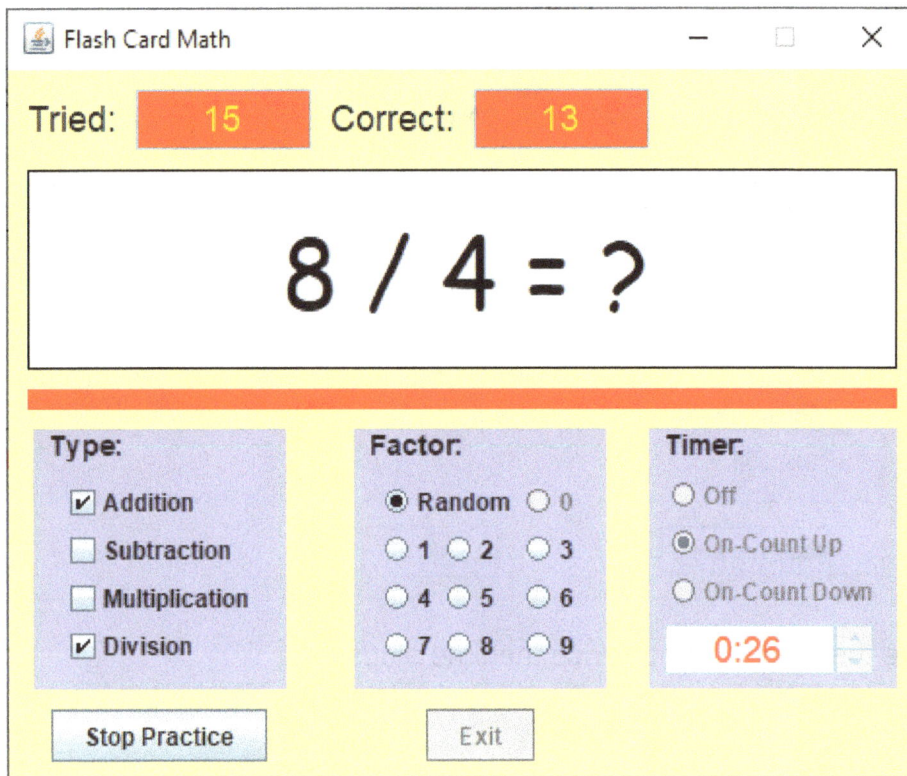

Click **Stop Practice** at some point. You should also make sure the program automatically stops after 30 minutes (go have lunch while the program runs).

Choose the **On-Count Down** option. Change the amount of allowed time using the vertical scroll bar. Make sure it reaches a maximum of 30:00 (it has a minimum of 0:30). Start the project. Make sure the time decrements correctly. Here's a run I made using a starting time of 1:00:

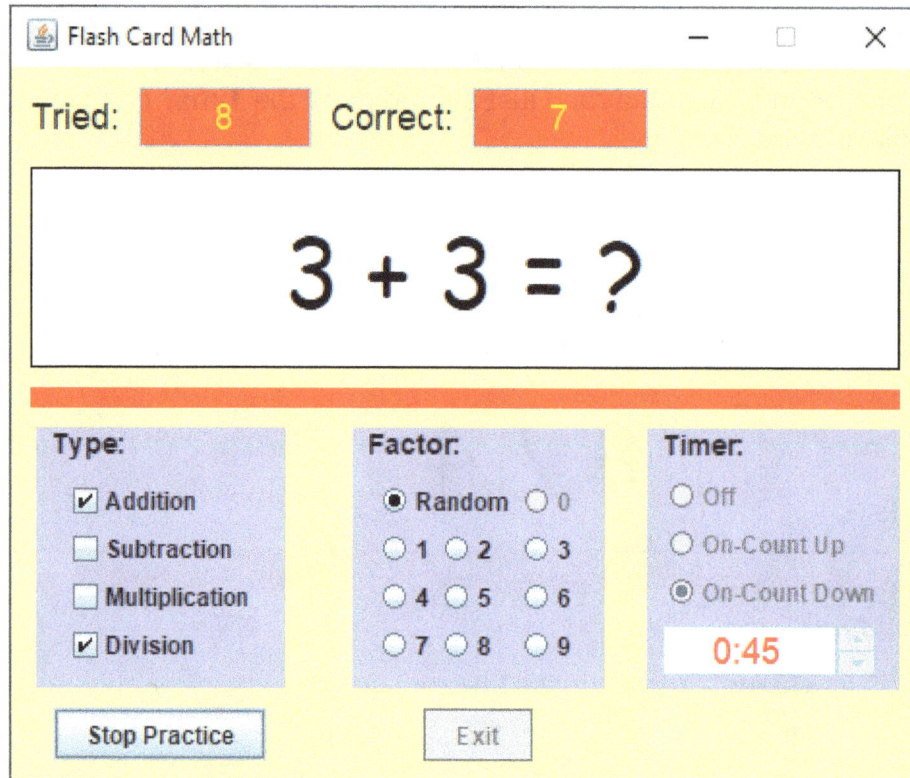

Make sure the program stops once the time elapses.

Code Design – Presenting Results

Once a user stops solving problems, we want to let he/she know how well they did in answering problems. The information of use would be:

- The number of problems tried
- The number of correct answers
- The percentage score
- If timing, amount of elapsed time and time spent (on average) on each problem

If timing up, the elapsed time is equal to **problemTime**. If timing down, the elapsed time is equal to the initial amount of time minus **problemTime**.

All of this information is readily available from the current variable set. The results are presented in the **startButtonActionPerformed** method (following clicking of **Stop Practice**). We will use a simple message box to relay the results. The modified **startButton** method (changes are shaded) that displays the results is:

```
private void startButtonActionPerformed(ActionEvent e)
{
  int score;
  String message = "";
  if (startButton.getText().equals("Start Practice"))
  {
    .
    .
    .
  }
  else
  {
    timerRadioButton[0].setEnabled(true);
    timerRadioButton[1].setEnabled(true);
    timerRadioButton[2].setEnabled(true);
    if (timerRadioButton[2].isSelected())
      timerScrollBar.setEnabled(true);
    problemsTimer.stop();
    startButton.setText( "Start Practice");
    exitButton.setEnabled(true);
    problemLabel.setText("");
    if (numberTried > 0)
    {
      score = (int)(100 * (double)(numberCorrect) /
numberTried);
      message = "Problems Tried: " +
String.valueOf(numberTried) + "\n";
```

```
        message += "Problems Correct: " +
String.valueOf(numberCorrect) + " (" +
String.valueOf(score) + "%)" + "\n";
      if (timerRadioButton[0].isSelected())
      {
        message += "Timer Off";
      }
      else
      {
        if (timerRadioButton[2].isSelected())
        {
          problemTime = 30 * timerScrollBar.getValue() -
problemTime;
        }
        message += "Elapsed Time: " + getTime(problemTime)
+ "\n";
        message += "Time Per Problem: " + new
DecimalFormat("0.00").format((double) (problemTime) /
numberTried) + " sec";
      }
      JOptionPane.showConfirmDialog(null, message,
"Results", JOptionPane.DEFAULT_OPTION,
JOptionPane.INFORMATION_MESSAGE);
    }
  }
}
```

Add the noted changes. The **DecimalFormat** method is used for formatting times. You need to add this import statement:

```
import java.text.*;
```

One last time – save and run the project. Solve some problems and see the results. Make sure the results display correctly whether timing or not. Here is a set of results I received while using the timing down option:

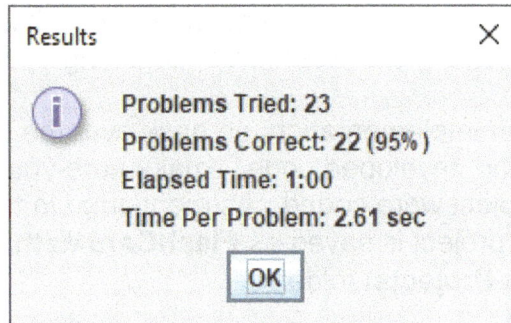

```
Results                                    ×

  i      Problems Tried: 23
         Problems Correct: 22 (95%)
         Elapsed Time: 1:00
         Time Per Problem: 2.61 sec

                    OK
```

Flash Card Math Quiz Project Review

The **Flash Card Math Quiz** project is now complete. Save and run the project and make sure it works as designed. Recheck that all options work and interact properly. Let your kids (or anyone else) have fun tuning up their basic math skills.

If there are errors in your implementation, go back over the steps of frame and code design. Go over the developed code – make sure you understand how different parts of the project were coded. As mentioned in the beginning of this chapter, the completed project is saved as **FlashCardMath** in the **\HomeJava\HomeJava Projects** folder.

While completing this project, new concepts and skills you should have gained include:

> ➤ Capabilities and proper use of the check box, radio button and panel controls.
> ➤ How to use scroll bars as input devices.
> ➤ Use of the **KeyPressed** event for "label" input.
> ➤ Using a message box to report results.

Flash Card Math Quiz
Project Enhancements

Possible enhancements to the flash card math project include:

> ➤ As implemented, the only feedback a user gets about entered answers is an update of the score. Some kind of audible feedback would be a big improvement (a positive sound for correct answer, a negative sound for a wrong answer). We discuss adding sounds to a project in Chapter 10 – you might like to look ahead.
> ➤ When a user stops answering problems, it would be nice to have a review mode where the problems missed are presented. You would need some way to save each problem that was answered incorrectly.
> ➤ Kids like rewards. As you gain more programming skills, a nice visual display of some sort for good work would be a fun addition.
> ➤ Currently, once a problem is answered, the next problem is immediately displayed. Some kind of delay (perhaps make it optional and adjustable) might be desired. You would need another timer object.

Flash Card Math Quiz Project
Java Code Listing

```java
/*
 * FlashCardMath.java
 */
package flashcardmath;
import javax.swing.*;
import java.awt.*;
import java.awt.event.*;
import java.util.Random;
import java.text.*;

public class FlashCardMath extends JFrame
{

    JLabel triedLabel = new JLabel();
    JTextField triedTextField = new JTextField();
    JLabel correctLabel = new JLabel();
    JTextField correctTextField = new JTextField();
    JLabel problemLabel = new JLabel();
    JLabel dividerLabel = new JLabel();
    JPanel typePanel = new JPanel();
    JCheckBox[] typeCheckBox = new JCheckBox[4];
    JPanel factorPanel = new JPanel();
    ButtonGroup factorButtonGroup = new ButtonGroup();
    JRadioButton[] factorRadioButton = new JRadioButton[11];
    JPanel timerPanel = new JPanel();
    ButtonGroup timerButtonGroup = new ButtonGroup();
    JRadioButton[] timerRadioButton = new JRadioButton[3];
    JTextField timerTextField = new JTextField();
    JScrollBar timerScrollBar = new JScrollBar();
    JButton startButton = new JButton();
    JButton exitButton = new JButton();
    Timer problemsTimer;

    Font myFont = new Font("Arial", Font.PLAIN, 18);

    Color lightBlue = new Color(192, 192, 255);

    Random myRandom = new Random();
    int numberTried, numberCorrect;
    int correctAnswer, numberDigits;
    String problem;
    String yourAnswer;
```

```
int digitNumber;
int problemTime;

public static void main(String args[])
{
  // create frame
  new FlashCardMath().setVisible(true);
}

public FlashCardMath()
{
  // frame constructor
  setTitle("Flash Card Math");
  getContentPane().setBackground(new Color(255, 255, 192));
  setResizable(false);

  addWindowListener(new WindowAdapter()
  {
    public void windowClosing(WindowEvent evt)
    {
      exitForm(evt);
    }
  });

  getContentPane().setLayout(new GridBagLayout());
  GridBagConstraints gridConstraints;

  triedLabel.setText("Tried:");
  triedLabel.setFont(myFont);
  gridConstraints = new GridBagConstraints();
  gridConstraints.gridx = 0;
  gridConstraints.gridy = 0;
  gridConstraints.anchor = GridBagConstraints.WEST;
  gridConstraints.insets = new Insets(10, 10, 0, 10);
  getContentPane().add(triedLabel, gridConstraints);

  triedTextField.setText("0");
  triedTextField.setPreferredSize(new Dimension(90,30));
  triedTextField.setEditable(false);
  triedTextField.setBackground(Color.RED);
  triedTextField.setForeground(Color.YELLOW);

triedTextField.setHorizontalAlignment(SwingConstants.CENTER);
  triedTextField.setFont(myFont);
  gridConstraints = new GridBagConstraints();
  gridConstraints.gridx = 1;
  gridConstraints.gridy = 0;
```

```java
    gridConstraints.insets = new Insets(10, 0, 0, 0);
    getContentPane().add(triedTextField, gridConstraints);

    correctLabel.setText("Correct:");
    correctLabel.setFont(myFont);
    gridConstraints = new GridBagConstraints();
    gridConstraints.gridx = 2;
    gridConstraints.gridy = 0;
    gridConstraints.anchor = GridBagConstraints.EAST;
    gridConstraints.insets = new Insets(10, 10, 0, 10);
    getContentPane().add(correctLabel, gridConstraints);

    correctTextField.setText("0");
    correctTextField.setPreferredSize(new Dimension(90,30));
    correctTextField.setEditable(false);
    correctTextField.setBackground(Color.RED);
    correctTextField.setForeground(Color.YELLOW);

correctTextField.setHorizontalAlignment(SwingConstants.CENTER
);
    correctTextField.setFont(myFont);
    gridConstraints = new GridBagConstraints();
    gridConstraints.gridx = 3;
    gridConstraints.gridy = 0;
    gridConstraints.insets = new Insets(10, 0, 0, 0);
    getContentPane().add(correctTextField, gridConstraints);

    problemLabel.setText("");

problemLabel.setBorder(BorderFactory.createLineBorder(Color.B
LACK));
    problemLabel.setPreferredSize(new Dimension(450, 100));
    problemLabel.setBackground(Color.WHITE);
    problemLabel.setOpaque(true);
    problemLabel.setFont(new Font("Comic Sans MS",
Font.PLAIN, 48));

problemLabel.setHorizontalAlignment(SwingConstants.CENTER);
    gridConstraints = new GridBagConstraints();
    gridConstraints.gridx = 0;
    gridConstraints.gridy = 1;
    gridConstraints.gridwidth = 5;
    gridConstraints.insets = new Insets(10, 10, 0, 10);
    getContentPane().add(problemLabel, gridConstraints);
    problemLabel.addKeyListener(new KeyAdapter()
    {
      public void keyPressed(KeyEvent e)
```

```
      {
        problemLabelKeyPressed(e);
      }
    });

    dividerLabel.setPreferredSize(new Dimension(450, 10));
    dividerLabel.setBackground(Color.RED);
    dividerLabel.setOpaque(true);
    gridConstraints = new GridBagConstraints();
    gridConstraints.gridx = 0;
    gridConstraints.gridy = 2;
    gridConstraints.gridwidth = 5;
    gridConstraints.insets = new Insets(10, 10, 10, 10);
    getContentPane().add(dividerLabel, gridConstraints);

    UIManager.put("TitledBorder.font", new Font("Arial",
Font.BOLD, 14));

    typePanel.setPreferredSize(new Dimension(130, 130));

typePanel.setBorder(BorderFactory.createTitledBorder("Type:")
);
    typePanel.setBackground(lightBlue);
    typePanel.setLayout(new GridBagLayout());
    gridConstraints = new GridBagConstraints();
    gridConstraints.gridx = 0;
    gridConstraints.gridy = 3;
    gridConstraints.gridwidth = 2;
    gridConstraints.anchor = GridBagConstraints.NORTH;
    getContentPane().add(typePanel, gridConstraints);

    for (int i = 0; i < 4; i++)
    {
      typeCheckBox[i] = new JCheckBox();
      typeCheckBox[i].setBackground(lightBlue);
      gridConstraints = new GridBagConstraints();
      gridConstraints.gridx = 0;
      gridConstraints.gridy = i;
      gridConstraints.anchor = GridBagConstraints.WEST;
      typePanel.add(typeCheckBox[i], gridConstraints);
      typeCheckBox[i].addActionListener(new ActionListener()
      {
        public void actionPerformed(ActionEvent e)
        {
          typeCheckBoxActionPerformed(e);
        }
      });
```

```
    }
    typeCheckBox[0].setText("Addition");
    typeCheckBox[1].setText("Subtraction");
    typeCheckBox[2].setText("Multiplication");
    typeCheckBox[3].setText("Division");
    typeCheckBox[0].setSelected(true);

    factorPanel.setPreferredSize(new Dimension(130, 130));

factorPanel.setBorder(BorderFactory.createTitledBorder("Facto
r:"));
    factorPanel.setBackground(lightBlue);
    factorPanel.setLayout(new GridBagLayout());
    gridConstraints = new GridBagConstraints();
    gridConstraints.gridx = 2;
    gridConstraints.gridy = 3;
    gridConstraints.gridwidth = 2;
    gridConstraints.anchor = GridBagConstraints.NORTH;
    getContentPane().add(factorPanel, gridConstraints);

    int x = 2;
    int y = 0;
    for (int i = 0; i < 11; i++)
    {
      factorRadioButton[i] = new JRadioButton();
      factorRadioButton[i].setText(String.valueOf(i));
      factorRadioButton[i].setBackground(lightBlue);
      factorButtonGroup.add(factorRadioButton[i]);
      gridConstraints = new GridBagConstraints();
      if (i < 10)
      {
        gridConstraints.gridx = x;
        gridConstraints.gridy = y;
      }
      else
      {
        gridConstraints.gridx = 0;
        gridConstraints.gridy = 0;
        gridConstraints.gridwidth = 2;
      }
      gridConstraints.anchor = GridBagConstraints.WEST;
      factorPanel.add(factorRadioButton[i], gridConstraints);
      factorRadioButton[i].addActionListener(new
ActionListener()
      {
        public void actionPerformed(ActionEvent e)
        {
```

```
                  factorRadioButtonActionPerformed(e);
          }
      });
      x++;
      if (x > 2)
      {
          x = 0;
          y++;
      }
    }
    factorRadioButton[10].setText("Random");
    factorRadioButton[10].setSelected(true);

    timerPanel.setPreferredSize(new Dimension(130, 130));

timerPanel.setBorder(BorderFactory.createTitledBorder("Timer:
"));
    timerPanel.setBackground(lightBlue);
    timerPanel.setLayout(new GridBagLayout());
    gridConstraints = new GridBagConstraints();
    gridConstraints.gridx = 4;
    gridConstraints.gridy = 3;
    gridConstraints.insets = new Insets(0, 0, 0, 10);
    gridConstraints.anchor = GridBagConstraints.NORTH;
    getContentPane().add(timerPanel, gridConstraints);

    for (int i = 0; i < 3; i++)
    {
        timerRadioButton[i] = new JRadioButton();
        timerRadioButton[i].setBackground(lightBlue);
        timerButtonGroup.add(timerRadioButton[i]);
        gridConstraints = new GridBagConstraints();
        gridConstraints.gridx = 0;
        gridConstraints.gridy = i;
        gridConstraints.gridwidth = 2;
        gridConstraints.anchor = GridBagConstraints.WEST;
        timerPanel.add(timerRadioButton[i], gridConstraints);
        timerRadioButton[i].addActionListener(new
ActionListener()
        {
          public void actionPerformed(ActionEvent e)
          {
            timerRadioButtonActionPerformed(e);
          }
        });
    }
    timerRadioButton[0].setText("Off");
```

```
    timerRadioButton[1].setText("On-Count Up");
    timerRadioButton[2].setText("On-Count Down");
    timerRadioButton[0].setSelected(true);


    timerTextField.setText("Off");
    timerTextField.setPreferredSize(new Dimension(90,25));
    timerTextField.setEditable(false);
    timerTextField.setBackground(Color.WHITE);
    timerTextField.setForeground(Color.RED);
timerTextField.setHorizontalAlignment(SwingConstants.CENTER);
    timerTextField.setFont(myFont);
    gridConstraints = new GridBagConstraints();
    gridConstraints.gridx = 0;
    gridConstraints.gridy = 3;
    gridConstraints.anchor = GridBagConstraints.WEST;
    gridConstraints.insets = new Insets(5, 0, 0, 0);
    timerPanel.add(timerTextField, gridConstraints);

    timerScrollBar.setPreferredSize(new Dimension(20, 25));
    timerScrollBar.setMinimum(1);
    timerScrollBar.setMaximum(60);
    timerScrollBar.setValue(1);
    timerScrollBar.setBlockIncrement(1);
    timerScrollBar.setUnitIncrement(1);
    timerScrollBar.setOrientation(JScrollBar.VERTICAL);
    timerScrollBar.setEnabled(false);
    gridConstraints = new GridBagConstraints();
    gridConstraints.gridx = 1;
    gridConstraints.gridy = 3;
    gridConstraints.anchor = GridBagConstraints.WEST;
    gridConstraints.insets = new Insets(5, 0, 0, 0);
    timerPanel.add(timerScrollBar, gridConstraints);
    timerScrollBar.addAdjustmentListener(new
AdjustmentListener()
    {
      public void adjustmentValueChanged(AdjustmentEvent e)
      {
        timerScrollBarAdjustmentValueChanged(e);
      }
    });

    startButton.setText("Start Practice");
    gridConstraints = new GridBagConstraints();
    gridConstraints.gridx = 0;
    gridConstraints.gridy = 4;
```

```
    gridConstraints.gridwidth = 2;
    gridConstraints.insets = new Insets(10, 0, 10, 0);
    getContentPane().add(startButton, gridConstraints);
    startButton.addActionListener(new ActionListener()
    {
      public void actionPerformed(ActionEvent e)
      {
        startButtonActionPerformed(e);
      }
    });

    exitButton.setText("Exit");
    gridConstraints = new GridBagConstraints();
    gridConstraints.gridx = 2;
    gridConstraints.gridy = 4;
    gridConstraints.gridwidth = 2;
    gridConstraints.insets = new Insets(10, 0, 10, 0);
    getContentPane().add(exitButton, gridConstraints);
    exitButton.addActionListener(new ActionListener()
    {
      public void actionPerformed(ActionEvent e)
      {
        exitButtonActionPerformed(e);
      }
    });

    problemsTimer = new Timer(1000, new ActionListener()
    {
      public void actionPerformed(ActionEvent e)
      {
        problemsTimerActionPerformed(e);
      }
    });

    pack();
    Dimension screenSize =
Toolkit.getDefaultToolkit().getScreenSize();
    setBounds((int) (0.5 * (screenSize.width - getWidth())),
(int) (0.5 * (screenSize.height - getHeight())), getWidth(),
getHeight());
  }

  private void exitForm(WindowEvent evt)
  {
    System.exit(0);
  }
```

```java
  private void typeCheckBoxActionPerformed(ActionEvent e)
  {
    int numberChecks;
    int clickedBox = 0;
    // determine which box was clicked
    String s = e.getActionCommand();
    if (s.equals("Addition"))
      clickedBox = 0;
    else if (s.equals("Subtraction"))
      clickedBox = 1;
    else if (s.equals("Multiplication"))
      clickedBox = 2;
    else if (s.equals("Division"))
      clickedBox = 3;
    // determine how many boxes are checked
    numberChecks = 0;
    if (typeCheckBox[0].isSelected())
      numberChecks++;
    if (typeCheckBox[1].isSelected())
      numberChecks++;
    if (typeCheckBox[2].isSelected())
      numberChecks++;
    if (typeCheckBox[3].isSelected())
    {
      numberChecks++;
      // make sure zero not selected factor
      if (factorRadioButton[0].isSelected())
        factorRadioButton[1].doClick();
      factorRadioButton[0].setEnabled(false);
    }
    else
    {
      factorRadioButton[0].setEnabled(true);
    }
    // if all boxes unchecked, recheck last clicked box
    if (numberChecks == 0)
      typeCheckBox[clickedBox].setSelected(true);
    problemLabel.requestFocus();
  }

  private void factorRadioButtonActionPerformed(ActionEvent
e)
  {
    problemLabel.requestFocus();
  }

  private void timerRadioButtonActionPerformed(ActionEvent e)
```

```
  {
    if (timerRadioButton[0].isSelected())
    {
      timerTextField.setText("Off");
      timerScrollBar.setEnabled(false);
    }
    else if (timerRadioButton[1].isSelected())
    {
      problemTime = 0;
      timerTextField.setText(getTime(problemTime));
      timerScrollBar.setEnabled(false);
    }
    else if (timerRadioButton[2].isSelected())
    {
      problemTime = 30 * timerScrollBar.getValue();
      timerTextField.setText(getTime(problemTime));
      timerScrollBar.setEnabled(true);
    }
  }

  private void timerScrollBarAdjustmentValueChanged
(AdjustmentEvent e)
  {
    timerTextField.setText(getTime(30 *
timerScrollBar.getValue()));
  }

  private void startButtonActionPerformed(ActionEvent e)
  {
    int score;
    String message = "";
    if (startButton.getText().equals("Start Practice"))
    {
      startButton.setText("Stop Practice");
      exitButton.setEnabled(false);
      numberTried = 0;
      numberCorrect = 0;
      triedTextField.setText("0");
      correctTextField.setText("0");
      timerRadioButton[0].setEnabled(false);
      timerRadioButton[1].setEnabled(false);
      timerRadioButton[2].setEnabled(false);
      timerScrollBar.setEnabled(false);
      if (!timerRadioButton[0].isSelected())
      {
        if (timerRadioButton[1].isSelected())
          problemTime = 0;
```

```
            else
              problemTime = 30 * timerScrollBar.getValue();
            timerTextField.setText(getTime(problemTime));
            problemsTimer.start();
          }
          problemLabel.setText(getProblem());
        }
        else
        {
          timerRadioButton[0].setEnabled(true);
          timerRadioButton[1].setEnabled(true);
          timerRadioButton[2].setEnabled(true);
          if (timerRadioButton[2].isSelected())
            timerScrollBar.setEnabled(true);
          problemsTimer.stop();
          startButton.setText( "Start Practice");
          exitButton.setEnabled(true);
          problemLabel.setText("");
          if (numberTried > 0)
          {
            score = (int)(100 * (double) (numberCorrect) /
numberTried);
            message = "Problems Tried: " +
String.valueOf(numberTried) + "\n";
            message += "Problems Correct: " +
String.valueOf(numberCorrect) + " (" + String.valueOf(score)
+ "%)" + "\n";
            if (timerRadioButton[0].isSelected())
            {
              message += "Timer Off";
            }
            else
            {
              if (timerRadioButton[2].isSelected())
              {
                problemTime = 30 * timerScrollBar.getValue() -
problemTime;
              }
              message += "Elapsed Time: " + getTime(problemTime)
+ "\n";
              message += "Time Per Problem: " + new
DecimalFormat("0.00").format((double) (problemTime) /
numberTried) + " sec";
            }
            JOptionPane.showConfirmDialog(null, message,
"Results", JOptionPane.DEFAULT_OPTION,
JOptionPane.INFORMATION_MESSAGE);
```

```
      }
    }
  }

  private void exitButtonActionPerformed(ActionEvent e)
  {
    System.exit(0);
  }

  private void problemLabelKeyPressed(KeyEvent e)
  {
    if (startButton.getText().equals("Start Practice"))
      return;
    // only allow number keys
    if (e.getKeyChar() >= '0' && e.getKeyChar() <= '9')
    {
      yourAnswer += e.getKeyChar();
      problemLabel.setText(problem + yourAnswer);
      if (digitNumber != numberDigits)
      {
        digitNumber++;
        problemLabel.setText(problemLabel.getText() + "?");
        return;
      }
      else
      {
        numberTried++;
        // check answer
        if (Integer.valueOf(yourAnswer).intValue() ==
correctAnswer)
        {
          numberCorrect++;
        }
        triedTextField.setText(String.valueOf(numberTried));

correctTextField.setText(String.valueOf(numberCorrect));
        problemLabel.setText(getProblem());
      }
    }
  }

  private void problemsTimerActionPerformed(ActionEvent e)
  {
    if (timerRadioButton[1].isSelected())
    {
      problemTime++;
      timerTextField.setText(getTime(problemTime));
```

```java
      if (problemTime >= 1800)
      {
        startButton.doClick();
        return;
      }
    }
    else
    {
      problemTime--;
      timerTextField.setText(getTime(problemTime));
      if (problemTime == 0)
      {
        startButton.doClick();
        return;
      }
    }
  }

  private String getProblem()
  {
    int pType, p, number, factor;
    p = 0;
    do
    {
      pType = myRandom.nextInt(4) + 1;
      if (pType == 1 && typeCheckBox[0].isSelected())
      {
        // Addition
        p = pType;
        number = myRandom.nextInt(10);
        factor = getFactor(1);
        correctAnswer = number + factor;
        problem = String.valueOf(number) + " + " +
String.valueOf(factor) + " = ";
      }
      else if (pType == 2 && typeCheckBox[1].isSelected())
      {
        // Subtraction
        p = pType;
        factor = getFactor(2);
        correctAnswer = myRandom.nextInt(10);
        number = correctAnswer + factor;
        problem = String.valueOf(number) + " - " +
String.valueOf(factor) + " = ";
      }
      else if (pType == 3 && typeCheckBox[2].isSelected())
      {
```

```
      // Multiplication
      p = pType;
      number = myRandom.nextInt(10);
      factor = getFactor(3);
      correctAnswer = number * factor;
      problem = String.valueOf(number) + " x " +
String.valueOf(factor) + " = ";
    }
    else if (pType == 4 && typeCheckBox[3].isSelected())
    {
      // Division
      p = pType;
      factor = getFactor(4);
      correctAnswer = myRandom.nextInt(10);
      number = correctAnswer * factor;
      problem = String.valueOf(number) + " / " +
String.valueOf(factor) + " = ";
    }
  }
  while (p == 0);
  yourAnswer = "";
  digitNumber = 1;
  problemLabel.requestFocus();
  if (correctAnswer < 10)
  {
    numberDigits = 1;
    return (problem + "?");
  }
  else
  {
    numberDigits = 2;
    return (problem + "??");
  }
}

private int getFactor(int p)
{
  if (factorRadioButton[10].isSelected())
  {
    //random
     if (p == 4)
       return (myRandom.nextInt(9) + 1);
     else
       return (myRandom.nextInt(10));
  }
  else
  {
```

```java
        for (int i = 0; i < 10; i++)
        {
          if (factorRadioButton[i].isSelected())
            return(i);
        }
          return (0);
    }
  }

  private String getTime(int s)
  {
    int min, sec;
    String ms, ss;
    min = (int) (s / 60);
    sec = s - 60 * min;
    ms = String.valueOf(min);
    ss = String.valueOf(sec);
    if (sec < 10)
      ss = "0" + ss;
    return (ms + ":" + ss);
  }

}
```

5

Multiple Choice Exam Project

Review and Preview

In this chapter, we build a project that quizzes a user on matching pairs of items – for example, states (or countries) and capital cities, words and meanings, books and authors, inventions and inventors. The **Multiple Choice Exam Project** allows you to select which item is given and which should be provided as the answer and whether the answers should be multiple choice or typed in. The project illustrates use of menus in Java projects, as well as reading information (using the open file dialog control) from files.

Multiple Choice Exam Project Preview

In this chapter, we will build a **multiple choice exam** program. Random items from a provided list are displayed to the user. The user picks the item that matches (or goes with the displayed item). For example, if a country is listed, the user may be asked for the capital city. Answers can be multiple choice or typed in.

The finished project is saved as **MultipleChoiceExam** in the **\HomeJava\HomeJava Projects** project group. Start NetBeans (or your IDE). Open the specified project group. Make **MultipleChoiceExam** the selected project. Run the project. You will see:

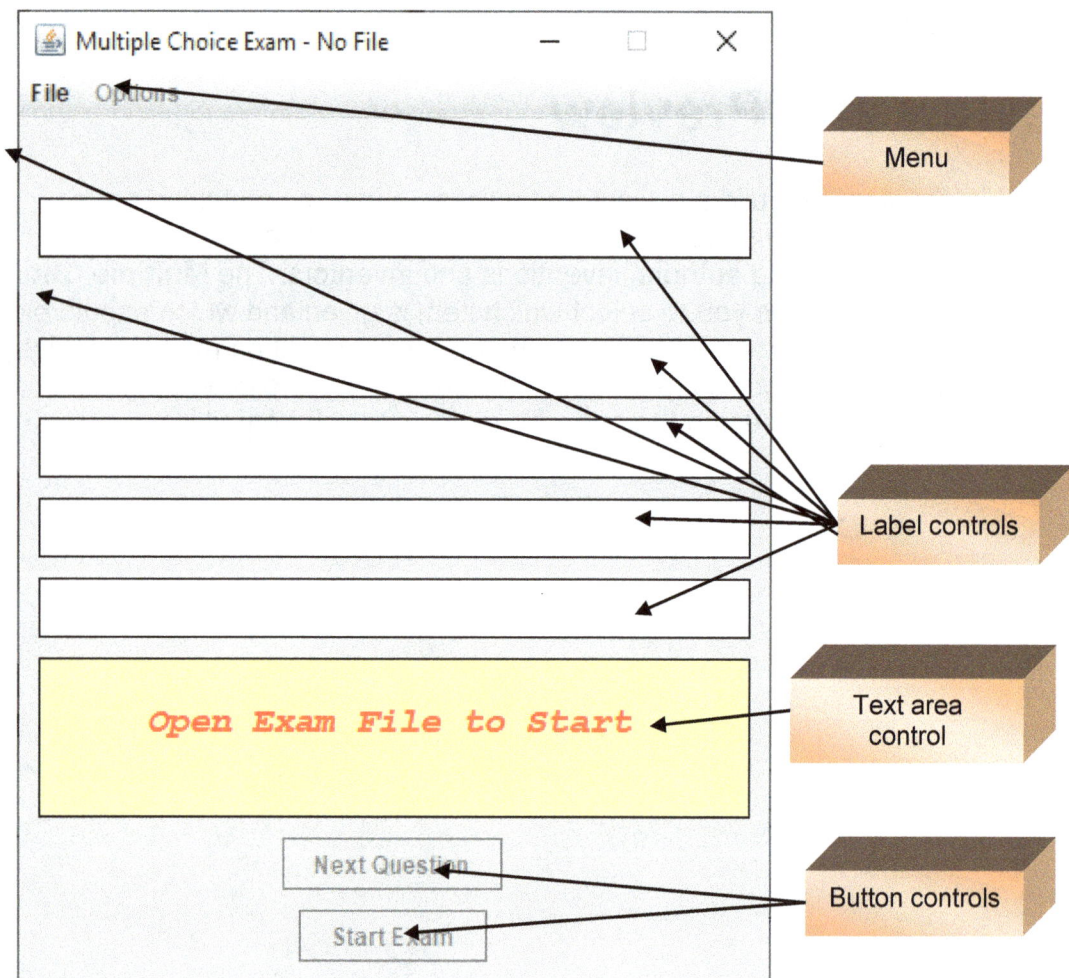

There are lots of controls here. A menu is used to control the program Two label controls (blank) are used for header information. Four white labels are used for multiple choice answers and a large yellow text area is used to provide comments to the user. There is also a text field control behind one of the label controls, used for entering typed-in answers. Two button controls are used to move from question to question and to start and stop the exam.

When started, the multiple choice exam program appears as:

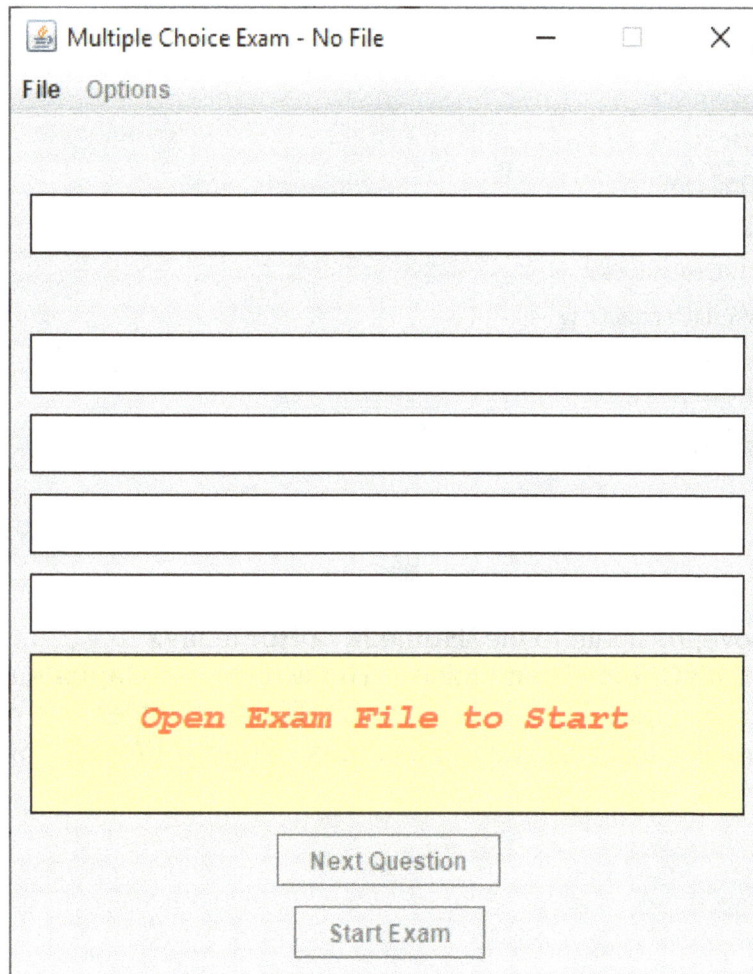

In the comment area you see "*Open Exam File to Start*". The information used for a multiple choice exam is stored in files you build (we will discuss how to do this). So, the first step is to open and load such a file. Choose the **File** menu item and click **Open**. An open file dialog box will appear:

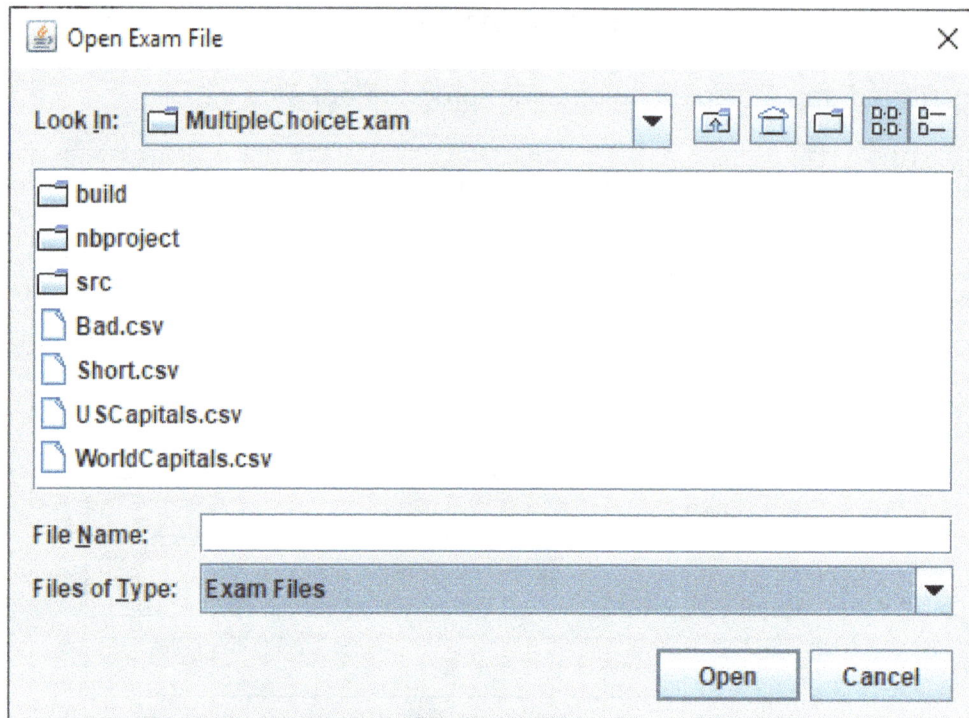

As shown above, navigate to the **\HomeJava\HomeJava Projects\MultipleChoiceExam** folder. The two files **USCapitals.csv** (listing states and capitals) and **WorldCapitals.csv** (listing countries and capitals) are example exam files included with these notes. Choose **WorldCapitals.csv** and click **Open**.

The file will open and the project form should now appear as:

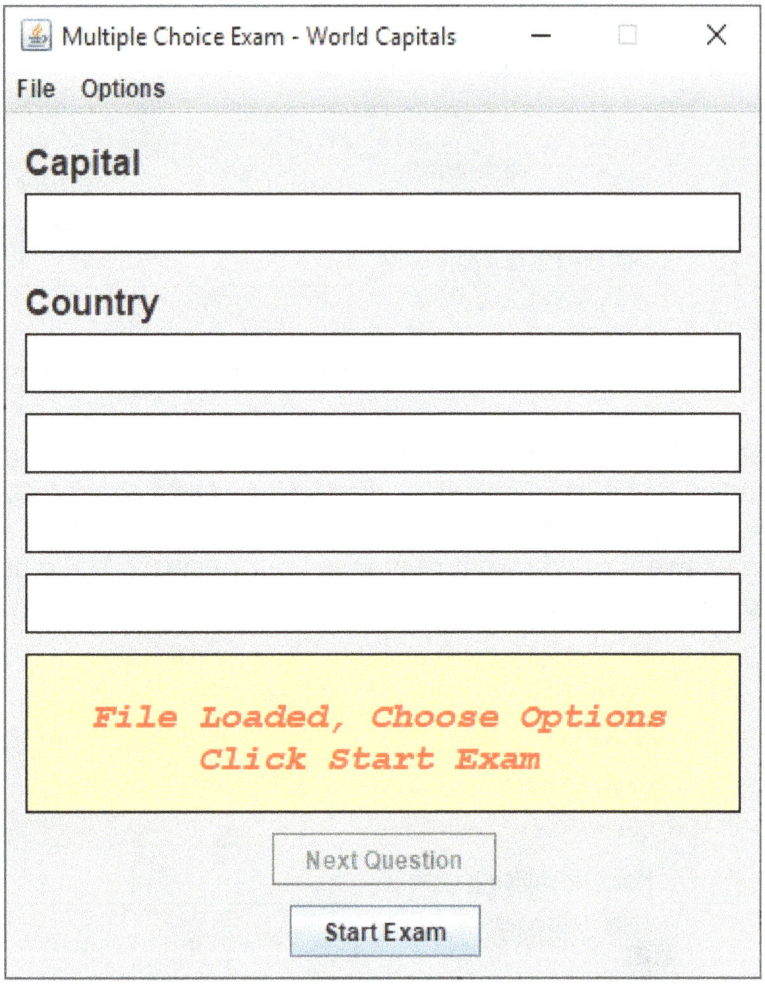

Notice headers (**Capital** and **Country**) are now listed on the form. The form has a caption (**Multiple Choice Exam – World Capitals**) with the exam title. The program is now asking you to select options before starting the exam.

Click the **Options** menu item and you will see four options with the default selections indicated by filled circles:

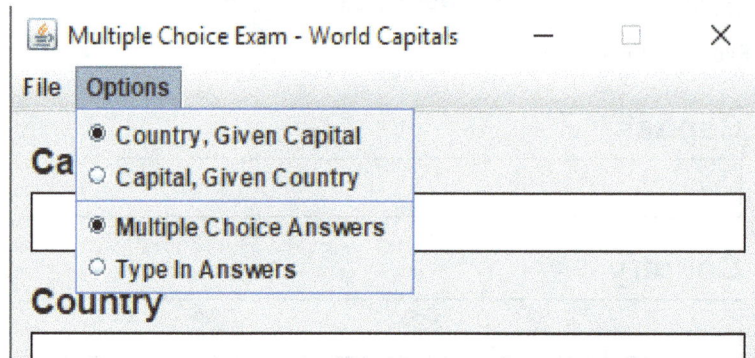

Two choices are to be made. In this example, you are asked whether you want to name the **Country**, given the **Capital**, or vice versa. Let's choose **Capital, Given Country**. The other choice is whether you want to be provided with a list of multiple choice answers or you want to type in your answer. Make sure a filled circle is next to **Multiple Choice Answers**. The choices should now appear as:

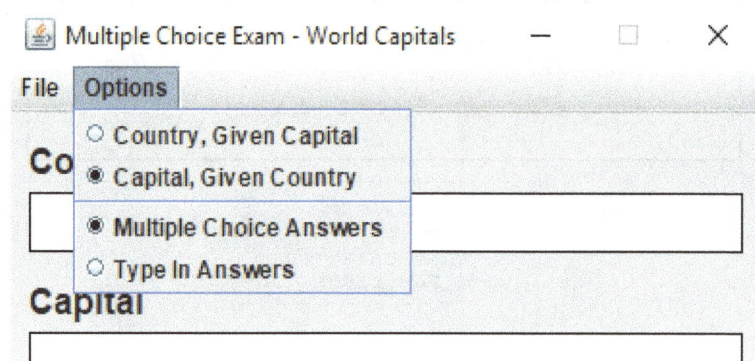

We're ready to start the exam. Click the button marked **Start Exam** and you will see:

Your entries will be different since the exam questions and possible answers are selected randomly. This question asks for the capital of **China** and four possible answers are listed. You click on your choice of capital. You will be told if you are correct or not and given the opportunity to answer another question. You are only given one chance to get the correct answer.

I know the capital of **China** is **Peking**. When I click that selection, I see:

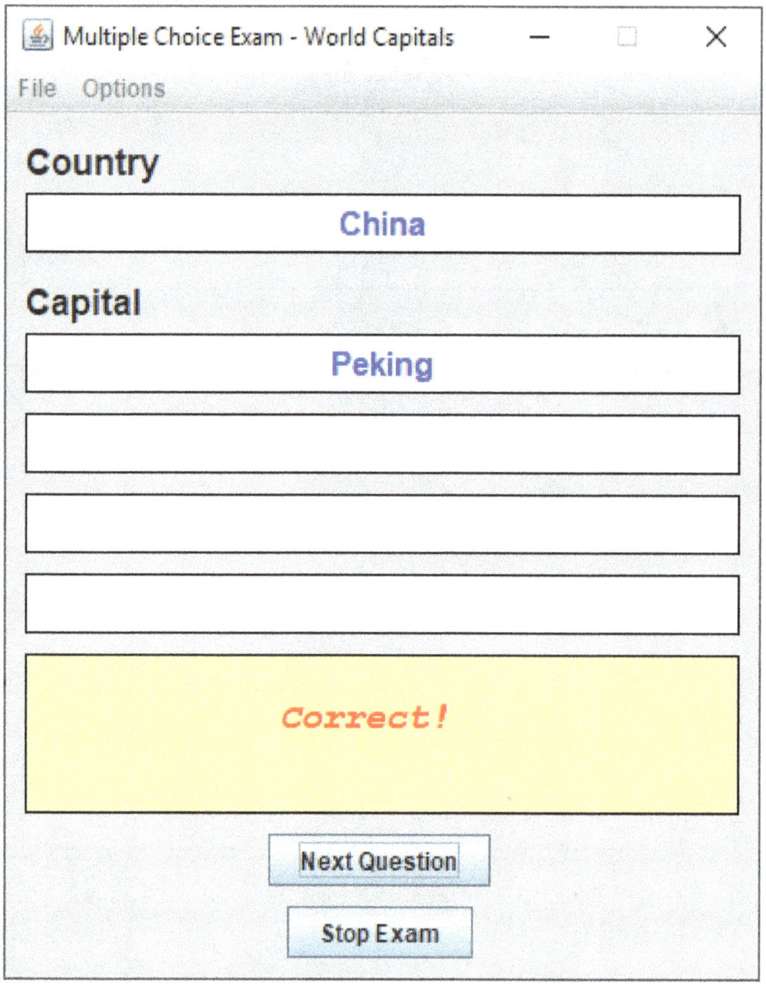

At this point, you have two choices – click **Next Question** to continue or click **Stop Exam** to stop. Try a few more questions.

At some point, when you answer incorrectly, you will see a screen similar to this:

So, with an incorrect answer, you are told so and given the correct answer. Keep answering questions as long as you'd like. When you finally click **Stop Exam**, you will be shown a message box with the exam results. Mine for a short exam is:

Click **OK** in the message box and your form returns to its initial configuration:

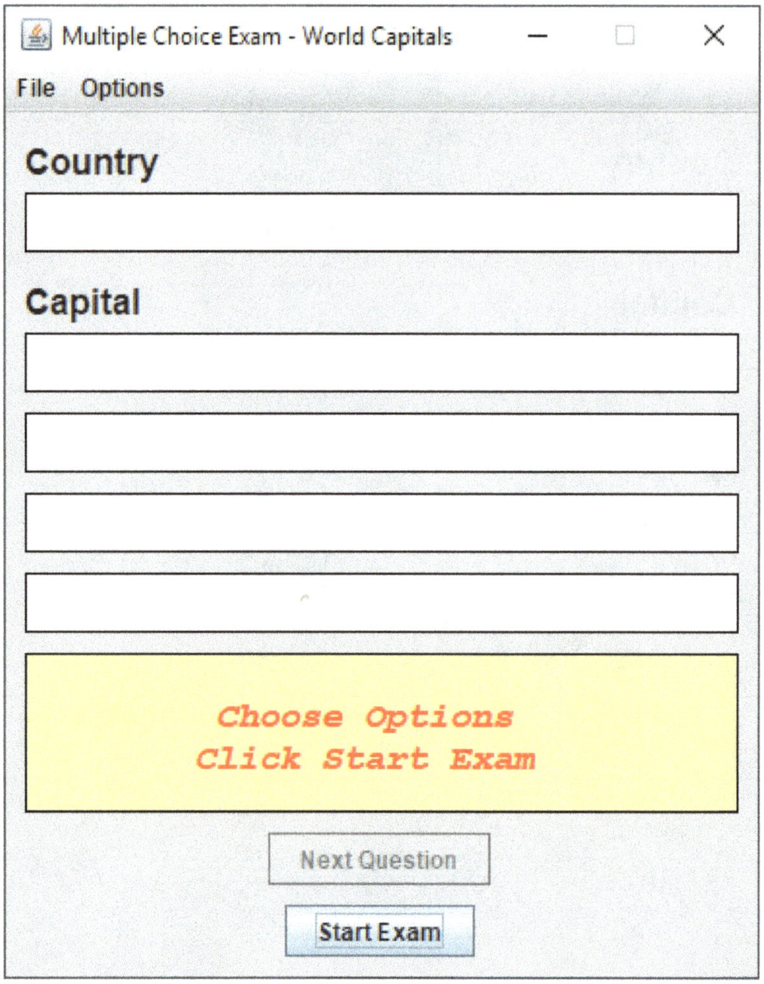

At this point, you can change any option and start a new exam, start a new exam with the same options or load a new exam file. Or, you can choose **Exit** in the **File** menu structure to stop the program.

Click the **Options** menu and choose **Type In Answer**. You will see:

The form has reconfigured – the four multiple choice answer areas (label controls) have been replaced by a single text field control where your answer is typed. Click **Start Exam**.

The first question is displayed (again, yours will be different):

The capital of **Greece** is **Athens**. If you type **Athens** in the text field area and press <**Enter**> you will be told this is a correct answer. The program allows your answers to be case-insensitive (we'll show you how to do this in the code design), so even if you type **athens**, you are credited with a correct answer.

When I type **athens** in the text box and press **<Enter>**, I see:

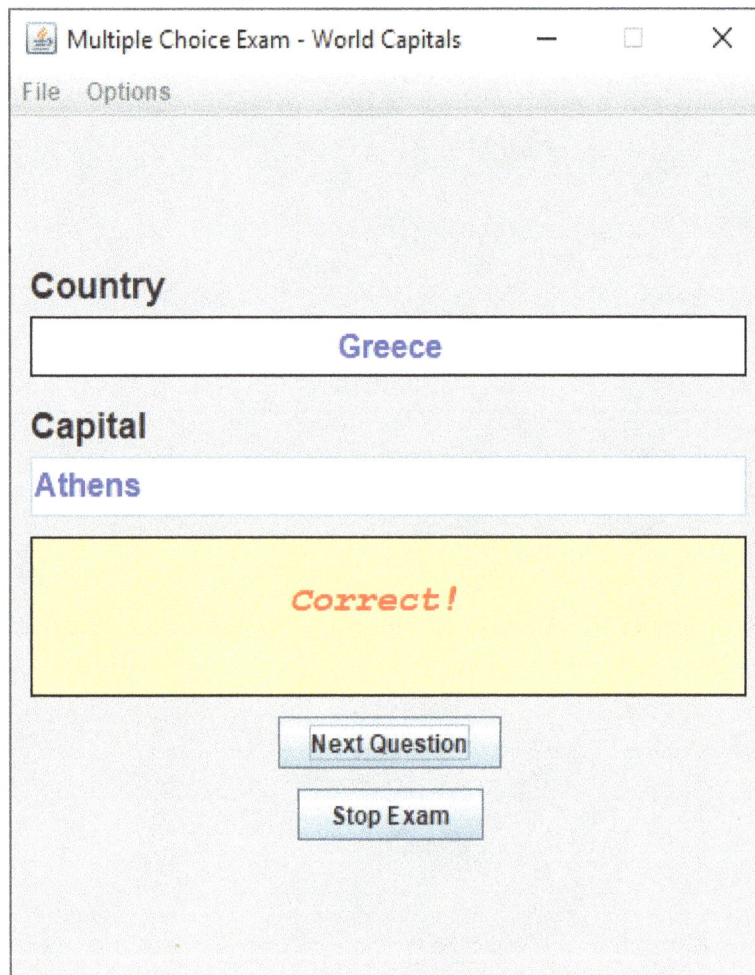

As mentioned, the answer is accepted and the 'capitalization' is corrected.

Now, let's look at a really neat feature of the program. Many times, when typing answers, you might know the answer but not the correct spelling. This happens a lot with kids – could you spell **Athens** when you were young? Rather than telling a user the answer is wrong, it would be nice to credit a user with the correct answer if the spelling is close. How do you do such magic, you ask? We'll see in the code design section. For now, let's just try it.

After getting credit for my **Greece** question, the next question presented was (again, your question will be different, but try misspelling an answer):

The capital of **Iceland** is **Reykjavik**, but who can spell that? What if I mistakenly spell it as **raykavick**:

When I press <**Enter**>, I see:

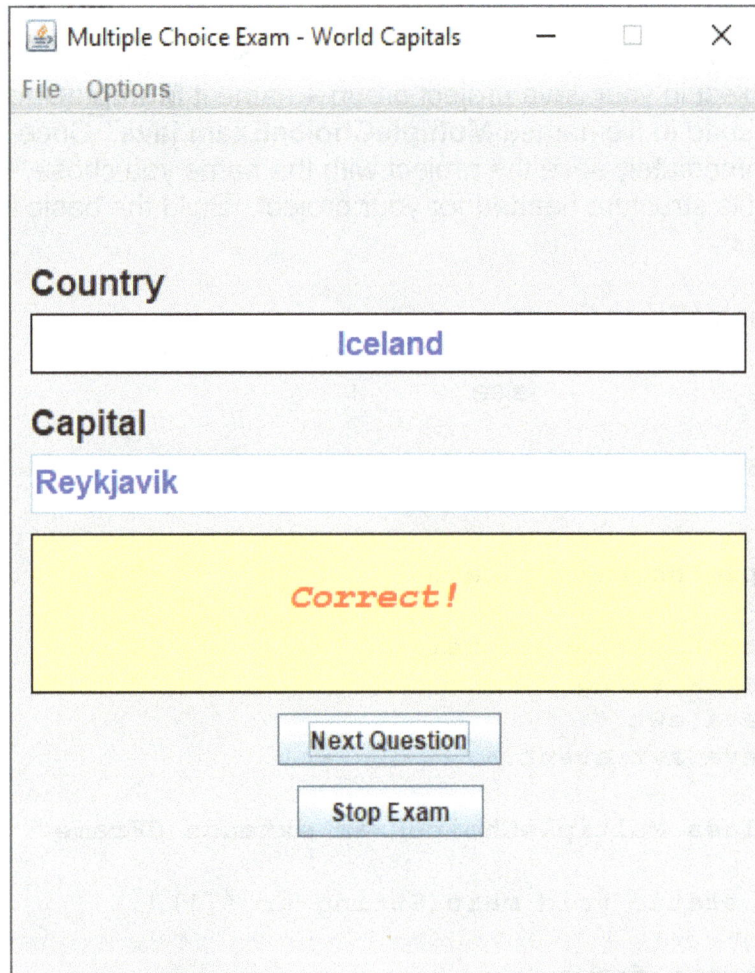

So, even though I misspelled the capital, I am given credit for a correct answer and shown the correct spelling. This little feature really helps alleviate user's frustration at not quite knowing how to spell an answer – this is especially useful with kids.

I think you see the idea of the program. Try as many questions, with as many different options, as you like. Maybe load in the **USCapitals.csv** file. When you are finally, finished choose **Exit** under the **File** menu to stop.

You will now build this project in several stages. We address **frame design**. We discuss the controls used to build the form and establish initial properties. And, we address **code design** in detail. We cover opening and loading exam files, establishing and switching configurations for different options, validation of both multiple choice and typed in answers and presenting results. And, we show how we did the trick to check for "close spelling"?

Multiple Choice Exam Frame Design

We begin building the **Multiple Choice Exam Project.** Let's build the frame. Start a new project in your Java project group – name it **MultipleChoiceExam**. Delete default code in file named **MultipleChoiceExam.java**. Once started, we suggest you immediately save the project with the name you chose. This sets up the folder and file structure needed for your project. Build the basic frame with these properties:

MultipleChoiceExam Frame:
title	Multiple Choice Exam – No File
resizable	false

The code is:

```java
/*
 * MultipleChoiceExam.java
 */
package multiplechoiceexam;
import javax.swing.*;
import java.awt.*;
import java.awt.event.*;

public class MultipleChoiceExam extends JFrame
{
  public static void main(String args[])
  {
    // create frame
    new MultipleChoiceExam().setVisible(true);
  }

  public MultipleChoiceExam()
  {
    // frame constructor
    setTitle("Multiple Choice Exam - No File");
    setResizable(false);

    addWindowListener(new WindowAdapter()
    {
      public void windowClosing(WindowEvent evt)
      {
        exitForm(evt);
      }
    });

    getContentPane().setLayout(new GridBagLayout());
```

```
    GridBagConstraints gridConstraints;

    pack();
    Dimension screenSize =
Toolkit.getDefaultToolkit().getScreenSize();
    setBounds((int) (0.5 * (screenSize.width -
getWidth())), (int) (0.5 * (screenSize.height -
getHeight())), getWidth(), getHeight());
  }

  private void exitForm(WindowEvent evt)
  {
    System.exit(0);
  }
}
```

This code builds the frame, sets up the layout manager and includes code to exit the application. Run the code to make sure the frame (at least, what there is of it at this point) appears and is centered on the screen:

Let's populate our frame with other controls. All code for creating the frame and placing controls (except declarations) goes in the **MultipleChoiceExam** constructor.

The **GridBagLayout** for the project frame is quite simple:

	gridx = 0
gridy = 0	**headGivenLabel**
gridy = 1	**givenLabel**
gridy = 2	**headAnswerLabel**
gridy = 3	**answerLabel[0]**
gridy = 4	**answerLabel[1]**
gridy = 5	**answerLabel[2]**
gridy = 6	**answerLabel[3]**
gridy = 7	**commentTextArea**
gridy = 8	**nextButton**
gridy = 9	**startButton**

headGivenLabel and **headAnswerLabel** are used for header information. **givenLabel** is used to list the 'given' item. **answerLabel[0]**, **answerLabel[1]**, **answerLabel[2]** and **answerLabel[3]** are used to list the multiple choice answers. In the same location as **answerLabel[0]** is a text field control (**answerText** Field) used to type-in answers. We will use code to make it appear when needed. The **commentTextArea** is used for comments. Lastly, one button (**startButton**) starts and stops the exams and one moves you from one question to the next (**nextButton**). We'll add a few controls at a time. Let's add the top three labels.

The control properties are:

headGivenLabel:

size	370, 30
font	Arial, Bold, Size 18
gridx	0
gridy	0
insets	10, 10, 0, 10

givenLabel:

size	370, 30
font	Arial, Bold, Size 16
border	Black line
background	White
foreground	Blue
opaque	true
horizontalAlignment	Center
gridx	0
gridy	1
insets	0, 10, 0, 10

headAnswerLabel:

size	370, 30:
font	Arial, Bold, Size 18
gridx	0
gridy	2
insets	10, 10, 0, 10

Declare these controls using:

```
JLabel headGivenLabel = new JLabel();
JLabel givenLabel = new JLabel();
JLabel headAnswerLabel = new JLabel();
```

Many controls will have the same size and font. Define two font objects and a size object to make life a little easier:

```
Font headerFont = new Font("Arial", Font.BOLD, 18);
Font examItemFont = new Font("Arial", Font.BOLD, 16);
Dimension itemSize = new Dimension(370, 30);
```

Now, the controls are added to the frame in the frame constructor using:

```
headGivenLabel.setPreferredSize(itemSize);
headGivenLabel.setFont(headerFont);
gridConstraints = new GridBagConstraints();
gridConstraints.gridx = 0;
gridConstraints.gridy = 0;
gridConstraints.insets = new Insets(10, 10, 0, 10);
getContentPane().add(headGivenLabel, gridConstraints);

givenLabel.setPreferredSize(itemSize);
givenLabel.setFont(examItemFont);
givenLabel.setBorder(BorderFactory.createLineBorder(Color.
BLACK));
givenLabel.setBackground(Color.WHITE);
givenLabel.setForeground(Color.BLUE);
givenLabel.setOpaque(true);
givenLabel.setHorizontalAlignment(SwingConstants.CENTER);
gridConstraints = new GridBagConstraints();
gridConstraints.gridx = 0;
gridConstraints.gridy = 1;
gridConstraints.insets = new Insets(0, 10, 0, 10);
getContentPane().add(givenLabel, gridConstraints);

headAnswerLabel.setPreferredSize(itemSize);
headAnswerLabel.setFont(headerFont);
gridConstraints = new GridBagConstraints();
gridConstraints.gridx = 0;
gridConstraints.gridy = 2;
gridConstraints.insets = new Insets(10, 10, 0, 10);
getContentPane().add(headAnswerLabel, gridConstraints);
```

Notice where the font objects and size object are used.

Save, run the project. You will see the added controls:

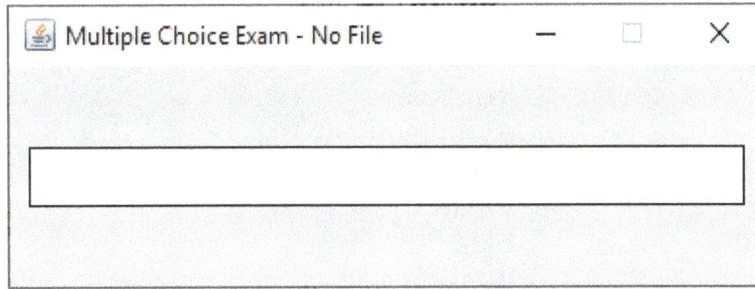

The two header labels are blank (**text** values will be established when we run the program).

Next, we add the four labels for multiple choice answers and the text field for typing in answers. The control properties are:

answerLabel[0]:

size	itemSize
font	examItemFont
border	Black line
background	White
foreground	Blue
opaque	true
horizontalAlignment	Center
gridx	0
gridy	3
insets	0, 10, 10, 10

answerLabel[1]:

size	itemSize
font	examItemFont
border	Black line
background	White
foreground	Blue
opaque	true
horizontalAlignment	Center
gridx	0
gridy	4
insets	0, 10, 10, 10

answerLabel[2]:

size	itemSize
font	examItemFont
border	Black line
background	White
foreground	Blue
opaque	true
horizontalAlignment	Center
gridx	0
gridy	5
insets	0, 10, 10, 10

answerLabel[3]:

size	itemSize
font	examItemFont
border	Black line
background	White
foreground	Blue
opaque	true
horizontalAlignment	Center
gridx	0
gridy	6
insets	0, 10, 10, 10

answerTextField:

size	itemSize
font	examItemFont
background	White
foreground	Blue
visible	false
gridx	0
gridy	3
insets	0, 10, 10, 10

Notice **answerTextField** and **answerLabel[0]** are in the same place on the grid. **answerTextField** has a **visible** property of **false**, hence it does not initially appear. Its appearance will be established based on selected options in the program.

Declare these controls using:

```
JLabel[] answerLabel = new JLabel[4];
JTextField answerTextField = new JTextField();
```

Add them to the frame with this code:

```
for (int i = 0; i < 4; i++)
{
  answerLabel[i] = new JLabel();
  answerLabel[i].setPreferredSize(itemSize);
  answerLabel[i].setFont(examItemFont);

answerLabel[i].setBorder(BorderFactory.createLineBorder(Co
lor.BLACK));
  answerLabel[i].setBackground(Color.WHITE);
  answerLabel[i].setForeground(Color.BLUE);
  answerLabel[i].setOpaque(true);
```

```
answerLabel[i].setHorizontalAlignment(SwingConstants.CENTE
R);
  gridConstraints = new GridBagConstraints();
  gridConstraints.gridx = 0;
  gridConstraints.gridy = i + 3;
  gridConstraints.insets = new Insets(0, 10, 10, 10);
  getContentPane().add(answerLabel[i], gridConstraints);
  answerLabel[i].addMouseListener(new MouseAdapter()
  {
    public void mousePressed(MouseEvent e)
    {
      answerLabelMousePressed(e);
    }
  });
}

answerTextField.setPreferredSize(itemSize);
answerTextField.setFont(examItemFont);
answerTextField.setBackground(Color.WHITE);
answerTextField.setForeground(Color.BLUE);
answerTextField.setVisible(false);
gridConstraints = new GridBagConstraints();
gridConstraints.gridx = 0;
gridConstraints.gridy = 3;
gridConstraints.insets = new Insets(0, 10, 10, 10);
getContentPane().add(answerTextField, gridConstraints);
answerTextField.addActionListener(new ActionListener ()
{
  public void actionPerformed(ActionEvent e)
  {
    answerTextFieldActionPerformed(e);
  }
});
```

The code above also adds a **MousePressed** method for the label controls (to detect clicking on the labels) and a **ActionPerformed** method for the text field (to allow checking typed answers). Add these empty methods:

```
private void answerLabelMousePressed(MouseEvent e)
{
}

private void answerTextFieldActionPerformed(ActionEvent e)
{
}
```

Save, run to see the newly added controls:

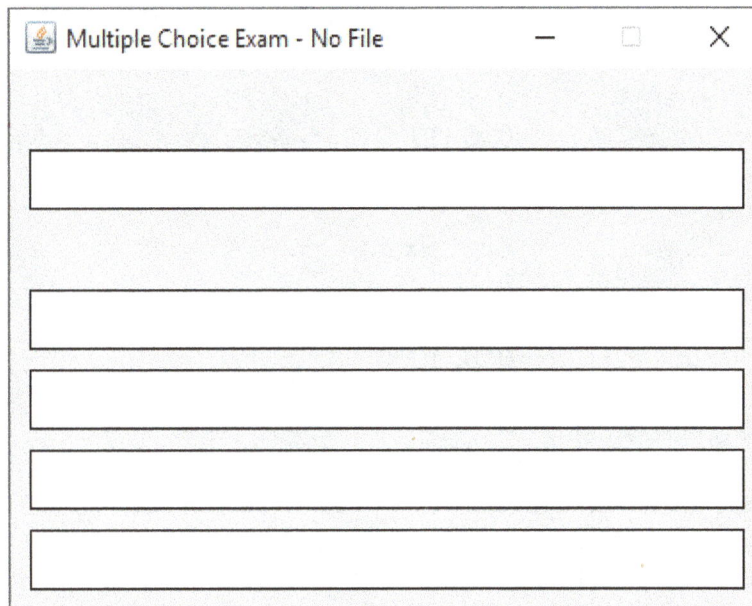

Let's add the final three controls. The properties are:

> **commentTextArea**:
>
> | | |
> |---|---|
> | size | 370, 80 |
> | font | Courier New, Bold, Italic, Size 18 |
> | border | Black line |
> | editable | false |
> | background | Color(255, 255, 192); |
> | foreground | Red |
> | gridx | 0 |
> | gridy | 7 |
> | insets | 0, 10, 10, 10 |
>
> **nextButton**:
>
> | | |
> |---|---|
> | text | Next Question |
> | gridx | 0 |
> | gridy | 8 |
> | insets | 0, 0, 10, 0 |
>
> **startButton**:
>
> | | |
> |---|---|
> | text | Start Exam |
> | gridx | 0 |
> | gridy | 9 |
> | insets | 0, 0, 10, 0 |

Declare these controls using:

```
JTextArea commentTextArea = new JTextArea();
JButton nextButton = new JButton();
JButton startButton = new JButton();
```

Add them to the frame using:

```
commentTextArea.setPreferredSize(new Dimension(370, 80));
commentTextArea.setFont(new Font("Courier New", Font.BOLD
+ Font.ITALIC, 18));
commentTextArea.setBorder(BorderFactory.createLineBorder(C
olor.BLACK));
commentTextArea.setEditable(false);
commentTextArea.setBackground(new Color(255, 255, 196));
commentTextArea.setForeground(Color.RED);
gridConstraints = new GridBagConstraints();
gridConstraints.gridx = 0;
gridConstraints.gridy = 7;
gridConstraints.insets = new Insets(0, 10, 10, 10);
getContentPane().add(commentTextArea, gridConstraints);

nextButton.setText("Next Question");
gridConstraints = new GridBagConstraints();
gridConstraints.gridx = 0;
gridConstraints.gridy = 8;
gridConstraints.insets = new Insets(0, 0, 10, 0);
getContentPane().add(nextButton, gridConstraints);
nextButton.addActionListener(new ActionListener()
{
  public void actionPerformed(ActionEvent e)
  {
    nextButtonActionPerformed(e);
  }
});

startButton.setText("Start Exam");
gridConstraints = new GridBagConstraints();
gridConstraints.gridx = 0;
gridConstraints.gridy = 9;
gridConstraints.insets = new Insets(0, 0, 10, 0);
getContentPane().add(startButton, gridConstraints);
startButton.addActionListener(new ActionListener()
{
  public void actionPerformed(ActionEvent e)
  {
    startButtonActionPerformed(e);
  }
});
```

The code above adds a **ActionPerformed** method for each button.. Add these empty methods:

```
private void nextButtonActionPerformed(ActionEvent e)
{
}

private void startButtonActionPerformed(ActionEvent e)
{
}
```

Save, run one more time:

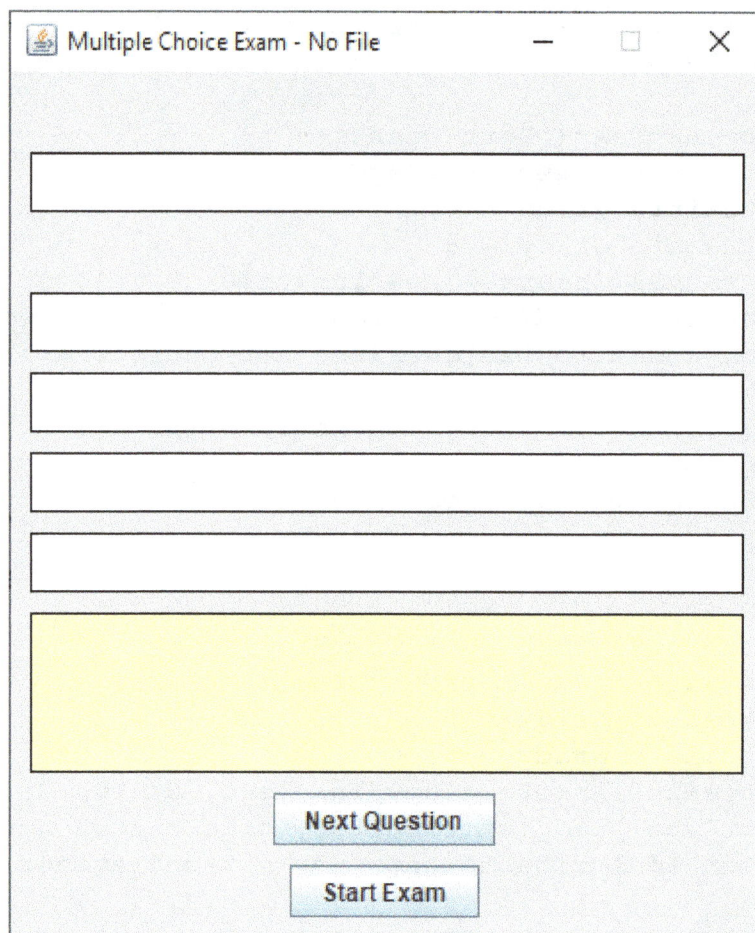

This completes the first part of the frame design. In the next section, we add a menu that allows us to control the program.

Frame Design – Menu Options

Menus are easily incorporated into Java GUI programs using three Swing objects: **menu bars**, **menus**, and **menu items**. The **JMenuBar** object is placed at the top of a frame and is used to hold the menu. The **JMenu** object is a labeled menu item, within the menu bar, that when clicked displays a pull-down menu. And, a **JMenuItem** is a simple menu item that when clicked results in some program action. **JMenuItem** objects appear in the pull-down menus of **JMenu** objects. Menu items can be simply text or even radio buttons and check boxes.

In the multiple choice exam project, we use one menu object (**fileMenu**) to open files and exit program and one object (**optionsMenu**) to allow choosing options. Our menu bar (**mainMenuBar**) structure will be:

Text	**Name**
File	fileMenu
Open	openMenuItem
(Separator)	
Exit	exitMenuItem
Options	optionsMenu
Header 1	header1MenuItem
Header 2	header2MenuItem
(Separator)	
Multiple Choice Answers	mcMenuItem
Type In Answers	typeMenuItem

Notice a separator in each menu object. The items under the **Objects** menu will be two sets of radio buttons (to allow distinct choices).

Declare the different menu items as class level objects:

```
// menu structure
JMenuBar mainMenuBar = new JMenuBar();
JMenu fileMenu = new JMenu("File");
JMenuItem openMenuItem = new JMenuItem("Open");
JMenuItem exitMenuItem = new JMenuItem("Exit");
JMenu optionsMenu = new JMenu("Options");
JRadioButtonMenuItem header1MenuItem = new
JRadioButtonMenuItem("Header 1", true);
JRadioButtonMenuItem header2MenuItem = new
JRadioButtonMenuItem("Header 2", false);
JRadioButtonMenuItem mcMenuItem = new
JRadioButtonMenuItem("Multiple Choice Answers", true);
JRadioButtonMenuItem typeMenuItem = new
JRadioButtonMenuItem("Type In Answers", false);
ButtonGroup nameGroup = new ButtonGroup();
ButtonGroup typeGroup = new ButtonGroup();
```

Establish the menu structure using this code in the frame constructor (each menu item has a corresponding **ActionPerformed** method):

```
// build menu structure
setJMenuBar(mainMenuBar);
mainMenuBar.add(fileMenu);
fileMenu.add(openMenuItem);
fileMenu.addSeparator();
fileMenu.add(exitMenuItem);
mainMenuBar.add(optionsMenu);
optionsMenu.add(header1MenuItem);
optionsMenu.add(header2MenuItem);
optionsMenu.addSeparator();
optionsMenu.add(mcMenuItem);
optionsMenu.add(typeMenuItem);
nameGroup.add(header1MenuItem);
nameGroup.add(header2MenuItem);
typeGroup.add(mcMenuItem);
typeGroup.add(typeMenuItem);
openMenuItem.addActionListener(new ActionListener()
{
  public void actionPerformed(ActionEvent e)
  {
    openMenuItemActionPerformed(e);
  }
});
exitMenuItem.addActionListener(new ActionListener()
{
```

```
   public void actionPerformed(ActionEvent e)
   {
     exitMenuItemActionPerformed(e);
   }
});
header1MenuItem.addActionListener(new ActionListener()
{
  public void actionPerformed(ActionEvent e)
  {
    header1MenuItemActionPerformed(e);
  }
});
header2MenuItem.addActionListener(new ActionListener()
{
  public void actionPerformed(ActionEvent e)
  {
    header2MenuItemActionPerformed(e);
  }
});
mcMenuItem.addActionListener(new ActionListener()
{
  public void actionPerformed(ActionEvent e)
  {
    mcMenuItemActionPerformed(e);
  }
});
typeMenuItem.addActionListener(new ActionListener()
{
  public void actionPerformed(ActionEvent e)
  {
   typeMenuItemActionPerformed(e);
  }
});
```

Add the six empty methods:

```java
private void openMenuItemActionPerformed(ActionEvent e)
{
}


private void exitMenuItemActionPerformed(ActionEvent e)
{
}


private void header1MenuItemActionPerformed(ActionEvent e)
{
}


private void header2MenuItemActionPerformed(ActionEvent e)
{
}


private void mcMenuItemActionPerformed(ActionEvent e)
{
}


private void typeMenuItemActionPerformed(ActionEvent e)
{
}
```

Save, run. The menu structure appears:

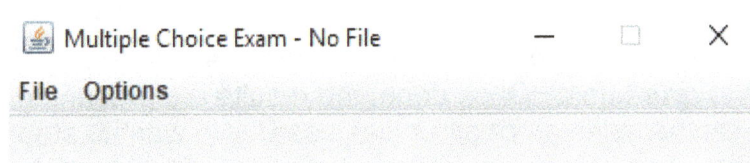

Click **File** to see:

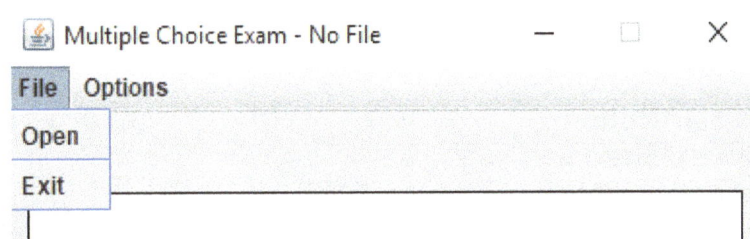

Notice the separator bar. Now click **Options**:

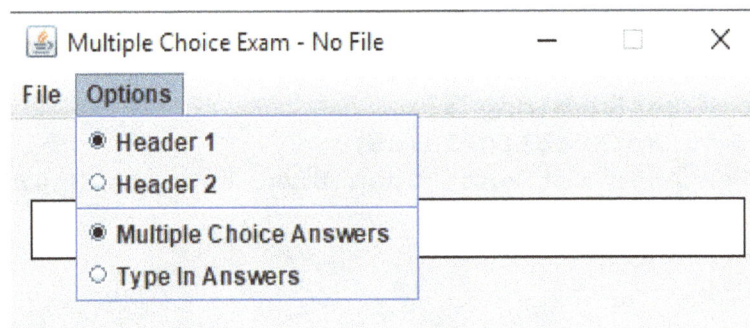

Notice the use of radio buttons to indicate choices. The **Header 1** and **Header 2** entries will be replaced when exam files are opened.

The frame is now complete. We will begin writing code for the application. We will write the code in several steps. As a first step, we write the code that gets the program in initial mode to allow opening an exam file.

Frame Design – Initialization

In the multiple choice exam project, the user opens an exam file, chooses options and proceeds to take a test. Once done, the results are presented. At that point, other options can be selected or other files used. We want to step the user through program use – this minimizes the possibility of errors. When the program starts, the first thing a user must do is open a file. We need to make sure the interface only allows access to the **File** menu option.

When the program first loads, these steps are taken:

> ➢ Disable **startButton**.
> ➢ Disable **nextButton**.
> ➢ Disable **optionsMenu**.
> ➢ Change **text** property of **commentTextArea** to **Open Exam File to Start**.

This initialization code is placed at the end of the frame constructor code:

```
// initialize form
startButton.setEnabled(false);
nextButton.setEnabled(false);
optionsMenu.setEnabled(false);
commentTextArea.setText("Open Exam File to Start");
```

Add this code to the project.

Save and run the project. The form will appear as:

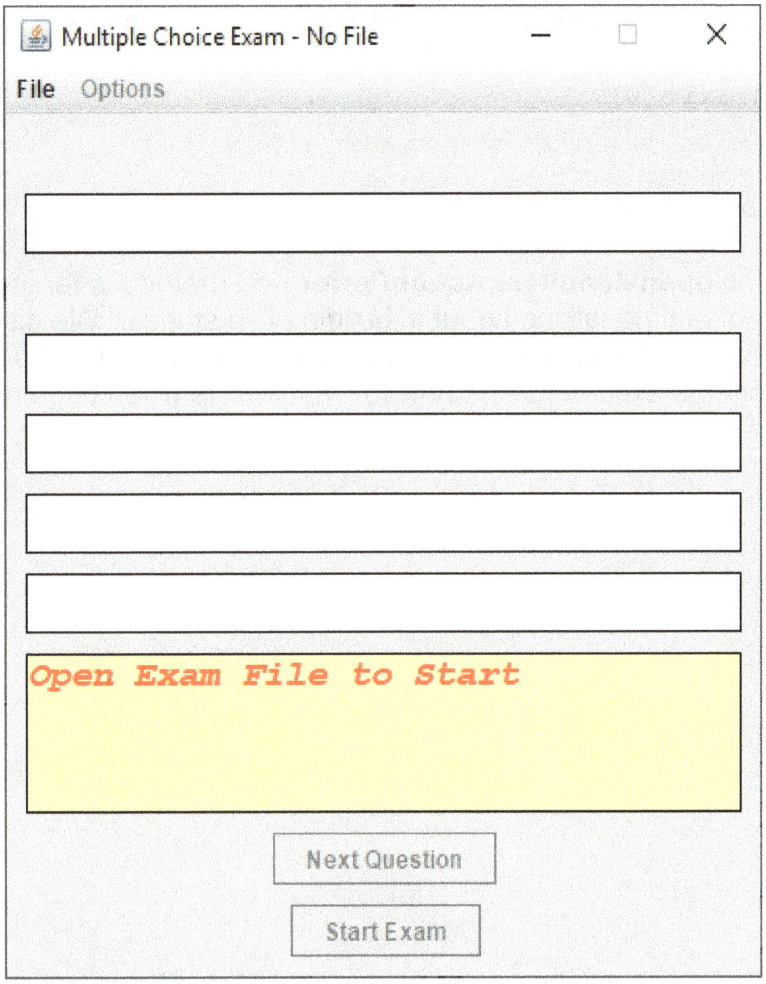

Notice at this point, the only thing a user can do is select the **File** menu option, where a file can be opened (**Open**) or the project can be stopped (**Exit**). We'll write code for both options. Also it would be nice if the text in the comment area were centered (both vertically and horizontally). Unfortunately, the text area control has no property for justifying text. But, we will fix this annoyance later with some clever coding.

The **exitMenuItem ActionPerformed** method is simple. The code is:

```
private void exitMenuItemActionPerformed(ActionEvent e)
{
   System.exit(0);
}
```

Add this method to the project.

The code for the **openMenuItem ActionPerformed** method is far more involved.
We'll spend a lot of time talking about it, building it in stages. We discuss file
format, ways to generate exam files, how to open exam files, how to read
information from the exam files and how to avoid errors when opening and reading
files.

Code Design – Exam File Format

The files used to store information for multiple choice exams have a specific format – you need to insure any files you generate conform to this standard. The files used are called **sequential files**, indicating they are just line after line of information.

To generate a file, you need to have two lists of matching terms (in our sample files, the lists are states and capitals and countries and capitals). Each term should have an identifying header. And each file (exam) should have a title. Once you have this information, the first line of the file is the exam title, followed by a comma (,). The second line is the two headers describing the listed terms, separated by a comma. Subsequent lines are the pairs of terms, each pair separated by a comma – the program will allow up to 100 matching pairs.

Using Windows Notepad (or some other text editor), open the **USCapitals.csv** file in the **\HomeJava\HomeJava Projects\MultipleChoiceExam** folder. When Notepad opens, choose **Open** under the **File** menu. Then, choose **All Files** under **Files of Type** in the **Open** dialog box (by default, only files with **txt** extensions are shown). Choose the file and click **Open**. Note the format:

```
USCapitals.csv - Notepad               —    □    ×

 File  Edit  Format  View  Help
US Capitals,
State,Capital
Alabama,Montgomery
Alaska,Juneau
Arizona,Phoenix
Arkansas,Little Rock
California,Sacramento
Colorado,Denver
Connecticut,Hartford
Delaware,Dover
```

The first line shows the title (**US Capitals**) with an ending comma (don't forget this comma when generating a file). The second line are the headers (**State** and **Capital**), separated by a comma. Following the headers are the 50 pairs of states and capitals, separated by commas. All files must be in this form. Let's see how you can generate such files.

Code Design – Generating Exam Files

You will eventually want to use exam files other than the two examples included. Hence, you need to know how to generate such files. First, you need to have your list of terms. Choose a title and the two headers. Once you have this information, you need to save it in the proper file format with a **csv** extension. The extension **csv** stands for **comma separated values** – that's why we saw all the commas in the **USCapitals.csv** file.

One way to generate an exam file is use a simple word processor such as the Windows **Notepad**. Start a new file and simply type in the information in the proper format like this:

```
Untitled - Notepad                    —    □    ×

File  Edit  Format  View  Help
Title,
Header1,Header2
Term1,Term2
Term1,Term2
Term1,Term2
Term1,Term2
Term1,Term2
Term1,Term2
Term1,Term2
Term1,Term2
```

There are very few restrictions on the information you can use in an exam file. Entries can be letters, numbers, spaces and nearly any "typeable" character. A major restriction is that the entries can have <u>no commas</u>. Since we use a comma as a **delimiter** (the character that separates one term from the other), any other comma in a line would result in an error.

When the file is complete, save it with a **csv** extension. Notepad, by default, will want to save your file with a **txt** extension. To bypass this, when the **Save** dialog opens, choose **All Files** in the **Save as type** drop-down as shown:

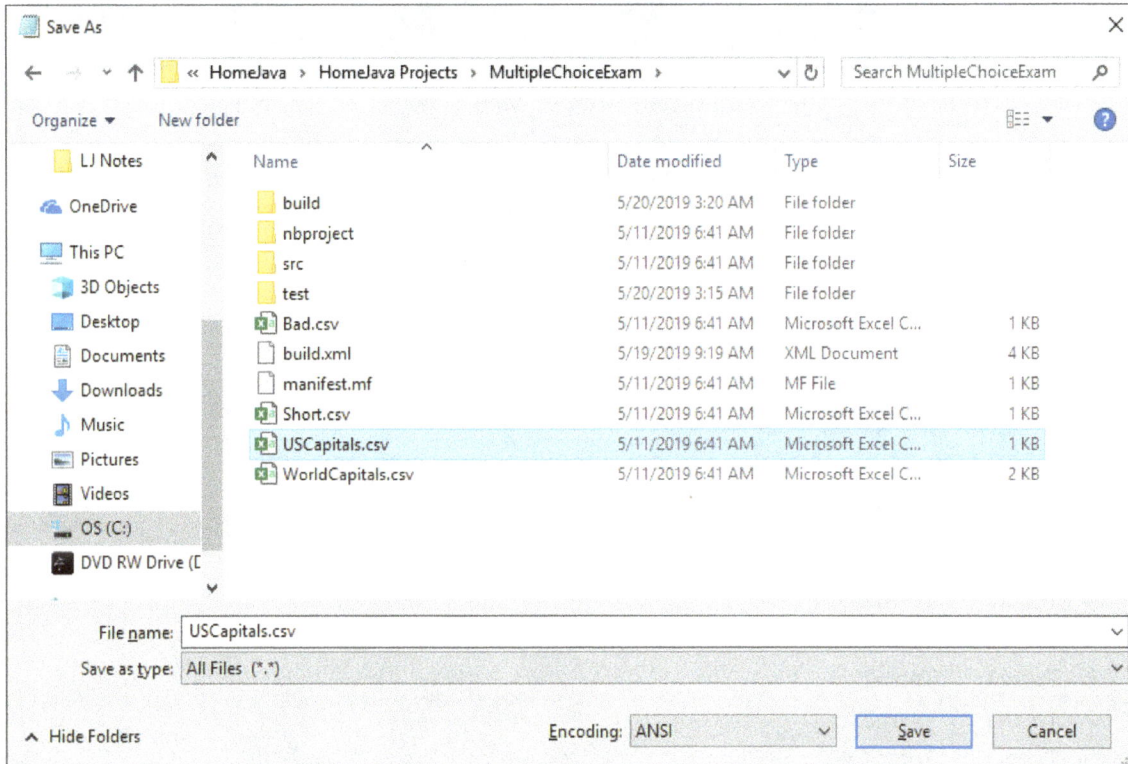

Type your file name with the **csv** extension and click **Save**.

A spreadsheet program such as Microsoft's **Excel** can also be used to generate an exam file. To do this, start Excel. A blank worksheet should appear. Type the information in the spreadsheet cells something like this:

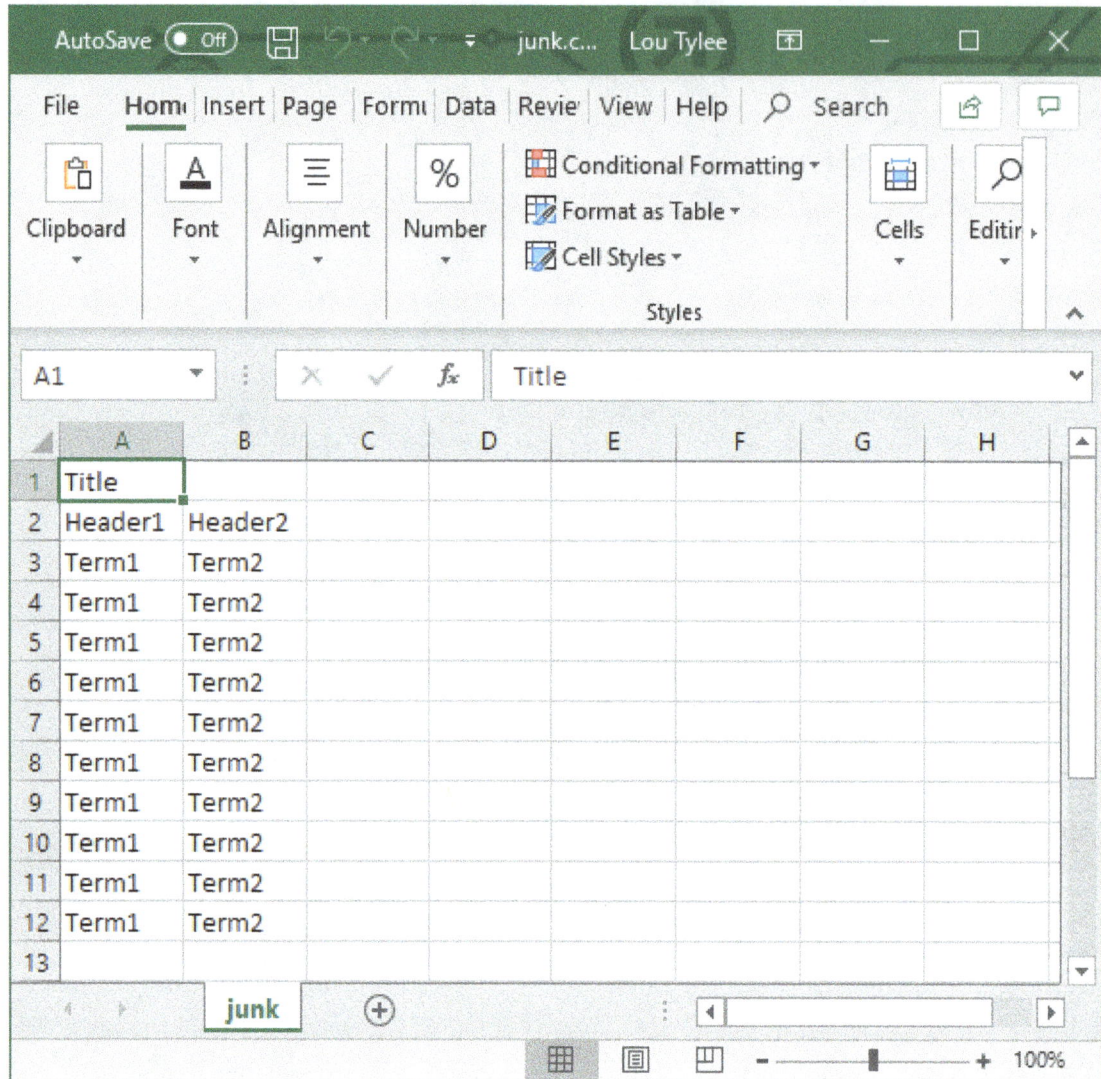

Once you've entered all your terms, choose **File**, then click **Save As**. When the **Save As** window appears, choose **CSV** under **Save as type** as shown below:

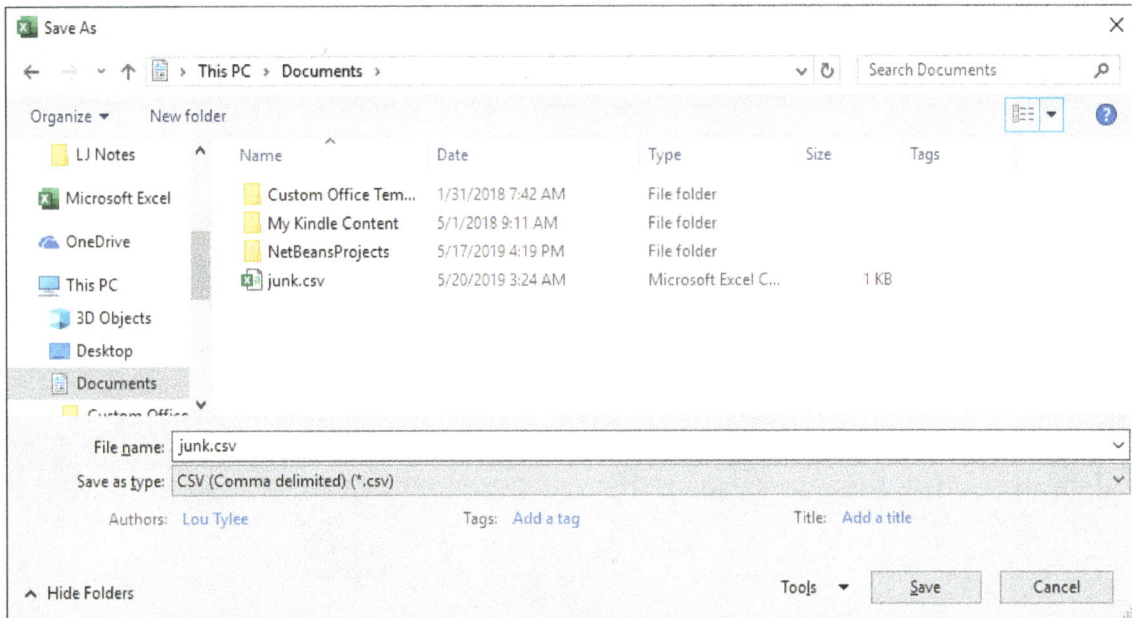

The information in the spreadsheet will be saved as a comma-separated file in the format used by the multiple choice exam project.

You can also open the example exam files in Excel. Choose **Open** under the **File** menu, then choose one of the samples – you have to set **Files of type** to **All Files** when selecting the file. Here's the **WorldCapitals.csv** file in Excel:

Now, let's see how to open exam files in our project.

Code Design – Opening an Exam File

When a user clicks the **Open** entry in the **File** menu, the project should ask the user for an exam file. When that file's name is provided, the program will open the file, read in the information and place that information in the proper program variables. Once this is done, the user can begin to take a quiz. All of this happens in the **openMenuItemActionPerformed** method. We will begin building that method. As a first step, let's look at the step of obtaining a file name from the user and opening the file for input.

The user needs to tell the program which exam file they want to use. The Swing file chooser (**JChooser**) object will be used to provide this name. The steps to do this are:

➢ Show the open file dialog box.
➢ If user picks a file name and clicks **Open**, proceed to open file and obtain values.
➢ If **Cancel** is clicked, do nothing.

Let's review **JFileChooser** relative to our task. File chooser **Properties**:

currentDirectory	The selected directory.
dialogTitle	Title that appears in the title area of the dialog.
dialogType	By default, an Open dialog (**JFileChooser.OPEN_DIALOG**), set to **JFileChooser.SAVE_DIALOG** for a save dialog control.
fileFilter	Used to limit types of files displayed.
selectedFile	The currently selected file.

File chooser **Methods**:

showOpenDialog	Displays the dialog box for opening files. Returned value indicates which button was clicked by user (**Open** or **Cancel**).
getCurrentDirectory	Retrieves the selected directory.
setDialogTitle	Sets the dialog title.
setDialogType	Sets the dialog type.
setFileFilter	Sets the filter to limit types of files displayed.
addChoosableFileFilter	Add a file filter to file chooser.
getSelectedFile	Retrieves the currently selected file.

To display the file chooser as an open dialog box, use the **showOpenDialog** method. If the chooser is named **openChooser**, the format is:

```
openChooser.showOpenDialog(this);
```

where **this** is a keyword referring to the current frame. The displayed dialog box is:

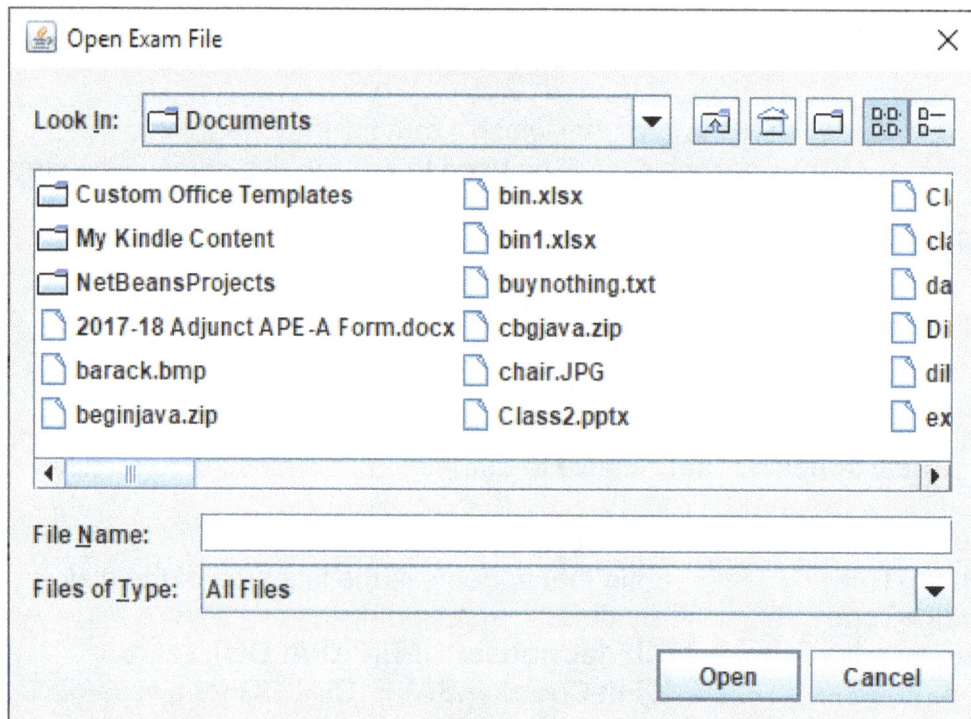

The user selects a file using the dialog control (or types a name in the **File Name** box). The file type is selected from the **Files of Type** box (values here set with the **Filter** property). Once selected, the **Open** button is clicked. **Cancel** can be clicked to cancel the open operation. The **showOpenDialog** method returns the clicked button. This method will return one of two values:

> **JFileChooser.APPROVE_OPTION** – Approve (**Open**) button clicked
> **JFileChooser.CANCEL_OPTION** – Cancel button clicked

If the user has selected the **Open** button, we can determine the selected file. This value is given by:

> `openChooser.getSelectedFile()`

The **fileFilter** property is set by the **FileNameExtensionFilter** constructor. The form for this constructor is

`FileNameExtensionFilter(description, extension1, extension2, ... )`

Here, description is the **description** that appears in the file chooser window, each **extension** is an acceptable file extension type to display. Each argument is a **string** type. To use this constructor, you need this **import** statement in your java class:

`import javax.swing.filechooser.*;`

Add this import statement to the project. In our project, we only want **csv** files. The snippet of code that accomplishes this is:

> `openChooser.addChoosableFileFilter(new`
> `FileNameExtensionFilter("Exam Files", "csv"));`

With this filter, only **csv** files will be displayed for opening.

We now look at opening the file for now. That's all we'll do for now – open the file. Assuming we know the name of the exam file, it is opened using Java **BufferedReader** and **FileReader** objects. These objects require the following import statement:

```
import java.io.*;
```

The syntax for opening a sequential file for input is:

```
BufferedReader inputFile = new BufferedReader(new
FileReader(fileName));
```

where **fileName** is a complete path to the file and **inputFile** is the returned file object.

Once opened, we can read information from the file. We will discuss how to do that next. When all values have been read from the sequential file, it is closed using:

```
inputFile.close();
```

Let's make sure we can open and close an exam file. The code in the
openMenuItemActionPerformed method that accomplishes the above tasks is:

```
private void openMenuItemActionPerformed(ActionEvent e)
{
  JFileChooser openChooser = new JFileChooser();
  openChooser.setDialogType(JFileChooser.OPEN_DIALOG);
  openChooser.setDialogTitle("Open Exam File");
  openChooser.addChoosableFileFilter(new
FileNameExtensionFilter("Exam Files", "csv"));
  if (openChooser.showOpenDialog(this) ==
JFileChooser.APPROVE_OPTION)
  {
    try
    {
      BufferedReader inputFile = new BufferedReader(new
FileReader(openChooser.getSelectedFile()));
      JOptionPane.showConfirmDialog(null,
openChooser.getSelectedFile() + " Opened", "Success!",
JOptionPane.DEFAULT_OPTION, JOptionPane.PLAIN_MESSAGE);
      inputFile.close();
    }
    catch (Exception ex)
    {
    }
  }
}
```

We use a temporary message box (**JOptionPane**) to tell us if the file opens
successfully:

Save and run the project. Choose the **Open** option under the **File** menu. You should see an open file dialog box:. Navigate to your project folder (or wherever you have the sample files)

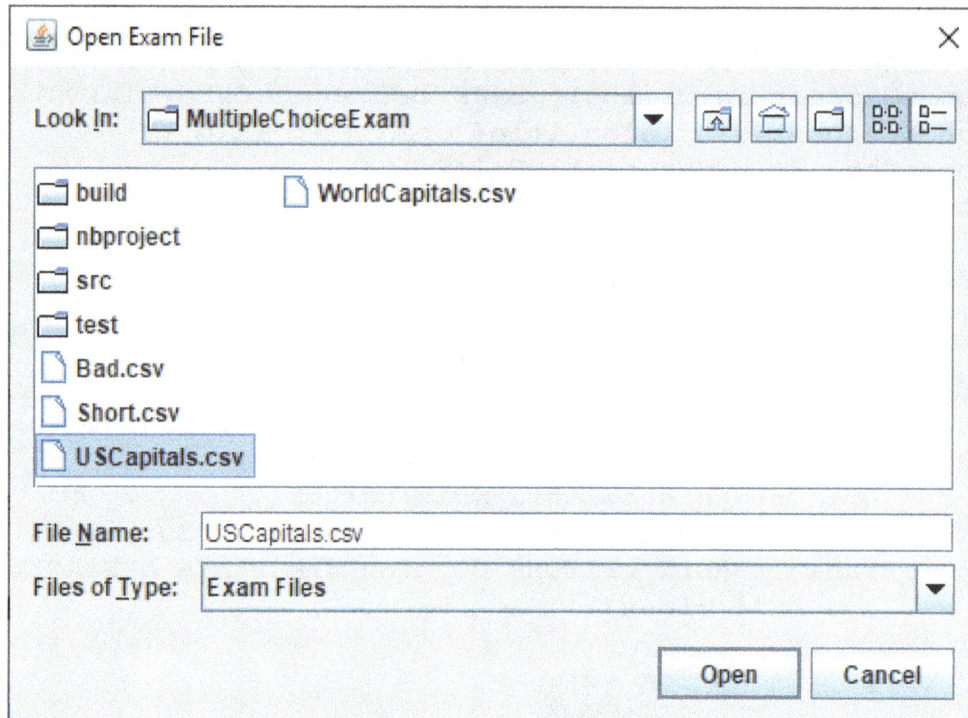

```
┌──────────────────────────────────────────────────────────────────┐
│ ☕ Open Exam File                                               ✕ │
│                                                                    │
│  Look In:  📁 MultipleChoiceExam        ▼   [▣] [⌂] [▢] [▦][☰]    │
│  ┌─────────────────────────────────────────────────────────────┐ │
│  │ 📁 build              📄 WorldCapitals.csv                   │ │
│  │ 📁 nbproject                                                 │ │
│  │ 📁 src                                                       │ │
│  │ 📁 test                                                      │ │
│  │ 📄 Bad.csv                                                   │ │
│  │ 📄 Short.csv                                                 │ │
│  │ 📄 USCapitals.csv                                            │ │
│  └─────────────────────────────────────────────────────────────┘ │
│                                                                    │
│  File Name:     USCapitals.csv                                    │
│  Files of Type: Exam Files                                    ▼   │
│                                                                    │
│                                        [ Open ]   [ Cancel ]      │
└──────────────────────────────────────────────────────────────────┘
```

Select an exam file and click **Open** to open the file. When I choose the example **USCapitals.csv** file, the message box I obtain is:

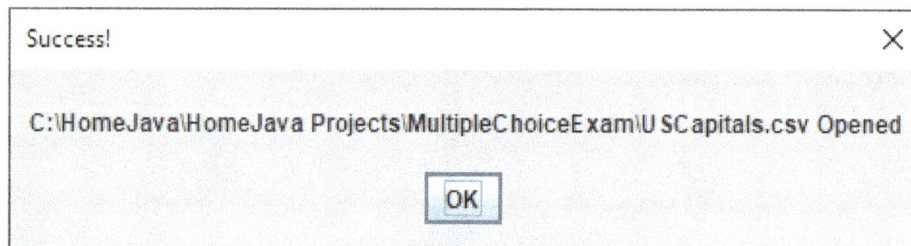

```
┌──────────────────────────────────────────────────────────────────┐
│ Success!                                                        ✕ │
│                                                                    │
│  C:\HomeJava\HomeJava Projects\MultipleChoiceExam\USCapitals.csv Opened │
│                             [ OK ]                                 │
│                                                                    │
└──────────────────────────────────────────────────────────────────┘
```

Try opening the other example file. Make sure the **Cancel** option in the open file dialog works properly, meaning nothing changes in the application if **Cancel** is selected. Stop the project and delete the line with the message box – we will no longer need that.

Code Design – Reading an Exam File

Once an exam file is open, we can read in the information from the file, line-by-line, and obtain needed program variables. Let's first declare those variables. The file will provide us with the exam title (**examTitle**), two headers (**header1**, **header2**) and lists of exam terms (**term1**, **term2**). We will use **String** type variables for all this information (the term lists will be stored in arrays). We will also need an **int** type variable (**numberTerms**) to know how many items are in the lists. Add these variable declarations as class level variables:

```
String examTitle;
String header1, header2;
int numberTerms;
String[] term1 = new String[100];
String[] term2 = new String[100];
```

We have arbitrarily set the limit on list length to be 100.

The steps to follow after opening an exam file are:

> ➤ Read in first line, obtain **examTitle**.
> ➤ Read in second line, obtain **header1** and **header2**
> ➤ Initialize **numberTerms** to 0.
> ➤ Increment **numberTerms**, read in **term1[numberTerms – 1]** and **term2[numberTerms – 1]**
> ➤ Continue reading lines until end of file is reached.

Note the term lists are stored in 0-based arrays (meaning the indices start at **0** and end at **numberTerms - 1**).

Let's see how to read the lines and get the needed variables. To read an entire line from a file opened as **inputFile**, use the **readLine** method:

```
myLine = inputFile.readLine();
```

where **myLine** will be the line represented as a **String** data type. In the exam file, this line (except for the first line) will have one variable, a comma, then another variable. To obtain the individual variables, we need to 'parse' the line. This means we will identify where the comma is in the line then extract one variable to the left of the comma and another variable to the right of the comma. This parsing is done with various string functions.

To determine the location of the comma in **myLine**, we use the **indexOf** method we have seen before. In the expression:

```
cl = myLine.indexOf(",");
```

The **int** variable **cl** will tell us which character in **myLine** is a comma. The characters of **myLine** are numbered from **0** to **myLine.Length - 1**, where the **length()** property is the number of characters in **myLine**. As an example, say **myLine** is given by:

```
myLine ="First,Second";
```

Note **myLine.length()** is **12**. If we apply the above **indexOf** method to this line, we will find **cl** is **5** (remember the first character is index 0, not 1).

To extract the two variables from this line, we use the **substring** method. This function allows you to extract substrings from a string. You need to specify the source string (**myLine**, in this case), the starting position (**start**) and the number of characters (**number**) to extract. The resulting **mySubstring** is obtained using:

```
mySubString = myLine.substring(start, number);
```

For multiple choice exam files, to extract the characters to the left of the comma (located at **cl**) in **myLine**, we start at character **0** and extract **cl** characters, or:

```
leftString = myLine.substring(0, cl);
```

To get the string to the right of the comma is easy. Simply specify the character you wish to start at and the function will return all characters from that point on. We want to start at cl + 1, so use:

```
rightString = myLine.substring(cl + 1);
```

To convince you that this works, let's return to the example with:

```
myLine ="First,Second";
```

where recall **cl** is **5** and **myLine.length()** is **12**. Using the **leftString** relation, we see:

```
leftString = myLine.substring(0, 5);
```

Starting at the first character (character index 0) and extracting five characters, we get:

```
leftString = "First";
```

Success. Now, using the **rightString** relation, we see:

```
rightString = myLine.substring(5 + 1);
rightString = myLine.substring(6);
```

Starting at the 7th character (character index 6) and extracting all characters, we get:

```
rightString = "Second";
```

It works!!

All we need to know now is how to determine when we've reached the end of the exam file, so we can close the file and continue. After each line is read, we call the **ready** property of the **BufferedReader** object. If true, there are still lines to read. When we reach the end of file, the property is **false**..

We can now write the code to implement the steps to read and establish the variable values. The modified **openMenuItemActionPerformed** method (changes are shaded) is:

```java
private void openMenuItemActionPerformed(ActionEvent e)
{
  String myLine;
  JFileChooser openChooser = new JFileChooser();
  openChooser.setDialogType(JFileChooser.OPEN_DIALOG);
  openChooser.setDialogTitle("Open Exam File");
  openChooser.addChoosableFileFilter(new
FileNameExtensionFilter("Exam Files", "csv"));
  if (openChooser.showOpenDialog(this) ==
JFileChooser.APPROVE_OPTION)
  {
    try
    {
      BufferedReader inputFile = new BufferedReader(new
FileReader(openChooser.getSelectedFile()));
      myLine = inputFile.readLine();
      examTitle = parseLeft(myLine);
      myLine = inputFile.readLine();
      header1 = parseLeft(myLine);
      header2 = parseRight(myLine);
      numberTerms = 0;
      do
      {
        numberTerms++;
        myLine = inputFile.readLine();
        term1[numberTerms - 1] = parseLeft(myLine);
        term2[numberTerms - 1] = parseRight(myLine);
      }
      while (inputFile.ready());
      inputFile.close();
    }
    catch (Exception ex)
    {
    }
  }
}
```

This code uses two general methods to parse the left (**parseLeft**) and right (**parseRight**) portions of the input line. These methods used the **substring** method:

```
private String parseLeft(String s)
{
  int cl;
  // find comma
  cl = s.indexOf(",");
  return (s.substring(0, cl));
}

private String parseRight(String s)
{
  int cl;
  // find comma
  cl = s.indexOf(",");
  return (s.substring(cl + 1));
}
```

You should be able to see all the steps in the code – we read the title, read the headers, then read in each set of variables. Save and run the project. Open and process an exam file. Nothing exciting will happen. The code will just run and the interface won't change.

Let's add the code that changes the frame so it is ready to start an exam. The steps are (assuming an exam file has been read correctly):

> Establish **text** property for frame.
> Set **text** properties for **header1MenuOption** and **header2MenuOption**.
> Set **text** properties for **headGivenLabel** and **headAnswerLabel** (based on **selected** properties of menu items under **Option** heading).
> Enable **startButton**.
> Enable **optionsMenu**.
> Set **text** property of **commentTextArea** to indicate the file is loaded.

The code for each of these steps also goes in the **openMenuItemActionPerformed** method. The changes are shaded:

```java
private void openMenuItemActionPerformed(ActionEvent e)
{
  String myLine;
  JFileChooser openChooser = new JFileChooser();
  openChooser.setDialogType(JFileChooser.OPEN_DIALOG);
  openChooser.setDialogTitle("Open Exam File");
  openChooser.addChoosableFileFilter(new
FileNameExtensionFilter("Exam Files", "csv"));
  if (openChooser.showOpenDialog(this) ==
JFileChooser.APPROVE_OPTION)
  {
    try
    {
      BufferedReader inputFile = new BufferedReader(new
FileReader(openChooser.getSelectedFile()));
      myLine = inputFile.readLine();
      examTitle = parseLeft(myLine);
      myLine = inputFile.readLine();
      header1 = parseLeft(myLine);
      header2 = parseRight(myLine);
      numberTerms = 0;
      do
      {
        numberTerms++;
        myLine = inputFile.readLine();
        term1[numberTerms - 1] = parseLeft(myLine);
        term2[numberTerms - 1] = parseRight(myLine);
      }
      while (inputFile.ready());
      inputFile.close();
      // establish frame title
      this.setTitle("Multiple Choice Exam - " +
examTitle);
      // set up menu items
      header1MenuItem.setText(header1 + ", Given " +
header2);
      header2MenuItem.setText(header2 + ", Given " +
header1);
      if (header1MenuItem.isSelected())
      {
        headGivenLabel.setText(header2);
        headAnswerLabel.setText(header1);
      }
      else
```

```
        {
          headGivenLabel.setText(header1);
          headAnswerLabel.setText(header2);
        }
        startButton.setEnabled(true);
        optionsMenu.setEnabled(true);
        commentTextArea.setText(File Loaded, Choose
Options\nClick Start Exam");
      }
    catch (Exception ex)
      {
      }
    }
  }
```

Save and run the project. Load in an exam file. When I loaded **USCapitals.csv**, the form looks like this:

The form is ready for a multiple choice exam, where you name the **State**, given the **Capital** (default options). At this point, the user can change options if desired, then click **Start Exam** to start an exam. We'll look at the code to do that soon, but first we need to address the possibilities of errors when trying to open and read an exam file. Before doing this, though, notice again the comment text is not nicely centered. Let's solve this problem.

Code Design – Centering Comment Text

The text area control used for comments has no provision for centering text (vertically or horizontally) which results in a bit of an ugly display. Let's use some string functions to build a method that centers up to two lines of text.

The general method (**centerTextArea**) that does the job is:

```
private String centerTextArea(String s)
{
  // centers up to two lines in text area
  int charsPerLine = 33;
  String sOut = "";
  int j = s.indexOf("\n");
  int nSpaces;
  if (j == -1)
  {
    // single line
    sOut = "\n" + spacePadding((int) ((charsPerLine -
s.length()) / 2)) + s;
  }
  else
  {
    // first line
    String l = s.substring(0, j);
    sOut = "\n" + spacePadding((int) ((charsPerLine -
l.length()) / 2)) + l;
    // second line
    l = s.substring(j + 1);
    sOut += "\n" + spacePadding((int) ((charsPerLine -
l.length()) / 2)) + l ;
  }
  return(sOut);
}
```

This method accepts the string to be centered (with perhaps two lines separated by a **\n** character). If there is a single line, it counts the characters and centers it based on a maximum width of **charsPerLine** (33 here, based on trial and error). If there are two lines, the two lines are extracted using the **\n** character as a delimiter. These two lines are then centered in the same manner as a single line.

Note the method uses another method (**spacePadding**) to form a string of spaces. This method is:

```
private String spacePadding(int n)
{
  String s = "";
  if (n != 0)
    for (int i = 0; i < n; i++)
      s += " ";
  return(s);
}
```

Add both methods to your project.

There are two places we currently need this method. Change the last line in the frame constructor to (change is shaded):

```
commentTextArea.setText(centerTextArea("Open Exam File to
Start"));
```

And the line just added in the **openMenuItemActionPerformed** method should be:

```
commentTextArea.setText(centerTextArea("File Loaded,
Choose Options\nClick Start Exam"));
```

Run the project. Note the initial text is now centered:

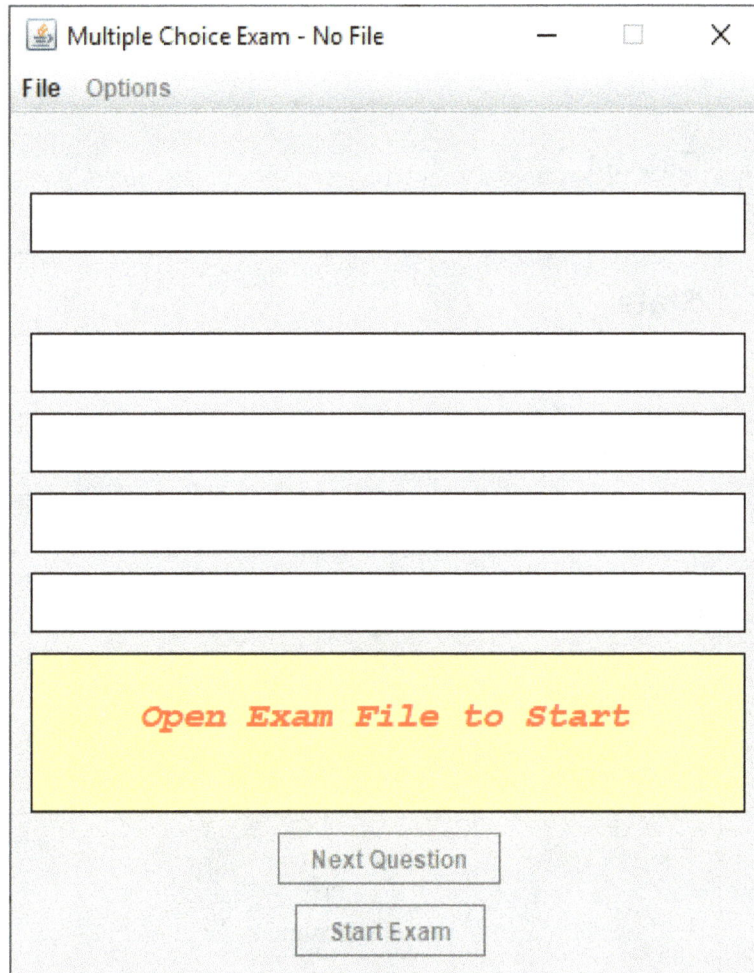

And open an exam file to see the next message:

I think you see these are nicer displays. It's always fun to do a little programming to solve a problem like this. Let's continue the code to get an exam up and going.

Code Design - Error Trapping and Handling

When working with files in a Java, things can go wrong. For example, in the multiple choice exam project, what if the selected exam file doesn't meet the specified format? Perhaps a comma is left off somewhere or a blank line is encountered. As written, the current project would go to the **catch** statement in the **try** loop with no indication of what happened. Or what if the user selects a **csv** file that looks like an exam file, but isn't? Again, the program will exit via the **catch** statement when it realizes it can't process the information in the file.

Also in the multiple choice exam project, we must make sure we have a minimum of five entries in the exam files. This insures we can generate multiple choices (when that option is selected). And, recall we have set the maximum number of entries to 100. This limit can be changed by resetting the array limits, but, no matter what the value, we need to insure we don't read in more than the maximum number of values when reading an exam file.

How do we handle the possibility of errors? Checking the limits on the number of allowed terms is relatively simple. If we don't have the minimum number of entries, we can present a message box to the user. If we exceed the maximum number of entries, we can just stop reading values. If an incorrectly formatted file is encountered, we will tell the user (using a message box) that the file is not acceptable and give them another chance to open a file. This is far preferable to the program just stopping, as it would now.

Here is the modified **openMenuItem ActionPerformed** method uses the **try/catch** block to check for file errors and code to check the minimum and maximum number of entries. As always, the changes are shaded:

```
private void openMenuItemActionPerformed(ActionEvent e)
{
  String myLine;
  JFileChooser openChooser = new JFileChooser();
  openChooser.setDialogType(JFileChooser.OPEN_DIALOG);
  openChooser.setDialogTitle("Open Exam File");
  openChooser.addChoosableFileFilter(new
FileNameExtensionFilter("Exam Files", "csv"));
  if (openChooser.showOpenDialog(this) ==
JFileChooser.APPROVE_OPTION)
  {
    try
    {
      BufferedReader inputFile = new BufferedReader(new
FileReader(openChooser.getSelectedFile()));
```

```java
      myLine = inputFile.readLine();
      examTitle = parseLeft(myLine);
      myLine = inputFile.readLine();
      header1 = parseLeft(myLine);
      header2 = parseRight(myLine);
      numberTerms = 0;
      do
      {
        numberTerms++;
        myLine = inputFile.readLine();
        term1[numberTerms - 1] = parseLeft(myLine);
        term2[numberTerms - 1] = parseRight(myLine);
      }
      while (inputFile.ready() && numberTerms < 100);
      if (numberTerms < 5)
      {
        JOptionPane.showConfirmDialog(null, "Must have at
least 5 entries in exam file.", "Exam File Error",
JOptionPane.DEFAULT_OPTION, JOptionPane.ERROR_MESSAGE);
        return;
      }
      inputFile.close();
      // establish frame title
      this.setTitle("Multiple Choice Exam - " +
examTitle);
      // set up menu items
      header1MenuItem.setText(header1 + ", Given " +
header2);
      header2MenuItem.setText(header2 + ", Given " +
header1);
      if (header1MenuItem.isSelected())
      {
        headGivenLabel.setText(header2);
        headAnswerLabel.setText(header1);
      }
      else
      {
        headGivenLabel.setText(header1);
        headAnswerLabel.setText(header2);
      }
      startButton.setEnabled(true);
      optionsMenu.setEnabled(true);
      commentTextArea.setText(centerTextArea("File Loaded,
Choose Options\nClick Start Exam"));
    }
    catch (Exception ex)
    {
```

```
        JOptionPane.showConfirmDialog(null, "Error reading
in input file - make sure file is correct format.",
"Multiple Choice Exam File Error",
JOptionPane.DEFAULT_OPTION, JOptionPane.ERROR_MESSAGE);
        return;
    }
  }
}
```

If an error occurs when opening/processing the file, a message box is presented (code in the **catch** block) and the method is exited (after closing the file). If fewer than 5 elements are read in, a message box is presented to the user and method exited. And, notice we have modified the **while** statement to now make sure we have no more than 100 entries.

To make sure this code works, you need some invalid files. I used Notepad to create one file in proper format, but with only a single entry:

```
Title,
Header1,Header2
Term1,Term2
```

I saved this file as **Short.csv**. I also created a file in improper format, leaving off a comma in one line:

```
Title,
Header1,Header2
Term1,Term2
Term1,Term2
Term1,Term2
Term1,Term2
Term1Term2
```

I saved this file as **Bad.csv**. You should do the same – create some test files. Whenever adding error handling to a project, you need to make sure it works! Both of these files are included in the **\HomeJava\HomeJava Projects\MultipleChoiceExam** folder.

Save and run the project. The interface should still look the same. Open one of the example exam files to make sure it still opens successfully. Now, try loading a file with too few entries. When I try my **Short.csv** file, I get this message:

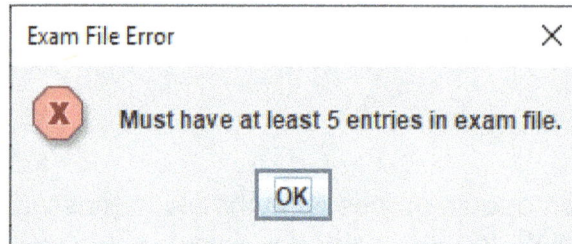

Exam File Error	✕
⊗ Must have at least 5 entries in exam file.	
OK	

And, attempting to open the invalid file (**Bad.csv**), I get:

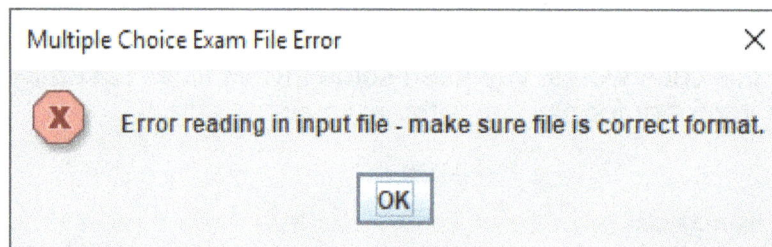

Multiple Choice Exam File Error	✕
⊗ Error reading in input file - make sure file is correct format.	
OK	

With either error, the user is returned to the program and allowed another chance at opening a file. This method of handling file errors is far preferable than just having the program stop with the user having no idea of what happened.

The **openMenuItemActionPerformed** method is now complete. Once an exam file is successfully opened, the user can change options and start an exam. We develop that code next.

Frame Design – Selecting Options

Once an exam file is opened, the user needs to make two decisions. First, they choose which term in the list they want to have as the 'given' value. The other term in the list will then be the answer. As answers, the user can be given multiple answers to choose from or the user can type in the correct answer. This is other option the user must choose. All options are selected under the **Option** heading in the menu structure. The code to switch from one option to the next is in the corresponding menu items' **ActionPerformed** methods.

Deciding which term will be 'given' involves changing the headers in two of the label controls. If the user chooses the menu option that says **header1, Given header2** (**header1MenuItem**), the steps are:

> Set **text** property of **headGivenLabel** to **header2**
> Set **text** property of **headAnswerLabel** to **header1**

Conversely, if the user chooses the menu option that says **header2, Given header1** (**header2MenuItem**), the steps are:

> Set **text** property of **headGivenLabel** to **header1**
> Set **text** property of **headAnswerLabel** to **header2**

The **header1MenuItem** and **optionsMenu2Header2 ActionPerformed** methods that correspond to these steps are:

```
private void header1MenuItemActionPerformed(ActionEvent e)
{
  // Set up for naming header1, given header2
  headGivenLabel.setText(header2);
  headAnswerLabel.setText(header1);
}

private void header2MenuItemActionPerformed(ActionEvent e)
{
  // Set up for naming header2, given header1
  headGivenLabel.setText(header1);
  headAnswerLabel.setText(header2);
}
```

Add these event methods.

Choosing between multiple choice and type in answers requires reconfiguration of the frame. The multiple choice option requires four label controls to present the possible answers, while the type in option requires a single text field for entry of the answer. The steps involved in choosing the **Multiple Choice Answers** option (**mcMenuItem**) are:

> ➢ Make four label controls for answer visible.
> ➢ Make text field control invisible.

And, conversely, if the **Type In Answer** option (**typeMenuItem**), the steps are:

> ➢ Make four label controls for answer invisible.
> ➢ Make text box control visible.

The **mcMenuItem** and **typeMenuItem ActionPerformed** methods that correspond to these steps are:

```
private void mcMenuItemActionPerformed(ActionEvent e)
{
  answerLabel[0].setVisible(true);
  answerLabel[1].setVisible(true);
  answerLabel[2].setVisible(true);
  answerLabel[3].setVisible(true);
  answerTextField.setVisible(false);
}

private void typeMenuItemActionPerformed(ActionEvent e)
{
  answerLabel[0].setVisible(false);
  answerLabel[1].setVisible(false);
  answerLabel[2].setVisible(false);
  answerLabel[3].setVisible(false);
  answerTextField.setVisible(true);
}
```

Add these methods.

Save and run the project. Open an example exam file. Make sure the newly coded options work correctly. When I load the **USCapitals.csv** file and select the **Capital, Given State** option, I see:

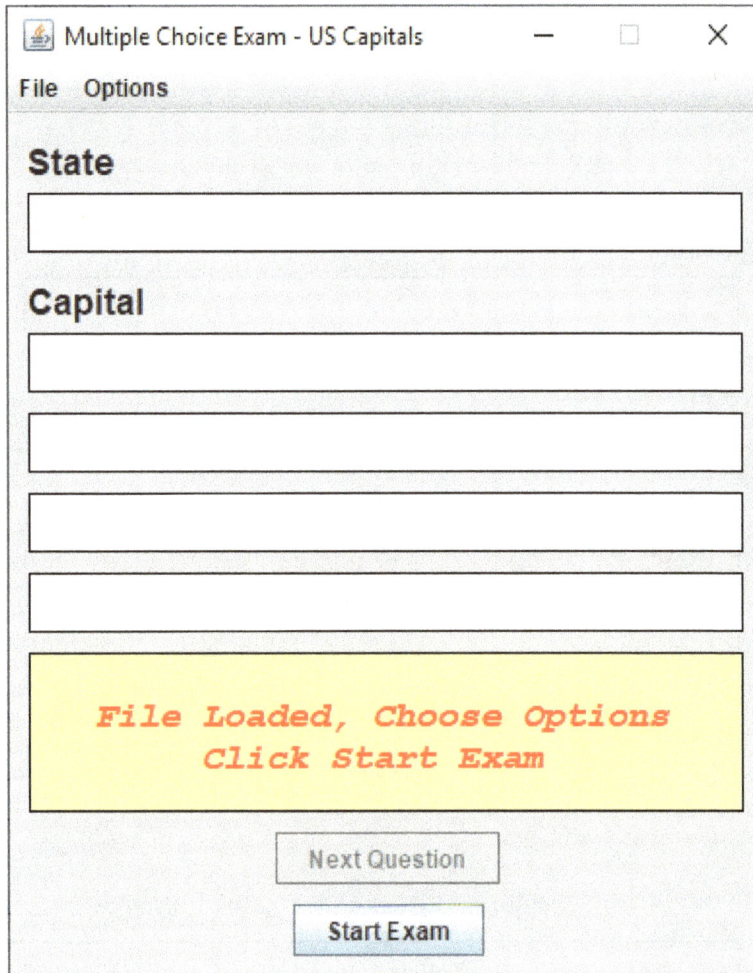

Note the proper headers.

By default, the multiple choice answer option is shown. Choosing the **Type In Answers** option changes the form to:

Make sure you can change back to the **Multiple Choice Answers** option.

We've completed the code for opening exam files and configuring the interface (by choosing options). It is now time to address the code to present an exam to the user.

Code Design – Start Exam

The idea of a multiple choice exam is to display a random question, obtain an answer from the user and check for correctness. Once an exam is complete, scoring results are provided.

An exam is started by clicking **Start Exam** (**startButton**). We want to make sure all the user can do at this point is answer a question. The following steps should occur:

> Change **text** property of **startButton** to **Stop Practice**
> Disable **nextButton**.
> Set number of questions tried and number correct to zero.
> Clear **text** property of **commentTextArea**.
> Disable **fileMenu**.
> Disable **optionsMenu**.
> Present question.
> Check answer and update score.

Once each question is answered, subsequent questions are presented.

The user answers questions until he/she clicks **Stop Exam** (also **startButton**). We want the interface to return to where options can be selected or a new file opened. The steps at this point are:

> Change **text** property of **startButton** to **Stop Practice**
> Disable **nextButton**.
> Present results.
> Clear **text** property of all controls used for answers.
> Set **text** property of **commentTextArea** to indicate a new exam can be started.
> Enable **fileMenu**.
> Enable **optionsMenu**.

Let's build a framework for the **startButton ActionPerformed** method that
implements most of these steps (we'll look at presenting results later). Declare
two class level variables to keep track of the number of questions tried and the
number correct:

```
int numberTried, numberCorrect;
```

The **startButton ActionPerformed** method that implements the listed steps
(again, except for results) is:

```java
private void startButtonActionPerformed(ActionEvent e)
{
  if (startButton.getText().equals("Start Exam"))
  {
    startButton.setText("Stop Exam");
    nextButton.setEnabled(false);
    // Reset the score
    numberTried = 0;
    numberCorrect = 0;
    commentTextArea.setText("");
    fileMenu.setEnabled(false);
    optionsMenu.setEnabled(false);
    nextQuestion();
  }
  else
  {
    startButton.setText("Start Exam");
    nextButton.setEnabled(false);
     givenLabel.setText("");
    answerLabel[0].setText("");
    answerLabel[1].setText("");
    answerLabel[2].setText("");
    answerLabel[3].setText("");
    answerTextField.setText("");
    commentTextArea.setText(centerTextArea("Choose
Options\nClick Start Exam"));
    fileMenu.setEnabled(true);
    optionsMenu.setEnabled(true);
  }
}
```

Add this code to the project.

This code uses a general method **nextQuestion** to generate a random question. Add this empty method to the project:

```
private void nextQuestion()
{

}
```

We'll write code for this method next, once we make sure the changes just made work.

Save and run the project. Open an exam file. When you click **Start Exam**, you should see:

Make sure when you click **Stop Exam**, the interface returns to its initial configuration.

Code Design - Question Generation

To generate a question, we examine the options selected by the user and produce a random question based on these selections. The code to generate such a question will be in the **nextQuestion** general method.

The steps involved in generating a random question are:

> ➤ Clear **text** property of **commentTextArea**.
> ➤ Select random item from term list as the "correct answer".
> ➤ Set **text** property of **givenLabel** to 'given' term.
> ➤ If **Multiple Choice Answers** is selected:
> o Generate four possible answers (one of which is the correct answer)
> o Display answers in label controls.
> ➤ If **Type In Answers** is selected:
> o Set **answerTextField editable** property to **true**.
> o Clear **answerTextField** text box.
> o Give **answerTextField** focus.

The code to select a question, set **givenLabel** and to set up for **type in answers** is straightforward, so we'll do this first. Add a class level variable to identify the array index of the correct answer and a random object to generate random questions:

```
int correctAnswer;
Random myRandom = new Random();
```

The **Random** object requires this import statement:

```
import java.util.Random;
```

The code for the **nextQuestion** method for these steps is:

```
private void nextQuestion()
{
  commentTextArea.setText("");
  // Generate the next question based on selected options
  correctAnswer = myRandom.nextInt(numberTerms);
  if (header1MenuItem.isSelected())
  {
    givenLabel.setText(term2[correctAnswer]);
  }
  else
  {
    givenLabel.setText(term1[correctAnswer]);
  }
  if (mcMenuItem.isSelected())
  {
    // Multiple choice answers
  }
  else
  {
    // Type-in answers
    answerTextField.setEditable(true);
    answerTextField.setText("");
    answerTextField.requestFocus();
  }
}
```

Add this code to the project.

Save and run the project if you'd like to see if you can type in answers (make sure you select this option). Here's an example with the **USCapitals.csv** file (you will see a different result because of the **Random** object):

We will see how to check an answer soon.

The code for presenting **multiple choice answers** is more detailed and we need to spend some time looking at it. The tricky part of this code is to select the four multiple choice options, one of which is the correct answer. The approach we follow is to first select four terms at random from the **numberTerms** possibilities, making sure we don't select the correct answer (index is **correctAnswer**). Once we have these four possibilities, we replace one at random with the correct answer. Let's look at the steps.

First, we need some way to know if we have already selected a previously chosen answer possibility. We will use a method level **boolean** array **termUsed**, dimensioned to **numberTerms** to tell us if a term has been used. Each element in this array is initialized to **false**, indicating all are available. The code snippet that accomplishes this task is:

```
boolean[] termUsed = new boolean[numberTerms];
for (int i = 0; i < numberTerms; i++)
{
  termUsed[i] = false;
}
```

A **do** loop is used to pick the four random answer possibilities. An **int** array **index**, dimensioned to 4, stores the four selected indices. The code snippet is:

```
int[] index = new int[4];
int j;
for (int i = 0; i < 4; i++)
{
  do
  {
    j = myRandom.nextInt(numberTerms);
  }
  while (termUsed[j] || j == correctAnswer);
  termUsed[j] = true;
  index[i] = j;
}
```

See how this works? For each of the four answers (selected with the **for** loop), a random index **j** is selected making sure the corresponding term has not been selected before and is not the **correctAnswer**.

Once the array **index** is established, one item in the array is replaced with **correctAnswer**. The line of code that accomplishes this replacement is:

```
index[myRandom.nextInt(4)] = correctAnswer;
```

Now, depending on which is term is given and which is the answer, the **index** array establishes the contents of the label controls used for multiple choice answers.

The modified **nextQuestion** method that incorporates the code for multiple choice answers (changes are shaded) is:

```
private void nextQuestion()
{
  boolean[] termUsed = new boolean[numberTerms];
  int[] index = new int[4];
  int j;
  commentTextArea.setText("");
  // Generate the next question based on selected options
  correctAnswer = myRandom.nextInt(numberTerms);
  if (header1MenuItem.isSelected())
  {
    givenLabel.setText(term2[correctAnswer]);
  }
  else
  {
    givenLabel.setText(term1[correctAnswer]);
  }
  if (mcMenuItem.isSelected())
  {
    // Multiple choice answers
    for (int i = 0; i < numberTerms; i++)
    {
      termUsed[i] = false;
    }
    // Pick four random possiblities
    for (int i = 0; i < 4; i++)
    {
      do
      {
        j = myRandom.nextInt(numberTerms);
      }
      while (termUsed[j] || j == correctAnswer);
      termUsed[j] = true;
      index[i] = j;
    }
    // Replace one with correct answer
```

```
      index[myRandom.nextInt(4)] = correctAnswer;
      // Display multiple choice answers in label boxes
      if (header1MenuItem.isSelected())
      {
        answerLabel[0].setText(term1[index[0]]);
        answerLabel[1].setText(term1[index[1]]);
        answerLabel[2].setText(term1[index[2]]);
        answerLabel[3].setText(term1[index[3]]);
      }
      else
      {
        answerLabel[0].setText(term2[index[0]]);
        answerLabel[1].setText(term2[index[1]]);
        answerLabel[2].setText(term2[index[2]]);
        answerLabel[3].setText(term2[index[3]]);
      }
    }
    else
    {
      // Type-in answers
      answerTextField.setEditable(true);
      answerTextField.setText("");
      answerTextField.requestFocus();
    }
  }
```

Make the noted modifications.

Save and run the project. Open an example exam file. Using default options and the **USCapitals.csv** file, clicking **Start Exam**, I see (you will see different results because of the **Random** object):

The given **Capital** is **Juneau**. Note the four possible **State** answers (three random and one the correct answer, **Alaska**). The multiple choice logic seems to be working. All you can do at this point is click **Stop Exam**. You can then click **Start Exam** to see another question (changing options if you wish). View as many questions, with different options, as you wish. Next, we'll see how to get answers to these questions – we consider both multiple choice and type in answers.

Code Design – Checking Multiple Choice Answers

Once a question is presented using multiple choice answers, the user is asked to click on the correct answer. That answer is then checked - we will only give the user one chance to get the answer right. The steps for checking a multiple choice answer:

> ➢ Make sure exam is in progress and question hasn't been answered already.
> ➢ Increment **numberTried**.
> ➢ Determine which label control was clicked.
> ➢ Check to see if **text** property of clicked label control matches the correct answer (correct answer depends on which term is given and which is answer).
> ➢ Update the score and provide feedback, presenting the correct answer.

The code corresponding to these steps is placed in a method named **answerLabelMousePressed**. This method will handle clicking on all four label controls used to display answers: **answerLabel[0]**, **answerLabel[1]**, **answerLabel[2]**, **answerLabel[3]**. The tricky part is – how to determine which of the four controls was clicked. An Internet search yielded the necessary logic. The mouse press method has a **MouseEvent** argument, **e**. The following method uses this argument and returns a **Point** object (**p**) that has the coordinates of the upper left corner of the clicked component (relative to the panel hosting the component):

```
Point p = e.getComponent().getLocation();
```

So, for our case, **p.x** and **p.y** represent the upper left corner of the clicked label control. The corresponding coordinates for the labels can be obtained using **getX** and **getY** methods.

The code for **answerLabelMousePressed** is:

```
private void answerLabelMousePressed(MouseEvent e)
{
  boolean correct = false;
  int labelSelected;
  // make sure exam has started and question has not been
answered
  if (startButton.getText().equals("Start Exam") ||
nextButton.isEnabled())
    return;
  // determine which label was clicked
  // get upper left corner of clicked label
  Point p = e.getComponent().getLocation();
  // determine index based on p
  for (labelSelected = 0; labelSelected < 20;
labelSelected++)
  {
    if (p.x == answerLabel[labelSelected].getX() && p.y ==
answerLabel[labelSelected].getY())
      break;
  }
  // If already answered, exit
  numberTried++;
  if (header1MenuItem.isSelected())
  {
    if
(answerLabel[labelSelected].getText().equals(term1[correct
Answer]))
      correct = true;
  }
  else
  {
    if
(answerLabel[labelSelected].getText().equals(term2[correct
Answer]))
      correct = true;
  }
  updateScore(correct);
}
```

Make sure you see how this works.

This code uses a general method **updateScore** to update the scoring and prepare the user interface for the next question. The method uses a single **boolean** argument that is **true** if the answer was answered correct, **false** is incorrect. The steps involved:

> ➤ If answer is correct: increment **numberCorrect** and set **text** property of **commentTextArea** to "**Correct!**"
> ➤ If answer is incorrect: set **text** property of **commentTextArea** to "**Sorry ... Correct Answer Shown**"
> ➤ If multiple choice answers are used: put correct answer in **answerLabel[0]**, clear all other label controls.
> ➤ If type in answers are used: put correct answer in **answerTextField**.
> ➤ Enable **startButton**.
> ➤ Enable **nextButton**.
> ➤ Give **nextButton** focus.

The code for **updateScore** is:

```
private void updateScore(boolean correct)
{
  // Check if answer is correct
  if (correct)
  {
    numberCorrect++;
    commentTextArea.setText(centerTextArea("Correct!"));
  }
  else
    commentTextArea.setText(centerTextArea("Sorry ...
Correct Answer Shown"));
  // Display correct answer
  if (mcMenuItem.isSelected())
  {
    if (header1MenuItem.isSelected())
      answerLabel[0].setText(term1[correctAnswer]);
    else
      answerLabel[0].setText(term2[correctAnswer]);
    answerLabel[1].setText("");
    answerLabel[2].setText("");
    answerLabel[3].setText("");
  }
  else
  {
    if (header1MenuItem.isSelected())
      answerTextField.setText(term1[correctAnswer]);
    else
      answerTextField.setText(term2[correctAnswer]);
  }
  startButton.setEnabled(true);
  nextButton.setEnabled(true);
  nextButton.requestFocus();
}
```

Add the **answerLabelMousePressed** and **updateScore** (this routine will also be used when checking typed in answers) code to the project.

Notice after displaying the correct answer, focus is given to **nextButton**. Clicking this button will present another question to the user. The code for the **nextButtonActionPerformed** method simply involves disabling the button, once clicked, then invoking the existing **nextQuestion** method:

```
private void nextButtonActionPerformed(ActionEvent e)
{
  // Generate next question
  nextButton.setEnabled(false);
  nextQuestion();
}
```

Enter this code and we are now ready to take exams with multiple choice answers

Save and run the project. Open an exam file. Select options (obviously choose multiple choice answers). For the example here, I use the **WorldCapitals.csv** file, providing capitals, given the country. The first question I see is:

```
┌─────────────────────────────────────────────────────────────┐
│ ☕ Multiple Choice Exam - World Capitals    —    ☐    ✕        │
│ File  Options                                                 │
│                                                               │
│ Country                                                       │
│ ┌───────────────────────────────────────────────────────┐   │
│ │                      India                             │   │
│ └───────────────────────────────────────────────────────┘   │
│ Capital                                                       │
│ ┌───────────────────────────────────────────────────────┐   │
│ │                    Stockholm                           │   │
│ └───────────────────────────────────────────────────────┘   │
│ ┌───────────────────────────────────────────────────────┐   │
│ │                     Manila                             │   │
│ └───────────────────────────────────────────────────────┘   │
│ ┌───────────────────────────────────────────────────────┐   │
│ │                   New Delhi                            │   │
│ └───────────────────────────────────────────────────────┘   │
│ ┌───────────────────────────────────────────────────────┐   │
│ │                    Ankara                              │   │
│ └───────────────────────────────────────────────────────┘   │
│ ┌───────────────────────────────────────────────────────┐   │
│ │                                                        │   │
│ │                                                        │   │
│ │                                                        │   │
│ └───────────────────────────────────────────────────────┘   │
│                    ┌──────────────────┐                       │
│                    │  Next Question   │                       │
│                    └──────────────────┘                       │
│                      ┌──────────────┐                         │
│                      │  Stop Exam   │                         │
│                      └──────────────┘                         │
└─────────────────────────────────────────────────────────────┘
```

When I click **New Delhi**, I see:

At this point, I can click **Next Question** for another question, or click **Stop Exam** to stop this test. Answer as many questions as you like.

At some point, answer incorrectly. When I do, I see:

```
┌─────────────────────────────────────────────┐
│ 🍵 Multiple Choice Exam - World Capitals  —  ☐  ✕ │
│ File  Options                                │
│                                              │
│  Country                                     │
│  ┌─────────────────────────────────────────┐ │
│  │              Denmark                    │ │
│  └─────────────────────────────────────────┘ │
│  Capital                                     │
│  ┌─────────────────────────────────────────┐ │
│  │            Copenhagen                   │ │
│  └─────────────────────────────────────────┘ │
│  ┌─────────────────────────────────────────┐ │
│  │                                         │ │
│  └─────────────────────────────────────────┘ │
│  ┌─────────────────────────────────────────┐ │
│  │                                         │ │
│  └─────────────────────────────────────────┘ │
│  ┌─────────────────────────────────────────┐ │
│  │                                         │ │
│  └─────────────────────────────────────────┘ │
│  ┌─────────────────────────────────────────┐ │
│  │                                         │ │
│  │   Sorry ... Correct Answer Shown        │ │
│  │                                         │ │
│  └─────────────────────────────────────────┘ │
│            ┌──────────────────┐              │
│            │  Next Question   │              │
│            └──────────────────┘              │
│            ┌──────────────────┐              │
│            │    Stop Exam     │              │
│            └──────────────────┘              │
└─────────────────────────────────────────────┘
```

So, with an incorrect answer, you are told so and given the correct answer. The only difference between the results of a correct and incorrect answer is the message displayed to the user (and the score, of course).

Code Design – Checking Type In Answers

We see it is a clear decision to check whether a multiple choice answer was correct. It's not so clear here, when typing in answers..

When a user types an answer, how do we know when they are done entering an answer? You could have a button to click that says **Check Answer** or have the user press a certain key. In this exam project, we will check the answer once a user presses the <**Enter**> key.

We need to consider case sensitivity when entering alphabetic entries. For example, in the **USCapitals.csv** file, the capital of the state of Washington (our home state) is saved as **Olympia**. If a user types **olympia** (all lower case), do we really want to tell the user the answer is incorrect? Or, what if they type **Olimpia**, a very close spelling? What do we do in this situation? We will solve both of these problems, addressing case-sensitivity first.

Once a user types an answer and presses <**Enter**>, we take these steps:

> ➢ Make sure an exam is in progress and question hasn't been answered already.
> ➢ Set **answerTextField editable** property to **false**.
> ➢ Increment **numberTried**.
> ➢ Convert **answerTextField.getText()** (user answer) to all upper case.
> ➢ Convert correct answer to all upper case.
> ➢ Compare upper case strings to see if they are equal.
> ➢ Update the score and provide feedback, presenting the correct answer.

The method **toUpperCase** converts a **string** value to all upper case. The function ignores any non-letter characters.

We place the code for these steps in the **answerTextFieldActionPerformed**
method (processing the code when the <**Enter**> key is pressed). The method is:

```
private void answerTextFieldActionPerformed(ActionEvent e)
{
  // Check type in answer
  boolean correct;
  String ucTypedAnswer, ucAnswer;
  // make sure exam has started and question has not been
answered
  if (startButton.getText().equals("Start Exam") ||
nextButton.isEnabled())
     return;
  answerTextField.setEditable(false);
  numberTried++;
  ucTypedAnswer = answerTextField.getText().toUpperCase();
  if (header1MenuItem.isSelected())
    ucAnswer = term1[correctAnswer].toUpperCase();
  else
    ucAnswer = term2[correctAnswer].toUpperCase();
  correct = false;
  if (ucTypedAnswer.equals(ucAnswer))
    correct = true;
  updateScore(correct);
}
```

Note the use of the **toUpperCase** method. This code also uses the general
method **updateScore** to update the score and controls after answering. Add the
answerTextFieldActionPerformed method to the project.

Save and run the project. Select an exam file (I used **WorldCapitals.csv**).
Choose the **Type In Answers** option. I also selected **Capitals, Given Country** as
an option. Click **Start Exam**. My first question appears as:

If I type **Copenhagen**, the correct answer with correct letter case, then press
<**Enter**>, I am told the answer is correct:

Click **Next Question**.

The next question is:

The capital of **Egypt** is **Cairo**. If you type **Cairo** in the text field area and press <**Enter**> you will be told this is a correct answer. Let's make sure the answers are not case-sensitive.

When I type **cairo** in the text area and click <**Enter**>, I see:

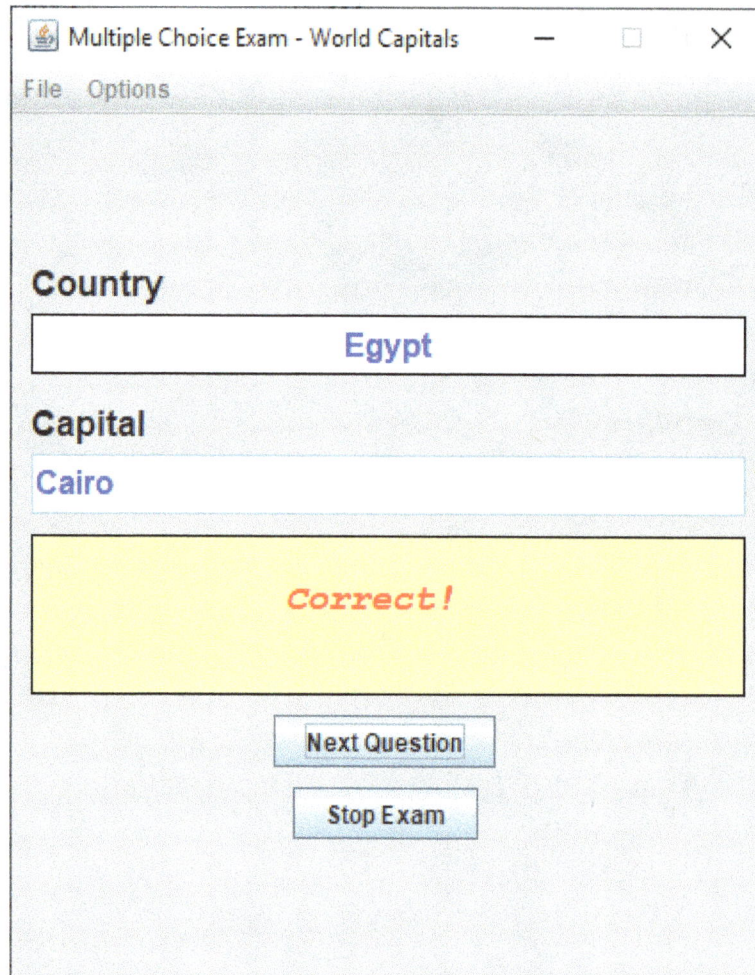

The answer is accepted and the 'capitalization' is corrected.

Continue trying correct and incorrect answers, checking to make sure case-insensitivity is properly incorporated into the project. Try typing an answer with spelling 'close to' the correct spelling. You will be told you are incorrect. This can be frustrating to the 'spelling challenged' and especially frustrating for children learning how to spell. If your spelling is 'close' you should be rewarded and gently corrected, not told you are wrong. Stop the exam and the project and we'll fix this problem.

Code Design – Checking Spelling

The techniques behind checking for 'close spelling' are called **Soundex** checks. Words, or terms, are assigned something called a **Soundex code**. Any two terms with the same Soundex code will have similar spellings. This is how spell checker programs work. When you misspell a word, you are presented with a list of words with similar Soundex codes from which to choose possible corrections. In our multiple choice exam project, if the Soundex code for a user typed response is equal to the Soundex code for the actual answer, we will credit the user with a correct answer.

The technique we use to determine Soundex codes is based on an article in an issue of **Byte** magazine from the early 1980's. As a historical footnote, early programmers were always eager to get the latest issue of **Byte**. It would contain programs you could type into your computer and try. These programs were usually written in the BASIC language. The code here is based on one of these programs. It's fun to go to a local library and look at old issues of **Byte** magazine. You'll find ads for computers with 8K (yes, I said 8K) of memory for just $500. And, you'll see 1/12th page ads for a little Bellevue, Washington, company just getting started in the computer business – yes, Microsoft.

To determine the **Soundex** code **s** (a **String** value) for a **String** value **w** (whose first character must be a letter), these steps are followed:

> ➢ Convert **w** to all upper case (call the result **wTemp**)
> ➢ Set the first character of **s** to the first character of **wTemp**.
> ➢ Cycle through all remaining characters in **wTemp**, one at a time.
> ➢ Assign letter characters in **wTemp** a corresponding numerical value from **0** to **9**, according to provided table. Numerical values are not given to any non-letter characters.
> ➢ If numerical value is non-zero and not equal to the previous character's numerical value, append that number to the end of the **Soundex** code **s**.

The numerical values associated with the 26 letters of the English alphabet are:

A = 0	B = 1	C = 2	D = 3	E = 0	F = 1	G = 2
H = 0	I = 0	J = 2	K = 2	L = 4	M = 5	N = 5
O = 0	P = 1	Q = 2	R = 6	S = 2	T = 3	U = 0
V = 1	W =0	X = 2	Y = 0	Z = 2		

Notice the vowels (A, E, I, O, U) and soft consonants (H, W, Y) have zero values.

You should see that a **Soundex** code will be a string starting with a letter, followed by a sequence of numbers (none of which are zero) with no identical consecutive numbers. Let's try it with an example to see how it works, then we'll write the code. We'll use the word 'beautiful'. We'll misspell it as 'buetifull'. First, convert both words to upper case. Initialize the Soundex codes for both to the first letter of the word (both will be **B**). So, obviously a condition for two Soundex codes to match is that the first letter of the two words being compared must be the same. Now, go through all subsequent letters in each capitalized word and assign the corresponding numerical value to the letters. The results are:

> **BEAUTIFUL**   **Code: B00030104**
> **BUETIFULL**   **Code: B00301044**

Remove the zeroes and repeated values to get the final codes:

> **BEAUTIFUL**   **Code: B314**
> **BUETIFULL**   **Code: B314**

The two codes match, hence have similar spellings. Can you find other words with the same code. Some I came up with are: bad ball (the space is ignored by Soundex), bedful, and bait pail. So, Soundex doesn't always work – call some one 'bait pail' instead of 'beautiful' and you'll see what I mean!

The code to compute a Soundex code will be in a general method **soundex**. The method will have a single **String** argument, **w**, the word the code is being computed for. The method returns a **String** argument which is the **soundex code** for **w**:

```
public String soundex(String w)
{
  // Generates Soundex code for w based on Unicode value
  // Allows answers whose spelling is close, but not exact
  String wTemp, s = "";
  int l;
  int wPrev, wSnd, cIndex;
  // Load soundex function array
  int[] wSound = {0, 1, 2, 3, 0, 1, 2, 0, 0, 2, 2, 4, 5,
5, 0, 1, 2, 6, 2, 3, 0, 1, 0, 2, 0, 2};
  wTemp = w.toUpperCase();
  l = w.length();
  if (l != 0)
  {
    s = String.valueOf(w.charAt(0));
    wPrev = 0;
    if (l > 1)
    {
      for (int i = 1; i < l; i++)
      {
        cIndex = (int) wTemp.charAt(i) - 65;
        if (cIndex >= 0 && cIndex <= 25)
        {
          wSnd = wSound[cIndex] + 48;
          if (wSnd != 48 && wSnd != wPrev)
          {
            s += String.valueOf((char) wSnd);
          }
          wPrev = wSnd;
        }
      }
    }
  }
  else
  s = "";
  }
  return(s);
}
```

The steps for finding a **Soundex** code are straightforward – the coding may not seem so. Let me explain what's going on here. First, the 26 numeric values are stored in a string array named **wSound**. **wSound[0]** represents the numeric value for an **A** up to **wSound[25]**, which represents the numeric value for a **Z**. The input word (**w**) is converted to all upper case (**wTemp**). The returned code (**s**) is initialized to the first character of **wTemp** (obtained using the **charAt** method).

The tricky part of the code is getting the numeric values for the subsequent characters in **wTemp**. The characters are related to their corresponding index in **wTemp** by their **Unicode** value (**65** for an **A**, up to **90** for a **Z**). So, the process is:

> ➢ Find the next **character** in **wTemp** using **charAt**.
> ➢ Find **Unicode** value for character and subtract 65, this is the array index (**cIndex**).
> ➢ Find character's numeric value (**wSnd**).
> ➢ Append **wSnd** to **s** if not a zero (0) and not equal to the last character currently in **s**.

Add the **soundex** method to the project.

To use the **soundex** method, we must modify a single line of code in the
answerTextFieldKeyPress method to not only check for exact spelling, but for
equal **Soundex** codes. The modified line is shaded:

```
private void answerTextFieldActionPerformed(ActionEvent e)
{
  // Check type in answer
  boolean correct;
  String ucTypedAnswer, ucAnswer;
  // make sure exam has started and question has not been
answered
  if (startButton.getText().equals("Start Exam") ||
nextButton.isEnabled())
    return;
  answerTextField.setEditable(false);
  numberTried++;
  ucTypedAnswer = answerTextField.getText().toUpperCase();
  if (header1MenuItem.isSelected())
    ucAnswer = term1[correctAnswer].toUpperCase();
  else
    ucAnswer = term2[correctAnswer].toUpperCase();
  correct = false;
  if (ucTypedAnswer.equals(ucAnswer) ||
soundex(ucTypedAnswer).equals(soundex(ucAnswer)))
    correct = true;
  updateScore(correct);
}
```

Make this change. Now, let's give the **Soundex** code a try!

Save and run the project. Select an exam file (I again used **WorldCapitals.csv**). Choose the **Type In Answers** option. I again selected **Capitals, Given Country** as an option. Click **Start Exam**. My first question appears as:

The capital of **Iceland** is **Reykjavik** (Soundex code is **R212**), but who can spell that? What if I mistakenly spell it as **raykavick**:

When I press <**Enter**>, I see:

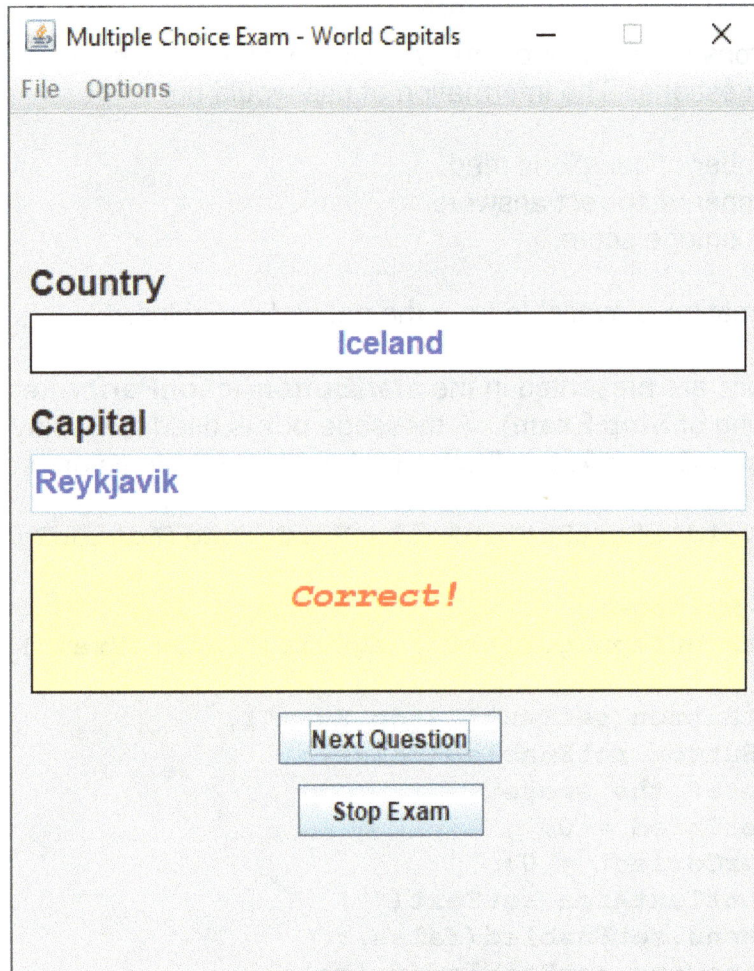

So, even though I misspelled the word, I am given credit for a correct answer and shown the correct spelling. This happens because the Soundex code for 'raykavick' is **R212**, the same code as 'Reykjavik'.

The program is nearly complete. Keep trying exams with different options to make sure everything works correctly. Play with the type in answers to see how well the Soundex codes work. How close does the spelling really need to be? Chose **File**, then **Exit** to stop the program when you want.

Code Design – Presenting Results

Once a user stops a particular exam, we want to let them know how well they did in answering questions. The information of use would be:

> ➢ The number of questions tried.
> ➢ The number of correct answers.
> ➢ The percentage score.

All of this information is available from the defined variables.

The exam results are presented in the **startButtonActionPerformed** method (following clicking of **Stop Exam**). A message box is used to display the results. The modified **startButtonActionPerformed** method (changes are shaded) is:

```java
private void startButtonActionPerformed(ActionEvent e)
{
  String message;
  if (startButton.getText().equals("Start Exam"))
  {
    startButton.setText("Stop Exam");
    nextButton.setEnabled(false);
    // Reset the score
    numberTried = 0;
    numberCorrect = 0;
    commentTextArea.setText("");
    fileMenu.setEnabled(false);
    optionsMenu.setEnabled(false);
    nextQuestion();
  }
  else
  {
    startButton.setText("Start Exam");
    nextButton.setEnabled(false);
    if (numberTried > 0)
    {
      message = "Questions Tried: " +
String.valueOf(numberTried) + "\n";
      message += "Questions Correct: " +
String.valueOf(numberCorrect) + "\n\n";
      message += "Your Score: " + new
DecimalFormat("0.0").format(100.0 * ((double)
numberCorrect / numberTried)) + "%";
      JOptionPane.showConfirmDialog(null, message,
examTitle + " Results", JOptionPane.DEFAULT_OPTION,
JOptionPane.INFORMATION_MESSAGE);
```

```
        }
    givenLabel.setText("");
    answerLabel[0].setText("");
    answerLabel[1].setText("");
    answerLabel[2].setText("");
    answerLabel[3].setText("");
    answerTextField.setText("");
    commentTextArea.setText(centerTextArea("Choose
Options\nClick Start Exam"));
    fileMenu.setEnabled(true);
    optionsMenu.setEnabled(true);
  }
}
```

Make the noted changes. The **DecimalFormat** method requires this import statement:

```
import java.text.*;
```

And, one last time, save and run the project. Load in an exam file. Take some kind of exam. Answer some questions – miss a few to make sure the scoring works. At some point, click **Stop Exam** and some results should appear. Here's a message box I received after taking an exam:

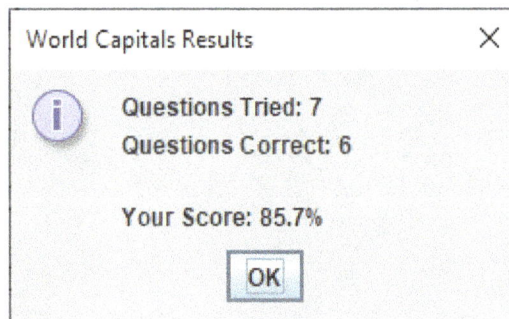

World Capitals Results   ✕

Questions Tried: 7
Questions Correct: 6

Your Score: 85.7%

OK

Multiple Choice Exam Project Review

The **Multiple Choice Exam** project is now complete. Save and run the project and make sure it works as designed. Recheck that all options work and interact properly. Create some exam files (or use the two examples) and have fun learning.

If there are errors in your implementation, go back over the steps of frame and code design. Go over the developed code – make sure you understand how different parts of the project were coded. As mentioned in the beginning of this chapter, the completed project is saved as **MultipleChoiceExam** in the **\HomeJava\HomeJava Projects** folder.

While completing this project, new concepts and skills you should have gained include:

> ➢ How to use the menus.
> ➢ How to use the open file dialog control to obtain a filename.
> ➢ Creating and saving an exam file.
> ➢ Opening a sequential file, inputting and parsing data lines.
> ➢ Error trapping techniques.
> ➢ Checking spelling using Soundex codes.

Multiple Choice Exam Project Enhancements

Possible enhancements to the multiple choice exam project include:

- ➤ The only feedback a user gets about entered answers is a displayed message. Some kind of audible feedback would be nice (a positive sound for correct answer, a negative sound for a wrong answer). We discuss adding sounds to a project in Chapter 10 – you might like to look ahead.
- ➤ Modify the program and scoring system to allow multiple tries at the answer. Award higher scores for fewer missed guesses. If using type in answers, you would need some kind of 'I Give Up' button or just give a specified number of guesses.
- ➤ The user only learns the results after an exam. Add some controls that always display the current results.
- ➤ Add an option that allows a user to review the entries in an exam file.
- ➤ Build an 'Exam Builder' tool that lets a user enter the needed information and save the exam file. You need to know how to save sequential files, a topic discussed in Chapter 8.
- ➤ Add printing capabilities where you can print out exams to take on your own time. We discuss printing in Chapter 9.

Multiple Choice Exam Project
Java Code Listing

```java
/*
 * MultipleChoiceExam.java
 */
package multiplechoiceexam;
import javax.swing.filechooser.*;
import javax.swing.*;
import java.awt.*;
import java.awt.event.*;
import java.io.*;
import java.util.Random;
import java.text.*;

public class MultipleChoiceExam extends JFrame
{
  JLabel headGivenLabel = new JLabel();
  JLabel givenLabel = new JLabel();
  JLabel headAnswerLabel = new JLabel();
  JLabel[] answerLabel = new JLabel[4];
  JTextField answerTextField = new JTextField();
  JTextArea commentTextArea = new JTextArea();
  JButton nextButton = new JButton();
  JButton startButton = new JButton();

  // menu structure
  JMenuBar mainMenuBar = new JMenuBar();
  JMenu fileMenu = new JMenu("File");
  JMenuItem openMenuItem = new JMenuItem("Open");
  JMenuItem exitMenuItem = new JMenuItem("Exit");
  JMenu optionsMenu = new JMenu("Options");
  JRadioButtonMenuItem header1MenuItem = new
JRadioButtonMenuItem("Header 1", true);
  JRadioButtonMenuItem header2MenuItem = new
JRadioButtonMenuItem("Header 2", false);
  JRadioButtonMenuItem mcMenuItem = new
JRadioButtonMenuItem("Multiple Choice Answers", true);
  JRadioButtonMenuItem typeMenuItem = new
JRadioButtonMenuItem("Type In Answers", false);
  ButtonGroup nameGroup = new ButtonGroup();
  ButtonGroup typeGroup = new ButtonGroup();

  Font headerFont = new Font("Arial", Font.BOLD, 18);
  Font examItemFont = new Font("Arial", Font.BOLD, 16);
```

```
Dimension itemSize = new Dimension(370, 30);

String examTitle;
String header1, header2;
int numberTerms;
String[] term1 = new String[100];
String[] term2 = new String[100];
int numberTried, numberCorrect;
int correctAnswer;
Random myRandom = new Random();

public static void main(String args[])
{
  // create frame
  new MultipleChoiceExam().setVisible(true);
}

public MultipleChoiceExam()
{
  // frame constructor
  setTitle("Multiple Choice Exam - No File");
  setResizable(false);

  addWindowListener(new WindowAdapter()
  {
    public void windowClosing(WindowEvent evt)
    {
      exitForm(evt);
    }
  });

  getContentPane().setLayout(new GridBagLayout());
  GridBagConstraints gridConstraints;

  headGivenLabel.setPreferredSize(itemSize);
  headGivenLabel.setFont(headerFont);
  gridConstraints = new GridBagConstraints();
  gridConstraints.gridx = 0;
  gridConstraints.gridy = 0;
  gridConstraints.insets = new Insets(10, 10, 0, 10);
  getContentPane().add(headGivenLabel, gridConstraints);

  givenLabel.setPreferredSize(itemSize);
  givenLabel.setFont(examItemFont);

givenLabel.setBorder(BorderFactory.createLineBorder(Color.BLA
CK));
```

```
      givenLabel.setBackground(Color.WHITE);
      givenLabel.setForeground(Color.BLUE);
      givenLabel.setOpaque(true);
      givenLabel.setHorizontalAlignment(SwingConstants.CENTER);
      gridConstraints = new GridBagConstraints();
      gridConstraints.gridx = 0;
      gridConstraints.gridy = 1;
      gridConstraints.insets = new Insets(0, 10, 0, 10);
      getContentPane().add(givenLabel, gridConstraints);

      headAnswerLabel.setPreferredSize(itemSize);
      headAnswerLabel.setFont(headerFont);
      gridConstraints = new GridBagConstraints();
      gridConstraints.gridx = 0;
      gridConstraints.gridy = 2;
      gridConstraints.insets = new Insets(10, 10, 0, 10);
      getContentPane().add(headAnswerLabel, gridConstraints);

      for (int i = 0; i < 4; i++)
      {
        answerLabel[i] = new JLabel();
        answerLabel[i].setPreferredSize(itemSize);
        answerLabel[i].setFont(examItemFont);

answerLabel[i].setBorder(BorderFactory.createLineBorder(Color
.BLACK));
        answerLabel[i].setBackground(Color.WHITE);
        answerLabel[i].setForeground(Color.BLUE);
        answerLabel[i].setOpaque(true);

answerLabel[i].setHorizontalAlignment(SwingConstants.CENTER);
        gridConstraints = new GridBagConstraints();
        gridConstraints.gridx = 0;
        gridConstraints.gridy = i + 3;
        gridConstraints.insets = new Insets(0, 10, 10, 10);
        getContentPane().add(answerLabel[i], gridConstraints);
        answerLabel[i].addMouseListener(new MouseAdapter()
        {
          public void mousePressed(MouseEvent e)
          {
            answerLabelMousePressed(e);
          }
        });
      }

      answerTextField.setPreferredSize(itemSize);
      answerTextField.setFont(examItemFont);
```

```
    answerTextField.setBackground(Color.WHITE);
    answerTextField.setForeground(Color.BLUE);
    answerTextField.setVisible(false);
    gridConstraints = new GridBagConstraints();
    gridConstraints.gridx = 0;
    gridConstraints.gridy = 3;
    gridConstraints.insets = new Insets(0, 10, 10, 10);
    getContentPane().add(answerTextField, gridConstraints);
    answerTextField.addActionListener(new ActionListener ()
    {
      public void actionPerformed(ActionEvent e)
      {
        answerTextFieldActionPerformed(e);
      }
    });

    commentTextArea.setPreferredSize(new Dimension(370, 80));
    commentTextArea.setFont(new Font("Courier New", Font.BOLD
+ Font.ITALIC, 18));

commentTextArea.setBorder(BorderFactory.createLineBorder(Colo
r.BLACK));
    commentTextArea.setEditable(false);
    commentTextArea.setBackground(new Color(255, 255, 192));
    commentTextArea.setForeground(Color.RED);
    gridConstraints = new GridBagConstraints();
    gridConstraints.gridx = 0;
    gridConstraints.gridy = 7;
    gridConstraints.insets = new Insets(0, 10, 10, 10);
    getContentPane().add(commentTextArea, gridConstraints);

    nextButton.setText("Next Question");
    gridConstraints = new GridBagConstraints();
    gridConstraints.gridx = 0;
    gridConstraints.gridy = 8;
    gridConstraints.insets = new Insets(0, 0, 10, 0);
    getContentPane().add(nextButton, gridConstraints);
    nextButton.addActionListener(new ActionListener()
    {
      public void actionPerformed(ActionEvent e)
      {
        nextButtonActionPerformed(e);
      }
    });

    startButton.setText("Start Exam");
    gridConstraints = new GridBagConstraints();
```

```java
gridConstraints.gridx = 0;
gridConstraints.gridy = 9;
gridConstraints.insets = new Insets(0, 0, 10, 0);
getContentPane().add(startButton, gridConstraints);
startButton.addActionListener(new ActionListener()
{
  public void actionPerformed(ActionEvent e)
  {
    startButtonActionPerformed(e);
  }
});

// build menu structure
setJMenuBar(mainMenuBar);
mainMenuBar.add(fileMenu);
fileMenu.add(openMenuItem);
fileMenu.addSeparator();
fileMenu.add(exitMenuItem);
mainMenuBar.add(optionsMenu);
optionsMenu.add(header1MenuItem);
optionsMenu.add(header2MenuItem);
optionsMenu.addSeparator();
optionsMenu.add(mcMenuItem);
optionsMenu.add(typeMenuItem);
nameGroup.add(header1MenuItem);
nameGroup.add(header2MenuItem);
typeGroup.add(mcMenuItem);
typeGroup.add(typeMenuItem);
openMenuItem.addActionListener(new ActionListener()
{
  public void actionPerformed(ActionEvent e)
  {
    openMenuItemActionPerformed(e);
  }
});
exitMenuItem.addActionListener(new ActionListener()
{
  public void actionPerformed(ActionEvent e)
  {
    exitMenuItemActionPerformed(e);
  }
});
header1MenuItem.addActionListener(new ActionListener()
{
  public void actionPerformed(ActionEvent e)
  {
    header1MenuItemActionPerformed(e);
```

```
      }
    });
    header2MenuItem.addActionListener(new ActionListener()
    {
      public void actionPerformed(ActionEvent e)
      {
        header2MenuItemActionPerformed(e);
      }
    });
    mcMenuItem.addActionListener(new ActionListener()
    {
      public void actionPerformed(ActionEvent e)
      {
        mcMenuItemActionPerformed(e);
      }
    });
    typeMenuItem.addActionListener(new ActionListener()
    {
      public void actionPerformed(ActionEvent e)
      {
        typeMenuItemActionPerformed(e);
      }
    });

    pack();
    Dimension screenSize =
Toolkit.getDefaultToolkit().getScreenSize();
    setBounds((int) (0.5 * (screenSize.width - getWidth())),
(int) (0.5 * (screenSize.height - getHeight())), getWidth(),
getHeight());
    // initialize form
    startButton.setEnabled(false);
    nextButton.setEnabled(false);
    optionsMenu.setEnabled(false);
    commentTextArea.setText(centerTextArea("Open Exam File to
Start"));
  }

  private void exitForm(WindowEvent evt)
  {
    System.exit(0);
  }

  private void answerLabelMousePressed(MouseEvent e)
  {
    boolean correct = false;
    int labelSelected;
```

```
    // make sure exam has started and question has not been
answered
    if (startButton.getText().equals("Start Exam") ||
nextButton.isEnabled())
      return;
    // determine which label was clicked
    // get upper left corner of clicked label
    Point p = e.getComponent().getLocation();
    // determine index based on p
    for (labelSelected = 0; labelSelected < 20;
labelSelected++)
    {
      if (p.x == answerLabel[labelSelected].getX() && p.y ==
answerLabel[labelSelected].getY())
        break;
    }
    // If already answered, exit
    numberTried++;
    if (header1MenuItem.isSelected())
    {
      if
(answerLabel[labelSelected].getText().equals(term1[correctAns
wer]))
        correct = true;
    }
    else
    {
      if
(answerLabel[labelSelected].getText().equals(term2[correctAns
wer]))
        correct = true;
    }
    updateScore(correct);
  }

  private void answerTextFieldActionPerformed(ActionEvent e)
  {
    // Check type in answer
    boolean correct;
    String ucTypedAnswer, ucAnswer;
    // make sure exam has started and question has not been
answered
    if (startButton.getText().equals("Start Exam") ||
nextButton.isEnabled())
      return;
    answerTextField.setEditable(false);
    numberTried++;
```

```
    ucTypedAnswer = answerTextField.getText().toUpperCase();
    if (header1MenuItem.isSelected())
      ucAnswer = term1[correctAnswer].toUpperCase();
    else
      ucAnswer = term2[correctAnswer].toUpperCase();
    correct = false;
    if (ucTypedAnswer.equals(ucAnswer) ||
soundex(ucTypedAnswer).equals(soundex(ucAnswer)))
      correct = true;
    updateScore(correct);
  }

  private void nextButtonActionPerformed(ActionEvent e)
  {
    // Generate next question
    nextButton.setEnabled(false);
    nextQuestion();
  }

  private void startButtonActionPerformed(ActionEvent e)
  {
    String message;
    if (startButton.getText().equals("Start Exam"))
    {
      startButton.setText("Stop Exam");
      nextButton.setEnabled(false);
      // Reset the score
      numberTried = 0;
      numberCorrect = 0;
      commentTextArea.setText("");
      fileMenu.setEnabled(false);
      optionsMenu.setEnabled(false);
      nextQuestion();
    }
    else
    {
      startButton.setText("Start Exam");
      nextButton.setEnabled(false);
      if (numberTried > 0)
      {
        message = "Questions Tried: " +
String.valueOf(numberTried) + "\n";
        message += "Questions Correct: " +
String.valueOf(numberCorrect) + "\n\n";
        message += "Your Score: " + new
DecimalFormat("0.0").format(100.0 * ((double) numberCorrect /
numberTried)) + "%";
```

```
      JOptionPane.showConfirmDialog(null, message,
examTitle + " Results", JOptionPane.DEFAULT_OPTION,
JOptionPane.INFORMATION_MESSAGE);
    }
    givenLabel.setText("");
    answerLabel[0].setText("");
    answerLabel[1].setText("");
    answerLabel[2].setText("");
    answerLabel[3].setText("");
    answerTextField.setText("");
    commentTextArea.setText(centerTextArea("Choose
Options\nClick Start Exam"));
    fileMenu.setEnabled(true);
    optionsMenu.setEnabled(true);
  }
}

private void openMenuItemActionPerformed(ActionEvent e)
{
  String myLine;
  JFileChooser openChooser = new JFileChooser();
  openChooser.setDialogType(JFileChooser.OPEN_DIALOG);
  openChooser.setDialogTitle("Open Exam File");
  openChooser.addChoosableFileFilter(new
FileNameExtensionFilter("Exam Files", "csv"));
  if (openChooser.showOpenDialog(this) ==
JFileChooser.APPROVE_OPTION)
  {
    try
    {
      BufferedReader inputFile = new BufferedReader(new
FileReader(openChooser.getSelectedFile()));
      myLine = inputFile.readLine();
      examTitle = parseLeft(myLine);
      myLine = inputFile.readLine();
      header1 = parseLeft(myLine);
      header2 = parseRight(myLine);
      numberTerms = 0;
      do
      {
        numberTerms++;
        myLine = inputFile.readLine();
        term1[numberTerms - 1] = parseLeft(myLine);
        term2[numberTerms - 1] = parseRight(myLine);
      }
      while (inputFile.ready() && numberTerms < 100);
      if (numberTerms < 5)
```

```
       {
           JOptionPane.showConfirmDialog(null, "Must have at
least 5 entries in exam file.", "Exam File Error",
JOptionPane.DEFAULT_OPTION, JOptionPane.ERROR_MESSAGE);
           return;
       }
       inputFile.close();
       // establish frame title
       this.setTitle("Multiple Choice Exam - " + examTitle);
       // set up menu items
       header1MenuItem.setText(header1 + ", Given " +
header2);
       header2MenuItem.setText(header2 + ", Given " +
header1);
       if (header1MenuItem.isSelected())
       {
         headGivenLabel.setText(header2);
         headAnswerLabel.setText(header1);
       }
       else
       {
         headGivenLabel.setText(header1);
         headAnswerLabel.setText(header2);
       }
       startButton.setEnabled(true);
       optionsMenu.setEnabled(true);
       commentTextArea.setText(centerTextArea("File Loaded,
Choose Options\nClick Start Exam"));
     }
     catch (Exception ex)
     {
         JOptionPane.showConfirmDialog(null, "Error reading
in input file - make sure file is correct format.", "Multiple
Choice Exam File Error", JOptionPane.DEFAULT_OPTION,
JOptionPane.ERROR_MESSAGE);
         return;
     }
   }
 }

 private void exitMenuItemActionPerformed(ActionEvent e)
 {
   System.exit(0);
 }

 private void header1MenuItemActionPerformed(ActionEvent e)
 {
```

```java
  // Set up for naming header1, given header2
  headGivenLabel.setText(header2);
  headAnswerLabel.setText(header1);
}

private void header2MenuItemActionPerformed(ActionEvent e)
{
  // Set up for naming header2, given header1
  headGivenLabel.setText(header1);
  headAnswerLabel.setText(header2);
}

private void mcMenuItemActionPerformed(ActionEvent e)
{
  answerLabel[0].setVisible(true);
  answerLabel[1].setVisible(true);
  answerLabel[2].setVisible(true);
  answerLabel[3].setVisible(true);
  answerTextField.setVisible(false);
}

private void typeMenuItemActionPerformed(ActionEvent e)
{
  answerLabel[0].setVisible(false);
  answerLabel[1].setVisible(false);
  answerLabel[2].setVisible(false);
  answerLabel[3].setVisible(false);
  answerTextField.setVisible(true);
}

private String parseLeft(String s)
{
    int cl;
    // find comma
    cl = s.indexOf(",");
    return (s.substring(0, cl));
}

private String parseRight(String s)
{
    int cl;
    // find comma
    cl = s.indexOf(",");
    return (s.substring(cl + 1));
}

private String centerTextArea(String s)
```

```
   {
     // centers up to two lines in text area
     int charsPerLine = 33;
     String sOut = "";
     int j = s.indexOf("\n");
     int nSpaces;
     if (j == -1)
     {
       // single line
       sOut = "\n" + spacePadding((int) ((charsPerLine -
s.length()) / 2)) + s;
     }
     else
     {
       // first line
       String l = s.substring(0, j);
       sOut = "\n" + spacePadding((int) ((charsPerLine -
l.length()) / 2)) + l;
       // second line
       l = s.substring(j + 1);
       sOut += "\n" + spacePadding((int) ((charsPerLine -
l.length()) / 2)) + l ;
     }
     return(sOut);
   }

  private String spacePadding(int n)
  {
    String s = "";
    if (n != 0)
      for (int i = 0; i < n; i++)
        s += " ";
    return(s);
  }

  private void nextQuestion()
  {
    boolean[] termUsed = new boolean[numberTerms];
    int[] index = new int[4];
    int j;
    commentTextArea.setText("");
    // Generate the next question based on selected options
    correctAnswer = myRandom.nextInt(numberTerms);
    if (header1MenuItem.isSelected())
    {
      givenLabel.setText(term2[correctAnswer]);
    }
```

```java
else
{
  givenLabel.setText(term1[correctAnswer]);
}
if (mcMenuItem.isSelected())
{
  // Multiple choice answers
  for (int i = 0; i < numberTerms; i++)
  {
    termUsed[i] = false;
  }
  // Pick four random possiblities
  for (int i = 0; i < 4; i++)
  {
    do
    {
      j = myRandom.nextInt(numberTerms);
    }
    while (termUsed[j] || j == correctAnswer);
    termUsed[j] = true;
    index[i] = j;
  }
  // Replace one with correct answer
  index[myRandom.nextInt(4)] = correctAnswer;
  // Display multiple choice answers in label boxes
  if (header1MenuItem.isSelected())
  {
    answerLabel[0].setText(term1[index[0]]);
    answerLabel[1].setText(term1[index[1]]);
    answerLabel[2].setText(term1[index[2]]);
    answerLabel[3].setText(term1[index[3]]);
  }
  else
  {
    answerLabel[0].setText(term2[index[0]]);
    answerLabel[1].setText(term2[index[1]]);
    answerLabel[2].setText(term2[index[2]]);
    answerLabel[3].setText(term2[index[3]]);
  }
}
else
{
  // Type-in answers
  answerTextField.setEditable(true);
  answerTextField.setText("");
  answerTextField.requestFocus();
}
```

```
  }

  private void updateScore(boolean correct)
  {
    // Check if answer is correct
    if (correct)
    {
      numberCorrect++;
      commentTextArea.setText(centerTextArea("Correct!"));
    }
    else
      commentTextArea.setText(centerTextArea("Sorry ...
Correct Answer Shown"));
    // Display correct answer
    if (mcMenuItem.isSelected())
    {
      if (header1MenuItem.isSelected())
        answerLabel[0].setText(term1[correctAnswer]);
      else
        answerLabel[0].setText(term2[correctAnswer]);
      answerLabel[1].setText("");
      answerLabel[2].setText("");
      answerLabel[3].setText("");
    }
    else
    {
      if (header1MenuItem.isSelected())
        answerTextField.setText(term1[correctAnswer]);
      else
        answerTextField.setText(term2[correctAnswer]);
    }
    startButton.setEnabled(true);
    nextButton.setEnabled(true);
    nextButton.requestFocus();
  }

  public String soundex(String w)
  {
    // Generates Soundex code for W based on Unicode value
    // Allows answers whose spelling is close, but not exact
    String wTemp, s = "";
    int l;
    int wPrev, wSnd, cIndex;
    // Load soundex function array
    int[] wSound = {0, 1, 2, 3, 0, 1, 2, 0, 0, 2, 2, 4, 5, 5,
0, 1, 2, 6, 2, 3, 0, 1, 0, 2, 0, 2};
    wTemp = w.toUpperCase();
```

```
    l = w.length();
    if (l != 0)
    {
      s = String.valueOf(w.charAt(0));
      wPrev = 0;
      if (l > 1)
      {
        for (int i = 1; i < l; i++)
        {
          cIndex = (int) wTemp.charAt(i) - 65;
          if (cIndex >= 0 && cIndex <= 25)
          {
            wSnd = wSound[cIndex] + 48;
            if (wSnd != 48 && wSnd != wPrev)
            {
              s += String.valueOf((char) wSnd);
            }
            wPrev = wSnd;
          }
        }
      }
      else
      s = "";
    }
    return(s);
  }
}
```

6

Blackjack Card Game Project

Review and Preview

The first popular computer games appeared in the early 1970's with the introduction of timeshare computing. There was a classic set of DEC (Digital Equipment Corporation) programs written in BASIC for timeshare users. The set included gambling games, simulations and the ever-popular Star Trek game.

In this chapter, we build a Blackjack card game. The **Blackjack Card Game Project** allows a single player to compete against the computer dealer. The project uses card images and discusses the math and logic involved in shuffling and displaying a deck of cards. You will indeed see that the odds are stacked against you so keep you real money in your wallet!

Blackjack Card Game Project Preview

In this chapter, we will build a **Blackjack card game** program. This program allows a single player to compete against the computer dealer. The idea of Blackjack is to score higher than the dealer's hand without exceeding twenty-one points. Cards count their value, except face cards (Jacks, Queens, Kings) count for ten, and Aces count for either one or eleven (you pick). If you beat the dealer, you get 10 points. If you get Blackjack (21 with just two cards) and beat the dealer, you get 15 points. If the dealer beats you, you lose 10 points.

The finished project is saved as **Blackjack** in the **\HomeJava\HomeJava Projects** project group. Start NetBeans (or your IDE). Open the specified project group. Make **Blackjack** the selected project. Run the project. You will see:

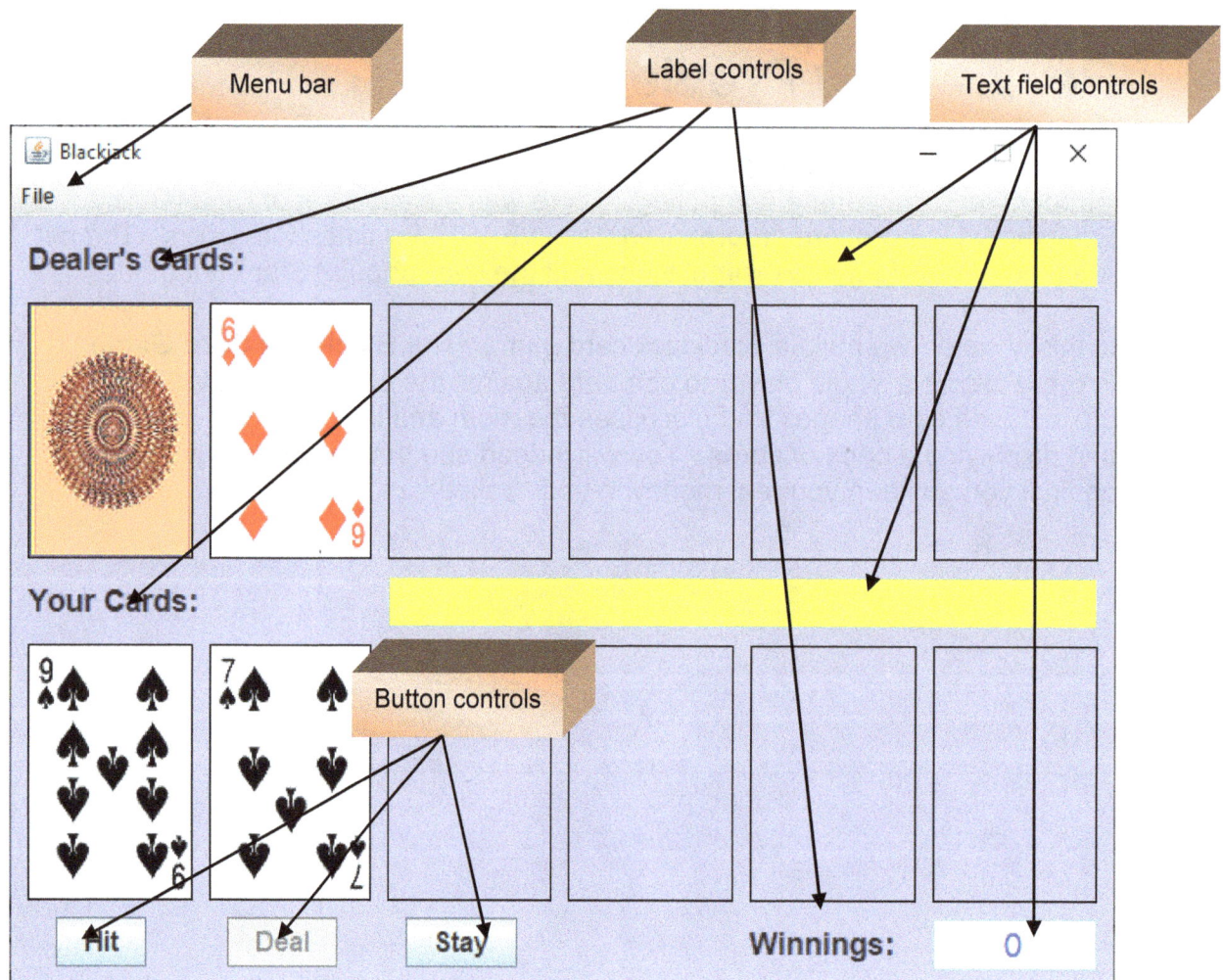

A menu bar is used to control the program Label controls are used for header information and text fields used to provide feedback and winnings information to the player. Three button controls are used by the player to 'talk to' the dealer. The cards are displayed using label controls – **ImageIcon** objects represent the graphic card depictions.

Defining the interface for this project is straightforward - the code behind the interface is not trivial. There are lots of rules involved with playing Blackjack and we need to determine some way to display the cards. We will build the code slowly. For now, let's review the rules used in this version of Blackjack and see how the program works.

Blackjack starts by giving two cards (from a standard 52 card deck – reshuffles are done when only a few cards remain) to the dealer (one face down) and two cards to the player (you). The player decides whether to **Hit** (receive another card) or **Stay** (stop receiving cards). The player can choose as many extra cards as desired. If the player's score exceeds 21 before staying, it is a loss (-10 points) and we say the player **busted**. If the player does not exceed 21, it becomes the dealer's turn. The dealer must add cards to his score until 16 is exceeded. When this occurs, if the dealer also exceeds 21 (**busts**) or if his score is less than the player's, he loses (+10 points for you). If the dealer's score is greater than the player's score (and under 21), the dealer wins (-10 points for you). If the dealer and the player have the same score, it is called a **push** (no points added or subtracted). The dealer must always take an Ace to be 11 points, unless it causes him to bust.

If either the player or dealer get 'Blackjack' which is defined as 21 points with just two cards (an Ace and a card worth 10 points), they automatically win. If the dealer gets Blackjack, the player loses 10 points. If the player gets Blackjack, he wins 15 points. If both the dealer and the player get Blackjack, it's a push.

A special rule for this version of Blackjack (not used in casinos) involves the number of cards received. Theoretically, you can have eleven cards given to you and still not bust! We don't want to display that many cards since it would be a rare occurrence. You can see in the interface, we limit the display to six cards. So, a special rule in this implementation is that, if the player gets six cards and has 21 or fewer points, the player is declared a winner. Similarly, if the player has fewer than six cards and the dealer is able to draw six cards without exceeding 16 points (since the dealer must stop adding cards after 16 points), the dealer wins, regardless of score.

Like we said – there are lots of rules here. Let's see these rules in action. The running Blackjack program appears as (you will see different cards – the results are random):

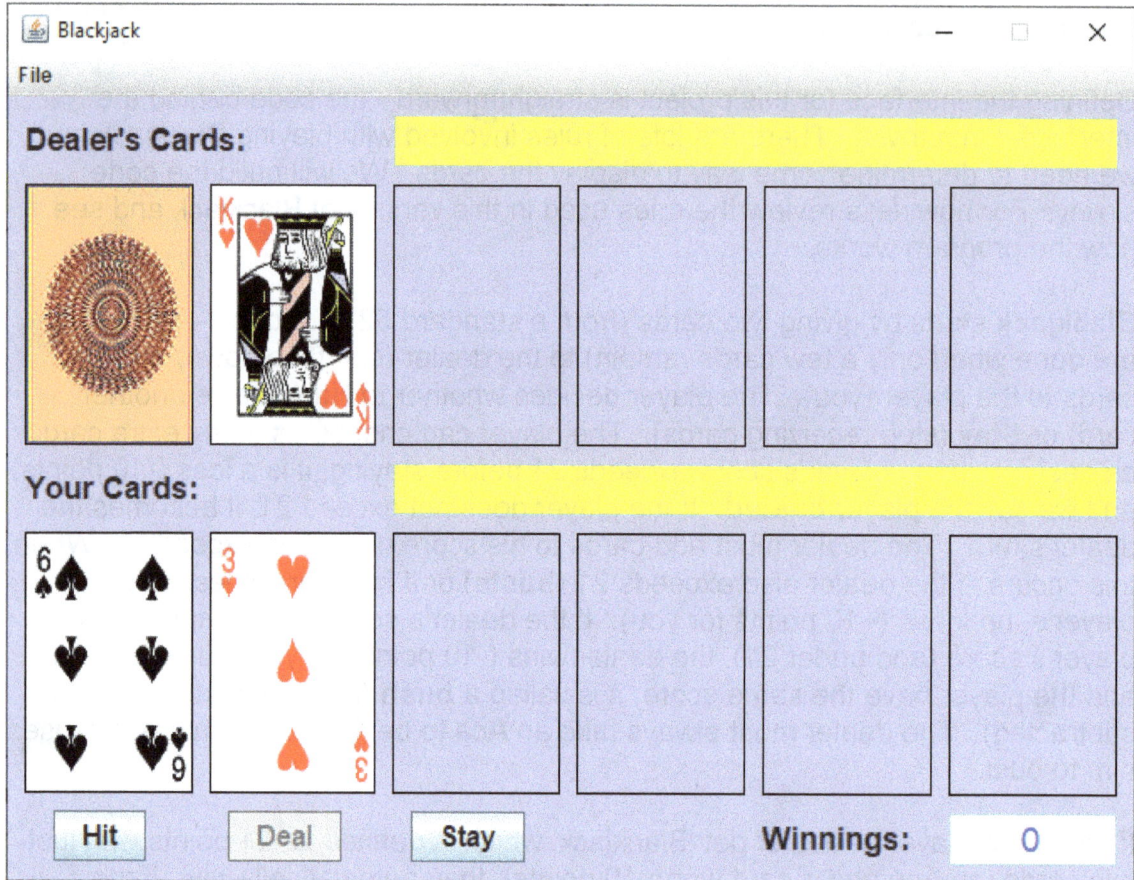

Notice the card graphics displayed in the label controls. In card lingo, the displayed cards are referred to **hands**. The dealer plays one hand, while the player plays the other hand. One of the dealer's cards is face down – the other is a King. I have a 6 and a 3 showing (9 points). I can either get another card (**Hit**) or stop (**Stay**). I think you'd agree that **Hit** is the correct choice since I'm far from 21.

When I click **Hit**, I receive a 5, giving me 14 points:

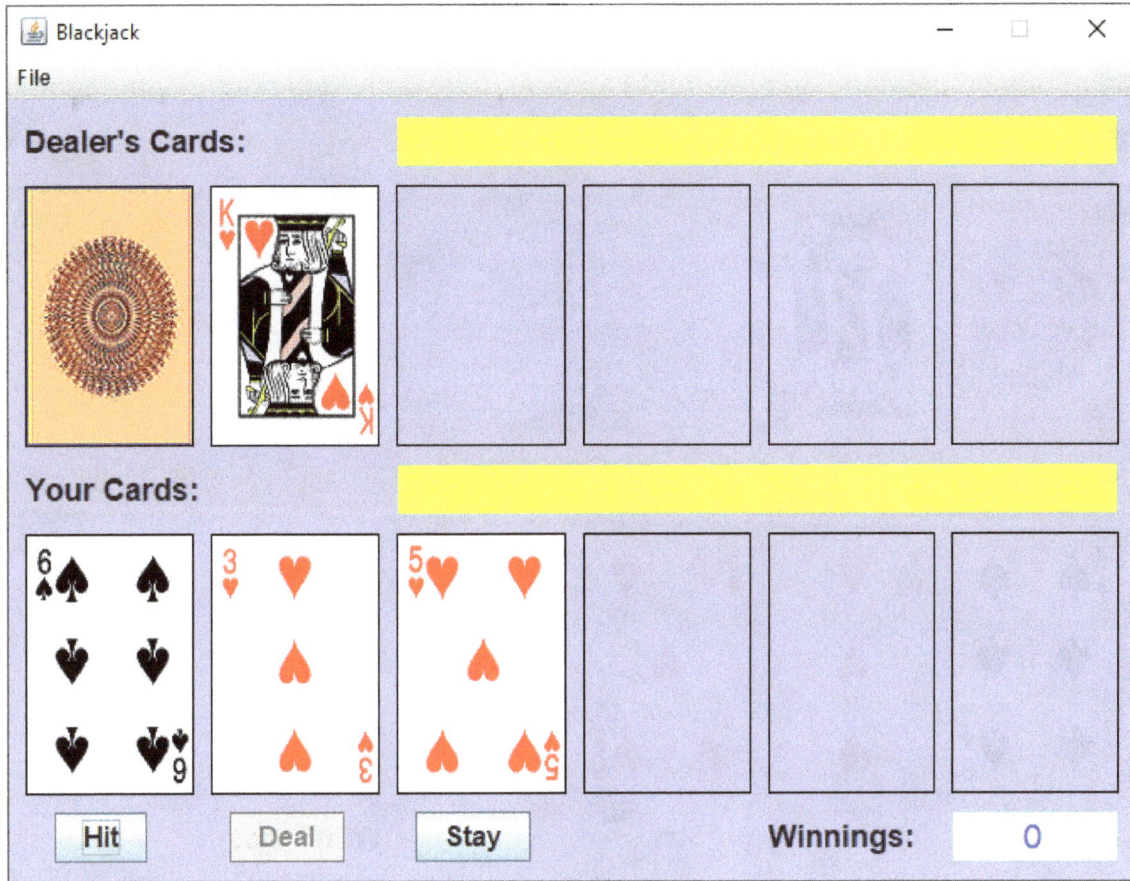

I click **Hit** one more time to see:

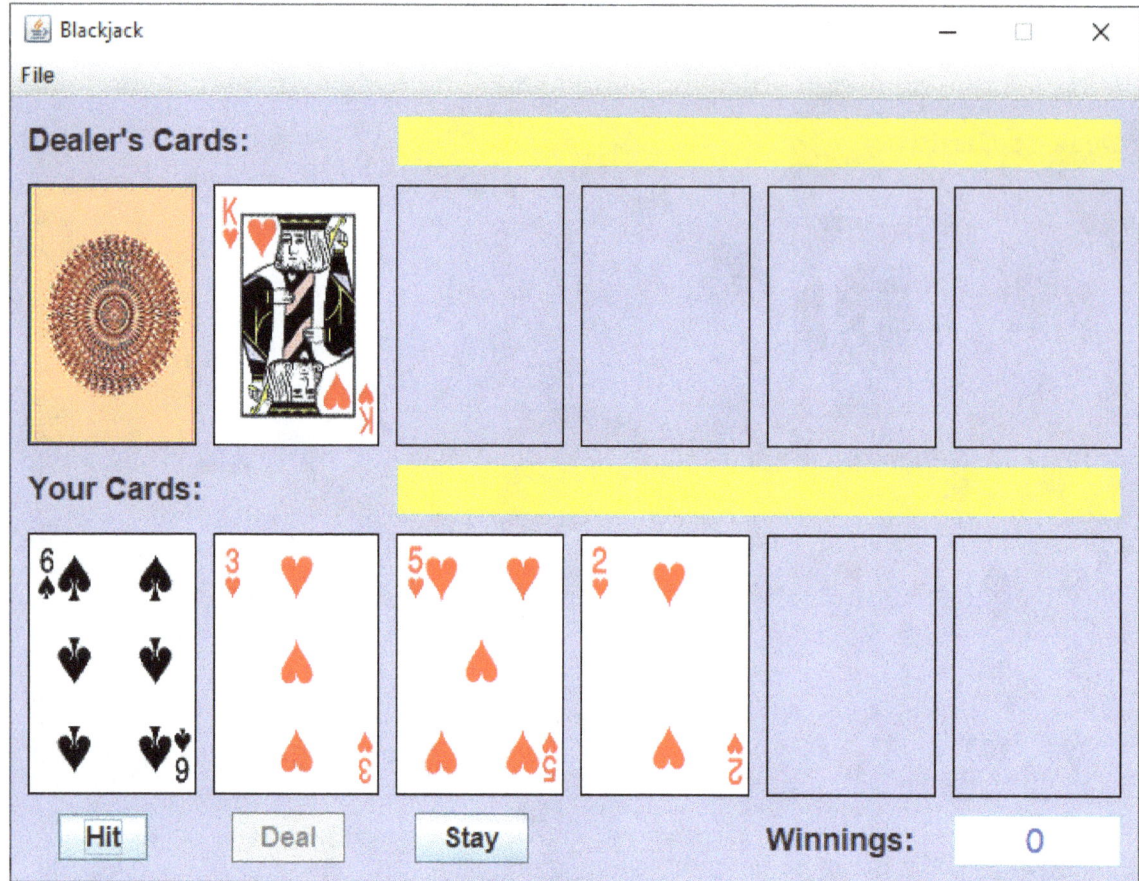

The 2 gives me 16 points. I'm getting nervous – a good time to **Stay**.

After clicking **Stay**, the dealer plays out his cards according to the prescribed rules:

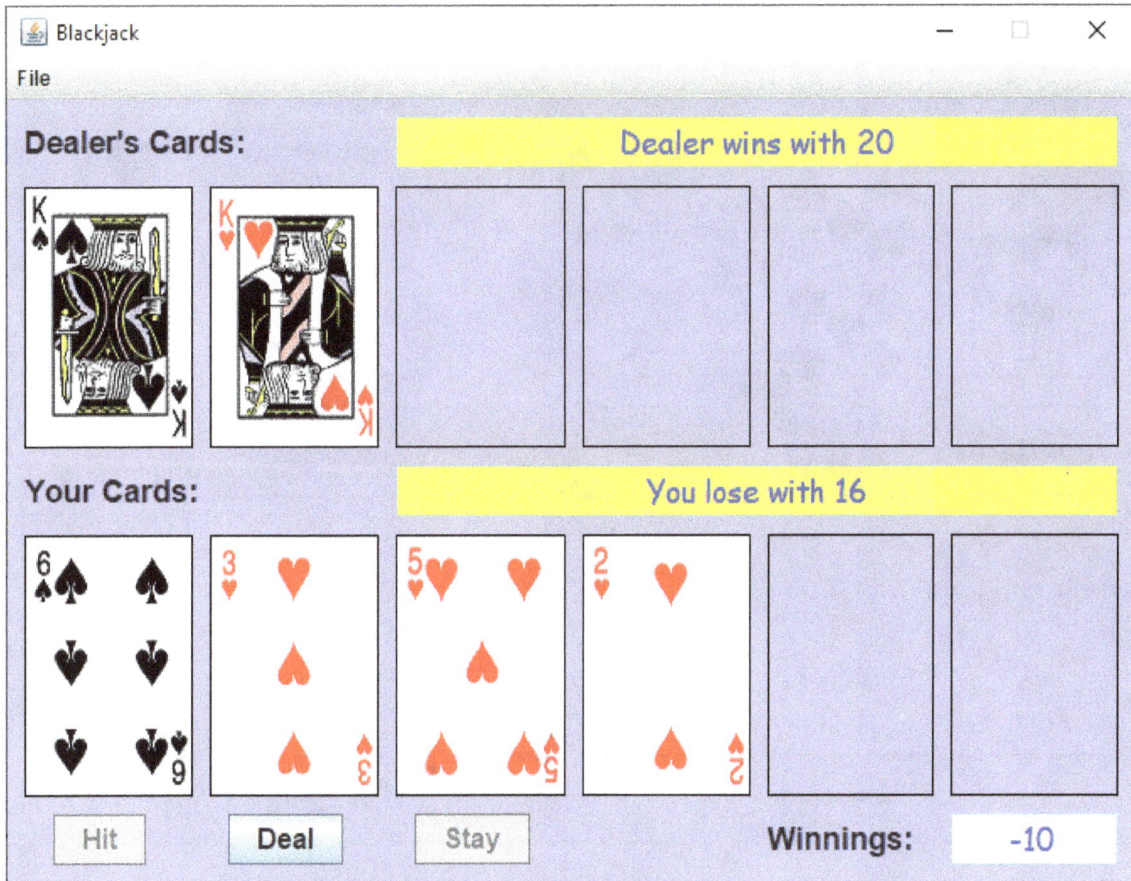

The first card is 'flipped' over revealing a King, giving the dealer 20 points. The dealer wins. I lose 10 points! Not a good start. Notice the text field controls telling me the results and displaying my winnings. Click **Deal** to play another hand.

After a few more hands, I see:

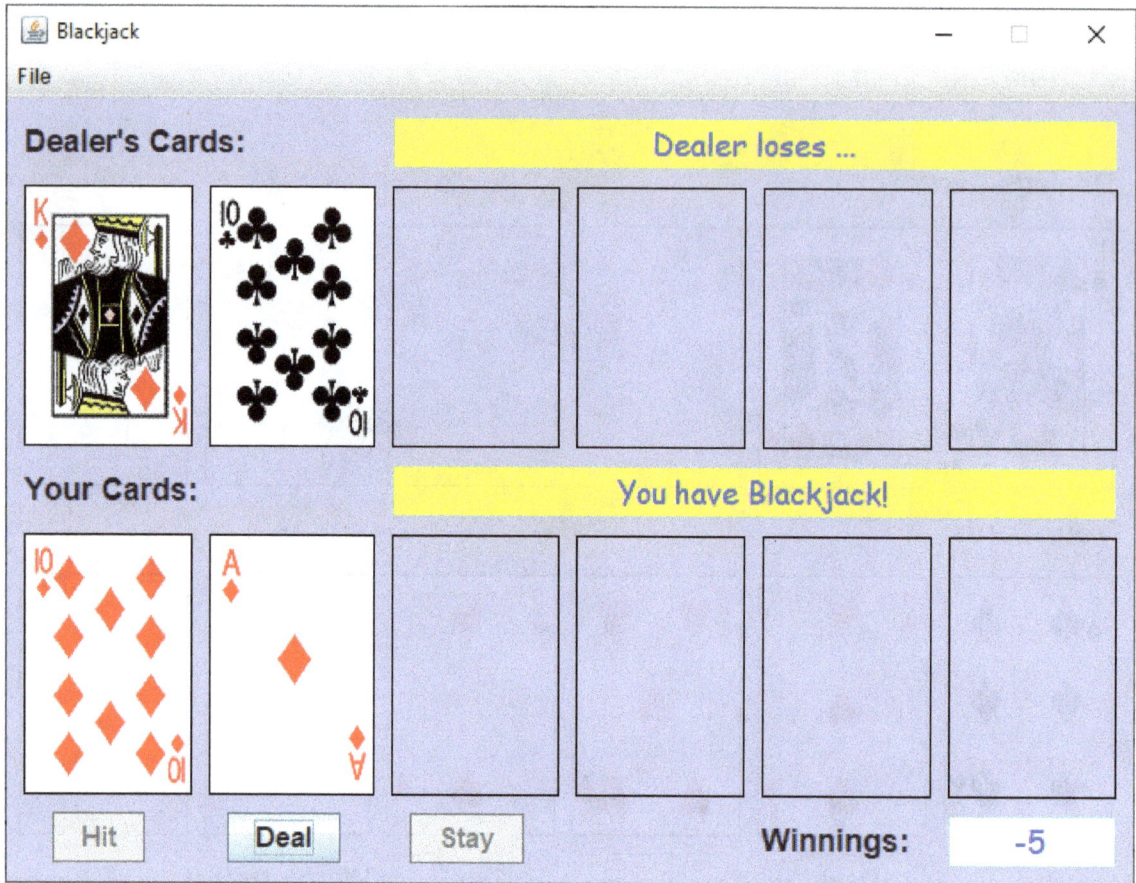

I have Blackjack – I win!

I click **Deal** again.

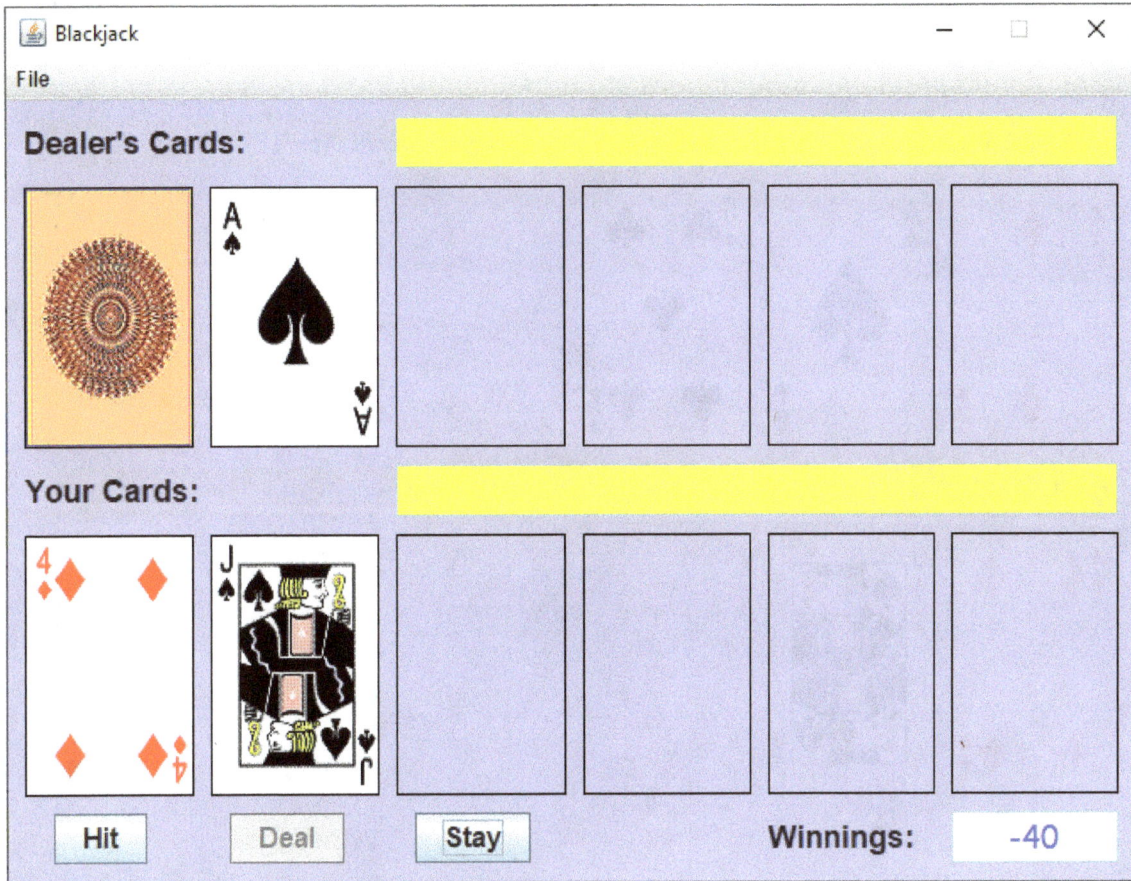

I have 14 points. I choose not to take a hit.

I click **Stay** and the dealer plays out:

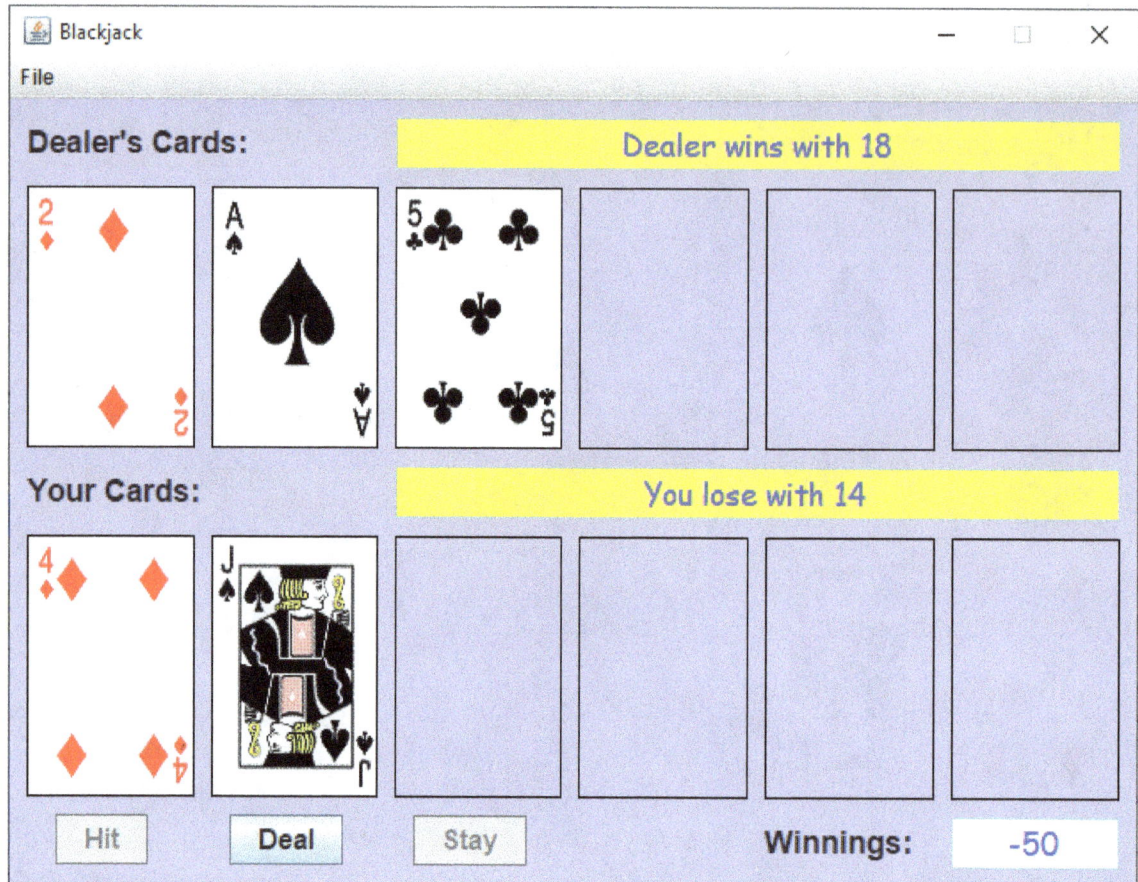

The face-down card is revealed to be a 2. The dealer has 3 or 13 points (an Ace can be 1 or 11). He must take another card – a 5. This brings the dealer score to 18. The dealer has beaten my 14 points. My winnings drop.

After playing a few more hands (not doing so well, since my **Winnings** are now -**90**), I got these cards.:

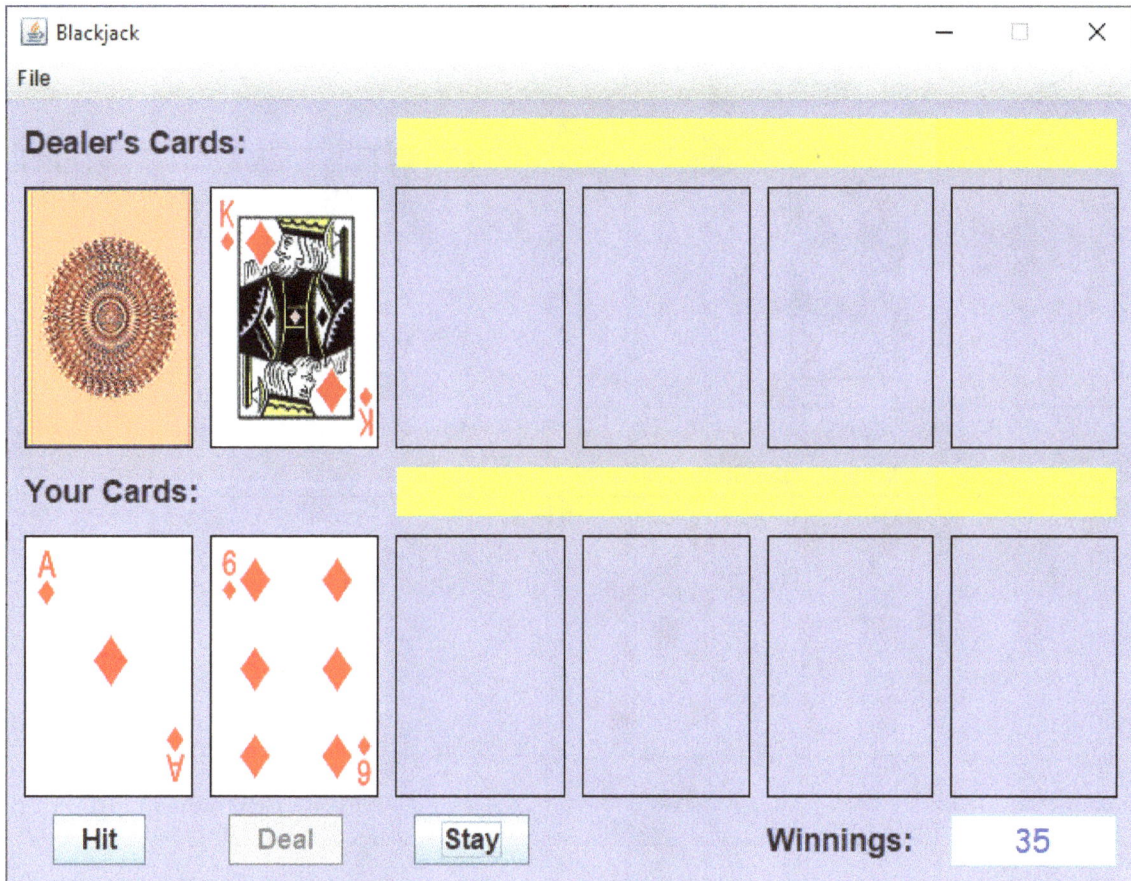

Recall, an Ace can be either 1 or 11 points. Choosing 1 in this case gives me 7 points (1 + 6). I choose to **Hit**.

After a **Hit**, I see:

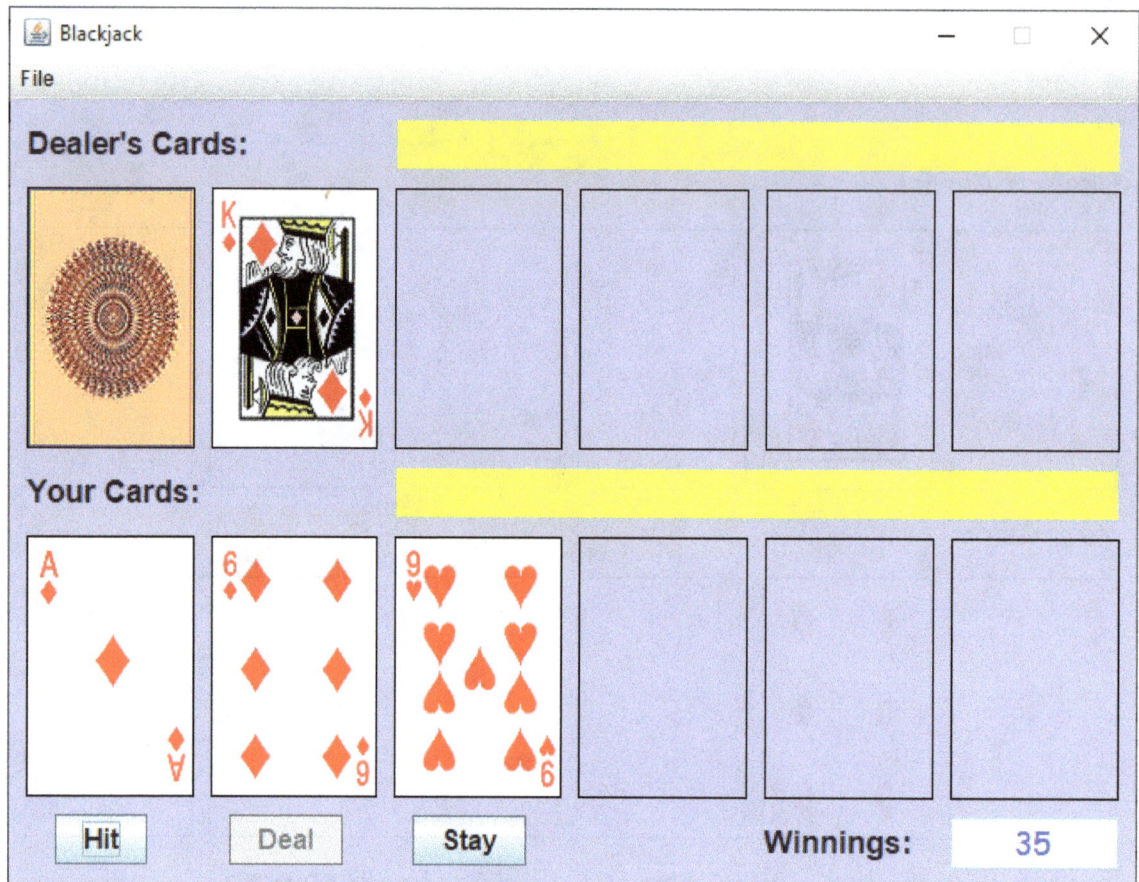

Leaving the Ace at 1 point, I have 16 (1 + 6 + 9). I choose to **Stay**.

After clicking **Stay**, the dealer flips over the face down card:

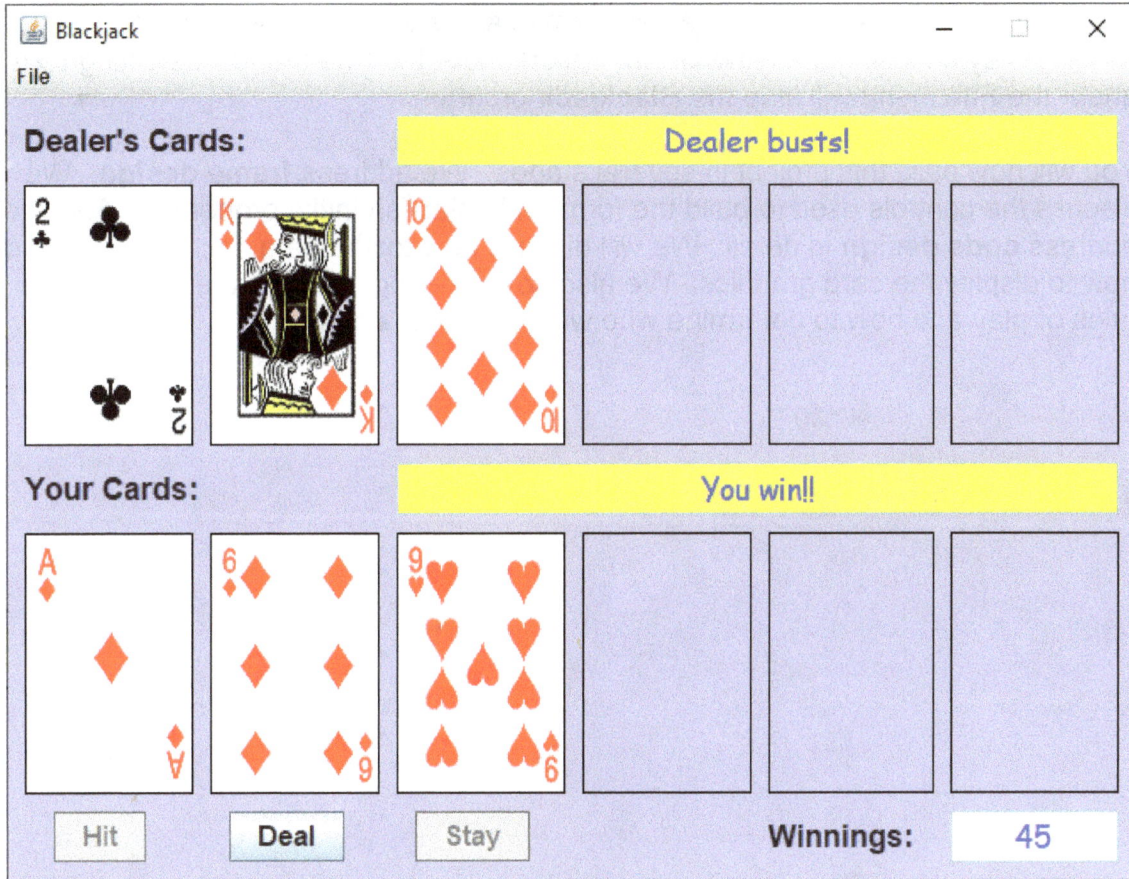

The dealer reveals his first card as a 2. The dealer adds a 10 and busts (22 points, over 21). I win!

Continue playing hands until you understand how the rules of the game, especially those that the dealer uses, are applied. Try to figure out some good strategy for playing Blackjack. At any point, a new game can be started (resetting the winnings) by choosing the **New Game** option under the **File** menu. Selecting **Exit** under the **File** menu will stop the **Blackjack** program.

You will now build this project in several stages. We address **frame design**. We discuss the controls used to build the form and establish initial properties. And, we address **code design** in detail. We will discuss how to shuffle a deck of cards and how to display the card graphics. We also cover the logic behind the complicated rules of play and how to determine who wins (or if it is a push).

Blackjack Form Design

We begin building the **Blackjack** project. Let's build the frame. Start a new project in your Java project group – name it **Blackjack**. Delete default code in file named **Blackjack.java**. Once started, we suggest you immediately save the project with the name you chose. This sets up the folder and file structure needed for your project. Build the basic frame with these properties:

Blackjack Frame:
title   Blackjack
background   Color(192, 192, 255), a light blue
resizable   false

The code is:

```
/*
 * Blackjack.java
 */
package blackjack;
import javax.swing.*;
import java.awt.*;
import java.awt.event.*;

public class Blackjack extends JFrame
{
  public static void main(String args[])
  {
    // create frame
    new Blackjack().setVisible(true);
  }

  public Blackjack()
  {
    // frame constructor
    setTitle("Blackjack");
    getContentPane().setBackground(new Color(192, 192,
255));
    setResizable(false);

    addWindowListener(new WindowAdapter()
    {
      public void windowClosing(WindowEvent evt)
      {
        exitForm(evt);
      }
    });
```

```
    getContentPane().setLayout(new GridBagLayout());
    GridBagConstraints gridConstraints;

    pack();
    Dimension screenSize =
Toolkit.getDefaultToolkit().getScreenSize();
    setBounds((int) (0.5 * (screenSize.width -
getWidth())), (int) (0.5 * (screenSize.height -
getHeight())), getWidth(), getHeight());
  }

  private void exitForm(WindowEvent evt)
  {
    System.exit(0);
  }
}
```

This code builds the frame, sets up the layout manager and includes code to exit the application. Run the code to make sure the frame (at least, what there is of it at this point) appears and is centered on the screen:

Let's populate our frame with other controls. All code for creating the frame and placing controls (except declarations) goes in the **Blackjack** constructor.

First, let's define the simple menu. We use a single menu object (**fileMenu**) to start a new game and to exit program. Our menu bar (**mainMenuBar**) structure will be:

Text	Name
File	fileMenu
New Game	newMenuItem
(Separator)	
Exit	exitMenuItem

Declare the different menu items as class level objects:

```
// menu structure
JMenuBar mainMenuBar = new JMenuBar();
JMenu fileMenu = new JMenu("File");
JMenuItem newMenuItem = new JMenuItem("New Game");
JMenuItem exitMenuItem = new JMenuItem("Exit");
```

Establish the menu structure using this code in the frame constructor (each menu item has a corresponding **ActionPerformed** method):

```
// build menu structure
setJMenuBar(mainMenuBar);
mainMenuBar.add(fileMenu);
fileMenu.add(newMenuItem);
fileMenu.addSeparator();
fileMenu.add(exitMenuItem);
newMenuItem.addActionListener(new ActionListener()
{
  public void actionPerformed(ActionEvent e)
  {
    newMenuItemActionPerformed(e);
  }
});
exitMenuItem.addActionListener(new ActionListener()
{
  public void actionPerformed(ActionEvent e)
  {
    exitMenuItemActionPerformed(e);
  }
});
```

Add the empty methods:

```
private void newMenuItemActionPerformed(ActionEvent e)
{
}

private void exitMenuItemActionPerformed(ActionEvent e)
{
}
```

Save, run. Make sure the menu structure appears:

Click **File** to see:

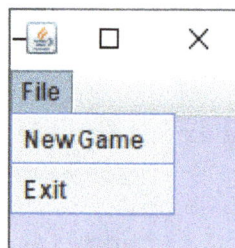

Let's add the controls.

The **GridBagLayout** for the project frame is fairly large (we show it in two segments to fit in the margins):

	gridx = 0	gridx = 1
gridy = 0	dealerLabel	
gridy = 1	dealerCard[0]	dealerCard[1]
gridy = 2	playerLabel	
gridy = 3	playerCard[0]	playerCard[1]
gridy = 4	hitButton	dealButton

	gridx = 2	gridx = 3	gridx = 4	gridx = 5
gridy = 0	dealerTextField			
gridy = 1	dealerCard[2]	dealerCard[3]	dealerCard[4]	dealerCard[5]
gridy = 2	playerTextField			
gridy = 3	playerCard[2]	playerCard[3]	playerCard[4]	playerCard[5]
gridy = 4	stayButton		winningsLabel	winningsTextField

dealerLabel, **playerLabel** and **winningsLabel** are used for titling information. **dealerTextField** and **playerTextField** are used to say who won and who lost. And, **winningsTextfield** displays your winnings. The first six label controls (**dealerCard** array) are used to display the dealer cards, while the other six (**playerCard** array)display the player (your) cards. The three button controls (**hitButton**, **dealButton**, **stayButton**) are used to indicate if you wish to take a hit, stay or deal a new hand. Let's add the dealer controls first.

The control properties are:

dealerLabel:
text	Dealer's Cards
font	Arial, Bold, Size 18
gridx	0
gridy	0
gridwidth	2
anchor	WEST
insets	10, 10, 10, 0

dealerTextField:
size	430, 30
font	Comic Sans MS, Plain, Size 18
background	Color(255, 255, 128), a light yellow
foreground	Blue
horizontalAlignment	Center
editable	false
gridx	2
gridy	0
gridwidth	4
insets	0, 10, 0, 10

dealerCard[0]:
size	100, 50
border	Black line
gridx	0
gridy	1
insets	0, 10, 0, 0

dealerCard[1]:
size	100, 50
border	Black line
gridx	1
gridy	1
insets	0, 10, 0, 0

dealerCard[2]:
size	100, 50
border	Black line
gridx	2
gridy	1
insets	0, 10, 0, 0

dealerCard[3]:

size	100, 50
border	Black line
gridx	3
gridy	1
insets	0, 10, 0, 0

dealerCard[4]:

size	100, 50
border	Black line
gridx	4
gridy	1
insets	0, 10, 0, 0

dealerCard[5]:

size	100, 50
border	Black line
gridx	5
gridy	1
insets	0, 10, 0, 10

Declare these controls using:

```
JLabel dealerLabel = new JLabel();
JTextField dealerTextField = new JTextField();
JLabel[] dealerCard = new JLabel[6];
```

Now, the controls are added to the frame in the frame constructor using:

```
dealerLabel.setText("Dealer's Cards:");
dealerLabel.setFont(new Font("Arial", Font.BOLD, 18));
gridConstraints = new GridBagConstraints();
gridConstraints.gridx = 0;
gridConstraints.gridy = 0;
gridConstraints.gridwidth = 2;
gridConstraints.anchor = GridBagConstraints.WEST;
gridConstraints.insets = new Insets(10, 10, 10, 0);
getContentPane().add(dealerLabel, gridConstraints);
```

```
dealerTextField.setPreferredSize(new Dimension(430, 30));
dealerTextField.setFont(new Font("Comic Sans MS",
Font.PLAIN, 18));
dealerTextField.setBackground(new Color(255, 255, 128));
dealerTextField.setForeground(Color.BLUE);
dealerTextField.setHorizontalAlignment(SwingConstants.CENT
ER);
dealerTextField.setEditable(false);
gridConstraints = new GridBagConstraints();
gridConstraints.gridx = 2;
gridConstraints.gridy = 0;
gridConstraints.gridwidth = 4;
gridConstraints.insets = new Insets(10, 10, 10, 10);
getContentPane().add(dealerTextField, gridConstraints);

for (int i = 0; i < 6; i++)
{
  dealerCard[i] = new JLabel();
  dealerCard[i].setPreferredSize(new Dimension(100, 150));

dealerCard[i].setBorder(BorderFactory.createLineBorder(Col
or.BLACK));
  gridConstraints = new GridBagConstraints();
  gridConstraints.gridx = i;
  gridConstraints.gridy = 1;
  gridConstraints.insets = new Insets(0, 10, 0, 0);
  if (i == 5)
gridConstraints.insets = new Insets(0, 10, 0, 10);
  getContentPane().add(dealerCard[i], gridConstraints);
}
```

Save, run the project. You will see the added controls:

Using nearly identical code, we can add the player controls. Set the properties:

playerLabel:

text	Player's Cards
font	Arial, Bold, Size 18
gridx	0
gridy	2
gridwidth	2
anchor	WEST
insets	10, 10, 10, 0

playerTextField:

size	430, 30
font	Comic Sans MS, Plain, Size 18
background	Color(255, 255, 128), a light yellow
foreground	Blue
horizontalAlignment	Center
editable	false
gridx	2
gridy	2
gridwidth	4
insets	0, 10, 0, 10

playerCard[0]:

size	100, 50
border	Black line
gridx	0
gridy	3
insets	0, 10, 0, 0

playerCard[1]:

size	100, 50
border	Black line
gridx	1
gridy	3
insets	0, 10, 0, 0

playerCard[2]:

size	100, 50
border	Black line
gridx	2
gridy	3
insets	0, 10, 0, 0

playerCard[3]:

size	100, 50
border	Black line
gridx	3
gridy	3
insets	0, 10, 0, 0

playerCard[4]:

size	100, 50
border	Black line
gridx	4
gridy	3
insets	0, 10, 0, 0

playerCard[5]:

size	100, 50
border	Black line
gridx	5
gridy	3
insets	0, 10, 0, 10

Declare these controls using:

```
JLabel playerLabel = new JLabel();
JTextField playerTextField = new JTextField();
JLabel[] playerCard = new JLabel[6];
```

The controls are added to the frame in the frame constructor using:

```
playerLabel.setText("Your Cards:");
playerLabel.setFont(new Font("Arial", Font.BOLD, 18));
gridConstraints = new GridBagConstraints();
gridConstraints.gridx = 0;
gridConstraints.gridy = 2;
gridConstraints.gridwidth = 2;
gridConstraints.anchor = GridBagConstraints.WEST;
gridConstraints.insets = new Insets(10, 10, 10, 0);
getContentPane().add(playerLabel, gridConstraints);

playerTextField.setPreferredSize(new Dimension(430, 30));
playerTextField.setFont(new Font("Comic Sans MS",
Font.PLAIN, 18));
playerTextField.setBackground(new Color(255, 255, 128));
playerTextField.setForeground(Color.BLUE);
playerTextField.setHorizontalAlignment(SwingConstants.CENT
ER);
playerTextField.setEditable(false);
gridConstraints = new GridBagConstraints();
gridConstraints.gridx = 2;
gridConstraints.gridy = 2;
gridConstraints.gridwidth = 4;
gridConstraints.insets = new Insets(10, 10, 10, 10);
getContentPane().add(playerTextField, gridConstraints);
```

```
for (int i = 0; i < 6; i++)
{
  playerCard[i] = new JLabel();
  playerCard[i].setPreferredSize(new Dimension(100, 150));

playerCard[i].setBorder(BorderFactory.createLineBorder(Col
or.BLACK));
  gridConstraints = new GridBagConstraints();
  gridConstraints.gridx = i;
  gridConstraints.gridy = 3;
  gridConstraints.insets = new Insets(0, 10, 0, 0);
  if (i == 5)
gridConstraints.insets = new Insets(0, 10, 0, 10);
  getContentPane().add(playerCard[i], gridConstraints);
}
```

Save, run the project. You will see the newly added player controls:

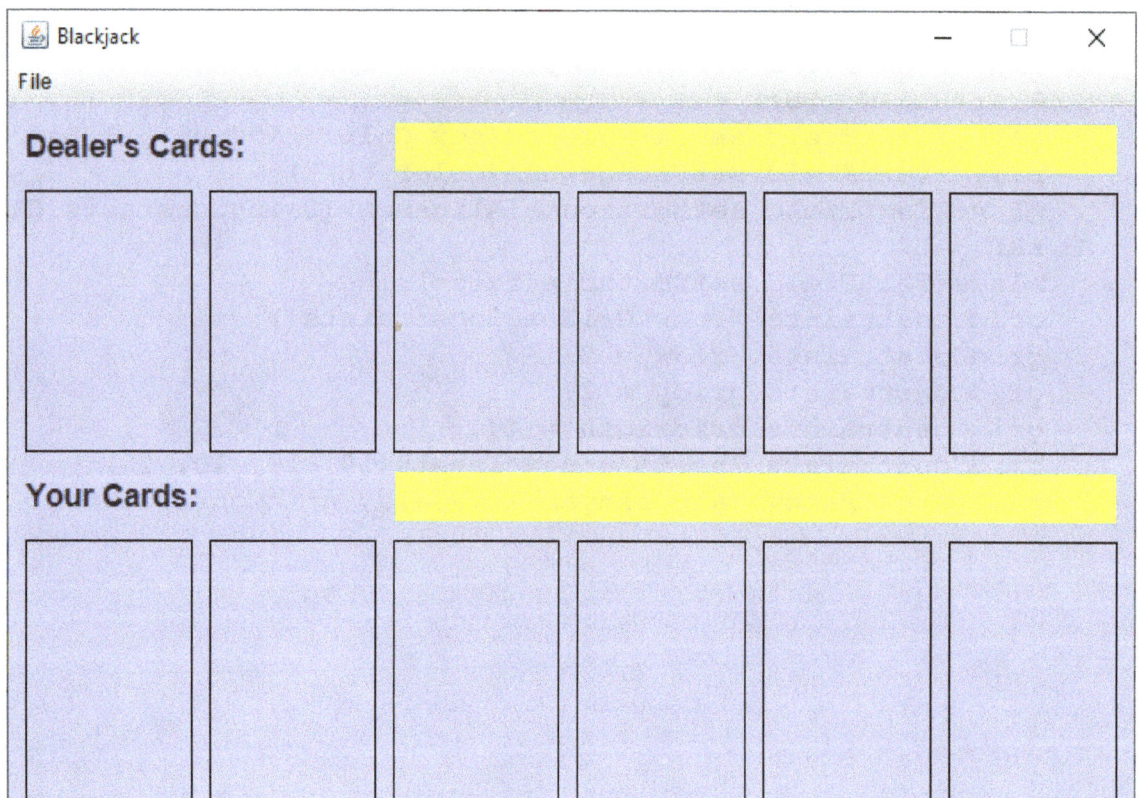

Let's finish by adding the button controls and winnings label and text field. The properties are:

hitButton:

text	Hit
font	Arial, Bold, Size 16
gridx	0
gridy	4
insets	10, 0, 10, 0

dealButton:

text	Deal
font	Arial, Bold, Size 16
gridx	1
gridy	4
insets	10, 0, 10, 0

stayButton:

text	Stay
font	Arial, Bold, Size 16
gridx	2
gridy	4
insets	10, 0, 10, 0

winningsLabel:

text	Winnings
font	Arial, Bold, Size 18
gridx	4
gridy	4
anchor	WEST
insets	10, 10, 10, 0

winningsTextField:

text	0
size	100, 30
font	Comic Sans MS, Plain, Size 18
background	White
foreground	Blue
horizontalAlignment	Center
editable	false
gridx	5
gridy	4
insets	10, 0, 10, 0

Declare these controls using:

```
JButton hitButton = new JButton();
JButton dealButton = new JButton();
JButton stayButton = new JButton();
JLabel winningsLabel = new JLabel();
JTextField winningsTextField = new JTextField();
```

Add them to the frame using:

```
hitButton.setText("Hit");
hitButton.setFont(new Font("Arial", Font.BOLD, 16));
gridConstraints = new GridBagConstraints();
gridConstraints.gridx = 0;
gridConstraints.gridy = 4;
gridConstraints.insets = new Insets(10, 0, 10, 0);
getContentPane().add(hitButton, gridConstraints);
hitButton.addActionListener(new ActionListener()
{
  public void actionPerformed(ActionEvent e)
  {
    hitButtonActionPerformed(e);
  }
});

dealButton.setText("Deal");
dealButton.setFont(new Font("Arial", Font.BOLD, 16));
gridConstraints = new GridBagConstraints();
gridConstraints.gridx = 1;
gridConstraints.gridy = 4;
gridConstraints.insets = new Insets(10, 0, 10, 0);
getContentPane().add(dealButton, gridConstraints);
dealButton.addActionListener(new ActionListener()
{
  public void actionPerformed(ActionEvent e)
  {
    dealButtonActionPerformed(e);
  }
});
```

```
stayButton.setText("Stay");
stayButton.setFont(new Font("Arial", Font.BOLD, 16));
gridConstraints = new GridBagConstraints();
gridConstraints.gridx = 2;
gridConstraints.gridy = 4;
gridConstraints.insets = new Insets(10, 0, 10, 0);
getContentPane().add(stayButton, gridConstraints);
stayButton.addActionListener(new ActionListener()
{
  public void actionPerformed(ActionEvent e)
  {
    stayButtonActionPerformed(e);
  }
});

winningsLabel.setText("Winnings:");
winningsLabel.setFont(new Font("Arial", Font.BOLD, 18));
gridConstraints = new GridBagConstraints();
gridConstraints.gridx = 4;
gridConstraints.gridy = 4;
gridConstraints.anchor = GridBagConstraints.WEST;
gridConstraints.insets = new Insets(10, 10, 10, 0);
getContentPane().add(winningsLabel, gridConstraints);

winningsTextField.setText("0");
winningsTextField.setPreferredSize(new Dimension(100,
30));
winningsTextField.setFont(new Font("Comic Sans MS",
Font.PLAIN, 18));
winningsTextField.setBackground(Color.WHITE);
winningsTextField.setForeground(Color.BLUE);
winningsTextField.setHorizontalAlignment(SwingConstants.CE
NTER);
winningsTextField.setEditable(false);
gridConstraints = new GridBagConstraints();
gridConstraints.gridx = 5;
gridConstraints.gridy = 4;
gridConstraints.insets = new Insets(10, 0, 10, 0);
getContentPane().add(winningsTextField, gridConstraints);
```

The code above adds a **ActionPerformed** method for each button.. Add these empty methods:

```
private void hitButtonActionPerformed(ActionEvent e)
{
}

private void dealButtonActionPerformed(ActionEvent e)
{
}

private void stayButtonActionPerformed(ActionEvent e)
{
}
```

Save, run one more time:

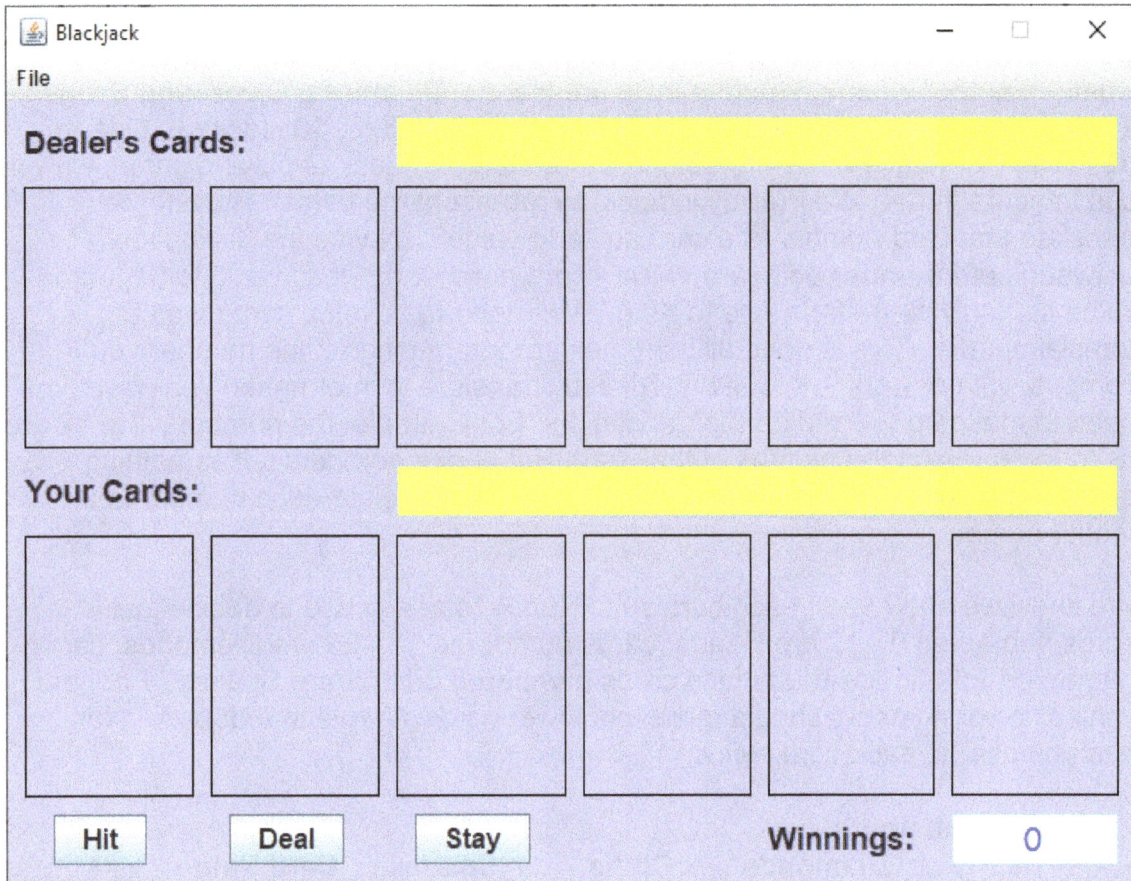

This completes the frame design.

We will begin writing code for the application. Many tasks are repeated in the Blackjack card game. We need to shuffle a deck of cards, deal a new hand, display cards for the dealer and player as play continues, and end a hand when a winner is declared. The approach we take is to build the code in modules that perform these repeated tasks. As we build the modules (general methods), we use them to write code for the event methods. One drawback to this modular approach is that we will have to write lots of code before anything can be tested. You may want to occasionally compile new code as it's built to make sure you don't get any unexpected errors. As a first step, we write the code that defines a deck of cards.

Code Design – Card Definition

Defining a card consists of answering two questions: what is the card suit and what is the card value? The four suits are Hearts, Diamonds, Clubs, and Spades. The thirteen card values are: Ace (A), 2, 3, 4, 5, 6, 7, 8, 9, 10, Jack (J), Queen (Q), King (K). Since there are 52 cards in a standard deck of playing cards, we will use integers from 0 to 51 (array indices) to represent the cards. How do we translate that card number to a card suit and value? (Notice the distinction between card **number** and card **value** - card number ranges from 0 to 51, card value can only range from Ace to King.) We need to develop some type of translation rule. This is done all the time in programming. If the number you compute with or work with does not directly translate to information you need, you need to make up rules to do the translation. For example, the numbers 1 to 12 are used to represent the months of the year. But, these numbers tell us nothing about the names of the month - we need a rule to translate each number to a month name.

We know we need 13 of each card suit. Hence, an easy rule to decide suit is: cards numbered 0 - 12 are Hearts, cards numbered 13 - 25 are Diamonds, cards numbered 26 - 38 are Clubs, and cards numbered 39 - 51 are Spades. For card values, lower numbers should represent lower cards. A rule that does this for each number in each card suit is:

| Card Numbers | | | | |
Hearts	Diamonds	Clubs	Spades	Card Value
0	13	26	39	A
1	14	27	40	2
2	15	28	41	3
3	16	29	42	4
4	17	30	43	5
5	18	31	44	6
6	19	32	45	7
7	20	33	46	8
8	21	34	47	9
9	22	35	48	10
10	23	36	49	J
11	24	37	50	Q
12	25	38	51	K

As examples, notice card number 11 is a Queen of Hearts. Card number 30 is a 5 of Clubs. These card numbers will be used to establish the graphics file associated with the card.

As mentioned, a card number is used to establish the graphics file that represents the corresponding card. In the **\HomeJava\HomeJava Projects\Card Graphics** folder are 52 graphics files (**gif** files) that represent the 52 playing cards. These files are named **CARD00.GIF** to **CARD51.GIF**. And, yes, the file numbers (the last two digits in the name) correspond to the card numbers we've assigned. So **CARD11.GIF** is a Queen of Hearts and **CARD30.GIF** is a 5 of Clubs. So, once we know a card number, we know which file is used to display that card. Just how are these files used in the Blackjack program?

Two approaches can be taken to display cards in the Blackjack program. The first is that whenever a card must be displayed in a label control, we could load the appropriate file into a label control using the **ImageIcon** constructor. In this approach, every time a card is needed, the program would have to find the file and load it from disk. This approach would require multiple accesses to disk files, slowing down the program. The second approach (and the one we use) is to preload all graphics files (still using the **ImageIcon** constructor) into an array of **ImageIcon** objects. Then, when a card must be displayed, we simply set the **icon** property of the label control displaying a card to the **ImageIcon** object representing the card. This is a much faster approach and only requires opening the graphics files one time. The preloading of images is done at the end of the frame's constructor code.

Before coding this, we address where the graphics files should be located in the project file structure. The accepted standard for storing needed files (graphics files, sound files, data files, configuration files) is to place them in the project folder. We will keep all the graphics files in this folder. Copy the 52 card graphics (plus the file **CARDBACK.GIF**, which holds the graphics to represent the back of a card) into your project's folder. If you want, open and view the **\HomeJava\HomeJava Projects\Blackjack** folder to see these files in the included project.

We will define 53 **ImageIcon** objects for card display – one for the card back (**cardBack**) and an array of 52 images (**cardImage**) for the individual cards. These will be class level variables in our program. Add these declarations to your project:

```
ImageIcon cardBack;
ImageIcon[] cardImage = new ImageIcon[52];
```

Now, the frame constructor code that establishes each **ImageIcon** object is:

```
String cn;
// load card images and determine points for each
cardBack = new ImageIcon("CARDBACK.GIF");
for (int cardNumber = 0; cardNumber < 52; cardNumber++)
{
  cn = String.valueOf(cardNumber);
  if (cardNumber < 10)
cn = "0" + cn;
  cardImage[cardNumber] = new ImageIcon("CARD" + cn +
".GIF");
}
```

In this code, we first set **cardBack**. Then, for all 52 cards, we form the appropriate file name using string functions and load the 52 **cardImage** values from files.

Add this new code at the end of the frame constructor, then save and run the project. If the program runs without errors (the frame appears), this tells you that all needed files are properly located in your project folder. If there are errors, you need to correct them. Want to really see if things worked? Add this temporary line at the end of the frame constructor:

```
dealerCard[0].setIcon(cardImage[11]);
```

This should display the Queen of Hearts in the first dealer card. Give it a try. If things work, you will see:

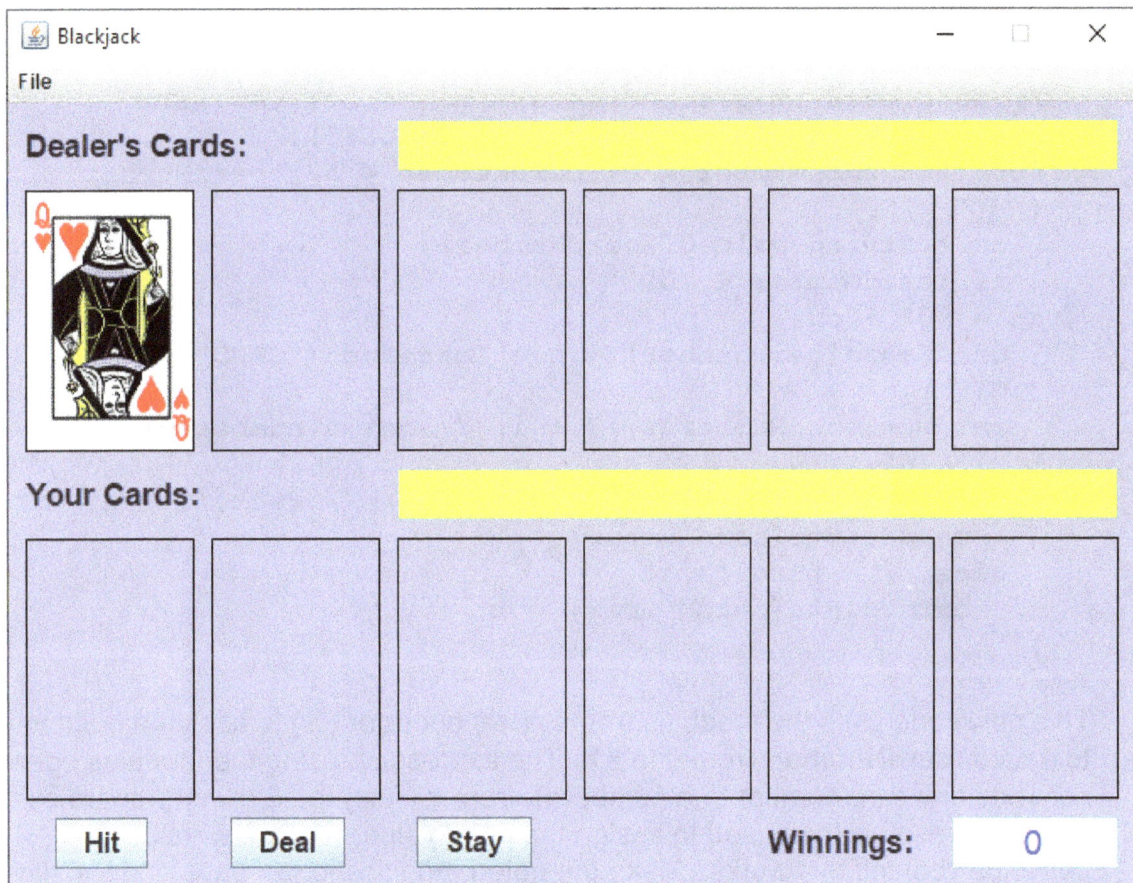

Remove the line you just added.

At this point, we have an array (**cardImage**) of the graphics used to represent each of the 52 cards. In Blackjack, each card also has a point value. An Ace (initially, at least) is worth 1 point, the cards 2 through 10 have point values equal to their card value. And, the face cards (Jack, Queen, King) are each worth 10 points. A class level array (**cardPoints**) is used to hold the point value for each card. Add this declaration:

```
int[] cardPoints = new int[52];
```

Modify the frame constructor code to establish the elements of this array (changes are shaded):

```
String cn;
// load card images and determine points for each
cardBack = new ImageIcon("CARDBACK.GIF");
for (int cardNumber = 0; cardNumber < 52; cardNumber++)
{
  cn = String.valueOf(cardNumber);
  if (cardNumber < 10)
cn = "0" + cn;
  cardImage[cardNumber] = new ImageIcon("CARD" + cn +
".GIF");
  int i = cardNumber % 13 + 1; // get a number from 1 (A)
to 13 (K)
  if (i == 11 || i == 12 || i == 13) // Jack, Queen, King
    cardPoints[cardNumber] = 10;
  else // A through 10
    cardPoints[cardNumber] = i;
}
```

This new code uses the modulus (remainder) operator (%) to assign a point value to a card (**cardNumber**) from 0 to 51. The expression using the modulus operator converts any card number to a number (**i**) from 1 (Ace) to 13 (King), regardless of suit. The result is then used to assign the point value. Try a few values to convince yourself this works. Make the noted modifications. Save and run the project, if you'd like.

We now have all the information we need to define a card. The array **cardImage** has images for specific cards, while the array **cardPoints** has the corresponding point values. The index on the array, called the **card number**, ranges from 0 to 51 (Ace of Hearts to King of Spades). Let's learn how to "shuffle" these cards.

Code Design – Card Shuffle

With 52 cards, we need to randomly sort the integers from 0 to 51 to "simulate" the shuffling process. How do we do this?

Usually when we need a computer version of something we can do without a computer, it is fairly easy to write down the steps taken and duplicate them in code. When we shuffle a deck of cards, we separate the deck in two parts, then interleaf the cards as we fan each part, making that familiar shuffling noise. I don't know how you could write code to do this. We'll take another approach which is hard or tedious to do off the computer, but is easy to do on a computer.

We perform what is called a "one card shuffle." In a one card shuffle, you pull a single card (at random) out of the deck and lay it aside on a pile. Repeat this 52 times and the cards are shuffled. Try it! I think you see this idea is simple, but doing a one card shuffle with a real deck of cards would be awfully time-consuming. We'll use the idea of a one card shuffle here, with a slight twist. Rather than lay the selected card on a pile, we will swap it with the bottom card in the stack of cards remaining to be shuffled. This takes the selected card out of the deck and replaces it with the remaining bottom card. The result is the same as if we lay it aside.

Here's how the shuffle works with n numbers:

> ➢ Start with a list of n consecutive integers.
> ➢ Randomly pick one item from the list. Swap that item with the last item. You now have one fewer items in the list to be sorted (called the remaining list), or n is now n - 1.
> ➢ Randomly pick one item from the remaining list. Swap it with the item on the bottom of the remaining list. Again, your remaining list now has one fewer items.
> ➢ Repeatedly remove one item from the remaining list and swap it with the item on the bottom of the remaining list until you have run out of items. When done, the list will have been replaced with the original list in random order.

The code to do a one card shuffle, or sort n integers, is placed in a general method named **sortIntegers**. The single argument is **n** the number of integers to sort. The method returns an array containing the randomly sorted integers. The returned array is zero-based, returning random integers from 0 to n - 1, not 1 to n. If you need integers from 1 to n, just simply add 1 to each value in the returned array! The code is:

```java
private int[] sortIntegers(int n)
{
   /*
    *   Returns n randomly sorted integers 0 -> n - 1
    */
   int[] sortedArray = new int[n];
   int temp, s;
   Random sortRandom = new Random();
   //  initialize array from 0 to n - 1
   for (int i = 0; i < n; i++)
   {
      sortedArray[i] = i;
   }
   //  i is number of items remaining in list
   for (int i = n; i >= 1; i--)
   {
      s = sortRandom.nextInt(i);
      temp = sortedArray[s];
      sortedArray[s] = sortedArray[i - 1];
      sortedArray[i - 1] = temp;
   }
   return(sortedArray);
}
```

You should be able to see each step of the shuffle method. This method is general (sorting n integers) and can be used in other projects requiring random lists of integers. Since we are using a random number, we need the following import statement:

```java
import java.util.Random;
```

Add the **sortIntegers** method (and the import statement) to your Blackjack project. It will be used every time we need to shuffle the 52 cards. In the project, we will use a class level array **card** (dimensioned to 52) to hold the randomly sorted integers (the shuffled cards). A class level variable **currentCard** will be used to indicate the current index of the **card** array being used. Add these declarations to your project:

```
int[] card = new int[52];
int currentCard;
```

The snippet of code that does a shuffle is:

```
card = sortIntegers(52);
currentCard = 0;
```

In this code, we obtain the shuffled cards in **card** and set **currentCard** to zero so we are 'pointing' to the first card (array index zero) in the deck.

We can now use the shuffling process and card descriptions to begin building modules to play the Blackjack game.

Code Design – Start New Game

To start a new **Blackjack** game, a user chooses **New Game** from the **File** menu. The steps in this method are:

> ➤ Set winnings to zero and reset winnings display.
> ➤ Shuffle cards.
> ➤ Start a new hand.

A class level variable **winnings** is used to track the player's winnings. Add this declaration to the project:

```
int winnings;
```

The code for the **newMenuItemActionPerformed** method is:

```
private void newMenuItemActionPerformed(ActionEvent e)
{
  // start new game - clear winnings and start over
  winnings = 0;
  winningsTextField.setText("0");
  card = sortIntegers(52);
  currentCard = 0;
  newHand();
}
```

Add this method to the project – the steps are obvious. This method uses a general method **newHand** to start a new hand of Blackjack. We will code that next, but let's take care of a couple of other tasks first.

Add the **exitMenuItemActionPerformed** method:

```
private void exitMenuItemActionPerformed(ActionEvent e)
{
  System.exit(0);
}
```

When the Blackjack program first begins, we also want to start a new game. Add this single line at the end of the frame constructor:

```
newMenuItem.doClick();
```

This line will cause the **newMenuItemActionPerformed** method to be executed:

Now, we'll code the **newHand** method.

Code Design – Start New Hand

Each "round" of Blackjack begins with a new hand. In a new hand, two dealer cards (one face down) and two player cards are displayed and the interface is set so the player can begin playing his hand. Many steps are required to start a new hand:

> ➢ Clear all cards.
> ➢ Clear dealer and player comments.
> ➢ Enable **Hit** button.
> ➢ Enable **Stay** button.
> ➢ Disable **Deal** button.
> ➢ Reshuffle if necessary (if more than 35 cards have been used).
> ➢ Add two cards to dealer hand.
> ➢ Add two cards to player hand.
> ➢ Check if either hand is a Blackjack. If so, end the hand.

Six class level variables are used to know the status of the dealer and player hands. Add these declarations:

```
int numberCardsDealer, acesDealer, scoreDealer;
int numberCardsPlayer, acesPlayer, scorePlayer;
```

numberCardsDealer tells us how many cards are currently in the dealer's hand, **acesDealer** tells us how many of those cards are Aces, and **scoreDealer** tells us the dealer point total. We track Aces separately since their score can be either a 1 or 11. **numberCardsPlayer** tells us how many cards are currently in the player's hand, **acesPlayer** tells us how many of those cards are Aces, and **scorePlayer** tells us the player point total. In the **newHand** method, all of these will be initialized at zero, prior to adding cards to the hands.

The **newHand** general method that implements the listed steps is:

```
private void newHand()
{
  // Deal a new hand
  // Clear table of cards
  for (int i = 0; i < 6; i++)
  {
    dealerCard[i].setIcon(null);
    playerCard[i].setIcon(null);
  }
  dealerTextField.setText("");
  playerTextField.setText("");
  hitButton.setEnabled(true);
  stayButton.setEnabled(true);
  dealButton.setEnabled(false);
  // reshuffle occasionally
  if (currentCard > 34)
  {
    card = sortIntegers(52);
    currentCard = 0;
  }
  // Get two dealer cards
  scoreDealer = 0;
  acesDealer = 0;
  numberCardsDealer = 0;
  addDealerCard();
  addDealerCard();
  // Get two player cards
  scorePlayer = 0;
  acesPlayer = 0;
  numberCardsPlayer = 0;
  addPlayerCard();
  addPlayerCard();
  // Check for blackjacks
  if (scoreDealer == 11 && acesDealer == 1)
    scoreDealer = 21;
  if (scorePlayer == 11 && acesPlayer == 1)
    scorePlayer = 21;
  if (scoreDealer == 21 && scorePlayer == 21)
    endHand("Dealer has Blackjack!", "And, you have
Blackjack .. a push!", 0);
  else if (scoreDealer == 21)
    endHand("Dealer has Blackjack!", "You lose ...", -10);
  else if (scorePlayer == 21)
    endHand("Dealer loses ...", "You have Blackjack!",
15);
```

```
}
```

Let's look at the **newHand** method in a little detail. The cards are cleared by setting the label control **icon** properties to **null**. A reshuffle is done when **currenCard** is greater than **34**. The dealer hand status variables are set to zero and two cards are added to the dealer hand using a general method **addDealerCard**. Similarly for the player's hand, two cards are added using **addPlayerCard**. We will write these methods soon (they update the three status variables for the dealer and player).

The last part of the method checks each hand for Blackjack (having an Ace and a card worth 10 points, a 10, a Jack, a Queen, or a King). If either has a Blackjack, the general method **endHand** is called. In this method, appropriate messages are displayed and the player's winnings are updated. The messages and winnings change are passed as arguments to the method.

Add the **newHand** method to your project. We still can't test the project. We still need three more methods which we'll code next – **endHand**, **addDealerCard**, **addPlayerCard**.

Code Design – End Hand

When a hand has ended, we want to tell the player whether he/she won and update their winnings. A new hand can then be dealt. The steps involved in ending a hand are:

> ➢ Display the dealer's face down card (just to make sure it is showing)
> ➢ Display dealer and player comments.
> ➢ Update **winnings** and display new value.
> ➢ Disable **Hit** button.
> ➢ Disable **Stay** button.
> ➢ Enable **Deal** button.

Since the first dealer card is shown face down (unless there is a Blackjack or until the player stays or busts), we need a variable to hold that card's image (**dealerFaceDown**). This variable will be established in the **addDealerCard** method. Add this declaration to your project:

```
ImageIcon dealerFaceDown;
```

The **endHand** general method that accomplishes the above tasks is:

```
private void endHand(String dealerComment, String
playerComment, int change)
{
  // make sure dealer cards are seen
  dealerCard[0].setIcon(dealerFaceDown);
  dealerTextField.setText(dealerComment);
  playerTextField.setText(playerComment);
  // Hand has ended - update winnings
  winnings += change;
  winningsTextField.setText(String.valueOf(winnings));
  hitButton.setEnabled(false);
  stayButton.setEnabled(false);
  dealButton.setEnabled(true);
}
```

Note (as seen in **newHand**) the dealer and player comments along with the amount to update the player's winnings are passed as arguments to the method. Add this method to the project.

Just two more methods and we can see if all this works! We need to add cards to the dealer and player hands.

Code Design – Display Dealer Card

Here, we build a general method to add a card to the dealer's hand and display that card. The **currentCard** variable, used with the **card** array, identifies the card added to the dealer's hand. Recall three class level variables (**numberCardsDealer**, **acesDealer**, **scoreDealer**) are used to provide specifics about the dealer's hand. Also, recall **dealerFaceDown** saves the dealer's face down card.

Knowing **currentCard**, the steps involved in adding a card to the dealer's hand are:

> ➢ Determine **cardNumber** from the **card** array.
> ➢ Increment **numberCardsDealer**.
> ➢ If displaying first card:
>> o Set **dealerFaceDown** to **cardImage[cardNumber]**.
>> o Set **dealerCard[0] icon** to **cardBack**.
> ➢ If display second through sixth card:
>> o Set appropriate dealer card label control **icon** to **cardImage[cardNumber]**.
> ➢ Increment dealer's score by **cardPoint[cardNumber]**
> ➢ Increment **acesDealer**, if card is an Ace.
> ➢ Increment **currentCard**.

In these steps, if we are adding the first card, we save the image and display the card back. For other cards, the appropriate image is displayed. We then update the score, noting if an Ace has been added. As a last step, the current card index is incremented by one. At all times, we know the status of the dealer's hand (number of cards, number of aces and score).

The steps of the process to add a card to the dealer's hand are coded in a general method named **addDealerCard**:

```
private void addDealerCard()
{
  int cardNumber;
  cardNumber = card[currentCard];
  // Adds a card to dealer hand
  numberCardsDealer++;
  switch (numberCardsDealer)
  {
    case 1:
      dealerFaceDown = cardImage[cardNumber];
      dealerCard[0].setIcon(cardBack);
      break;
    case 2:
      dealerCard[1].setIcon(cardImage[cardNumber]);
      break;
    case 3:
      dealerCard[2].setIcon(cardImage[cardNumber]);
      break;
    case 4:
      dealerCard[3].setIcon(cardImage[cardNumber]);
      break;
    case 5:
      dealerCard[4].setIcon(cardImage[cardNumber]);
      break;
    case 6:
      dealerCard[5].setIcon(cardImage[cardNumber]);
      break;
  }
  scoreDealer += cardPoints[cardNumber];
  if (cardPoints[cardNumber] == 1)
    acesDealer++;
  currentCard++;
}
```

Add this method to your project. Notice the score (**scoreDealer**) always considers Aces as a single point. This may change when final hands are considered.

Code Design – Display Player Card

The method to add a card to the player's hand is similar to the code just developed. The only difference is that there is never a 'face-down' card in the player's hand. The **currentCard** variable, used with the **card** array, identifies the card added to the player's hand. Three class level variables (**numberCardsPlayer**, **acesPlayer**, **scorePlayer**) are used to provide specifics about the player's hand.

Knowing **currentCard**, the steps involved in adding a card to the player's hand are:

> ➢ Determine **cardNumber** from the **card** array.
> ➢ Increment **numberCardsPlayer**.
> ➢ Set appropriate player card label control **icon** to **cardImage[cardNumber]**.
> ➢ Increment player's score by **cardPoints[cardNumber]**
> ➢ Increment **acesPlayer**, if card is an Ace.
> ➢ Increment **currentCard**.

In these steps, the appropriate image is displayed. We then update the score, noting if an Ace has been added. As a last step, the current card index is incremented by one. At all times, we know the status of the player's hand (number of cards, number of aces and score).

The steps of the process to add a card to the player's hand are coded in a general method named **addPlayerCard**:

```
private void addPlayerCard()
{
  int cardNumber;
  cardNumber = card[currentCard];
  // Adds a card to player hand
  numberCardsPlayer++;
  switch (numberCardsPlayer)
  {
    case 1:
      playerCard[0].setIcon(cardImage[cardNumber]);
      break;
    case 2:
      playerCard[1].setIcon(cardImage[cardNumber]);
      break;
    case 3:
      playerCard[2].setIcon(cardImage[cardNumber]);
      break;
    case 4:
      playerCard[3].setIcon(cardImage[cardNumber]);
      break;
    case 5:
      playerCard[4].setIcon(cardImage[cardNumber]);
      break;
    case 6:
      playerCard[5].setIcon(cardImage[cardNumber]);
      break;
  }
  scorePlayer += cardPoints[cardNumber];
  if (cardPoints[cardNumber] == 1)
    acesPlayer++;
  currentCard++;
}
```

Add this method to your project. Again, notice the score (**scorePlayer**) always considers Aces as a single point. This may change when final hands are considered.

After all the code we have added, we are finally at a point to try running the project. Save and run the project to make sure there are no syntax errors in the code. If there are no errors, the frame with the first hand should appear. Here's what I see:

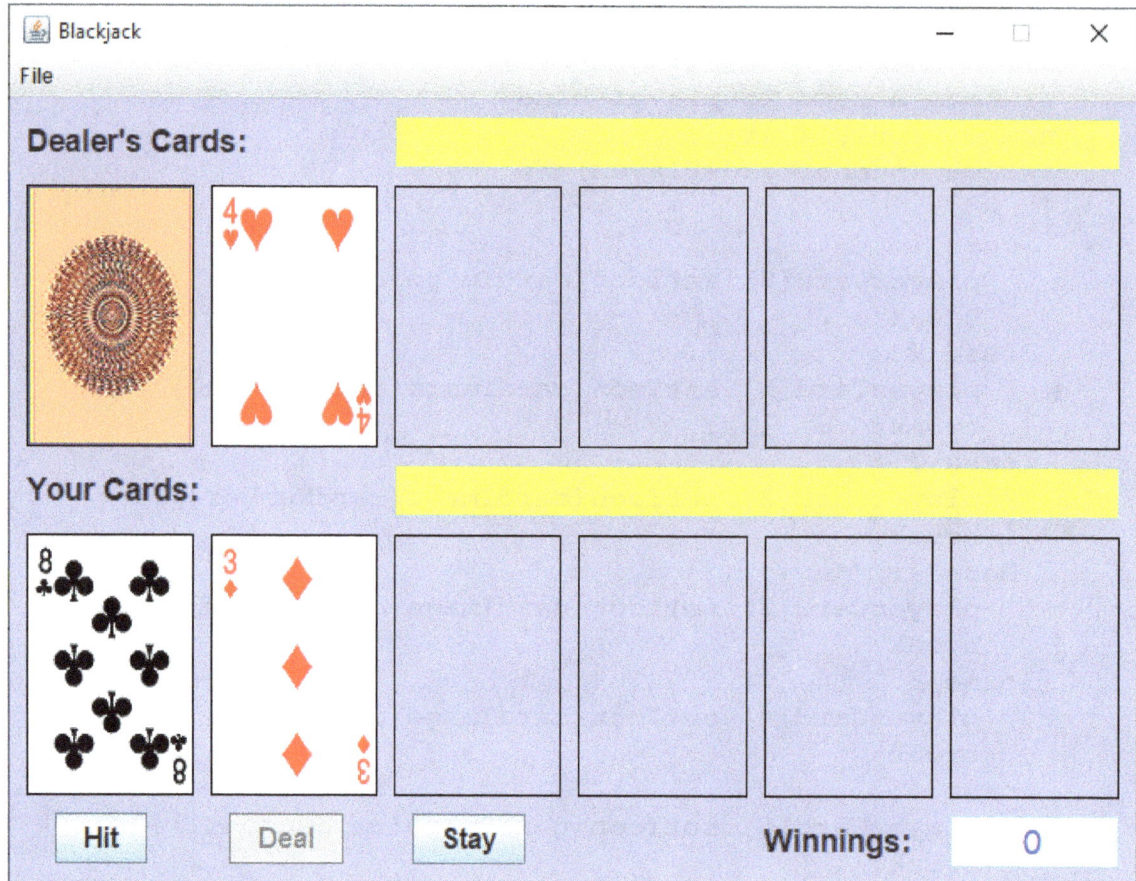

You should see something similar, unless there is a Blackjack. If one of the first hands is a Blackjack, you will see messages to say so and the frame will be set so a new hand can be dealt (the **Deal** button will be enabled).

If you encounter syntax errors in trying to run the project, you need to go back over all the code and see what went wrong. Hopefully, by taking things slow and step-by-step, fixing problems should be straightforward. In the current mode, the user can click **Hit** or **Stay**. If there is a Blackjack, the user can click **Deal**. The last remaining programming tasks are to code the **ActionPerformed** events for these three buttons. The general methods we have written will help in this additional coding. The **Deal** button has the simplest coding, so we'll do it first.

Code Design – Deal New Hand

When a hand has ended, the user can either start a new game, exit the program or deal a new hand. We have already coded methods for starting a new game and exiting the program. Here we write code for dealing a new hand, once the user clicks the **Deal** button.

The code for the **dealButtonActionPerformed** method is made simple because of all the code we have already developed. It is a single line of code that calls the existing **newHand** method:

```
private void dealButtonActionPerformed(ActionEvent e)
{
  newHand();
}
```

Add this method to the project.

Code Design – Player 'Hit'

When a player chooses the **Hit** button, a new card is added to his/her hand and the results evaluated. The steps are:

> ➢ Add a player card.
> ➢ If player's score exceeds 21, end hand announcing player has busted.
> ➢ If player has 6 cards, end hand announcing player has won.

As mentioned earlier in this chapter, this last step is a special rule used in our version of Blackjack.

The code is placed in the **hitButtonActionPerformed** method:

```
private void hitButtonActionPerformed(ActionEvent e)
{
 // Add a card if player requests
  addPlayerCard();
  if (scorePlayer > 21)
    endHand("Dealer wins", "You busted!", -10);
  else if (numberCardsPlayer == 6)
    endHand("No dealer play", "You win - 6 cards and not
over 21!", 10);
}
```

Add this method to the project.

Save and run the project. Try the **Hit** button. Keep adding cards until you bust (exceed 21) or get 6 cards. You can't choose to **Stay** – we need to write some code behind that method. Once you bust or get 6 cards, you can click **Deal** to try again. You won't be able to test the **Hit** button if there is an initial Blackjack. In this case, click the **Deal** button until hands without a Blackjack appear. Then try the **Hit** button.

Code Design – Player 'Stay'

We save the most detailed event– clicking the **Stay** button - for last. Lots of things need to happen in this code. We need to determine player's final score, then allow the dealer to play out his hand according to the fixed set of rules. There are lots of decisions to be made. The method steps are:

> ➤ Disable **Hit** button.
> ➤ Disable **Stay** button.
> ➤ Determine player's highest possible score without exceeding 21 (accounting for any aces).
> ➤ Display the dealer's face down card.
> ➤ Play dealer's hand (repeat all steps until hand is ended):
>   ○ Determine dealer's highest possible score without exceeding 21 (accounting for any aces).
>   ○ If dealer's score is above 16, determine winner and end hand.
>   ○ If dealer has six cards and still under 16, end hand and declare dealer the winner.
>   ○ Add card to dealer's hand.
>   ○ If above 21, end hand and declare player the winner.

As you can see most of the logic is in playing the dealer's hand. Also, notice the special "six card" rule we use.

Determining either the player's or dealer's score (considering the possibility of Aces) is a little tricky. Let's look at a snippet of code that does the task for the player:

```
if (acesPlayer != 0 && scorePlayer <= 11)
{
  scorePlayer += 10;
  acesPlayer--;
}
```

Recall the running score (**scorePlayer**) always considers Aces as one point. If the player has no Aces, there is no score adjustment. Otherwise 10 points is added to the score, if that adjusted score would not exceed 21. If a player has multiple Aces, only one can count for 11 points (would exceed 21, otherwise). Similar code is used for the dealer score.

The **stayButtonActionPerformed** method is:

```java
private void stayButtonActionPerformed(ActionEvent e)
{
  boolean dealerDone = false;
  int scoreTemp, acesTemp;
  hitButton.setEnabled(false);
  stayButton.setEnabled(false);
  // Check for aces in player hand and adjust score
  // to highest possible
  if (acesPlayer != 0 && scorePlayer <= 11)
  {
    scorePlayer += 10;
    acesPlayer--;
  }
  // Uncover dealer face down card and play dealer hand
  dealerCard[0].setIcon(dealerFaceDown);
  do
  {
    scoreTemp = scoreDealer;
    acesTemp = acesDealer;
    // Check for aces and adjust score
    if (acesTemp != 0 && scoreDealer <= 11)
    {
      scoreTemp += 10;
      acesTemp--;
    }
    // add card unless score above 16 or dealer has 6
cards
    if (scoreTemp > 16)
    {
      if (scoreTemp > scorePlayer)
        endHand("Dealer wins with " +
String.valueOf(scoreTemp), "You lose with " +
String.valueOf(scorePlayer), -10);
      else if (scoreTemp == scorePlayer)
        endHand("Dealer has " + String.valueOf(scoreTemp),
"So do you ... a push!", 0);
      else
        endHand("Dealer loses with " +
String.valueOf(scoreTemp), "You win with " +
String.valueOf(scorePlayer), 10);
      dealerDone = true;
      continue;
    }
    else if (numberCardsDealer == 6)
    {
```

```
      endHand("Dealer wins ... 6 cards and not over 16!",
"You lose ...", -10);
      dealerDone = true;
      continue;
    }
    else
    {
      addDealerCard();
      // dealer loses if busted
      if (scoreDealer > 21)
      {
        endHand("Dealer busts!", "You win!!", 10);
        dealerDone = true;
        continue;
      }
    }
  }
  while (!dealerDone);
}
```

We use a boolean variable **dealerDone** to let us know when the dealer is done playing his cards. Notice the code to determine player and dealer scores. For the dealer, we use temporary variables (**scoreTemp** and **acesTemp**) to represent the dealer score. We don't want to destroy the values of **scoreDealer** and **acesDealer** in case more cards may be added. A **do/while** structure is implemented to allow the dealer to continue to add cards to his hand until the hand ends. Notice whenever a call to **endHand** is encountered, it is followed by setting **dealerDone** to **true** and a **continue** statement to move to the **while** statement so the dealer no longer adds cards. Add this final method to the project.

Save and run the project. You should now have a complete, running version of the Blackjack game. Have fun playing it! See if you can come up with some kind of winning strategy. Here's the first game I played. I won after taking a couple of hits and staying:

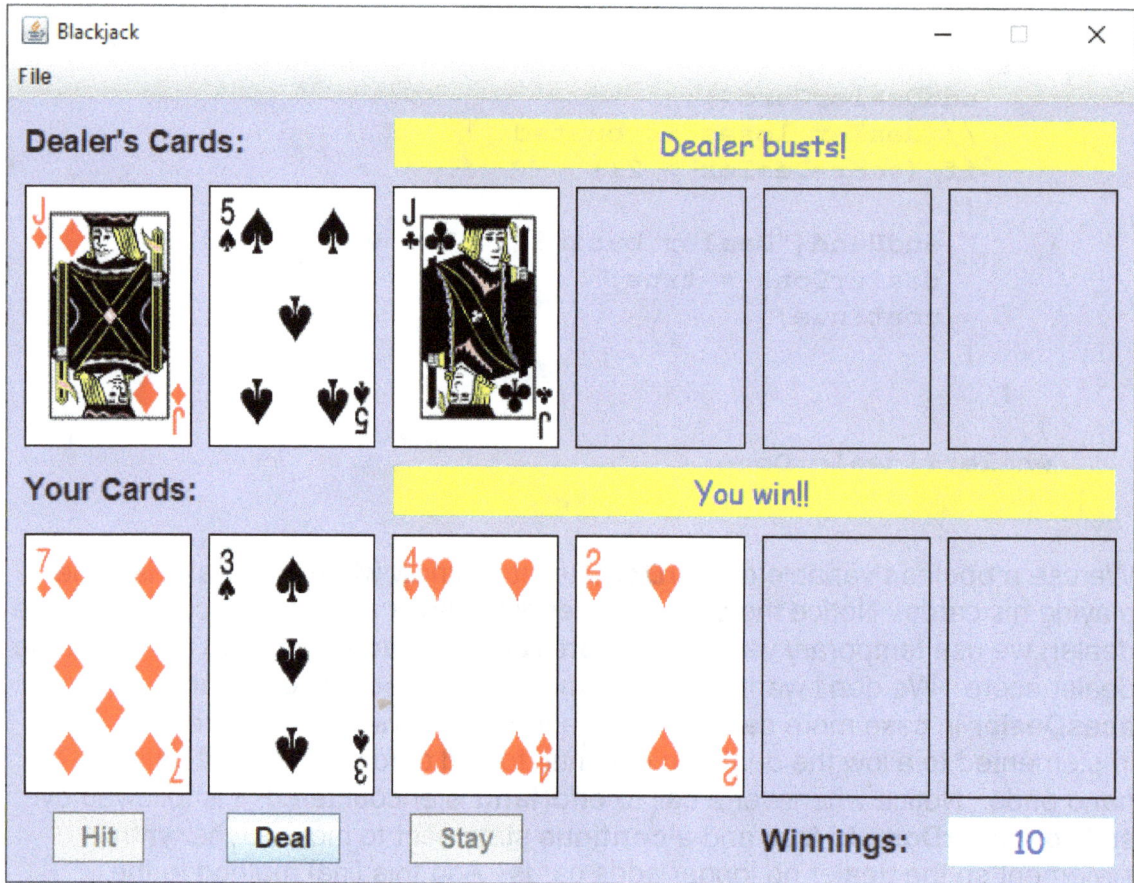

My luck ran out in the next hand though – the Dealer got Blackjack:

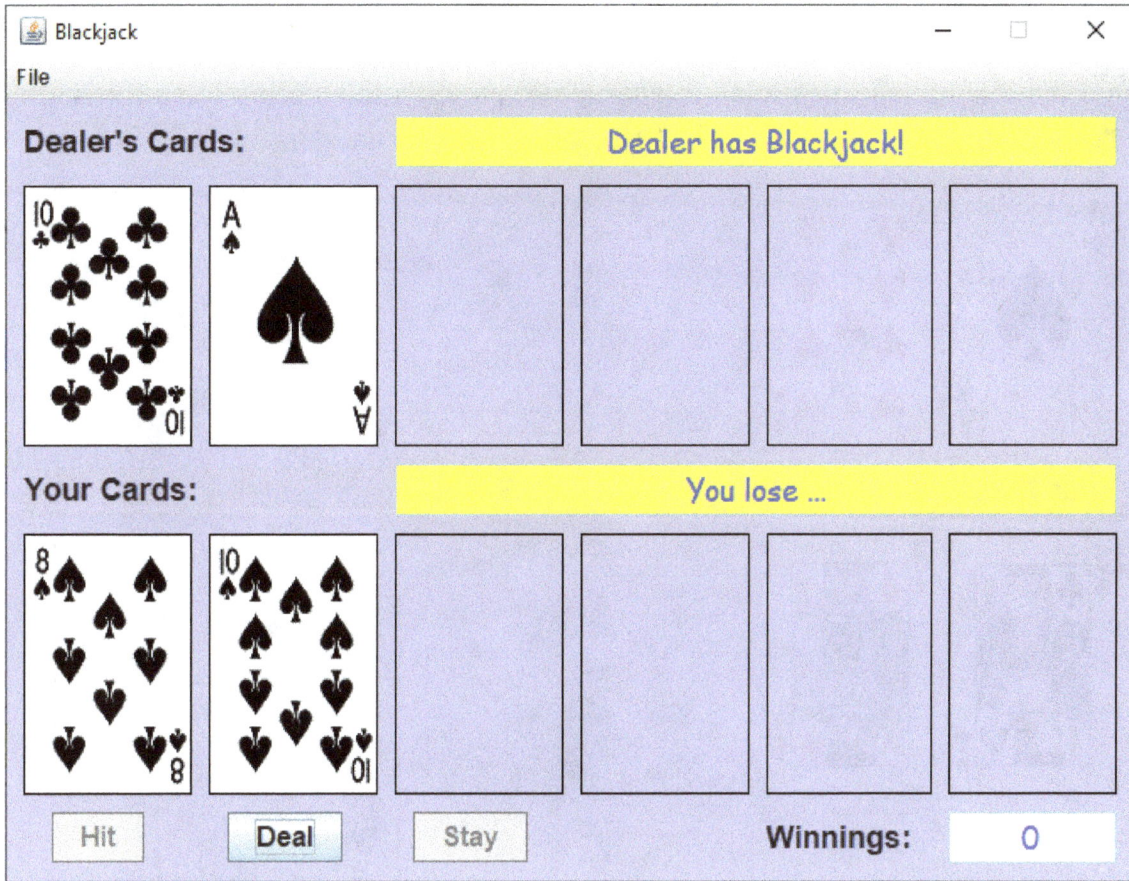

In a later game, the dealer and I tied (a push):

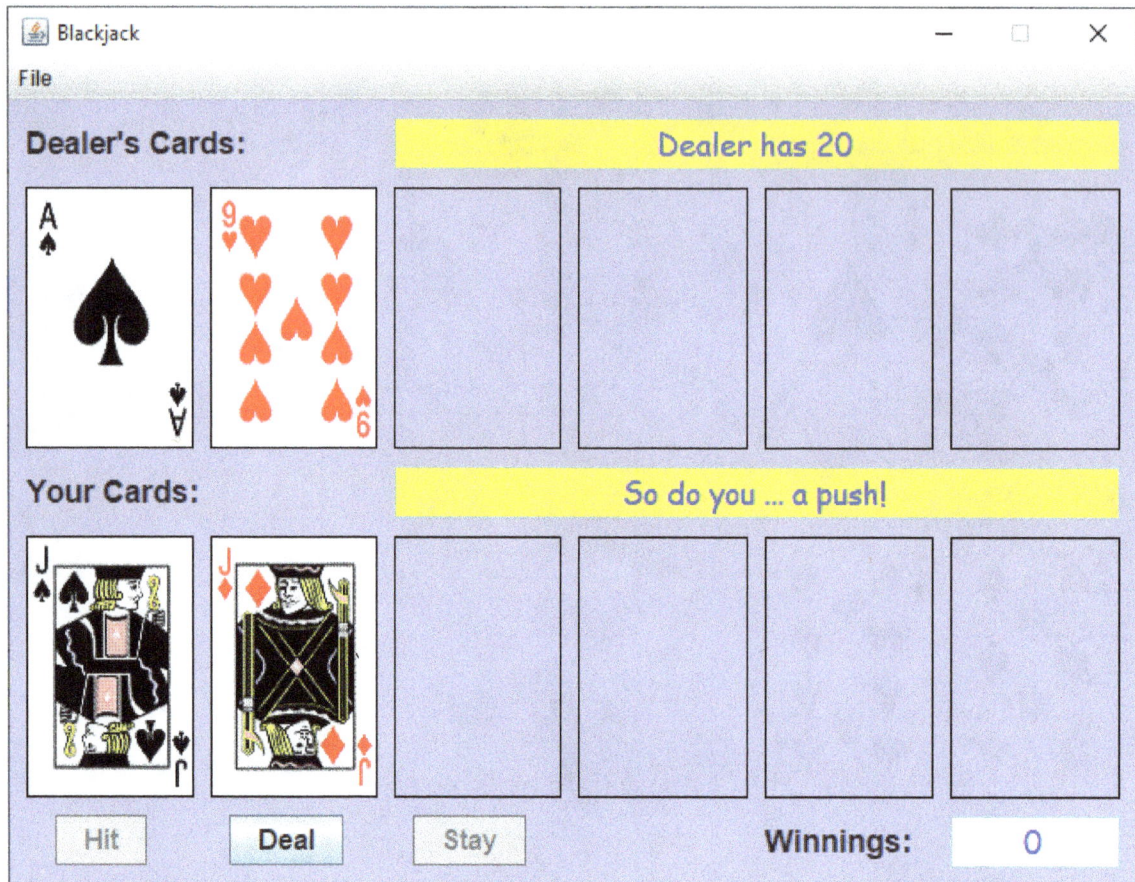

And, in one game, I got Blackjack!!

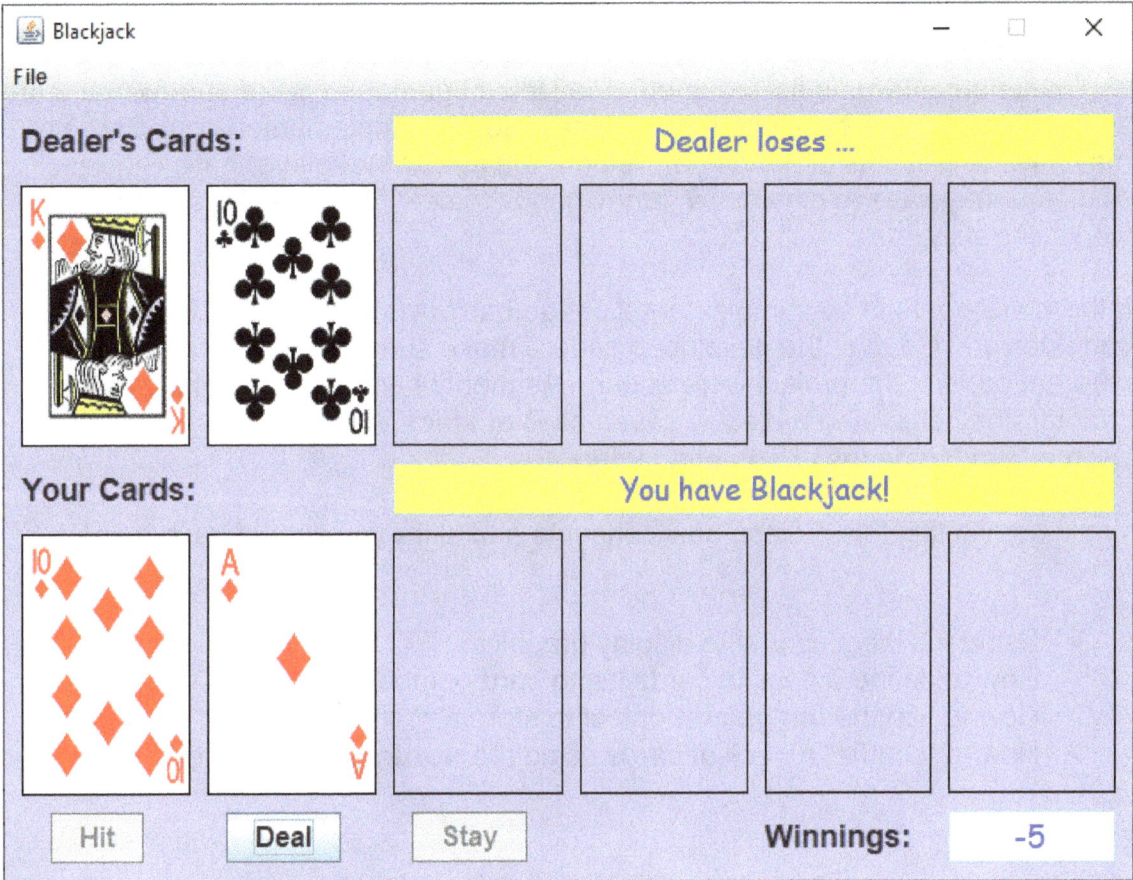

Blackjack Card Game Project Review

The **Blackjack Card Game Project** is now complete. Save and run the project and make sure it works as designed. Play lots of games to make sure winners are always declared correctly and that the dealer logic is implemented correctly. You may have to play lots of hands before both the dealer and player have Blackjack. And, you may have to play many, many hands to see if the special "six card" rule works correctly.

If there are errors in your implementation, go back over the steps of frame and code design. Go over the developed code – make sure you understand how different parts of the project were coded. As mentioned in the beginning of this chapter, the completed project is saved as **Blackjack** in the **\HomeJava\HomeJava Projects** folder.

While completing this project, new concepts and skills you should have gained include:

> ➢ Using the label control to display graphics.
> ➢ How to define a deck of cards using card number indices.
> ➢ How to use the **ImageIcon** object to store a graphics file.
> ➢ How to "shuffle" a deck of cards using the **sortIntegers** method.

Blackjack Card Game Project Enhancements

Possible enhancements to the Blackjack card game project include:

> ➢ As you probably know, Blackjack is a gambling game. The idea is for you (the player) to win as much money as possible from the dealer. Our version of Blackjack is a simplification of the casino version. The casino version allows betting – our version doesn't (you either win or lose 10 points with each hand; well, you win 15 if you get a Blackjack). Unfortunately, Casinos tend to make a lot of profit from uneducated players. Our purpose here is to educate you on how the odds are stacked against you. We recommend you enjoy this game at home and keep your hard earned money in your wallet!

> ➢ Casinos also allow you, in certain cases, to double your bet after a hand has been dealt. And, if your two initial cards are the same, you can split them and play two hands. Not being a gambler, I don't know all the specifics behind "double-down" and "splitting." Ask some who does or consult a gambling guide. If you want, implement these modifications to the program.

> ➢ Some casinos have different rules for dealer play. In our version, an Ace must always take on its highest value (without exceeding 21 of course). In other versions, the dealer has discretion. Perhaps, you would like to give the dealer in your program this discretion.

> ➢ To make play more difficult, some casinos play Blackjack with more than one deck of cards. Maybe have the number of card decks being used be an option in your program. In such a case, or even in the current configuration, it might be nice to announce to the player when a reshuffle of the cards is done.

Now that you know the high risks involved with gambling, let's move on to a more practical application.

Blackjack Card Game Project
Java Code Listing

```java
/*
 * Blackjack.java
 */
package blackjack;
import javax.swing.*;
import java.awt.*;
import java.awt.event.*;
import java.util.Random;

public class Blackjack extends JFrame
{

    // menu structure
  JMenuBar mainMenuBar = new JMenuBar();
  JMenu fileMenu = new JMenu("File");
  JMenuItem newMenuItem = new JMenuItem("New Game");
  JMenuItem exitMenuItem = new JMenuItem("Exit");

  JLabel dealerLabel = new JLabel();
  JTextField dealerTextField = new JTextField();
  JLabel[] dealerCard = new JLabel[6];
  JLabel playerLabel = new JLabel();
  JTextField playerTextField = new JTextField();
  JLabel[] playerCard = new JLabel[6];
  JButton hitButton = new JButton();
  JButton dealButton = new JButton();
  JButton stayButton = new JButton();
  JLabel winningsLabel = new JLabel();
  JTextField winningsTextField = new JTextField();

  ImageIcon cardBack;
  ImageIcon[] cardImage = new ImageIcon[52];
  ImageIcon dealerFaceDown;
  int[] cardPoints = new int[52];
  int[] card = new int[52];
  int currentCard;
  int winnings;
  int numberCardsDealer, acesDealer, scoreDealer;
  int numberCardsPlayer, acesPlayer, scorePlayer;

  public static void main(String args[])
  {
```

```
  // create frame
  new Blackjack().setVisible(true);
}

public Blackjack()
{
  // frame constructor
  setTitle("Blackjack");
  getContentPane().setBackground(new Color(192, 192, 255));
  setResizable(false);

  addWindowListener(new WindowAdapter()
  {
    public void windowClosing(WindowEvent evt)
    {
      exitForm(evt);
    }
  });

  getContentPane().setLayout(new GridBagLayout());
  GridBagConstraints gridConstraints;

  // build menu structure
  setJMenuBar(mainMenuBar);
  mainMenuBar.add(fileMenu);
  fileMenu.add(newMenuItem);
  fileMenu.addSeparator();
  fileMenu.add(exitMenuItem);
  newMenuItem.addActionListener(new ActionListener()
  {
    public void actionPerformed(ActionEvent e)
    {
      newMenuItemActionPerformed(e);
    }
  });
  exitMenuItem.addActionListener(new ActionListener()
  {
    public void actionPerformed(ActionEvent e)
    {
      exitMenuItemActionPerformed(e);
    }
  });

  dealerLabel.setText("Dealer's Cards:");
  dealerLabel.setFont(new Font("Arial", Font.BOLD, 18));
  gridConstraints = new GridBagConstraints();
  gridConstraints.gridx = 0;
```

```
      gridConstraints.gridy = 0;
      gridConstraints.gridwidth = 2;
      gridConstraints.anchor = GridBagConstraints.WEST;
      gridConstraints.insets = new Insets(10, 10, 10, 0);
      getContentPane().add(dealerLabel, gridConstraints);

      dealerTextField.setPreferredSize(new Dimension(430, 30));
      dealerTextField.setFont(new Font("Comic Sans MS",
Font.PLAIN, 18));
      dealerTextField.setBackground(new Color(255, 255, 128));
      dealerTextField.setForeground(Color.BLUE);

dealerTextField.setHorizontalAlignment(SwingConstants.CENTER)
;
      dealerTextField.setEditable(false);
      gridConstraints = new GridBagConstraints();
      gridConstraints.gridx = 2;
      gridConstraints.gridy = 0;
      gridConstraints.gridwidth = 4;
      gridConstraints.insets = new Insets(10, 10, 10, 10);
      getContentPane().add(dealerTextField, gridConstraints);

      for (int i = 0; i < 6; i++)
      {
        dealerCard[i] = new JLabel();
        dealerCard[i].setPreferredSize(new Dimension(100,
150));

dealerCard[i].setBorder(BorderFactory.createLineBorder(Color.
BLACK));
        gridConstraints = new GridBagConstraints();
        gridConstraints.gridx = i;
        gridConstraints.gridy = 1;
        gridConstraints.insets = new Insets(0, 10, 0, 0);
        if (i == 5)
          gridConstraints.insets = new Insets(0, 10, 0, 10);
        getContentPane().add(dealerCard[i], gridConstraints);
      }

      playerLabel.setText("Your Cards:");
      playerLabel.setFont(new Font("Arial", Font.BOLD, 18));
      gridConstraints = new GridBagConstraints();
      gridConstraints.gridx = 0;
      gridConstraints.gridy = 2;
      gridConstraints.gridwidth = 2;
      gridConstraints.anchor = GridBagConstraints.WEST;
      gridConstraints.insets = new Insets(10, 10, 10, 0);
```

```java
   getContentPane().add(playerLabel, gridConstraints);

   playerTextField.setPreferredSize(new Dimension(430, 30));
   playerTextField.setFont(new Font("Comic Sans MS",
Font.PLAIN, 18));
   playerTextField.setBackground(new Color(255, 255, 128));
   playerTextField.setForeground(Color.BLUE);

playerTextField.setHorizontalAlignment(SwingConstants.CENTER)
;
   playerTextField.setEditable(false);
   gridConstraints = new GridBagConstraints();
   gridConstraints.gridx = 2;
   gridConstraints.gridy = 2;
   gridConstraints.gridwidth = 4;
   gridConstraints.insets = new Insets(10, 10, 10, 10);
   getContentPane().add(playerTextField, gridConstraints);

   for (int i = 0; i < 6; i++)
   {
     playerCard[i] = new JLabel();
     playerCard[i].setPreferredSize(new Dimension(100,
150));

playerCard[i].setBorder(BorderFactory.createLineBorder(Color.
BLACK));
     gridConstraints = new GridBagConstraints();
     gridConstraints.gridx = i;
     gridConstraints.gridy = 3;
     gridConstraints.insets = new Insets(0, 10, 0, 0);
     if (i == 5)
       gridConstraints.insets = new Insets(0, 10, 0, 10);
     getContentPane().add(playerCard[i], gridConstraints);
   }

   hitButton.setText("Hit");
   hitButton.setFont(new Font("Arial", Font.BOLD, 16));
   gridConstraints = new GridBagConstraints();
   gridConstraints.gridx = 0;
   gridConstraints.gridy = 4;
   gridConstraints.insets = new Insets(10, 0, 10, 0);
   getContentPane().add(hitButton, gridConstraints);
   hitButton.addActionListener(new ActionListener()
   {
     public void actionPerformed(ActionEvent e)
     {
       hitButtonActionPerformed(e);
```

```
      }
    });

    dealButton.setText("Deal");
    dealButton.setFont(new Font("Arial", Font.BOLD, 16));
    gridConstraints = new GridBagConstraints();
    gridConstraints.gridx = 1;
    gridConstraints.gridy = 4;
    gridConstraints.insets = new Insets(10, 0, 10, 0);
    getContentPane().add(dealButton, gridConstraints);
    dealButton.addActionListener(new ActionListener()
    {
      public void actionPerformed(ActionEvent e)
      {
        dealButtonActionPerformed(e);
      }
    });

    stayButton.setText("Stay");
    stayButton.setFont(new Font("Arial", Font.BOLD, 16));
    gridConstraints = new GridBagConstraints();
    gridConstraints.gridx = 2;
    gridConstraints.gridy = 4;
    gridConstraints.insets = new Insets(10, 0, 10, 0);
    getContentPane().add(stayButton, gridConstraints);
    stayButton.addActionListener(new ActionListener()
    {
      public void actionPerformed(ActionEvent e)
      {
        stayButtonActionPerformed(e);
      }
    });

    winningsLabel.setText("Winnings:");
    winningsLabel.setFont(new Font("Arial", Font.BOLD, 18));
    gridConstraints = new GridBagConstraints();
    gridConstraints.gridx = 4;
    gridConstraints.gridy = 4;
    gridConstraints.anchor = GridBagConstraints.WEST;
    gridConstraints.insets = new Insets(10, 10, 10, 0);
    getContentPane().add(winningsLabel, gridConstraints);

    winningsTextField.setText("0");
    winningsTextField.setPreferredSize(new Dimension(100,
30));
    winningsTextField.setFont(new Font("Comic Sans MS",
Font.PLAIN, 18));
```

```
    winningsTextField.setBackground(Color.WHITE);
    winningsTextField.setForeground(Color.BLUE);

winningsTextField.setHorizontalAlignment(SwingConstants.CENTE
R);
    winningsTextField.setEditable(false);
    gridConstraints = new GridBagConstraints();
    gridConstraints.gridx = 5;
    gridConstraints.gridy = 4;
    gridConstraints.insets = new Insets(10, 0, 10, 0);
    getContentPane().add(winningsTextField, gridConstraints);

    pack();
    Dimension screenSize =
Toolkit.getDefaultToolkit().getScreenSize();
    setBounds((int) (0.5 * (screenSize.width - getWidth())),
(int) (0.5 * (screenSize.height - getHeight())), getWidth(),
getHeight());

    String cn;
    // load card images and determine points for each
    cardBack = new ImageIcon("CARDBACK.GIF");
    for (int cardNumber = 0; cardNumber < 52; cardNumber++)
    {
      cn = String.valueOf(cardNumber);
      if (cardNumber < 10)
        cn = "0" + cn;
      cardImage[cardNumber] = new ImageIcon("CARD" + cn +
".GIF");
      int i = cardNumber % 13 + 1; // get a number from 1 (A)
to 13 (K)
      if (i == 11 || i == 12 || i == 13) // Jack, Queen, King
        cardPoints[cardNumber] = 10;
      else // A through 10
        cardPoints[cardNumber] = i;
    }
    newMenuItem.doClick();
  }

  private void exitForm(WindowEvent evt)
  {
    System.exit(0);
  }

  private void newMenuItemActionPerformed(ActionEvent e)
  {
    // start new game - clear winnings and start over
```

```
      winnings = 0;
      winningsTextField.setText("0");
      card = sortIntegers(52);
      currentCard = 0;
      newHand();
   }

   private void exitMenuItemActionPerformed(ActionEvent e)
   {
      System.exit(0);
   }

   private void hitButtonActionPerformed(ActionEvent e)
   {
    // Add a card if player requests
      addPlayerCard();
      if (scorePlayer > 21)
        endHand("Dealer wins", "You busted!", -10);
      else if (numberCardsPlayer == 6)
        endHand("No dealer play", "You win - 6 cards and not
over 21!", 10);
   }

   private void dealButtonActionPerformed(ActionEvent e)
   {
      newHand();
   }

   private void stayButtonActionPerformed(ActionEvent e)
   {
      boolean dealerDone = false;
      int scoreTemp, acesTemp;
      hitButton.setEnabled(false);
      stayButton.setEnabled(false);
      // Check for aces in player hand and adjust score
      // to highest possible
      if (acesPlayer != 0 && scorePlayer <= 11)
      {
        scorePlayer += 10;
        acesPlayer--;
      }
      // Uncover dealer face down card and play dealer hand
      dealerCard[0].setIcon(dealerFaceDown);
      do
      {
        scoreTemp = scoreDealer;
        acesTemp = acesDealer;
```

```
    // Check for aces and adjust score
    if (acesTemp != 0 && scoreDealer <= 11)
    {
      scoreTemp += 10;
      acesTemp--;
    }
    // add card unless score above 16 or dealer has 6 cards
    if (scoreTemp > 16)
    {
      if (scoreTemp > scorePlayer)
        endHand("Dealer wins with " +
String.valueOf(scoreTemp), "You lose with " +
String.valueOf(scorePlayer), -10);
      else if (scoreTemp == scorePlayer)
        endHand("Dealer has " + String.valueOf(scoreTemp),
"So do you ... a push!", 0);
      else
        endHand("Dealer loses with " +
String.valueOf(scoreTemp), "You win with " +
String.valueOf(scorePlayer), 10);
      dealerDone = true;
      continue;
    }
    else if (numberCardsDealer == 6)
    {
      endHand("Dealer wins ... 6 cards and not over 16!",
"You lose ...", -10);
      dealerDone = true;
      continue;
    }
    else
    {
      addDealerCard();
      // dealer loses if busted
      if (scoreDealer > 21)
      {
        endHand("Dealer busts!", "You win!!", 10);
        dealerDone = true;
        continue;
      }
    }
  }
  while (!dealerDone);
}

private int[] sortIntegers(int n)
{
```

```java
  /*
   *  Returns n randomly sorted integers 0 -> n - 1
   */
  int[] sortedArray = new int[n];
  int temp, s;
  Random sortRandom = new Random();
  //  initialize array from 0 to n - 1
  for (int i = 0; i < n; i++)
  {
    sortedArray[i] = i;
  }
  //  i is number of items remaining in list
  for (int i = n; i >= 1; i--)
  {
    s = sortRandom.nextInt(i);
    temp = sortedArray[s];
    sortedArray[s] = sortedArray[i - 1];
    sortedArray[i - 1] = temp;
  }
  return(sortedArray);
}

private void newHand()
{
  // Deal a new hand
  // Clear table of cards
  for (int i = 0; i < 6; i++)
  {
    dealerCard[i].setIcon(null);
    playerCard[i].setIcon(null);
  }
  dealerTextField.setText("");
  playerTextField.setText("");
  hitButton.setEnabled(true);
  stayButton.setEnabled(true);
  dealButton.setEnabled(false);
  // reshuffle occasionally
  if (currentCard > 34)
  {
    card = sortIntegers(52);
    currentCard = 0;
  }
  // Get two dealer cards
  scoreDealer = 0;
  acesDealer = 0;
  numberCardsDealer = 0;
  addDealerCard();
```

```
    addDealerCard();
    // Get two player cards
    scorePlayer = 0;
    acesPlayer = 0;
    numberCardsPlayer = 0;
    addPlayerCard();
    addPlayerCard();
    // Check for blackjacks
    if (scoreDealer == 11 && acesDealer == 1)
      scoreDealer = 21;
    if (scorePlayer == 11 && acesPlayer == 1)
      scorePlayer = 21;
    if (scoreDealer == 21 && scorePlayer == 21)
      endHand("Dealer has Blackjack!", "And, you have
Blackjack .. a push!", 0);
    else if (scoreDealer == 21)
      endHand("Dealer has Blackjack!", "You lose ...", -10);
    else if (scorePlayer == 21)
      endHand("Dealer loses ...", "You have Blackjack!", 15);
  }

  private void endHand(String dealerComment, String
playerComment, int change)
  {
    // make sure dealer cards are seen
    dealerCard[0].setIcon(dealerFaceDown);
    dealerTextField.setText(dealerComment);
    playerTextField.setText(playerComment);
    // Hand has ended - update winnings
    winnings += change;
    winningsTextField.setText(String.valueOf(winnings));
    hitButton.setEnabled(false);
    stayButton.setEnabled(false);
    dealButton.setEnabled(true);
  }
  private void addDealerCard()
  {
    int cardNumber;
    cardNumber = card[currentCard];
    // Adds a card to dealer hand
    numberCardsDealer++;
    switch (numberCardsDealer)
    {
      case 1:
        dealerFaceDown = cardImage[cardNumber];
        dealerCard[0].setIcon(cardBack);
        break;
```

```java
      case 2:
        dealerCard[1].setIcon(cardImage[cardNumber]);
        break;
      case 3:
        dealerCard[2].setIcon(cardImage[cardNumber]);
        break;
      case 4:
        dealerCard[3].setIcon(cardImage[cardNumber]);
        break;
      case 5:
        dealerCard[4].setIcon(cardImage[cardNumber]);
        break;
      case 6:
        dealerCard[5].setIcon(cardImage[cardNumber]);
        break;
    }
    scoreDealer += cardPoints[cardNumber];
    if (cardPoints[cardNumber] == 1)
      acesDealer++;
    currentCard++;
  }

  private void addPlayerCard()
  {
    int cardNumber;
    cardNumber = card[currentCard];
    // Adds a card to player hand
    numberCardsPlayer++;
    switch (numberCardsPlayer)
    {
      case 1:
        playerCard[0].setIcon(cardImage[cardNumber]);
        break;
      case 2:
        playerCard[1].setIcon(cardImage[cardNumber]);
        break;
      case 3:
        playerCard[2].setIcon(cardImage[cardNumber]);
        break;
      case 4:
        playerCard[3].setIcon(cardImage[cardNumber]);
        break;
      case 5:
        playerCard[4].setIcon(cardImage[cardNumber]);
        break;
      case 6:
        playerCard[5].setIcon(cardImage[cardNumber]);
```

```
        break;
    }
    scorePlayer += cardPoints[cardNumber];
    if (cardPoints[cardNumber] == 1)
      acesPlayer++;
    currentCard++;
  }


}
```

7

Weight Monitor Project

Review and Preview

Everyone these days seems to be watching their weight. In this project, we build a program that tracks your weight each day and helps you monitor progress toward goals.

The **Weight Monitor Project** lets you choose a date from a calendar and enter your weight on that day. Plots of your daily weight are provided along with a computation of the trend in your weight. New controls (tab control, list, save file dialog) are introduced as is sequential file input and output. The project also introduces use of date selection controls and graphics used to draw and display the weight curves.

Weight Monitor Project Preview

In this chapter, we will build a **weight monitor** program. This program allows you to enter your weight each day, then examine a plot to observe trends.

The finished project is saved as **WeightMonitor** in the **\HomeJava\HomeJava Projects** project group. Start NetBeans (or your IDE). Open the specified project group. Make **WeightMonitor** the selected project. Run the project. You will see:

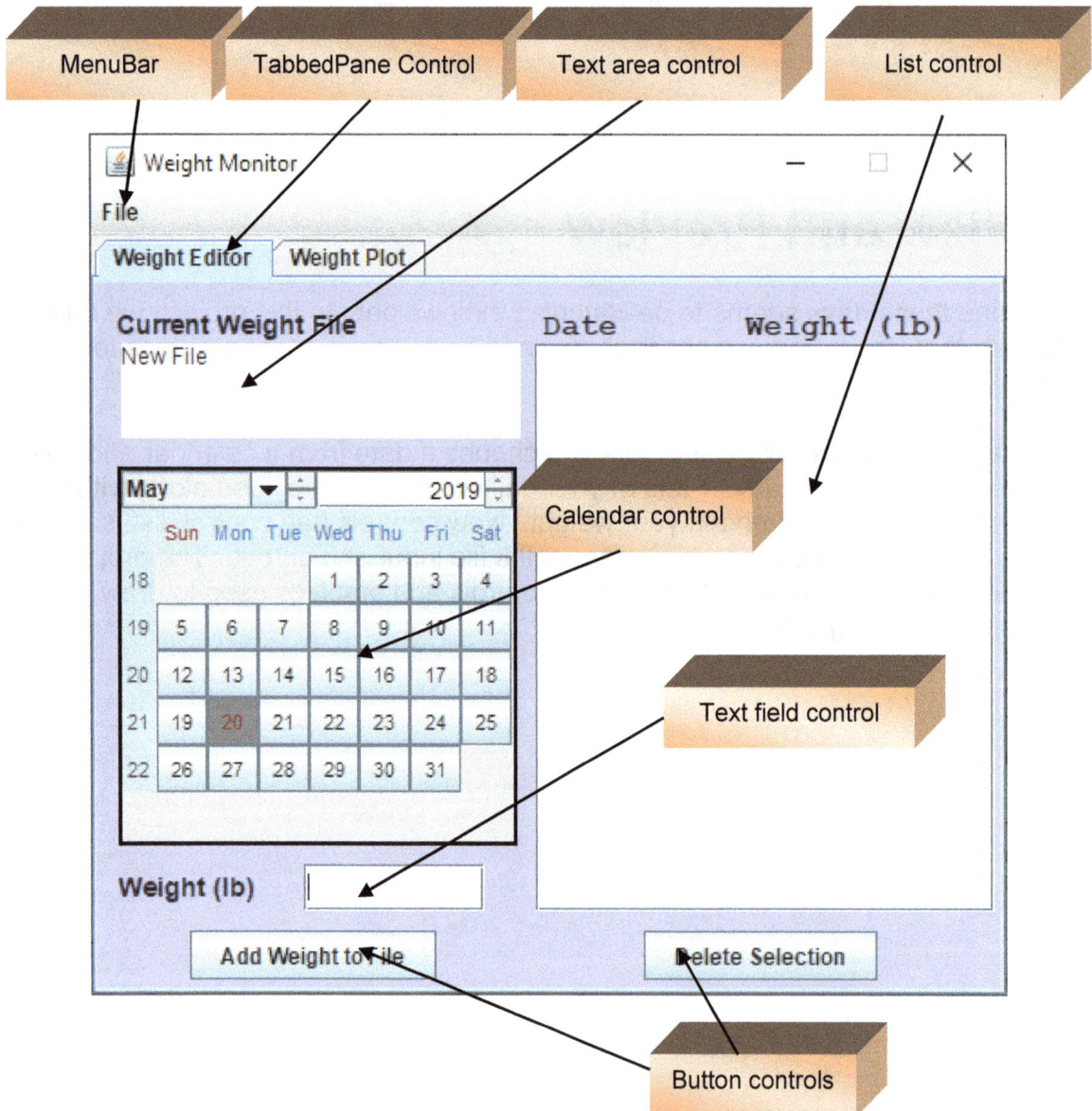

This project is built using a tabbed pane control which allows multiple pages (tabs) of information on a single form. There are two tabs: **Weight Editor**, **Weight Plot**. Each tab has a single panel control upon which other controls are placed. We initially see the controls on the **Weight Editor** tab panel. Labels (used for titling) are unidentified. A text area control displays the most recent weight file. A calendar control is used to select the date and a text box used to enter a weight value. Button controls are used to add and delete entries from the weight file, which are displayed in the list control.

Click the **Weight Plot** tab and you will see:

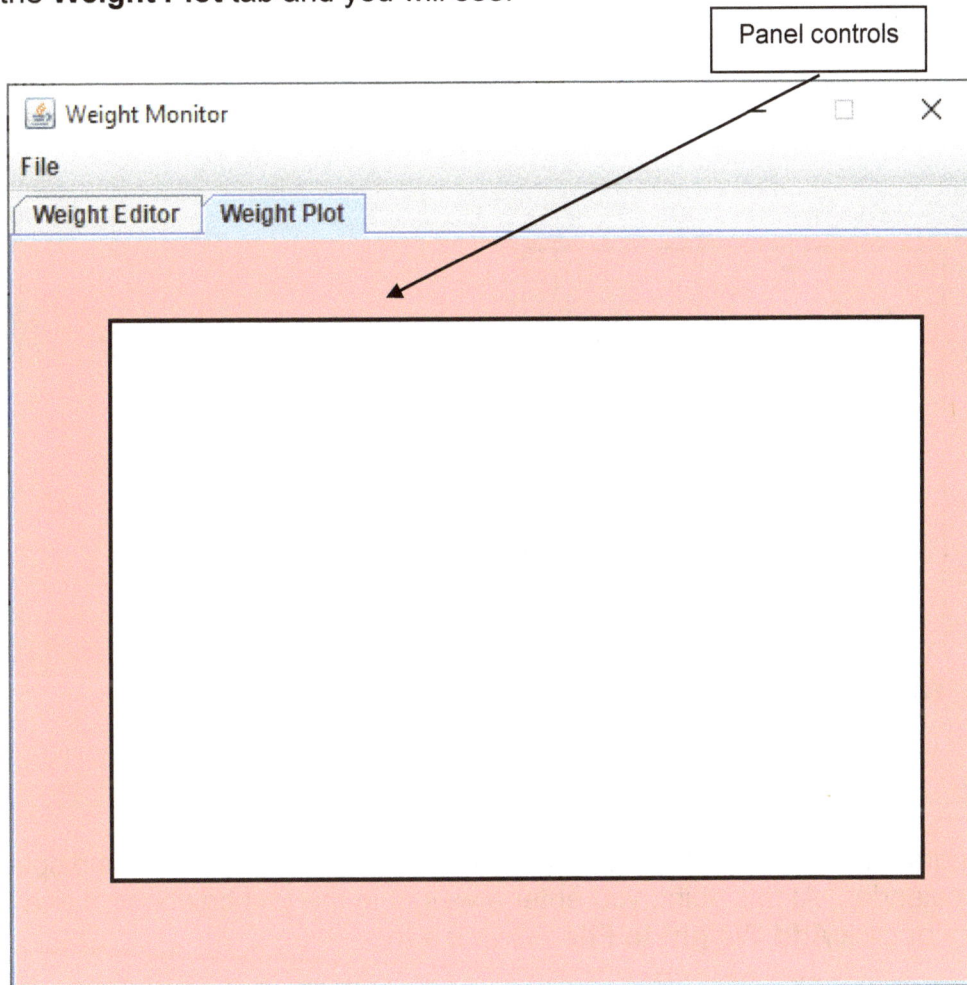

On this tab is a single panel with a blank rectangular region (will be used to show the weight plot).

The normal way to use the weight monitor is to run the program, open an existing weight file, modify it with new entries, view the trends, resave the file and exit. A nice feature of the weight monitor program is that, when it begins, it will automatically open the last opened/saved file (saving you that step for daily recording). The weight monitor program appears in an initial condition (since no file has been saved yet). Return to the **Weight Monitor** tab:

The program indicates we are working with a new file. Today's date is displayed on the calendar. At this point, you enter a weight in the text box control and press **<Enter>** or click **Add Weight to File**. Give it a try.

When I enter my weight, I see:

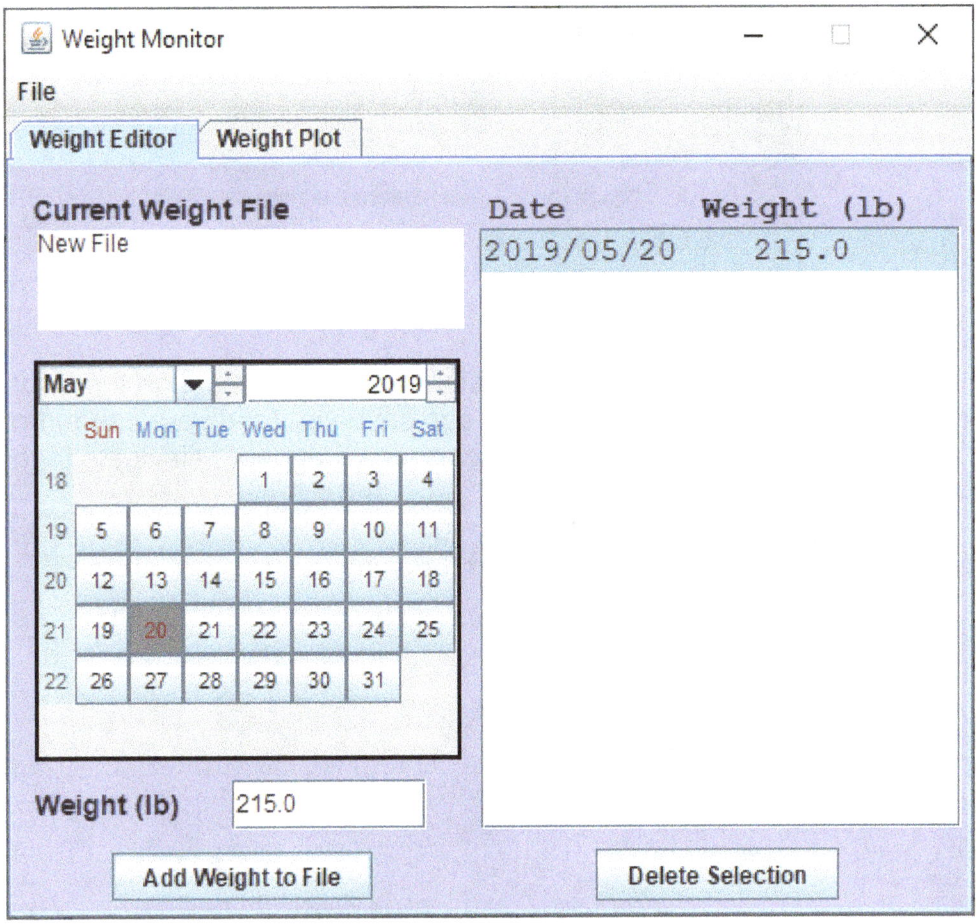

Notice the date (displayed as **year/month/day** and weight have been added to the list control. And, that's what the program does – it records your weight each day. By running the program periodically, you will have a log of your weight that you can plot and view any trends. Try adding more values (by selecting other dates on the calendar) if you'd like. A file is saved using the **Save Weight File** option under the **File** menu. The **File** menu can also be used to start a new with file or open previously saved weight files.

In the **\HomeJava\HomeJava Projects\WeightMonitor** folder is a sample weight file named **sample.wgt**. Use the **Open Weight File** option under the **File** menu to open that file. You will see a message box:

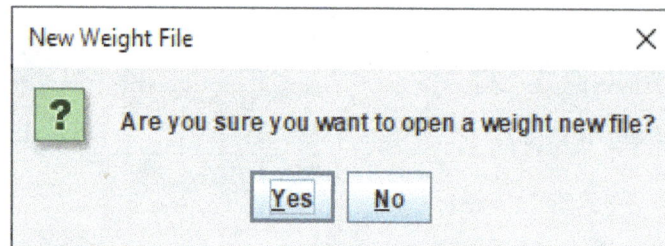

```
New Weight File                               ×

  [?]    Are you sure you want to open a weight new file?

                    Yes      No
```

Answer **Yes**. The program always asks before you want to change the displayed information. Such protective mechanisms can save you (and your users) from losing important data. An open file dialog control will appear. Navigate to the **sample.wgt** file and click **Open**.

Here's my **Weight Editor** tab after opening the sample file:

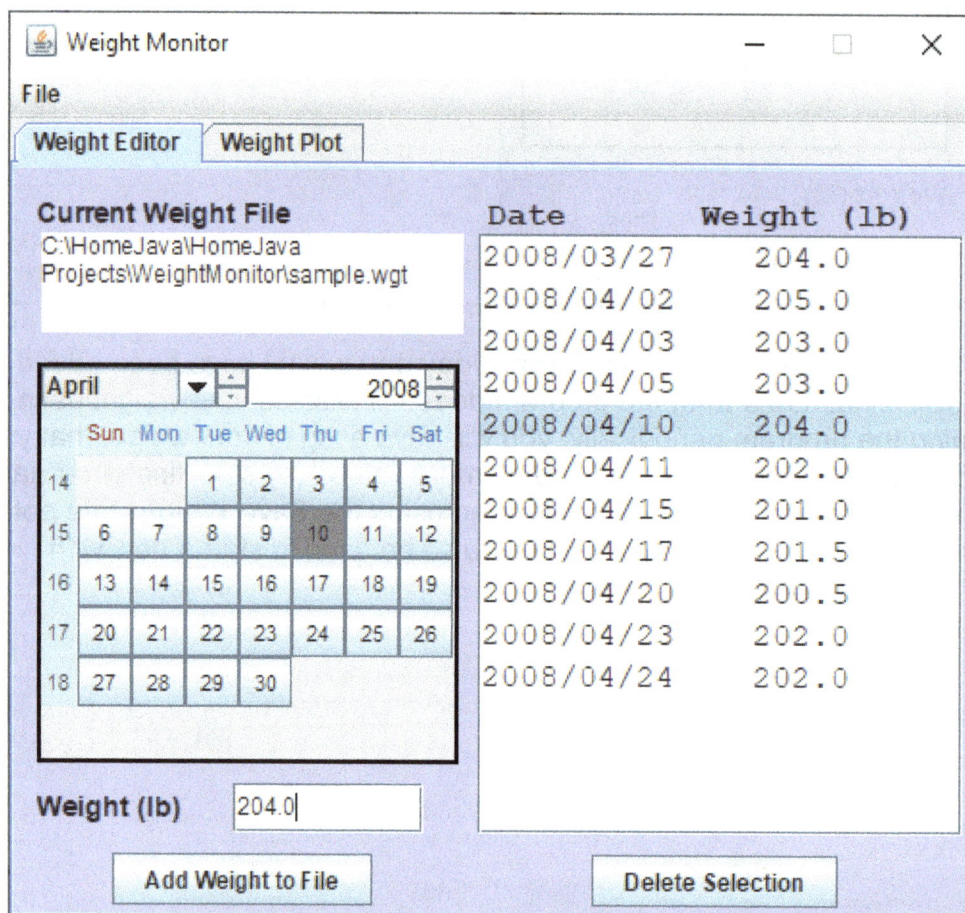

Date	Weight (lb)
2008/03/27	204.0
2008/04/02	205.0
2008/04/03	203.0
2008/04/05	203.0
2008/04/10	204.0
2008/04/11	202.0
2008/04/15	201.0
2008/04/17	201.5
2008/04/20	200.5
2008/04/23	202.0
2008/04/24	202.0

Current Weight File
C:\HomeJava\HomeJava Projects\WeightMonitor\sample.wgt

April ▼   2008

Sun	Mon	Tue	Wed	Thu	Fri	Sat
14		1	2	3	4	5
15	6	7	8	9	10	11	12
16	13	14	15	16	17	18	19
17	20	21	22	23	24	25	26
18	27	28	29	30			

Weight (lb)   204.0

Add Weight to File   Delete Selection

The weight monitor program allows you to **add** (we've seen how to do that), **delete** or **modify** entries. To delete an entry, select that entry in the list control and click **Delete Selection**. To edit an entry, select that entry in the list; the corresponding date will appear on the calendar control and the weight in the text box. Make any changes and click **Add Weight to File**. The calendar control and list entries are always coordinated (assuming there is a list entry matching the selected date). See that coordination in the example above (the April 10 entry is shown). Try adding, deleting and modifying weight entries, if you want. At some point, click the **Weight Plot** tab.

Here's what I see on the **Weight Plot** tab (I didn't modify any of the entries):

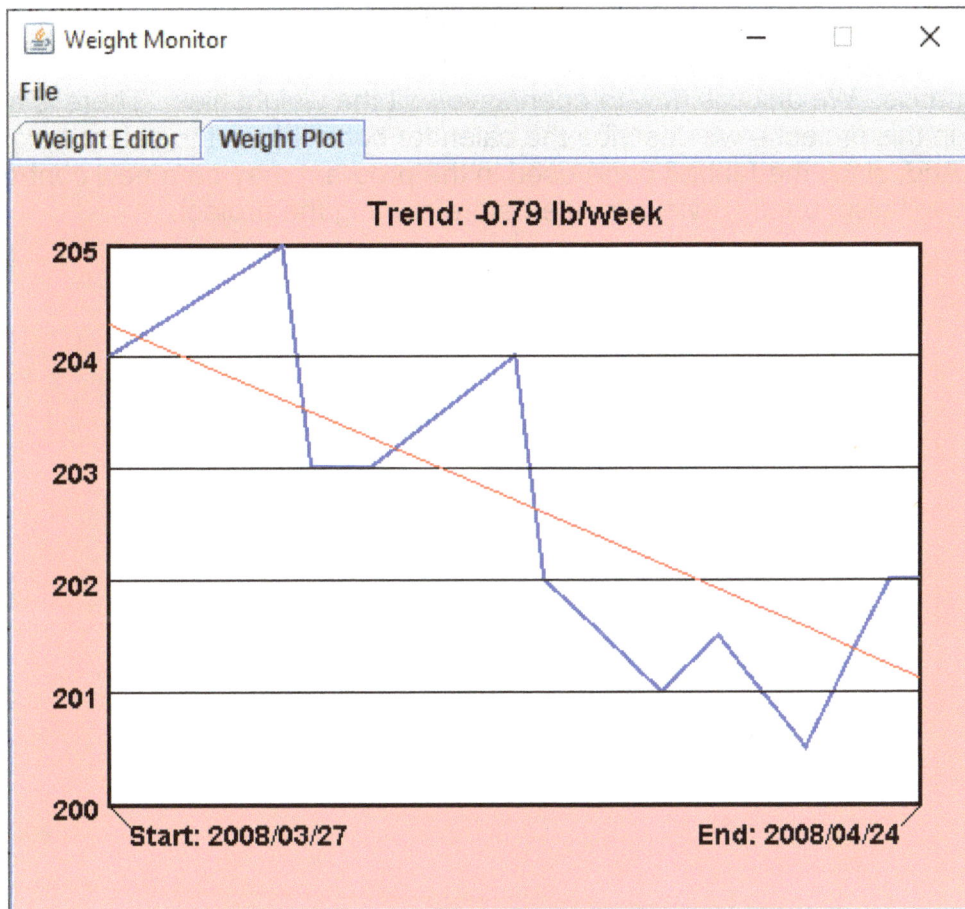

The program has provided a nice line plot of the recorded weights over the specified time period. At the top of the plot, I am shown an indication of the trend in my weight (going down at 0.79 pounds each week – a good trend).

That's what you do with the weight monitor project. Periodically enter your weight in a saved file using the **Weight Editor** tab. View your weight trends using the **Weight Plot** tab. To stop the program, select **Exit** under the **File** menu. The program will automatically save the last file opened and/or saved. After stopping, if you restart the program (assuming you opened the sample weight file), the weight monitor will automatically display the **sample.wgt** file (the last file opened/saved). Play with the program some more if you want. Start a new file, select some dates, enter some weights, view your plot. Save your file.

You will now build this project in several stages. We first address **frame design**. We discuss the controls used to build each tab page on the frame and establish initial properties. And, we address **code design** in detail. We will discuss graphics methods in detail. These are the methods we use to draw the weight curves and curve labeling information. We will discuss how to do date mathematics. We discuss how to open/save/edit the weight files. There is a new control in this project – we describe the calendar control (used to select weight date). And, since the tabbed pane used in the program may be a new control to you, we will also briefly review its use before starting the project.

TabbedPane Control

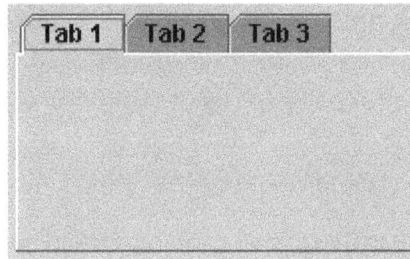

The **tabbed pane** control provides an easy way to present several panels of information in a single frame - it is similar to having a multi-frame application. This is the same interface seen in many commercial GUI applications.

The tabbed pane control provides a group of tabs, each holding a **panel** control. The process for using a tabbed pane control is to create a separate panel for each tab. The panels are then added to the tabbed pane using the **addTab** method. For example, to add a panel named **myPanel** to a tabbed pane control named **myTabbedPane**, you would use:

```
myTabbedPane.addTab(tabTitle, myPanel);
```

where **tabTitle** is a string value representing the text that will appear on the tab associated with **myPanel**. The panels "grow" to fit the declared size of the tabbed pane control or the tabbed pane can "grow" to fit the largest panel added to it.

Only one tab can be active at a time. Navigation from one tab to the next is simple: just click on the corresponding tab. Using this control is easy. Since most of the coding is in the panels attached to the tabbed pane, there are relatively few properties and methods associated with the tabbed pane. Do some study on your own if you'd like to learn more about this control.

Calendar Controls

The Java Swing library does not have a control that allows selection of a date. A quick search of the Internet will find several Java controls that perform such a task. The calendar controls we present here are described at this website:

http://www.toedter.com/

There are two controls: **JDateChooser** (a drop-down selector) and **JCalendar** (a monthly calendar display that allows a user to select a date). Here, we just use **JCalendar**. Both feature a very easy to use interface – just point and click. These controls are useful for ordering information, making reservations or choosing the current date. Use of these controls is similar, with identical properties and identical methods.

The calendar control is made up of three components a **MonthChooser**, a **DayChooser** and a **YearChooser**:

Operation is simple. A month is selected either from the drop-down box or by clicking the spinner arrows. A day is selected by clicking the desired box. A year is selected using the spinner arrows or by typing a value. By default, a calendar for the current month is displayed initially.

The date chooser control is a drop-down box:

When you click the drop-down arrow, the calendar control described above appears, allowing date selection.

Calendar/DateChooser **Properties**:

font	Font name, style, size.
background	Calendar background color.

Calendar/Date Chooser **Methods**:

setFont	Sets font name, style, size.
setBackground	Sets the calendar background color.
getDate	Returns current date.
getDayChooser	Returns calendar DayChooser
getMonthChooser	Returns calendar MonthChooser.
getYearChooser	Returns calendar YearChooser.
setDate	Sets specified date.

Calendar/Date Chooser **Event**:

propertyChange	Event (**PropertyChangeEvent**) triggered when the selected date changes. Added with **PropertyChangeListener** (requires importation of **java.beans.*** files).

To add a listener for such a **propertyChange** event to a calendar control named **myCalendar**, use:

```
myCalendar.addPropertyChangeListener(new
PropertyChangeListener()
{
  public void propertyChange(PropertyChangeEvent e)
  {
    myCalendarPropertyChange(e);
  }
});
```

And, the corresponding event code would be placed in a **myCalendarPropertyChange** method:

```
private void myCalendarPropertyChange(PropertyChangeEvent
e)
{
   [method code]
}
```

Two tasks you usually want to do with a calendar control are to retrieve the displayed date and to set the date. To retrieve the displayed date for a calendar control named **myCalendar**, use:

```
myCalendar.getDate();
```

This returns a Java **Date** type (we will talk about these later in this chapter). A calendar date is established using:

```
myCalendar.setDate(myDate);
```

Typical use of **date chooser** control:

> Declare and create calendar control, assigning an identifiable **name**. For **myDateChooser**, the code is:

```
JDateChooser myDateChooser = new JDateChooser();
```

> Place control in layout manager.
> Initialize date if desired (default display is today's date).
> Add listener for and monitor **propertyChange** event for changes in value.
> Use **getDate** method to determine selected date.
> You may also choose to change the **font** and **background** properties of the date chooser control.

Typical use of **calendar** control:

> Declare and create calendar control, assigning an identifiable **name**. For **myCalendar**, the code is:

```
JCalendar myCalendar = new JCalendar();
```

> Place control in layout manager.
> Initialize date if desired (default display is today's date).
> Add listener for and monitor **propertyChange** event for changes in value.
> Use **getDate** method to determine selected date.
> You may also choose to change the **font** and **background** properties of the calendar control.

The **JDateChooser** and **JCalendar** controls are provided in what is called a **jar** (Java archive) file that you download from the Internet. This is a library file that contains any code you need to use the controls. To add the controls to your computer, go to the above referenced website. On the page, you will find a link to download the zipped file. The zip file (current version is **jcalendar-1.3.2.zip**) can also be found in the **\HomeJava\HomeJava Projects** folder. Download the file and extract (unzip) the files to a directory on your computer (I used **c:\JCalendar**). Many files will be written to your computer, including documentation and source files. The actual jar file (**jcalendar-1.3.2.jar**) will be in the **lib** subfolder.

You need to make your project aware of the fact you will be using such a jar file. Once we get the framework built for the weight monitor, we will take these steps.

Weight Monitor Frame Design

We begin building the **Weight Monitor Project.** Let's build the frame. Start a new project in your Java project group – name it **WeightMonitor**. Delete default code in file named **WeightMonitor.java**. Once started, we suggest you immediately save the project with the name you chose. This sets up the folder and file structure needed for your project. Build the basic frame with these properties:

Weight Monitor Frame:
title   Weight Monitor
resizable   false

The code is:

```
/*
 * WeightMonitor.java
 */
package weightmonitor;
import javax.swing.*;
import java.awt.*;
import java.awt.event.*;

public class WeightMonitor extends JFrame
{
  public static void main(String args[])
  {
    // create frame
    new WeightMonitor().setVisible(true);
  }

  public WeightMonitor()
  {
    // frame constructor
    setTitle("Weight Monitor");
    setResizable(false);

    addWindowListener(new WindowAdapter()
    {
      public void windowClosing(WindowEvent evt)
      {
        exitForm(evt);
      }
    });

    getContentPane().setLayout(new GridBagLayout());
    GridBagConstraints gridConstraints;
```

```
    pack();
    Dimension screenSize =
Toolkit.getDefaultToolkit().getScreenSize();
    setBounds((int) (0.5 * (screenSize.width -
getWidth())), (int) (0.5 * (screenSize.height -
getHeight())), getWidth(), getHeight());
  }

  private void exitForm(WindowEvent evt)
  {
    System.exit(0);
  }
}
```

This code builds the frame, sets up the layout manager and includes code to exit the application. Run the code to make sure the frame (at least, what there is of it at this point) appears and is centered on the screen:

Let's populate our frame with other controls. All code for creating the frame and placing controls (except declarations) goes in the **WeightMonitor** constructor.

First, let's define the menu. We use a single menu object (**fileMenu**) to start a new file, open a file, save a file and to exit program. Our menu bar (**mainMenuBar**) structure will be:

Text	**Name**
File	fileMenu
New Weight File	newMenuItem
Open Weight File	openMenuItem
Save Weight File	saveMenuItem
(Separator)	
Exit	exitMenuItem

Declare the different menu items as class level objects:

```java
// menu structure
JMenuBar mainMenuBar = new JMenuBar();
JMenu fileMenu = new JMenu("File");
JMenuItem newMenuItem = new JMenuItem("New Weight File");
JMenuItem openMenuItem = new JMenuItem("Open Weight
File");
JMenuItem saveMenuItem = new JMenuItem("Save Weight
File");
JMenuItem exitMenuItem = new JMenuItem("Exit");
```

Establish the menu structure using this code in the frame constructor (each menu item has a corresponding **ActionPerformed** method):

```java
// build menu structure
setJMenuBar(mainMenuBar);
mainMenuBar.add(fileMenu);
fileMenu.add(newMenuItem);
fileMenu.add(openMenuItem);
fileMenu.add(saveMenuItem);
fileMenu.addSeparator();
fileMenu.add(exitMenuItem);
newMenuItem.addActionListener(new ActionListener()
{
  public void actionPerformed(ActionEvent e)
  {
    newMenuItemActionPerformed(e);
  }
});
openMenuItem.addActionListener(new ActionListener()
{
  public void actionPerformed(ActionEvent e)
  {
    openMenuItemActionPerformed(e);
  }
});
saveMenuItem.addActionListener(new ActionListener()
{
  public void actionPerformed(ActionEvent e)
  {
    saveMenuItemActionPerformed(e);
  }
});
exitMenuItem.addActionListener(new ActionListener()
{
  public void actionPerformed(ActionEvent e)
  {
    exitMenuItemActionPerformed(e);
  }
});
```

Add the empty methods:

```
private void newMenuItemActionPerformed(ActionEvent e)
{
}

private void openMenuItemActionPerformed(ActionEvent e)
{
}

private void saveMenuItemActionPerformed(ActionEvent e)
{
}

private void exitMenuItemActionPerformed(ActionEvent e)
{
}
```

Save, run. Make sure the menu structure appears:

Click **File** to see:

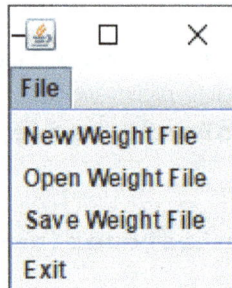

Let's add controls.

The **GridBagLayout** for the project frame is very simple, just one control (a tabbed pane)::

	gridx = 0
gridy = 0	weightTabbedPane

The tab control (**weightTabbedPane**) will host the two tab pages (each with panel controls, **editorPanel** and **plotPanel**). Before adding this basic starting framework, we do some proactive work.

The **plotPanel** will display a plot of weight versus time. For graphics to be persistent (we will explain what this means), we need a special panel class with a **paintComponent** method (where the graphics methods are used). We need such a class here too. We define the **WeightPlotPanel** class using this code (added after the **WeightMonitor** class):

```
class WeightPlotPanel extends JPanel
{
  public void paintComponent(Graphics g)
  {
    Graphics2D g2D = (Graphics2D) g;
    super.paintComponent(g2D);

    g2D.dispose();
  }
}
```

All graphics used for the weight plot will go in the **paintComponent** method for this class (this will be done after developing all the code for the editor panel).

Now, the control properties are:

weightTabbedPane:
size   500, 400
gridx   0
gridy   0

editorPanel:
background   Color(192, 192, 255)

weightPanel:
background   Color(255, 192, 192)

Declare the tab control and panels using:

```
JTabbedPane weightTabbedPane = new JTabbedPane();
JPanel editorPanel = new JPanel();
WeightPlotPanel plotPanel = new WeightPlotPanel();
```

Note the **plotPanel** is from the newly added **WeightPlotPanel** class.

Now, the tabbed pane and panels are added to the frame in the frame constructor using:

```
weightTabbedPane.setPreferredSize(new Dimension(500,
400));
weightTabbedPane.addTab("Weight Editor", editorPanel);
weightTabbedPane.addTab("Weight Plot", plotPanel);
gridConstraints = new GridBagConstraints();
gridConstraints.gridx = 0;
gridConstraints.gridy = 0;
getContentPane().add(weightTabbedPane, gridConstraints);

editorPanel.setBackground(new Color(192, 192, 255));
editorPanel.setLayout(new GridBagLayout());
plotPanel.setBackground(new Color(255, 192, 192));
```

Notice we give the editor panel a **GridBagLayout** for control placement.

Save, run the project. You will see the blank **Weight Editor** tab:

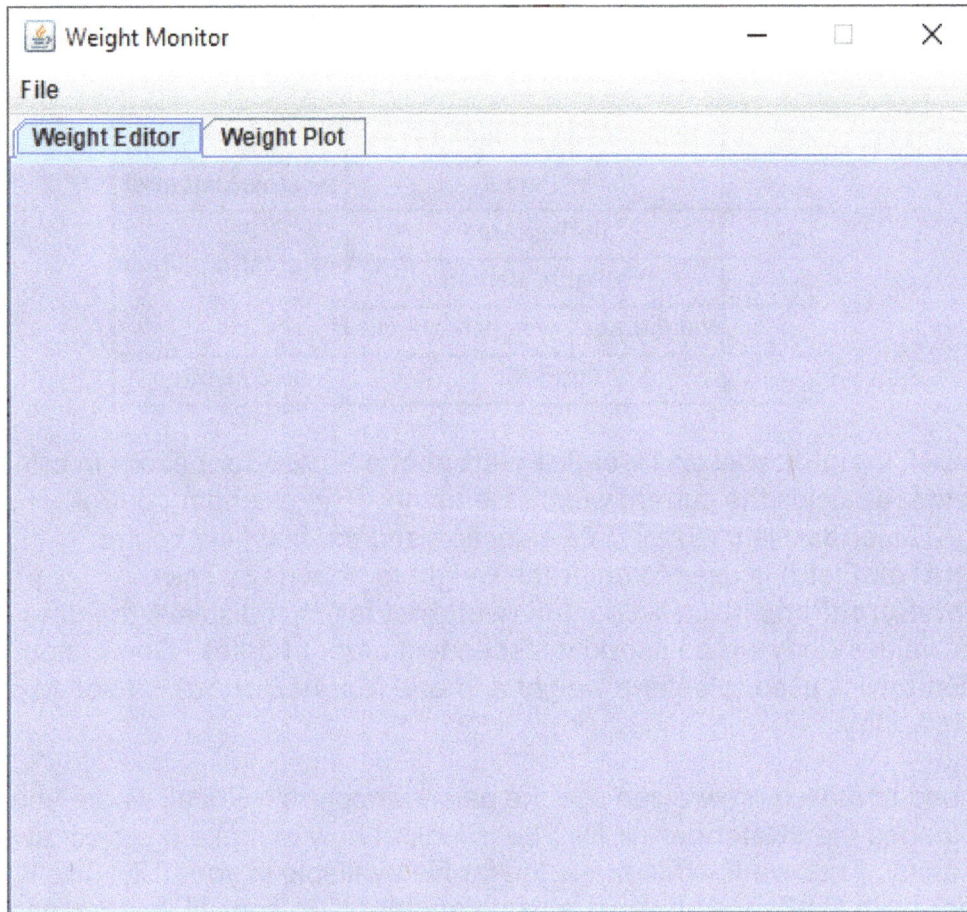

Click **Weight Plot** to see that blank panel if you wish. Let's add controls to the **Weight Editor** tab.

Frame Design – Weight Editor Panel

Let's build this first tab panel. The **GridBagLayout** for the project frame is::

	gridx = 0	gridx = 1	gridx = 2
gridy = 0	fileLabel		weightsListLabel
gridy = 1	fileTextArea		weightsScrollPane
gridy = 2	weightCalendar		
gridy = 3	weightLabel	weightTextField	
gridy = 4	addButton		deleteButton

fileLabel, **weightLabel** and **weightsListLabel** are used for header information.
fileTextArea holds the current weight file name. The calendar control
(**weightCalendar**) is used for date selection and the text field control
(**weightTextField**) is used to enter the weight for that day. The
weightsScrollPane holds list control (**weightsList**) that displays the date and
weight values (they will be sorted in ascending order of date). One button
(**addButton**) is used to enter a weight and one (**deleteButton**) is used to delete a
selected entry.

We need to make sure we can use the calendar control. Recall where you
downloaded the **JCalendar** jar file. Let's look at how to make a project aware of
such a file. First, we need to make the jar file available in your IDE. We'll show
you how with NetBeans. If you are using another IDE, consult its documentation
to see how to add jar files to a project. Make sure **WeightMonitor** is the selected
project.

In the menu, choose **Tools**, then **Libraries** to see:

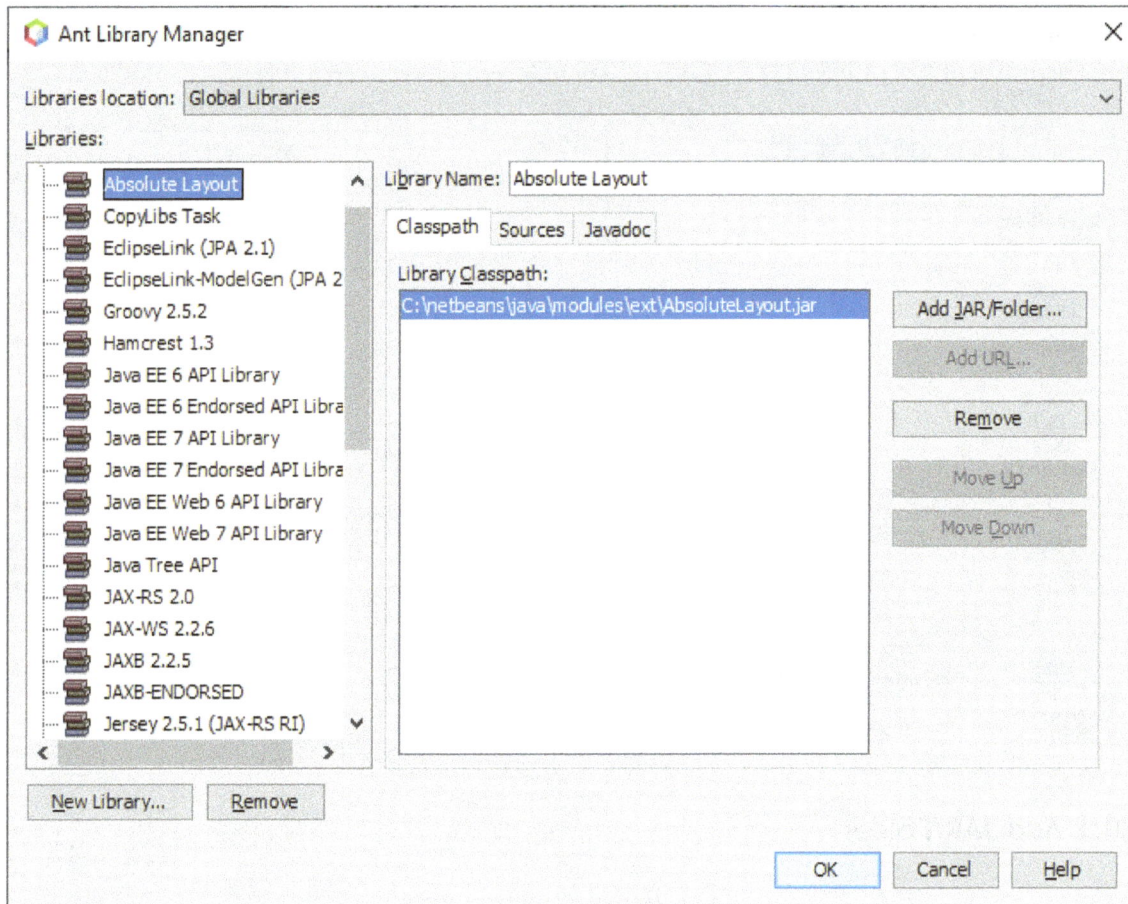

Click **New Library** and name it **Calendar**:

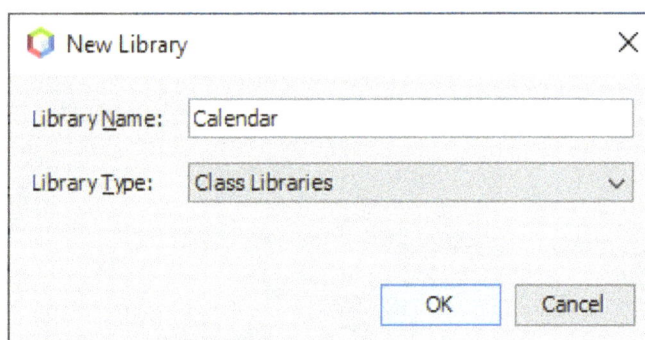

Click **OK** to accept name.

In next window, click **Add JAR/Folder**. Navigate to jar location:

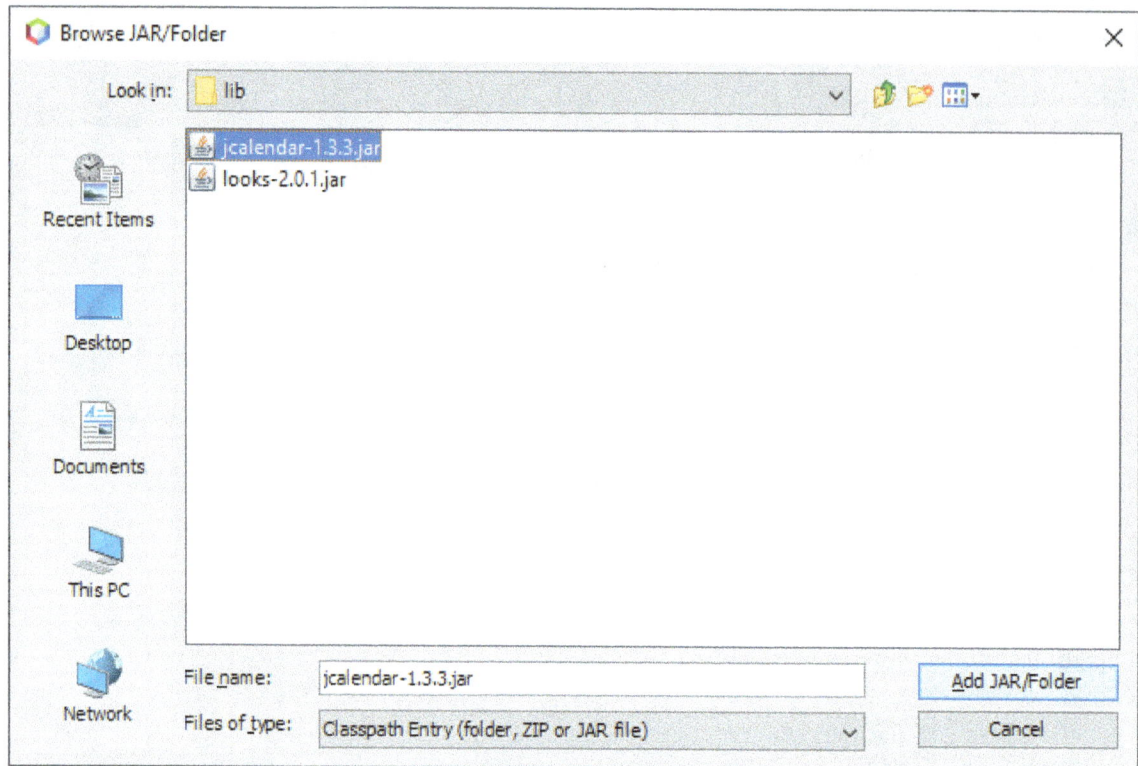

Browse JAR/Folder		×
Look in:	lib	

jcalendar-1.3.3.jar
looks-2.0.1.jar

Recent Items

Desktop

Documents

This PC

Network

File name:	jcalendar-1.3.3.jar	Add JAR/Folder
Files of type:	Classpath Entry (folder, ZIP or JAR file)	Cancel

Click **Add JAR/Folder.**

Library is now there:

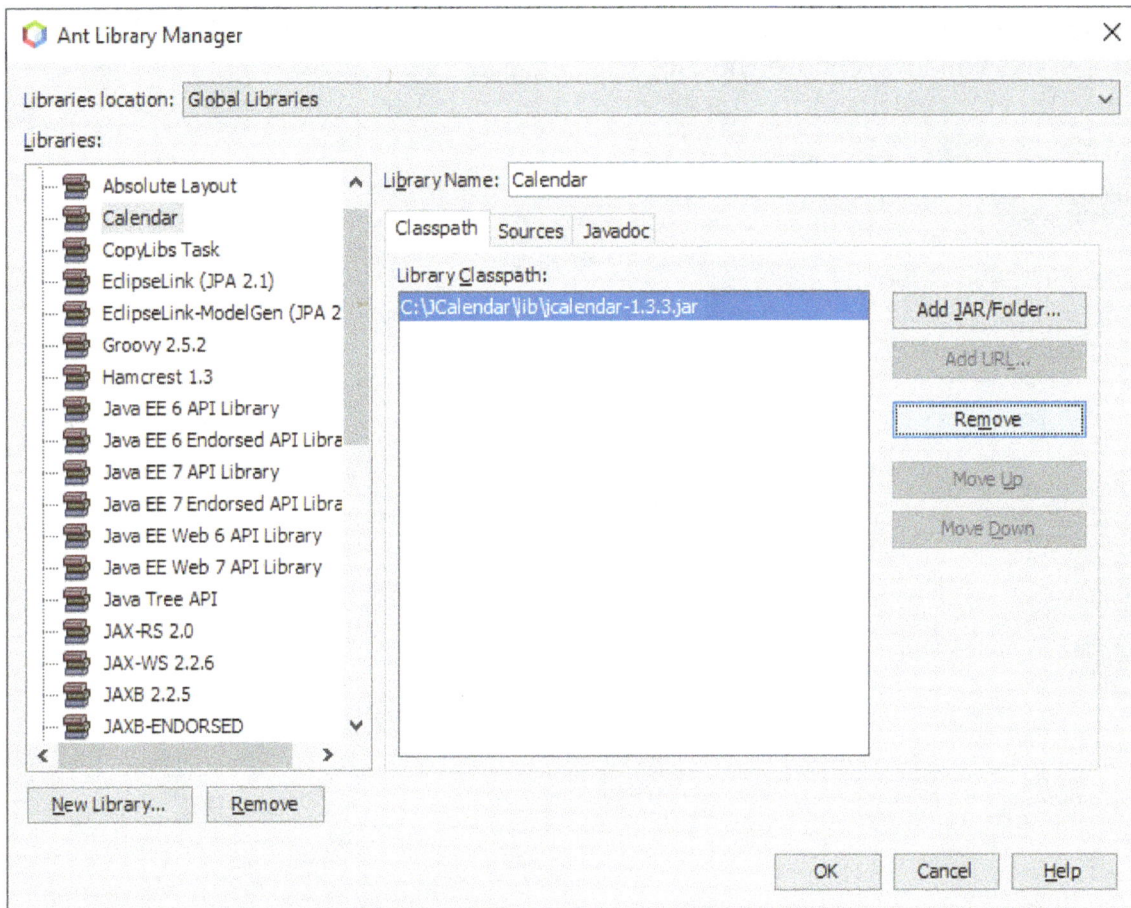

The **Calendar** library can now be added to any project that needs it. Click **OK**.

To add an archived library to a project, follow these steps:

In file view area, right-click the project name and click **Properties**. In the properties window, choose the **Libraries** category:

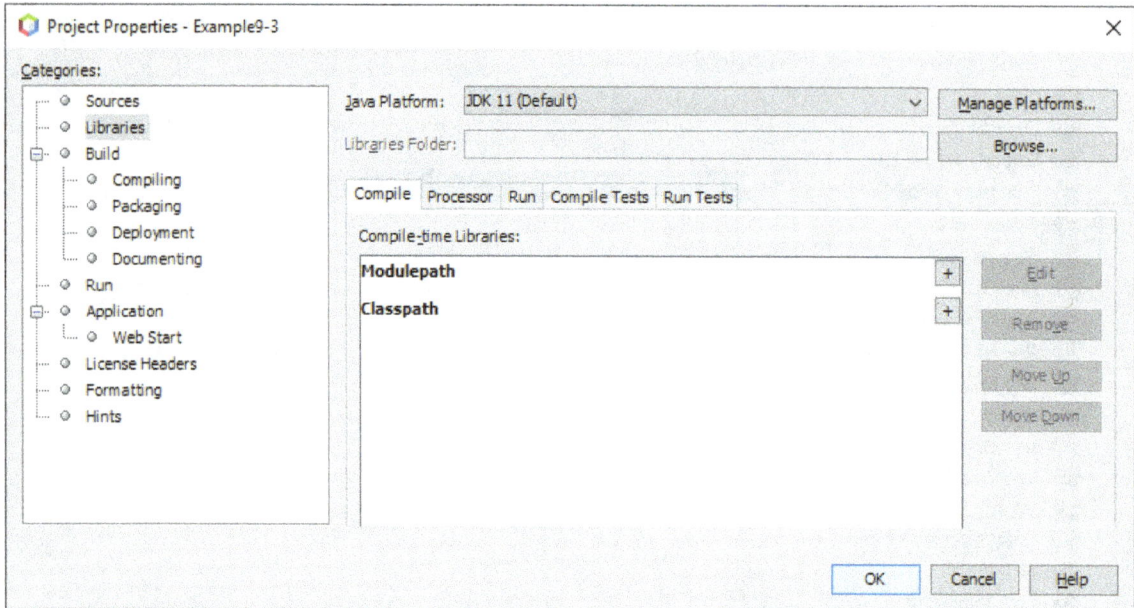

Click the + sign to the right of **Classpath** and select **Add Library** to see

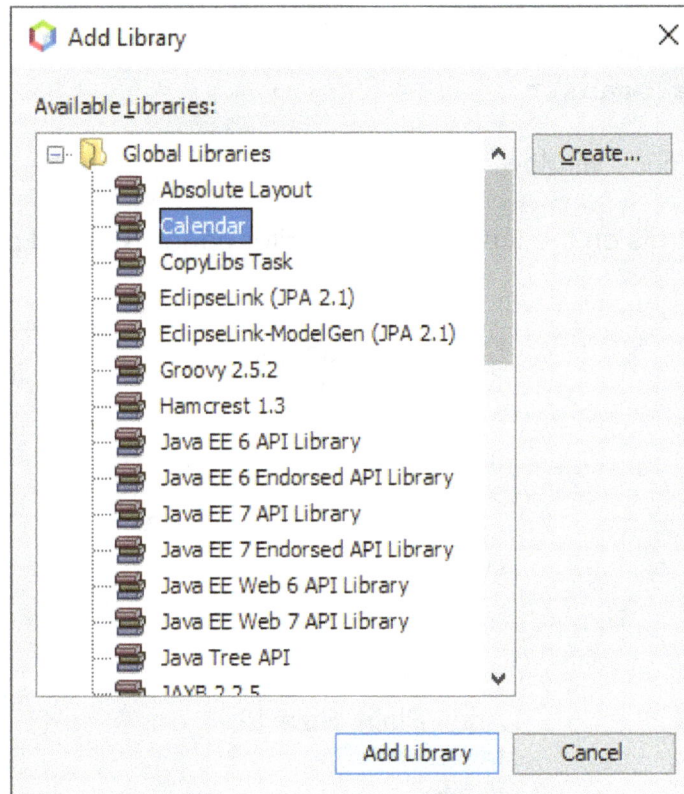

Choose **Calendar**, then click **Add Library**. Click **OK** when returned to the **Properties** window.

The calendar tools can now be used in the weight monitor project with the addition of these **import** statements:

```
import com.toedter.calendar.*;
import java.beans.*;
```

Add these to the code window.

Let's add the controls on the left side of the editor panel. Control properties are:

fileLabel:

text	Current Weight File
font	Arial, Bold, Size 14
gridx	0
gridy	0
gridwidth	2
insets	10, 10, 0, 0
anchor	WEST

fileTextArea:

size	220, 50
font	Arial, Plain, Size 12
editable	false
background	White
lineWrap	true
wrapStyleWord	true
gridx	0
gridy	1
gridwidth	2
insets	0, 10, 10, 0

weightCalendar:

size	220, 200
border	Black line, width 2
gridx	0
gridy	2
gridwidth	2
insets	5, 10, 0, 5

weightLabel:

text	Weight (lb)
font	Arial, Bold, Size 14
gridx	0
gridy	3
insets	10, 10, 0, 0
anchor	WEST

weightTextField:

size	100, 25
font	Arial, Plain, Size 12
gridx	1
gridy	3
insets	10, 5, 0, 0

addButton:

text	Add Weights to File
gridx	0
gridy	4
gridwidth	2
insets	10, 0, 0, 0

Declare these controls using:

```
JLabel fileLabel = new JLabel();
JTextArea fileTextArea = new JTextArea();
JCalendar weightCalendar = new JCalendar();
JLabel weightLabel = new JLabel();
JTextField weightTextField = new JTextField();
JButton addButton = new JButton();
```

Add the controls to the panel with this code (in the frame constructor):

```
fileLabel.setText("Current Weight File");
fileLabel.setFont(new Font("Arial", Font.BOLD, 14));
gridConstraints = new GridBagConstraints();
gridConstraints.gridx = 0;
gridConstraints.gridy = 0;
gridConstraints.gridwidth = 2;
gridConstraints.insets = new Insets(10, 10, 0, 0);
gridConstraints.anchor = GridBagConstraints.WEST;
editorPanel.add(fileLabel, gridConstraints);

fileTextArea.setPreferredSize(new Dimension(220, 50));
fileTextArea.setFont(new Font("Arial", Font.PLAIN, 12));
fileTextArea.setEditable(false);
fileTextArea.setBackground(Color.WHITE);
fileTextArea.setLineWrap(true);
fileTextArea.setWrapStyleWord(true);
gridConstraints = new GridBagConstraints();
gridConstraints.gridx = 0;
gridConstraints.gridy = 1;
gridConstraints.gridwidth = 2;
gridConstraints.insets = new Insets(0, 10, 10, 0);
editorPanel.add(fileTextArea, gridConstraints);
```

```
weightCalendar.setPreferredSize(new Dimension(220, 200));
weightCalendar.setBorder(BorderFactory.createLineBorder(Co
lor.BLACK, 2));
gridConstraints = new GridBagConstraints();
gridConstraints.gridx = 0;
gridConstraints.gridy = 2;
gridConstraints.gridwidth = 2;
gridConstraints.insets = new Insets(5, 10, 0, 5);
editorPanel.add(weightCalendar, gridConstraints);
weightCalendar.addPropertyChangeListener(new
PropertyChangeListener()
{
  public void propertyChange(PropertyChangeEvent e)
  {
    weightCalendarPropertyChange(e);
  }
});

weightLabel.setText("Weight (lb)");
weightLabel.setFont(new Font("Arial", Font.BOLD, 14));
gridConstraints = new GridBagConstraints();
gridConstraints.gridx = 0;
gridConstraints.gridy = 3;
gridConstraints.insets = new Insets(10, 10, 0, 0);
gridConstraints.anchor = GridBagConstraints.WEST;
editorPanel.add(weightLabel, gridConstraints);

weightTextField.setPreferredSize(new Dimension(100, 25));
weightTextField.setFont(new Font("Arial", Font.PLAIN,
12));
gridConstraints = new GridBagConstraints();
gridConstraints.gridx = 1;
gridConstraints.gridy = 3;
gridConstraints.insets = new Insets(10, 5, 0, 0);
editorPanel.add(weightTextField, gridConstraints);
weightTextField.addActionListener(new ActionListener ()
{
  public void actionPerformed(ActionEvent e)
  {
    weightTextFieldActionPerformed(e);
  }
});
```

```
addButton.setText("Add Weight to File");
gridConstraints.gridx = 0;
gridConstraints.gridy = 4;
gridConstraints.gridwidth = 2;
gridConstraints.insets = new Insets(10, 0, 0, 0);
editorPanel.add(addButton, gridConstraints);
addButton.addActionListener(new ActionListener()
{
  public void actionPerformed(ActionEvent e)
  {
   addButtonActionPerformed(e);
  }
});
```

Three methods were added with this code, one to detect changes in selected dates (**weightCalendarPropertyChange**), one to detect changes in an entered weight value (**weightTextFieldActionPerformed**) and one to detect button clicks (**addButtonActionPerformed**). Add these empty methods:

```
private void
weightCalendarPropertyChange(PropertyChangeEvent e)
{
}

private void weightTextFieldActionPerformed(ActionEvent e)
{
}

private void addButtonActionPerformed(ActionEvent e)
{
}
```

Save, run the project to see the results:

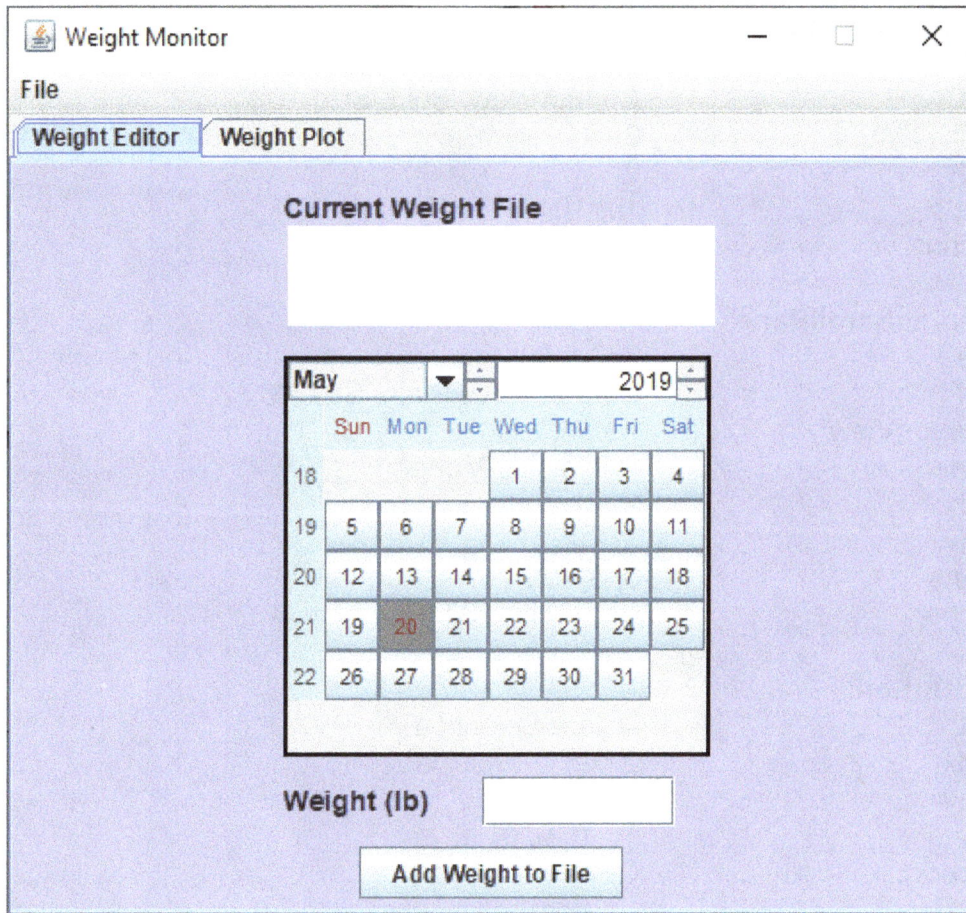

The controls will move to the left when we complete the panel. We do that now.

Let's add the controls on the right side of the editor panel. Control properties are:

weightsListLabel:
text	Date Weight (lb)
font	Courier New, Bold, Size 16
gridx	2
gridy	0
insets	10, 10, 0, 0
anchor	WEST

weightsScrollPane:
size	250, 300
font	Courier New, Plain, Size 16
viewportView	weightsList
model	weightsListModel
gridx	2
gridy	1
insets	0, 5, 0, 0
anchor	NORTHWEST

addButton:
text	Delete Selection
gridx	2
gridy	4
insets	10, 0, 0, 0
anchor	CENTER

Declare these controls (and the list and list model needed by the scroll pane) using:

```
JLabel weightsListLabel = new JLabel();
JScrollPane weightsScrollPane = new JScrollPane();
JList weightsList = new JList();
DefaultListModel weightsListModel = new
DefaultListModel();
JButton deleteButton = new JButton();
```

Add the controls to the panel with this code (in the frame constructor):

```
weightsListLabel.setText("Date    Weight (lb)");
weightsListLabel.setFont(new Font("Courier New",
Font.BOLD, 16));
gridConstraints = new GridBagConstraints();
gridConstraints.gridx = 2;
gridConstraints.gridy = 0;
gridConstraints.insets = new Insets(10, 10, 0, 0);
gridConstraints.anchor = GridBagConstraints.WEST;
editorPanel.add(weightsListLabel, gridConstraints);

weightsScrollPane.setPreferredSize(new Dimension(250,
300));
weightsList.setFont(new Font("Courier New", Font.PLAIN,
16));
weightsScrollPane.setViewportView(weightsList);
weightsList.setModel(weightsListModel);
gridConstraints = new GridBagConstraints();
gridConstraints.gridx = 2;
gridConstraints.gridy = 1;
gridConstraints.gridheight = 3;
gridConstraints.insets = new Insets(0, 5, 0, 0);
gridConstraints.anchor = GridBagConstraints.NORTHWEST;
editorPanel.add(weightsScrollPane, gridConstraints);
weightsList.addListSelectionListener(new
ListSelectionListener()
{
  public void valueChanged(ListSelectionEvent e)
  {
    weightsListValueChanged(e);
  }
});

deleteButton.setText("Delete Selection");
gridConstraints.gridx = 2;
gridConstraints.gridy = 4;
gridConstraints.insets = new Insets(10, 0, 0, 0);
gridConstraints.anchor = GridBagConstraints.CENTER;
editorPanel.add(deleteButton, gridConstraints);
deleteButton.addActionListener(new ActionListener()
{
  public void actionPerformed(ActionEvent e)
  {
    deleteButtonActionPerformed(e);
  }
});
```

Two methods were added with this code, one to detect changes in the list control (**weightsListValueChanged**) and one to detect button clicks (**deleteButtonActionPerformed**). Add these empty methods:

```
private void weightsListValueChanged(ListSelectionEvent e)
{
}

private void deleteButtonActionPerformed(ActionEvent e)
{
}
```

The list selection method requires this import statement:

```
import javax.swing.event.*;
```

Save, run the project to see the finished **Weight Editor** panel:

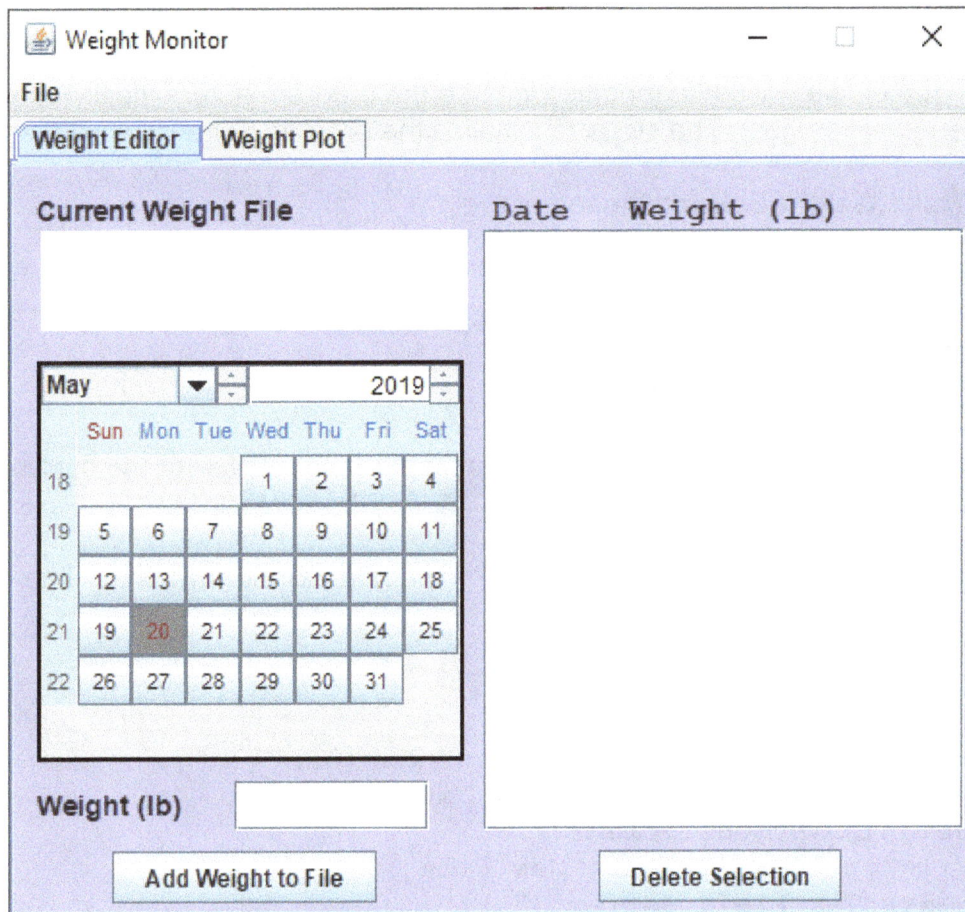

We will begin writing code for this tab page. As always, the code will be written in steps. We'll begin by writing code that starts a new weight file and initializes the application in its starting mode.

Code Design – New Weight File

When the project first begins, we want a new file to be established for weight values. (Later, we will make modifications so the program automatically opens the last opened/saved file.) The steps to initialize the program for a new file are:

> ➤ Make **Weight Editor** tab page active.
> ➤ Set calendar date to current day.
> ➤ Clear list control.
> ➤ Set **text** property of **fileTextArea** to **New File**.
> ➤ Blank out **weightTextField**.
> ➤ Give focus to **weightTextField**.

With these steps, the program is ready to accept the first entry for the current date.

We put these initialization steps in a general method named **initialize**. The code is:

```
private void initialize()
{
  weightTabbedPane.setSelectedIndex(0);
  weightCalendar.setDate(new Date());
  weightsListModel.clear();
  fileTextArea.setText("New File");
  weightTextField.setText("");
  weightTextField.requestFocus();
}
```

The **Date** object (sets the initial date) requires this import statement:

```
import java.util.*;
```

This general method should be called when the frame is first created. Add this single line at the end of the frame constructor code.

```
initialize();
```

This method should also be called when the user selects **New Weight File** in the **File** menu. Before calling it, though, the user should be asked if he/she really wants to start a new file. The code for the corresponding **newMenuItemActionPerformed** method is:

```
private void newMenuItemActionPerformed(ActionEvent e)
{
   if (JOptionPane.showConfirmDialog(null, "Are you sure
you want to start a new weight file?", "New File",
JOptionPane.YES_NO_OPTION, JOptionPane.QUESTION_MESSAGE)
== JOptionPane.YES_OPTION)
   {
      initialize();
   }
}
```

And, let's take care of the **exitMenuItemActionPerformed** method while we're at it. The code is a little different here than usual. Usually we just close the application if a user clicks **Exit**. Here, though, we want to save some information when the program stops (that code will be added later). We want to save this information whether the user clicks the **Exit** button or clicks the **X** in the upper right corner of the frame. When a user clicks the **X**, code in the **exitForm** method is executed. Hence, we will simply have the **exitMenuItemActionPerformed** method call this method to insure the same code (in the **exitForm** method) is executed:

```
private void exitMenuItemActionPerformed(ActionEvent e)
{
   exitForm(null);
}
```

In general, it is a good idea to have your 'exit' button method call the **exitForm** method to make sure the program is always exited in a consistent manner. Also, you should make sure you have saved any edits before clicking **Exit**. You could put a message box here asking the user if they really mean to exit. I've chosen not to.

Add these methods (**initialize**, **newMenuItemActionPerformed**, **exitMenuItemActionPerformed**) to the project. Add the reference to the **initialize** method in the frame constructor.

Save and run the application to make sure things initialize correctly. The frame should appear as:

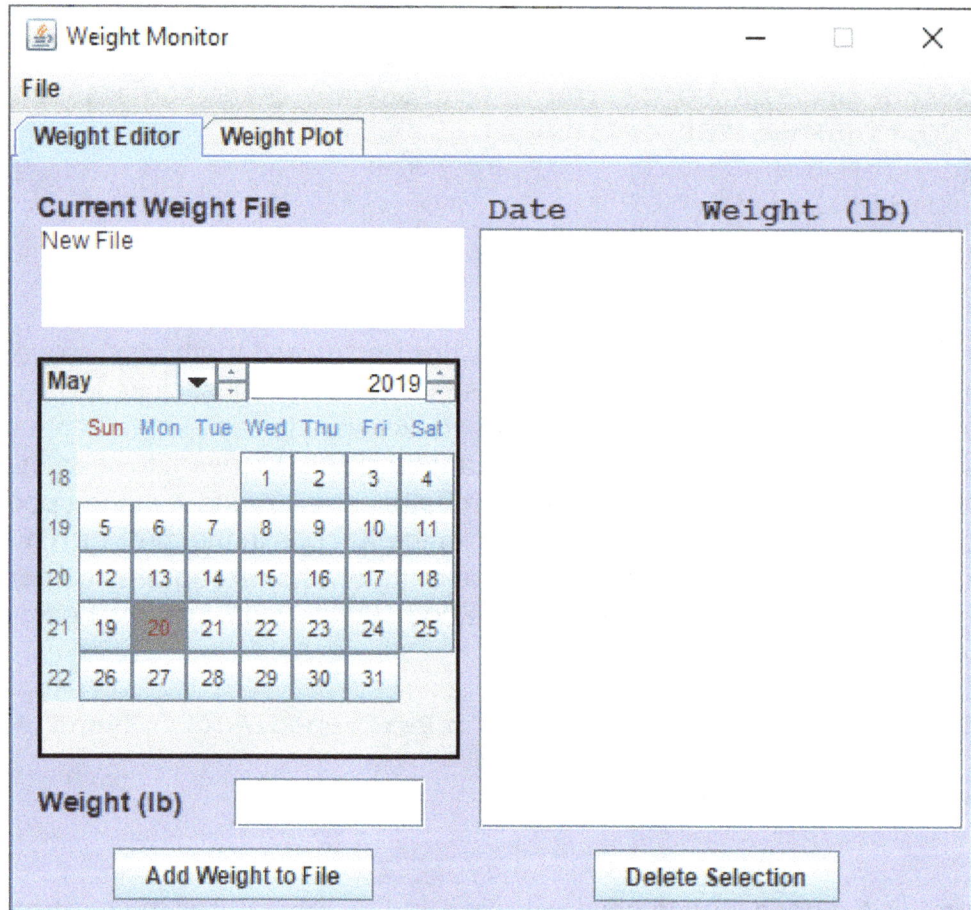

On your frame, the current date will appear. Try the **New Weight File** option under the **File** menu. This message box should appear asking you if you're sure:

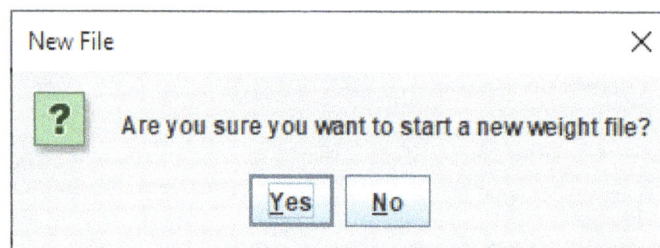

Make sure the **Exit** option works.

Code Design – Entering Weights

When the program opens, the user selects a date from the calendar (if not the current date) and enters a corresponding weight in the text field control. The user then clicks **Add Weight to File** to have that entry placed in the list control. Here, we write the code that accomplishes this task.

Once a user selects a date and enters a weight, we need to process the following steps to add the entry to the list control:

> ➢ See if entry already exists in list for selected date; if so, delete the entry to avoid a repeat.
> ➢ Add new date and new weight to list.
> ➢ Highlight (select) new entry in list.

The code to implement these steps will be in the **addButtonActionPerformed** method. Before writing code to process these steps, let's look at how the information will be formatted in the list control.

We want the date and weight information to be neatly represented in a single line of information in the list control. The format we choose is to have each line be 19 characters long (I picked this number because it fit nicely in the space provided). The first 10 columns of the line will be the date in a **yyyy/mm/dd** format (where **yyyy** is the year number, **mm** is the month number, and **dd** the day number). Using this format insures the lines are can be sorted in ascending date order. The weight (with a single decimal place) will be right justified in the remaining 9 columns. A fixed width font (**Courier New**) is used. As an example, if the weight is 202 on April 24, 2005, the line in the list control will be:

```
2005/04/24     202.0
```

There are four spaces between the date and the weight, making the line the required 19 characters long. Formatting the weight is straightforward. Let's look at how to get the date in this string format (**yyyy/mm/dd**).

The calendar control uses the **Date** data type to represent a date. This type is used to hold a date <u>and</u> a time. Here, we only want the date. To initialize a **Date** variable (**myDate**) to a specific date, use:

```
Date myDate = new Date(year, month, day);
```

where **year** is the desired year (less 1900, that is, a value of 0 represents the year 1900) (**int** type), **month** the desired month (**int** type), and **day** the desired day (**int** type). The month 'numbers' run from 0 (January) to 11 (December), not 1 to 12. As an example, if you use:

```
myDate = new Date(50, 6, 19);
```

then, display the result, you would get:

```
Wed Jul 19 00:00:00 GMT-08:00 1950
```

This is my birthday (July 19, 1950), by the way. The time is set to a default value since only a date was specified.

Individual parts of a **Date** object can be retrieved. For our example:

```
myDate.getYear()    // returns 50
myDate.getMonth()   // returns 6
myDate.getDate()    // returns 19
```

To retrieve the actual year, add 1900 to the value returned by **getYear**. To retrieve the month (1 – 12), add 1 to the value returned by **getMonth**. Note, to retrieve the day number, the method is **getDate**, not **getDay** – **getDay** returns the day of the week (a number from 0 to 6).

We will write two general methods to work with dates. One takes a **Date** object and converts it to the desired string format (**dateToString**) and one that takes the string format and converts it to a **Date** object (**stringToDate**). The two methods are:

```
private String dateToString(Date dd)
{
  String yString = String.valueOf(dd.getYear() + 1900);
  int m = dd.getMonth() + 1;
  String mString = new DecimalFormat("00").format(m);
  int d = dd.getDate();
  String dString = new DecimalFormat("00").format(d);
  return(yString + "/" + mString + "/" + dString);
}

private Date stringToDate(String s)
{
  int y = Integer.valueOf(s.substring(0, 4)).intValue() -
1900;
  int m = Integer.valueOf(s.substring(5, 7)).intValue() -
1;
  int d = Integer.valueOf(s.substring(8, 10)).intValue();
  return(new Date(y, m, d));
}
```

Notice we use zero-padding for months and days, that is if the month is 6, we write it as 06. Add these methods to your project.

We can use these date methods to format a data line with the date and weight. The function is named **formLine**. It requires a date (in **yyyy/mm/dd String** format) and weight (**String** type) as input arguments. It returns the data line as a **String** type:

```
private String formLine(String d, String w)
{
  int lineLength = 19;
  String s = d;
  w = new
DecimalFormat("0.0").format(Double.valueOf(w).doubleValue(
));
  for (int i = 0; i < lineLength - 10 - w.length(); i++)
    s += " ";
  s += w;
  return (s);
}
```

You should recognize the steps in forming the line. Note how we determine how many spaces to add between the date (10 characters long) and the weight. The **DecimalFormat** method needs this import statement:

```
import java.text.*;
```

With the **formLine** function, we can add a date and weight to the list control. We also need the capability of 'parsing' out date and weight values from a list line. The two methods that do this are **getDate** and **getWeight**. Each method has the list data line (19 characters long) as the input argument. **getDate** returns the date (in the desired **yyyy/mm/dd String** format) and **getWeight** returns the weight (**String** type). Those methods are:

```
private String getDate(String s)
{
  s = s.substring(0, 10);
  return(s);
}
```

```
private String getWeight(String s)
{
  s = s.substring(10);
  return (s.trim());
}
```

One more method is needed. The last step in adding a line to the list is to highlight the newly added line. This involves searching through the list and finding the line with the matching date (using the **getDate** method). The method **findDate** takes a date (**String** type) as input and returns the index (**int** type) of the line in the list with that date. A negative one (-1) is returned if no matching line is found. The code that does the search is:

```
private int findDate(String d)
{
  if (!weightsListModel.isEmpty())
  {
    for (int i = 0; i < weightsListModel.getSize(); i++)
    {
      if
(getDate(weightsListModel.getElementAt(i).toString()).equa
ls(d))
         return (i);
    }
  }
  return (-1);
}
```

With these new methods, we can now write the **addButtonActionPerformed** method that implements the previously outlined steps:

```java
private void addButtonActionPerformed(ActionEvent e)
{
  int i;
  // add to list (check to see if date already there)
  i = findDate(dateToString(weightCalendar.getDate()));
  if (i != -1)
    weightsListModel.removeElementAt(i);
  String item =
formLine(dateToString(weightCalendar.getDate()),
weightTextField.getText());
  // bubble sort to see where item goes in list to
maintain order
  if (weightsListModel.isEmpty() ||
item.compareTo(weightsListModel.getElementAt(weightsListMo
del.size() - 1).toString()) > 0)
  {
    // if list empty or greater than last item, item goes
at end
    weightsListModel.addElement(item);
    weightsList.setSelectedIndex(weightsListModel.size() -
1);
  }
  else
  {
    for (i = weightsListModel.size() - 1; i >= 0; i--)
    {
      if
((weightsListModel.getElementAt(i).toString().compareTo(it
em)) < 0)
      {
        break;
      }
    }
    weightsListModel.insertElementAt(item, i + 1);
    weightsList.setSelectedIndex(i + 1);
  }
}
```

The list control has no sorting capability – we use code to place entries in proper position. We using something called a **bubble sort** to do this. The idea is simple. First, if the list is empty or the new entry is 'greater than' the last entry, we put the new entry at the end. Else, we go through the existing list from bottom to top (**bubbling** up), find where the new entry fits and add it at the proper position. In either case, we highlight the added entry using the **setSelectedIndex** method. Add **addButtonActionPerformed**, **formLine**, **GetDate, getWeight, findDate** methods to your project.

Save and run the project. Type a weight in the text box control and click the **Add Weight to File**. When I type my weight in for today, I see:

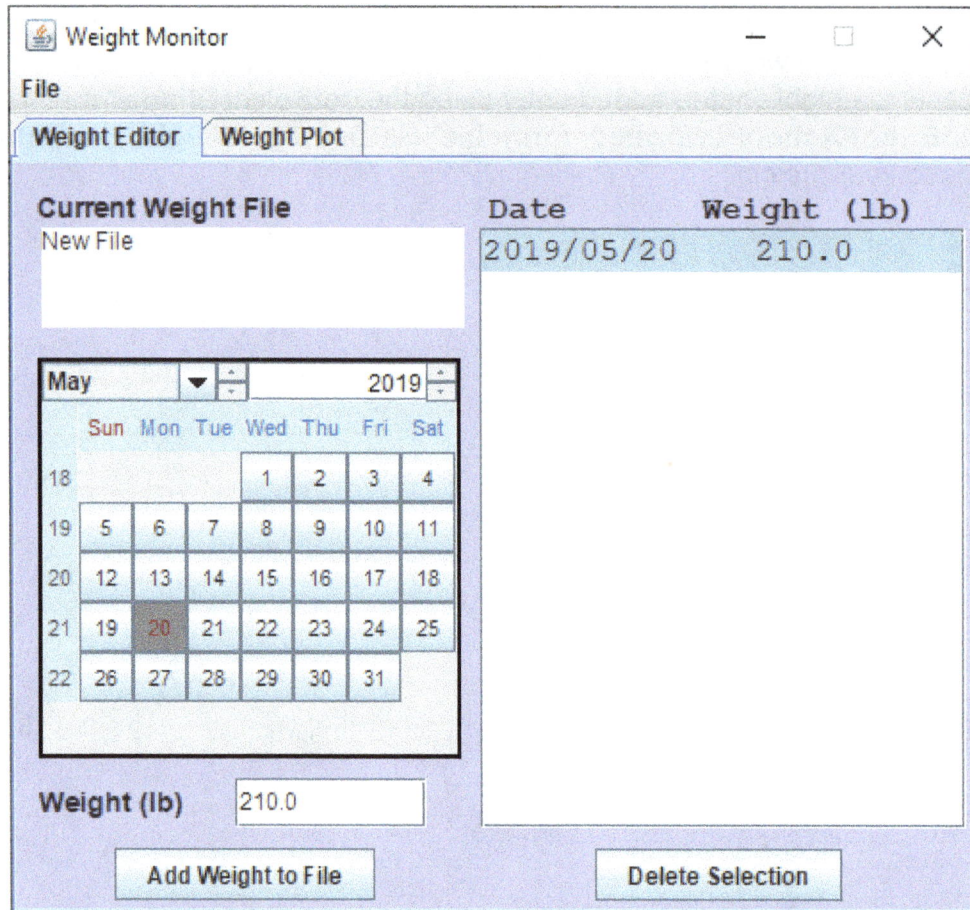

Note the proper formatting in the list control. Pick some other dates on the calendar and enter other weights if you'd like. Stop the project when you're done.

You may or may not have noted that when entering a weight in the text box, there are no restrictions on what you can type or if you type any entry. In the **Loan Assistant** project (Chapter 3), we developed this method (**validateDecimalNumber**) that validates decimal number entries in text field controls:

```java
private boolean validateDecimalNumber(JTextField tf)
{
  // checks to see if text field contains
  // valid decimal number with only digits and a single
decimal point
  String s = tf.getText().trim();
  boolean hasDecimal = false;
  boolean valid = true;
  if (s.length() == 0)
  {
    valid = false;
  }
  else
  {
    for (int i = 0; i < s.length(); i++)
    {
      char c = s.charAt(i);
      if (c >= '0' && c <= '9')
      {
        continue;
      }
      else if (c == '.' && !hasDecimal)
      {
        hasDecimal = true;
      }
      else
      {
        // invalid character found
        valid = false;
      }
    }
  }
  tf.setText(s);
  if (!valid)
  {
    tf.requestFocus();
  }
  return (valid);
}
```

Add this to your project.

We can now use this method in the **addButtonActionPerformed** method to validate entries before adding them to the list control. The shaded code shows the needed modifications:

```
private void addButtonActionPerformed(ActionEvent e)
{
  int i;
  if (!validateDecimalNumber(weightTextField))
  {
    JOptionPane.showConfirmDialog(null, "Empty or invalid
weight entry.\nPlease correct.", "Weight Input Error",
JOptionPane.DEFAULT_OPTION,
JOptionPane.INFORMATION_MESSAGE);
    return;
  }
  // add to list (check to see if date already there)
  .
  .
  .
}
```

We would also like this method to be executed when the user presses <**Enter**> after typing a weight. To do this, add a single line to the **weightTextFieldActionPerformed** method:

```
private void weightTextFieldActionPerformed(ActionEvent e)
{
  addButton.doClick();
}
```

Add these changes to the project to make sure the validation works as desired. When you type an incorrect entry you should see:

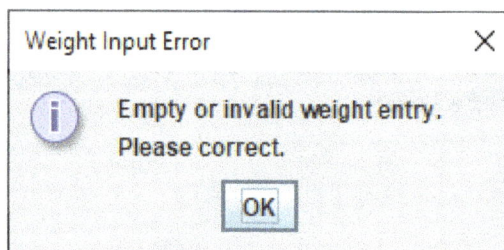

Make sure weight entries are added to the list when the <**Enter**> key is pressed.

Code Design – Editing Weights

We have the capability to enter weights for selected dates. We should also have the capability to edit existing entries in list control, in case of incorrect entries.

The most drastic editing feature is to delete an entry in the list control. To do this, the user selects the entry to delete, then clicks the button marked **Delete Selection**. The code for this process goes in the **deleteButtonActionPerformed** method:

```
private void deleteButtonActionPerformed(ActionEvent e)
{
  // remove selected item

weightsListModel.removeElementAt(weightsList.getSelectedIndex());
}
```

Note, we have not given the user an option to change his/her mind about deleting. You might like to do this using a message box.

Now, let's look at a less drastic editing step – changing a previously entered weight value. When a user clicks an entry in the list control, he/she should be given the ability to edit the entry. Conversely, when the user clicks a date on the calendar, if there is an corresponding entry in the list, editing should be available. Note both editing tasks require some coordination between the calendar date and the selected list entry.

When a user selects a list control line to edit, the following should occur:

> ➢ Parse the date from the selected line and establish that date on the calendar control.
> ➢ Parse the weight from the selected line and place it in **weightTextField**.
> ➢ Give focus to **weightTextField**.

After this, the user can change the weight and click **Add Weight to File** (or press **<Enter>**) to register the change.

The code for the above steps will go in the **weightsListValueChanged** method. The corresponding method is:

```
private void weightsListValueChanged(ListSelectionEvent e)
{
  // display corresponding date
  if (weightsList.getSelectedIndex() >= 0)
  {
    // form Date object from String

weightCalendar.setDate(stringToDate(weightsList.getSelecte
dValue().toString()));

weightTextField.setText(getWeight(weightsList.getSelectedV
alue().toString()));
    weightTextField.requestFocus();
  }
}
```

Add this method to the project.

When a user selects a date from the calendar control, the following should occur:

> ➤ Check to see if there is a corresponding date entry in list control.
> ➤ If corresponding entry is found:
>   ○ Select (highlight) entry in list.
>   ○ Parse the weight from the selected line and place it in **weightTextField**.
>   ○ Give focus to **weightTextField**.
> ➤ If corresponding entry is not found:
>   ○ Unselect all items in list.
>   ○ Blank out **weightTextField**.
>   ○ Give focus to **weightTextField**.

In either case, the user can enter a weight for the selected date and click **Add Weight to File** (or press <**Enter**>) to register the change.

The code for responding to a date selection is placed in the **calWeights DateChanged** method. That code is:

```
private void
weightCalendarPropertyChange(PropertyChangeEvent e)
{
  // show corresponding list box element (if there is one)
  int i;
  i = findDate(dateToString(weightCalendar.getDate()));
  if (i != -1)
  {
    weightsList.setSelectedIndex(i);

weightTextField.setText(getWeight(weightsList.getSelectedV
alue().toString()));
  }
  else
  {
    weightsList.clearSelection();
    weightTextField.setText("");
  }
  weightTextField.requestFocus();
}
```

Place this method in the project. Notice use of the **findDate** method to highlight the corresponding line (if it is there).

Save and run the project. Click a few dates on the calendar control and add some weights. Then, try the editing features. Click a date on the calendar – see if there is a matching line in the list control. Click a line in the list control – the date should be highlighted in the calendar control and the weight available for edit in the text box. Here's such a case in a run I made:

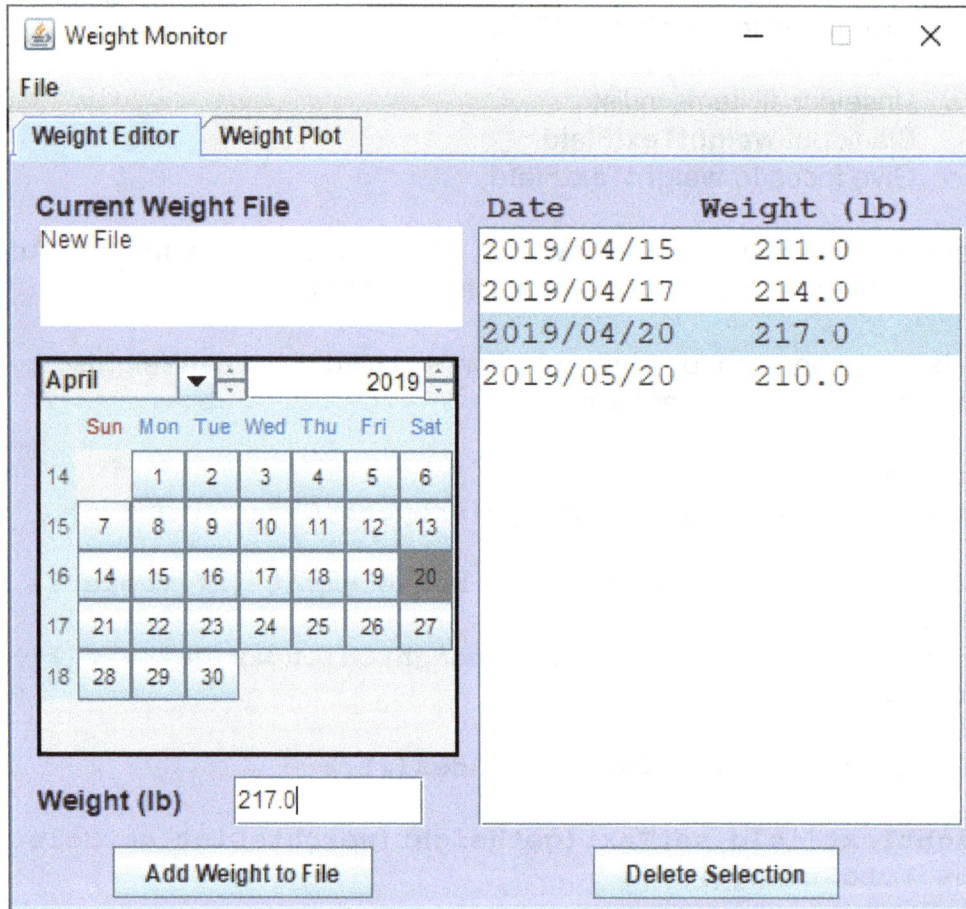

We now have full editing capability for the weight monitor project. We still need the capability to save any entries we might make. And we need the ability to read any saved values. We will use sequential files to save the date and weight values.

Code Design – Saving Weight Files

We now write the code that saves date and weight information to a sequential file. We will save each individual line from the list control on separate lines in the file.

When the user selects the **Save Weight File** option under the **File** menu, the following steps should be taken:

> ➢ Make sure there is at least one entry in the list.
> ➢ Display save file dialog (using **JChooser**) to obtain file name.
> ➢ If user clicks **Save**, then:
> > o Check if we are overwriting an existing file.
> > o Add extension to filename.
> > o Open file for output.
> > o Write each line in list control to file..
> > o Close file.
> ➢ If user clicks **Cancel**, do nothing.

We reviewed the **JChooser** control in Chapter 5 (**Multiple Choice Exam Proejct**).

Let's look at saving a weight file. Assuming we know the name of the file, it is created using Java **PrintWriter**, **BufferedWriter** and **FileWriter** objects. These objects require the following import statement:

```
import java.io.*;
```

Add this to your project. The syntax for opening a sequential file for output is:

```
PrintWriter outputFile = new PrintWriter(new
BufferedWriter(new FileWriter(myFile)));
```

where **myFile** is the name (a **String**) of the file to open and **outputFile** is the returned **PrintWriter** object used to write variables to disk.

A word of warning - when you open a file using the **PrintWriter** method, if the file already exists, it will be erased immediately! So, make sure you really want to overwrite the file. We will take steps to give the user a second chance before overwriting an existing weight file.

Information (variables or text) is written to a sequential file in an appended fashion. Separate Java statements are required for each appending. In this project, we write each line from the list control to the file. If a line is **myLine**, the syntax is:

```
outputFile.println(myLine);
```

When done writing to a sequential file, it must be flushed (information placed on disk) and closed. The syntax for our example file is:

```
outputFile.flush();
outputFile.close();
```

Once a file is closed, it is saved on the disk under the path (if different from the project path) and filename used to open the file.

We put the code to write the weight data to a file (**fn**) in a general method **saveWeightFile**:

```
private void saveWeightFile(String fn)
{
  try
  {
    PrintWriter outputFile = new PrintWriter(new
BufferedWriter(new FileWriter(fn)));
    fileTextArea.setText(fn);
    for (int i = 0; i < weightsListModel.getSize(); i++)
    {

outputFile.println(weightsListModel.getElementAt(i).toStri
ng());
    }
    outputFile.flush();
    outputFile.close();
  }
  catch (Exception ex)
  {
    JOptionPane.showConfirmDialog(null, "An error occurred
saving the weight file.", "File Error",
JOptionPane.DEFAULT_OPTION, JOptionPane.ERROR_MESSAGE);
  }
}
```

This code opens the file (**fn**) and cycles through all the lines in the list control, writing them to the file.

 The code to obtain and validate the filename selected by a user then call the above method goes in the **saveMenuItemActionPerformed** method:

```
private void saveMenuItemActionPerformed(ActionEvent e)
{
  if (weightsListModel.isEmpty())
  {
    JOptionPane.showConfirmDialog(null, "You need to enter
at least one weight value.", "File Error",
JOptionPane.DEFAULT_OPTION, JOptionPane.ERROR_MESSAGE);
    return;
  }
  JFileChooser saveChooser = new JFileChooser();
  saveChooser.setDialogType(JFileChooser.SAVE_DIALOG);
  saveChooser.setDialogTitle("Save Weight File");
  saveChooser.addChoosableFileFilter(new
FileNameExtensionFilter("Weight Files", "wgt"));
```

```
    if (saveChooser.showSaveDialog(this) ==
JFileChooser.APPROVE_OPTION)
  {
    // see if file already exists
    if (saveChooser.getSelectedFile().exists())
    {
      int response;
      response = JOptionPane.showConfirmDialog(null,
saveChooser.getSelectedFile().toString() + "exists.
Overwrite?", "Confirm Save", JOptionPane.YES_NO_OPTION,
JOptionPane.QUESTION_MESSAGE);
      if (response == JOptionPane.NO_OPTION)
      {
        return;
      }
    }
    // make sure file has wgt extension
    // strip off any extension that might be there
    // then tack on wgt
    String fileName =
saveChooser.getSelectedFile().toString();
    int dotlocation = fileName.indexOf(".");
    if (dotlocation == -1)
    {
      // no extension
      fileName += ".wgt";
    }
    else
    {
      // make sure extension is wgt
      fileName = fileName.substring(0, dotlocation) +
".wgt";
    }
    saveWeightFile(fileName);
  }
}
```

You also need this import statement for the file filter:

```
import javax.swing.filechooser.*;
```

Step through this to understand its operation. We first check to see if the selected file already exists. If it does, a message box appears. Then, we make sure the **wgt** extension is added to the file. Once a valid name (**fileName**) is available, the **saveWeightFile** method is called. Add this method to the project.

Save and run the project. Click some dates and enter some weights. Here are some values I entered:

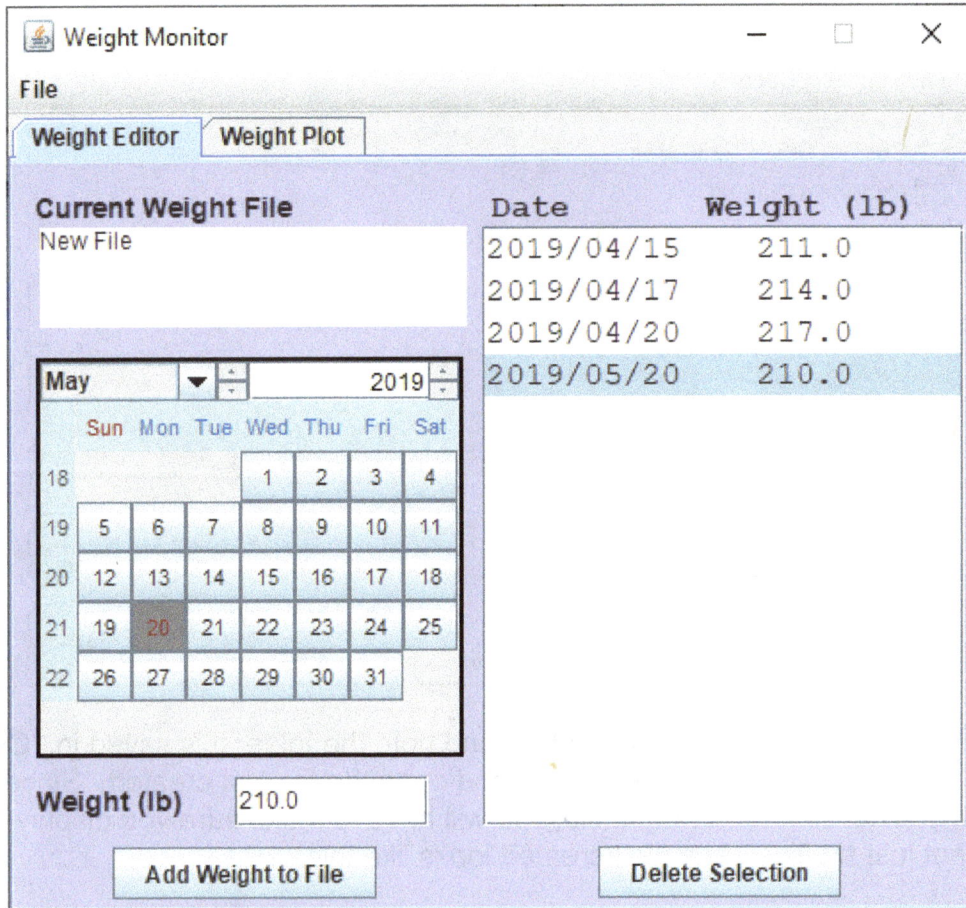

Choose **Save Weight File** from the **File** menu. You will see:

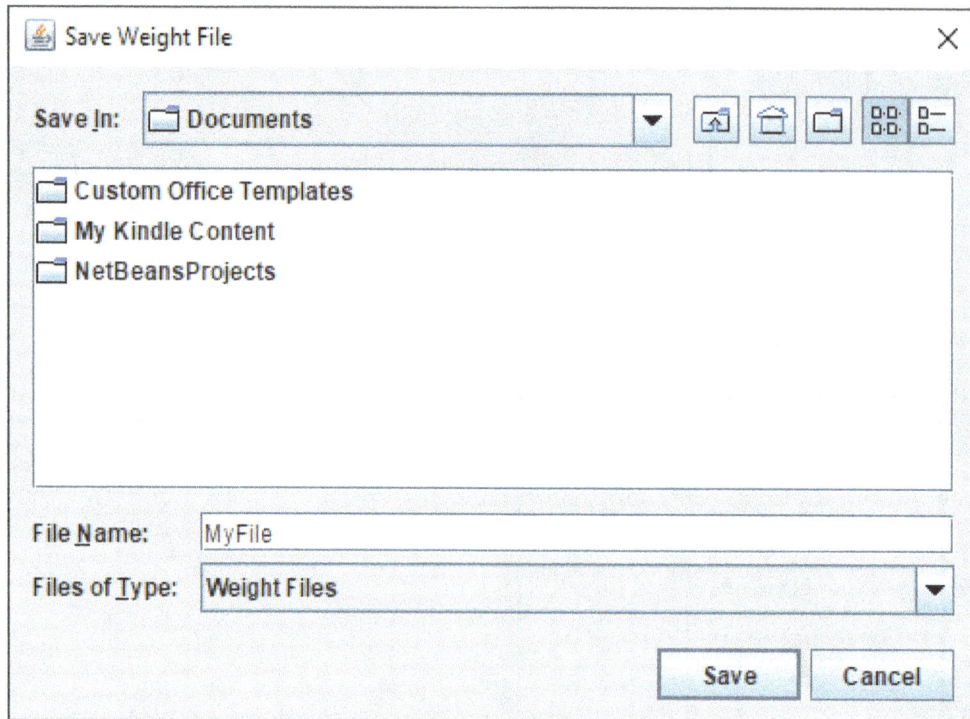

Give a name to your file (I chose **myfile**) and note the folder it is saved in. Click **Save**. Start a text editor (like **Notepad**) and open the file just created. Since we use a **wgt** extension for a weight file, you will have to make sure you display all file types, not just **txt** files. The file I created looks like this:

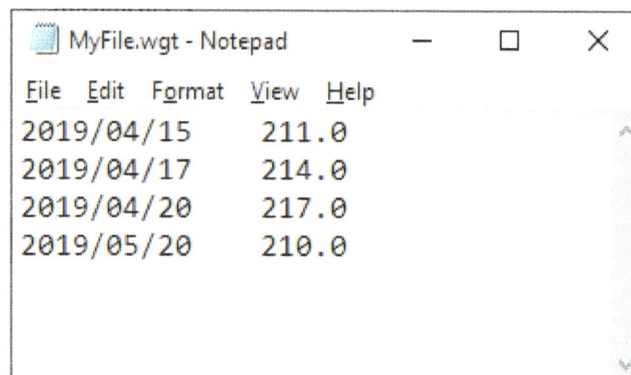

Note the file looks just like the list control entries.

Select **File** and Save **Weight File** from the menu again. Select the file you just saved:

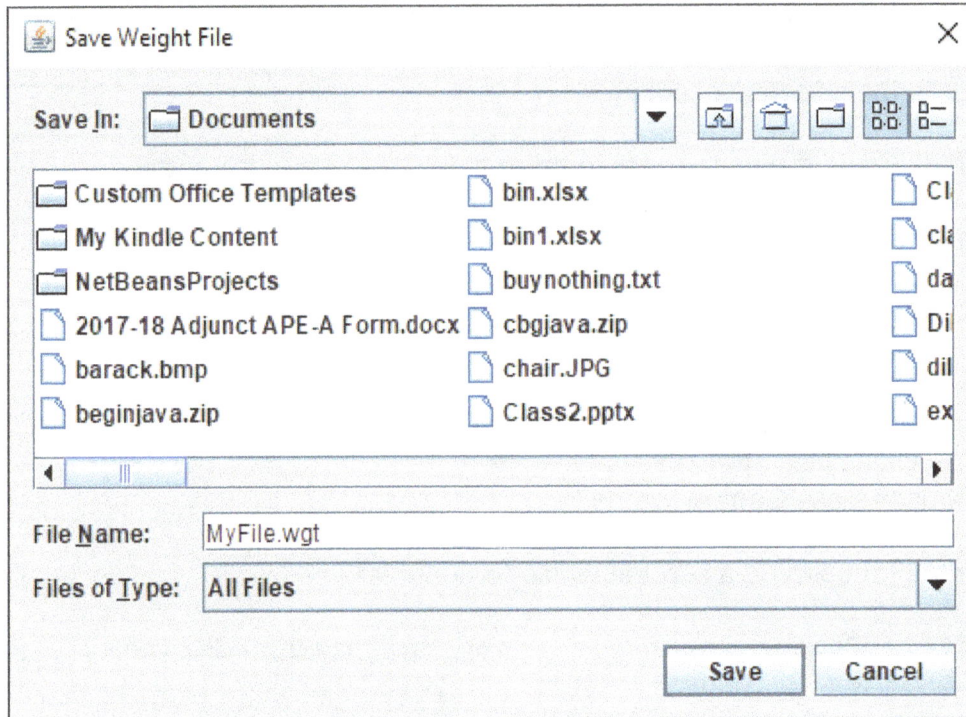

Click **Save**. This message will appear warning you that you are about to overwrite and existing file:

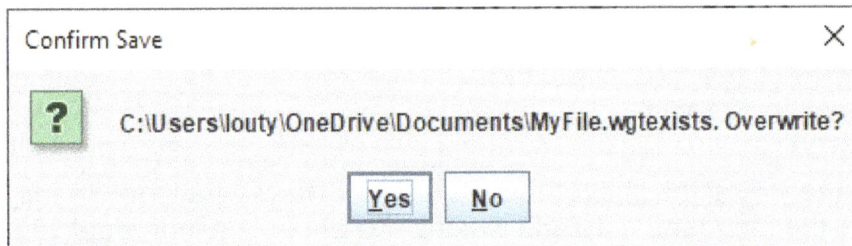

Code Design – Opening Weight Files

Now, with a capability to save weight files, we need code to open and read information from those files. When the user selects **Open Weight File** from the **File** menu, the following occurs:

> ➢ Make sure the user wants to open a new file; if not, do nothing.
> ➢ Display open file dialog to obtain file name.
> ➢ If user clicks **Open**, then:
> > o Initialize the panel.
> > o Open file for input.
> > o Set **text** property of **fileTextArea**.
> > o Read each date and weight pair.
> > o Add entry to list control using **formLine** method.
> > o Close file.
> ➢ If user clicks **Cancel**, do nothing.

The syntax for opening a sequential file for input is:

```
BufferedReader inputFile = new BufferedReader(new
FileReader(fileName));
```

where **fileName** is a complete path to the file and **inputFile** is the returned file object.

Once opened, we read information from the file. To read an entire line from a file opened as **inputFile**, use the **readLine** method:

```
myLine = inputFile.readLine();
```

where **myLine** will be the line represented as a **String** data type. In the weight file, this has the formatted date and weight. To obtain the individual variables, we need to 'parse' the line with the **getDate** and **getWeight** methods When all values have been read from the sequential file, it is closed using:

```
inputFile.close();
```

A general method **openWeightFile** is used to open and read a known file (**fn**):

```
private void openWeightFile(String fn)
{
  try
  {
    initialize();
    BufferedReader inputFile = new BufferedReader(new
FileReader(fn));
    fileTextArea.setText(fn);
    do
    {
      String s = inputFile.readLine();
      weightsListModel.addElement(s);
    }
    while (inputFile.ready());
    inputFile.close();
    // see if current date is in file
    int i =
findDate(dateToString(weightCalendar.getDate()));
    if (i != -1)
      weightsList.setSelectedIndex(i);
  }
  catch (Exception ex)
  {
    JOptionPane.showConfirmDialog(null, "An error occurred
opening the weight file.", "File Error",
JOptionPane.DEFAULT_OPTION, JOptionPane.ERROR_MESSAGE);
  }
}
```

The code reads in each line and places it in the list control. Note how the **ready** method is used to read until the end-of-file is reached. Once done, if today's date is in the listing, that element is selected in the list control. Add this method to your project.

The code to obtain a filename and call this method goes in the
mnuFileOpenActionPerformed method:

```java
private void openMenuItemActionPerformed(ActionEvent e)
{
  if (JOptionPane.showConfirmDialog(null, "Are you sure
you want to open a weight new file?", "New Weight File",
JOptionPane.YES_NO_OPTION, JOptionPane.QUESTION_MESSAGE)
== JOptionPane.YES_OPTION)
  {
    JFileChooser openChooser = new JFileChooser();
    openChooser.setDialogType(JFileChooser.OPEN_DIALOG);
    openChooser.setDialogTitle("Open Weight File");
    openChooser.addChoosableFileFilter(new
FileNameExtensionFilter("Weight Files", "wgt"));
    if (openChooser.showOpenDialog(this) ==
JFileChooser.APPROVE_OPTION)
    {

openWeightFile(openChooser.getSelectedFile().toString());
    }
  }
}
```

Save and run the project. Choose **Open Weight File** under the **File** menu. You will see the message box:

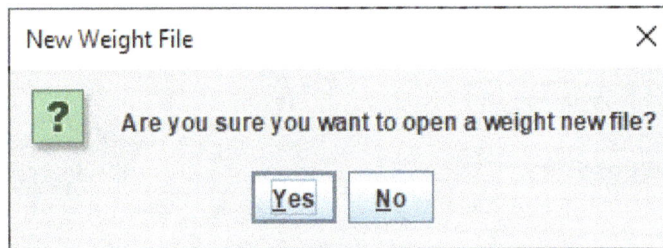

New Weight File   ✕

?   Are you sure you want to open a weight new file?

Yes   No

Click **Yes** and the open file dialog box will appear:

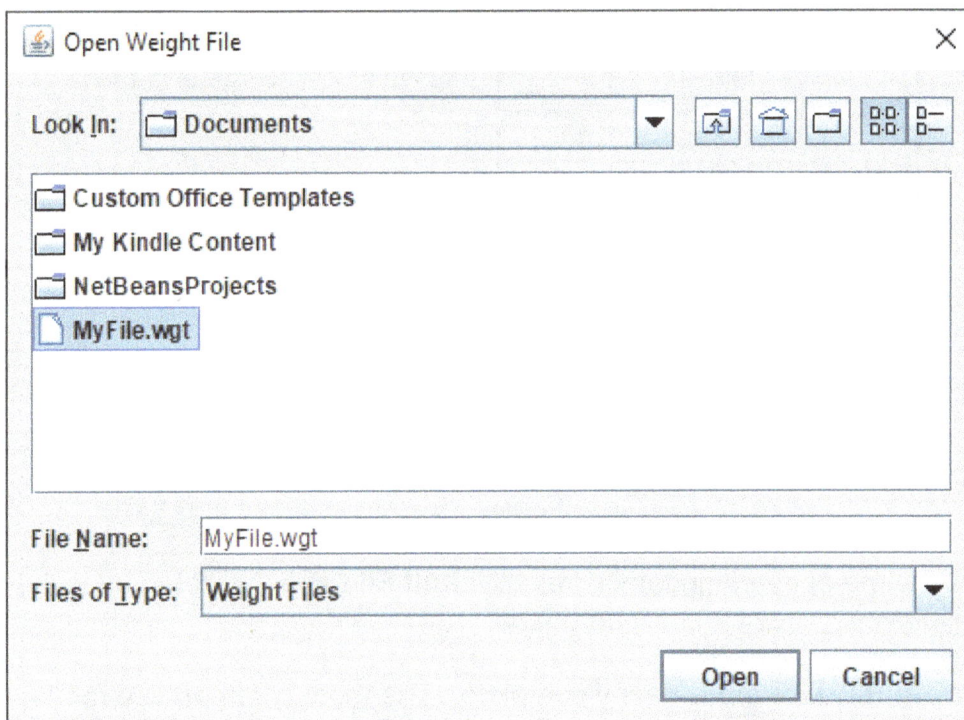

Open Weight File   ✕

Look In: Documents

Custom Office Templates
My Kindle Content
NetBeansProjects
MyFile.wgt

File Name: MyFile.wgt

Files of Type: Weight Files

Open   Cancel

Navigate to the file you just created and click **Open**. The dates and weights you entered will appear.

Here is what I see when I open the file I created (**myfile.wgt**):

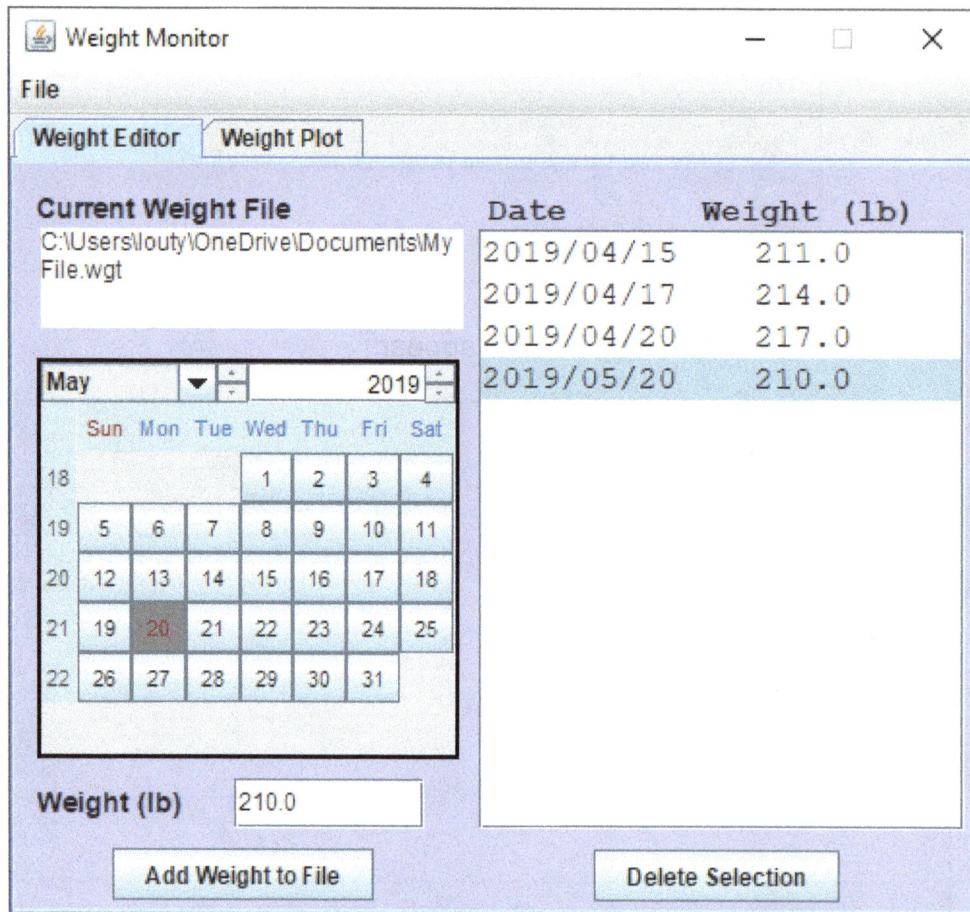

The file name appears under **Current Weight File** and the date and weight values are displayed. They can now be edited.

The **Weight Editor** tab is nearly complete. The most common use for the weight monitor program is to enter your daily weight. This involves starting the program, opening your weight file, making any new entries, saving the file, then exiting. You might also view a plot of your weight (using the **Weight Plot** tab we develop next). After a while, you get tired of opening the same file each time you run the program. It would be nice if your file opened automatically and the date and weight values were displayed. And, you get tired of remembering to save your file before exiting. It would be nice if the program would just automatically save the last file your were working with.

We can solve both of these problems. To do this, we use a configuration file. Such a file is used to save information needed to initialize a program. In our case, we want to use a configuration file to save the last file opened so that file is automatically opened/saved the next time we run the weight monitor program.

Code Design – Configuration File

We want to use a configuration file (named **weight.ini**) to save the name of the last weight file opened and/or saved in the weight monitor project. When the application ends (**exitForm** method), we need code to save the configuration file and specified weight file. That's why we call **exitForm** in the **exitMenuItemActionPerformed** method (rather than just close the form). That way, no matter how the application is stopped, either with the **Exit** menu item or by clicking the **X** in the upper right corner of the frame, the code in the **exitForm** event method (writing the configuration file) will be executed.

Conversely, when the application starts, we need code in the frame constructor method to open the configuration file and then open the specified weight file. Let's do the save steps first.

Establish a class level variable (**String** type) to hold the last file opened and/or saved:

```
String lastFile = "";
```

We initialize it to a blank.

Modify the **saveWeightFile** general method to establish a value for **lastFile** (new lines are shaded):

```
private void saveWeightFile(String fn)
{
  try
  {
    PrintWriter outputFile = new PrintWriter(new
BufferedWriter(new FileWriter(fn)));
    fileTextArea.setText(fn);
    for (int i = 0; i < weightsListModel.getSize(); i++)
    {

outputFile.println(weightsListModel.getElementAt(i).toStri
ng());
    }
    outputFile.flush();
    outputFile.close();
    lastFile = fn;
  }
  catch (Exception ex)
  {
    JOptionPane.showConfirmDialog(null, "An error occurred
saving the weight file.", "File Error",
JOptionPane.DEFAULT_OPTION, JOptionPane.ERROR_MESSAGE);
    lastFile = "";
  }
}
```

No value is established if there is an error in saving the file.

The **exitForm** method saves the configuration file and uses **SaveWeightFile** to automatically save **lastFile**. That method is (changes are shaded; only last line currently exists):

```
private void exitForm(WindowEvent evt)
{
  // Write out initialization file
  try
  {
    PrintWriter outputFile = new PrintWriter(new
BufferedWriter(new FileWriter("weight.ini")));
    outputFile.println(lastFile);
    outputFile.close();
  }
  catch (Exception ex)
  {
  }
  // save last file
  if (!lastFile.equals(""))
    saveWeightFile(lastFile);
  System.exit(0);
}
```

With these changes, when the program ends, the configuration file is saved, as is the last opened weight file. Make the noted changes.

Let's do the converse operation – open the configuration file and accompanying weight file. Modify the **openWeightFile** general method to establish a value for **lastFile** (new lines are shaded):

```java
private void openWeightFile(String fn)
{
  try
  {
    initialize();
    BufferedReader inputFile = new BufferedReader(new
FileReader(fn));
    fileTextArea.setText(fn);
    do
    {
      String s = inputFile.readLine();
      weightsListModel.addElement(s);
    }
    while (inputFile.ready());
    inputFile.close();
    lastFile = fn;
    // see if current date is in file
    int i =
findDate(dateToString(weightCalendar.getDate()));
    if (i != -1)
      weightsList.setSelectedIndex(i);
  }
  catch (Exception ex)
  {
    JOptionPane.showConfirmDialog(null, "An error occurred
opening the weight file.", "File Error",
JOptionPane.DEFAULT_OPTION, JOptionPane.ERROR_MESSAGE);
    lastFile = "";
  }
}
```

Again, no value is established if there is an error in opening the file.

The code to open the configuration file and use the **openWeightFile** method to automatically open **lastFile** goes in the frame constructor code. Add these lines at the end of that code (new code is shaded; one line is original):

```
// open .ini file
try
{
  BufferedReader inputFile = new BufferedReader(new
FileReader("weight.ini"));
  lastFile = inputFile.readLine();
  inputFile.close();
}
catch (Exception ex)
{
  // initialization file not found
  lastFile = "";
}
if (!lastFile.equals(""))
  openWeightFile(lastFile);
else
  initialize();
```

With these changes, when the program begins, the configuration file is opened and the last saved weight file opened and those values displayed.

The **Weight Editor** panel is now complete. Let's try it. Save and run the project. The form will appear in its initial configuration since no **lastFile** value has been saved yet (there is no **weight.ini** file). Click **Open Weight File** under the **File** menu. In the **\HomeJava\HomeJava Projects\WeightMonitor** folder is a sample weight file named **sample.wgt**. Open that file. You should see:

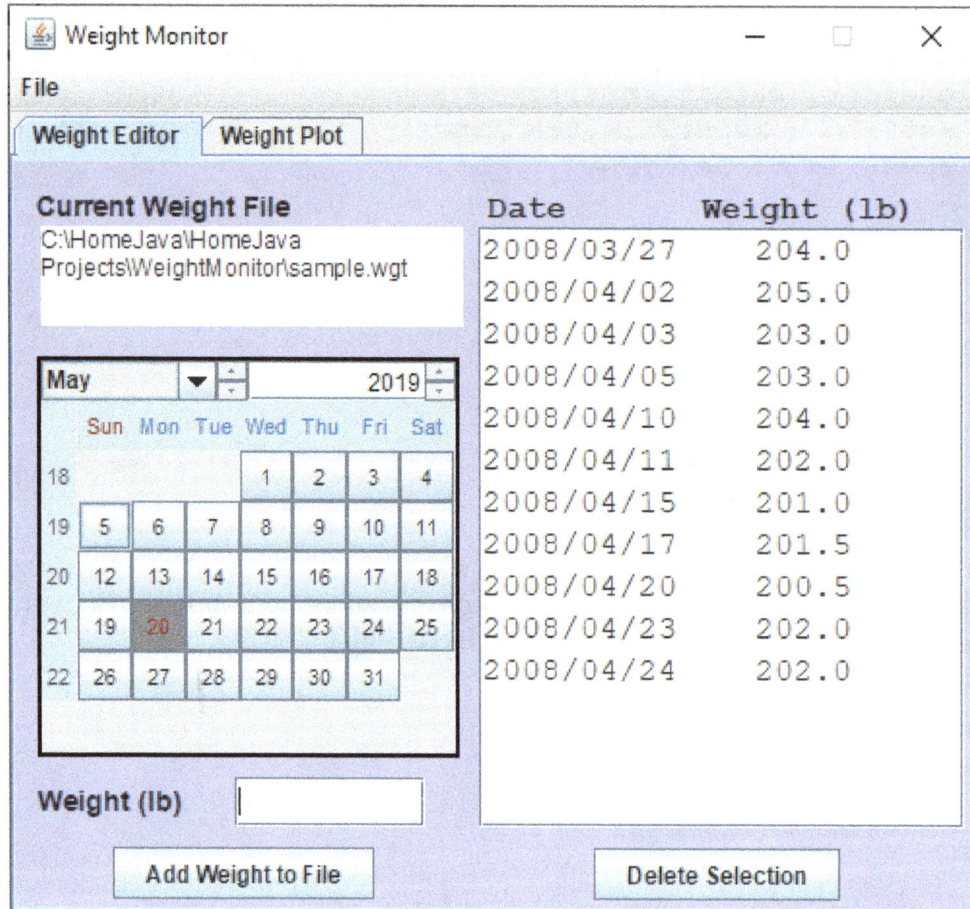

Edit some values if you want or add some values. Now, stop the project – the weight file will be automatically saved. And, at this point, the **weight.ini** file is written to your project's folder. Look in that folder to make sure it's there. Open it and you should see:

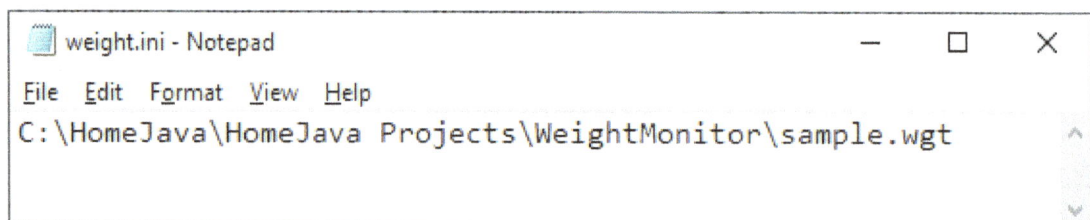

Now, run the project again. The data in the sample file (with any changes you made) should appear:

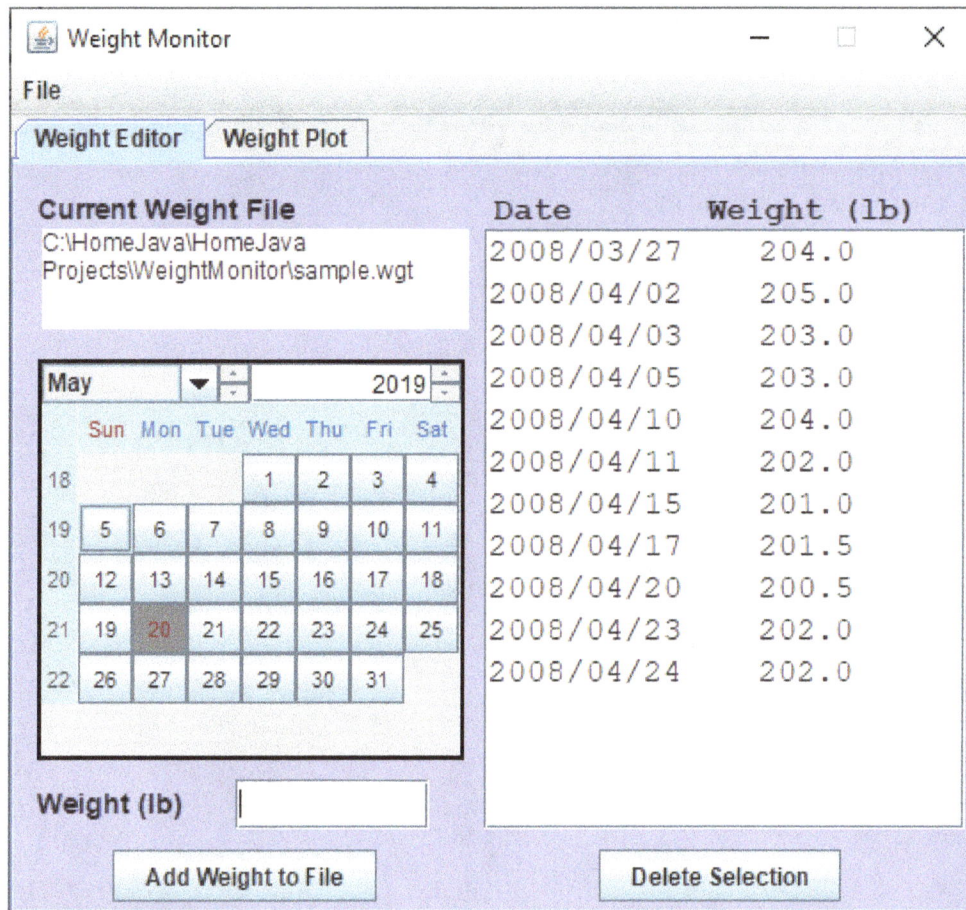

Now, whenever you run the weight monitor project, it will automatically begin using the last set of weight values you were editing. When you stop, any changes you made are automatically saved. This is usually what you want to do. You can always override this automatic feature if you want. If the values displayed upon opening are not correct, simply open the correct file using **Open** option in the **File** menu. Similarly, a file can be saved at any time using the **Save** option. Now, let's take a look at plotting these weight values.

Frame Design – Weight Plot Panel

Run the weight monitor program and click the **Weight Plot** tab. You see:

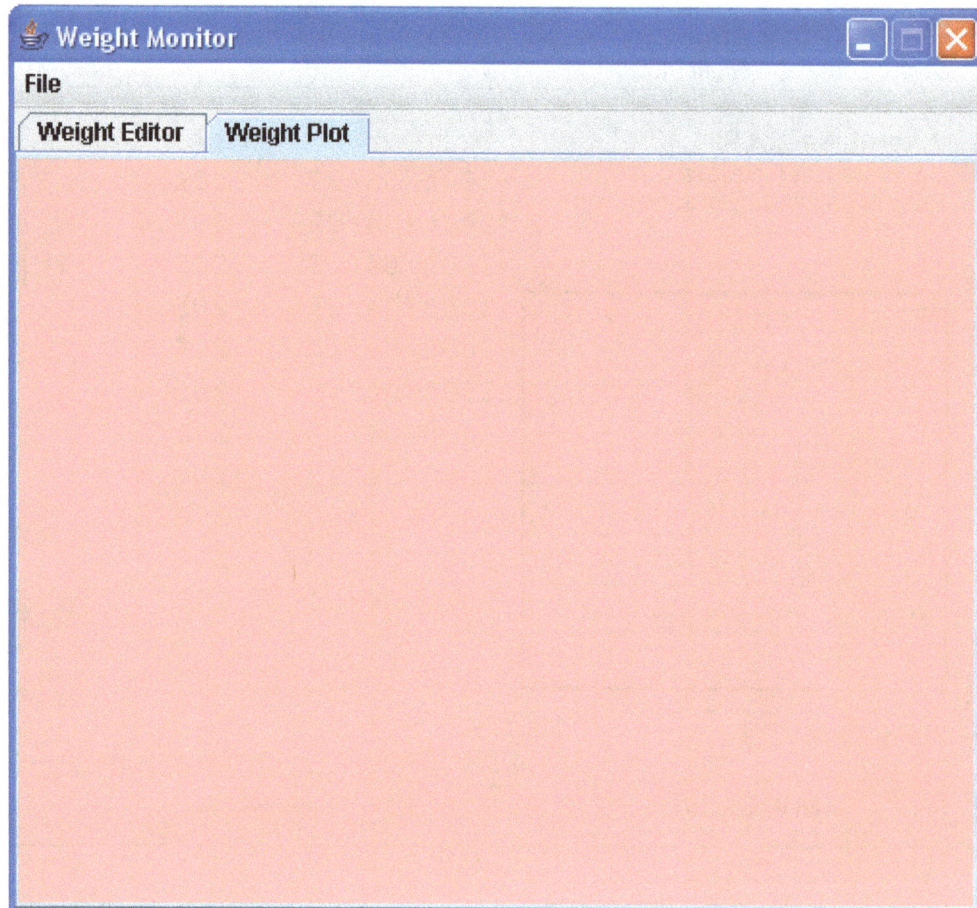

This is the empty **plotPanel** added long ago to the tabbed pane control. Recall **plotPanel** was constructed using our defined **WeightPlotPanel** class. That class has a **paintComponent** method where all graphics methods will reside.

Let's look at what the finished product will look like (originally, I sketched this on a piece of paper to get the general idea of where things go):

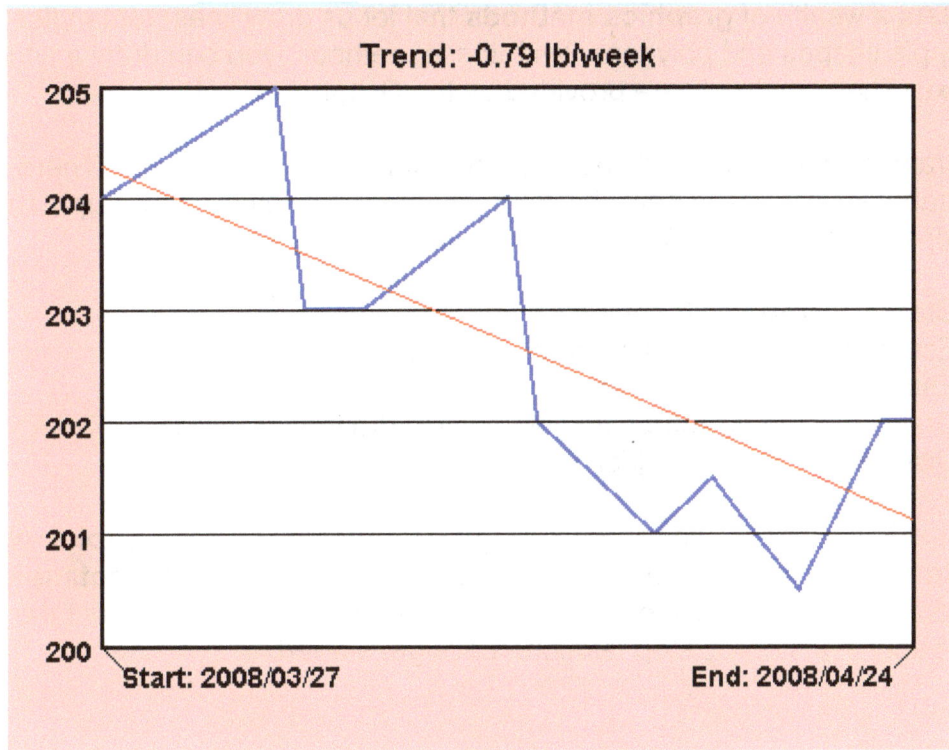

We have a white rectangular region hosting the plot (two lines, one straight and one jagged are shown). There are grid lines, horizontal and vertical axis labels and a heading title. To draw the information on this panel, we use graphics methods.

We need to learn several tasks:

1. Drawing a framed, filled rectangle for the plot area.
2. Drawing lines for the plot grid.
3. Drawing text information (yes, it is drawn) for plot labeling.
4. Drawing text/lines for legend.
5. Drawing weight plot.

We will look at how to accomplish each task. First, we give a general overview of **graphics methods** and the **graphics object**.

Graphics Methods

Java offers a wealth of **graphics methods** that let us draw lines, rectangles, ellipses, pie shapes and polygons. With these methods, you can draw anything – even text! These methods are provided by the **Graphics2D** class.

Using graphics objects is a little detailed, but worth the time to learn. There is a new vocabulary with many new objects to study. We'll cover every step. The basic approach to drawing with graphics objects will always be:

> ➢ Create a **Graphics2D** object.
> ➢ Establish the **Stroke** and **Paint** objects needed for drawing.
> ➢ Establish the object for drawing.
> ➢ Draw object to **Graphics2D** object using drawing methods
> ➢ Dispose of graphics object when done.

In the next few sections, we will learn about **Graphics2D** objects, **Stroke** objects and **Paint** objects (use of **colors**). We'll learn how to draw and fill **rectangles**, how to draw **lines**, and how to draw **text**. As we learn, we will construct the display panel in a step-by-step fashion. Let's get started.

Graphics2D Object

As mentioned, graphics methods (drawing methods) are applied to graphics objects. **Graphics2D objects** provide the "surface" for drawing methods. In this project, we will use the panel control for drawing.

A **Graphics2D object** (**g2D**) is created using:

```
Graphics g2D = (Graphics2D) hostControl.getGraphics();
```

where **hostControl** is the control hosting the graphics object. Note the **getGraphics** method returns a **Graphics** object that must be cast (converted) to a **Graphics2D** object. Placement of this statement depends on scope. Place it in a method for method level scope. Place it with other class level declarations for class level scope.

Once a graphics object is created, all graphics methods are applied to this object. Hence, to apply a drawing method named **drawingMethod** to the **g2D** object, use:

```
g2D.drawingMethod(arguments);
```

where **arguments** are any needed arguments.

Once you are done drawing to an object and need it no longer, it should be properly disposed to clear up system resources. The syntax for disposing of our example graphics object uses the **dispose** method:

```
g2D.dispose();
```

Stroke and Paint Objects

The attributes of lines (either lines or borders of shapes) drawn using **Graphics2D** objects are specified by the **stroke**. Stroke can be used to establish line style, such as solid, dashed or dotted lines, line thickness and line end styles. By default, a solid line, one pixel in width is drawn. In this class, we will only look at how to change the line thickness. Stroke is changed using the **setStroke** method. To set the thickness (**width**) of the line for a graphics object **g2D**, use a **BasicStroke** object:

```
g2D.setStroke(new BasicStroke(width));
```

After this method, all lines will be drawn with the new **width** attribute.

To change the color of lines being drawn, use the **setPaint** method. For our example graphics object, the color is changed using:

```
g2D.setPaint(color);
```

where **color** is either a built-in color or one set using RGB values. After this line of code, all lines are drawn with the new color.

The **setPaint** method can also be used to establish the color and pattern used to fill a graphics region.

Shapes and Drawing Methods

We will learn to draw various **shapes**. Shapes will include lines and rectangles. The classes used to do this drawing are in the **java.awt.geom.*** package, so we need to include an import statement for this package:

```
import java.awt.geom.*;
```

Shape objects are specified with the **user coordinates** of the hosting panel control (**myPanel**):

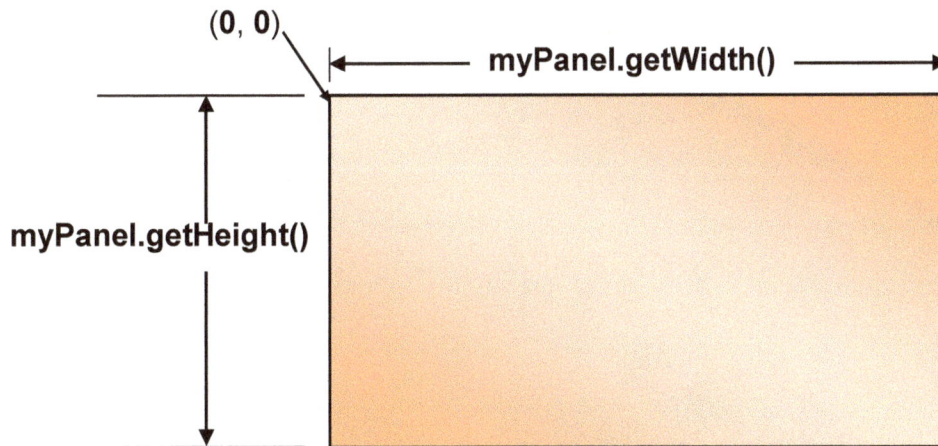

The host dimensions, **myPanel.getWidth()** and **myPanel.getHeight()** represent the "graphics" region of the control hosting the graphics object.

Points are referred to by a Cartesian pair, **(x, y)**. In the diagram, note the **x** (horizontal) coordinate runs from left to right, starting at **0** and extending to **myPanel.getWidth() - 1**. The **y** (vertical) coordinate goes from top to bottom, starting at **0** and ending at **myPanel.getHeight() - 1**. All measurements are integers and in units of **pixels**.

Once a **shape** object is created (we will see how to do that next), the shape is drawn using the draw method. For a shape **myShape** using our example graphics object (**g2D**), the code is:

```
g2D.draw(myShape);
```

The shape will be drawn using the current **stroke** and **paint** attributes.

For shape objects that encompass some two-dimensional region, that region can be filled using the fill method. For our example, the code is:

```
g2D.fill(myShape);
```

The shape will be filled using the current **paint** attribute.

Let's define our first two shapes – a **line** – yes, a line is a shape and a rectangle. This will allow us to draw the weight plot area in the display panel.

Line2D Shape

The first shape we learn to draw is a line, or the **Line2D** shape. This shape is used to connect two Cartesian points with a straight-line segment:

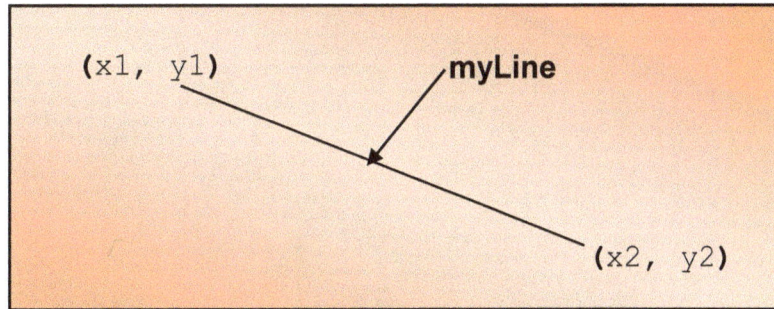

If we wish to connect the point (**x1**, **y1**) with (**x2**, **y2**), the shape (**myLine**) is created using:

```
Line2D.Double myLine = new Line2D.Double(x1, y1, x2, y2);
```

Each coordinate value is a **double** type (there is also a **Line2D.Float** shape, where each coordinate is a **float** type). Once created, the line is drawn (in a previously created Graphics2D object, **g2D**) using the **draw** method:

```
g2D.draw(myLine);
```

The line will be drawn using the current **stroke** and **paint** attributes.

Rectangle2D Shape

We now look at two-dimensional shapes. We want to draw a rectangle, represented by the **Rectangle2D** shape. To specify an rectangle, you specify the upper left corner (**x, y**), the width (**w**) and the height (**h**) of the rectangle:

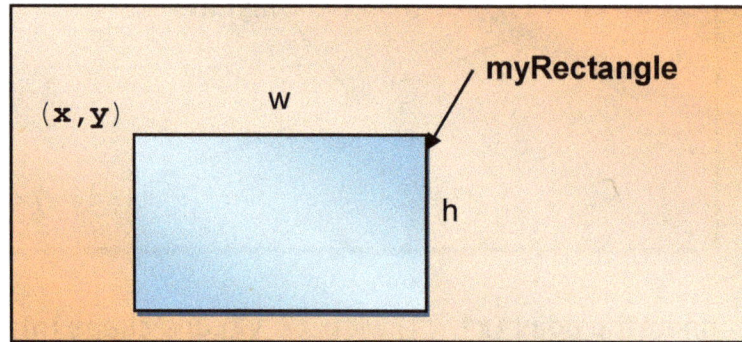

If the rectangle is named **myRectangle**, the corresponding shape is created using:

```
Rectangle2D.Double myRectangle = new Rectangle2D.Double(x,
y, w, h);
```

Each argument value is a **double** type (there is also a **Rectangle2D.Float** shape, where each argument is a **float** type). Once created, the rectangle is drawn (in a previously created Graphics2D object, **g2D**) using the **draw** method:

```
g2D.draw(myRectangle);
```

The rectangle will be drawn using the current **stroke** and **paint** attributes.

Say we have a panel (**myPanel**) of dimension (300, 200). To draw a black rectangle (**myRectangle**) in that panel, with a line width of 1 (the default stroke), starting at (40, 40), with width 150 and height 100, the Java code would be:

```
Graphics2D g2D = (Graphics2D) myPanel.getGraphics();
Rectangle2D.Double myRectangle = new
Rectangle2D.Double(40, 40, 150, 100);
g2D.setPaint(Color.BLACK);
g2D.draw(myRectangle);
g2D.dispose();
```

This produces:

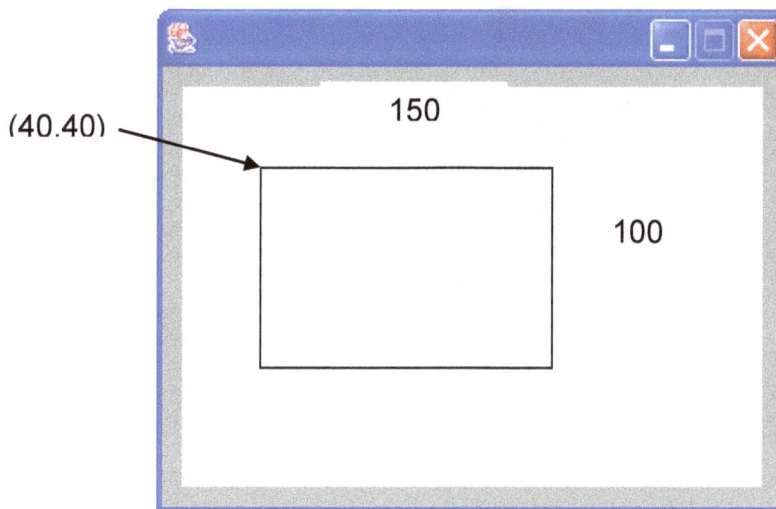

The rectangle we just drew is pretty boring. It would be nice to have the capability to fill it with a color and/or pattern. Filling of shapes in Java2D is done with the **fill** method. To fill the rectangle, use:

```
g2D.fill(myRectangle);
```

The rectangle will be filled with the current **paint** attribute. For now, we will just fill the shapes with solid colors.

To fill our example rectangle with red, we use this code:

```
Graphics2D g2D = (Graphics2D) myPanel.getGraphics();
Rectangle2D.Double myRectangle = new
Rectangle2D.Double(40, 40, 150, 100);
g2D.setPaint(Color.RED);
g2D.fill(myRectangle);
g2D.dispose();
```

This produces:

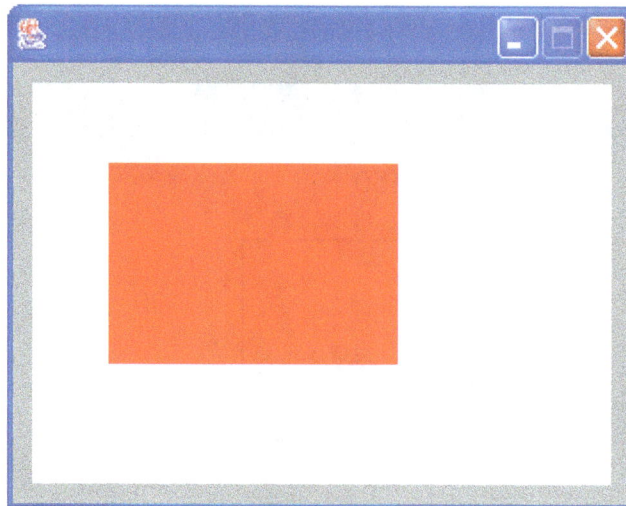

Notice the fill method fills the entire region with the selected color. If you had previously used the **draw** method to form a bordered rectangle, the fill will blot out that border. If you want a bordered, filled region, do the **fill** operation **first**, **then** the **draw** operation.

Persistent Graphics

It looks like we have enough information to draw the plot area (a filled rectangle with some black grid lines) on the **displayPanel**. Before doing that, we need to address one problem – graphics persistence.

Java graphics objects have <u>no</u> memory. They only display what has been last drawn on them. If you reduce your frame to an icon (or it becomes obscured by another frame) and restore it, the graphics object cannot remember what was displayed previously – it will be cleared. Similarly, if you switch from an active Java application to some other application, your Java form may become partially or fully obscured. When you return to your Java application, the obscured part of any graphics object will be erased. Again, there is no memory. Notice in both these cases, however, all controls are automatically restored to the form. Your application remembers these, fortunately! The controls are persistent. We also want **persistent graphics**.

To maintain persistent graphics, we need to build memory into our graphics objects using code. In this code, we must be able to recreate, when needed, the current state of a graphics object. This 'custom' code is placed in the host control's **paintComponent** method. This event method is called whenever an obscured object becomes unobscured. The **paintComponent** method will be called for each object when a frame is first activated and when a frame is restored from an icon or whenever an obscured object is viewable again.

How do we access the **paintComponent** method for a control? For such access, we need to create a separate **class** for the control that **extends** the particular control. Creating the class is a simple. We define a **GraphicsPanel** class (a **JPanel** control hosting a graphics object, each panel needing persistent graphics would use a different name) using the following code framework:

```
class GraphicsPanel extends JPanel
{
  public void paintComponent(Graphics g)
  {
     [Painting code goes here]
  }
}
```

This class is placed after the main class in a program. A **GraphicsPanel** object is then declared and created using:

```
GraphicsPanel myPanel = new GraphicsPanel();
```

With this declaration, the "painting" of the control is now handled by the **paintComponent** method. Notice this method passes a **Graphics** object **g**. The first step in painting the component is to cast this object to a **Graphics2D** object:

```
Graphics2D g2D = (Graphics2D) g;
```

After this, we place code in the **paintComponent** method that describes the current state of the graphics object. In particular, make sure the first statement is:

```
super.paintComponent(g2D);
```

This will reestablish any background color (the keyword **super** refers to the 'inherited' control, the panel in this case).

Maintaining persistent graphics does require a bit of work on your part. You need to always know what is in your graphics object and how to recreate the object, when needed. This usually involves developing some program variables that describe how to recreate the graphics object. And, you usually need to develop some ad hoc rules for recreation. As you build your first few **paintComponent** events, you will begin to develop your own ways for maintaining persistent graphics. At certain times, you'll need to force a "repaint" of your control. To do this, for a host control named **hostControl** use:

```
hostControl.repaint();
```

You will often need to have your **paintComponent** method access variables from your main class. If your main class is named **mainClass** and you want the value of **myVariable**, the variable is accessed using:

```
mainClass.myVariable
```

Any variables accessed in this manner must have class level scope and, when declared, be prefaced with the keyword **static**. This is due to the way the **paintComponent** method works.

This all may sound difficult, but it really isn't. We've already added our graphics panel (**WeightPlotPanel**) and it's **paintComponent** method. Let's see how to use it.

Code Design – Panel Plot Area

Again, let's look at our future:

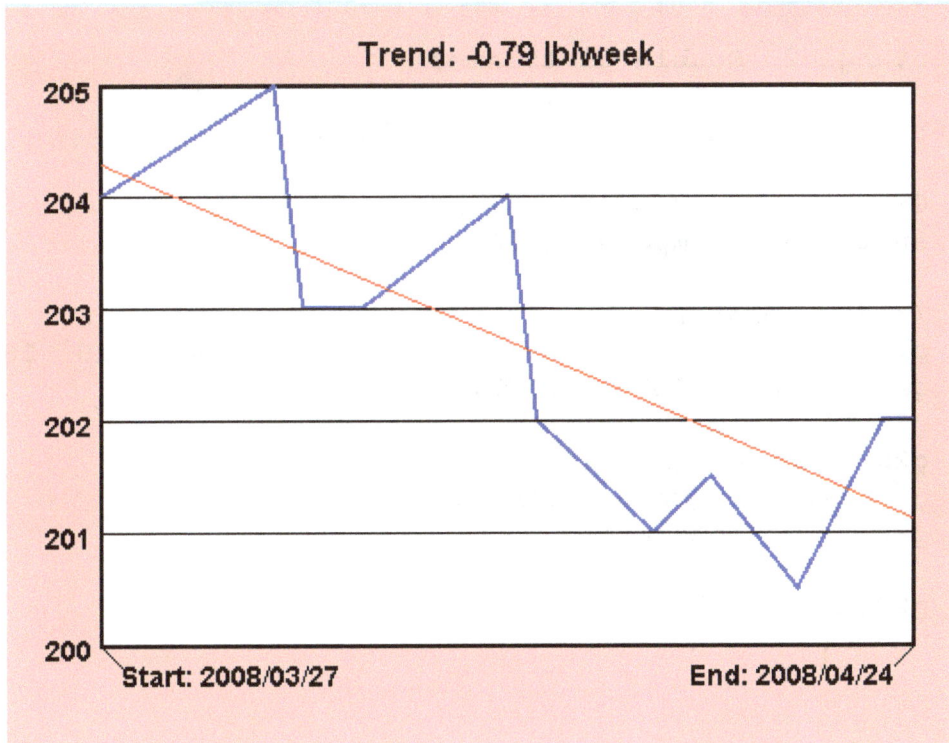

Since this is our first drawing, we'll take it in steps. As a first step, we will define the plot frame (**plotFrame**) rectangular region where the plot will be drawn. Add the import statement (to the **WeightMonitor** class) needed for graphics:

```
import java.awt.geom.*;
```

All graphics code will go in the **WeightPlotPanel** class. Add the shaded code to define and draw **plotFrame**:

```
class WeightPlotPanel extends JPanel
{

  Rectangle2D.Double plotFrame;

  public void paintComponent(Graphics g)
  {
    Graphics2D g2D = (Graphics2D) g;
    super.paintComponent(g2D);

    // draw plot frame
    plotFrame = new Rectangle2D.Double(50, 40, 420, 280);
    g2D.setPaint(Color.WHITE);
    g2D.fill(plotFrame);
    g2D.setStroke(new BasicStroke(2));
    g2D.setPaint(Color.BLACK);
    g2D.draw(plotFrame);

    g2D.dispose();
  }
}
```

Save, run to see the newly create **plotFrame** element:

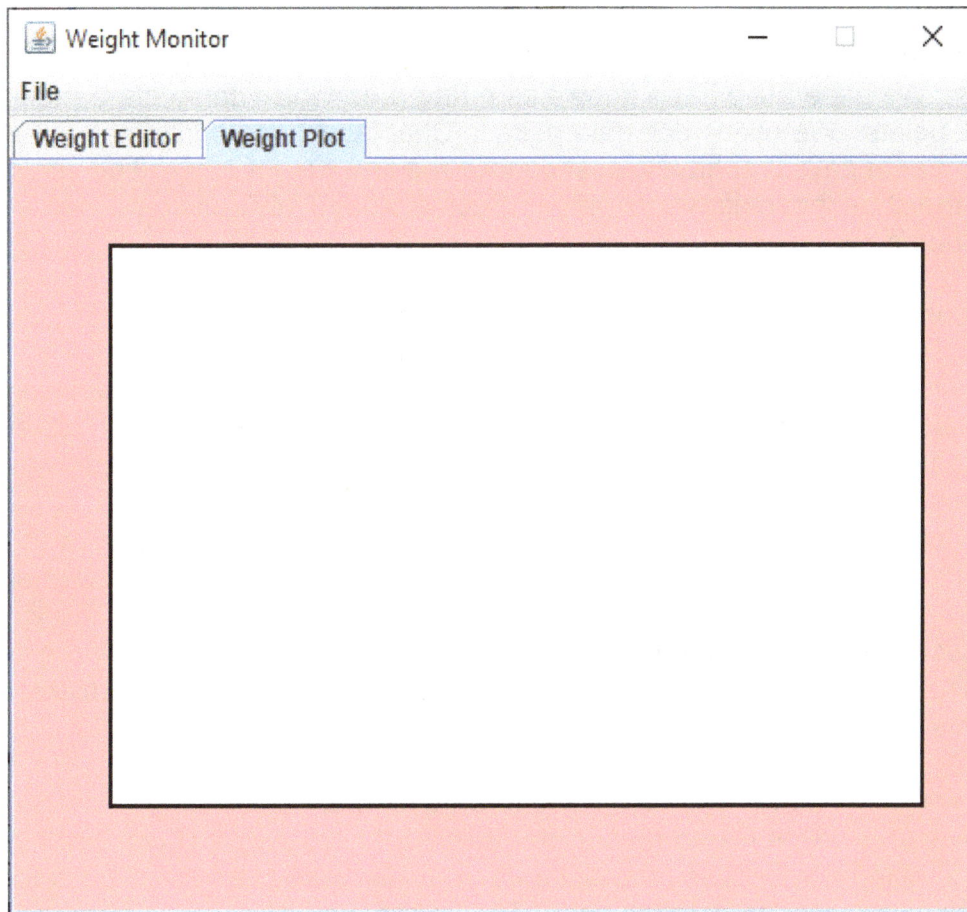

As usual, we will write the code for this panel in several steps. There are two primary tasks in drawing the weight plot. The first is to "connect the points" entered in the list control to draw the plot in a panel control. The second is to put useful labeling information around the plot. Let's look at the plot drawing task first. All remaining code will go in the **WeightPlotPanel** class **paintComponent** method.

Code Design – Weight Plot

When a user clicks the **Weight Plot** tab, we want to display a plot of the input weights. We generate what is known as a **line plot**, which connects Cartesian pairs of points. We used such data pairs in Chapter 7. The horizontal axis will be the number of days that have elapsed since the first weight entry. The vertical axis will be the corresponding weight value. Such a plot will give us some idea of any trends noted over time.

The steps to generate such a plot are fairly simple:

> ➤ Cycle through all values in the list control, extracting the date and weight values. Store the number of elapsed days (difference between 'current' date and first date) in an array **d**. Store the corresponding weight values in an array **w**.
> ➤ Loop through all array elements, connecting consecutive points (with **d** as the horizontal point and **w** as the vertical point) using the **Line2D** shape.

In our work, both **d** and **w** will be **zero-based arrays** (to match up with the items of the list control). Hence, each array will have **weightsListModel.getSize()** elements, numbered from **0** to **weightsListModel.getSize()– 1**.

 In the weight plot, the horizontal value (a date difference) will range from **0** (the first day in the weight file) to **d[weightsListModel.getSize() – 1]** (we'll call this d_{max}, the difference between the last date in the list control and the first date). This value increases from left to right. The vertical value will range from the minimum weight value (w_{min}) to the maximum weight value (w_{max}) - we will need to find these extremes. This value increases from bottom to top. Hence, to plot our data, we need to compute where each (**d**, **w**) pair in our weight plot fits within the dimensions of **plotFrame**. This is a straightforward coordinate conversion computation.

Let's look at the horizontal axis first. The horizontal (**x** axis) in **plotFrame** is **plotFrame.getWidth()** pixels wide. The far left pixel is at **x = plotFrame.getX()** and the far right is at **x = plotFrame.getX() + plotFrame.getWidth()**. **x** increases from left to right:

plotFrame.getX()   **x**   **plotFrame.getX() + plotFrame.getWidth()**

The horizontal weight plot value (**d**) runs from a minimum, **0**, at the left to a maximum, **dmax,** at the right. Thus, the first pixel on the horizontal axis of our weight plot will be **0** and the last will be **dmax**:

0   **d**   **dmax**

With these two depictions, we can compute the **x** value corresponding to a given **d** value using simple **proportions,** taking the distance from some point on each axis to the minimum and dividing by the total distance. The process is also called **linear interpolation**. These proportions show:

$$\frac{d - 0}{d_{max} - 0} = \frac{x - plotFrame.getX()}{plotFrame.getWidth()}$$

Solving this for **x** yields the desired conversion from a days value on the horizontal axis (**d**) to a graphics object value for plotting:

x = plotFrame.getX() + d(plotFrame.getX())/d$_{max}$

You can see this is correct at each extreme value. When **d = 0, x = plotFrame.getX()**. When **d = dmax, x = plotFrame.getX() + plotFrame.getWidth()**.

Now, we find the corresponding conversion for the vertical (**y**) axis. We'll place the two axes side-by-side for easy comparison (graphics object on left, weight axis on right):

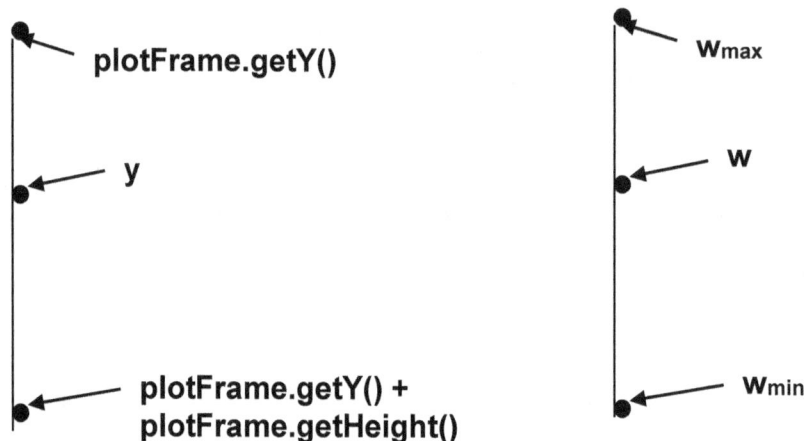

The vertical (**y** axis) in **plotFrame** is **plotFrame.getHeight( )**pixels high. The topmost pixel is at **y = plotFrame.getY()** and the bottom is at **y = plotFrame.getY() + plotFrame.getHeight()**. **y** increases from top to bottom. The vertical data (weight axis, **w**) in our weight plot, runs from a minimum, w_{min}, at the bottom, to a maximum, w_{max}, at the top. Thus, the top pixel on the vertical axis will be w_{max} and the bottom will be w_{min} (note the weight axis increases up, rather than down).

With these two depictions, we can compute the **y** value corresponding to a given **w** value using linear interpolation. The computations show:

$$\frac{w - w_{min}}{w_{max} - w_{min}} = \frac{y - (\texttt{plotFrame.getY()}+\texttt{plotFrame.getHeight()})}{\texttt{plotFrame.getHeight()}}$$

Solving this for **y** yields the desired conversion from a weight value on the vertical axis (**w**) to a graphics object value for plotting (this requires a bit algebra, but it's straightforward):

y = plotFrame.getY() + (w_{max} - w)(plotFrame.getHeight())/(w_{max} − w_{min})

Again, check the extremes. When **w = w_{min}, y = plotFrame.getY() + plotFrame.getHeight()**. When **w = w_{max}, y = plotFrame.getY()**. It looks good.

We will use two general methods to do these coordinate conversions. First, for the horizontal axis, we use **cToX**. This method has two input arguments: the **d** value and the maximum **d** value, **dmax**. Both values are of **double** data type. The method returns the **plotFrame**coordinate (an **int** type):

```
private int dToX(double d, double dmax)
{
   return ((int)(d * (plotFrame.getWidth() - 1) / dmax +
plotFrame.getX()));
}
```

Note this is used with the panel control where the plot will be drawn (**plotPanel**).

For the vertical axis, we use **wToY**. This method has three input arguments: the **w** value, the minimum **w** value, **wmin**, and the maximum value, **wmax**. All values are of **double** data type. The method returns the **plotPanel** coordinate (an **int** type):

```
private int wToY(double w, double wmin, double wmax)
{
   return ((int)((wmax - w) * (plotFrame.getHeight() - 1) /
(wmax - wmin) + plotFrame.getY()));
}
```

Add both these methods to the **WeightPlotClass**.

With the ability to transform coordinates, we can now rewrite the steps to generate a weight plot:

- ➢ Cycle through all values in the list control, extracting the date and weight values. Store the number of elapsed days (difference between 'current' date and first date) in an array **d**. Store the corresponding weight values in an array **w**. These are both zero-based arrays. While extracting values, determine the minimum and maximum weight values (**wmin** and **wmax**).
- ➢ Loop through all array elements. For each point, convert the **d** and **w** values to graphics object coordinates, then connect the current point with the previous point using a **Line2D** object.

The code to create the weight plot in the **WeightPlotPanel** class will need objects, variables and methods from the main class (**WeightMonitor**). In the previous chapter, we saw that any main class variables or objects that need access in another class should be prefaced with the keyword **static**. To access such a variable, we use the syntax:

```
MainClass.variable
```

Main class variables that require the **static** modifier are:

```
static DefaultListModel weightsListModel = new
DefaultListModel();
```

Make the changes.

In a similar fashion, any methods in the main class that need to be accessed in the 'secondary' class need to be declared **static**, with **public** rather than private access. This is a simple change, merely needing a modification of the header line. Once done, these methods can be accessed using:

```
MainClass.method(arguments)
```

The modified headers for main class methods that require such access are:

```
static public Date stringToDate(String s)

static public String getDate(String s)

static public String getWeight(String s)
```

Make the noted changes

With this knowledge, the code to implement the above plotting steps is:

```
// draw weight plot
int lSize = WeightMonitor.weightsListModel.getSize();
double[] d = new double[lSize];
double[] w = new double[lSize];
double wmin, wmax;
String s;
if (lSize < 2)
  return;
g2D.setStroke(new BasicStroke(2));
g2D.setPaint(Color.BLUE);
wmin = 1000.0;
wmax = 0.0;
long t1 =
WeightMonitor.stringToDate(WeightMonitor.getDate(WeightMon
itor.weightsListModel.getElementAt(0).toString())).getTime
();
for (int i = 0; i < lSize; i++)
{
  s =
WeightMonitor.weightsListModel.getElementAt(i).toString();
  long t2 =
WeightMonitor.stringToDate(WeightMonitor.getDate(s)).getTi
me();
  d[i] = (double) ((t2 - t1) / (24 * 3600 * 1000));
  w[i] =
Double.valueOf(WeightMonitor.getWeight(s)).doubleValue();
  wmin = Math.min(w[i], wmin);
  wmax = Math.max(w[i], wmax);
}
for (int i = 1; i < lSize; i++)
{
  // connect current point to previous point
  Line2D.Double weightLine = new Line2D.Double(dToX(d[i -
1], d[lSize - 1]), wToY(w[i - 1], wmin, wmax), dToX(d[i],
d[lSize - 1]), wToY(w[i], wmin, wmax));
  g2D.draw(weightLine);
}
```

Add this code to the **paintComponent** method for the **WeightPlotPanel** class..

Let's look at this code in detail. If there are fewer than 2 points, we return the user to the **Weight Editor** tab and exit the method, since you need two points to draw a line. Next, the **d** and **w** array values are obtained from the list items and the minimum and maximum weight values are found. To draw the plot, we cycle through all points in the array, connecting the current point with the previous point. Make sure you understand these steps. Notice how we use time in milliseconds to compute date differences in days (**t2 – t1**)

Save and run the project. If you opened the sample weight file before, the weight values for that file will be displayed. If they are not displayed, open the **sample.wgt** file found in the **\HomeJava\HomeJava Projects\WeightMonitor** folder. You should see:

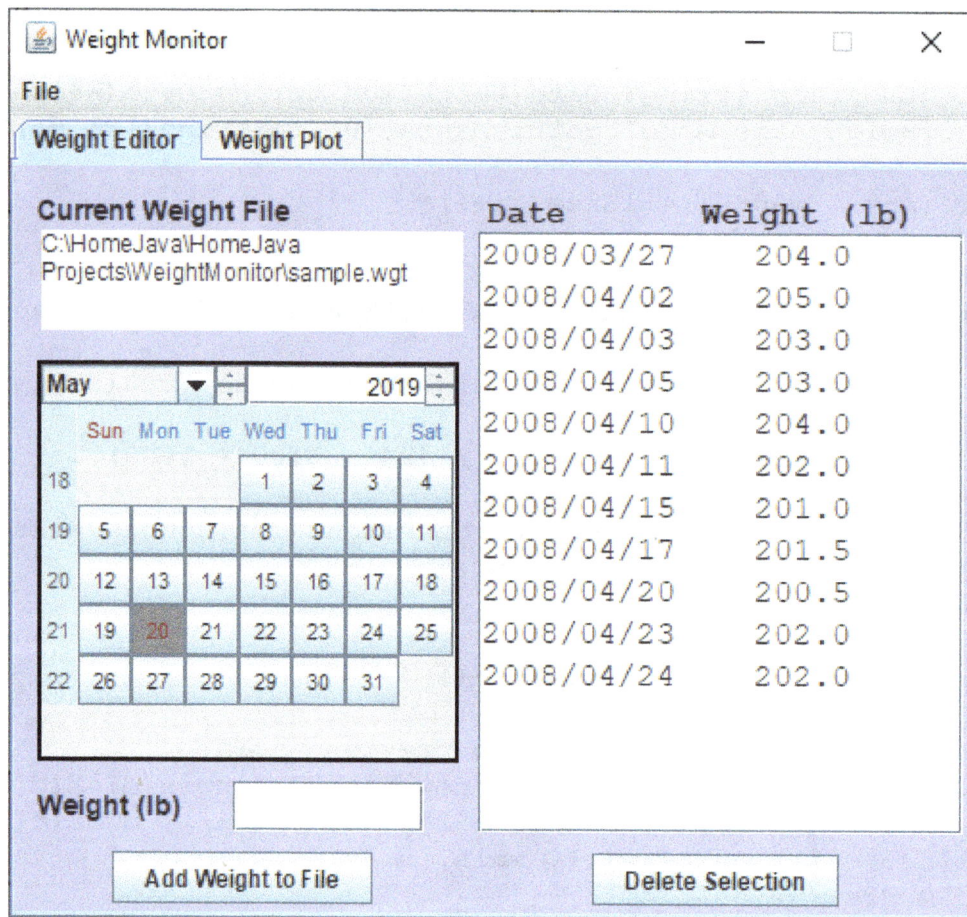

Now, click the **Weight Plot** tab and you will see this data in a line plot:

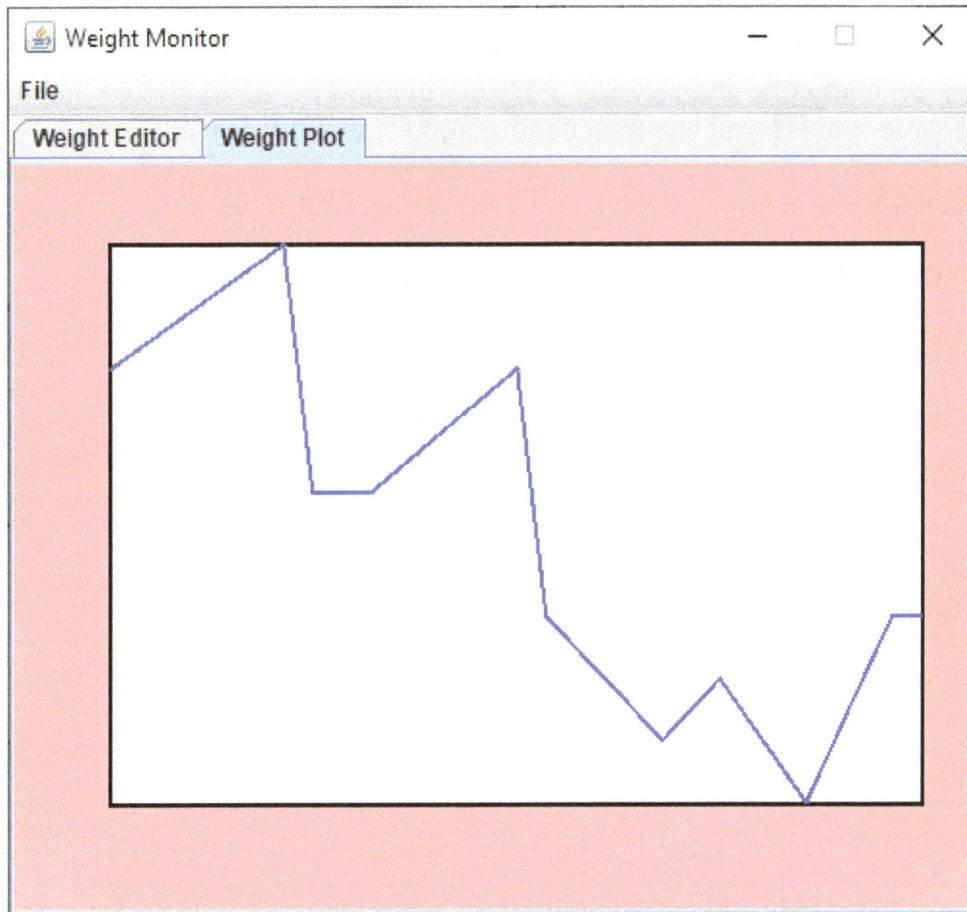

Success!

As drawn, the weight plot (though informative) is pretty boring. It lacks grid lines indicating weight values. And, it lacks labeling information to tell us what we're looking at. We need labels on the vertical axis telling us the weight range. We need labels on the horizontal axis telling us the represented date range. Let's make things nicer.

Code Design – Grid Lines

With horizontal grid lines, we would be better able to determine plotted weight values. How many grid lines should there be and how far apart should they be spaced? We will use grid line spacing that results in a "nice" plot.

If you look back at the weight values in the **Weight Editor** tab, you will see that the weights range from a minimum of 200.5 to 205.0. So, as drawn, the bottom of the vertical axis in the plot is 200.5 and the top is 205.0. Notice the line plot hits these extremes in a few points. With this example, we could choose a grid line spacing of 0.5 pounds. That would result in 10 weight value labels (200.5, 201.0, 201.5, 202.0, 202.5, 203.0, 203.5, 204.0, 204.5, 205.0) and 8 grid lines (we don't need grid lines at the bottom or top of the plot). Such a plot would be pretty cluttered, not a "nice" plot. Let's develop some rules for nicer grid line spacing. We'll use whole numbers for spacing and whole number for labels. And, we'll try to make sure the weight plot never touches either vertical extreme.

Here's the rules I use (you may come up with some others):

> ➢ Round maximum weight up to next integer value.
> ➢ Round minimum weight down to next integer value.
> ➢ If difference between maximum and minimum is less than 5 pounds, set grid line spacing to 1 pound.
> ➢ If difference between maximum and minimum is less than 10 pounds, set grid line spacing to 2 pounds.
> ➢ If difference between maximum and minimum is less than 25 pounds, set grid line spacing to 5 pounds.
> ➢ If difference between maximum and minimum is less than 50 pounds, set grid line spacing to 10 pounds.
> ➢ For larger differences, use a grid line spacing of 20 pounds.
> ➢ Adjust maximum value to next highest integer multiple of the grid line spacing (if necessary).
> ➢ Adjust minimum value to next lowest integer multiple of the grid line spacing (if necessary).

Once the grid line spacing is determined, the grid lines can be drawn using the **Line2D** object. As stated, grid lines are drawn at each vertical position, except the bottom and top.

The modified **paintComponent** code segment that computes grid line spacing and draws the grid lines is (changes are shaded):

```
// draw weight plot
int lSize = WeightMonitor.weightsListModel.getSize();
double[] d = new double[lSize];
double[] w = new double[lSize];
double wmin, wmax;
String s;
int intervals;
double gridSpacing, wLegend;
if (lSize < 2)
  return;
g2D.setStroke(new BasicStroke(2));
g2D.setPaint(Color.BLUE);
wmin = 1000.0;
wmax = 0.0;
long t1 =
WeightMonitor.stringToDate(WeightMonitor.getDate(WeightMon
itor.weightsListModel.getElementAt(0).toString())).getTime
();
for (int i = 0; i < lSize; i++)
{
  s =
WeightMonitor.weightsListModel.getElementAt(i).toString();
  long t2 =
WeightMonitor.stringToDate(WeightMonitor.getDate(s)).getTi
me();
  d[i] = (double) ((t2 - t1) / (24 * 3600 * 1000));
  w[i] =
Double.valueOf(WeightMonitor.getWeight(s)).doubleValue();
  wmin = Math.min(w[i], wmin);
  wmax = Math.max(w[i], wmax);
}
// adjust Wmin/Wmax for 'nice' intervals
if (wmin == wmax)
  wmin = wmax - 1;
wmax = (double) ((int)(wmax + 0.5)); // round up
wmin = (double) ((int)(wmin - 0.5)); // round down
if (wmax - wmin <= 5.0)
  gridSpacing = 1.0;
else if (wmax - wmin <= 10.0)
  gridSpacing = 2.0;
else if (wmax - wmin <= 25.0)
  gridSpacing = 5.0;
else if (wmax - wmin <= 50.0)
  gridSpacing = 10.0;
```

```
else
  gridSpacing = 20.0;
if (wmax % (int)gridSpacing != 0)
  wmax = gridSpacing * (int)(wmax / gridSpacing) +
gridSpacing;
if (wmin % (int)gridSpacing != 0)
  wmin = gridSpacing * (int)(wmin / gridSpacing);
intervals = (int)((wmax - wmin) / gridSpacing);
for (int i = 1; i < lSize; i++)
{
  // connect current point to previous point
  Line2D.Double weightLine = new Line2D.Double(dToX(d[i -
1], d[lSize - 1]), wToY(w[i - 1], wmin, wmax), dToX(d[i],
d[lSize - 1]), wToY(w[i], wmin, wmax));
  g2D.draw(weightLine);
}
```

```
// draw grid lines
g2D.setStroke(new BasicStroke(1));
g2D.setPaint(Color.BLACK);
wLegend = wmin;
for (int i = 0; i <= intervals; i++)
{
  if (i > 0 && i < intervals)
  {
    // draw grid line (except at top and bottom)
    Line2D.Double gridLine = new
Line2D.Double(plotFrame.getX(), wToY(wLegend, wmin, wmax),
plotFrame.getX() + plotFrame.getWidth(), wToY(wLegend,
wmin, wmax));
    g2D.draw(gridLine);
  }
  wLegend += gridSpacing;
}
```

In this code, **gridSpacing** is the spacing between grid lines and **intervals** is the number of grid intervals between **wmin** and **wmax**. **wLegend** is the weight value at the current grid line (it starts at **wmin** and increases by **gridSpacing** after drawing a grid line). The grid lines are drawn with a black pen with 1 pixel width. You should see all the grid spacing calculation steps. Make the indicated changes in your project.

Save and run the project. Make sure the **sample.wgt** file is opened. Click the
Weight Plot tab. Here's the modified plot:

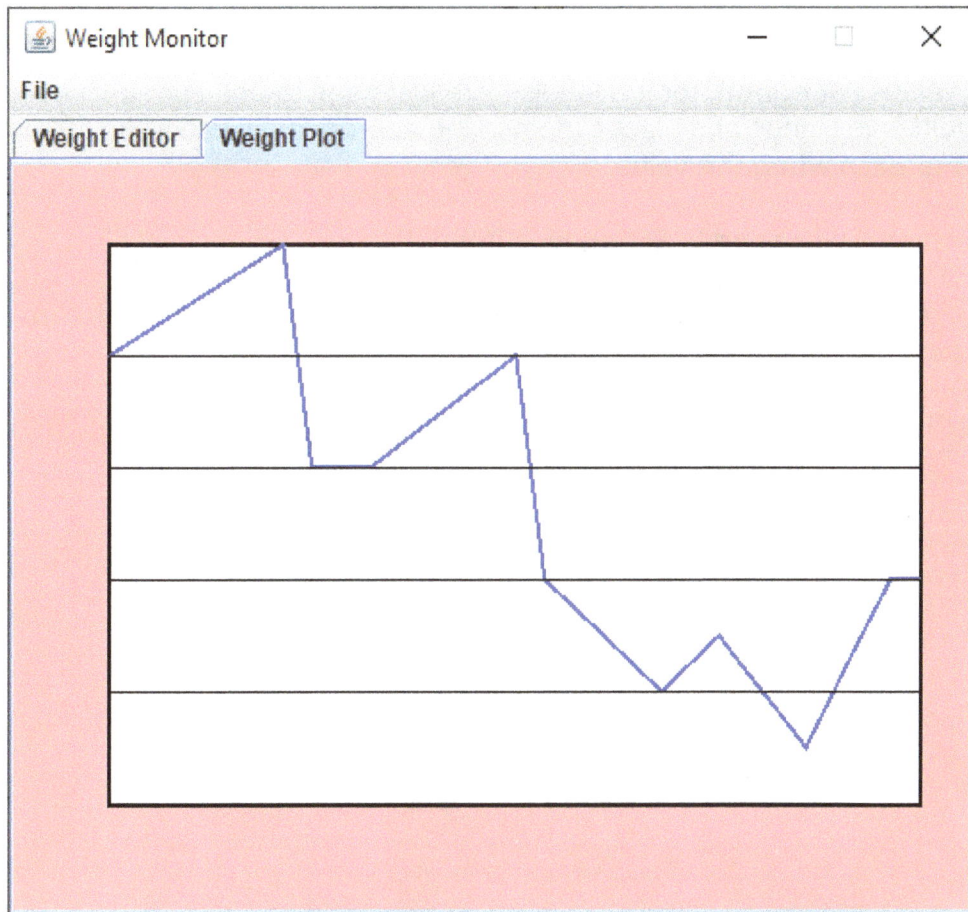

Notice the grid lines (they're spaced apart by 1 pound, by the way). This is a nicer
plot. It's still not "nice enough." There's no indication of what the grid line spacing
is. We don't know what the weight range is. We don't know what the date range
is. All that information is provided with plot labeling.

Code Design – Plot Labels

We will add labels (not label controls, just text information for labeling) for the weight axis first. When drawing the grid lines, we wrote code that specified the weight values (**wLegend**) for the labels. We just need to add code that converts these values to strings and places them in the appropriate location on the plot tab page. For each **wLegend** value:

> ➤ Convert **wLegend** to **String** type (formatted with no decimal places)
> ➤ Determine width and height of string.
> ➤ Position string in proper vertical location and right justified to left side of plot.

The **getStringBounds** method will be used to find the width and height of the string. The **wToY** method helps position the string label vertically.

Each label will be "drawn" outside the **plotFrame** area. Here's a sketch that shows you how one label (for a weight value **w**) is positioned:

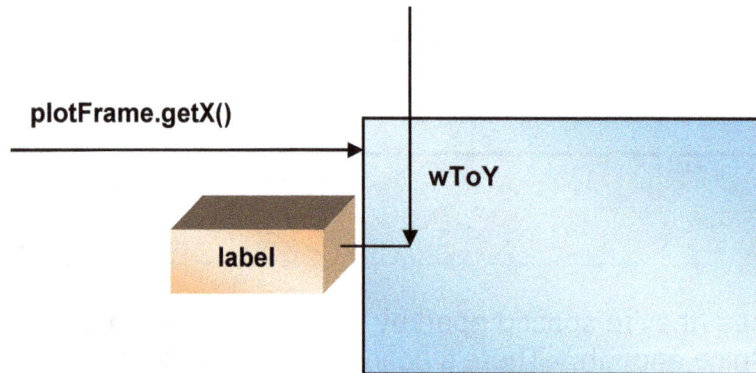

To horizontally position **label**, you use (the 5 gives a little padding):

```
x = (int) (plotFrame.getX() - label.getWidth() - 5);
```

To vertically position **label**, use:

```
y = (int) (wtoY(w, wmin, wmax) + 0.5 *
label.getHeight()));
```

The pair (**x, y**) are used to position the string label using **drawString** on **weightPanel**. The width and height of the label are found using the **getStringBounds** method.

The code to 'draw' the labels is placed in the code where the grid lines are drawn. This modified code segment (changes are shaded):

```java
// draw grid lines and labels
Font labelFont = new Font("Arial", Font.BOLD, 14);
g2D.setFont(labelFont);
Rectangle2D labelRect;
String lblText;
g2D.setStroke(new BasicStroke(1));
g2D.setPaint(Color.BLACK);
wLegend = wmin;
for (int i = 0; i <= intervals; i++)
{
  lblText = String.valueOf((int) wLegend);
  labelRect = labelFont.getStringBounds(lblText,
g2D.getFontRenderContext());
  g2D.drawString(lblText, (int) (plotFrame.getX() -
labelRect.getWidth() - 5), (int) (wToY(wLegend, wmin,
wmax) + 0.5 * labelRect.getHeight()));
  if (i > 0 && i < intervals)
  {
    // draw grid line (except at top and bottom)
    Line2D.Double gridLine = new
Line2D.Double(plotFrame.getX(), wToY(wLegend, wmin, wmax),
plotFrame.getX() + plotFrame.getWidth(), wToY(wLegend,
wmin, wmax));
    g2D.draw(gridLine);
  }
  wLegend += gridSpacing;
}
```

Make the noted changes to the segment of code in the **paintComponent** method.

Save and run the project. The values for **sample.wgt** should appear. Click the **Weight Plot** tab:

Our plot now has very nice labels.

Now, we add labels to the horizontal weight plot axis. Recall this axis tells us how many days have elapsed since we started the weight file. We could label the axis with such day values, choosing an appropriate horizontal spacing. Instead of doing this, we will simply label the axis with the starting date and the ending date. We feel this is more meaningful information. The form of the labeling will be:

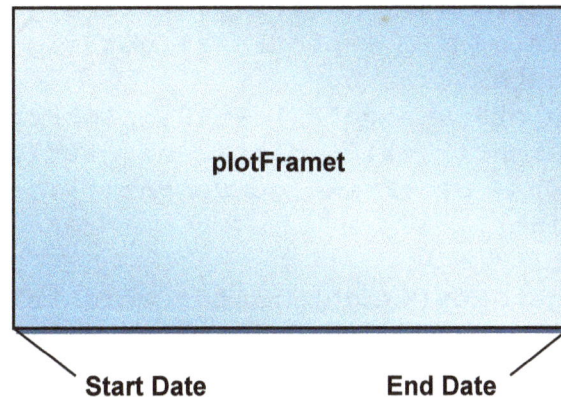

Start Date   **End Date**

That is, we will display the two dates and draw lines indicating where these dates fall on the plot. Recall the **start** date is given by:

```
getDate(weightsListModel.getElementAt(0).toString())
```

and the **end** date is given by

```
getDate(weightsListModel.getElementAt(weightsListModel.get
Size() - 1).toString())
```

The code to generate these labels also goes at the end of the current
paintComponent method.:

```
// draw horizontal axis labels (using label font)
String dateText = "Start: " +
WeightMonitor.getDate(WeightMonitor.weightsListModel.getEl
ementAt(0).toString());
g2D.drawString(dateText, (int) (plotFrame.getX() + 10),
 (int) (plotFrame.getY() + plotFrame.getHeight() + 20));
Line2D.Double dateLine = new
Line2D.Double(plotFrame.getX() + 10, plotFrame.getY() +
plotFrame.getHeight() + 10, plotFrame.getX(),
plotFrame.getY() + plotFrame.getHeight());
g2D.draw(dateLine);
dateText = "End: " +
WeightMonitor.getDate(WeightMonitor.weightsListModel.getEl
ementAt(WeightMonitor.weightsListModel.getSize() -
1).toString());
Rectangle2D dateRect = labelFont.getStringBounds(dateText,
g2D.getFontRenderContext());
g2D.drawString(dateText, (int) (plotFrame.getX() +
plotFrame.getWidth() - dateRect.getWidth() - 10), (int)
 (plotFrame.getY() + plotFrame.getHeight() + 20));
dateLine = new Line2D.Double(plotFrame.getX() +
plotFrame.getWidth() - 10, plotFrame.getY() +
plotFrame.getHeight() + 10, plotFrame.getX() +
plotFrame.getWidth(), plotFrame.getY() +
plotFrame.getHeight());
g2D.draw(dateLine);
```

You should be able to see how the labels are formed and positioned. Add the
new code.

Save and run the project. Click **Weight Plot** (using the **sample.wgt** values) and you should see:

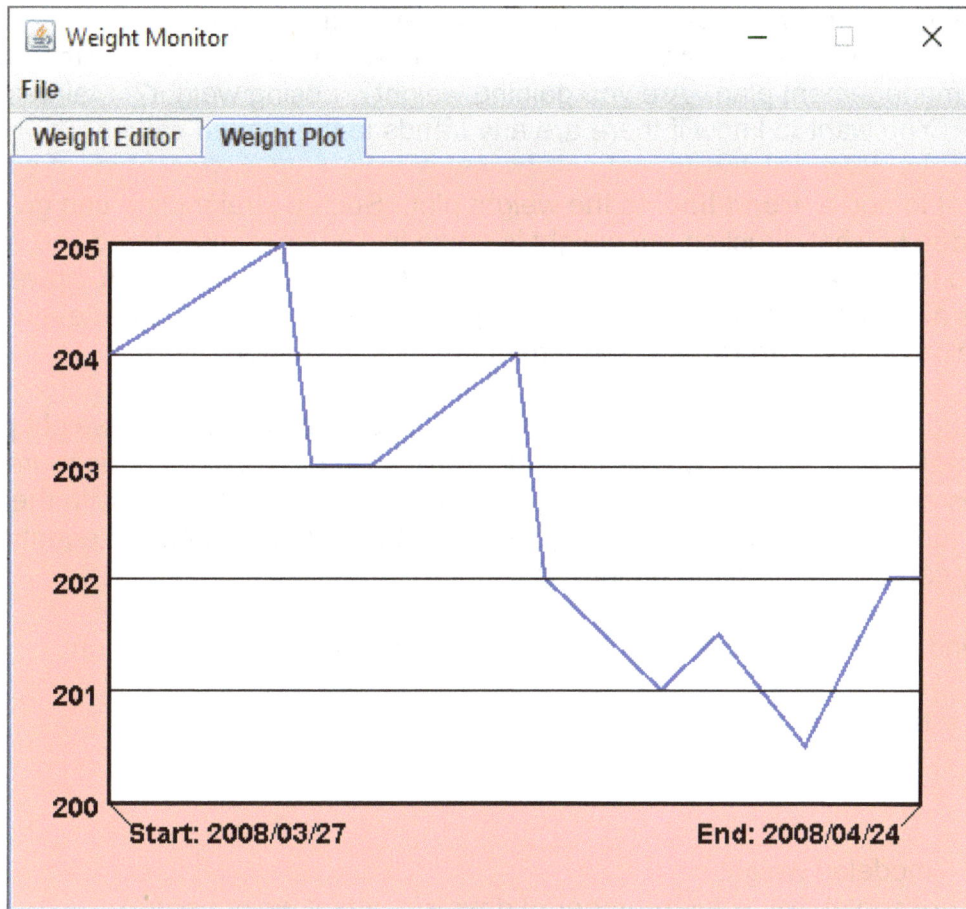

Don't you agree the plot looks much nicer with labels?

Code Design – Weight Plot Trend

We're almost done with our weight monitor project. Just one more change. When you track your weight with a plot, you want to know how you're doing with your weight management plan. Are you gaining weight? Losing weight? Maintaining weight? You want to know if there are any trends in the plotted values.

We want to add a '**trend line**' to the weight plot. Such a straight line can give us some idea of what direction our weight is going in. A very simple trend line would be to connect the first point in the plot to the last point. This approach, however, ignores all other points in the plot. The approach we take will consider every point in the plot, but, be forewarned, some mathematics is needed.

The trend line we use will represent a "best fit" to all the points in the weight plot. Mathematically speaking, we do a **linear regression** on the data. This regression involves calculus and solving linear equations, so we won't bore you with the details (unless you want to see them). We'll just give you the needed equations so they can be added to the project code.

Our trend line 'models' the weight values using the straight line equation:

$$w_m = td + w_0$$

where:

w_m – modeled weight
d – horizontal axis value (number of days since first weight entry)
t – trend value (pounds/day), called the slope of the line
w_0 – modeled weight when $d = 0$

With the above model, the trend line connects two Cartesian end points: $(0, w_0)$ and $(d_{max}, td_{max} + w_0)$. So, to draw the trend line, we need to know values for t and w_0 (we know d_{max}). Values for these two terms are found using the d and w arrays currently used to create the weight plots. The equations for t and w_0, using these arrays are (these equations come from the linear regression we mentioned):

$$t = \frac{N \sum_{k=0}^{N-1} d[k]w[k] - \sum d[k] \sum w[k]}{N \sum d^2[k] - (\sum d[k])^2}$$

$$w_0 = \frac{\sum d^2[k] \sum w[k] - \sum d[k] \sum d[k]w[k]}{N \sum d^2[k] - (\sum d[k])^2}$$

where recall the Greek sigma in the above equations indicates you add up all the corresponding elements next to the sigma. Also, N is the number of elements in each array (**weightsListModel.getSize()**).

I know the above equations are messy, but they yield a very nice trend line and are straightforward to program. You simply declare a variable for each of the summation terms and form the sums as you establish the two arrays d and w. Then a little math gives you values for t and w_0.

For those interested in the mathematics involved in deriving these relations, I'll outline them for you. For those not interested, leave this paragraph now. The idea behind linear regression is to minimize the squared error between the modeled weight points and the actual weight points. That error (**e**) is given by:

$$\mathbf{e} = \sum_{k=0}^{N-1} \{w[k] - (td[k] + w_0)\}^2$$

We want e to as small as possible, seeking the so-called least square error solution. For e to be minimum the partial derivative of e with respect to t and the partial derivative with respect to w_0 must be zero. Those derivatives are (here's where the calculus shows up):

2      $\{w[k] - (td[k] + w_0)\}d[k] = 0$ (partial derivative with respect to t)

2      $\{w[k] - (td[k] + w_0)\} = 0$ (partial derivative with respect to w_0)

If we rearrange these equations a bit, we get:

t $d^2[k] + w_0$ $d[k] =$ $d[k]w[k]$

t $d[k] + w_0 N =$ $w[k]$

We have two linear equations with two unknowns (**t** and $\mathbf{w_0}$). We can use Cramer's rule to solve these equations to yield the previously seen relations for **t** and $\mathbf{w_0}$.

The code to compute and draw the trend line is interspersed at various locations in the **paintComponent** method. In addition to drawing the trend line, we add a label at the top of the plot to indicate a "weekly" trend value (**7 * t**), showing how much weight you are losing or gaining each week. The modified method is (changes are shaded; we show the entire paintComponent method, now that it is complete):

```
public void paintComponent(Graphics g)
{
  Graphics2D g2D = (Graphics2D) g;
  super.paintComponent(g2D);

  // draw plot frame
  plotFrame = new Rectangle2D.Double(50, 40, 420, 280);
  g2D.setPaint(Color.WHITE);
  g2D.fill(plotFrame);
  g2D.setStroke(new BasicStroke(2));
  g2D.setPaint(Color.BLACK);
  g2D.draw(plotFrame);

  // draw weight plot
  int lSize = WeightMonitor.weightsListModel.getSize();
  double[] d = new double[lSize];
  double[] w = new double[lSize];
  double wmin, wmax;
  String s;
  int intervals;
  double gridSpacing, wLegend;
  double sumD, sumD2, sumW, sumDW;
  double t, w0;
  if (lSize < 2)
    return;
  g2D.setStroke(new BasicStroke(2));
  g2D.setPaint(Color.BLUE);
  wmin = 1000.0;
  wmax = 0.0;
  sumD = 0.0;
  sumD2 = 0.0;
  sumW = 0.0;
  sumDW = 0.0;
  long t1 =
WeightMonitor.stringToDate(WeightMonitor.getDate(WeightMon
itor.weightsListModel.getElementAt(0).toString())).getTime
();
  for (int i = 0; i < lSize; i++)
  {
    s =
WeightMonitor.weightsListModel.getElementAt(i).toString();
```

```
    long t2 =
WeightMonitor.stringToDate(WeightMonitor.getDate(s)).getTi
me();
    d[i] = (double) ((t2 - t1) / (24 * 3600 * 1000));
    w[i] =
Double.valueOf(WeightMonitor.getWeight(s)).doubleValue();
    wmin = Math.min(w[i], wmin);
    wmax = Math.max(w[i], wmax);
    // values for trend line
    sumD += d[i];
    sumD2 += d[i] * d[i];
    sumW += w[i];
    sumDW += d[i] * w[i];
  }
  // adjust Wmin/Wmax for 'nice' intervals
  if (wmin == wmax)
    wmin = wmax - 1;
  wmax = (double) ((int)(wmax + 0.5)); // round up
  wmin = (double) ((int)(wmin - 0.5)); // round down
  if (wmax - wmin <= 5.0)
    gridSpacing = 1.0;
  else if (wmax - wmin <= 10.0)
    gridSpacing = 2.0;
  else if (wmax - wmin <= 25.0)
    gridSpacing = 5.0;
  else if (wmax - wmin <= 50.0)
    gridSpacing = 10.0;
  else
    gridSpacing = 20.0;
  if (wmax % (int)gridSpacing != 0)
    wmax = gridSpacing * (int)(wmax / gridSpacing) +
gridSpacing;
  if (wmin % (int)gridSpacing != 0)
    wmin = gridSpacing * (int)(wmin / gridSpacing);
  intervals = (int)((wmax - wmin) / gridSpacing);
  for (int i = 1; i < lSize; i++)
  {
    // connect current point to previous point
    Line2D.Double weightLine = new Line2D.Double(dToX(d[i
- 1], d[lSize - 1]), wToY(w[i - 1], wmin, wmax),
dToX(d[i], d[lSize - 1]), wToY(w[i], wmin, wmax));
    g2D.draw(weightLine);
  }

  // draw grid lines and labels
  Font labelFont = new Font("Arial", Font.BOLD, 14);
  g2D.setFont(labelFont);
```

```
Rectangle2D labelRect;
String lblText;
g2D.setStroke(new BasicStroke(1));
g2D.setPaint(Color.BLACK);
wLegend = wmin;
for (int i = 0; i <= intervals; i++)
{
  lblText = String.valueOf((int) wLegend);
  labelRect = labelFont.getStringBounds(lblText,
g2D.getFontRenderContext());
  g2D.drawString(lblText, (int) (plotFrame.getX() -
labelRect.getWidth() - 5), (int) (wToY(wLegend, wmin,
wmax) + 0.5 * labelRect.getHeight()));
  if (i > 0 && i < intervals)
  {
    // draw grid line (except at top and bottom)
    Line2D.Double gridLine = new
Line2D.Double(plotFrame.getX(), wToY(wLegend, wmin, wmax),
plotFrame.getX() + plotFrame.getWidth(), wToY(wLegend,
wmin, wmax));
    g2D.draw(gridLine);
  }
  wLegend += gridSpacing;
}

// draw horizontal axis labels (using label font)
String dateText = "Start: " +
WeightMonitor.getDate(WeightMonitor.weightsListModel.getEl
ementAt(0).toString());
  g2D.drawString(dateText, (int) (plotFrame.getX() + 10),
(int) (plotFrame.getY() + plotFrame.getHeight() + 20));
  Line2D.Double dateLine = new
Line2D.Double(plotFrame.getX() + 10, plotFrame.getY() +
plotFrame.getHeight() + 10, plotFrame.getX(),
plotFrame.getY() + plotFrame.getHeight());
  g2D.draw(dateLine);
  dateText = "End: " +
WeightMonitor.getDate(WeightMonitor.weightsListModel.getEl
ementAt(WeightMonitor.weightsListModel.getSize() -
1).toString());
  Rectangle2D dateRect =
labelFont.getStringBounds(dateText,
g2D.getFontRenderContext());
  g2D.drawString(dateText, (int) (plotFrame.getX() +
plotFrame.getWidth() - dateRect.getWidth() - 10), (int)
(plotFrame.getY() + plotFrame.getHeight() + 20));
```

```
      dateLine = new Line2D.Double(plotFrame.getX() +
plotFrame.getWidth() - 10, plotFrame.getY() +
plotFrame.getHeight() + 10, plotFrame.getX() +
plotFrame.getWidth(), plotFrame.getY() +
plotFrame.getHeight());
   g2D.draw(dateLine);


   // trend computations
   t = (lSize * sumDW - sumD * sumW) / (lSize * sumD2 -
sumD * sumD);
   w0 = (sumD2 * sumW - sumD * sumDW) / (lSize * sumD2 -
sumD * sumD);
   // draw line
   Line2D.Double trendLine = new
Line2D.Double(plotFrame.getX(), wToY(w0, wmin, wmax),
dToX(d[lSize - 1], d[lSize - 1]), wToY(t * d[lSize - 1] +
w0, wmin, wmax));
   g2D.setPaint(Color.RED);
   g2D.draw(trendLine);
   String title = "Trend: ";
   if (t > 0)
     title += "+";
   title += new DecimalFormat("0.00").format(7 * t) + "
lb/week";
   Font titleFont = new Font("Arial", Font.BOLD, 16);
   Rectangle2D titleRect = titleFont.getStringBounds(title,
g2D.getFontRenderContext());
   g2D.setFont(titleFont);
   g2D.setPaint(Color.BLACK);
   g2D.drawString(title, (int) (plotFrame.getX() + 0.5 *
(plotFrame.getWidth() - titleRect.getWidth())), (int)
(plotFrame.getY() - 10));

   g2D.dispose();
}
```

This is the final version of the **paintComponent** event. Make the noted changes.
You should see how the trend line is computed and drawn. Also notice how the
trend value is printed at the top of the plot.

Save and run the project. Click **Weight Plot** one last time using **sample.wgt** and you will see a nice red trend line and corresponding label indicating I'm losing nearly a pound a week:

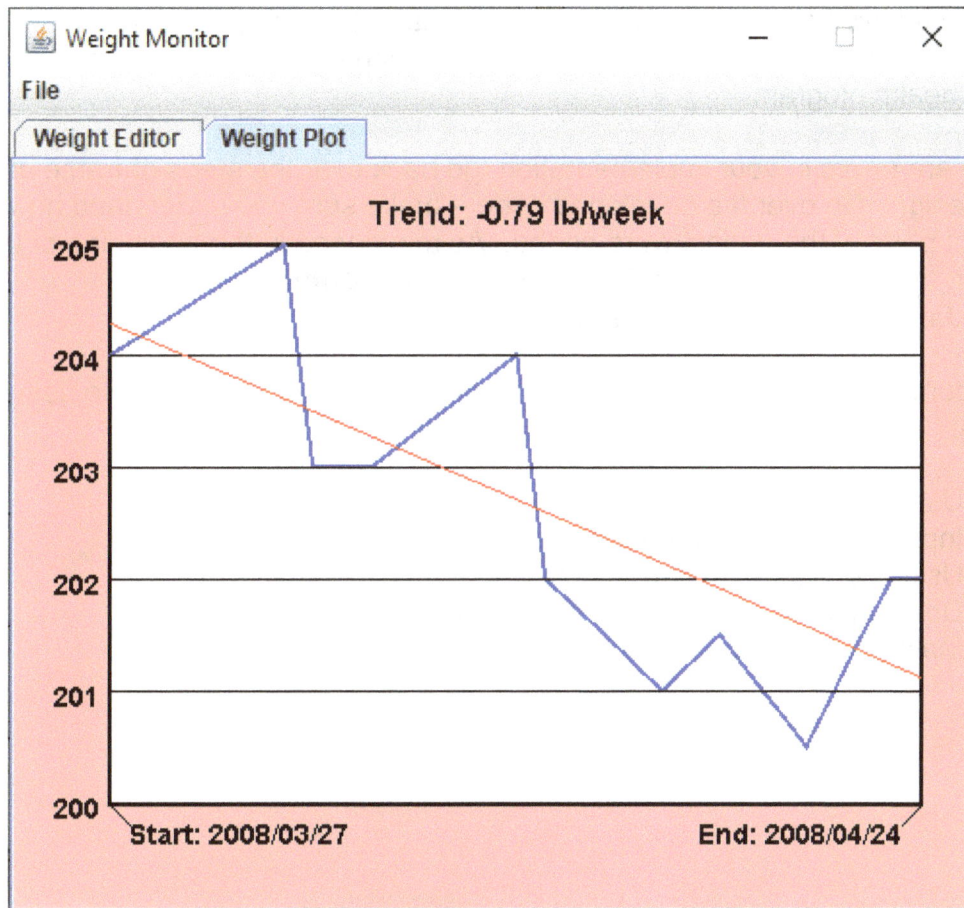

Weight Monitor Project Review

The **Weight Monitor Project** is now complete. Save and run the project and make sure it works as designed. Use the program to track your weight each day (or let your family try it). Hopefully the program can become an integral part of an overall health program.

If there are errors in your implementation, go back over the steps of frame and code design. Go over the developed code – make sure you understand how different parts of the project were coded. As mentioned in the beginning of this chapter, the completed project is saved as **WeightMonitor** in the **\HomeJava\HomeJava Projects** project group.

While completing this project, new concepts and skills you should have gained include:

> ➢ Use of the tabbed pane control.
> ➢ Input/output of variables with sequential files.
> ➢ Using configuration files in projects.
> ➢ Doing unit conversions need for plotting.
> ➢ Making "nice" intervals for plots.

Weight Monitor Project Enhancements

Possible enhancements to the weight monitor project include:

> ➤ We discuss printing in the next chapter. Once you understand how to print, you might like to add such capabilities to the weight monitor project. Print out your date/weight values. Print out the weight plot, including trend line.
>
> ➤ Many times, you are trying to achieve a certain weight goal. Modify the program to allow a user to enter a desired goal and a desired goal date. Provide computations that show how well the user to doing in trying the reach this goal. Draw a "goal" line on the weight plot.
>
> ➤ As implemented, weights need to be in pounds. Most of the world uses kilograms for weight. Add the capability to choose either unit for weight. You'll have to decide if you want to change any current values to the new units or just keep file in one particular set of units.

Weight Monitor Project Java Code Listing

```java
/*
 * WeightMonitor.java
 */
package weightmonitor;
import javax.swing.*;
import javax.swing.filechooser.*;
import javax.swing.event.*;
import java.awt.*;
import java.awt.event.*;
import com.toedter.calendar.*;
import java.beans.*;
import java.util.*;
import java.text.*;
import java.io.*;
import java.awt.geom.*;


public class WeightMonitor extends JFrame
{

   // menu structure
   JMenuBar mainMenuBar = new JMenuBar();
   JMenu fileMenu = new JMenu("File");
   JMenuItem newMenuItem = new JMenuItem("New Weight File");
   JMenuItem openMenuItem = new JMenuItem("Open Weight File");
   JMenuItem saveMenuItem = new JMenuItem("Save Weight File");
   JMenuItem exitMenuItem = new JMenuItem("Exit");

   JTabbedPane weightTabbedPane = new JTabbedPane();
   JPanel editorPanel = new JPanel();
   WeightPlotPanel plotPanel = new WeightPlotPanel();

   JLabel fileLabel = new JLabel();
   JTextArea fileTextArea = new JTextArea();
   JCalendar weightCalendar = new JCalendar();
   JLabel weightLabel = new JLabel();
   JTextField weightTextField = new JTextField();
   JButton addButton = new JButton();
   JLabel weightsListLabel = new JLabel();
   JScrollPane weightsScrollPane = new JScrollPane();
   JList weightsList = new JList();
   static DefaultListModel weightsListModel = new
DefaultListModel();
   JButton deleteButton = new JButton();
```

```java
String lastFile = "";

public static void main(String args[])
{
  // create frame
  new WeightMonitor().setVisible(true);
}

public WeightMonitor()
{
  // frame constructor
  setTitle("Weight Monitor");
  setResizable(false);

  addWindowListener(new WindowAdapter()
  {
    public void windowClosing(WindowEvent evt)
    {
      exitForm(evt);
    }
  });

  getContentPane().setLayout(new GridBagLayout());
  GridBagConstraints gridConstraints;

  // build menu structure
  setJMenuBar(mainMenuBar);
  mainMenuBar.add(fileMenu);
  fileMenu.add(newMenuItem);
  fileMenu.add(openMenuItem);
  fileMenu.add(saveMenuItem);
  fileMenu.addSeparator();
  fileMenu.add(exitMenuItem);
  newMenuItem.addActionListener(new ActionListener()
  {
    public void actionPerformed(ActionEvent e)
    {
      newMenuItemActionPerformed(e);
    }
  });
  openMenuItem.addActionListener(new ActionListener()
  {
    public void actionPerformed(ActionEvent e)
    {
      openMenuItemActionPerformed(e);
    }
```

```java
    });
    saveMenuItem.addActionListener(new ActionListener()
    {
      public void actionPerformed(ActionEvent e)
      {
        saveMenuItemActionPerformed(e);
      }
    });
    exitMenuItem.addActionListener(new ActionListener()
    {
      public void actionPerformed(ActionEvent e)
      {
        exitMenuItemActionPerformed(e);
      }
    });

    weightTabbedPane.setPreferredSize(new Dimension(500,
400));
    weightTabbedPane.addTab("Weight Editor", editorPanel);
    weightTabbedPane.addTab("Weight Plot", plotPanel);
    gridConstraints = new GridBagConstraints();
    gridConstraints.gridx = 0;
    gridConstraints.gridy = 0;
    getContentPane().add(weightTabbedPane, gridConstraints);

    editorPanel.setBackground(new Color(192, 192, 255));
    editorPanel.setLayout(new GridBagLayout());
    plotPanel.setBackground(new Color(255, 192, 192));

    fileLabel.setText("Current Weight File");
    fileLabel.setFont(new Font("Arial", Font.BOLD, 14));
    gridConstraints = new GridBagConstraints();
    gridConstraints.gridx = 0;
    gridConstraints.gridy = 0;
    gridConstraints.gridwidth = 2;
    gridConstraints.insets = new Insets(10, 10, 0, 0);
    gridConstraints.anchor = GridBagConstraints.WEST;
    editorPanel.add(fileLabel, gridConstraints);

    fileTextArea.setPreferredSize(new Dimension(220, 50));
    fileTextArea.setFont(new Font("Arial", Font.PLAIN, 12));
    fileTextArea.setEditable(false);
    fileTextArea.setBackground(Color.WHITE);
    fileTextArea.setLineWrap(true);
    fileTextArea.setWrapStyleWord(true);
    gridConstraints = new GridBagConstraints();
    gridConstraints.gridx = 0;
```

```
    gridConstraints.gridy = 1;
    gridConstraints.gridwidth = 2;
    gridConstraints.insets = new Insets(0, 10, 10, 0);
    editorPanel.add(fileTextArea, gridConstraints);

    weightCalendar.setPreferredSize(new Dimension(220, 200));

weightCalendar.setBorder(BorderFactory.createLineBorder(Color
.BLACK, 2));
    gridConstraints = new GridBagConstraints();
    gridConstraints.gridx = 0;
    gridConstraints.gridy = 2;
    gridConstraints.gridwidth = 2;
    gridConstraints.insets = new Insets(5, 10, 0, 5);
    editorPanel.add(weightCalendar, gridConstraints);
    weightCalendar.addPropertyChangeListener(new
PropertyChangeListener()
    {
      public void propertyChange(PropertyChangeEvent e)
      {
        weightCalendarPropertyChange(e);
      }
    });

    weightLabel.setText("Weight (lb)");
    weightLabel.setFont(new Font("Arial", Font.BOLD, 14));
    gridConstraints = new GridBagConstraints();
    gridConstraints.gridx = 0;
    gridConstraints.gridy = 3;
    gridConstraints.insets = new Insets(10, 10, 0, 0);
    gridConstraints.anchor = GridBagConstraints.WEST;
    editorPanel.add(weightLabel, gridConstraints);

    weightTextField.setPreferredSize(new Dimension(100, 25));
    weightTextField.setFont(new Font("Arial", Font.PLAIN,
12));
    gridConstraints = new GridBagConstraints();
    gridConstraints.gridx = 1;
    gridConstraints.gridy = 3;
    gridConstraints.insets = new Insets(10, 5, 0, 0);
    editorPanel.add(weightTextField, gridConstraints);
    weightTextField.addActionListener(new ActionListener ()
    {
      public void actionPerformed(ActionEvent e)
      {
        weightTextFieldActionPerformed(e);
      }
```

```
    });

    addButton.setText("Add Weight to File");
    gridConstraints.gridx = 0;
    gridConstraints.gridy = 4;
    gridConstraints.gridwidth = 2;
    gridConstraints.insets = new Insets(10, 0, 0, 0);
    editorPanel.add(addButton, gridConstraints);
    addButton.addActionListener(new ActionListener()
    {
      public void actionPerformed(ActionEvent e)
      {
        addButtonActionPerformed(e);
      }
    });

    weightsListLabel.setText("Date        Weight (lb)");
    weightsListLabel.setFont(new Font("Courier New",
Font.BOLD, 16));
    gridConstraints = new GridBagConstraints();
    gridConstraints.gridx = 2;
    gridConstraints.gridy = 0;
    gridConstraints.insets = new Insets(10, 10, 0, 0);
    gridConstraints.anchor = GridBagConstraints.WEST;
    editorPanel.add(weightsListLabel, gridConstraints);

    weightsScrollPane.setPreferredSize(new Dimension(250,
300));
    weightsList.setFont(new Font("Courier New", Font.PLAIN,
16));
    weightsScrollPane.setViewportView(weightsList);
    weightsList.setModel(weightsListModel);
    gridConstraints = new GridBagConstraints();
    gridConstraints.gridx = 2;
    gridConstraints.gridy = 1;
    gridConstraints.gridheight = 3;
    gridConstraints.insets = new Insets(0, 5, 0, 0);
    gridConstraints.anchor = GridBagConstraints.NORTHWEST;
    editorPanel.add(weightsScrollPane, gridConstraints);
    weightsList.addListSelectionListener(new
ListSelectionListener()
    {
      public void valueChanged(ListSelectionEvent e)
      {
        weightsListValueChanged(e);
      }
    });
```

```
    deleteButton.setText("Delete Selection");
    gridConstraints.gridx = 2;
    gridConstraints.gridy = 4;
    gridConstraints.insets = new Insets(10, 0, 0, 0);
    gridConstraints.anchor = GridBagConstraints.CENTER;
    editorPanel.add(deleteButton, gridConstraints);
    deleteButton.addActionListener(new ActionListener()
    {
      public void actionPerformed(ActionEvent e)
      {
        deleteButtonActionPerformed(e);
      }
    });

    pack();
    Dimension screenSize =
Toolkit.getDefaultToolkit().getScreenSize();
    setBounds((int) (0.5 * (screenSize.width - getWidth())),
(int) (0.5 * (screenSize.height - getHeight())), getWidth(),
getHeight());

    // open .ini file
    try
    {
      BufferedReader inputFile = new BufferedReader(new
FileReader("weight.ini"));
      lastFile = inputFile.readLine();
      inputFile.close();
    }
    catch (Exception ex)
    {
      // initialization file not found
      lastFile = "";
    }
    if (!lastFile.equals(""))
      openWeightFile(lastFile);
    else
      initialize();

  }

  private void exitForm(WindowEvent evt)
  {
    System.out.print(lastFile);
    // Write out initialization file
    try
```

```
      {
        PrintWriter outputFile = new PrintWriter(new
BufferedWriter(new FileWriter("weight.ini")));
        outputFile.println(lastFile);
        outputFile.close();
      }
      catch (Exception ex)
      {

      }
      // save last file
      if (!lastFile.equals(""))
        saveWeightFile(lastFile);
      System.exit(0);
    }

  private void newMenuItemActionPerformed(ActionEvent e)
    {
      if (JOptionPane.showConfirmDialog(null, "Are you sure you
want to start a new weight file?", "New File",
JOptionPane.YES_NO_OPTION, JOptionPane.QUESTION_MESSAGE) ==
JOptionPane.YES_OPTION)
      {
        initialize();
      }
    }


  private void openMenuItemActionPerformed(ActionEvent e)
    {

      if (JOptionPane.showConfirmDialog(null, "Are you sure you
want to open a weight new file?", "New Weight File",
JOptionPane.YES_NO_OPTION, JOptionPane.QUESTION_MESSAGE) ==
JOptionPane.YES_OPTION)
      {
        JFileChooser openChooser = new JFileChooser();
        openChooser.setDialogType(JFileChooser.OPEN_DIALOG);
        openChooser.setDialogTitle("Open Weight File");
        openChooser.addChoosableFileFilter(new
  FileNameExtensionFilter("Weight Files", "wgt"));
        if (openChooser.showOpenDialog(this) ==
JFileChooser.APPROVE_OPTION)
        {

openWeightFile(openChooser.getSelectedFile().toString());
        }
      }
```

```
    }

  private void saveMenuItemActionPerformed(ActionEvent e)
  {
    if (weightsListModel.isEmpty())
    {
      JOptionPane.showConfirmDialog(null, "You need to enter
at least one weight value.", "File Error",
JOptionPane.DEFAULT_OPTION, JOptionPane.ERROR_MESSAGE);
      return;
    }
    JFileChooser saveChooser = new JFileChooser();
    saveChooser.setDialogType(JFileChooser.SAVE_DIALOG);
    saveChooser.setDialogTitle("Save Weight File");
    saveChooser.addChoosableFileFilter(new
  FileNameExtensionFilter("Weight Files", "wgt"));
    if (saveChooser.showSaveDialog(this) ==
JFileChooser.APPROVE_OPTION)
    {
      // see if file already exists
      if (saveChooser.getSelectedFile().exists())
      {
        int response;
        response = JOptionPane.showConfirmDialog(null,
saveChooser.getSelectedFile().toString() + "exists.
Overwrite?", "Confirm Save", JOptionPane.YES_NO_OPTION,
JOptionPane.QUESTION_MESSAGE);
        if (response == JOptionPane.NO_OPTION)
        {
          return;
        }
      }
      // make sure file has wgt extension
      // strip off any extension that might be there
      // then tack on wgt
      String fileName =
saveChooser.getSelectedFile().toString();
      int dotlocation = fileName.indexOf(".");
      if (dotlocation == -1)
      {
        // no extension
        fileName += ".wgt";
      }
      else
      {
        // make sure extension is txt
```

```
        fileName = fileName.substring(0, dotlocation) +
".wgt";
      }
      saveWeightFile(fileName);
    }
  }

  private void exitMenuItemActionPerformed(ActionEvent e)
  {
    exitForm(null);
  }

  private void
weightCalendarPropertyChange(PropertyChangeEvent e)
  {
    // show corresponding list box element (if there is one)
    int i;
    i = findDate(dateToString(weightCalendar.getDate()));
    if (i != -1)
    {
      weightsList.setSelectedIndex(i);

weightTextField.setText(getWeight(weightsList.getSelectedValu
e().toString())));
    }
    else
    {
      weightsList.clearSelection();
      weightTextField.setText("");
    }
    weightTextField.requestFocus();
  }

  private void weightTextFieldActionPerformed(ActionEvent e)
  {
    addButton.doClick();
  }

  private void addButtonActionPerformed(ActionEvent e)
  {
    int i;
    if (!validateDecimalNumber(weightTextField))
    {
      JOptionPane.showConfirmDialog(null, "Empty or invalid
weight entry.\nPlease correct.", "Weight Input Error",
JOptionPane.DEFAULT_OPTION, JOptionPane.INFORMATION_MESSAGE);
      return;
```

```
    }
    // add to list (check to see if date already there)
    i = findDate(dateToString(weightCalendar.getDate()));
    if (i != -1)
      weightsListModel.removeElementAt(i);
    String item =
formLine(dateToString(weightCalendar.getDate()),
weightTextField.getText());
    // bubble sort to see where item goes in list to maintain
order
    if (weightsListModel.isEmpty() ||
item.compareTo(weightsListModel.getElementAt(weightsListModel
.size() - 1).toString()) > 0)
    {
      // if list empty or greater than last item, item goes
at end
      weightsListModel.addElement(item);
      weightsList.setSelectedIndex(weightsListModel.size() -
1);
    }
    else
    {
      for (i = weightsListModel.size() - 1; i >= 0; i--)
      {
        if
((weightsListModel.getElementAt(i).toString().compareTo(item)
) < 0)
        {
          break;
        }
      }
      weightsListModel.insertElementAt(item, i + 1);
      weightsList.setSelectedIndex(i + 1);
    }
  }

  private void weightsListValueChanged(ListSelectionEvent e)
  {
    // display corresponding date
    if (weightsList.getSelectedIndex() >= 0)
    {
      // form Date object from String

weightCalendar.setDate(stringToDate(weightsList.getSelectedVa
lue().toString()));
```

```java
weightTextField.setText(getWeight(weightsList.getSelectedValu
e().toString()));
      weightTextField.requestFocus();
    }
  }

  private void deleteButtonActionPerformed(ActionEvent e)
  {
    // remove selected item

weightsListModel.removeElementAt(weightsList.getSelectedIndex
());
  }

  private void initialize()
  {
    weightTabbedPane.setSelectedIndex(0);
    weightCalendar.setDate(new Date());
    weightsListModel.clear();
    fileTextArea.setText("New File");
    weightTextField.setText("");
    weightTextField.requestFocus();
  }

  private String dateToString(Date dd)
  {
    String yString = String.valueOf(dd.getYear() + 1900);
    int m = dd.getMonth() + 1;
    String mString = new DecimalFormat("00").format(m);
    int d = dd.getDate();
    String dString = new DecimalFormat("00").format(d);
    return(yString + "/" + mString + "/" + dString);
  }

  static public Date stringToDate(String s)
  {
    int y = Integer.valueOf(s.substring(0, 4)).intValue() -
1900;
    int m = Integer.valueOf(s.substring(5, 7)).intValue() -
1;
    int d = Integer.valueOf(s.substring(8, 10)).intValue();
    return(new Date(y, m, d));
  }

  private String formLine(String d, String w)
  {
```

```
    int lineLength = 19;
    String s = d;
    w = new
DecimalFormat("0.0").format(Double.valueOf(w).doubleValue());
    for (int i = 0; i < lineLength - 10 - w.length(); i++)
      s += " ";
    s += w;
    return (s);
  }

  static public String getDate(String s)
  {
    s = s.substring(0, 10);
    return(s);
  }

  static public String getWeight(String s)
  {
    s = s.substring(10);
    return (s.trim());
  }

  private int findDate(String d)
  {
    if (!weightsListModel.isEmpty())
    {
      for (int i = 0; i < weightsListModel.getSize(); i++)
      {
        if
(getDate(weightsListModel.getElementAt(i).toString()).equals(
d))
          return (i);
    }
  }
    return (-1);
  }

  private boolean validateDecimalNumber(JTextField tf)
  {
    // checks to see if text field contains
    // valid decimal number with only digits and a single
decimal point
    String s = tf.getText().trim();
    boolean hasDecimal = false;
    boolean valid = true;
    if (s.length() == 0)
    {
```

```
        valid = false;
      }
    else
    {
      for (int i = 0; i < s.length(); i++)
      {
        char c = s.charAt(i);
        if (c >= '0' && c <= '9')
        {
          continue;
        }
        else if (c == '.' && !hasDecimal)
        {
          hasDecimal = true;
        }
        else
        {
          // invalid character found
          valid = false;
        }
      }
    }
    tf.setText(s);
    if (!valid)
    {
      tf.requestFocus();
    }
    return (valid);
  }

  private void saveWeightFile(String fn)
  {
    try
    {
      PrintWriter outputFile = new PrintWriter(new
BufferedWriter(new FileWriter(fn)));
      fileTextArea.setText(fn);
      for (int i = 0; i < weightsListModel.getSize(); i++)
      {

outputFile.println(weightsListModel.getElementAt(i).toString(
));
      }
      outputFile.flush();
      outputFile.close();
      lastFile = fn;
    }
```

```
      catch (Exception ex)
      {
        JOptionPane.showConfirmDialog(null, "An error occurred
saving the weight file.", "File Error",
JOptionPane.DEFAULT_OPTION, JOptionPane.ERROR_MESSAGE);
        lastFile = "";
      }
  }

  private void openWeightFile(String fn)
  {
    try
    {
      initialize();
      BufferedReader inputFile = new BufferedReader(new
FileReader(fn));
      fileTextArea.setText(fn);
      do
      {
        String s = inputFile.readLine();
        weightsListModel.addElement(s);
      }
      while (inputFile.ready());
      inputFile.close();
      lastFile = fn;
      // see if current date is in file
      int i =
findDate(dateToString(weightCalendar.getDate()));
      if (i != -1)
        weightsList.setSelectedIndex(i);
    }
    catch (Exception ex)
    {
      JOptionPane.showConfirmDialog(null, "An error occurred
opening the weight file.", "File Error",
JOptionPane.DEFAULT_OPTION, JOptionPane.ERROR_MESSAGE);
      lastFile = "";
    }
  }
}

class WeightPlotPanel extends JPanel
{

  Rectangle2D.Double plotFrame;

  public void paintComponent(Graphics g)
```

```java
{
  Graphics2D g2D = (Graphics2D) g;
  super.paintComponent(g2D);

  // draw plot frame
  plotFrame = new Rectangle2D.Double(50, 40, 420, 280);
  g2D.setPaint(Color.WHITE);
  g2D.fill(plotFrame);
  g2D.setStroke(new BasicStroke(2));
  g2D.setPaint(Color.BLACK);
  g2D.draw(plotFrame);

  // draw weight plot
  int lSize = WeightMonitor.weightsListModel.getSize();
  double[] d = new double[lSize];
  double[] w = new double[lSize];
  double wmin, wmax;
  String s;
  int intervals;
  double gridSpacing, wLegend;
  double sumD, sumD2, sumW, sumDW;
  double t, w0;
  if (lSize < 2)
    return;
  g2D.setStroke(new BasicStroke(2));
  g2D.setPaint(Color.BLUE);
  wmin = 1000.0;
  wmax = 0.0;
  sumD = 0.0;
  sumD2 = 0.0;
  sumW = 0.0;
  sumDW = 0.0;
  long t1 =
WeightMonitor.stringToDate(WeightMonitor.getDate(WeightMonito
r.weightsListModel.getElementAt(0).toString())).getTime();
  for (int i = 0; i < lSize; i++)
  {
    s =
WeightMonitor.weightsListModel.getElementAt(i).toString();
    long t2 =
WeightMonitor.stringToDate(WeightMonitor.getDate(s)).getTime(
);
    d[i] = (double) ((t2 - t1) / (24 * 3600 * 1000));
    w[i] =
Double.valueOf(WeightMonitor.getWeight(s)).doubleValue();
    wmin = Math.min(w[i], wmin);
    wmax = Math.max(w[i], wmax);
```

```
   // values for trend line
   sumD += d[i];
   sumD2 += d[i] * d[i];
   sumW += w[i];
   sumDW += d[i] * w[i];
}
// adjust Wmin/Wmax for 'nice' intervals
if (wmin == wmax)
   wmin = wmax - 1;
wmax = (double) ((int)(wmax + 0.5)); // round up
wmin = (double) ((int)(wmin - 0.5)); // round down
if (wmax - wmin <= 5.0)
   gridSpacing = 1.0;
else if (wmax - wmin <= 10.0)
   gridSpacing = 2.0;
else if (wmax - wmin <= 25.0)
   gridSpacing = 5.0;
else if (wmax - wmin <= 50.0)
   gridSpacing = 10.0;
else
   gridSpacing = 20.0;
if (wmax % (int)gridSpacing != 0)
   wmax = gridSpacing * (int)(wmax / gridSpacing) +
gridSpacing;
if (wmin % (int)gridSpacing != 0)
   wmin = gridSpacing * (int)(wmin / gridSpacing);
intervals = (int)((wmax - wmin) / gridSpacing);
for (int i = 1; i < lSize; i++)
{
   // connect current point to previous point
   Line2D.Double weightLine = new Line2D.Double(dToX(d[i -
1], d[lSize - 1]), wToY(w[i - 1], wmin, wmax), dToX(d[i],
d[lSize - 1]), wToY(w[i], wmin, wmax));
   g2D.draw(weightLine);
}

// draw grid lines and labels
Font labelFont = new Font("Arial", Font.BOLD, 14);
g2D.setFont(labelFont);
Rectangle2D labelRect;
String lblText;
g2D.setStroke(new BasicStroke(1));
g2D.setPaint(Color.BLACK);
wLegend = wmin;
for (int i = 0; i <= intervals; i++)
{
   lblText = String.valueOf((int) wLegend);
```

```
    labelRect = labelFont.getStringBounds(lblText,
g2D.getFontRenderContext());
    g2D.drawString(lblText, (int) (plotFrame.getX() -
labelRect.getWidth() - 5), (int) (wToY(wLegend, wmin, wmax) +
0.5 * labelRect.getHeight()));
    if (i > 0 && i < intervals)
    {
       // draw grid line (except at top and bottom)
       Line2D.Double gridLine = new
Line2D.Double(plotFrame.getX(), wToY(wLegend, wmin, wmax),
plotFrame.getX() + plotFrame.getWidth(), wToY(wLegend, wmin,
wmax));
       g2D.draw(gridLine);
    }
    wLegend += gridSpacing;
  }


  // draw horizontal axis labels (using label font)
  String dateText = "Start: " +
WeightMonitor.getDate(WeightMonitor.weightsListModel.getEleme
ntAt(0).toString());
    g2D.drawString(dateText, (int) (plotFrame.getX() + 10),
(int) (plotFrame.getY() + plotFrame.getHeight() + 20));
    Line2D.Double dateLine = new
Line2D.Double(plotFrame.getX() + 10, plotFrame.getY() +
plotFrame.getHeight() + 10, plotFrame.getX(),
plotFrame.getY() + plotFrame.getHeight());
    g2D.draw(dateLine);
    dateText = "End: " +
WeightMonitor.getDate(WeightMonitor.weightsListModel.getEleme
ntAt(WeightMonitor.weightsListModel.getSize() -
1).toString());
    Rectangle2D dateRect =
labelFont.getStringBounds(dateText,
g2D.getFontRenderContext());
    g2D.drawString(dateText, (int) (plotFrame.getX() +
plotFrame.getWidth() - dateRect.getWidth() - 10), (int)
(plotFrame.getY() + plotFrame.getHeight() + 20));
    dateLine = new Line2D.Double(plotFrame.getX() +
plotFrame.getWidth() - 10, plotFrame.getY() +
plotFrame.getHeight() + 10, plotFrame.getX() +
plotFrame.getWidth(), plotFrame.getY() +
plotFrame.getHeight());
    g2D.draw(dateLine);

  // trend computations
```

```java
      t = (lSize * sumDW - sumD * sumW) / (lSize * sumD2 - sumD
* sumD);
      w0 = (sumD2 * sumW - sumD * sumDW) / (lSize * sumD2 -
sumD * sumD);
      // draw line
      Line2D.Double trendLine = new
Line2D.Double(plotFrame.getX(), wToY(w0, wmin, wmax),
dToX(d[lSize - 1], d[lSize - 1]), wToY(t * d[lSize - 1] + w0,
wmin, wmax));
      g2D.setPaint(Color.RED);
      g2D.draw(trendLine);
      String title = "Trend: ";
      if (t > 0)
         title += "+";
      title += new DecimalFormat("0.00").format(7 * t) + "
lb/week";
      Font titleFont = new Font("Arial", Font.BOLD, 16);
      Rectangle2D titleRect = titleFont.getStringBounds(title,
g2D.getFontRenderContext());
      g2D.setFont(titleFont);
      g2D.setPaint(Color.BLACK);
      g2D.drawString(title, (int) (plotFrame.getX() + 0.5 *
(plotFrame.getWidth() - titleRect.getWidth())), (int)
(plotFrame.getY() - 10));

      g2D.dispose();
   }

   private int dToX(double d, double dmax)
   {
      return ((int)(d * (plotFrame.getWidth() - 1) / dmax +
plotFrame.getX()));
   }

   private int wToY(double w, double wmin, double wmax)
   {
      return ((int)((wmax - w) * (plotFrame.getHeight() - 1) /
(wmax - wmin) + plotFrame.getY()));
   }


}
```

8

Home Inventory Manager Project

Review and Preview

The **Home Inventory Manager Project** helps you keep track of your valuable belongings. For every item in your inventory, the program stores a description, location, serial number, purchase information, and even a photo! A printed inventory is available - very useful for insurance purposes. We introduce some object-oriented programming concepts and how to print from a project.

Home Inventory Manager Project Preview

In this chapter, we will build a **home inventory manager** program. This program lets you keep a record of your belongings.

The finished project is saved as **HomeInventory** in the **\HomeJava\HomeJava Projects** project group. Start NetBeans (or your IDE). Open the specified project group. Make **HomeInventory** the selected project. Run the project. You will see:

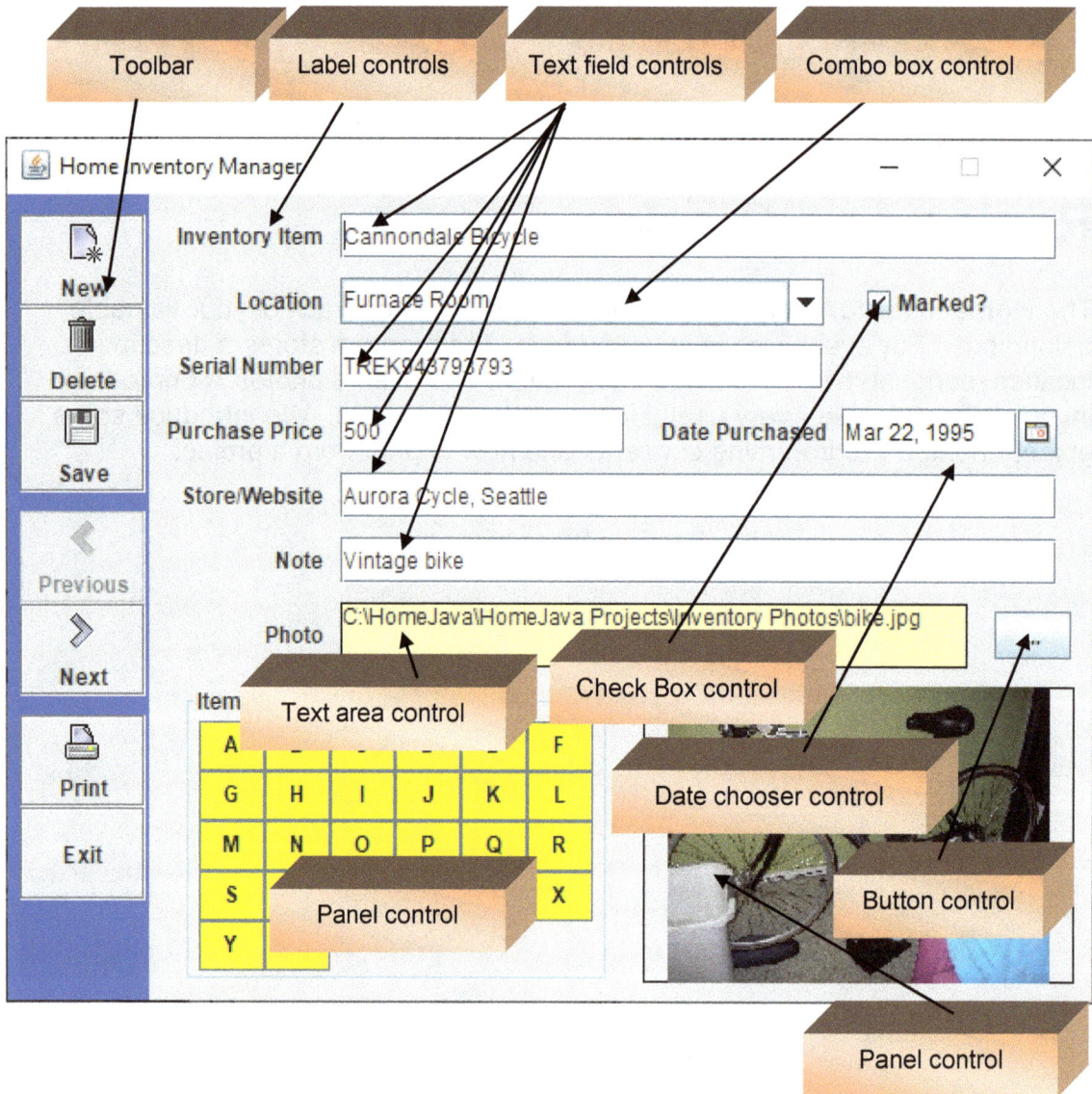

A toolbar control is used to add, delete and save items from the inventory. It is also used to navigate from one item to the next. The primary way to enter information about an inventory item is with several text field controls. A combo box is used to specify location, while a date chooser is used to select purchase date. A check box control indicates if an item is marked with identifying information. A button control (with an ellipsis) selects a photo to display in the panel control. A panel control holds 26 buttons for searching.

The program has a built-in sample inventory file – the first item in that file is displayed (items are listed alphabetically by **Inventory Item**):

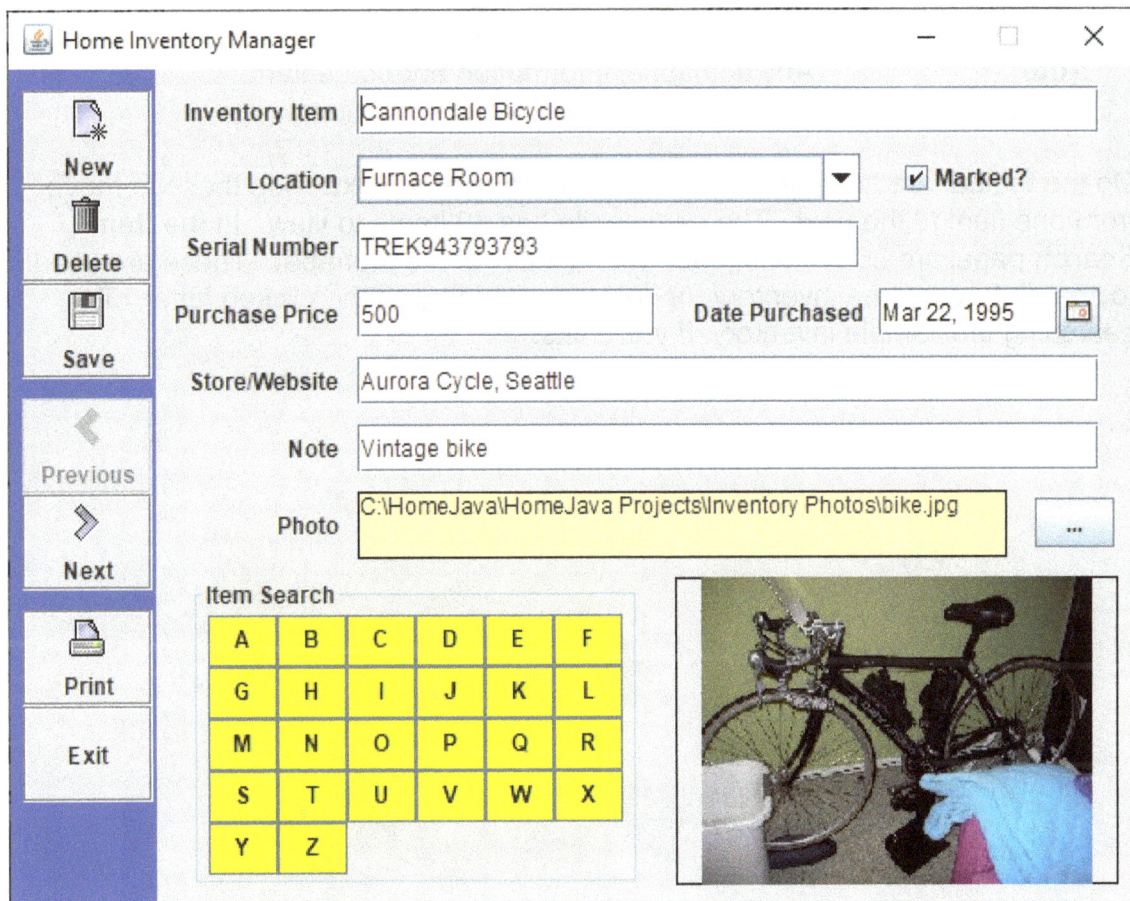

You will, of course, be able to replace the built-in file with your own belongings, but for now, let's see how the program works.

The idea of the program is to enter and/or view descriptive information about each item in your inventory. You can enter:

Inventory Item	A description of the item (required)
Location	Description of where item is located
Marked	Indicates if item is marked with some kind of identifying information (social security number, driver's license number, phone number)
Serial Number	Item serial number
Purchase Price	How much you paid for the item.
Date Purchased	When you purchased the item.
Store/Website	Where you purchased the item.
Note	Any additional information about the item.
Photo	View a stored JPEG photo of the item.

On the toolbar are two buttons marked **Previous** and **Next**. Use these to move from one item to the next. The sample file has 10 items to view. In the **Item Search** panel are 26 buttons, each with a letter of the alphabet. These are used to search through the inventory for items beginning with the clicked letter. Try searching the sample inventory, if you'd like.

Another nice feature of the project is the ability to get a printed record of your inventory. Click the toolbar button marked **Print** (don't worry, nothing will print). You will see:

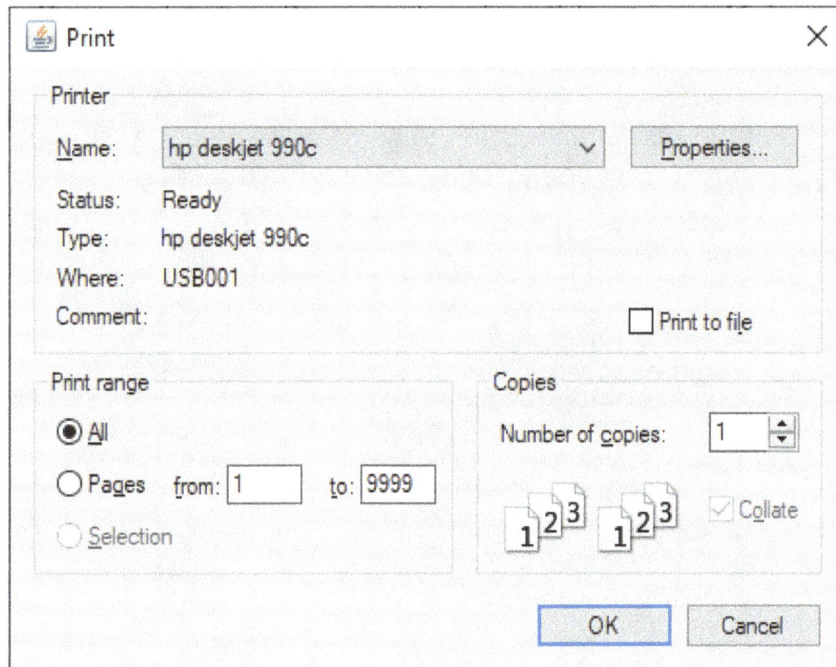

This is the standard print dialog where you select printing options (including what printer to use). Click **Cancel**.

A primary task of the home inventory manager is to add, edit, save and delete inventory items. To add an item, you click the **Add** button in the toolbar. You then enter the necessary information and click the **Save** button. To edit an existing item, you first display the item to edit. Make the desired changes and click **Save**. To delete an item, you display the item, then click the **Delete** toolbar button. Let's try the editing features.

Navigate to one of the existing items in the sample file (use the **Previous** or **Next** buttons or try a search). I moved to **Toby**, my ever faithful dog:

We'll delete this item, then rebuild it to demonstrate how to enter information. Click the **Delete** button – choose **Yes** when asked if you really want Toby to go away. The display will show the next item in the inventory. Click the **New** button to start a new item.

The blank inventory screen appears as:

At this point, you simply work your way down the form entering the desired information at the desired locations. When done, you click **Save** and the item is added to your inventory. We'll add Toby back to the file.

Under **Inventory Item**, type **Toby** and press <**Enter**>. This is the only required piece of information – all other entries are optional. For **Location**, click the drop-down arrow in the combo box. A list of choices is presented. Choose one of these items or type your own. If you type an entry that's not in the combo box, it will be added and saved for future items. Choose **Under the other desk** for Toby (he's always there). Put a check mark next to **Marked**? Make up a **Serial Number** for Toby – I used **DOOFUS123**. We got Toby for free, so his **Purchase Price** is **0.00**. We got Toby on **June 6, 2001**. Under **Date Purchased**, click the drop-down arrow. On the calendar that appears, navigate to this date and click it. Under **Store/Website**, type **Olympia SPCA** (he's a pound puppy) and under **Note**, type **Priceless**.

At this point, the form should look like this:

The last step is adding a photo.

Click the button with the ellipsis (**...**) next to the **Photo** label area. An open file dialog box will appear:

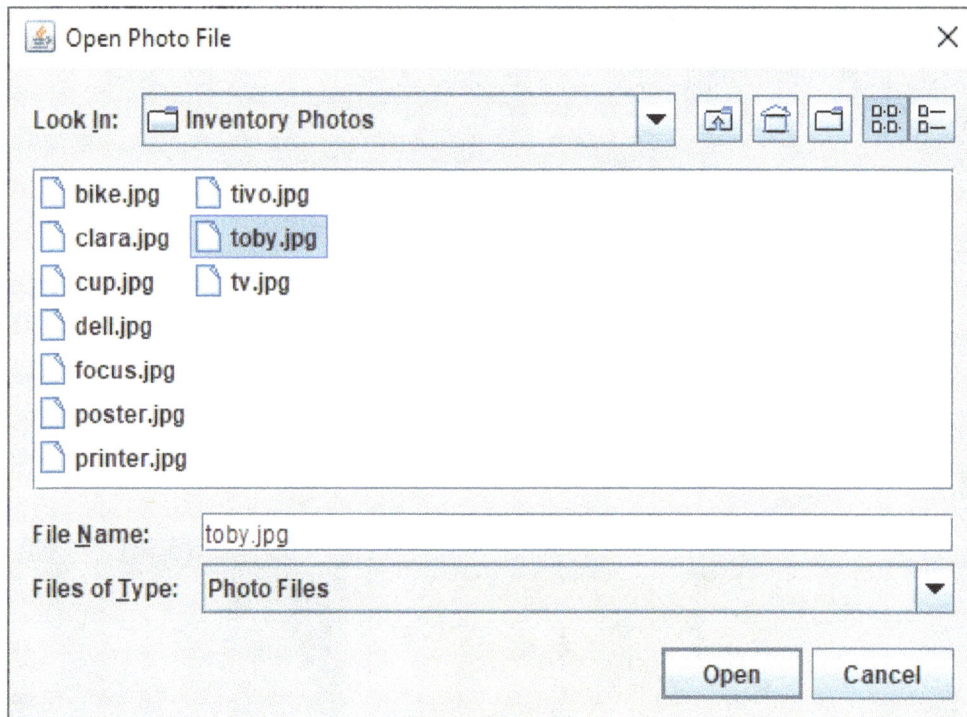

The photo can be any JPEG file (what a digital camera uses). You simply navigate to a photo location and click **Open**. The samples for these notes are in the **\HomeJava\HomeJava Projects\Inventory Photos** folder. Move to that folder and select **toby.jpg** as shown. Click **Open** and the photo will appear.

The final **Toby** inventory item page looks like this:

Notice the photo and the file name listed under **Photo**. At this point, click **Save** and Toby is back in the list (properly sorted alphabetically).

That's the idea of the program. Fill in an entry page for each item in your inventory and click **Save**. Click **Exit** on the toolbar when done. Upon exiting the program, all your inventory items are saved to a file (the built-in file currently holding the sample entries). This same file is automatically opened when you rerun the program, so your items are always available for additions, changes and deletions.

We will now build this program in several stages. We discuss **frame design**. We discuss the controls used to build the frame and establish initial properties. We see how to add a toolbar to the project. And, we address **code design** in detail. We introduce object-oriented programming (OOP) concepts to store the inventory data. We discuss how to read and write the inventory file, how to perform the various editing features, how to load a photo file, how to create the buttons used in the search function, and how to print out the inventory.

Home Inventory Manager Frame Design

We begin building the **Home Inventory Project.** Let's build the frame. Start a new project in your Java project group – name it **HomeInventory**. Delete default code in file named **HomeInventory.java**. Once started, we suggest you immediately save the project with the name you chose. This sets up the folder and file structure needed for your project. Build the basic frame with these properties:

> **Home Inventory** Frame:
>
> | title | Home Inventory Manager |
> | resizable | false |

The code is:

```java
/*
 * HomeInventory.java
 */
package homeinventory;
import javax.swing.*;
import java.awt.*;
import java.awt.event.*;

public class HomeInventory extends JFrame
{
  public static void main(String args[])
  {
    // create frame
    new HomeInventory().setVisible(true);
  }

  public HomeInventory()
  {
    // frame constructor
    setTitle("Home Inventory Manager");
    setResizable(false);
    addWindowListener(new WindowAdapter()
    {
      public void windowClosing(WindowEvent evt)
      {
        exitForm(evt);
      }
    });

    getContentPane().setLayout(new GridBagLayout());
```

```
    GridBagConstraints gridConstraints;

    pack();
    Dimension screenSize =
Toolkit.getDefaultToolkit().getScreenSize();
    setBounds((int) (0.5 * (screenSize.width -
getWidth())), (int) (0.5 * (screenSize.height -
getHeight())), getWidth(), getHeight());
  }

  private void exitForm(WindowEvent evt)
  {
    System.exit(0);
  }
}
```

This code builds the frame, sets up the layout manager and includes code to exit the application. Run the code to make sure the frame (at least, what there is of it at this point) appears and is centered on the screen:

Let's populate our frame with other controls. All code for creating the frame and placing controls (except declarations) goes in the **HomeInventory** constructor.

The are lots of controls in this project. The **GridBagLayout** for the frame is::

	gridx = 0	gridx = 1	gridx = 2	gridx = 3	gridx = 4	gridx = 5	gridx = 6
gridy = 0		itemLabel	itemTextField				
gridy = 1		locationLabel	locationTextField			markedCheckBox	
gridy = 2		serialLabel	serialTextField				
gridy = 3	inventoryToolbar	priceLabel	priceTextField	dateLabel	dateDateChooser		
gridy = 4		storeLabel	storeTextField				
gridy = 5		noteLabel	noteTextField				
gridy = 6		photoLabel	photoTextArea				photoButton
gridy = 7		searchPanel			photoPanel		

The label controls are used for titling. **photoTextArea** holds the plot file name. The text fields are used to input item information. The combo box control (**locationCombo**) is used to select location information. The check box (**markedCheckBox**) indicates if an item is marked. The date chooser (**dateDateChooser**) selects purchase date. The button (**photoButton**) is used to select the photo file. The photo is displayed in **photoPanel**. The other panel (**searchPanel**) will hold buttons used for searching. The tool bar (**inventoryToolbar**) is used to edit items and navigate from one item to the next.

As noted, there are lots of controls. We will discuss adding controls in a few steps. First, we discuss the toolbar. Then, we cover the controls used to input inventory information. Lastly, we add the **searchPanel** (and associated button controls) and the **photoPanel**.

Frame Design – Toolbar

The toolbar (**JToolbar**) is used to edit the inventory items and navigate through them. It is also used to print the items and exit the program. Let's preview what it should look like:

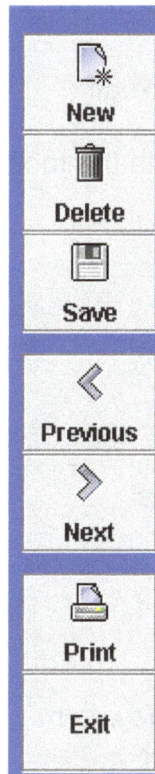

The toolbar will have seven buttons: one to create a **new** item (**newButton**), one to **delete** an item (**deleteButton**), one to **save** an item (**saveButton**), one to view the **previous** item (**previousButton**) one to view the **next** item (**nextButton**), one to **print** the inventory (**printButton**) and one to **exit** the program (**exitButton**). Separators are used at the top, after the **save** button and after the **next** button.

All but the last button has an image. The images used are in the
\HomeJava\HomeJava Projects\HomeInventory folder. Copy these images to
your project folder. The six images are:

new.gif	delete.gif	save.gif
previous.gif	next.gif	print.gif

The control properties associated with the toolbar:

inventoryToolbar:
floatable	false
background	Blue
orientation	Vertical
gridx	0
gridy	0
gridheight	8
fill	Vertical

newbutton:
image	new.gif
text	New
size	70, 50
toolTipText	Add New Item
horizontalTextPosition	Center
verticalTextPosition	Bottom

deletebutton:
image	delete.gif
text	Delete
size	70, 50
toolTipText	Delete Current Item
horizontalTextPosition	Center
verticalTextPosition	Bottom

savebutton:
image	save.gif
text	Save
size	70, 50
toolTipText	Save Current Item
horizontalTextPosition	Center
verticalTextPosition	Bottom

previousbutton:
image	previous.gif
text	Previous
size	70, 50
toolTipText	Display Previous Item
horizontalTextPosition	Center
verticalTextPosition	Bottom

nextbutton:
image	next.gif
text	Next
size	70, 50
toolTipText	Display Next Item
horizontalTextPosition	Center
verticalTextPosition	Bottom

printbutton:
image	print.gif
text	Print
size	70, 50
toolTipText	Print Inventory List
horizontalTextPosition	Center
verticalTextPosition	Bottom

exitButton:
text	Exit
size	70, 50
toolTipText	Exit Program

Declare the controls as class level objects:

```
// Toolbar
JToolBar inventoryToolBar = new JToolBar();
JButton newButton = new JButton(new ImageIcon("new.gif"));
JButton deleteButton = new JButton(new
ImageIcon("delete.gif"));
JButton saveButton = new JButton(new
ImageIcon("save.gif"));
JButton previousButton = new JButton(new
ImageIcon("previous.gif"));
JButton nextButton = new JButton(new
ImageIcon("next.gif"));
JButton printButton = new JButton(new
ImageIcon("print.gif"));
JButton exitButton = new JButton();
```

Add the controls (and separators) to the frame/toolbar using this code in the frame constructor:

```
inventoryToolBar.setFloatable(false);
inventoryToolBar.setBackground(Color.BLUE);
inventoryToolBar.setOrientation(SwingConstants.VERTICAL);
gridConstraints = new GridBagConstraints();
gridConstraints.gridx = 0;
gridConstraints.gridy = 0;
gridConstraints.gridheight = 8;
gridConstraints.fill = GridBagConstraints.VERTICAL;
getContentPane().add(inventoryToolBar, gridConstraints);

inventoryToolBar.addSeparator();
```

```
Dimension bSize = new Dimension(70, 50);
newButton.setText("New");
sizeButton(newButton, bSize);
newButton.setToolTipText("Add New Item");
newButton.setHorizontalTextPosition(SwingConstants.CENTER)
;
newButton.setVerticalTextPosition(SwingConstants.BOTTOM);
inventoryToolBar.add(newButton);
newButton.addActionListener(new ActionListener()
{
  public void actionPerformed(ActionEvent e)
  {
    newButtonActionPerformed(e);
  }
});

deleteButton.setText("Delete");
sizeButton(deleteButton, bSize);
deleteButton.setToolTipText("Delete Current Item");
deleteButton.setHorizontalTextPosition(SwingConstants.CENT
ER);
deleteButton.setVerticalTextPosition(SwingConstants.BOTTOM
);
inventoryToolBar.add(deleteButton);
deleteButton.addActionListener(new ActionListener()
{
  public void actionPerformed(ActionEvent e)
  {
    deleteButtonActionPerformed(e);
  }
});

saveButton.setText("Save");
sizeButton(saveButton, bSize);
saveButton.setToolTipText("Save Current Item");
saveButton.setHorizontalTextPosition(SwingConstants.CENTER
);
saveButton.setVerticalTextPosition(SwingConstants.BOTTOM);
inventoryToolBar.add(saveButton);
saveButton.addActionListener(new ActionListener()
{
  public void actionPerformed(ActionEvent e)
  {
    saveButtonActionPerformed(e);
  }
});
```

```java
inventoryToolBar.addSeparator();

previousButton.setText("Previous");
sizeButton(previousButton, bSize);
previousButton.setToolTipText("Display Previous Item");
previousButton.setHorizontalTextPosition(SwingConstants.CENTER);
previousButton.setVerticalTextPosition(SwingConstants.BOTTOM);
inventoryToolBar.add(previousButton);
previousButton.addActionListener(new ActionListener()
{
  public void actionPerformed(ActionEvent e)
  {
    previousButtonActionPerformed(e);
  }
});

nextButton.setText("Next");
sizeButton(nextButton, bSize);
nextButton.setToolTipText("Display Next Item");
nextButton.setHorizontalTextPosition(SwingConstants.CENTER);
nextButton.setVerticalTextPosition(SwingConstants.BOTTOM);
inventoryToolBar.add(nextButton);
nextButton.addActionListener(new ActionListener()
{
  public void actionPerformed(ActionEvent e)
  {
    nextButtonActionPerformed(e);
  }
});

inventoryToolBar.addSeparator();
```

```
printButton.setText("Print");
sizeButton(printButton, bSize);
printButton.setToolTipText("Print Inventory List");
printButton.setHorizontalTextPosition(SwingConstants.CENTE
R);
printButton.setVerticalTextPosition(SwingConstants.BOTTOM)
;
inventoryToolBar.add(printButton);
printButton.addActionListener(new ActionListener()
{
  public void actionPerformed(ActionEvent e)
  {
    printButtonActionPerformed(e);
  }
});

exitButton.setText("Exit");
sizeButton(exitButton, bSize);
exitButton.setToolTipText("Exit Program");
inventoryToolBar.add(exitButton);
exitButton.addActionListener(new ActionListener()
{
  public void actionPerformed(ActionEvent e)
  {
exitButtonActionPerformed(e);
  }
});
```

Note each toolbar button is the same size (70 x 50). We defined a variable (**bSize**) to represent the size and used a general method (**sizeButton**) to set the size.. Add this method to your project:

```
private void sizeButton(JButton b, Dimension d)
{
  b.setPreferredSize(d);
  b.setMinimumSize(d);
  b.setMaximumSize(d);
}
```

Each button has an **ActionPerformed** method. Add these empty methods:

```java
private void newButtonActionPerformed(ActionEvent e)
{
}

private void deleteButtonActionPerformed(ActionEvent e)
{
}

private void saveButtonActionPerformed(ActionEvent e)
{
}

private void previousButtonActionPerformed(ActionEvent e)
{
}

private void nextButtonActionPerformed(ActionEvent e)
{
}

private void printButtonActionPerformed(ActionEvent e)
{
}

private void exitButtonActionPerformed(ActionEvent e)
{
}
```

Save and run the project. You should see the completed toolbar on the left side of the frame:

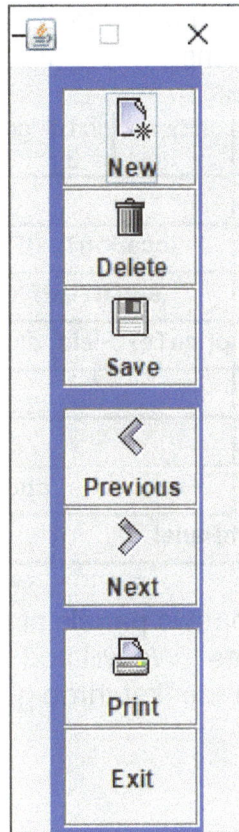

Frame Design – Entry Controls

We show the frame **GridBagLayout** again to allow placement of all the controls used to input information about items:

	gridx = 0	gridx = 1	gridx = 2	gridx = 3	gridx = 4	gridx = 5	gridx = 6
gridy = 0		itemLabel	itemTextField				
gridy = 1		locationLabel	locationTextField		markedCheckBox		
gridy = 2		serialLabel	serialTextField				
gridy = 3	inventoryToolbar	priceLabel	priceTextField	dateLabel	dateDateChooser		
gridy = 4		storeLabel	storeTextField				
gridy = 5		noteLabel	noteTextField				
gridy = 6		photoLabel	photoTextArea				photoButton
gridy = 7		searchPanel			photoPanel		

We will now add everything but the two panels at the bottom of the grid. There are many controls and many properties. We will add them in stages to keep things manageable. First the controls in the first three grid rows.

The control properties are:

itemLabel:
text	Inventory Item
gridx	1
gridy	0
insets	10, 10, 0, 10
anchor	EAST

itemTextField:
size	400, 25
gridx	2
gridy	0
gridwidth	5
insets	10, 0, 0, 10
anchor	WEST

locationLabel:

text	Location
gridx	1
gridy	1
insets	10, 10, 0, 10
anchor	EAST

locationComboBox:

size	270, 25
font	Arial, Plain, Size 12
editable	true
background	White
gridx	2
gridy	1
gridwidth	3
insets	10, 0, 0, 10
anchor	WEST

markedCheckBox:

text	Marked?
gridx	5
gridy	1
insets	10, 10, 0, 0
anchor	WEST

serialLabel:
text	Serial Number
gridx	1
gridy	2
insets	10, 10, 0, 10
anchor	EAST

serialTextField:
size	270, 25
gridx	2
gridy	2
gridwidth	3
insets	10, 0, 0, 10
anchor	WEST

Declare the controls as class level objects:

```
// Frame
JLabel itemLabel = new JLabel();
JTextField itemTextField = new JTextField();
JLabel locationLabel = new JLabel();
JComboBox locationComboBox = new JComboBox();
JCheckBox markedCheckBox = new JCheckBox();
JLabel serialLabel = new JLabel();
JTextField serialTextField = new JTextField();
```

Add the controls to the frame using:

```
itemLabel.setText("Inventory Item");
gridConstraints = new GridBagConstraints();
gridConstraints.gridx = 1;
gridConstraints.gridy = 0;
gridConstraints.insets = new Insets(10, 10, 0, 10);
gridConstraints.anchor = GridBagConstraints.EAST;
getContentPane().add(itemLabel, gridConstraints);

itemTextField.setPreferredSize(new Dimension(400, 25));
gridConstraints = new GridBagConstraints();
gridConstraints.gridx = 2;
gridConstraints.gridy = 0;
gridConstraints.gridwidth = 5;
gridConstraints.insets = new Insets(10, 0, 0, 10);
gridConstraints.anchor = GridBagConstraints.WEST;
getContentPane().add(itemTextField, gridConstraints);
```

```
locationLabel.setText("Location");
gridConstraints = new GridBagConstraints();
gridConstraints.gridx = 1;
gridConstraints.gridy = 1;
gridConstraints.insets = new Insets(10, 10, 0, 10);
gridConstraints.anchor = GridBagConstraints.EAST;
getContentPane().add(locationLabel, gridConstraints);

locationComboBox.setPreferredSize(new Dimension(270, 25));
locationComboBox.setFont(new Font("Arial", Font.PLAIN,
12));
locationComboBox.setEditable(true);
locationComboBox.setBackground(Color.WHITE);
gridConstraints = new GridBagConstraints();
gridConstraints.gridx = 2;
gridConstraints.gridy = 1;
gridConstraints.gridwidth = 3;
gridConstraints.insets = new Insets(10, 0, 0, 10);
gridConstraints.anchor = GridBagConstraints.WEST;
getContentPane().add(locationComboBox, gridConstraints);

markedCheckBox.setText("Marked?");
gridConstraints = new GridBagConstraints();
gridConstraints.gridx = 5;
gridConstraints.gridy = 1;
gridConstraints.insets = new Insets(10, 10, 0, 0);
gridConstraints.anchor = GridBagConstraints.WEST;
getContentPane().add(markedCheckBox, gridConstraints);

serialLabel.setText("Serial Number");
gridConstraints = new GridBagConstraints();
gridConstraints.gridx = 1;
gridConstraints.gridy = 2;
gridConstraints.insets = new Insets(10, 10, 0, 10);
gridConstraints.anchor = GridBagConstraints.EAST;
getContentPane().add(serialLabel, gridConstraints);

serialTextField.setPreferredSize(new Dimension(270, 25));
gridConstraints = new GridBagConstraints();
gridConstraints.gridx = 2;
gridConstraints.gridy = 2;
gridConstraints.gridwidth = 3;
gridConstraints.insets = new Insets(10, 0, 0, 10);
gridConstraints.anchor = GridBagConstraints.WEST;
getContentPane().add(serialTextField, gridConstraints);
```

Run to see the newly added controls:

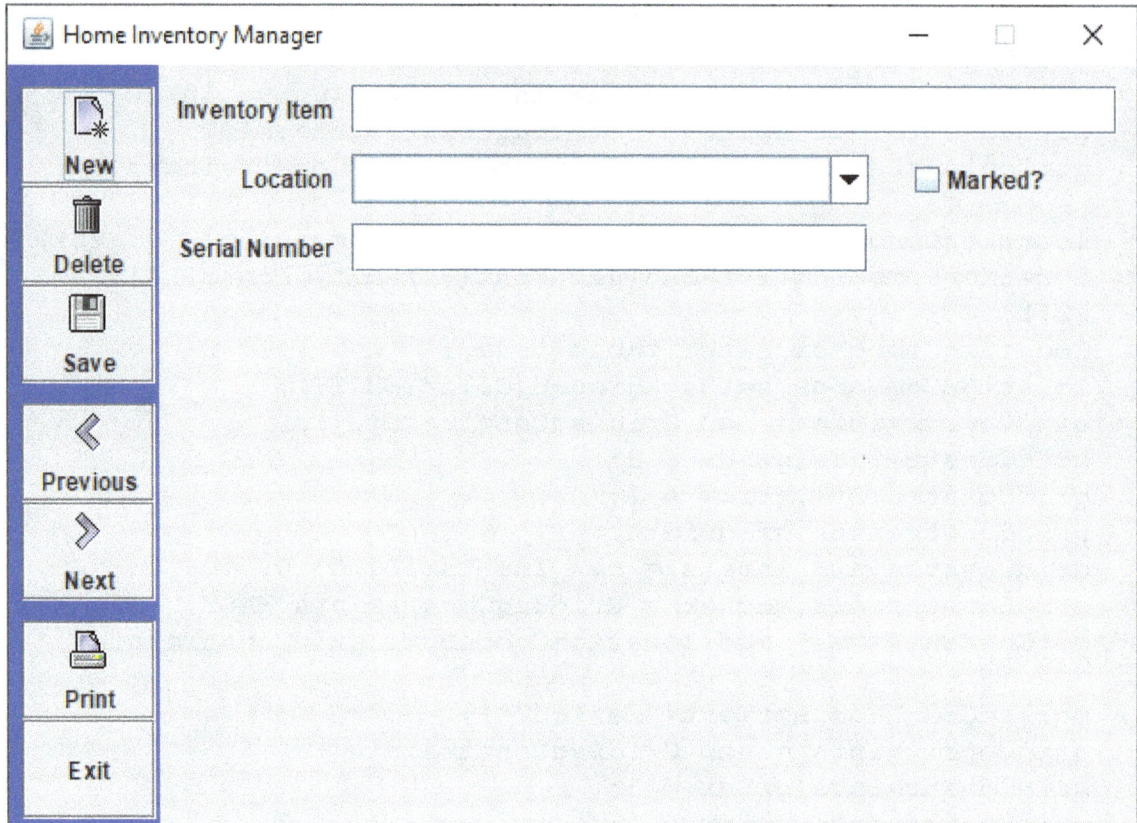

Let's add the remaining input controls. One of these is the same date chooser control used in the **Weight Monitor** project. In that chapter, we added a reference to the **jcalendar-1.3.2.jar** library to our NetBeans IDE. We need to add this library to our project. Make sure **HomeInventory** is the selected project. In the file view area, right-click the project name (**HomeInventory**) and click **Properties**. In the properties window, choose the **Libraries** category:

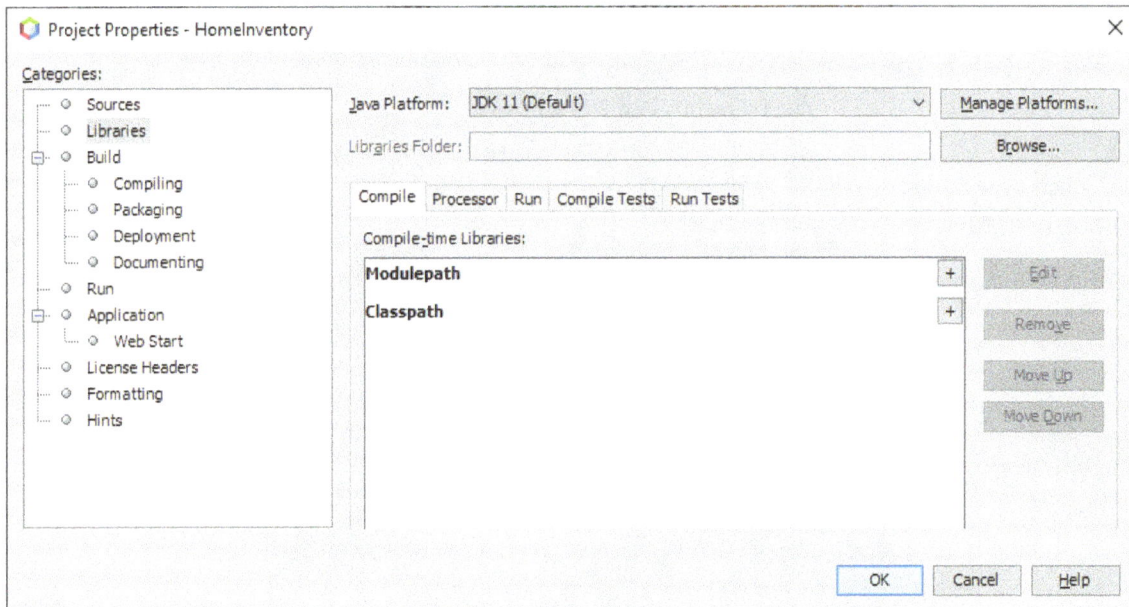

Click the **+** next to **Classpath**, then choose **Add Library** to see

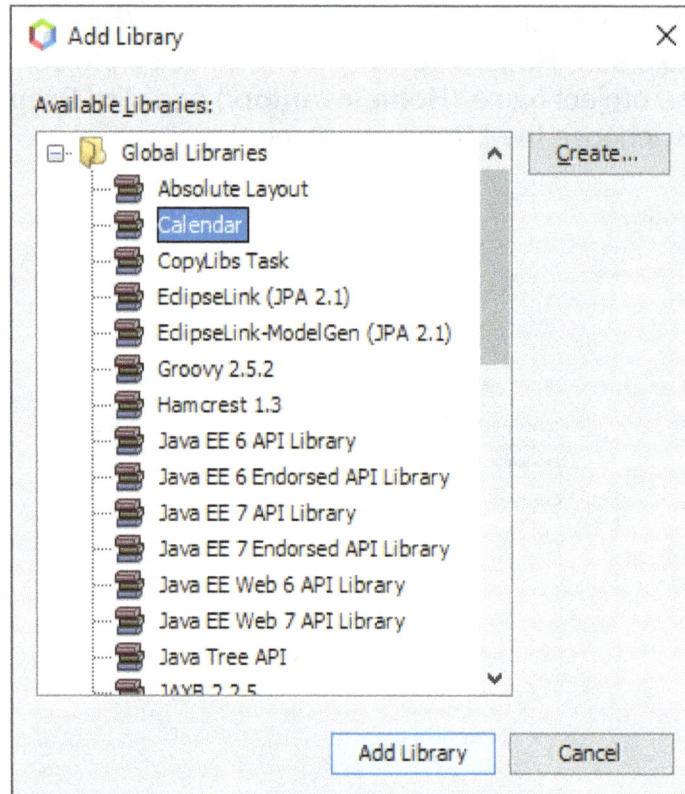

Choose **Calendar**, then click **Add Library**. Click **OK** when returned to the **Properties** window. The calendar tools can now be used in the weight monitor project with the addition of these **import** statements:

```
import com.toedter.calendar.*;
import java.beans.*;
```

Add these to the code window.

The control properties are:

priceLabel:

text	Purchase Price
gridx	1
gridy	3
insets	10, 10, 0, 10
anchor	EAST

priceTextField:

size	160, 25
gridx	2
gridy	3
gridwidth	1
insets	10, 0, 0, 10
anchor	WEST

dateLabel:

text	Date Purchased
gridx	4
gridy	3
insets	10, 10, 0, 0
anchor	EAST

dateDateChooser:

size	120, 25
gridx	5
gridy	3
gridwidth	2
insets	10, 0, 0, 10
anchor	WEST

storeLabel:

text	Store/Website
gridx	1
gridy	4
insets	10, 10, 0, 10
anchor	EAST

storeTextField:
size	400, 25
gridx	2
gridy	4
gridwidth	5
insets	10, 0, 0, 10
anchor	WEST

noteLabel:
text	Note
gridx	1
gridy	5
insets	10, 10, 0, 10
anchor	EAST

noteTextField:
size	400, 25
gridx	2
gridy	5
gridwidth	5
insets	10, 0, 0, 10
anchor	WEST

photoLabel:
text	Photo
gridx	1
gridy	6
insets	10, 10, 0, 10
anchor	EAST

photoTextArea:

size	350, 35
font	Arial, Plain, Size 12
editable	false
lineWrap	true
wrapStyleWord	true
background	Color(255, 255, 192)
border	Black line
gridx	2
gridy	6
gridwidth	4
insets	10, 0, 0, 10
anchor	WEST

photoButton:

text	...
gridx	6
gridy	6
insets	10, 0, 0, 10
anchor	WEST

These controls are declared using:

```
JLabel priceLabel = new JLabel();
JTextField priceTextField = new JTextField();
JLabel dateLabel = new JLabel();
JDateChooser dateDateChooser = new JDateChooser();
JLabel storeLabel = new JLabel();
JTextField storeTextField = new JTextField();
JLabel noteLabel = new JLabel();
JTextField noteTextField = new JTextField();
JLabel photoLabel = new JLabel();
JTextArea photoTextArea = new JTextArea();
JButton photoButton = new JButton();
```

The controls are added to the frame using:

```
priceLabel.setText("Purchase Price");
gridConstraints = new GridBagConstraints();
gridConstraints.gridx = 1;
gridConstraints.gridy = 3;
gridConstraints.insets = new Insets(10, 10, 0, 10);
gridConstraints.anchor = GridBagConstraints.EAST;
getContentPane().add(priceLabel, gridConstraints);

priceTextField.setPreferredSize(new Dimension(160, 25));
gridConstraints = new GridBagConstraints();
gridConstraints.gridx = 2;
gridConstraints.gridy = 3;
gridConstraints.gridwidth = 2;
gridConstraints.insets = new Insets(10, 0, 0, 10);
gridConstraints.anchor = GridBagConstraints.WEST;
getContentPane().add(priceTextField, gridConstraints);

dateLabel.setText("Date Purchased");
gridConstraints = new GridBagConstraints();
gridConstraints.gridx = 4;
gridConstraints.gridy = 3;
gridConstraints.insets = new Insets(10, 10, 0, 0);
gridConstraints.anchor = GridBagConstraints.WEST;
getContentPane().add(dateLabel, gridConstraints);

dateDateChooser.setPreferredSize(new Dimension(120, 25));
gridConstraints = new GridBagConstraints();
gridConstraints.gridx = 5;
gridConstraints.gridy = 3;
gridConstraints.gridwidth = 2;
gridConstraints.insets = new Insets(10, 0, 0, 10);
gridConstraints.anchor = GridBagConstraints.WEST;
getContentPane().add(dateDateChooser, gridConstraints);

storeLabel.setText("Store/Website");
gridConstraints = new GridBagConstraints();
gridConstraints.gridx = 1;
gridConstraints.gridy = 4;
gridConstraints.insets = new Insets(10, 10, 0, 10);
gridConstraints.anchor = GridBagConstraints.EAST;
getContentPane().add(storeLabel, gridConstraints);
```

```
storeTextField.setPreferredSize(new Dimension(400, 25));
gridConstraints = new GridBagConstraints();
gridConstraints.gridx = 2;
gridConstraints.gridy = 4;
gridConstraints.gridwidth = 5;
gridConstraints.insets = new Insets(10, 0, 0, 10);
gridConstraints.anchor = GridBagConstraints.WEST;
getContentPane().add(storeTextField, gridConstraints);

noteLabel.setText("Note");
gridConstraints = new GridBagConstraints();
gridConstraints.gridx = 1;
gridConstraints.gridy = 5;
gridConstraints.insets = new Insets(10, 10, 0, 10);
gridConstraints.anchor = GridBagConstraints.EAST;
getContentPane().add(noteLabel, gridConstraints);

noteTextField.setPreferredSize(new Dimension(400, 25));
gridConstraints = new GridBagConstraints();
gridConstraints.gridx = 2;
gridConstraints.gridy = 5;
gridConstraints.gridwidth = 5;
gridConstraints.insets = new Insets(10, 0, 0, 10);
gridConstraints.anchor = GridBagConstraints.WEST;
getContentPane().add(noteTextField, gridConstraints);

photoLabel.setText("Photo");
gridConstraints = new GridBagConstraints();
gridConstraints.gridx = 1;
gridConstraints.gridy = 6;
gridConstraints.insets = new Insets(10, 10, 0, 10);
gridConstraints.anchor = GridBagConstraints.EAST;
getContentPane().add(photoLabel, gridConstraints);
```

```
photoTextArea.setPreferredSize(new Dimension(350, 35));
photoTextArea.setFont(new Font("Arial", Font.PLAIN, 12));
photoTextArea.setEditable(false);
photoTextArea.setLineWrap(true);
photoTextArea.setWrapStyleWord(true);
photoTextArea.setBackground(new Color(255, 255, 192));
photoTextArea.setBorder(BorderFactory.createLineBorder(Col
or.BLACK));
gridConstraints = new GridBagConstraints();
gridConstraints.gridx = 2;
gridConstraints.gridy = 6;
gridConstraints.gridwidth = 4;
gridConstraints.insets = new Insets(10, 0, 0, 10);
gridConstraints.anchor = GridBagConstraints.WEST;
getContentPane().add(photoTextArea, gridConstraints);

photoButton.setText("...");
gridConstraints = new GridBagConstraints();
gridConstraints.gridx = 6;
gridConstraints.gridy = 6;
gridConstraints.insets = new Insets(10, 0, 0, 10);
gridConstraints.anchor = GridBagConstraints.WEST;
getContentPane().add(photoButton, gridConstraints);
photoButton.addActionListener(new ActionListener ()
{
  public void actionPerformed(ActionEvent e)
  {
    photoButtonActionPerformed(e);
  }
});
```

The button control has an **ActionPerformed** method. Add the empty method

```
private void photoButtonActionPerformed(ActionEvent e)
{
}
```

Run to see more controls:

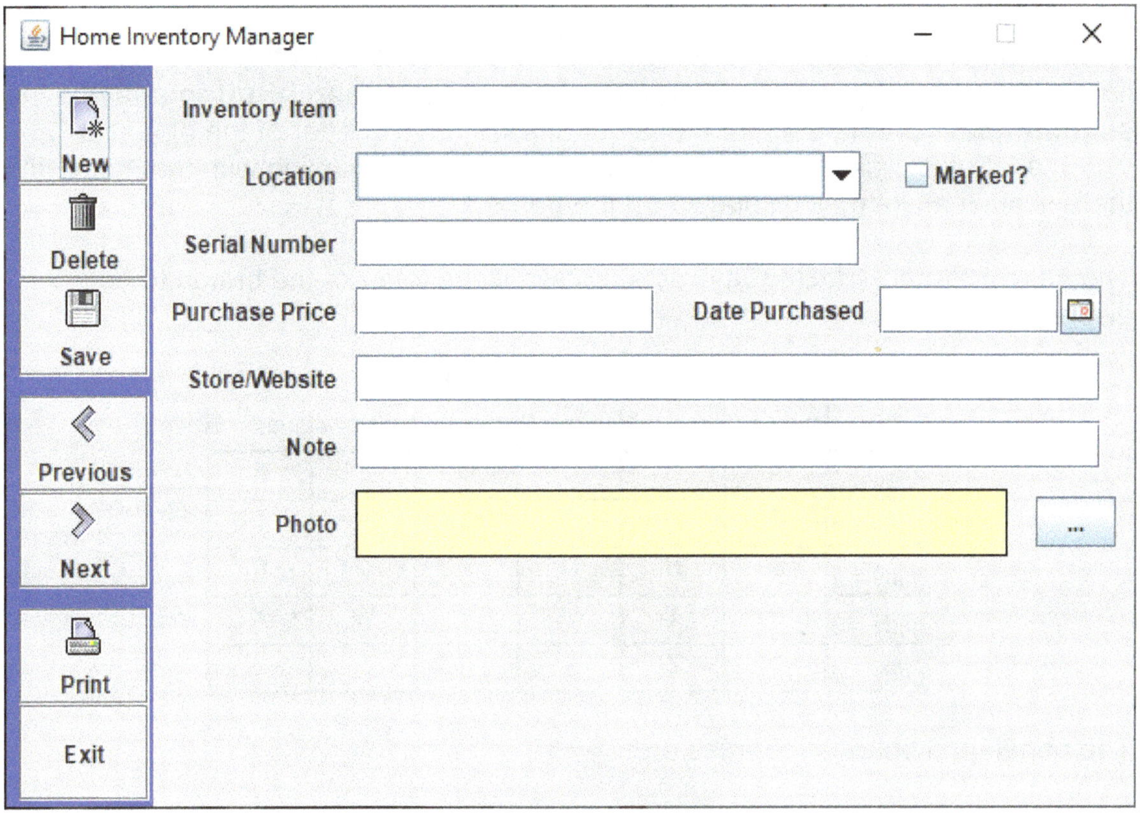

Frame Design – Search Panel

As an inventory list grows, you will want the capability to search for particular items. In this project, we use 26 small button controls (**searchButton** array) in the **searchPanel** control. Each of these buttons will have a letter of the alphabet. When a letter is clicked, the first item in the inventory beginning with that letter (if there is such an item) is displayed on the frame.

The **searchPanel GridBagLayout** is (shown is the letter of the button to be displayed):

	gridx = 0	gridx = 1	gridx = 2	gridx = 3	gridx = 4	gridx = 5
gridy = 0	A	B	C	D	E	F
gridy = 1	G	H	I	J	K	L
gridy = 2	M	N	O	P	Q	R
gridy = 3	S	T	U	V	W	X
gridy = 4	Y	Z				

The panel and button properties are:

searchPanel:

size	240, 160
title	Item Search
gridx	1
gridy	7
gridwidth	3
insets	10, 0, 10, 0
anchor	CENTER

searchButton:

font	Arial, Bold, Size 12
margin	-10, -10, -10, -10
size	37, 27
background	Yellow

We only list generic button properties. The grid above shows the corresponding letter and location. Using negative margins allows room for the text. The button size (37 x 27) was found by trial and error.

Declare the panel and buttons using:

```
JPanel searchPanel = new JPanel();
JButton[] searchButton = new JButton[26];
```

Add them to the panel using:

```
searchPanel.setPreferredSize(new Dimension(240, 160));
searchPanel.setBorder(BorderFactory.createTitledBorder("It
em Search"));
searchPanel.setLayout(new GridBagLayout());
gridConstraints = new GridBagConstraints();
gridConstraints.gridx = 1;
gridConstraints.gridy = 7;
gridConstraints.gridwidth = 3;
gridConstraints.insets = new Insets(10, 0, 10, 0);
gridConstraints.anchor = GridBagConstraints.CENTER;
getContentPane().add(searchPanel, gridConstraints);

int x = 0, y = 0;
// create and position 26 buttons
for (int i = 0; i < 26; i++)
{
  // create new button
  searchButton[i] = new JButton();
  // set text property
   searchButton[i].setText(String.valueOf((char) (65 +
i)));
  searchButton[i].setFont(new Font("Arial", Font.BOLD,
12));
  searchButton[i].setMargin(new Insets(-10, -10, -10, -
10));
  sizeButton(searchButton[i], new Dimension(37, 27));
  searchButton[i].setBackground(Color.YELLOW);
  gridConstraints = new GridBagConstraints();
  gridConstraints.gridx = x;
  gridConstraints.gridy = y;
  searchPanel.add(searchButton[i], gridConstraints);
  // add method
  searchButton[i].addActionListener(new ActionListener ()
  {
    public void actionPerformed(ActionEvent e)
    {
      searchButtonActionPerformed(e);
    }
  });
  x++;
```

```
   // six buttons per row
   if (x % 6 == 0)
   {
x = 0;
y++;
   }
}
```

Note the buttons are sized using the previously added **sizeButton** method.

Each button has the same **ActionPerformed** method. Add this empty framework:

```
private void searchButtonActionPerformed(ActionEvent e)
{
}
```

Save and run the project. The search buttons should now appear on the frame in the search panel control:

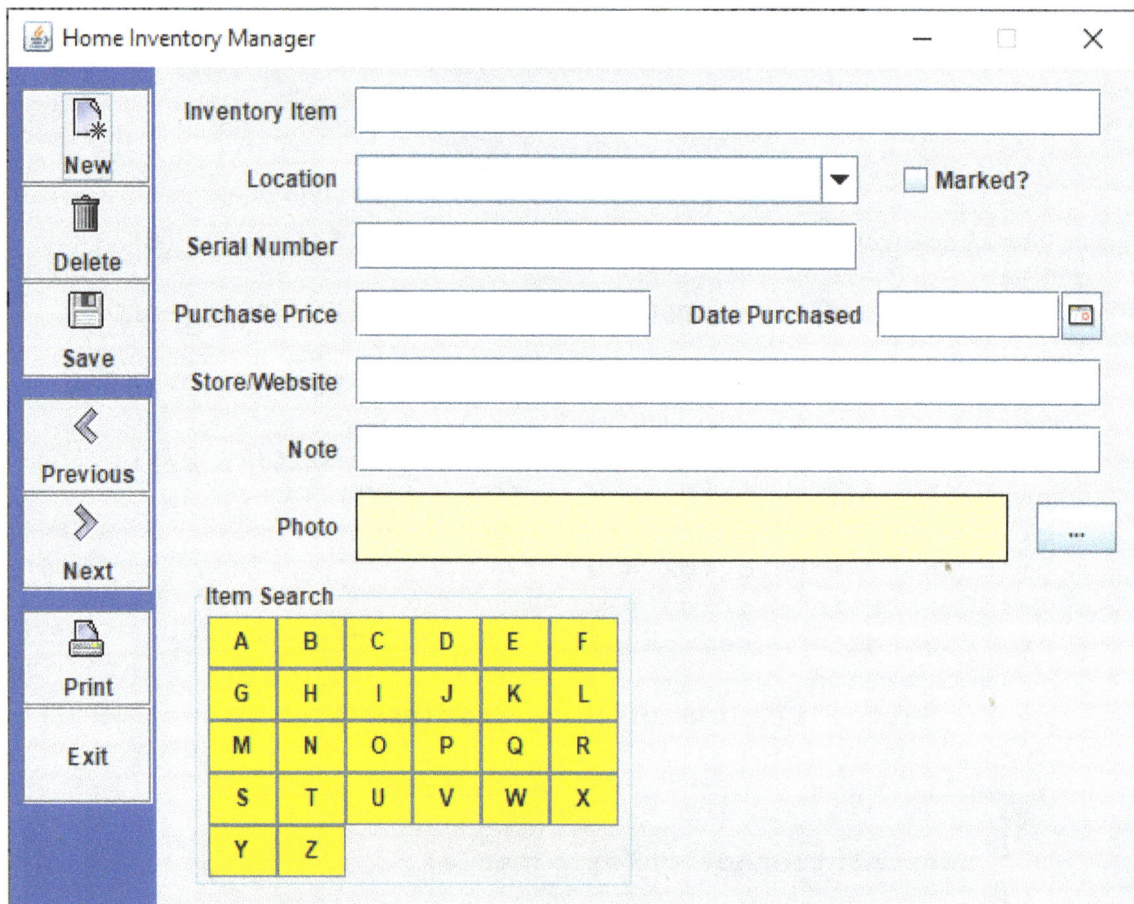

Frame Design – Photo Panel

We complete the frame design by adding the panel (**photoPanel**) that will display inventory photos. We will use a graphic method to place a scaled version of any photo we load into the panel. As such, we need a special panel class with a **paintComponent** method (where the graphics methods are used). We define the **PhotoPanel** class using this code (added after the **HomeInventory** class):

```
class PhotoPanel extends JPanel
{
  public void paintComponent(Graphics g)
  {
    Graphics2D g2D = (Graphics2D) g;
    super.paintComponent(g2D);

    g2D.dispose();
  }
}
```

All graphics methods will go in the **paintComponent** method for this class. Add this class to your project.

Now, the panel properties are:

photoPanel:
size	240, 160
gridx	4
gridy	7
gridwidth	3
insets	10, 0, 10, 10
anchor	CENTER

The panel is declared using:

```
PhotoPanel photoPanel = new PhotoPanel();
```

and added to the frame using:

```
photoPanel.setPreferredSize(new Dimension(240, 160));
gridConstraints = new GridBagConstraints();
gridConstraints.gridx = 4;
gridConstraints.gridy = 7;
gridConstraints.gridwidth = 3;
gridConstraints.insets = new Insets(10, 0, 10, 10);
gridConstraints.anchor = GridBagConstraints.CENTER;
getContentPane().add(photoPanel, gridConstraints);
```

Let's add a border to the panel. Add the shaded code to the panel
paintComponent method.

```
class PhotoPanel extends JPanel
{
  public void paintComponent(Graphics g)
  {
    Graphics2D g2D = (Graphics2D) g;
    super.paintComponent(g2D);

    // draw border
    g2D.setPaint(Color.BLACK);
    g2D.draw(new Rectangle2D.Double(0, 0, getWidth() - 1,
getHeight() - 1));

    g2D.dispose();
  }
}
```

You need to add this import statement to the project (for the graphics code):

```
import java.awt.geom.*;
```

Run the project one more time to see the last control, the framed photo panel:

At long last, all the controls are in place. We now start writing the code. There are many steps. First, let's address proper ordering of the controls for input.

Frame Design – Tab Order and Focus

This project has many controls for user input. We want to make sure it's clear to the user just what information is needed and when. We want the input to 'flow' from the top of the form to the bottom. Run the project. You will see that the **New** button has focus. We would prefer the cursor starting in the **itemTextField** control so the user can start typing input. And, if you tab through the controls, you will see that the toolbar buttons and search buttons (and other controls) can receive focus, even though we don't want this behavior.

Remove the ability to focus on all the toolbar buttons (**newButton, deleteButton, saveButton, previousButton, nextButton, printButton, exitButton**), the search buttons (**searchButton** array), the **markedCheckBox** and the **photoTextArea** controls. To do this, set the **focusable** property of each (use the **setFocusable** method) to **false**. This involves a single line of code for each control in the frame constructor code.

Now, run the project again. The tab sequence starts at the Inventory Item text field (**itemTextField**) and sequentially works down through all the input controls (text fields, combo box, date chooser) to the note text field (**noteTextField**), then the photo button (**photoButton**). We choose to skip the check box.

Another feature for the input is that whenever the user presses <**Enter**> after entering a value (in the combo box or text fields) or clicks a date in the date chooser, the control focus should move to the next control. This feature is implemented in the **ActionPerformed** methods for the combo box control and the five text fields and the **PropertyChange** method for the date control. Let's start at the top of the frame and work our way down, in proper tab order. First, the **itemTextFieldActionPerformed** method. Add a listener in the frame constructor code:

```
itemTextField.addActionListener(new ActionListener ()
{
  public void actionPerformed(ActionEvent e)
  {
    itemTextFieldActionPerformed(e);
  }
});
```

Then add the corresponding method:

```
private void itemTextFieldActionPerformed(ActionEvent e)
{
  locationComboBox.requestFocus();
}
```

This method moves focus to the combo box (**locationComboBox**). Add it's listener:

```
locationComboBox.addActionListener(new ActionListener ()
{
  public void actionPerformed(ActionEvent e)
  {
    locationComboBoxActionPerformed(e);
  }
});
```

and corresponding method:

```
private void locationComboBoxActionPerformed(ActionEvent e)
{
  serialTextField.requestFocus();
}
```

Focus moves to **serialTextField**. Add a listener:

```
serialTextField.addActionListener(new ActionListener ()
{
  public void actionPerformed(ActionEvent e)
  {
    serialTextFieldActionPerformed(e);
  }
});
```

Then, the corresponding method:

```
private void serialTextFieldActionPerformed(ActionEvent e)
{
  priceTextField.requestFocus();
}
```

Focus moves to **priceTextField**. Add a listener:

```
priceTextField.addActionListener(new ActionListener ()
{
  public void actionPerformed(ActionEvent e)
  {
    priceTextFieldActionPerformed(e);
  }
});
```

Then, the corresponding method:

```
private void priceTextFieldActionPerformed(ActionEvent e)
{
  dateDateChooser.requestFocus();
}
```

Focus moves to **dateDateChooser**. Add a listener for property change:

```
dateDateChooser.addPropertyChangeListener(new
PropertyChangeListener()
{
  public void propertyChange(PropertyChangeEvent e)
  {
    dateDateChooserPropertyChange(e);
  }
});
```

Then, the corresponding method:

```
private void
dateDateChooserPropertyChange(PropertyChangeEvent e)
{
  storeTextField.requestFocus();
}
```

Focus moves to **storeTextField**. Add a listener:

```
storeTextField.addActionListener(new ActionListener ()
{
  public void actionPerformed(ActionEvent e)
  {
    storeTextFieldActionPerformed(e);
  }
});
```

Then, the corresponding method:

```
private void storeTextFieldActionPerformed(ActionEvent e)
{
  noteTextField.requestFocus();
}
```

Focus moves to **noteTextField**. Add a listener:

```
noteTextField.addActionListener(new ActionListener ()
{
  public void actionPerformed(ActionEvent e)
  {
    noteTextFieldActionPerformed(e);
  }
});
```

And method:

```
private void noteTextFieldActionPerformed(ActionEvent e)
{
  photoButton.requestFocus();
}
```

So, the focus ends up, as desired, on the photo button (**photoButton**). Double-check that all this added code is in the proper place. The listeners are created in the frame constructor code and the methods are added with all the other **HomeInventory** class methods.

Save and run the project. Press <**Enter**> in each control to make sure the focus transfers properly. One exception is the date chooser – you need to select a date to have the focus move to the next control. You will see this bit of work will be well worth it when you start entering information onto the form. We'll start writing code to process entries soon. First, let's look at how we'll structure all the information used to describe an inventory item.

Introduction to Object-Oriented Programming

Each inventory item requires nine individual pieces of information. Each item and the data type represented are:

> ➤ Description (**String** type)
> ➤ Location (**String** type)
> ➤ Marked indicator (**boolean** type)
> ➤ Serial number (**String** type)
> ➤ Purchase Price (**String** type)
> ➤ Purchase Date (**String** type)
> ➤ Purchase Location (**String** type)
> ➤ Note (**String** type)
> ➤ Photo file (**String** type)

One way to store all this information is to use nine different arrays, one for each quantity, each element of the array representing a single item in the inventory. Using arrays would be "doable," but messy. It would be especially messy to write code for swapping inventory items (needed to make sure items remain in alphabetical order). Each swap would require swapping nine different array elements. And, what if we later want to add more information to an inventory item? We would need to remember everywhere these arrays were referenced in code to make the needed changes. There must be a better way to structure all this information. And there is.

We say Java is an **object-oriented** language. At this point in this course, we have used many of the built-in objects included with Java. We have used button objects, text field objects, label objects and many other controls. We have used graphics objects, stroke objects, paint objects, and shape objects. Having used these objects, we are familiar with such concepts as **declaring** an object, **constructing** an object and using an object's **properties** and **methods**.

We have seen that objects are just things that have attributes (properties) with possible actions (methods). We'll use the idea here to create our own "inventory item" objects. Our objects will only have properties (specified above) and no methods. You will see how creating such objects saves us lots of work.

Before getting started, you may be asking the question "If Java is an object-oriented language, why have we waited so long to start talking about using our own objects?" And, that's a good question. Many books on Java dive right into building objects. We feel it's best to see objects and use objects before trying to create your own. Java is a great language for doing this. The wealth of existing, built-in objects helps you learn about OOP before needing to build your own.

Now, let's review some of the vocabulary of object-oriented programming. These are terms you've seen before in working with the built-in objects of Java. A **class** provides a general description of an **object**. All objects are created from this class description. The first step in creating an object is adding a class to a Java project. Every application we have built in this course is a class itself. Note the top line of every application has the keyword **class**.

The **class** provides a framework for describing three primary components:

> **Properties** – attributes describing the objects
> **Constructors** – methods that initialize the object
> **Methods** – procedures describing things an object can do

Once a class is defined, an object can be created or **instantiated** from the class. This simply means we use the class description to create a copy of the object we can work with. Once the instance is created, we **construct** the finished object for our use.

One last important term to define, related to OOP, is **inheritance**. This is a capability that allows one object to 'borrow' properties and methods from another object. This prevents the classic 'reinventing the wheel' situation. Inheritance is one of the most powerful features of OOP. In this chapter, we will only look at using a simple object, with just some properties. In the next chapter, we will look at adding methods and using inheritance in a project.

Code Design – InventoryItem Class

The first step in creating our own object is to define the class from which the object will be created. This step (and all following steps) is best illustrated by example. And our example will be our inventory item object. We will be creating **InventoryItem** objects that have nine properties, one for each previously-listed piece of information input on the form.

We need to add a class to our project to allow the definition of our **InventoryItem** objects. We could add the class in the existing frame file. However, doing so would defeat a primary advantage of objects, that being re-use. Hence, we will create a separate file to hold our class. To do this, in **NetBeans**, right-click the project name (**Home Inventory**) and add a new Java class file to the project. Name that file **InventoryItem**. Put it in the **homeinventory** source folder. Delete the default code in the file and type these lines:

```
package homeinventory;
public class InventoryItem
{

}
```

All code needed to define properties, constructors and methods for this class will be between the curly braces defining this class.

Add nine property declarations so the file looks like this:

```
package homeinventory;
public class InventoryItem
{
  public String description;
  public String location;
  public boolean marked;
  public String serialNumber;
  public String purchasePrice;
  public String purchaseDate;
  public String purchaseLocation;
  public String note;
  public String photoFile;
}
```

You should see how each property relates to the information on the frame. The keyword **public** indicates the variable is available to any class.

To declare an **InventoryItem** object named **myItem** (in our inventory application) use this line of code:

```
InventoryItem myItem;
```

To construct this object, use this line of code:

```
myItem = new InventoryItem();
```

This line just says "give me a new inventory item." Our **InventoryItem** object is now complete, ready for use. This uses the **default** constructor automatically included with every class. The default constructor simply creates an object with no defined properties.

Once we have created an object, we can refer to properties using the usual notation:

```
objectName.propertyName
```

So, to set the **description** property of our example inventory item, we would use:

```
myItem.description = "This is my inventory item";
```

Let's see how to use our **InventoryItem** class in the home inventory manager project. In this project, we will use an array of inventory items to keep track of things.

Code Design – Inventory File Input

We can now use the **InventoryItem** class to define how we will save inventory information in our project. First, we look at how to input that information from a file. We have chosen to store the inventory information in a built-in, "hard-wired" file. The program looks for a file named **inventory.txt** in the project folder. If the file can't be found, the program begins with an empty inventory and, once items are added, these items are written to a new copy of **inventory.txt**.

The file (**inventory.txt**) keeps track of each item in the inventory. The file also stores the items in the combo box used to specify item location. In later code, we will look at how to modify these items, so new ones are saved. The **inventory.txt** file is sequential and stores one piece of information on each line. The first line is the number of inventory items in the file. After this line are 9 lines for each item in the inventory (each line saving one property for the **InventoryItem** object). After each item is described in the file is a line containing the number of items in the combo box control (**locationComboBox**). Following this line are the corresponding combo box items. In the **\HomeJava\HomeJava Projects** folder is the sample provided with these notes (seen in the project preview). Open this file in a text editor and you will see:

```
inventory.txt - Notepad                    —    □    ×
File  Edit  Format  View  Help
10
Cannondale Bicycle
Furnace Room
TREK943793793
true
500
03/22/1995
Aurora Cycle, Seattle
Vintage bike
C:\HomeJava\HomeJava Projects\Inventory Photos\bike.jpg
Clara
Under my desk
KING5430
true
```

You see this file has 10 entries and there will be 9 lines per entry. You can see the first entry (**Cannondale Bicycle**) and the beginning of the second (**Clara**).

Scroll down to the bottom to see:

```
inventory.txt - Notepad                          —    □    ✕

File  Edit  Format  View  Help
C:\HomeJava\HomeJava Projects\Inventory Photos\tv.jpg
11
Always Lost
Basement Office
Driveway
Family Room
Furnace Room
My Office
Under my desk
Under the other desk

Living Room
Under the desk
```

After the last entry are the eight (8) items used in the combo box control. Let's write the code to read this file.

When the home inventory manager project begins, the program should read in the **inventory.txt** file to store the inventory item information. Here's where we'll use the **InventoryItem** object. The steps are:

> ➢ Open **inventory.txt** for input.
> ➢ Read in the number of entries.
> ➢ For each entry in the file:
>   ○ Create a new **InventoryItem** object.
>   ○ Read in the nine object properties.
> ➢ When done reading inventory items, read in the number of items in combo box control.
> ➢ Read in combo box items.
> ➢ Close file.

Make sure your are now working with the **HomeInventory.java** file. We will use the file objects to read the file, so add this import statement at the top of the code window:

```
import java.io.*;
```

The code associated with the above steps goes at the end of the frame constructor method so it is executed when the program first begins. Define three class level variables:

```
final int maximumEntries = 300;
int numberEntries;
InventoryItem[] myInventory = new
InventoryItem[maximumEntries];
```

maximumEntries is the maximum number of inventory items allowed, **numberEntries** is the number of entries in our inventory and **myInventory** is a 0-based array of **InventoryItem** objects used to store the information. With these variables, the code to open and read the **inventory.txt** file is:

```
int n;
// open file for entries
try
{
  BufferedReader inputFile = new BufferedReader(new
FileReader("inventory.txt"));
  numberEntries =
Integer.valueOf(inputFile.readLine()).intValue();
  if (numberEntries != 0)
  {
    for (int i = 0; i < numberEntries; i++)
    {
      myInventory[i] = new InventoryItem();
      myInventory[i].description = inputFile.readLine();
      myInventory[i].location = inputFile.readLine();
      myInventory[i].serialNumber = inputFile.readLine();
      myInventory[i].marked =
Boolean.valueOf(inputFile.readLine()).booleanValue();
      myInventory[i].purchasePrice = inputFile.readLine();
      myInventory[i].purchaseDate = inputFile.readLine();
      myInventory[i].purchaseLocation =
inputFile.readLine();
      myInventory[i].note = inputFile.readLine();
      myInventory[i].photoFile = inputFile.readLine();
    }
  }
  // read in combo box elements
  n = Integer.valueOf(inputFile.readLine()).intValue();
  if (n != 0)
  {
    for (int i = 0; i < n; i++)
    {
      locationComboBox.addItem(inputFile.readLine());
```

```
      }
    }
    inputFile.close();
  }
catch (Exception ex)
{
    numberEntries = 0;
}
if (numberEntries == 0)
{
    newButton.setEnabled(false);
    deleteButton.setEnabled(false);
    nextButton.setEnabled(false);
    previousButton.setEnabled(false);
    printButton.setEnabled(false);
}
```

Let's take a look at this code. All the code is in a **try/catch** structure in case the input file cannot be opened. If the file is successfully opened, we read **numberEntries**, then read each subsequent entry, creating a new **InventoryItem** object for each entry. Once the inventory items have been input, the combo box items are read in. If **numberEntries** is zero when done (meaning the file couldn't be opened or truly had zero elements), we set the toolbar buttons so only a new item can be entered. Add this method to your project.

Let's try this code. Copy the sample **inventory.txt** file into your project folder. Save and run the project. If the file opens and reads successfully, you should see a blank form with all toolbar buttons enabled (try clicking the drop-down in the combo box to see the items added). Here's my frame:

If only the **Save** button is enabled, there was an error in reading the file. If this occurs, make sure the file is in the correct folder and double-check the code.

Code Design – Viewing Inventory Item

We can now read in the input file, but it's not very satisfying not being able to see the results. We remedy that now by writing code to display the properties of an inventory item (including the photo). The code simply sets the correct frame control with the corresponding property.

We will use a general method **showEntry** to display the properties of a single inventory item. The method will have an **int** argument, specifying the entry number (from **1** to **numberEntries**) to display. The method is:

```java
private void showEntry(int j)
{
  // display entry j (1 to numberEntries)
  itemTextField.setText(myInventory[j - 1].description);
  locationComboBox.setSelectedItem(myInventory[j -
1].location);
  markedCheckBox.setSelected(myInventory[j - 1].marked);
  serialTextField.setText(myInventory[j -
1].serialNumber);
  priceTextField.setText(myInventory[j -
1].purchasePrice);
  dateDateChooser.setDate(stringToDate(myInventory[j -
1].purchaseDate));
  storeTextField.setText(myInventory[j -
1].purchaseLocation);
  noteTextField.setText(myInventory[j - 1].note);
  showPhoto(myInventory[j - 1].photoFile);
  itemTextField.requestFocus();
}
```

This code simply transfers the properties of the **myInventory InventoryItem** object into the appropriate controls. When done, it gives focus to the first text field (**itemTextField**).

The **showEntry** method uses a general method, **stringToDate**. We store the purchase date as a **String** type in the data file. We use a **month/day/year** representation, always using two digits for the month and day. The date chooser control requires dates to be of **Date** type. Hence, we need the capability of converting strings to dates, and dates to strings. We did the same thing in the biorhythm tracker project. The **stringToDate** and **dateToString** methods that do this task are:

```
private Date stringToDate(String s)
{
  int m = Integer.valueOf(s.substring(0, 2)).intValue() -
1;
  int d = Integer.valueOf(s.substring(3, 5)).intValue();
  int y = Integer.valueOf(s.substring(6)).intValue() -
1900;
  return(new Date(y, m, d));
}

private String dateToString(Date dd)
{
  String yString = String.valueOf(dd.getYear() + 1900);
  int m = dd.getMonth() + 1;
  String mString = new DecimalFormat("00").format(m);
  int d = dd.getDate();
  String dString = new DecimalFormat("00").format(d);
  return(mString + "/" + dString + "/" + yString);
}
```

These routines require these import statements:

```
import java.util.*;
import java.text.*;
```

To show a photo, we use another general method **showPhoto**. The code to actually display the photo goes in the **paintComponent** method for the **PhotoPanel** class. We will write code for this method soon. The **showPhoto** method simply accepts the photo file name (**photoFile**) as a **String** argument and displays the name. A **try/catch** structure is used in case there is an error loading a photo file:

```java
private void showPhoto(String photoFile)
{
  if (!photoFile.equals(""))
  {
    try
    {
      photoTextArea.setText(photoFile);
    }
    catch (Exception ex)
    {
      photoTextArea.setText("");
    }
  }
  else
  {
    photoTextArea.setText("");
  }
  photoPanel.repaint();
}
```

Place all of these methods (**showEntry**, **stringToDate**, **dateToString** and **showPhoto**) in your project. Add the two new **import** statements.

We need to modify the frame constructor code to call the display routine. First, add another class level variable declaration:

```
int currentEntry;
```

currentEntry will always point to the current entry in the inventory file (going from **1** to **numberEntries**). The modified code that uses this variable to display the entry is (changes are shaded, much unmodified code is not shown):

```
int n;
// open file for entries
try
{
   BufferedReader inputFile = new BufferedReader(new
FileReader("inventory.txt"));
      .
      .
      .
   }
   inputFile.close();
   currentEntry = 1;
   showEntry(currentEntry);
}
catch (Exception ex)
{
   numberEntries = 0;
   currentEntry = 0;
}
if (numberEntries == 0)
{
   newButton.setEnabled(false);
   deleteButton.setEnabled(false);
   nextButton.setEnabled(false);
   previousButton.setEnabled(false);
   printButton.setEnabled(false);
}
```

Make the noted changes.

Save and run the project. You should now see the first item in the inventory displayed (except for photo):

Code Design – Viewing Photo

The photo is displayed in **photoPanel** (using code in the **paintComponent** method). We use the **drawImage** graphics method to display the photo. This method allows us to scale any photo to fit within the display region. If our graphics region is **g2D**, the **drawImage** method is:

```
g2D.drawImage(myImage, x, y, w, h, null);
```

In this method, the image (**myImage**) will be positioned at (**x**, **y**) with width **w** and height **h**. We will adjust the width and height arguments to maintain the width-to-height ratio of the corresponding photo.

A word about photo location. The example file assumes the inventory photos are located in a folder named **c:\HomeJava\HomeJava Projects\Inventory Photos**. Your copy of the photos may or may not be in such a folder, depending on where you installed your version of these notes and projects. If they are in such a folder, great! If not, you have a few choices: (1) create such a folder and copy the photos to that folder, (2) hand edit the **inventory.txt** file to change the file names to your particular folder, (3) ignore the location and let the program run, knowing the photos won't display. You choose. Once the program is fully functional, you can load each picture individually from folders on your computer. Then, when the data file is saved, those locations are saved correctly for your machine.

Add the shaded code to the **PhotoPanel** class **paintComponent** method:

```java
public void paintComponent(Graphics g)
{
   Graphics2D g2D = (Graphics2D) g;
   super.paintComponent(g2D);

   // draw border
   g2D.setPaint(Color.BLACK);
   g2D.draw(new Rectangle2D.Double(0, 0, getWidth() - 1,
getHeight() - 1));

   // show photo
   Image photoImage = new
ImageIcon(HomeInventory.photoTextArea.getText()).getImage(
);
   int w = getWidth();
   int h = getHeight();
   double rWidth = (double) getWidth() / (double)
photoImage.getWidth(null);
   double rHeight = (double) getHeight() / (double)
photoImage.getHeight(null);
   if (rWidth > rHeight)
   {
     // leave height at display height, change width by
amount height is changed
     w = (int) (photoImage.getWidth(null) * rHeight);
   }
   else
   {
     // leave width at display width, change height by
amount width is changed
     h = (int) (photoImage.getHeight(null) * rWidth);
   }
   // center in panel
   g2D.drawImage(photoImage, (int) (0.5 * (getWidth() -
w)), (int) (0.5 * (getHeight() - h)), w, h, null);

   g2D.dispose();
}
```

In this code, we first create an **Image** object (**photoImage**) from the photo file. We then determine photo scaling so that the width-to-height ration of the original photo is maintained. Lastly, we use the **drawImage** method to position the photo on the **photoPanel**. Note the code requires access to the **photoTextArea** control in the **HomeInventory** class. Because of this, the **photoTextArea** declaration must be prefaced with **static**:

```
static JTextArea photoTextArea = new JTextArea();
```

Make this simple change.

Run the project. You should see the first inventory item (including photo, assuming you solved any "photo location" problem you may have had):

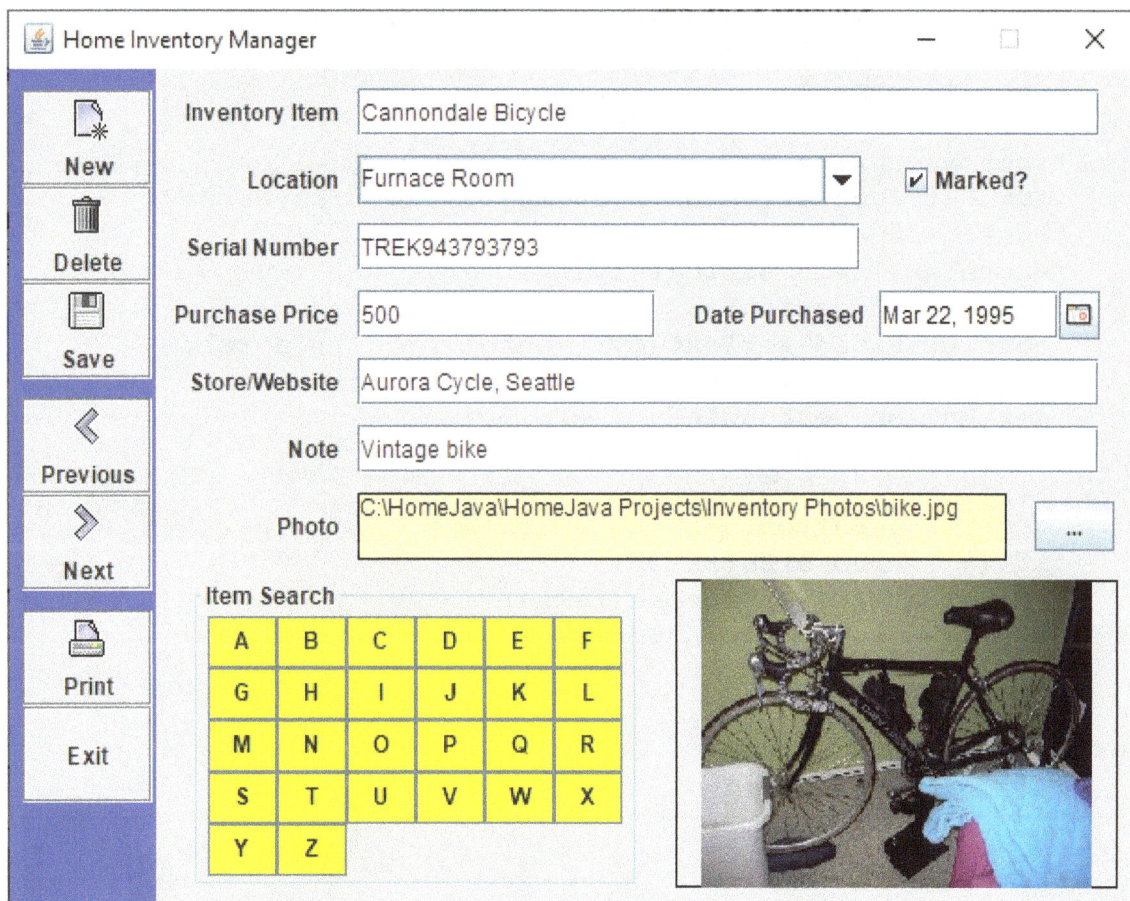

At this point, we would like to be able to move to the next item, or move backward. Let's write the code to do that.

Code Design – Item Navigation

First, we modify the **showEntry** method to establish proper **enabled** properties for the two toolbar buttons (**previousButton** and **nextButton**) used to move among the inventory items. We set these properties based on whether we're at the beginning, at the end or in the middle of the item list (changes are shaded):

```java
private void showEntry(int j)
{
  // display entry j (1 to numberEntries)
  itemTextField.setText(myInventory[j - 1].description);
  locationComboBox.setSelectedItem(myInventory[j - 1].location);
  markedCheckBox.setSelected(myInventory[j - 1].marked);
  serialTextField.setText(myInventory[j - 1].serialNumber);
  priceTextField.setText(myInventory[j - 1].purchasePrice);
  dateDateChooser.setDate(stringToDate(myInventory[j - 1].purchaseDate));
  storeTextField.setText(myInventory[j - 1].purchaseLocation);
  noteTextField.setText(myInventory[j - 1].note);
  showPhoto(myInventory[j - 1].photoFile);
  nextButton.setEnabled(true);
  previousButton.setEnabled(true);
  if (j == 1)
    previousButton.setEnabled(false);
  if (j == numberEntries)
    nextButton.setEnabled(false);
  itemTextField.requestFocus();
}
```

Make these changes.

Now, we need code for the **ActionPerformed** methods on the **previousButton** and **nextButton** buttons. In each case, we adjust **currentEntry** in the proper direction and display the item. The methods are:

```
private void previousButtonActionPerformed(ActionEvent e)
{
  currentEntry--;
  showEntry(currentEntry);
}

private void nextButtonActionPerformed(ActionEvent e)
{
  currentEntry++;
  showEntry(currentEntry);
}
```

Add these methods to your project.

And, while we're at it, add the **exitButtonActionPerformed** method to your project:

```
private void exitButtonActionPerformed(ActionEvent e)
{
  exitForm(null);
}
```

We call the **exitForm** method.

Again, save and run the project. You should now be able to view all 10 items in the sample file by using the **Previous** and **Next** buttons in the toolbar. Give it a try. Here's my dog Toby:

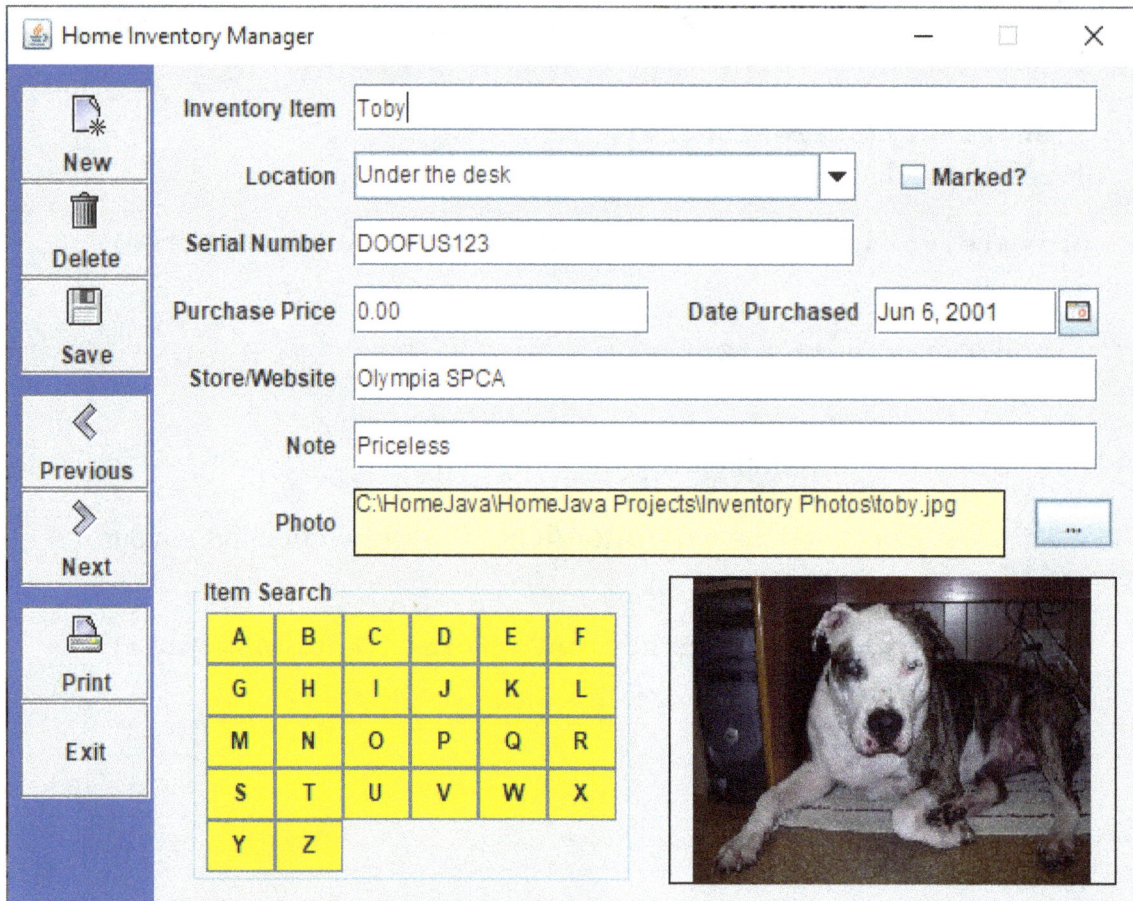

Try the **Exit** button.

Code Design – Inventory File Output

If inventory entries are edited or new items added (we'll see how to do this next), we want to save all entries back to the **inventory.txt** file. We do this output in the **exitForm** method. That method is essentially the same as the code in the frame constructor with the **readLine** lines replaced by **println** statements:

```
private void exitForm(WindowEvent evt)
{
  // write entries back to file
  try
  {
    PrintWriter outputFile = new PrintWriter(new
BufferedWriter(new FileWriter("inventory.txt")));
    outputFile.println(numberEntries);
    if (numberEntries != 0)
    {
      for (int i = 0; i < numberEntries; i++)
      {
        outputFile.println(myInventory[i].description);
        outputFile.println(myInventory[i].location);
        outputFile.println(myInventory[i].serialNumber);
        outputFile.println(myInventory[i].marked);
        outputFile.println(myInventory[i].purchasePrice);
        outputFile.println(myInventory[i].purchaseDate);

outputFile.println(myInventory[i].purchaseLocation);
        outputFile.println(myInventory[i].note);
        outputFile.println(myInventory[i].photoFile);
      }
    }
    // write combo box entries
    outputFile.println(locationComboBox.getItemCount());
    if (locationComboBox.getItemCount() != 0)
    {
      for (int i = 0; i < locationComboBox.getItemCount();
i++)
        outputFile.println(locationComboBox.getItemAt(i));
    }
    outputFile.close();
  }
  catch (Exception ex)
  {

  }
  System.exit(0);
```

```
}
```

All but the last line is new code. Add this method to your project. Note the code to write the combo box items back to file also.

Save and run the project. The input file will be read and the items displayed. Stop the project. The file will be written back to disk. Currently, the same file will be written back. This is because we have no editing capability.

Code Design – Input Validation

Before adding editing capability, we need to address a couple of input validation issues. First, let's discuss the **purchasePrice** property. We could make sure this is a numeric input, using validation code used in the loan assistant project. I choose not to do this for a couple of reasons. First, the value is never used with any math functions, so we really don't care if it's a number. Second, it allows the user to write something like 'Free' or 'Gift' in the text field and have it properly saved.

Next, we address the **location** property. The value for this property is obtained from the **locationComboBox** control. Two selection possibilities exist: (1) choose from an existing location, (2) type in a new location. If a new location is typed in, it is added to the list portion of the combo box, so it can be saved for future edits (in the **inventory.txt** file). So, we need code to check a typed entry versus the existing list to see if the new entry needs to be added to the list box. The code to do this goes in the **locationComboBoxActionPerformed** method. Make the shaded changes to this method:

```
private void locationComboBoxActionPerformed(ActionEvent
e)
{
  // If in list - exit method
  if (locationComboBox.getItemCount() != 0)
  {
    for (int i = 0; i < locationComboBox.getItemCount();
i++)
    {
      if
(locationComboBox.getSelectedItem().toString().equals(loca
tionComboBox.getItemAt(i).toString()))
      {
        serialTextField.requestFocus();
        return;
      }
    }
  }
  // If not found, add to list box

locationComboBox.addItem(locationComboBox.getSelectedItem(
));
  serialTextField.requestFocus();
}
```

You should be able to follow the logic of what's going on here. Add this method to the project.

Lastly, we address how to load a photo into the photo panel control on the frame. When the user clicks the button with an ellipsis (**photoButton**) next to the **Photo** text area control, the open file dialog control (using **JChooser**) should appear allowing the user to select a file. The **FileNameExtensionFilter** method is used to set the filter. Add this import statement:

```
import javax.swing.filechooser.*;
```

Once a file is selected, the photo panel control should display the photo. We have already written code to do most of these steps in the **showPhoto** method we use to display an already stored photo file. So, the **photoButtonActionPerformed** method is:

```
private void photoButtonActionPerformed(ActionEvent e)
  {
  JFileChooser openChooser = new JFileChooser();
  openChooser.setDialogType(JFileChooser.OPEN_DIALOG);
  openChooser.setDialogTitle("Open Photo File");
  openChooser.addChoosableFileFilter(new
FileNameExtensionFilter("Photo Files", "jpg"));
  if (openChooser.showOpenDialog(this) ==
JFileChooser.APPROVE_OPTION)
     showPhoto(openChooser.getSelectedFile().toString());
  }
```

Add this method to the project.

Save and run the project to make sure the code compiles. You can try the new validations with the existing inventory items. Click the photo button. The dialog will appear:

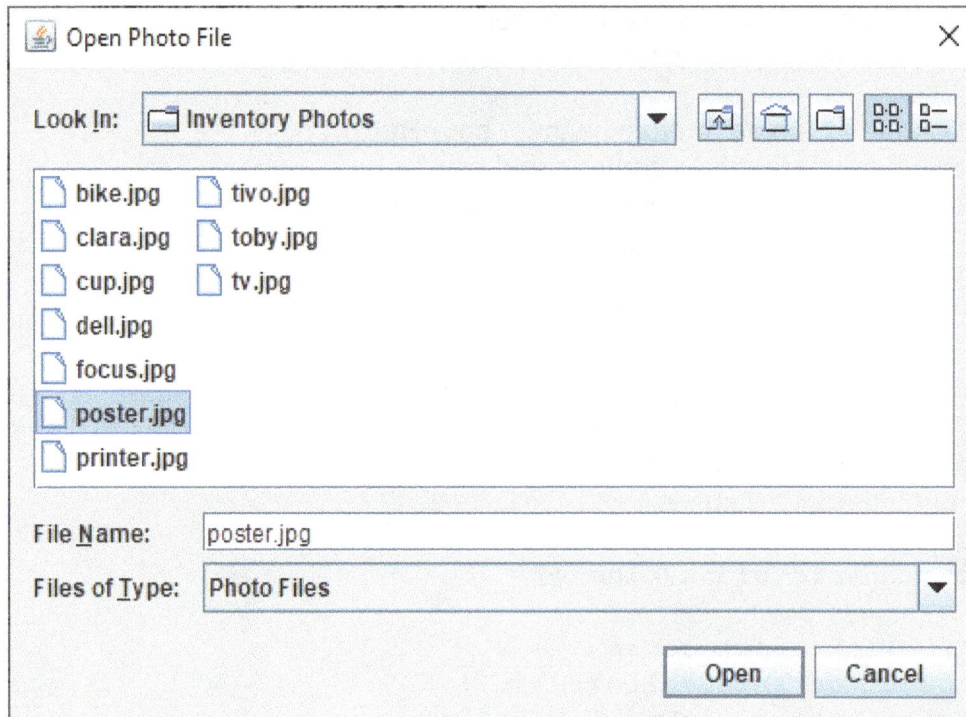

You can change a photo, if you choose. Any changes to an item won't be saved (changes to the combo box will be saved). We now add editing capability to allow saving changes to existing and new inventory items.

Code Design – New Inventory Item

When the project first begins (with an empty input file) or when the user clicks the **New** button in the toolbar, we want the form to be in a state to accept a new set of inventory information. The steps are:

> ➤ Disable all toolbar buttons, except **saveButton**.
> ➤ Blank out all text field controls and combo box.
> ➤ Uncheck check box control (**markedCheckBox**).
> ➤ Set calendar to today's date.
> ➤ Blank out **photoPanel** paneland **photoTextField** label.
> ➤ Give **itemTextField** focus.

The code for these steps is placed in a general method **blankValues**. We use a method because it is needed here, to start a new item, and later in the delete method (in case we delete the last item in the inventory). The method to implement the above steps is:

```
private void blankValues()
{
  // blank input screen
  newButton.setEnabled(false);
  deleteButton.setEnabled(false);
  saveButton.setEnabled(true);
  previousButton.setEnabled(false);
  nextButton.setEnabled(false);
  printButton.setEnabled(false);
  itemTextField.setText("");
  locationComboBox.setSelectedItem("");
  markedCheckBox.setSelected(false);
  serialTextField.setText("");
  priceTextField.setText("");
  dateDateChooser.setDate(new Date());
  storeTextField.setText("");
  noteTextField.setText("");
  photoTextArea.setText("");
  photoPanel.repaint();
  itemTextField.requestFocus();
}
```

Add this method to your project.

With this general method, the **newButton Click** event is coded simply as:

```
private void newButtonActionPerformed(ActionEvent e)
{
   blankValues();
}
```

Add this method to your project.

Now we need code to save entries for a new inventory item. When the user clicks the **Save** button on the toolbar, the following steps occur:

> Make sure there is an entry in **itemTextField** (the only required input). Capitalize the first character (to insure proper ordering).
> Increment **numberEntries**.
> Determine entry location in **myInventory** array (alphabetically, using **itemTextField Text** property)
> Once location is determined, move all items "below" location down one position in **myInventory** array.
> Establish properties for new array entry.
> Display new entry.
> Disable **newButton**, if we've reached the maximum number of entries.
> Enable **deleteButton** and **printButton**.

The tricky part of the code associated with these steps involves moving elements in the **myInventory** array. Let me explain. With normal Java variables **a**, **b**, **c** if you write:

```
a = b;
b = c;
```

a will be replaced by the value in b. When b is replaced by c, a is unchanged, retaining the original value for b.

What if **a**, **b**, **c** are objects (such as elements of the **myInventory** array) and we write the same code:

```
a = b;
b = c;
```

With objects, a will be assigned the same memory location as b, not a copy of its value. When b is then assigned to c, a will also change to c since it shares the same memory location. To avoid this, we need one additional step following the assignment of b to a. The modified code is:

```
a = b;
b = new Object();
b = c;
```

In this code, once b is assigned to a, we create a new object for b, giving it a new memory location prior to assigning it to c. This "breaks" the connection between memory locations for a and b. This modified code gives us the desired result of a having the original value for b and b having the new value for c.

The code for saving an entry is placed in the **saveButtonActionPerformed** method:

```
private void saveButtonActionPerformed(ActionEvent e)
{
  // check for description
  itemTextField.setText(itemTextField.getText().trim());
  if (itemTextField.getText().equals(""))
  {
    JOptionPane.showConfirmDialog(null, "Must have item
description.", "Error", JOptionPane.DEFAULT_OPTION,
JOptionPane.ERROR_MESSAGE);
    itemTextField.requestFocus();
    return;
  }
  // capitalize first letter
  String s = itemTextField.getText();
  itemTextField.setText(s.substring(0, 1).toUpperCase() +
s.substring(1));
  numberEntries++;
  // determine new current entry location based on
description
  currentEntry = 1;
  if (numberEntries != 1)
  {
    do
    {
```

```
      if
(itemTextField.getText().compareTo(myInventory[currentEntr
y - 1].description) < 0)
        break;
      currentEntry++;
    }
    while (currentEntry < numberEntries);
  }
  // move all entries below new value down one position
unless at end
  if (currentEntry != numberEntries)
  {
    for (int i = numberEntries; i >= currentEntry + 1; i--
)
    {
      myInventory[i - 1] = myInventory[i - 2];
      myInventory[i - 2] = new InventoryItem();
    }
  }
  myInventory[currentEntry - 1] = new InventoryItem();
  myInventory[currentEntry - 1].description =
itemTextField.getText();
  myInventory[currentEntry - 1].location =
locationComboBox.getSelectedItem().toString();
  myInventory[currentEntry - 1].marked =
markedCheckBox.isSelected();
  myInventory[currentEntry - 1].serialNumber =
serialTextField.getText();
  myInventory[currentEntry - 1].purchasePrice =
priceTextField.getText();
  myInventory[currentEntry - 1].purchaseDate =
dateToString(dateDateChooser.getDate());
  myInventory[currentEntry - 1].purchaseLocation =
storeTextField.getText();
  myInventory[currentEntry - 1].photoFile =
photoTextArea.getText();
  myInventory[currentEntry - 1].note =
noteTextField.getText();
  showEntry(currentEntry);
  if (numberEntries < maximumEntries)
    newButton.setEnabled(true);
  else
    newButton.setEnabled(false);
  deleteButton.setEnabled(true);
  printButton.setEnabled(true);
}
```

Study this code. If there is no entry in **itemTextField**, a message box is displayed. If there is an entry, capitalize the first character, to obtain proper ordering. We then determine the location of the new entry in the list of current entries. Once that position (**currentEntry**) is found, all other array elements are moved down one position (paying attention to how we "equate" objects). A new **InventoryItem** is created at **currentEntry - 1** (recall we're using a 0-based array) and the control values placed in the appropriate object properties. Based on the number of entries, toolbar button status is modified. Add this method to your project.

One option the user has while adding a new inventory item is to click on the **Exit** button in the toolbar, essentially stopping the program. We want to add a message box to the program to make sure if this happens, the user really means to exit. This message box could be placed in the **exitButtonActionPerformed** event (which closes the form, invoking the **exitForm** method). Recall, however, a user can also exit a program by clicking the **X** in the upper right corner of the form, also invoking the **exitForm** method. So, to intercept all exit requests, we place this new message box in the **exitForm** method. The modified method is (changes are shaded, unmodified code writing properties back to file is not shown):

```
private void exitForm(WindowEvent evt)
{
    if (JOptionPane.showConfirmDialog(null, "Any unsaved
changes will be lost.\nAre you sure you want to exit?", "Exit
Program", JOptionPane.YES_NO_OPTION,
JOptionPane.QUESTION_MESSAGE) == JOptionPane.NO_OPTION)
        return;
    // write entries back to file
    try
    {
        PrintWriter outputFile = new PrintWriter(new
BufferedWriter(new FileWriter("inventory.txt")));
        outputFile.println(numberEntries);
        .
        .
}
```

We need to make one change to make this code work. By default, when this method is called, the frame is closed and cannot be reopened. To avoid this, add this line of code in the frame constructor when the frame is first created:

```
setDefaultCloseOperation(JFrame.DO_NOTHING_ON_CLOSE);
```

Add these code modifications to your project.

Save and run the project. You should now have the capability to add and save a new item to the inventory. Let's try it. Click the **New** toolbar button to see a blank form ready for input (only the **Save** button and **Exit** buttons are enabled):

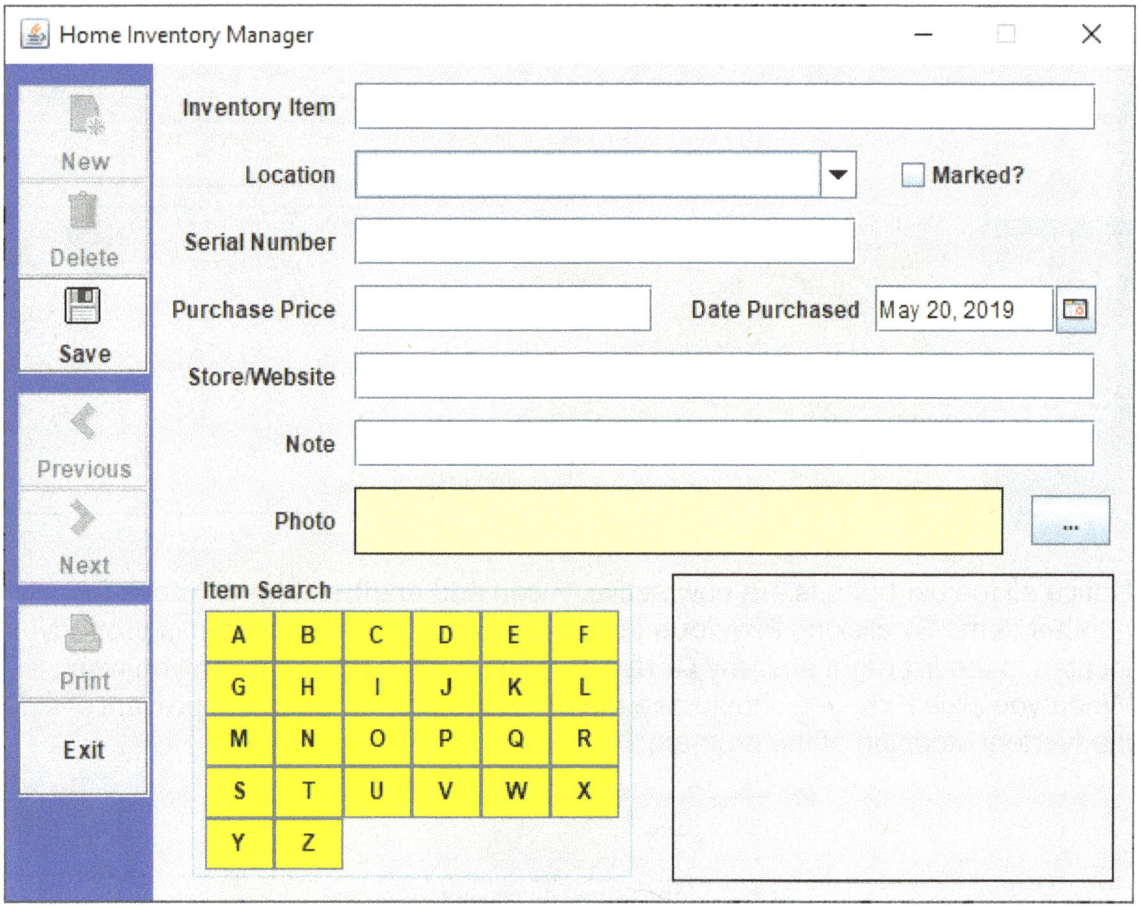

Type in some entries. Try the combo box selections (type a new one if you want). Add a photo if you have one. When done, click **Save** to make sure the item is properly sorted.

I added a **Couch** to my inventory (no photo). After clicking **Save**, I see:

Notice all toolbar buttons are now active. I can add another item or move to another item. By clicking **Previous** and **Next**, I can see that the item is properly located in the list (right after my **Coffee Cup**). Stop the project when you want. When you click **Exit**, you should see the message box we added to prevent inadvertent stopping of the program:

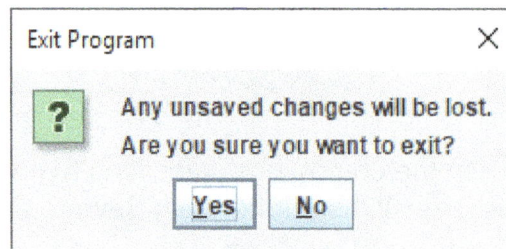

Make sure both the **Yes** and **No** options work correctly. Stop, then rerun the project. Make sure any added items are now in the inventory.

Code Design – Deleting Inventory Items

After entering a new item (or when viewing an existing item), the **Delete** toolbar button is enabled, but there is no code "behind" the button. Let's write that code.

When a user clicks the **Delete** button while displaying an entry, the following should happen:

> ➢ Ask the user if he/she really wants to delete the entry.
> ➢ Move all items "below" displayed entry up one position in **myInventory** array. This removes the entry from the array.
> ➢ Decrement **numberEntries**.
> ➢ If entry deleted is last item, set form up for new entry.
> ➢ If more entries remain after deletion, display entry preceding deleted entry.

The code for the above steps is placed in the **deleteButtonActionPerformed** method:

```
private void deleteButtonActionPerformed(ActionEvent e)
{
  if (JOptionPane.showConfirmDialog(null, "Are you sure
you want to delete this item?", "Delete Inventory Item",
JOptionPane.YES_NO_OPTION, JOptionPane.QUESTION_MESSAGE)
== JOptionPane.NO_OPTION)
    return;
  deleteEntry(currentEntry);
  if (numberEntries == 0)
  {
    currentEntry = 0;
    blankValues();
  }
  else
  {
    currentEntry--;
    if (currentEntry == 0)
      currentEntry = 1;
    showEntry(currentEntry);
  }
}
```

Notice if we delete the last item in the inventory, the form is 'blanked.' Otherwise, the entry preceding the deleted entry (if there is one) is displayed. Add this method to your project.

The above code uses a general method **deleteEntry** to remove an entry from the **myInventory** array. The code for this method is (the **int** argument indicates which item to remove):

```
private void deleteEntry(int j)
{
  // delete entry j
  if (j != numberEntries)
  {
    // move all entries under j up one level
    for (int i = j; i < numberEntries; i++)
    {
      myInventory[i - 1] = new InventoryItem();
      myInventory[i - 1] = myInventory[i];
    }
  }
  numberEntries--;
}
```

Again, notice the special way to "equate" objects. Add this method to your project.

Save and run the project with these changes. Make sure you can delete any entries you added earlier. You will see this message box when you try to delete an entry:

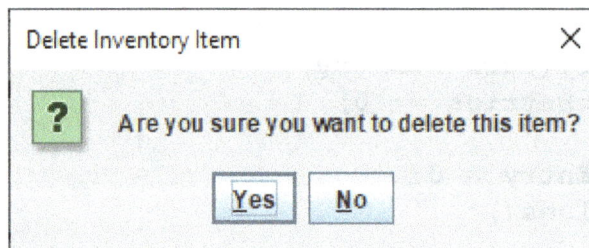

Make sure both the **Yes** and **No** options work. I was able to successfully delete my **Couch** from the inventory.

Code Design – Editing Inventory Items

There is one problem you may notice. If you edit a current entry in the inventory and click **Save**, a new item is added to the inventory, rather than a simple update of the existing item. We need to modify the save method to be able to handle editing an existing item.

The approach we take is that if we are editing an existing item and click **Save**, we first delete it, then treat the modified item as if it is a new item. This allows us to use the existing save code and also properly sorts the edited item (if the **Description** property changed). The modified **saveButtonActionPerformed** method is (changes are shaded, much unmodified code not shown):

```
private void saveButtonActionPerformed(ActionEvent e)
{
  // check for description
  itemTextField.setText(itemTextField.getText().trim());
  if (itemTextField.getText().equals(""))
  {
    JOptionPane.showConfirmDialog(null, "Must have item
description.", "Error", JOptionPane.DEFAULT_OPTION,
JOptionPane.ERROR_MESSAGE);
    itemTextField.requestFocus();
    return;
  }
  if (newButton.isEnabled())
  {
    // delete edit entry then resave
    deleteEntry(currentEntry);
  }
     .
     .
     .
}
```

In this code, we use the **enabled** status of **newButton** to determine if we are saving an existing item (**enabled** is **true**) or a new item (**enabled** is **false**). Add these changes to your project.

Save and run the project. You now have full editing capability in the home inventory manager project. You can view inventory items, add new items to your inventory, delete items, or modify existing items. All information can now be properly saved.

We still need to add search and print capabilities to our project. But, first we need to address one "small" annoyance. If you edit an existing item and then click **New**, **Previous**, or **Next** without clicking **Save**, your changes are lost. (You can also click **Exit**, but we have already added code for that event to give the user a chance to reconsider). It would be nice if the program would "save us from ourselves" and ask us if we'd like to save the changes before moving on. This is a straightforward modification. We essentially need to know if anything was changed for a particular item. If changes were made and we attempt to move away from that item (click **New**, **Previous** or **Next**) without clicking **Save**, we can display a message box asking if the changes should be saved.

We will use a general method, **checkSave**, to see if a save might be needed. Modify the **newButton**, **previousButton** and **nextButton ActionPerformed** methods to call this method (changes are shaded):

```java
private void newButtonActionPerformed(ActionEvent e)
{
  checkSave();
  blankValues();
}

private void previousButtonActionPerformed(ActionEvent e)
{
  checkSave();
  currentEntry--;
  showEntry(currentEntry);
}

private void nextButtonActionPerformed(ActionEvent e)
{
  checkSave();
  currentEntry++;
  showEntry(currentEntry);
}
```

The general method **checkSave** used by each of these methods is:

```
private void checkSave()
{
  boolean edited = false;
  if (!myInventory[currentEntry -
1].description.equals(itemTextField.getText()))
    edited = true;
  else if (!myInventory[currentEntry -
1].location.equals(locationComboBox.getSelectedItem().toSt
ring()))
    edited = true;
  else if (myInventory[currentEntry - 1].marked !=
markedCheckBox.isSelected())
    edited = true;
  else if (!myInventory[currentEntry -
1].serialNumber.equals(serialTextField.getText()))
    edited = true;
  else if (!myInventory[currentEntry -
1].purchasePrice.equals(priceTextField.getText()))
    edited = true;
  else if (!myInventory[currentEntry -
1].purchaseDate.equals(dateToString(dateDateChooser.getDat
e())))
    edited = true;
  else if (!myInventory[currentEntry -
1].purchaseLocation.equals(storeTextField.getText()))
    edited = true;
  else if (!myInventory[currentEntry -
1].note.equals(noteTextField.getText()))
    edited = true;
  else if (!myInventory[currentEntry -
1].photoFile.equals(photoTextArea.getText()))
    edited = true;
  if (edited)
  {
    if (JOptionPane.showConfirmDialog(null, "You have
edited this item. Do you want to save the changes?", "Save
Item", JOptionPane.YES_NO_OPTION,
JOptionPane.QUESTION_MESSAGE) == JOptionPane.YES_OPTION)
      saveButton.doClick();
  }
}
```

This method has a local **boolean** variable **edited** that tells us if the current inventory item has been modified. It is initialized at **false**. It then sequentially goes through all the input controls. If any of the values displayed in the controls disagree with the stored values, the user has changed something and **edited** is set to **true**. If **edited** is **true**, the user is asked if they would like to save the entry.

Make the specified changes to your project. Save and run the project. Add a new inventory item, make some entries describing the item and click **Save**. Now modify something about your new item and click **New**, **Previous** or **Next**. You should see this message box:

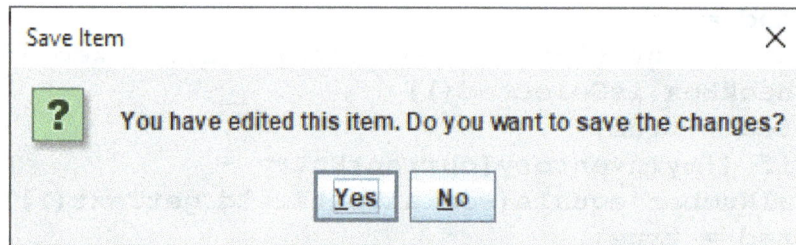

You decide whether to save the changes or not. If you do, notice you don't have to click the **Save** button; it is done for you in code.

Code Design – Inventory Item Search

When a user clicks one of the search button controls (**searchButton** array), the following happens:

> ➢ Determine which search button was clicked.
> ➢ Find first item in inventory list that begins with 'clicked' letter – display that item.
> ➢ If no matching item found, display a message box.

The code to implement these steps is straightforward and is placed in the **searchLabelActionPerformed** method:

```java
private void searchButtonActionPerformed(ActionEvent e)
{
  int i;
  if (numberEntries == 0)
      return;
  // search for item letter
  String letterClicked = e.getActionCommand();
  i = 0;
  do
  {
    if (myInventory[i].description.substring(0,
1).equals(letterClicked))
    {
      currentEntry = i + 1;
      showEntry(currentEntry);
      return;
    }
    i++;
  }
  while (i < numberEntries);
  JOptionPane.showConfirmDialog(null, "No " +
letterClicked + " inventory items.", "None Found",
JOptionPane.DEFAULT_OPTION,
JOptionPane.INFORMATION_MESSAGE);
}
```

Add this method to your project.

Save and run the project. Notice how the search labels are properly created and positioned. When I click the 'T' search label using the sample inventory, I see:

Notice we see the first **T** entry (**TIVO**). To see entries 'around' this choice, use the **Previous** and **Next** buttons. Click on 'R' and you'll see:

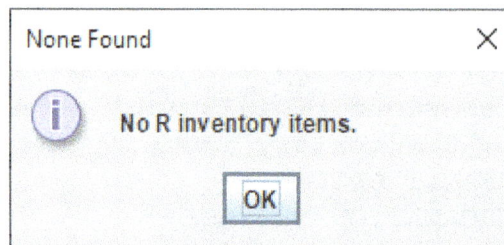

Printing with Java

One last capability we will add to our home inventory project is printing. A printed copy of our items would be helpful for archival purposes and for any potential insurance claims. Printing is one of the more tedious programming tasks within Java. But, fortunately, it is straightforward and there are dialog controls that help with the tasks. We will introduce lots of new topics here. All steps will be reviewed.

To perform printing in Java, we need this import statement:

```
import java.awt.print.*;
```

The **PrinterJob** class from this imported package controls the printing process. This class is used to start or cancel a printing job. It can also be used to display dialog boxes when needed. The **Printable** interface from this package is used to represent the item (document) to be printed.

The steps to print a document (which may include text and graphics) using the **PrinterJob** class are:

> ➢ Declare and create a **PrinterJob** object.
> ➢ Point the **PrinterJob** object to a **Printable** class (containing code to print the desired document) using the **setPrintable** method of the **PrinterJob** object.
> ➢ Print the document using the **print** method of the **PrinterJob** object.

These steps are straightforward. To declare and create a **PrinterJob** object named **myPrinterJob**, use:

```
PrinterJob myPrinterJob = PrinterJob.getPrinterJob();
```

If the **Printable** class is named **MyDocument**, the **PrinterJob** is associated with this class using:

```
myPrinterJob.setPrintable(new MyDocument);
```

Once associated, the printing is accomplished using the **print** method:

```
myPrinterJob.print();
```

This print method must be enclosed in a **try/catch** (catching a **PrinterException**) block.

The key to printing is the establishment of the **Printable** interface, called **MyDocument** here. This class describes the document to be printed and is placed after the main class. The form of this class is:

```
class MyDocument implements Printable
{
  public int print(Graphics g, PageFormat pf, int
pageIndex)
  {
    Graphics2D g2D = (Graphics2D) g;
        .
        .
        .
  }
}
```

This class has a single method, **print**, which is called whenever the **PrinterJob** object needs information to do its job. In this method, you 'construct' each page (using Java code) that is to be printed. You'll see the code in this method is familiar.

Note the **print** method has three arguments. The first argument is a **Graphics** object **g**. Something familiar! The **Printable** interface provides us with a graphics object to 'draw' each page we want to print. We cast this to a **Graphics2D** object, noting this is the same graphics object we used in Chapters 7 and 8 to draw lines, curves, rectangles, and text. And, all the methods we learned there apply here! We'll look at how to do this in detail next. The second argument is a **PageFormat** object **pf**, which describes the size and orientation of the paper being used. Finally, the **pageIndex** argument is the number of the page to print. This argument is zero-based, meaning the first page has a value of zero.

The **print** method can return one of two constant values:

> **PAGE_EXISTS**   returned if **pageIndex** refers to an existing page
> **NO_SUCH_PAGE**   returned if **pageIndex** refers to a non-existing page

It is <u>very</u> important that **NO_SUCH_PAGE** is returned at some point or your program will assume there are an infinite number of pages to print!!

Another important thing to remember is that the **print** method may be called more than once per printed page, as the output is buffered to the printer. So, don't build in any assumptions about how often **print** is called for a given page.

Summarizing the printing steps, here is basic Java code (**PrintingExample**) to print a document described by a class **MyDocument**:

```java
import javax.swing.*;
import java.awt.*;
import java.awt.print.*;

public class PrintingExample
{
  public static void main(String[] args)
  {
    PrinterJob myPrinterJob = PrinterJob.getPrinterJob();
    myPrinterJob.setPrintable(new MyDocument());
    try
    {
      myPrinterJob.print();
    }
    catch (PrinterException ex)
    {
      JOptionPane.showConfirmDialog(null, ex.getMessage(),
"Print Error", JOptionPane.DEFAULT_OPTION,
JOptionPane.ERROR_MESSAGE);
    }
  }
}

class MyDocument implements Printable
{
  public int print(Graphics g, PageFormat pf, int
pageIndex)
  {
    Graphics2D g2D = (Graphics2D) g;
      .
      .
      .
  }
}
```

Let's see how to develop code for the **Printable** interface **print** method to do some printing.

Printing Document Pages

The **Printable** interface provides (in its **print** method) a graphics object (**g**, which we cast to a **Graphics2D** object, **g2D**) for 'drawing' our pages. And, that's just what we do using familiar graphics methods. For each page in our printed document, we draw the desired text information (**drawString** method), any shapes (**draw** method), or graphics (using the **drawImage** we used to 'draw' the inventory photo).

Once a page is completely drawn to the graphics object, we 'tell' the **PrinterJob** object to print it. We repeat this process for each page we want to print. As noted, the **pageIndex** argument (in conjunction with the **return** value) of the print method helps with this effort. This does require a little bit of work on your part. You must know how many pages your document has and what goes on each page.

Let's look at the coordinates and dimensions of the graphics object for a single page.

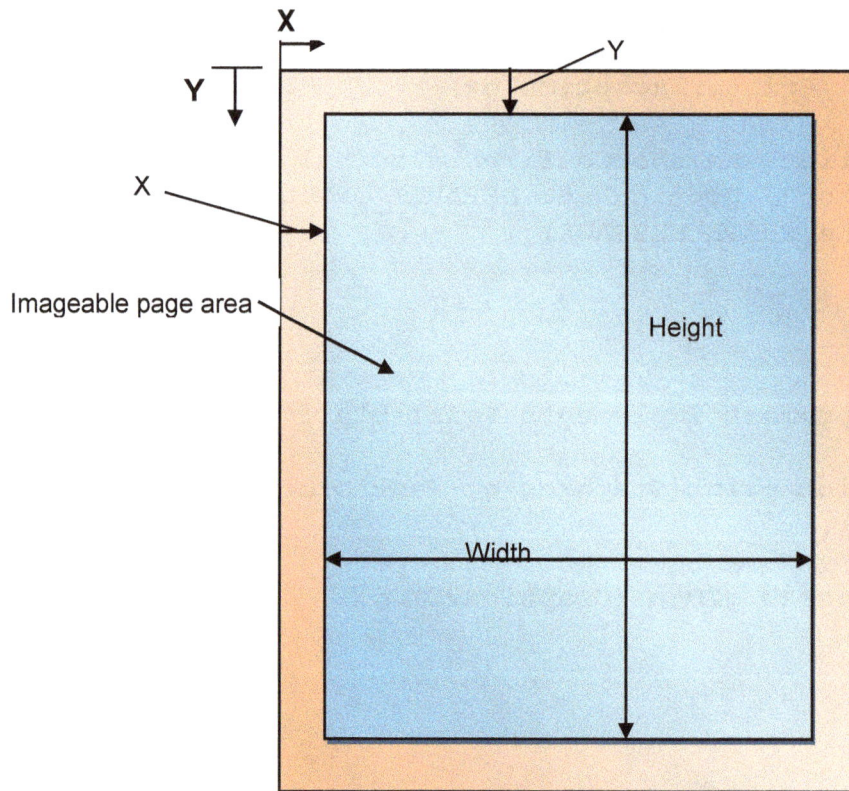

This becomes our palette for positioning items on a page. Horizontal position is governed by **X** (increases from 0 to the right) and vertical position is governed by **Y** (increases from 0 to the bottom). All dimensions are type **double**, in units of 1/72 inch. A standard sheet of 8.5 inch by 11-inch paper (with zero margins) would have a width and height of 612 and 792, respectively.

The **imageable area** rectangle is described by the **PageFormat** argument (**pf**) of the **Printable** class **print** method. The origin can be determined using:

```
pf.getImageableX();
pf.getImageableY();
```

These values define the right and top margins, respectively. The width and height of the imageable area, respectively, are found using:

```
pf.getImageableWidth();
pf.getImageableHeight();
```

The returned values are **double** types in units of 1/72 inch.

The process for each page is to decide "what goes where" and then position the desired information using the appropriate graphics method. Any of the graphics methods we have learned can be used to put information on the graphic object.

To place text on the graphics object (**g2D**), use the **drawString** method introduced in Chapter 7. To place the string **myString** at position (**x, y**), the syntax is:

```
g2D.drawString(myString, x, y);
```

The string is printed using the current font and paint attributes. With this statement, you can place any text, anywhere you like, with any font and paint. You just need to make the desired specifications. Each line of text on a printed page will require a **drawString** statement. Note x and y in this method are **int** types, not **double**, hence type casting of page dimensions is usually needed.

Also in Chapter 7, we saw how to determine the width and height of strings (knowing the font object **myFont**). This is helpful for both vertical and horizontal placement of text on a page. This information is returned in a **Rectangle2D** structure (**stringRect**), using:

```
Rectangle2D stringRect = myFont.getStringBounds(myString,
g2D.getFontRenderContext());
```

The height and width of the returned **stringRect** structure yield the string size (in units of 1/72 inch). These two properties are useful for justifying (left, right, center, vertical) text strings.

Many times, you use lines in a document to delineate various sections. To draw a line on the graphics object, use the **draw** method and **Line2D** shape (from Chapter 7):

```
Line2D.Double myLine = new Line2D.Double(x1, y1, x2, y2);
g2D.draw(myLine);
```

This statement will draw a line from (**x1, y1**) to (**x2, y2**) using the current **stroke** and **paint** attributes.

 Finally, the **drawImage** method is used to position an image (**myImage**) object on a page. This is the same method we used earlier to place the inventory photo on **photoPanel**. The syntax is:

```
g2D.drawImage(myImage, x, y, width, height,null);
```

The upper left corner of **myImage** will be at (**x, y**) with the specified **width** and **height**. Any image will be scaled to fit the specified region.

We've seen all of these graphics methods before, so their use should be familiar. You should note that each item on a printed page requires at least one line of code. That results in lots of coding for printing. So, if you're writing lots of code in your print routines, you're probably doing it right.

Recall when doing persistent graphics using a **paintComponent** method in another clas, any variable needed by that method needed to be prefaced by the keyword **static**. That is also needed here. Any class level object referred to in the **print** method of the **Printable** class must also be declared with a **static** preface.

Many print jobs just involve the user clicking a button marked '**Print**' and the results appear on the printed page with no further interaction. If more interaction is desired, there is a methods associated with the **PrinterJob** class that helps specify desired printing job properties: **printDialog**.

The **printDialog** method displays a dialog box that allows the user to select which printer to use, choose page orientation, printed page range and number of copies. This is the same dialog box that appears in many applications. The Windows version of the print dialog is:

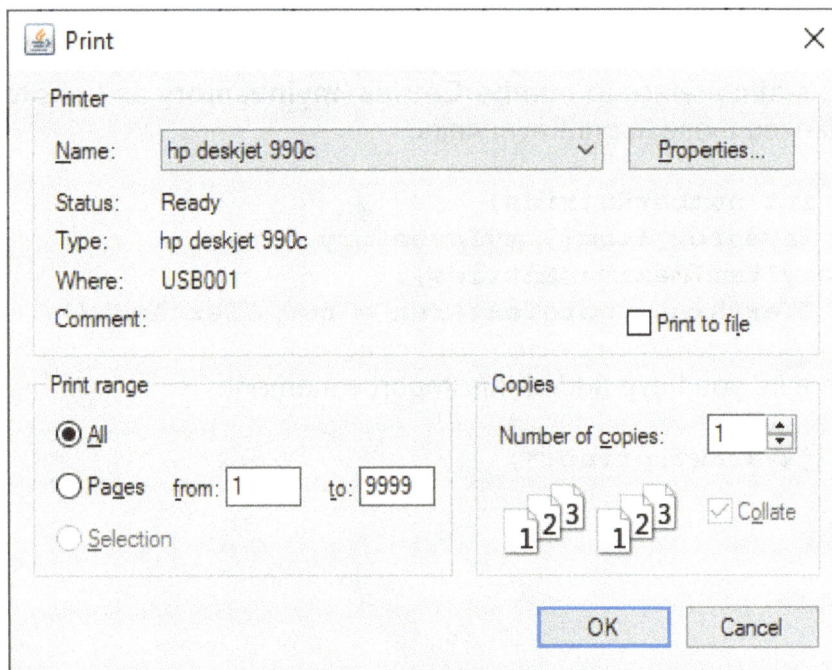

The **printDialog** method returns **true** if the user clicked the **OK** button to leave the dialog and **false** otherwise. After the method returns a value, you don't have to do anything to retrieve the parameters the user selected. The **PrinterJob** object is automatically updated with the selections!

Code Design – Printing the Inventory

The format used for the printed inventory is straightforward – modify it as you see fit. Each page will have a simple header (giving the page number) and will hold two items from the inventory. Each property for each item (including the picture) will be printed. Items will be separated by a single straight line.

The code to establish the print document and display the printed inventory goes in the **printButtonActionPerformed** method. But, first, we need two class (**HomeInventory** class) level variable declarations to keep track of the printing process:

```
static final int entriesPerPage = 2;
static int lastPage;
```

They are prefaced with **static** because they will be used in the **PrintJob** class. Also add the **static** preface to **numberEntries**, **myInventory** and **photoTextArea** since we will need these to print everything:

```
static int numberEntries;
static InventoryItem[] myInventory = new
InventoryItem[maximumEntries];
static JTextArea photoTextArea = new JTextArea();
```

Lastly, make sure you have added this import statement:

```
import java.awt.print.*;
```

The **printButtonActionPerformed** method is then:

```
private void printButtonActionPerformed(ActionEvent e)
{
  lastPage = (int) (1 + (numberEntries - 1) /
entriesPerPage);

  PrinterJob inventoryPrinterJob =
PrinterJob.getPrinterJob();
  inventoryPrinterJob.setPrintable(new
InventoryDocument());
  if (inventoryPrinterJob.printDialog())
  {
    try
    {
      inventoryPrinterJob.print();
    }
    catch (PrinterException ex)
    {
      JOptionPane.showConfirmDialog(null, ex.getMessage(),
"Print Error", JOptionPane.DEFAULT_OPTION,
JOptionPane.ERROR_MESSAGE);
    }
  }
}
```

We determine the **lastPage** to print and create the **PrinterJob** object (**inventoryPrinterJob**). This object 'points' to the **Printable** class, **InventoryDocument**. A print dialog is displayed. If the user chooses **OK**, the **print** method is called Add this method and the variable declarations to your project.

The **Printable** class to accomplish the printing is (place this after the **HomeInventory** and **PhotoPanel** classes)::

```
class InventoryDocument implements Printable
{
  public int print(Graphics g, PageFormat pf, int
pageIndex)
   {
     Graphics2D g2D = (Graphics2D) g;
     if ((pageIndex + 1) > HomeInventory.lastPage)
     {
       return NO_SUCH_PAGE;
     }
     int i, iEnd;
     // here you decide what goes on each page and draw it
     // header
     g2D.setFont(new Font("Arial", Font.BOLD, 14));
     g2D.drawString("Home Inventory Items - Page " +
String.valueOf(pageIndex + 1), (int) pf.getImageableX(),
(int) (pf.getImageableY() + 25));
     // get starting y
     int dy = (int) g2D.getFont().getStringBounds("S",
g2D.getFontRenderContext()).getHeight();
     int y = (int) (pf.getImageableY() + 4 * dy);
     iEnd = HomeInventory.entriesPerPage * (pageIndex + 1);
     if (iEnd > HomeInventory.numberEntries)
        iEnd = HomeInventory.numberEntries;
     for (i = 0 + HomeInventory.entriesPerPage * pageIndex;
i < iEnd; i++)
     {
       // dividing line
       Line2D.Double dividingLine = new
Line2D.Double(pf.getImageableX(), y, pf.getImageableX() +
pf.getImageableWidth(), y);
       g2D.draw(dividingLine);
       y += dy;
       g2D.setFont(new Font("Arial", Font.BOLD, 12));

g2D.drawString(HomeInventory.myInventory[i].description,
(int) pf.getImageableX(), y);
       y += dy;
       g2D.setFont(new Font("Arial", Font.PLAIN, 12));
       g2D.drawString("Location: " +
HomeInventory.myInventory[i].location, (int)
(pf.getImageableX() + 25), y);
       y += dy;
       if (HomeInventory.myInventory[i].marked)
```

```
        g2D.drawString("Item is marked with identifying
information.", (int) (pf.getImageableX() + 25), y);
      else
        g2D.drawString("Item is NOT marked with
identifying information.", (int) (pf.getImageableX() +
25), y);
      y += dy;
      g2D.drawString("Serial Number: " +
HomeInventory.myInventory[i].serialNumber, (int)
(pf.getImageableX() + 25), y);
      y += dy;
      g2D.drawString("Price: $" +
HomeInventory.myInventory[i].purchasePrice + ", Purchased
on: " + HomeInventory.myInventory[i].purchaseDate, (int)
(pf.getImageableX() + 25), y);
      y += dy;
      g2D.drawString("Purchased at: " +
HomeInventory.myInventory[i].purchaseLocation, (int)
(pf.getImageableX() + 25), y);
      y += dy;
      g2D.drawString("Note: " +
HomeInventory.myInventory[i].note, (int)
(pf.getImageableX() + 25), y);
      y += dy;
      try
      {
        // maintain original width/height ratio
        Image inventoryImage = new
ImageIcon(HomeInventory.myInventory[i].photoFile).getImage
();
        double ratio = (double)
(inventoryImage.getWidth(null)) / (double)
inventoryImage.getHeight(null);
        g2D.drawImage(inventoryImage, (int)
(pf.getImageableX() + 25), y, (int) (100 * ratio), 100,
null);
      }
      catch (Exception ex)
      {
        // have place to go in case image file doesn't
open
      }
      y += 2 * dy + 100;
    }
    return PAGE_EXISTS;
  }
}
```

Yes, there's lots of code here, but the steps are straightforward:

> ➤ Print the header.
> ➤ For next two items in inventory:
> > ○ Draw dividing line.
> > ○ Print on separate lines: **Description**, **Location**, **Marked Statement**, **Serial Number**, **Purchase Price**, **Purchase Date**, **Purchase Location**, and any **Note**.
> > ○ Print picture (maintaining original height-to-width ratio).
> ➤ Check to see if more pages are to be printed.

You should see all of these steps in the above code. Note specifically how the vertical print location is updated using the text height.

Save, run the project one last time. Click the **Print** button on the toolbar. For the example inventory, the print dialog should appear:

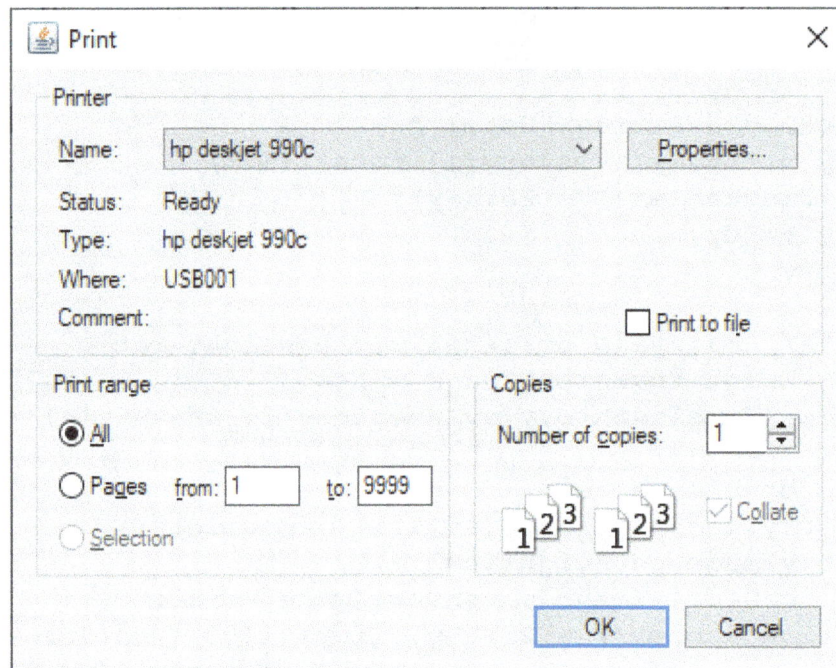

You can choose how many (if not all) pages to print here and click OK, if your wish. A nicely formatted printing of your inventory will be obtained.

Home Inventory Manager Project Review

The **Home Inventory Manager Project** is now complete. Save and run the project and make sure it works as designed. Use the program to keep track of your belongings. You'll want to delete the **inventory.txt** file currently in your project folder and start over adding your own items and establishing your own combo box elements.

If there are errors in your implementation, go back over the steps of frame and code design. Go over the developed code – make sure you understand how different parts of the project were coded. As mentioned in the beginning of this chapter, the completed project is saved as **HomeInventory** in the **\HomeJava\HomeJava Projects** project group.

While completing this project, new concepts and skills you should have gained include:

> ➤ Use of combo box control.
> ➤ Basic object-oriented programming concepts and how to define your own classes and objects.
> ➤ How to add printing to a project, including use of the print dialog control.

Home Inventory Manager
Project Enhancements

Possible enhancements to the home inventory manager project include:

> ➤ After clicking the **New** toolbar button, you must add an item to the inventory and click **Save**. There is no **Cancel** option – add such an option.
> ➤ The implemented search is rather basic. Add a search capability that looks through all the information in the inventory for certain terms or parts of terms. Use the **SoundEx** function from the **Multiple Choice Exam Project** to do "sound-alike" searches.
> ➤ Modify the project to allow opening and saving of separate inventory files. That is, replace the built-in file (inventory.txt) with one you open/save using the dialog controls.

Home Inventory Manager Project
Java Code Listing

There are two files, **HomeInventory.java** and **InventoryItem.**
HomeInventory.java:

```java
/*
 * HomeInventory.java
 */

package homeinventory;
import javax.swing.*;
import javax.swing.filechooser.*;
import java.awt.*;
import java.awt.event.*;
import java.beans.*;
import com.toedter.calendar.*;
import java.awt.geom.*;
import java.io.*;
import java.util.*;
import java.text.*;
import java.awt.print.*;


public class HomeInventory extends JFrame
{

  // Toolbar
  JToolBar inventoryToolBar = new JToolBar();
  JButton newButton = new JButton(new ImageIcon("new.gif"));
  JButton deleteButton = new JButton(new
ImageIcon("delete.gif"));
  JButton saveButton = new JButton(new
ImageIcon("save.gif"));
  JButton previousButton = new JButton(new
ImageIcon("previous.gif"));
  JButton nextButton = new JButton(new
ImageIcon("next.gif"));
  JButton printButton = new JButton(new
ImageIcon("print.gif"));
  JButton exitButton = new JButton();

  // Frame
  JLabel itemLabel = new JLabel();
  JTextField itemTextField = new JTextField();
```

```java
JLabel locationLabel = new JLabel();
JComboBox locationComboBox = new JComboBox();
JCheckBox markedCheckBox = new JCheckBox();
JLabel serialLabel = new JLabel();
JTextField serialTextField = new JTextField();
JLabel priceLabel = new JLabel();
JTextField priceTextField = new JTextField();
JLabel dateLabel = new JLabel();
JDateChooser dateDateChooser = new JDateChooser();
JLabel storeLabel = new JLabel();
JTextField storeTextField = new JTextField();
JLabel noteLabel = new JLabel();
JTextField noteTextField = new JTextField();
JLabel photoLabel = new JLabel();
static JTextArea photoTextArea = new JTextArea();
JButton photoButton = new JButton();
JPanel searchPanel = new JPanel();
JButton[] searchButton = new JButton[26];
PhotoPanel photoPanel = new PhotoPanel();

static final int maximumEntries = 300;
static int numberEntries;
static InventoryItem[] myInventory = new
InventoryItem[maximumEntries];
int currentEntry;
static final int entriesPerPage = 2;
static int lastPage;


public static void main(String args[])
{
  // create frame
  new HomeInventory().setVisible(true);
}

public HomeInventory()
{
  // frame constructor
  setTitle("Home Inventory Manager");
  setResizable(false);

  setDefaultCloseOperation(JFrame.DO_NOTHING_ON_CLOSE);
  addWindowListener(new WindowAdapter()
  {
    public void windowClosing(WindowEvent evt)
    {
```

```
        exitForm(evt);
      }
    });

    getContentPane().setLayout(new GridBagLayout());
    GridBagConstraints gridConstraints;

    inventoryToolBar.setFloatable(false);
    inventoryToolBar.setBackground(Color.BLUE);
    inventoryToolBar.setOrientation(SwingConstants.VERTICAL);
    gridConstraints = new GridBagConstraints();
    gridConstraints.gridx = 0;
    gridConstraints.gridy = 0;
    gridConstraints.gridheight = 8;
    gridConstraints.fill = GridBagConstraints.VERTICAL;
    getContentPane().add(inventoryToolBar, gridConstraints);

    inventoryToolBar.addSeparator();

    Dimension bSize = new Dimension(70, 50);
    newButton.setText("New");
    sizeButton(newButton, bSize);
    newButton.setToolTipText("Add New Item");

newButton.setHorizontalTextPosition(SwingConstants.CENTER);
    newButton.setVerticalTextPosition(SwingConstants.BOTTOM);
    newButton.setFocusable(false);
    inventoryToolBar.add(newButton);
    newButton.addActionListener(new ActionListener()
    {
      public void actionPerformed(ActionEvent e)
      {
        newButtonActionPerformed(e);
      }
    });

    deleteButton.setText("Delete");
    sizeButton(deleteButton, bSize);
    deleteButton.setToolTipText("Delete Current Item");

deleteButton.setHorizontalTextPosition(SwingConstants.CENTER)
;

deleteButton.setVerticalTextPosition(SwingConstants.BOTTOM);
    deleteButton.setFocusable(false);
    inventoryToolBar.add(deleteButton);
    deleteButton.addActionListener(new ActionListener()
```

```java
    {
      public void actionPerformed(ActionEvent e)
      {
        deleteButtonActionPerformed(e);
      }
    });

    saveButton.setText("Save");
    sizeButton(saveButton, bSize);
    saveButton.setToolTipText("Save Current Item");

saveButton.setHorizontalTextPosition(SwingConstants.CENTER);

saveButton.setVerticalTextPosition(SwingConstants.BOTTOM);
    saveButton.setFocusable(false);
    inventoryToolBar.add(saveButton);
    saveButton.addActionListener(new ActionListener()
    {
      public void actionPerformed(ActionEvent e)
      {
        saveButtonActionPerformed(e);
      }
    });

    inventoryToolBar.addSeparator();

    previousButton.setText("Previous");
    sizeButton(previousButton, bSize);
    previousButton.setToolTipText("Display Previous Item");

previousButton.setHorizontalTextPosition(SwingConstants.CENTE
R);

previousButton.setVerticalTextPosition(SwingConstants.BOTTOM)
;
    previousButton.setFocusable(false);
    inventoryToolBar.add(previousButton);
    previousButton.addActionListener(new ActionListener()
    {
      public void actionPerformed(ActionEvent e)
      {
        previousButtonActionPerformed(e);
      }
    });

    nextButton.setText("Next");
    sizeButton(nextButton, bSize);
```

```java
        nextButton.setToolTipText("Display Next Item");

nextButton.setHorizontalTextPosition(SwingConstants.CENTER);

nextButton.setVerticalTextPosition(SwingConstants.BOTTOM);
        nextButton.setFocusable(false);
        inventoryToolBar.add(nextButton);
        nextButton.addActionListener(new ActionListener()
        {
          public void actionPerformed(ActionEvent e)
          {
            nextButtonActionPerformed(e);
          }
        });

        inventoryToolBar.addSeparator();

        printButton.setText("Print");
        sizeButton(printButton, bSize);
        printButton.setToolTipText("Print Inventory List");

printButton.setHorizontalTextPosition(SwingConstants.CENTER);

printButton.setVerticalTextPosition(SwingConstants.BOTTOM);
        printButton.setFocusable(false);
        inventoryToolBar.add(printButton);
        printButton.addActionListener(new ActionListener()
        {
          public void actionPerformed(ActionEvent e)
          {
            printButtonActionPerformed(e);
          }
        });

        exitButton.setText("Exit");
        sizeButton(exitButton, bSize);
        exitButton.setToolTipText("Exit Program");
        exitButton.setFocusable(false);
        inventoryToolBar.add(exitButton);
        exitButton.addActionListener(new ActionListener()
        {
          public void actionPerformed(ActionEvent e)
          {
            exitButtonActionPerformed(e);
          }
        });
```

```
itemLabel.setText("Inventory Item");
gridConstraints = new GridBagConstraints();
gridConstraints.gridx = 1;
gridConstraints.gridy = 0;
gridConstraints.insets = new Insets(10, 10, 0, 10);
gridConstraints.anchor = GridBagConstraints.EAST;
getContentPane().add(itemLabel, gridConstraints);

itemTextField.setPreferredSize(new Dimension(400, 25));
gridConstraints = new GridBagConstraints();
gridConstraints.gridx = 2;
gridConstraints.gridy = 0;
gridConstraints.gridwidth = 5;
gridConstraints.insets = new Insets(10, 0, 0, 10);
gridConstraints.anchor = GridBagConstraints.WEST;
getContentPane().add(itemTextField, gridConstraints);
itemTextField.addActionListener(new ActionListener ()
{
  public void actionPerformed(ActionEvent e)
  {
    itemTextFieldActionPerformed(e);
  }
});

locationLabel.setText("Location");
gridConstraints = new GridBagConstraints();
gridConstraints.gridx = 1;
gridConstraints.gridy = 1;
gridConstraints.insets = new Insets(10, 10, 0, 10);
gridConstraints.anchor = GridBagConstraints.EAST;
getContentPane().add(locationLabel, gridConstraints);

locationComboBox.setPreferredSize(new Dimension(270,
25));
locationComboBox.setFont(new Font("Arial", Font.PLAIN,
12));
locationComboBox.setEditable(true);
locationComboBox.setBackground(Color.WHITE);
gridConstraints = new GridBagConstraints();
gridConstraints.gridx = 2;
gridConstraints.gridy = 1;
gridConstraints.gridwidth = 3;
gridConstraints.insets = new Insets(10, 0, 0, 10);
gridConstraints.anchor = GridBagConstraints.WEST;
getContentPane().add(locationComboBox, gridConstraints);
locationComboBox.addActionListener(new ActionListener ()
{
```

```
    public void actionPerformed(ActionEvent e)
    {
      locationComboBoxActionPerformed(e);
    }
});

markedCheckBox.setText("Marked?");
markedCheckBox.setFocusable(false);
gridConstraints = new GridBagConstraints();
gridConstraints.gridx = 5;
gridConstraints.gridy = 1;
gridConstraints.insets = new Insets(10, 10, 0, 0);
gridConstraints.anchor = GridBagConstraints.WEST;
getContentPane().add(markedCheckBox, gridConstraints);

serialLabel.setText("Serial Number");
gridConstraints = new GridBagConstraints();
gridConstraints.gridx = 1;
gridConstraints.gridy = 2;
gridConstraints.insets = new Insets(10, 10, 0, 10);
gridConstraints.anchor = GridBagConstraints.EAST;
getContentPane().add(serialLabel, gridConstraints);

serialTextField.setPreferredSize(new Dimension(270, 25));
gridConstraints = new GridBagConstraints();
gridConstraints.gridx = 2;
gridConstraints.gridy = 2;
gridConstraints.gridwidth = 3;
gridConstraints.insets = new Insets(10, 0, 0, 10);
gridConstraints.anchor = GridBagConstraints.WEST;
getContentPane().add(serialTextField, gridConstraints);
serialTextField.addActionListener(new ActionListener ()
{
    public void actionPerformed(ActionEvent e)
    {
      serialTextFieldActionPerformed(e);
    }
});

priceLabel.setText("Purchase Price");
gridConstraints = new GridBagConstraints();
gridConstraints.gridx = 1;
gridConstraints.gridy = 3;
gridConstraints.insets = new Insets(10, 10, 0, 10);
gridConstraints.anchor = GridBagConstraints.EAST;
getContentPane().add(priceLabel, gridConstraints);
```

```
priceTextField.setPreferredSize(new Dimension(160, 25));
gridConstraints = new GridBagConstraints();
gridConstraints.gridx = 2;
gridConstraints.gridy = 3;
gridConstraints.gridwidth = 2;
gridConstraints.insets = new Insets(10, 0, 0, 10);
gridConstraints.anchor = GridBagConstraints.WEST;
getContentPane().add(priceTextField, gridConstraints);
priceTextField.addActionListener(new ActionListener ()
{
  public void actionPerformed(ActionEvent e)
  {
    priceTextFieldActionPerformed(e);
  }
});

dateLabel.setText("Date Purchased");
gridConstraints = new GridBagConstraints();
gridConstraints.gridx = 4;
gridConstraints.gridy = 3;
gridConstraints.insets = new Insets(10, 10, 0, 0);
gridConstraints.anchor = GridBagConstraints.WEST;
getContentPane().add(dateLabel, gridConstraints);

dateDateChooser.setPreferredSize(new Dimension(120, 25));
gridConstraints = new GridBagConstraints();
gridConstraints.gridx = 5;
gridConstraints.gridy = 3;
gridConstraints.gridwidth = 2;
gridConstraints.insets = new Insets(10, 0, 0, 10);
gridConstraints.anchor = GridBagConstraints.WEST;
getContentPane().add(dateDateChooser, gridConstraints);
dateDateChooser.addPropertyChangeListener(new
PropertyChangeListener()
{
  public void propertyChange(PropertyChangeEvent e)
  {
    dateDateChooserPropertyChange(e);
  }
});

storeLabel.setText("Store/Website");
gridConstraints = new GridBagConstraints();
gridConstraints.gridx = 1;
gridConstraints.gridy = 4;
gridConstraints.insets = new Insets(10, 10, 0, 10);
gridConstraints.anchor = GridBagConstraints.EAST;
```

```
getContentPane().add(storeLabel, gridConstraints);

storeTextField.setPreferredSize(new Dimension(400, 25));
gridConstraints = new GridBagConstraints();
gridConstraints.gridx = 2;
gridConstraints.gridy = 4;
gridConstraints.gridwidth = 5;
gridConstraints.insets = new Insets(10, 0, 0, 10);
gridConstraints.anchor = GridBagConstraints.WEST;
getContentPane().add(storeTextField, gridConstraints);
storeTextField.addActionListener(new ActionListener ()
{
  public void actionPerformed(ActionEvent e)
  {
    storeTextFieldActionPerformed(e);
  }
});


noteLabel.setText("Note");
gridConstraints = new GridBagConstraints();
gridConstraints.gridx = 1;
gridConstraints.gridy = 5;
gridConstraints.insets = new Insets(10, 10, 0, 10);
gridConstraints.anchor = GridBagConstraints.EAST;
getContentPane().add(noteLabel, gridConstraints);

noteTextField.setPreferredSize(new Dimension(400, 25));
gridConstraints = new GridBagConstraints();
gridConstraints.gridx = 2;
gridConstraints.gridy = 5;
gridConstraints.gridwidth = 5;
gridConstraints.insets = new Insets(10, 0, 0, 10);
gridConstraints.anchor = GridBagConstraints.WEST;
getContentPane().add(noteTextField, gridConstraints);
noteTextField.addActionListener(new ActionListener ()
{
  public void actionPerformed(ActionEvent e)
  {
    noteTextFieldActionPerformed(e);
  }
});

photoLabel.setText("Photo");
gridConstraints = new GridBagConstraints();
gridConstraints.gridx = 1;
gridConstraints.gridy = 6;
```

```
    gridConstraints.insets = new Insets(10, 10, 0, 10);
    gridConstraints.anchor = GridBagConstraints.EAST;
    getContentPane().add(photoLabel, gridConstraints);

    photoTextArea.setPreferredSize(new Dimension(350, 35));
    photoTextArea.setFont(new Font("Arial", Font.PLAIN, 12));
    photoTextArea.setEditable(false);
    photoTextArea.setLineWrap(true);
    photoTextArea.setWrapStyleWord(true);
    photoTextArea.setBackground(new Color(255, 255, 192));

photoTextArea.setBorder(BorderFactory.createLineBorder(Color.
BLACK));
    photoTextArea.setFocusable(false);
    gridConstraints = new GridBagConstraints();
    gridConstraints.gridx = 2;
    gridConstraints.gridy = 6;
    gridConstraints.gridwidth = 4;
    gridConstraints.insets = new Insets(10, 0, 0, 10);
    gridConstraints.anchor = GridBagConstraints.WEST;
    getContentPane().add(photoTextArea, gridConstraints);

    photoButton.setText("...");
    gridConstraints = new GridBagConstraints();
    gridConstraints.gridx = 6;
    gridConstraints.gridy = 6;
    gridConstraints.insets = new Insets(10, 0, 0, 10);
    gridConstraints.anchor = GridBagConstraints.WEST;
    getContentPane().add(photoButton, gridConstraints);
    photoButton.addActionListener(new ActionListener ()
    {
      public void actionPerformed(ActionEvent e)
      {
        photoButtonActionPerformed(e);
      }
    });

    searchPanel.setPreferredSize(new Dimension(240, 160));

searchPanel.setBorder(BorderFactory.createTitledBorder("Item
Search"));
    searchPanel.setLayout(new GridBagLayout());
    gridConstraints = new GridBagConstraints();
    gridConstraints.gridx = 1;
    gridConstraints.gridy = 7;
    gridConstraints.gridwidth = 3;
    gridConstraints.insets = new Insets(10, 0, 10, 0);
```

```java
gridConstraints.anchor = GridBagConstraints.CENTER;
getContentPane().add(searchPanel, gridConstraints);

int x = 0, y = 0;
// create and position 26 buttons
for (int i = 0; i < 26; i++)
{
  // create new button
  searchButton[i] = new JButton();
  // set text property
  searchButton[i].setText(String.valueOf((char) (65 +
i)));
  searchButton[i].setFont(new Font("Arial", Font.BOLD,
12));
  searchButton[i].setMargin(new Insets(-10, -10, -10, -
10));
  sizeButton(searchButton[i], new Dimension(37, 27));
  searchButton[i].setBackground(Color.YELLOW);
  searchButton[i].setFocusable(false);
  gridConstraints = new GridBagConstraints();
  gridConstraints.gridx = x;
  gridConstraints.gridy = y;
  searchPanel.add(searchButton[i], gridConstraints);
  // add method
  searchButton[i].addActionListener(new ActionListener ()
  {
    public void actionPerformed(ActionEvent e)
    {
      searchButtonActionPerformed(e);
    }
  });
  x++;
  // six buttons per row
  if (x % 6 == 0)
  {
    x = 0;
    y++;
  }
}

photoPanel.setPreferredSize(new Dimension(240, 160));
gridConstraints = new GridBagConstraints();
gridConstraints.gridx = 4;
gridConstraints.gridy = 7;
gridConstraints.gridwidth = 3;
gridConstraints.insets = new Insets(10, 0, 10, 10);
gridConstraints.anchor = GridBagConstraints.CENTER;
```

```java
      getContentPane().add(photoPanel, gridConstraints);

      pack();
      Dimension screenSize =
Toolkit.getDefaultToolkit().getScreenSize();
      setBounds((int) (0.5 * (screenSize.width - getWidth())),
(int) (0.5 * (screenSize.height - getHeight())), getWidth(),
getHeight());

      int n;
      // open file for entries
      try
      {
        BufferedReader inputFile = new BufferedReader(new
FileReader("inventory.txt"));
        numberEntries =
Integer.valueOf(inputFile.readLine()).intValue();
        if (numberEntries != 0)
        {
          for (int i = 0; i < numberEntries; i++)
          {
            myInventory[i] = new InventoryItem();
            myInventory[i].description = inputFile.readLine();
            myInventory[i].location = inputFile.readLine();
            myInventory[i].serialNumber = inputFile.readLine();
            myInventory[i].marked =
Boolean.valueOf(inputFile.readLine()).booleanValue();
            myInventory[i].purchasePrice =
inputFile.readLine();
            myInventory[i].purchaseDate = inputFile.readLine();
            myInventory[i].purchaseLocation =
inputFile.readLine();
            myInventory[i].note = inputFile.readLine();
            myInventory[i].photoFile = inputFile.readLine();
          }
        }
        // read in combo box elements
        n = Integer.valueOf(inputFile.readLine()).intValue();
        if (n != 0)
        {
          for (int i = 0; i < n; i++)
          {
            locationComboBox.addItem(inputFile.readLine());
          }
        }
        inputFile.close();
        currentEntry = 1;
```

```
        showEntry(currentEntry);
    }
    catch (Exception ex)
    {
      numberEntries = 0;
      currentEntry = 0;
    }
    if (numberEntries == 0)
    {
      newButton.setEnabled(false);
      deleteButton.setEnabled(false);
      nextButton.setEnabled(false);
      previousButton.setEnabled(false);
      printButton.setEnabled(false);
    }


  }

  private void exitForm(WindowEvent evt)
  {
    if (JOptionPane.showConfirmDialog(null, "Any unsaved
changes will be lost.\nAre you sure you want to exit?", "Exit
Program", JOptionPane.YES_NO_OPTION,
JOptionPane.QUESTION_MESSAGE) == JOptionPane.NO_OPTION)
      return;
    // write entries back to file
    try
    {
      PrintWriter outputFile = new PrintWriter(new
BufferedWriter(new FileWriter("inventory.txt")));
      outputFile.println(numberEntries);
      if (numberEntries != 0)
      {
        for (int i = 0; i < numberEntries; i++)
        {
          outputFile.println(myInventory[i].description);
          outputFile.println(myInventory[i].location);
          outputFile.println(myInventory[i].serialNumber);
          outputFile.println(myInventory[i].marked);
          outputFile.println(myInventory[i].purchasePrice);
          outputFile.println(myInventory[i].purchaseDate);

outputFile.println(myInventory[i].purchaseLocation);
          outputFile.println(myInventory[i].note);
          outputFile.println(myInventory[i].photoFile);
        }
      }
```

```java
      // write combo box entries
      outputFile.println(locationComboBox.getItemCount());
      if (locationComboBox.getItemCount() != 0)
      {
        for (int i = 0; i < locationComboBox.getItemCount();
i++)
          outputFile.println(locationComboBox.getItemAt(i));
      }
      outputFile.close();
    }
    catch (Exception ex)
    {

    }
    System.exit(0);
  }


  private void newButtonActionPerformed(ActionEvent e)
  {
    checkSave();
    blankValues();
  }

  private void deleteButtonActionPerformed(ActionEvent e)
  {
    if (JOptionPane.showConfirmDialog(null, "Are you sure you
want to delete this item?", "Delete Inventory Item",
JOptionPane.YES_NO_OPTION, JOptionPane.QUESTION_MESSAGE) ==
JOptionPane.NO_OPTION)
      return;
    deleteEntry(currentEntry);
    if (numberEntries == 0)
    {
      currentEntry = 0;
      blankValues();
    }
    else
    {
      currentEntry--;
      if (currentEntry == 0)
        currentEntry = 1;
      showEntry(currentEntry);
    }
  }

  private void saveButtonActionPerformed(ActionEvent e)
```

```
{
  // check for description
  itemTextField.setText(itemTextField.getText().trim());
  if (itemTextField.getText().equals(""))
  {
    JOptionPane.showConfirmDialog(null, "Must have item
description.", "Error", JOptionPane.DEFAULT_OPTION,
JOptionPane.ERROR_MESSAGE);
    itemTextField.requestFocus();
    return;
  }
  if (newButton.isEnabled())
  {
    // delete edit entry then resave
    deleteEntry(currentEntry);
  }
  // capitalize first letter
  String s = itemTextField.getText();
  itemTextField.setText(s.substring(0, 1).toUpperCase() +
s.substring(1));
  numberEntries++;
  // determine new current entry location based on
description
  currentEntry = 1;
  if (numberEntries != 1)
  {
    do
    {
      if
(itemTextField.getText().compareTo(myInventory[currentEntry -
1].description) < 0)
        break;
      currentEntry++;
    }
    while (currentEntry < numberEntries);
  }
  // move all entries below new value down one position
unless at end
  if (currentEntry != numberEntries)
  {
    for (int i = numberEntries; i >= currentEntry + 1; i--)
    {
      myInventory[i - 1] = myInventory[i - 2];
      myInventory[i - 2] = new InventoryItem();
    }
  }
  myInventory[currentEntry - 1] = new InventoryItem();
```

```
      myInventory[currentEntry - 1].description =
itemTextField.getText();
      myInventory[currentEntry - 1].location =
locationComboBox.getSelectedItem().toString();
      myInventory[currentEntry - 1].marked =
markedCheckBox.isSelected();
      myInventory[currentEntry - 1].serialNumber =
serialTextField.getText();
      myInventory[currentEntry - 1].purchasePrice =
priceTextField.getText();
      myInventory[currentEntry - 1].purchaseDate =
dateToString(dateDateChooser.getDate());
      myInventory[currentEntry - 1].purchaseLocation =
storeTextField.getText();
      myInventory[currentEntry - 1].photoFile =
photoTextArea.getText();
      myInventory[currentEntry - 1].note =
noteTextField.getText();
    showEntry(currentEntry);
    if (numberEntries < maximumEntries)
      newButton.setEnabled(true);
    else
      newButton.setEnabled(false);
    deleteButton.setEnabled(true);
    printButton.setEnabled(true);
  }

  private void previousButtonActionPerformed(ActionEvent e)
  {
    checkSave();
    currentEntry--;
    showEntry(currentEntry);
  }

  private void nextButtonActionPerformed(ActionEvent e)
  {
    checkSave();
    currentEntry++;
    showEntry(currentEntry);
  }

  private void printButtonActionPerformed(ActionEvent e)
  {
    lastPage = (int) (1 + (numberEntries - 1) /
entriesPerPage);
```

```
   PrinterJob inventoryPrinterJob =
PrinterJob.getPrinterJob();
   inventoryPrinterJob.setPrintable(new
InventoryDocument());
   if (inventoryPrinterJob.printDialog())
   {
     try
      {
       inventoryPrinterJob.print();
     }
     catch (PrinterException ex)
     {
       JOptionPane.showConfirmDialog(null, ex.getMessage(),
"Print Error", JOptionPane.DEFAULT_OPTION,
JOptionPane.ERROR_MESSAGE);
     }
   }
 }

 private void exitButtonActionPerformed(ActionEvent e)
 {
   exitForm(null);
 }

 private void photoButtonActionPerformed(ActionEvent e)
 {
   JFileChooser openChooser = new JFileChooser();
   openChooser.setDialogType(JFileChooser.OPEN_DIALOG);
   openChooser.setDialogTitle("Open Photo File");
    openChooser.addChoosableFileFilter(new
 FileNameExtensionFilter("Photo Files", "jpg"));
   if (openChooser.showOpenDialog(this) ==
JFileChooser.APPROVE_OPTION)
      showPhoto(openChooser.getSelectedFile().toString());
 }

 private void searchButtonActionPerformed(ActionEvent e)
 {
   int i;
   if (numberEntries == 0)
       return;
   // search for item letter
   String letterClicked = e.getActionCommand();
   i = 0;
   do
   {
```

```java
        if (myInventory[i].description.substring(0,
1).equals(letterClicked))
        {
          currentEntry = i + 1;
          showEntry(currentEntry);
          return;
        }
        i++;
      }
      while (i < numberEntries);
      JOptionPane.showConfirmDialog(null, "No " + letterClicked
+ " inventory items.", "None Found",
JOptionPane.DEFAULT_OPTION, JOptionPane.INFORMATION_MESSAGE);
    }

    private void itemTextFieldActionPerformed(ActionEvent e)
    {
      locationComboBox.requestFocus();
    }

    private void locationComboBoxActionPerformed(ActionEvent e)
    {
      // If in list - exit method
      if (locationComboBox.getItemCount() != 0)
      {
        for (int i = 0; i < locationComboBox.getItemCount();
i++)
        {
          if
(locationComboBox.getSelectedItem().toString().equals(locatio
nComboBox.getItemAt(i).toString()))
          {
            serialTextField.requestFocus();
            return;
          }
        }
      }
      // If not found, add to list box

locationComboBox.addItem(locationComboBox.getSelectedItem());
      serialTextField.requestFocus();
    }

    private void serialTextFieldActionPerformed(ActionEvent e)
    {
      priceTextField.requestFocus();
    }
```

```
  private void priceTextFieldActionPerformed(ActionEvent e)
  {
    dateDateChooser.requestFocus();
  }

  private void
dateDateChooserPropertyChange(PropertyChangeEvent e)
  {
    storeTextField.requestFocus();
  }

  private void storeTextFieldActionPerformed(ActionEvent e)
  {
    noteTextField.requestFocus();
  }

  private void noteTextFieldActionPerformed(ActionEvent e)
  {
    photoButton.requestFocus();
  }


  private void sizeButton(JButton b, Dimension d)
  {
    b.setPreferredSize(d);
    b.setMinimumSize(d);
    b.setMaximumSize(d);
  }

  private void showEntry(int j)
  {
    // display entry j (1 to numberEntries)
    itemTextField.setText(myInventory[j - 1].description);
    locationComboBox.setSelectedItem(myInventory[j -
1].location);
    markedCheckBox.setSelected(myInventory[j - 1].marked);
    serialTextField.setText(myInventory[j - 1].serialNumber);
    priceTextField.setText(myInventory[j - 1].purchasePrice);
    dateDateChooser.setDate(stringToDate(myInventory[j -
1].purchaseDate));
    storeTextField.setText(myInventory[j -
1].purchaseLocation);
    noteTextField.setText(myInventory[j - 1].note);
    showPhoto(myInventory[j - 1].photoFile);
    nextButton.setEnabled(true);
    previousButton.setEnabled(true);
```

```java
    if (j == 1)
      previousButton.setEnabled(false);
    if (j == numberEntries)
      nextButton.setEnabled(false);
    itemTextField.requestFocus();
  }

  private Date stringToDate(String s)
  {
    int m = Integer.valueOf(s.substring(0, 2)).intValue() -
1;
    int d = Integer.valueOf(s.substring(3, 5)).intValue();
    int y = Integer.valueOf(s.substring(6)).intValue() -
1900;
    return(new Date(y, m, d));
  }


  private String dateToString(Date dd)
  {
    String yString = String.valueOf(dd.getYear() + 1900);
    int m = dd.getMonth() + 1;
    String mString = new DecimalFormat("00").format(m);
    int d = dd.getDate();
    String dString = new DecimalFormat("00").format(d);
    return(mString + "/" + dString + "/" + yString);
  }

  private void showPhoto(String photoFile)
  {
    if (!photoFile.equals(""))
    {
      try
      {
        photoTextArea.setText(photoFile);
      }
      catch (Exception ex)
      {
        photoTextArea.setText("");
      }
    }
    else
    {
      photoTextArea.setText("");
    }
    photoPanel.repaint();
  }
```

```java
  private void blankValues()
  {
    // blank input screen
    newButton.setEnabled(false);
    deleteButton.setEnabled(false);
    saveButton.setEnabled(true);
    previousButton.setEnabled(false);
    nextButton.setEnabled(false);
    printButton.setEnabled(false);
    itemTextField.setText("");
    locationComboBox.setSelectedItem("");
    markedCheckBox.setSelected(false);
    serialTextField.setText("");
    priceTextField.setText("");
    dateDateChooser.setDate(new Date());
    storeTextField.setText("");
    noteTextField.setText("");
    photoTextArea.setText("");
    photoPanel.repaint();
    itemTextField.requestFocus();
  }

  private void deleteEntry(int j)
  {
    // delete entry j
    if (j != numberEntries)
    {
      // move all entries under j up one level
      for (int i = j; i < numberEntries; i++)
      {
        myInventory[i - 1] = new InventoryItem();
        myInventory[i - 1] = myInventory[i];
      }
    }
    numberEntries--;
  }

  private void checkSave()
  {
    boolean edited = false;
    if (!myInventory[currentEntry -
1].description.equals(itemTextField.getText()))
      edited = true;
    else if (!myInventory[currentEntry -
1].location.equals(locationComboBox.getSelectedItem().toStrin
g()))
```

```
        edited = true;
    else if (myInventory[currentEntry - 1].marked !=
markedCheckBox.isSelected())
        edited = true;
    else if (!myInventory[currentEntry -
1].serialNumber.equals(serialTextField.getText()))
        edited = true;
    else if (!myInventory[currentEntry -
1].purchasePrice.equals(priceTextField.getText()))
        edited = true;
    else if (!myInventory[currentEntry -
1].purchaseDate.equals(dateToString(dateDateChooser.getDate()
)))
        edited = true;
    else if (!myInventory[currentEntry -
1].purchaseLocation.equals(storeTextField.getText()))
        edited = true;
    else if (!myInventory[currentEntry -
1].note.equals(noteTextField.getText()))
        edited = true;
    else if (!myInventory[currentEntry -
1].photoFile.equals(photoTextArea.getText()))
        edited = true;
    if (edited)
    {
        if (JOptionPane.showConfirmDialog(null, "You have
edited this item. Do you want to save the changes?", "Save
Item", JOptionPane.YES_NO_OPTION,
JOptionPane.QUESTION_MESSAGE) == JOptionPane.YES_OPTION)
            saveButton.doClick();
    }
  }
}

class PhotoPanel extends JPanel
{
  public void paintComponent(Graphics g)
  {
    Graphics2D g2D = (Graphics2D) g;
    super.paintComponent(g2D);

    // draw border
    g2D.setPaint(Color.BLACK);
    g2D.draw(new Rectangle2D.Double(0, 0, getWidth() - 1,
getHeight() - 1));
```

```
    // show photo
    Image photoImage = new
ImageIcon(HomeInventory.photoTextArea.getText()).getImage();
    int w = getWidth();
    int h = getHeight();
    double rWidth = (double) getWidth() / (double)
photoImage.getWidth(null);
    double rHeight = (double) getHeight() / (double)
photoImage.getHeight(null);
    if (rWidth > rHeight)
    {
      // leave height at display height, change width by
amount height is changed
      w = (int) (photoImage.getWidth(null) * rHeight);
    }
    else
    {
      // leave width at display width, change height by
amount width is changed
      h = (int) (photoImage.getHeight(null) * rWidth);
    }
    // center in panel
    g2D.drawImage(photoImage, (int) (0.5 * (getWidth() - w)),
(int) (0.5 * (getHeight() - h)), w, h, null);

    g2D.dispose();
  }
}

class InventoryDocument implements Printable
{
  public int print(Graphics g, PageFormat pf, int pageIndex)
  {
    Graphics2D g2D = (Graphics2D) g;
    if ((pageIndex + 1) > HomeInventory.lastPage)
    {
      return NO_SUCH_PAGE;
    }
    int i, iEnd;
    // here you decide what goes on each page and draw it
    // header
    g2D.setFont(new Font("Arial", Font.BOLD, 14));
    g2D.drawString("Home Inventory Items - Page " +
String.valueOf(pageIndex + 1), (int) pf.getImageableX(),
(int) (pf.getImageableY() + 25));
    // get starting y
```

```
      int dy = (int) g2D.getFont().getStringBounds("S",
g2D.getFontRenderContext()).getHeight();
    int y = (int) (pf.getImageableY() + 4 * dy);
    iEnd = HomeInventory.entriesPerPage * (pageIndex + 1);
    if (iEnd > HomeInventory.numberEntries)
      iEnd = HomeInventory.numberEntries;
    for (i = 0 + HomeInventory.entriesPerPage * pageIndex; i
< iEnd; i++)
      {
      // dividing line
      Line2D.Double dividingLine = new
Line2D.Double(pf.getImageableX(), y, pf.getImageableX() +
pf.getImageableWidth(), y);
      g2D.draw(dividingLine);
      y += dy;
      g2D.setFont(new Font("Arial", Font.BOLD, 12));

g2D.drawString(HomeInventory.myInventory[i].description,
(int) pf.getImageableX(), y);
      y += dy;
      g2D.setFont(new Font("Arial", Font.PLAIN, 12));
      g2D.drawString("Location: " +
HomeInventory.myInventory[i].location, (int)
(pf.getImageableX() + 25), y);
      y += dy;
      if (HomeInventory.myInventory[i].marked)
        g2D.drawString("Item is marked with identifying
information.", (int) (pf.getImageableX() + 25), y);
      else
        g2D.drawString("Item is NOT marked with identifying
information.", (int) (pf.getImageableX() + 25), y);
      y += dy;
      g2D.drawString("Serial Number: " +
HomeInventory.myInventory[i].serialNumber, (int)
(pf.getImageableX() + 25), y);
      y += dy;
      g2D.drawString("Price: $" +
HomeInventory.myInventory[i].purchasePrice + ", Purchased on:
" + HomeInventory.myInventory[i].purchaseDate, (int)
(pf.getImageableX() + 25), y);
      y += dy;
      g2D.drawString("Purchased at: " +
HomeInventory.myInventory[i].purchaseLocation, (int)
(pf.getImageableX() + 25), y);
      y += dy;
```

```
        g2D.drawString("Note: " +
HomeInventory.myInventory[i].note, (int) (pf.getImageableX()
+ 25), y);
        y += dy;
        try
        {
          // maintain original width/height ratio
          Image inventoryImage = new
ImageIcon(HomeInventory.myInventory[i].photoFile).getImage();
          double ratio = (double)
(inventoryImage.getWidth(null)) / (double)
inventoryImage.getHeight(null);
          g2D.drawImage(inventoryImage, (int)
(pf.getImageableX() + 25), y, (int) (100 * ratio), 100,
null);
        }
        catch (Exception ex)
        {
          // have place to go in case image file doesn't open
        }
        y += 2 * dy + 100;
      }


    return PAGE_EXISTS;


  }
}
```

InventoryItem.java:

```java
package homeinventory;
public class InventoryItem
{
  public String description;
  public String location;
  public boolean marked;
  public String serialNumber;
  public String purchasePrice;
  public String purchaseDate;
  public String purchaseLocation;
  public String note;
  public String photoFile;
}
```

9

Snowball Toss Game Project

Review and Preview

In the final project, we'll have some fun. In the **Snowball Toss Game Project**, two players toss snowballs at each other or a single player plays against the computer - the most hits wins! We introduce concepts needed for game programming – animation, collision detection, keyboard control, and sounds.

We also look at adding methods to custom objects and how to use inheritance. And, we'll look at how to give our computer a semblance of intelligence.

Snowball Toss Game Project Preview

In this chapter, we will build a **Snowball Toss Game** program. This program lets two players compete in throwing snowballs at each other. Or, optionally, a single player can play against a computer with adjustable 'smarts'.

 The finished project is saved as **Snowball Toss** in the **\HomeJava\HomeJava Projects** program group. Start NetBeans (or your IDE). Open the specified project group. Make **Snowball Toss** the selected project. Run the project. Press the **Options** button. You will see:

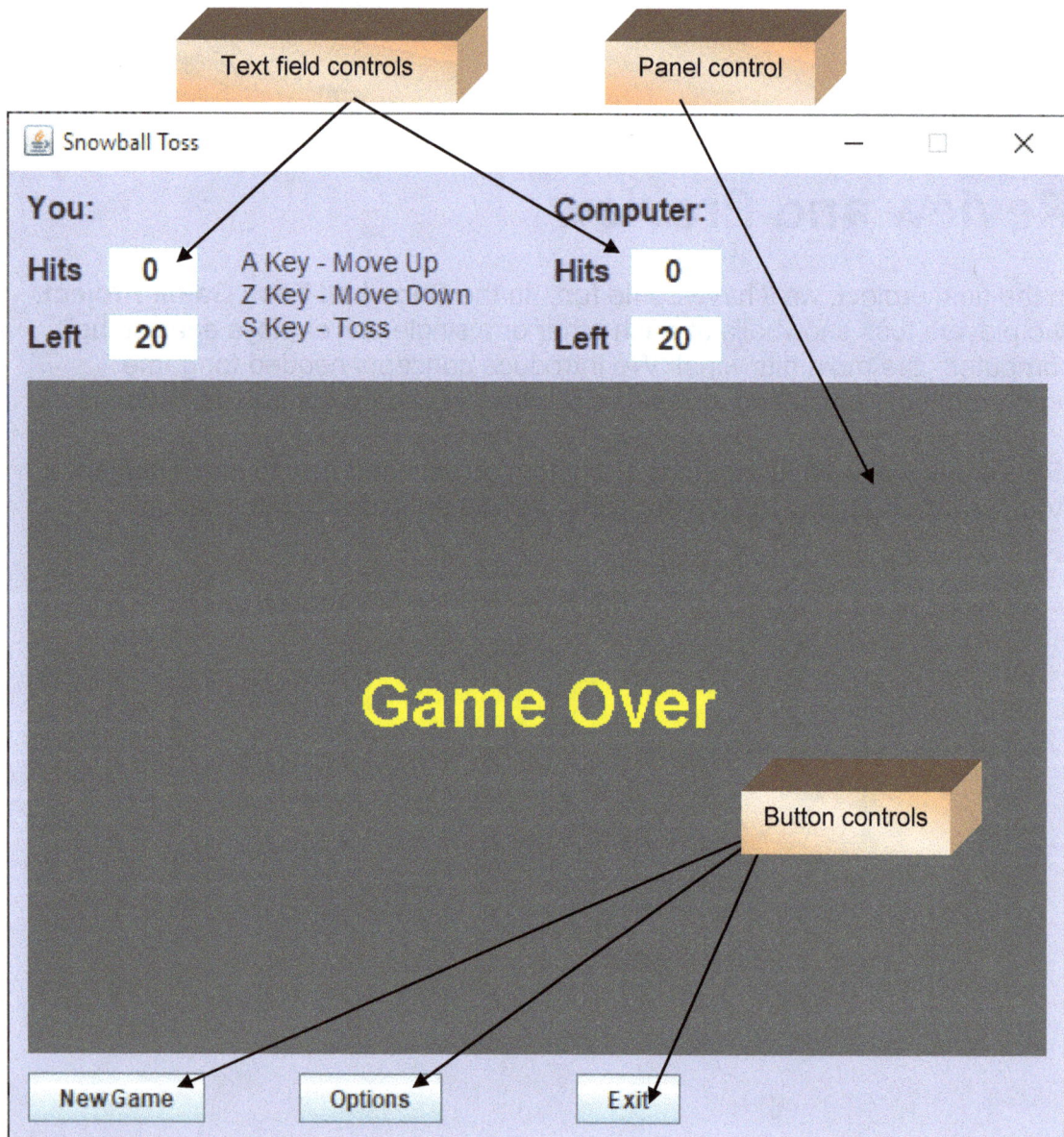

The label and text field controls at the top of the form provide game status (score, snowballs left to toss and keys to use to move players). The large gray panel with the **Game Over** message is the game field. Three button controls are used to start/stop the game, set options and stop the program.

Click **Options**. Another panel with radio buttons appears:

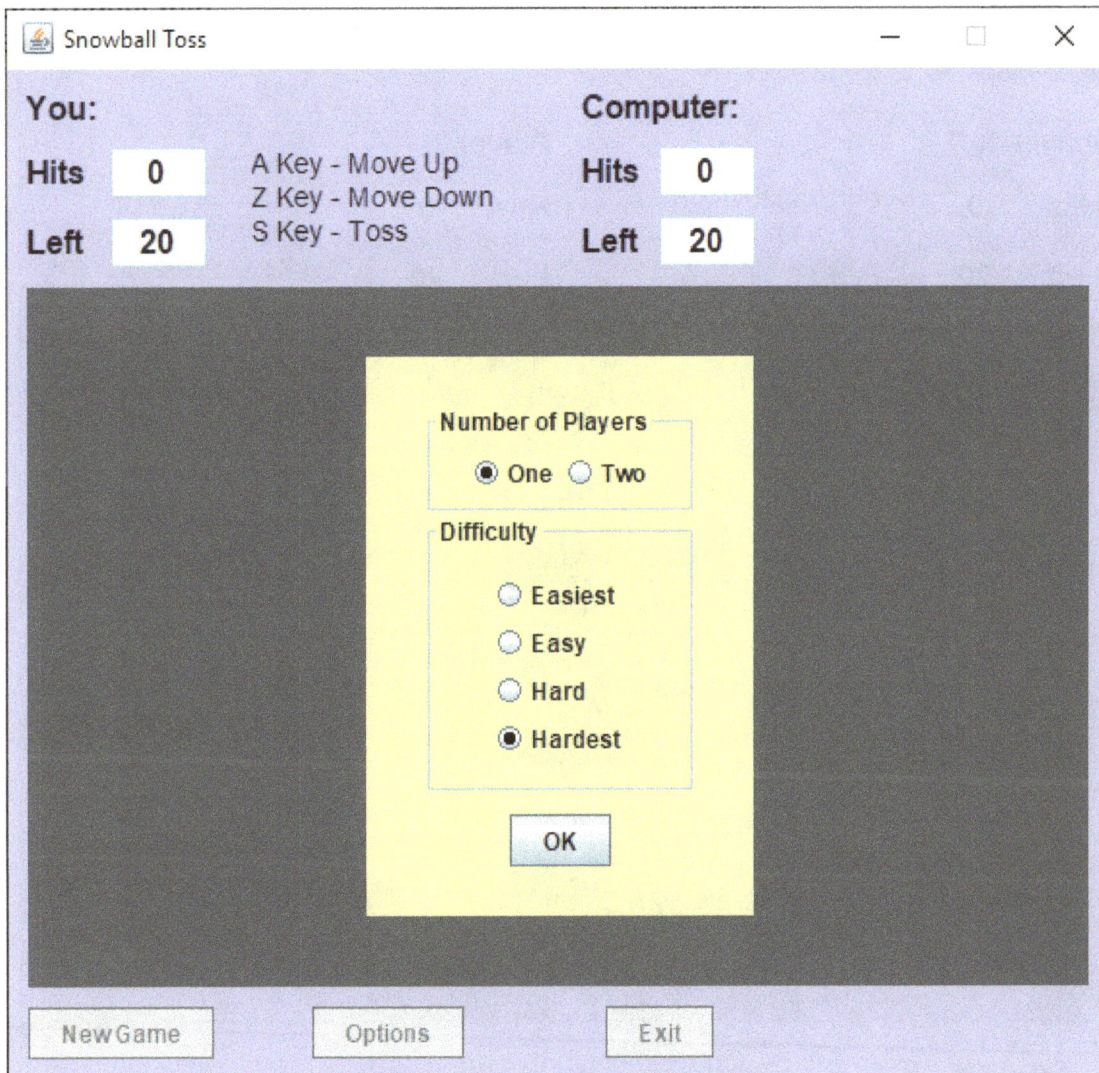

In the game, you can have two players competing against each other or one player against the computer. For now, choose **One Player**. With a single player, you can also choose **Difficulty** (setting the intelligence level of the computer) – select **Easiest**. Click **OK** to make the **Options** window disappear. Then, click **New Game**.

The game screen shows the two snowball tossing characters, one on each side of the screen (the players are identified by the label controls at the top of the form). Also shown are the player scores (**Hits**) and displays showing how many snowballs are left. The idea of the game is to move your 'tosser' up and down the screen, trying to hit the other player with a snowball. Zombie snowmen move in strange ways through the middle of the screen to act as cover and deflect some tosses:

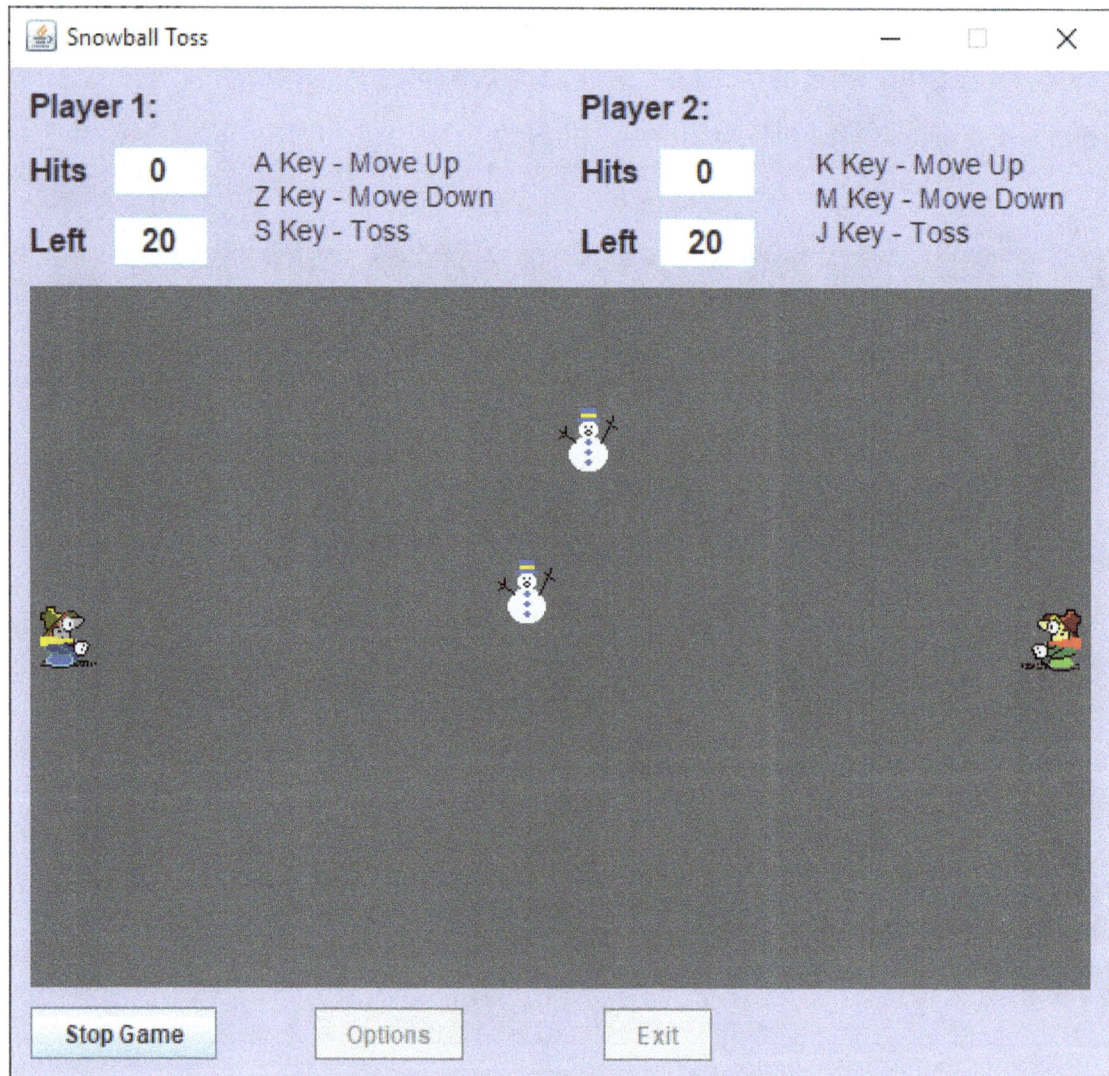

Watch out – the computer may make a toss at you.

Control of the players is via the keyboard. Player 1 (and the player when playing against the computer) uses the **A** key to move up, the **Z** key to move down, and the **S** key to toss a snowball. Player 2 uses the **K** key to move up, the **M** key to move down, and the **J** key to toss. These instructions are shown on the form. The game ends when all the snowballs have been thrown or when the **Stop** button is clicked.

Try moving your player up and down using the **A** and **Z** keys. When you want, take a toss at the other player by pressing the **S** key. You should hear a 'throwing' sound.   Here's a throw I made:

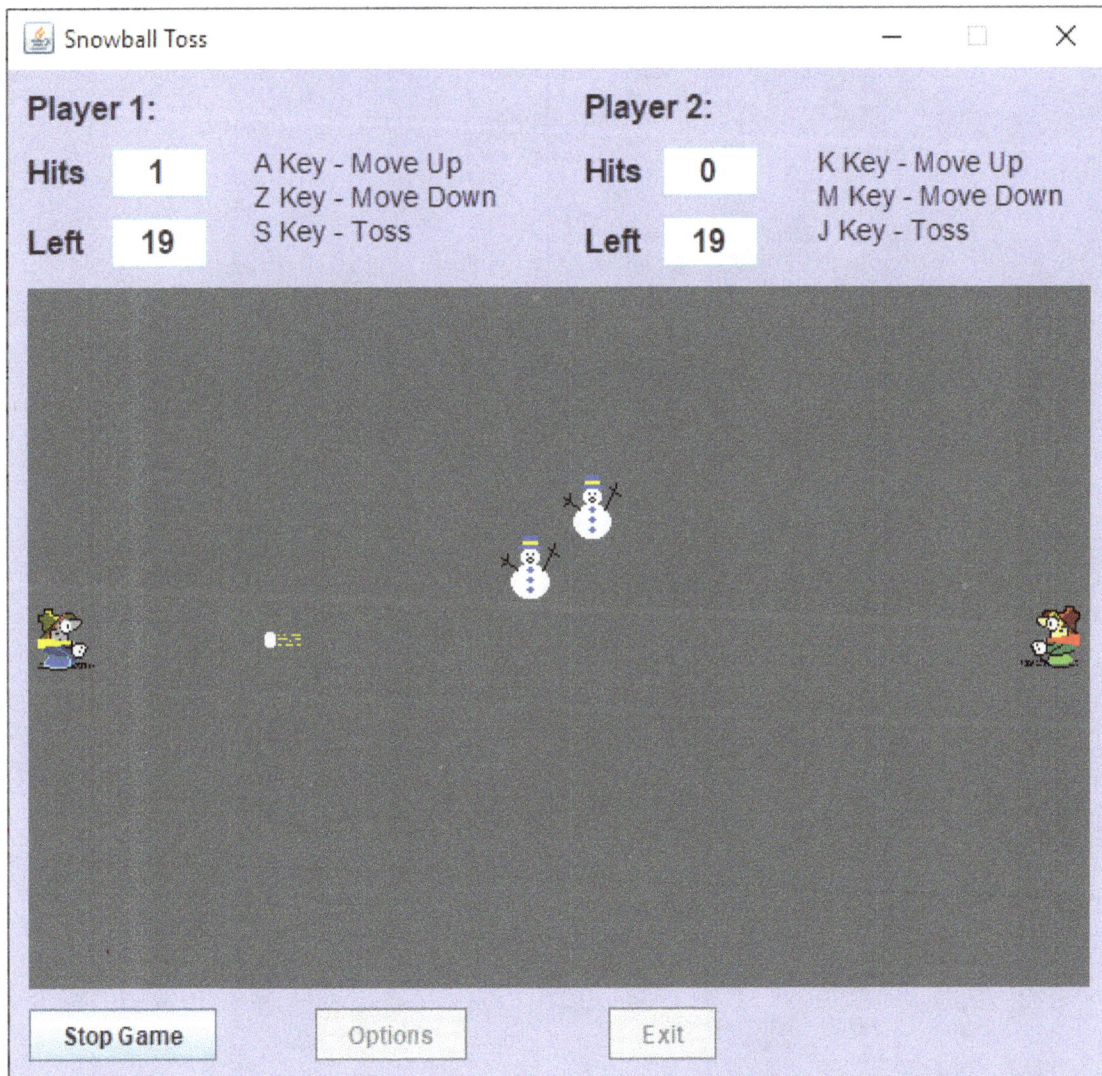

The snowball will move across the screen until it hits something or flies off the side of the form. If you hit the other player (resulting in an ouch sound), you earn one point. The player with the most points when the game stops is the winner.

That's all there is to this game. Conceptually, it is very simple. Just throw snowballs at each other until you're out of snowballs. Though simple, there are many topics we need to discuss to build the project.

The project will be built in several stages. We discuss **frame design**. We discuss the controls used to build the form and establish initial properties. We show how to configure the form based on selected options. And, we address **code design**. We discuss several areas of game programming: animation, keyboard events, collision detection and sounds. Lastly, we look at how to give the computer intelligence in making decisions needed to play the game.

Snowball Toss Game Frame Design

We begin building the **Snowball Toss Project.** Let's build the frame. Start a new project in your Java project group – name it **SnowballToss**. Delete default code in file named **SnowballToss.java**. Once started, we suggest you immediately save the project with the name you chose. This sets up the folder and file structure needed for your project. Build the basic frame with these properties:

SnowballToss Frame:

title	Snowball Toss
background	Color(192, 192, 255)
resizable	false

The code is:

```java
/*
 * SnowballToss.java
 */

package snowballtoss;
import javax.swing.*;
import java.awt.*;
import java.awt.event.*;

public class SnowballToss extends JFrame
{

  public static void main(String args[])
  {
    // create frame
    new SnowballToss().setVisible(true);
  }

  public SnowballToss()
  {
    // frame constructor
    setTitle("Snowball Toss");
    getContentPane().setBackground(new Color(192, 192,
255));
    setResizable(false);
    addWindowListener(new WindowAdapter()
    {
      public void windowClosing(WindowEvent evt)
      {
        exitForm(evt);
      }
```

```
    });

    getContentPane().setLayout(new GridBagLayout());
    GridBagConstraints gridConstraints;

    pack();
    Dimension screenSize =
Toolkit.getDefaultToolkit().getScreenSize();
    setBounds((int) (0.5 * (screenSize.width -
getWidth())), (int) (0.5 * (screenSize.height -
getHeight())), getWidth(), getHeight());
  }

  private void exitForm(WindowEvent evt)
  {
    System.exit(0);
  }
}
```

This code builds the frame, sets up the layout manager and includes code to exit the application. Run the code to make sure the frame (at least, what there is of it at this point) appears and is centered on the screen:

Let's populate our frame with other controls. All code for creating the frame and placing controls (except declarations) goes in the **SnowballToss** constructor.

The **GridBagLayout** for the frame is (in two segments)::

	gridx = 0	gridx = 1	gridx = 2
gridy = 0	player1Label		
gridy = 1	player1HitsLabel	player1HitsTextField	player1TextArea
gridy = 2	player1LeftLabel	player1LeftTextField	
gridy = 3	snowPanel		
gridy = 4	gameButton		optionsButton

	gridx = 3	gridx = 4	gridx = 5
gridy = 0	player2Label		
gridy = 1	player2HitsLabel	player2HitsTextField	player2TextArea
gridy = 2	player2LeftLabel	player2LeftTextField	
gridy = 3	snowPanel		
gridy = 4	exitButton		

All label and text field controls are used for titling and providing scoring and game play information. The large panel (**snowPanel**) is the game field. It also holds another panel control that allows options selection (we will code that panel soon). The three button controls are used to start/stop a game (**gameButton**), set options (**optionsButton**) and exit the program (**exitButton**). Default properties are set for a one player game with easiest difficulty.

As usual, we will discuss add controls in stages. First, we add the scoring labels and text controls for each player.. Then, we add the snowPanel along with the yet to be designed **optionsPanel**. Lastly, we add the three button controls.

Properties for the **Player 1** controls are:

player1Label:
text	You:
font	Arial, Bold, Size 16
gridx	0
gridy	0
gridwidth	2
insets	10, 10, 0, 0
anchor	WEST

player1HitsLabel:
text	Hits
font	Arial, Bold, Size 16
gridx	0
gridy	1
insets	10, 10, 0, 0
anchor	WEST

player1HitsTextField:
size	50, 25
text	0
font	Arial, Bold, Size 16
editable	false
background	White
horizontalAlignment	Center
gridx	1
gridy	1
insets	10, 10, 0, 0

player1LeftLabel:
text	Left
font	Arial, Bold, Size 16
gridx	0
gridy	2
insets	10, 10, 0, 0
anchor	WEST

player1LeftTextField:

size	50, 25
text	20
font	Arial, Bold, Size 16
editable	false
background	White
horizontalAlignment	Center
gridx	1
gridy	2
insets	10, 10, 0, 0

player1TextArea:

size	160, 60
text	A Key - Move Up\nZ Key - Move Down\nS Key - Toss
font	Arial, Plain, Size 14
editable	false
background	Color(192, 192, 255), same as frame
gridx	2
gridy	1
gridheight	2
insets	10, 20, 0, 0

Declare the controls as class level objects using:

```
JLabel player1Label = new JLabel();
JLabel player1HitsLabel = new JLabel();
JTextField player1HitsTextField = new JTextField();
JLabel player1LeftLabel = new JLabel();
JTextField player1LeftTextField = new JTextField();
JTextArea player1TextArea = new JTextArea();
```

Add the controls to the frame using (since many of the controls use the same font, we define a common object, **myFont**):

```
Font myFont = new Font("Arial", Font.BOLD, 16);

player1Label.setText("You:");
player1Label.setFont(myFont);
gridConstraints = new GridBagConstraints();
gridConstraints.gridx = 0;
gridConstraints.gridy = 0;
gridConstraints.gridwidth = 2;
gridConstraints.insets = new Insets(10, 10, 0, 0);
gridConstraints.anchor = GridBagConstraints.WEST;
getContentPane().add(player1Label, gridConstraints);

player1HitsLabel.setText("Hits");
player1HitsLabel.setFont(myFont);
gridConstraints = new GridBagConstraints();
gridConstraints.gridx = 0;
gridConstraints.gridy = 1;
gridConstraints.insets = new Insets(10, 10, 0, 0);
gridConstraints.anchor = GridBagConstraints.WEST;
getContentPane().add(player1HitsLabel, gridConstraints);

player1HitsTextField.setPreferredSize(new Dimension(50,
25));
player1HitsTextField.setText("0");
player1HitsTextField.setFont(myFont);
player1HitsTextField.setEditable(false);
player1HitsTextField.setBackground(Color.WHITE);
player1HitsTextField.setHorizontalAlignment(SwingConstants
.CENTER);
gridConstraints = new GridBagConstraints();
gridConstraints.gridx = 1;
gridConstraints.gridy = 1;
gridConstraints.insets = new Insets(10, 10, 0, 0);
getContentPane().add(player1HitsTextField,
gridConstraints);
```

```
player1LeftLabel.setText("Left");
player1LeftLabel.setFont(myFont);
gridConstraints = new GridBagConstraints();
gridConstraints.gridx = 0;
gridConstraints.gridy = 2;
gridConstraints.insets = new Insets(10, 10, 0, 0);
gridConstraints.anchor = GridBagConstraints.WEST;
getContentPane().add(player1LeftLabel, gridConstraints);

player1LeftTextField.setPreferredSize(new Dimension(50,
25));
player1LeftTextField.setText("20");
player1LeftTextField.setFont(myFont);
player1LeftTextField.setEditable(false);
player1LeftTextField.setBackground(Color.WHITE);
player1LeftTextField.setHorizontalAlignment(SwingConstants
.CENTER);
gridConstraints = new GridBagConstraints();
gridConstraints.gridx = 1;
gridConstraints.gridy = 2;
gridConstraints.insets = new Insets(10, 10, 0, 0);
getContentPane().add(player1LeftTextField,
gridConstraints);

player1TextArea.setPreferredSize(new Dimension(160, 60));
player1TextArea.setText("A Key - Move Up\nZ Key - Move
Down\nS Key - Toss");
player1TextArea.setFont(new Font("Arial", Font.PLAIN,
14));
player1TextArea.setEditable(false);
player1TextArea.setBackground(getContentPane().getBackgrou
nd());
gridConstraints = new GridBagConstraints();
gridConstraints.gridx = 2;
gridConstraints.gridy = 1;
gridConstraints.gridheight = 2;
gridConstraints.insets = new Insets(10, 20, 0, 0);
getContentPane().add(player1TextArea, gridConstraints);
```

Run to see these controls:

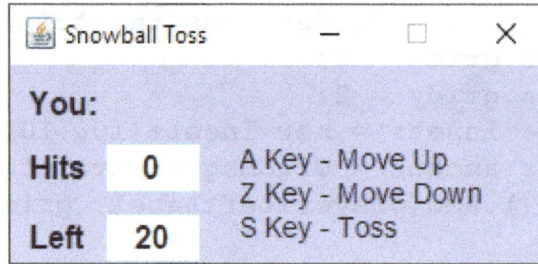

The **Player 2** controls are nearly identical to those we just added, so this is a good place to practice your cut and paste skills with the code. The properties are:

player2Label:
text	Computer:
font	Arial, Bold, Size 16
gridx	3
gridy	0
gridwidth	2
insets	10, 10, 0, 0
anchor	WEST

player2HitsLabel:
text	Hits
font	Arial, Bold, Size 16
gridx	3
gridy	1
insets	10, 10, 0, 0
anchor	WEST

player2HitsTextField:
size	50, 25
text	0
font	Arial, Bold, Size 16
editable	false
background	White
horizontalAlignment	Center
gridx	4
gridy	1
insets	10, 10, 0, 0

player2LeftLabel:

text	Left
font	Arial, Bold, Size 16
gridx	3
gridy	2
insets	10, 10, 0, 0
anchor	WEST

player2LeftTextField:

size	50, 25
text	20
font	Arial, Bold, Size 16
editable	false
background	White
horizontalAlignment	Center
gridx	4
gridy	2
insets	10, 10, 0, 0

player2TextArea:

size	160, 60
text	K Key - Move Up\nM Key - Move Down\nJ Key - Toss
font	Arial, Plain, Size 14
editable	false
background	Color(192, 192, 255), same as frame
gridx	5
gridy	1
gridheight	2
insets	10, 20, 0, 0

The controls are declared using:

```
JLabel player2Label = new JLabel();
JLabel player2HitsLabel = new JLabel();
JTextField player2HitsTextField = new JTextField();
JLabel player2LeftLabel = new JLabel();
JTextField player2LeftTextField = new JTextField();
JTextArea player2TextArea = new JTextArea();
```

The controls are added to the frame using:

```
player2Label.setText("Computer:");
player2Label.setFont(myFont);
gridConstraints = new GridBagConstraints();
gridConstraints.gridx = 3;
gridConstraints.gridy = 0;
gridConstraints.gridwidth = 2;
gridConstraints.insets = new Insets(10, 10, 0, 0);
gridConstraints.anchor = GridBagConstraints.WEST;
getContentPane().add(player2Label, gridConstraints);

player2HitsLabel.setText("Hits");
player2HitsLabel.setFont(myFont);
gridConstraints = new GridBagConstraints();
gridConstraints.gridx = 3;
gridConstraints.gridy = 1;
gridConstraints.insets = new Insets(10, 10, 0, 0);
gridConstraints.anchor = GridBagConstraints.WEST;
getContentPane().add(player2HitsLabel, gridConstraints);

player2HitsTextField.setPreferredSize(new Dimension(50,
25));
player2HitsTextField.setText("0");
player2HitsTextField.setFont(myFont);
player2HitsTextField.setEditable(false);
player2HitsTextField.setBackground(Color.WHITE);
player2HitsTextField.setHorizontalAlignment(SwingConstants
.CENTER);
gridConstraints = new GridBagConstraints();
gridConstraints.gridx = 4;
gridConstraints.gridy = 1;
gridConstraints.insets = new Insets(10, 10, 0, 0);
getContentPane().add(player2HitsTextField,
gridConstraints);

player2LeftLabel.setText("Left");
player2LeftLabel.setFont(myFont);
gridConstraints = new GridBagConstraints();
gridConstraints.gridx = 3;
gridConstraints.gridy = 2;
gridConstraints.insets = new Insets(10, 10, 0, 0);
gridConstraints.anchor = GridBagConstraints.WEST;
getContentPane().add(player2LeftLabel, gridConstraints);
```

```
player2LeftTextField.setPreferredSize(new Dimension(50,
25));
player2LeftTextField.setText("20");
player2LeftTextField.setFont(myFont);
player2LeftTextField.setEditable(false);
player2LeftTextField.setBackground(Color.WHITE);
player2LeftTextField.setHorizontalAlignment(SwingConstants
.CENTER);
gridConstraints = new GridBagConstraints();
gridConstraints.gridx = 4;
gridConstraints.gridy = 2;
gridConstraints.insets = new Insets(10, 10, 0, 0);
getContentPane().add(player2LeftTextField,
gridConstraints);

player2TextArea.setPreferredSize(new Dimension(140, 60));
player2TextArea.setText("K Key - Move Up\nM Key - Move
Down\nJ Key - Toss");
player2TextArea.setFont(new Font("Arial", Font.PLAIN,
14));
player2TextArea.setEditable(false);
player2TextArea.setBackground(getContentPane().getBackgrou
nd());
gridConstraints = new GridBagConstraints();
gridConstraints.gridx = 5;
gridConstraints.gridy = 1;
gridConstraints.gridheight = 2;
gridConstraints.insets = new Insets(10, 20, 0, 0);
getContentPane().add(player2TextArea, gridConstraints);
```

Run to see:

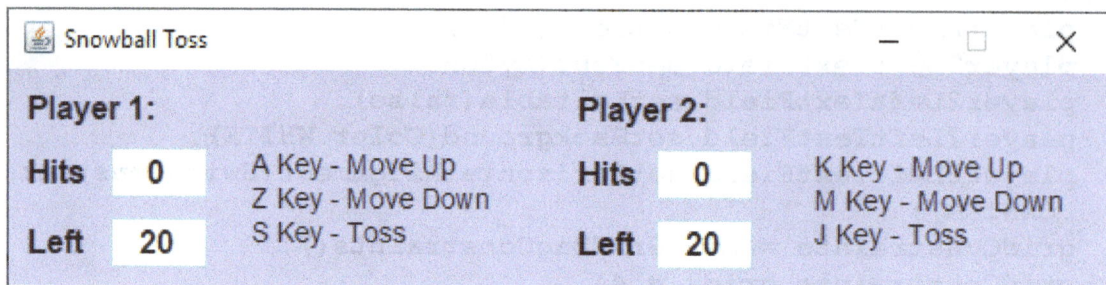

The labels and text fields will change when the user selects a different number of players. The scoring controls are complete. Let's add the game display (**snowPanel**) and associated options panels and controls.

The large panel in the middle of the frame (**snowPanel**) is used to display game play. It holds another panel (**optionsPanel**) used to establish options. Since we use **snowPanel** to host graphics, we will create a special class (**SnowPanel**) with a **paintComponent** method to place graphics methods. Add this class after the **SnowballToss** main class:

```
class SnowPanel extends JPanel
{
  public void paintComponent(Graphics g)
  {
    Graphics2D g2D = (Graphics2D) g;
    super.paintComponent(g2D);

    g2D.dispose();
  }
}
```

Properties for the two new panels are:

snowPanel:

size	550, 350
background	Gray
gridx	0 (on frame)
gridy	3 (on frame)
gridwidth	6 (on frame)
insets	10, 10, 10, 10

optionsPanel:

size	200, 280
background	Color(255, 255, 192)
gridx	0 (on snowPanel)
gridy	0 (on snowPanel)

The panels are declared using:

```
SnowPanel snowPanel = new SnowPanel();
static JPanel optionsPanel  = new JPanel();
```

We need to display the **optionsPanel** on the **snowPanel** so it needs the **static** declaration.

The panels are added to the frame with this code:

```
snowPanel.setPreferredSize(new Dimension(550, 350));
snowPanel.setBackground(Color.GRAY);
snowPanel.setLayout(new GridBagLayout());
gridConstraints = new GridBagConstraints();
gridConstraints.gridx = 0;
gridConstraints.gridy = 3;
gridConstraints.gridwidth = 6;
gridConstraints.insets = new Insets(10, 10, 10, 10);
getContentPane().add(snowPanel, gridConstraints);

optionsPanel.setPreferredSize(new Dimension(200, 280));
optionsPanel.setBackground(new Color(255, 255, 192));
optionsPanel.setLayout(new GridBagLayout());
gridConstraints = new GridBagConstraints();
gridConstraints.gridx = 0;
gridConstraints.gridy = 0;
snowPanel.add(optionsPanel, gridConstraints);
```

Add the shaded line to the **SnowPanel painttComponent** method to make sure the options panel shows up:

```
class SnowPanel extends JPanel
{
  public void paintComponent(Graphics g)
  {
    Graphics2D g2D = (Graphics2D) g;
    super.paintComponent(g2D);

    SnowballToss.optionsPanel.repaint();

    g2D.dispose();
  }
}
```

Save, run to see the added panels:

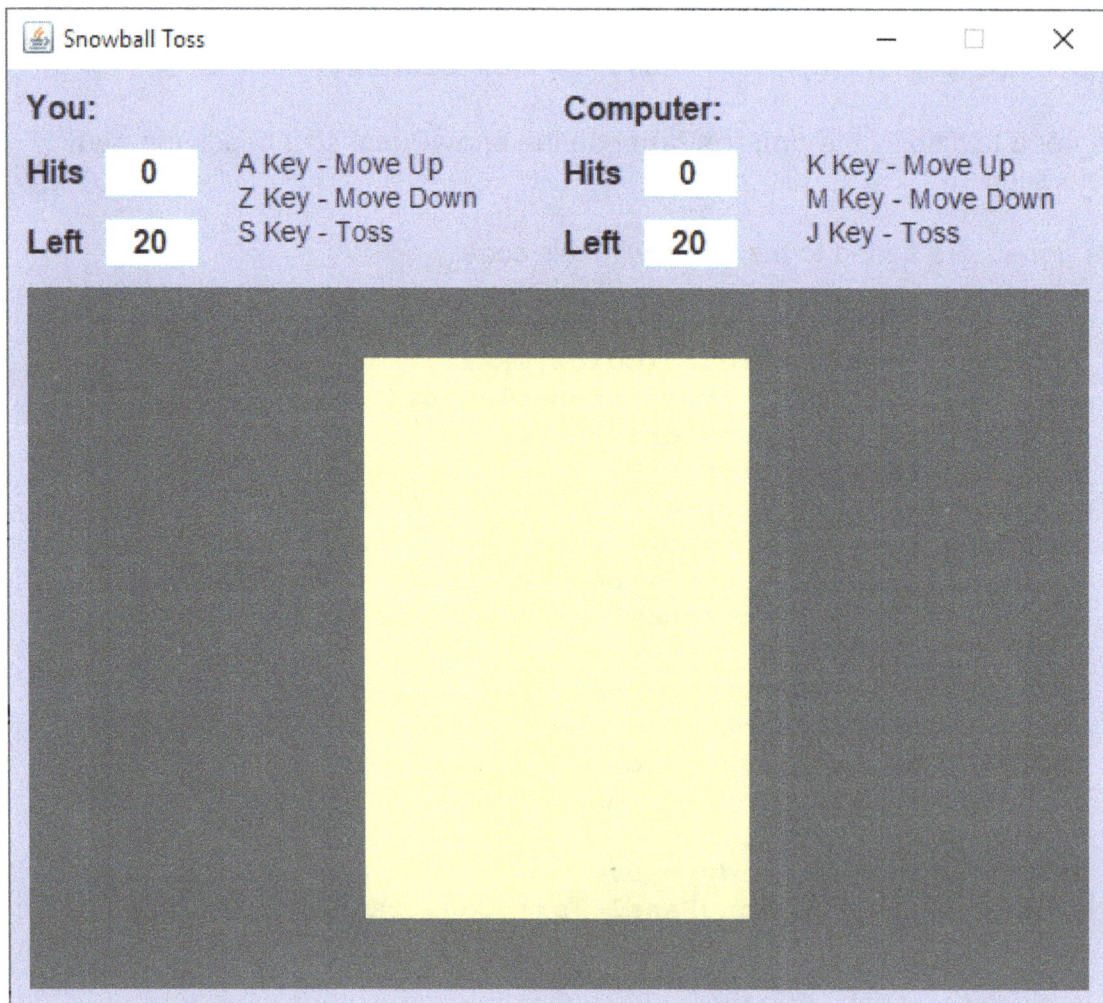

Next, we add controls to **optionsPanel** to allow selection of options.

The **GridBagLayout** for the options panel is:

	gridx = 0
gridy = 0	**playersPanel**
gridy = 1	**difficultyPanel**
gridy = 2	**okButton**

One panel (**playersPanel**) holds two radio buttons used to select the number of players. One panel (**difficultyPanel**) holds four radio buttons to select the game difficulty level, when playing against the computer. A small button (**okButton**) is used to close the options panel. We'll add all the controls (panels, radio buttons and ok button) at one time. You should have no trouble following the logic.

The control properties are:

playersPanel:

size	140, 55
title	Number of Players
background	Color(255, 255, 192)
gridx	0 (on optionsPanel)
gridy	0 (on optionsPanel)

onePlayerRadioButton:

text	One
background	Color(255, 255, 192)
selected	true
buttonGroup	playersButtons
gridx	0 (on playersPanel)
gridy	0 (on playersPanel)

twoPlayersRadioButton:

text	Two
background	Color(255, 255, 192)
buttonGroup	playersButtons
gridx	1 (on playersPanel)
gridy	0 (on playersPanel)

difficultyPanel:

size	140, 140
title	Difficulty
background	Color(255, 255, 192)
gridx	0 (on optionsPanel)
gridy	0 (on optionsPanel)

easiestRadioButton:

text	Easiest
background	Color(255, 255, 192)
selected	true
buttonGroup	difficultyButtons
gridx	0 (on difficultyPanel)
gridy	0 (on difficultyPanel)
anchor	WEST

easyRadioButton:

text	Easy
background	Color(255, 255, 192)
buttonGroup	difficultyButtons
gridx	0 (on difficultyPanel)
gridy	1 (on difficultyPanel)
anchor	WEST

hardRadioButton:

text	Hard
background	Color(255, 255, 192)
buttonGroup	difficultyButtons
gridx	0 (on difficultyPanel)
gridy	2 (on difficultyPanel)
anchor	WEST

hardestRadioButton:

text	Hardest
background	Color(255, 255, 192)
buttonGroup	difficultyButtons
gridx	0 (on difficultyPanel)
gridy	3 (on difficultyPanel)
anchor	WEST

okButton:

text	OK
gridx	0 (on optionsPanel)
gridy	2 (on optionsPanel)
insets	10, 0, 0, 0

The controls are declared using:

```
JPanel playersPanel  = new JPanel();
ButtonGroup playersButtons = new ButtonGroup();
JRadioButton onePlayerRadioButton = new JRadioButton();
JRadioButton twoPlayersRadioButton = new JRadioButton();
JPanel difficultyPanel  = new JPanel();
ButtonGroup difficultyButtons = new ButtonGroup();
JRadioButton easiestRadioButton = new JRadioButton();
JRadioButton easyRadioButton = new JRadioButton();
JRadioButton hardRadioButton = new JRadioButton();
JRadioButton hardestRadioButton = new JRadioButton();
JButton okButton = new JButton();
```

The controls are added to the various panel controls using:

```
playersPanel.setPreferredSize(new Dimension(140, 55));
playersPanel.setBorder(BorderFactory.createTitledBorder("N
umber of Players"));
playersPanel.setBackground(new Color(255, 255, 192));
playersPanel.setLayout(new GridBagLayout());
gridConstraints = new GridBagConstraints();
gridConstraints.gridx = 0;
gridConstraints.gridy = 0;
optionsPanel.add(playersPanel, gridConstraints);

onePlayerRadioButton.setText("One");
onePlayerRadioButton.setBackground(new Color(255, 255,
192));
onePlayerRadioButton.setSelected(true);
onePlayerRadioButton.setLayout(new GridBagLayout());
playersButtons.add(onePlayerRadioButton);
gridConstraints = new GridBagConstraints();
gridConstraints.gridx = 0;
gridConstraints.gridy = 0;
playersPanel.add(onePlayerRadioButton, gridConstraints);
onePlayerRadioButton.addActionListener(new ActionListener
()
{
  public void actionPerformed(ActionEvent e)
  {
    playersRadioButtonActionPerformed(e);
  }
});
```

```java
twoPlayersRadioButton.setText("Two");
twoPlayersRadioButton.setBackground(new Color(255, 255,
192));
twoPlayersRadioButton.setLayout(new GridBagLayout());
playersButtons.add(twoPlayersRadioButton);
gridConstraints = new GridBagConstraints();
gridConstraints.gridx = 1;
gridConstraints.gridy = 0;
playersPanel.add(twoPlayersRadioButton, gridConstraints);
twoPlayersRadioButton.addActionListener(new ActionListener
()
{
  public void actionPerformed(ActionEvent e)
  {
    playersRadioButtonActionPerformed(e);
  }
});

difficultyPanel.setPreferredSize(new Dimension(140, 140));
difficultyPanel.setBorder(BorderFactory.createTitledBorder
("Difficulty"));
difficultyPanel.setBackground(new Color(255, 255, 192));
difficultyPanel.setLayout(new GridBagLayout());
gridConstraints = new GridBagConstraints();
gridConstraints.gridx = 0;
gridConstraints.gridy = 1;
optionsPanel.add(difficultyPanel, gridConstraints);

easiestRadioButton.setText("Easiest");
easiestRadioButton.setBackground(new Color(255, 255,
192));
easiestRadioButton.setSelected(true);
easiestRadioButton.setLayout(new GridBagLayout());
difficultyButtons.add(easiestRadioButton);
gridConstraints = new GridBagConstraints();
gridConstraints.gridx = 0;
gridConstraints.gridy = 0;
gridConstraints.anchor = GridBagConstraints.WEST;
difficultyPanel.add(easiestRadioButton, gridConstraints);
easiestRadioButton.addActionListener(new ActionListener ()
{
  public void actionPerformed(ActionEvent e)
  {
    difficultyRadioButtonActionPerformed(e);
  }
});
```

```
easyRadioButton.setText("Easy");
easyRadioButton.setBackground(new Color(255, 255, 192));
easyRadioButton.setLayout(new GridBagLayout());
difficultyButtons.add(easyRadioButton);
gridConstraints = new GridBagConstraints();
gridConstraints.gridx = 0;
gridConstraints.gridy = 1;
gridConstraints.anchor = GridBagConstraints.WEST;
difficultyPanel.add(easyRadioButton, gridConstraints);
easyRadioButton.addActionListener(new ActionListener ()
{
  public void actionPerformed(ActionEvent e)
  {
    difficultyRadioButtonActionPerformed(e);
  }
});

hardRadioButton.setText("Hard");
hardRadioButton.setBackground(new Color(255, 255, 192));
hardRadioButton.setLayout(new GridBagLayout());
difficultyButtons.add(hardRadioButton);
gridConstraints = new GridBagConstraints();
gridConstraints.gridx = 0;
gridConstraints.gridy = 2;
gridConstraints.anchor = GridBagConstraints.WEST;
difficultyPanel.add(hardRadioButton, gridConstraints);
hardRadioButton.addActionListener(new ActionListener ()
{
  public void actionPerformed(ActionEvent e)
  {
    difficultyRadioButtonActionPerformed(e);
  }
});
```

```
hardestRadioButton.setText("Hardest");
hardestRadioButton.setBackground(new Color(255, 255,
192));
hardestRadioButton.setLayout(new GridBagLayout());
difficultyButtons.add(hardestRadioButton);
gridConstraints = new GridBagConstraints();
gridConstraints.gridx = 0;
gridConstraints.gridy = 3;
gridConstraints.anchor = GridBagConstraints.WEST;
difficultyPanel.add(hardestRadioButton, gridConstraints);
hardestRadioButton.addActionListener(new ActionListener ()
{
  public void actionPerformed(ActionEvent e)
  {
    difficultyRadioButtonActionPerformed(e);
  }
});

okButton.setText("OK");
gridConstraints = new GridBagConstraints();
gridConstraints.gridx = 0;
gridConstraints.gridy = 2;
gridConstraints.insets = new Insets(10, 0, 0, 0);
optionsPanel.add(okButton, gridConstraints);
okButton.addActionListener(new ActionListener ()
{
  public void actionPerformed(ActionEvent e)
  {
    okButtonActionPerformed(e);
  }
});
```

Each group of radio buttons and the **OK** button each have an **ActionPerformed** method. Add these empty methods to the project:

```
private void playersRadioButtonActionPerformed(ActionEvent
e)
{
}

private void
difficultyRadioButtonActionPerformed(ActionEvent e)
{
}

private void okButtonActionPerformed(ActionEvent e)
{
}
```

Save and run the project. The fully coded options panel is now seen:

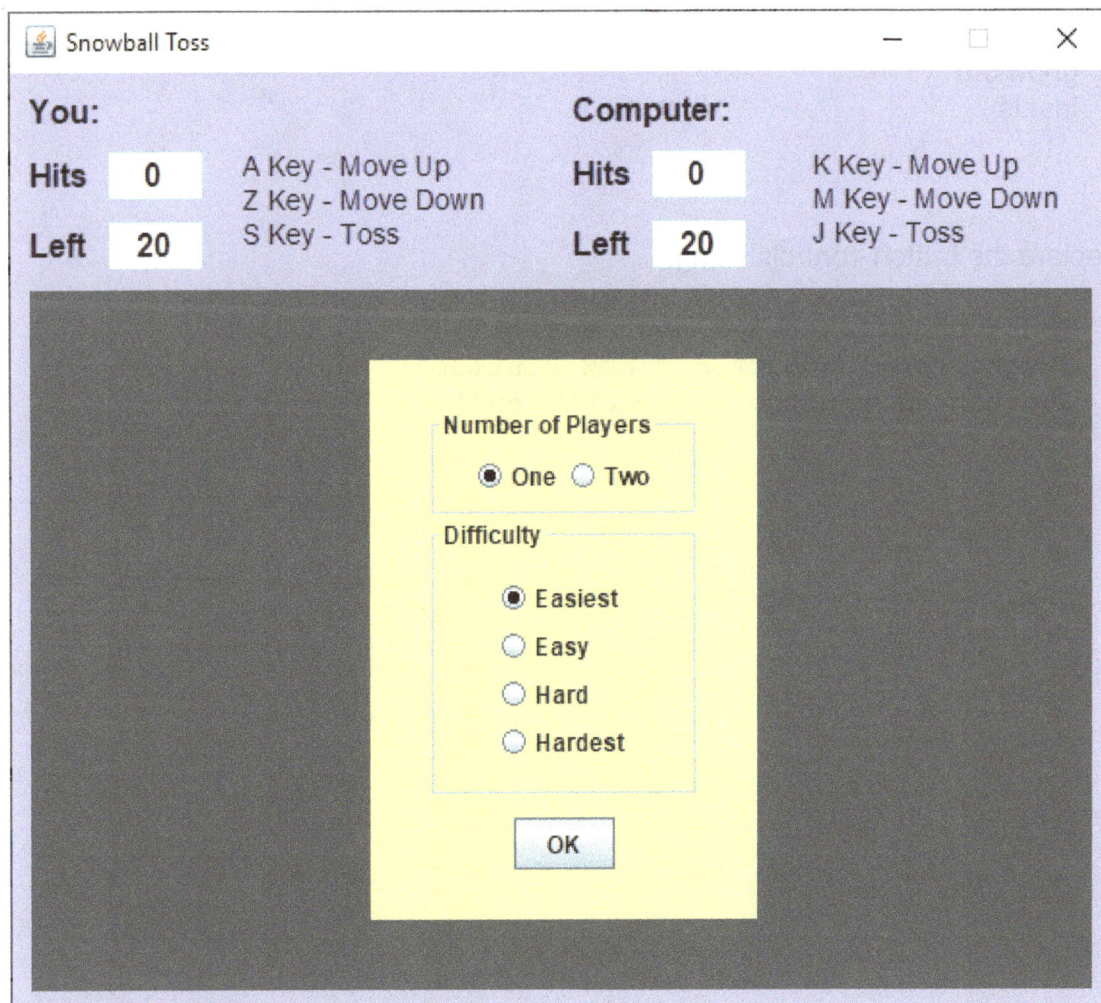

We complete the frame by adding the three button controls to the frame. The properties are:

gameButton:
text	New Game
gridx	0
gridy	4
gridwidth	2
insets	0, 10, 10, 0

optionsButton:
text	Options
gridx	2
gridy	4
insets	0, 0, 10, 0

exitButton:
text	Exit
gridx	3
gridy	4
gridwidth	2
insets	0, 0, 10, 0

Declare the button controls using:

```
JButton gameButton = new JButton();
JButton optionsButton = new JButton();
JButton exitButton = new JButton();
```

Add the button controls to the frame using this code:

```
gameButton.setText("New Game");
gridConstraints = new GridBagConstraints();
gridConstraints.gridx = 0;
gridConstraints.gridy = 4;
gridConstraints.gridwidth = 2;
gridConstraints.insets = new Insets(0, 10, 10, 0);
getContentPane().add(gameButton, gridConstraints);
gameButton.addActionListener(new ActionListener ()
{
  public void actionPerformed(ActionEvent e)
  {
    gameButtonActionPerformed(e);
  }
});

optionsButton.setText("Options");
gridConstraints = new GridBagConstraints();
gridConstraints.gridx = 2;
gridConstraints.gridy = 4;
gridConstraints.insets = new Insets(0, 0, 10, 0);
getContentPane().add(optionsButton, gridConstraints);
optionsButton.addActionListener(new ActionListener ()
{
  public void actionPerformed(ActionEvent e)
  {
    optionsButtonActionPerformed(e);
  }
});

exitButton.setText("Exit");
gridConstraints = new GridBagConstraints();
gridConstraints.gridx = 3;
gridConstraints.gridy = 4;
gridConstraints.gridwidth = 2;
gridConstraints.insets = new Insets(0, 0, 10, 0);
getContentPane().add(exitButton, gridConstraints);
exitButton.addActionListener(new ActionListener ()
{
  public void actionPerformed(ActionEvent e)
  {
    exitButtonActionPerformed(e);
  }
});
```

Each button has an **ActionPerformed** method. Add these empty methods to the code listing:

```
private void gameButtonActionPerformed(ActionEvent e)
{
}

private void optionsButtonActionPerformed(ActionEvent e)
{
}

private void exitButtonActionPerformed(ActionEvent e)
{
}
```

Run to see the completed frame:

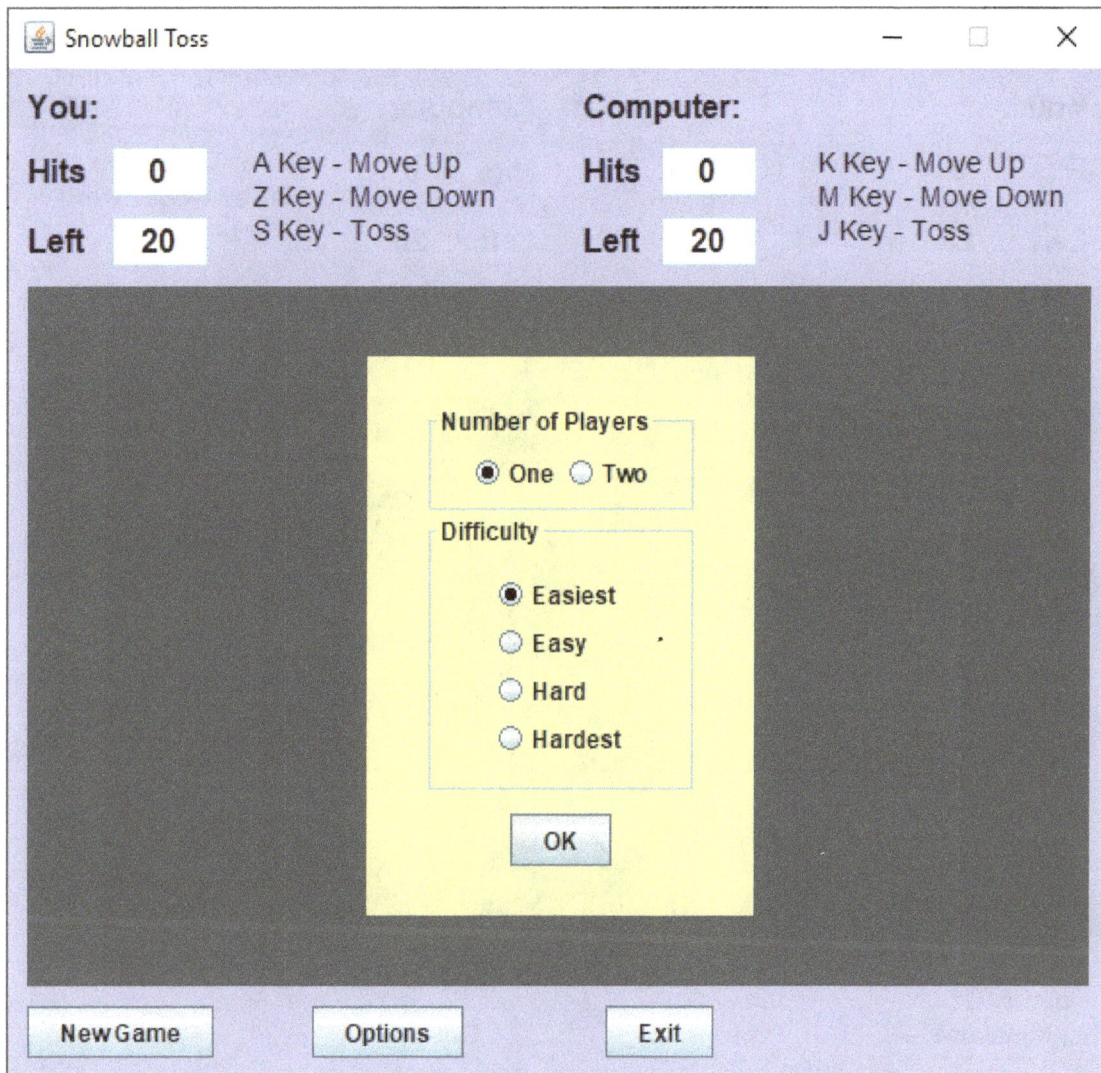

There is one slight problem. We don't want the options panel to appear initially (it shouldn't appear until the user clicks **Options**). So, add this one line in the code establishing the options panel:

```
optionsPanel.setVisible(false);
```

Run again and the frame is in the desired initial configuration (no options panel):

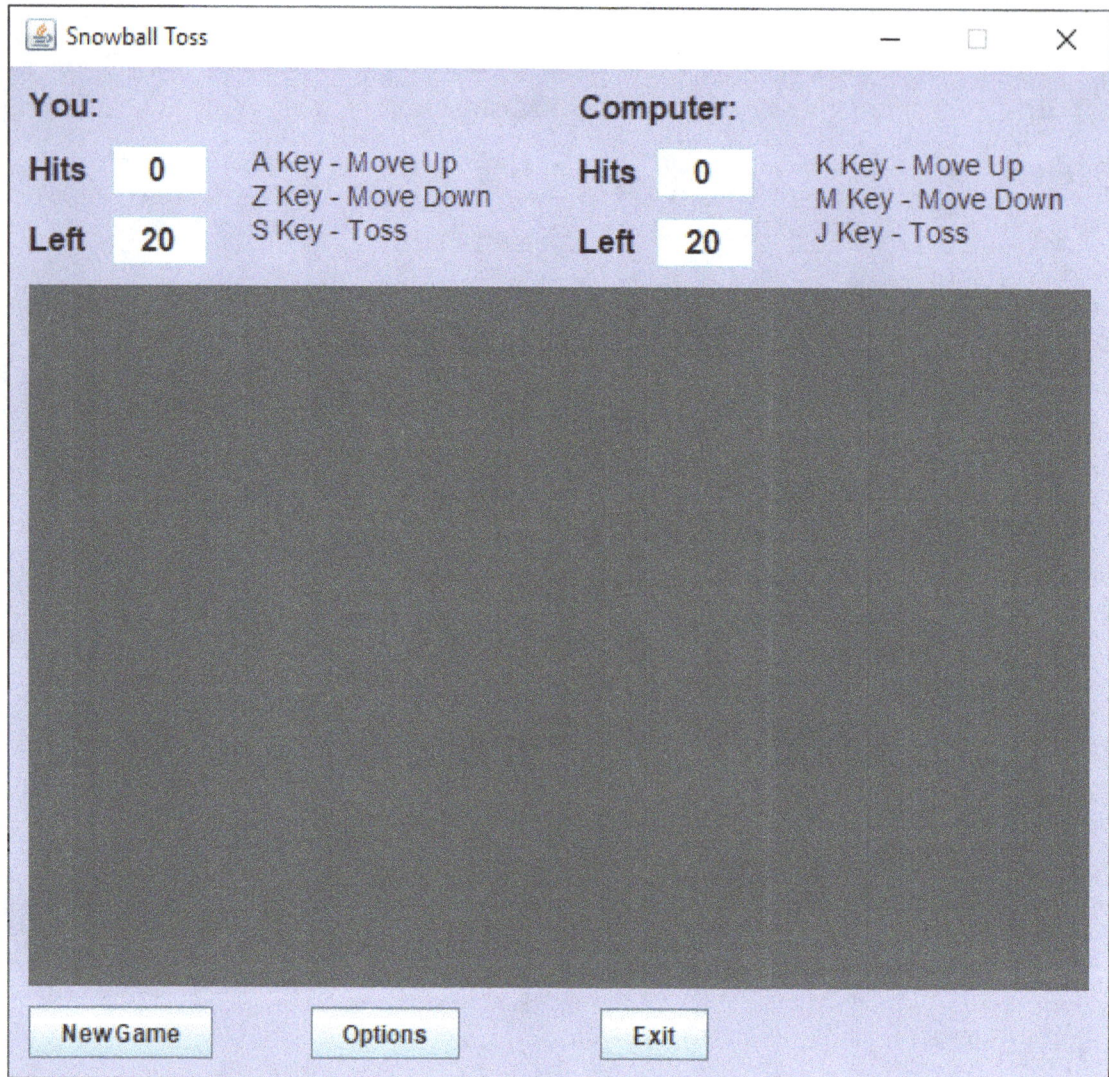

We now begin writing project code. We first write code that establishes frame status based on selected game options.

Frame Design – Choosing Options

When the game begins, a user usually chooses options (number of players and difficulty level). Based on these choices, the frame will display different information. When the user clicks the **Options** button (**optionsButton**), the following occurs:

> ➢ Disable **gameButton**.
> ➢ Disable **optionsButton**.
> ➢ Disable **exitButton**.
> ➢ Make **optionsPanel** visible.

The code for these steps goes in the **optionsButtonActionPerformed** method:

```
private void optionsButtonActionPerformed(ActionEvent e)
{
  gameButton.setEnabled(false);
  optionsButton.setEnabled(false);
  exitButton.setEnabled(false);
  optionsPanel.setVisible(true);
}
```

Add this method.

Once the options panel is displayed, the user can choose one or two players and game difficulty (if playing against the computer). We will use the **int** variable **numberPlayers** to store the number of players and the **int** variable **difficulty** to store the selected difficulty. Add these class level variable declarations to the project:

```
int numberPlayers, difficulty;
```

Add these two lines at the end of the frame constructor to initialize these variables to default values:

```
numberPlayers = 1;
difficulty = 1;
```

If the one player (**onePlayerRadioButton** button) is selected, you play against the computer and the following happens:

- ➢ Set **numberPlayers** to 1.
- ➢ Set **player1Label text** property to **You:**
- ➢ Set **player2Label text** property to **Computer:**
- ➢ Set **visible** property of **player2TextArea** to **false**
- ➢ Set **visible** property of **difficultyPanel** to **true**

If the two player (**twoPlayersRadioButton** button) is selected, you play against another person and the following happens:

- ➢ Set **numberPlayers** to 2.
- ➢ Set **player1Label text** property to **Player 1:**
- ➢ Set **player2Label text** property to **Player 2:**
- ➢ Set **visible** property of **player2TextArea** to **true**
- ➢ Set **visible** property of **difficultyPanel** to **false**

Notice game difficulty is only selected when playing against the computer (one player).

The code to implement these steps is placed in a method named
playersRadioButtonActionPerformed (which handles the **ActionPerformed**
method for both **onePlayerRadioButton** and **twoPlayersRadioButton**):

```
private void playersRadioButtonActionPerformed(ActionEvent
e)
{
  if (e.getActionCommand().equals("One"))
  {
    numberPlayers = 1;
    player1Label.setText("You:");
    player2Label.setText("Computer:");
    player2TextArea.setVisible(false);
    difficultyPanel.setVisible(true);
  }
  else
  {
    numberPlayers = 2;
    player1Label.setText("Player 1:");
    player2Label.setText("Player 2:");
    player2TextArea.setVisible(true);
    difficultyPanel.setVisible(false);
  }
}
```

Add this method to your project.

Similarly, a method named **difficultyRadioButtonActionPerformed** handles the **ActionPerformed** method for the four radio buttons in **difficultyPanel**. Based on which button is clicked, the **difficulty** variable is set:

```
private void
difficultyRadioButtonActionPerformed(ActionEvent e)
{
  String s = e.getActionCommand();
  if (s.equals("Easiest"))
    difficulty = 1;
  else if (s.equals("Easy"))
    difficulty = 2;
  else if (s.equals("Hard"))
    difficulty = 3;
  else if (s.equals("Hardest"))
    difficulty = 4;
}
```

Add this method to your project.

Once the user has selected options, he clicks the **OK** button (**okButton**) to close out the options panel. The code in the **okButtonActionPerformed** method is just the reverse of the code in the optionsButtonActionPerformed method (reversing the boolean properties):

```
private void okButtonActionPerformed(ActionEvent e)
{
  gameButton.setEnabled(true);
  optionsButton.setEnabled(true);
  exitButton.setEnabled(true);
  optionsPanel.setVisible(false);
}
```

Add this final options method to your project. At this point, game play can begin.

Save and run the project. The game screen will appear with default values (one player, easiest difficulty). Click **Options** to make the options panel appear:

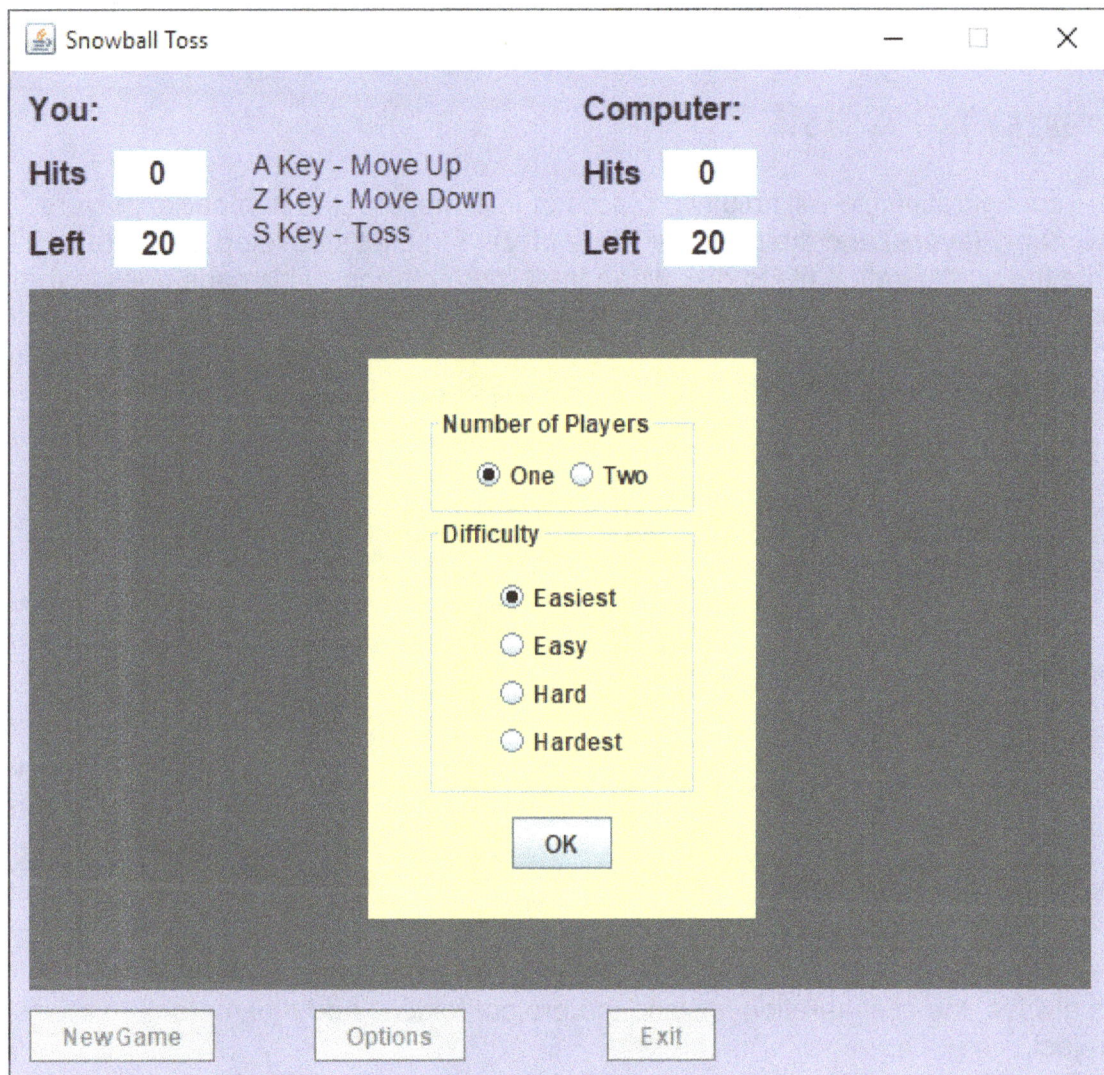

Changing the difficulty will not change the form appearance. Changing the number of players will. Choose two players – the header information should change to reflect two players and the **Difficulty** panel will disappear. Make sure everything works as planned.

Each time you play the game, you would like the options you used the last time you played the game to be "pre-selected." A configuration file can handle this task.

Code Design – Configuration File

Since we will be writing/reading files, we need to add this import statement at the top of the code window:

```
using System.IO;
```

The configuration file will hold two pieces of information: the number of players (**numberPlayers**) and the difficulty (**difficulty**). First, let's develop the code to write the configuration file to disk when the program ends. This code goes in the **exitForm** method (all but the last line is new code):

```
private void exitForm(WindowEvent evt)
{
  try
  {
    PrintWriter outputFile = new PrintWriter(new
BufferedWriter(new FileWriter("snowball.ini")));
    outputFile.println(numberPlayers);
    outputFile.println(difficulty);
    outputFile.flush();
    outputFile.close();
  }
  catch (Exception ex)
  {
  }
  System.exit(0);
}
```

As always, the configuration file is in the project folder. Add this method to your project.

Add this code to the **exitButtonActionPerformed** method, so we can stop the project and write the file:

```
private void exitButtonActionPerformed(ActionEvent e)
{
  exitForm(null);
}
```

The configuration file is opened and read in at the end of the frame constructor method. Based on the values read, we then simulate clicks on the appropriate radio buttons to choose options. The code that opens the configuration file and chooses the appropriate radio buttons is (changes are shaded):

```
try
{
  BufferedReader inputFile = new BufferedReader(new
FileReader("snowball.ini"));
  numberPlayers =
Integer.valueOf(inputFile.readLine()).intValue();
  difficulty =
Integer.valueOf(inputFile.readLine()).intValue();
  inputFile.close();
}
catch (Exception ex)
{
  numberPlayers = 1;
  difficulty = 1;
}
if (difficulty == 1)
  easiestRadioButton.doClick();
else if (difficulty == 2)
  easyRadioButton.doClick();
else if (difficulty == 3)
  hardRadioButton.doClick();
else
  hardestRadioButton.doClick();
if (numberPlayers == 1)
  onePlayerRadioButton.doClick();
else
  twoPlayersRadioButton.doClick();
```

Notice we use default values if the configuration file cannot be opened. We choose the difficulty option first, since this option is not enabled if the two player optioned is selected.

Save and run the project. Choose some options. Make sure the form is properly configured after choosing the options. Stop the project – click **Exit** or click the **X** in the upper right corner of the form. Run the project again to make sure your last set of selected options is still selected and the form looks correct. Before stopping the program for the last time, make sure the **Two Player** option is selected. We will use this for most of our design work.

We're now ready to start programming the graphics features of the snowball game – moving the tossers up and down the screen, throwing snowballs, and moving the zombie snowmen across the screen.

Animation with Java

Programming animated games in Java requires a specific set of skills. We need to know how to develop a graphic image, how to move (animate) that image and how to see if one image collides with another image. We also want to add sounds to our games. As we build the snowball toss game, we will discuss these new skills. We start with **animation**.

Animating an image in a graphic object involves two steps: (1) determine the image location, and (2) move the image to that location. The image region is rectangular. We use the Java **Rectangle2D** shape to specify such regions. The properties for this shape we will use are:

x	x-coordinate of the upper-left corner of the rectangle
y	y-coordinate of the upper-left corner of the rectangle
height	Width of the rectangle
width	Height of the rectangle

The **x** and **y** values are relative to the graphics object. A diagram shows everything:

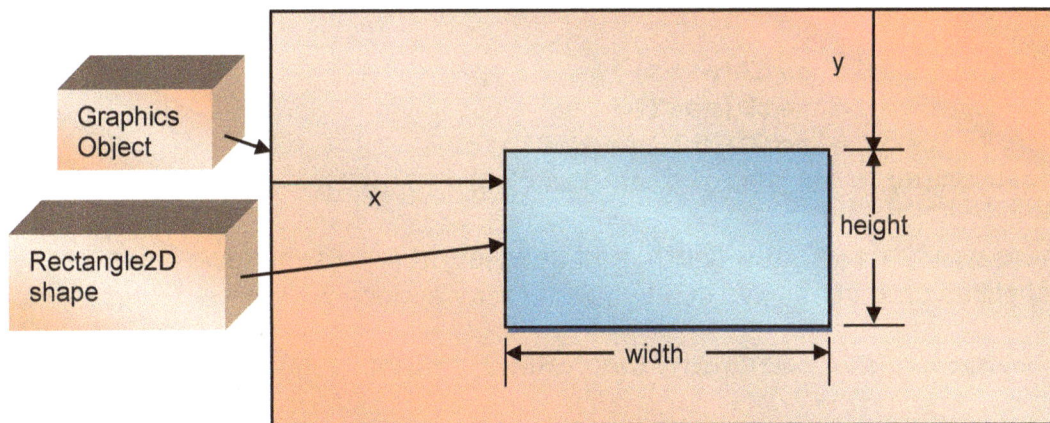

x, **y**, **width** and **height** can be changed at run-time.

There are two steps involved in creating a **rectangle shape**. We first declare the structure using the standard statement:

```
Rectangle2D.Double myRectangle;
```

Placement of this statement depends on scope. Place it in a method for method level scope. Place it with other class level declarations for class level scope. Once declared, the structure is created using the **Rectangle2D** constructor:

```
myRectangle = new Rectangle2D.Double(x, y, width, height);
```

where **x**, **y**, **width** and **height** are the desired integer measurements (in pixels).

Once established, the x, y, width and height properties can be retrieved using:

```
myRectangle.getX();
myRectangle.getY();
myRectangle.getWidth();
mRectangle.getHeight();
```

You can move and resize the rectangle in code, by changing any of four properties using:

```
myRectangle.setX(newX);
myRectangle.setY(newY);
myRectangle.setWidth(newWidth);
mRectangle.setHeight(newHeight);
```

where **newX**, **newY**, **newWidth**, and **newHeight** represent new values for the respective properties. We can set all of these at once with the **setRect** method:

```
myRectangle.setRect(newX, newY, newWidth, newHeight);
```

An image is drawn to a graphics object using the **drawImage** graphics method. Before using **drawImage**, you need two things: a **Graphics2D** object (**g2D**) to draw to and an **Image** object to draw. In our project, the graphics object is available in the **SnowPanel** class **paintComponent** method. The **Image** object is usually loaded from a graphics file.

The **drawImage** method is:

```
g2D.DrawImage(myImage, myRectangle.getX(),
myRectangle.getY(), null);
```

where **myRectangle** is a rectangle shape that positions **myImage** within **g2D**. **myRectangle** is specified by **x** the horizontal position, **y** the vertical position, the width **w** and height **h**:

```
myRectangle = new Rectangle2D.Double(x, y, w, h);
```

The width and height is the image size given by:

```
myImage.getWidth(null);
myImage.getHeight(null);
```

A picture illustrates what's going on with **drawImage**:

g2D (after drawing)

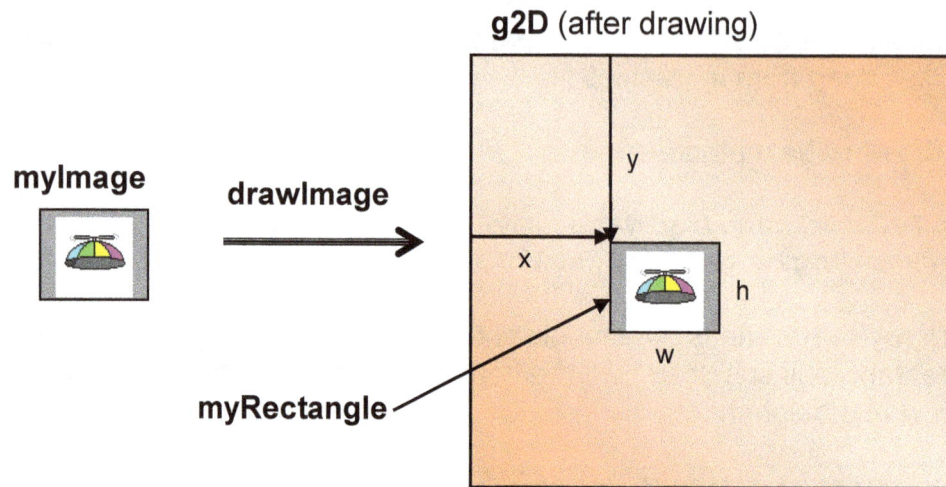

Note how the transfer of the rectangular region occurs. Successive image transfers gives the impression of motion, or animation

With our newly-gained knowledge of the **Rectangle2D** shape and the **drawImage** graphics method, we can summarize the steps needed to move (or animate) an image (**myImage**) in a graphics object named **g2D**. Assume the image is currently at location (**x, y**) and is **w** by **h** in size. Assume we want to move the image to a new location (**x + dx**, **y + dy**). The steps are:

➢ Update **Rectangle2D** structure to new location:

```
myRectangle.setRect(myRectangle.getX() + dx,
myRectangle.getY() + dy, myRectangle.getWidth(),
myRectangle.getHeight());
```

➢ Draw image at new location:

```
g2D.DrawImage(myImage, myRectangle.getX(),
myRectangle.getY(), null);
```

Successive application of each of these steps for each image in our graphics region results in a nice smooth animated motion.

We're ready to start writing code to animate our snowball toss game, but first we need to answer one question that might be lingering. In describing the **drawImage** method, we said the images we use are loaded from files. Your question might be – where do these files come from? The answer is you either need to find them from some source (the Internet is a good place to look) or create them yourself.

To create animation images, you could use a tool like the **Paint** program that ships with Windows. Draw your picture and save it as a bitmap file. Or you could use one of many available commercial paintbrush programs. In the snowball toss game, we use another tool to develop our images – a program called **IconEdit**.

Drawing Images with IconEdit

Icons are used in Windows Explorer, to represent programs in the Programs menu, to represent programs on the desktop and to identify an application removal tool. Icons are used throughout projects. We can create our own icons and use them. In fact, we do that in the Appendix to these notes, where we discuss distributing a Java project.

For now, we just want to look at a tool used to create such icons (a file with an **ico** extension) and use it to create the images we need for our snowball toss program. Icons are simply special cases of bitmap files that are 32 bits by 32 bits in size. Their size makes them very useful in games such as this.

A few years ago, *PC Magazine* offered a free utility called **IconEdit** that allows you to design and save icons. Included with these notes are this program and other files (directory **\HomeJava\HomeJava Projects\IconEdit**). To run **IconEdit**, click **Start** on the Windows task bar, and then click **Run**. Find the **IconEdit.exe** program (use **Browse** mode) and run it. You can also establish a shortcut to start **IconEdit** from your desktop, if desired. The following Editor window will appear when you choose the **New** option under the **File** menu:

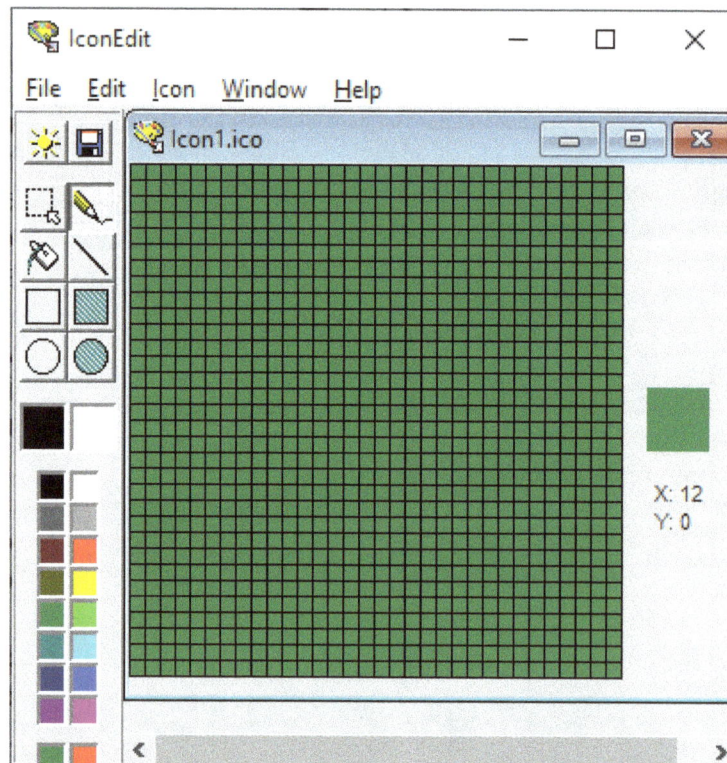

The basic idea of **IconEdit** is to draw an icon in the large 32 x 32 grid displayed. You can draw single points, lines, open rectangles and ovals, and filled rectangles and ovals. Various colors are available with simple mouse clicks. The displayed green color is a transparent color. As you draw in the large grid, the small grid to the right displays your finished icon. Once completed, the icon file can be saved for attaching to a form or use within an application.

We won't go into a lot of detail on using the **IconEdit** program here - I just want you to know it exists and can be used to create and save icon files. Its use is fairly intuitive. Consult the help (click **Help** in the menu) that comes with the program for details. Or, more specific usage details are given in the Appendix. One point you might like to ponder is that an application like this could easily be built with Java.

All graphics used in the snowball toss game were created using **IconEdit**. These files are included in the **\HomeJava\HomeJava Projects\SnowballToss**folder. Let's look at the files used to represent one of the two players. Start **IconEdit**. Choose **Open** under the **File** menu. An **Open Icon** dialog will appear. Navigate to the above folder. There are two files used to represent the players – **player1.ico** and **player2.ico**. Open **player1.ico** as shown:

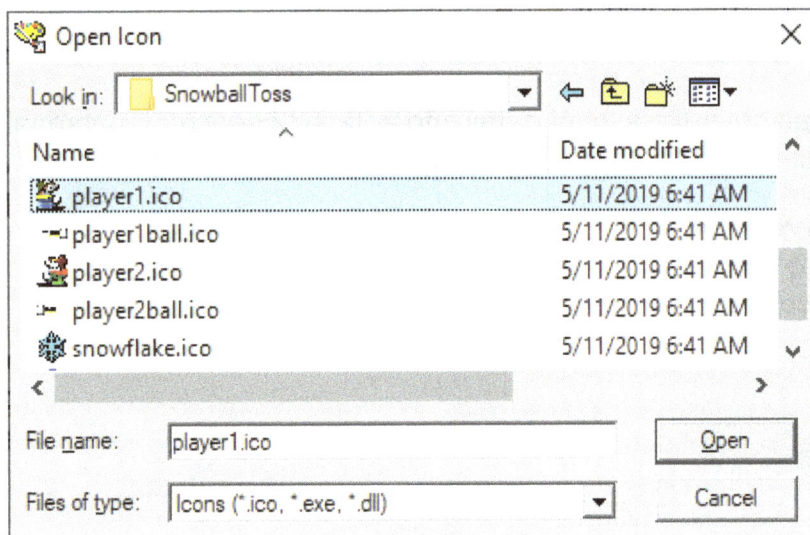

This cute little guy will appear:

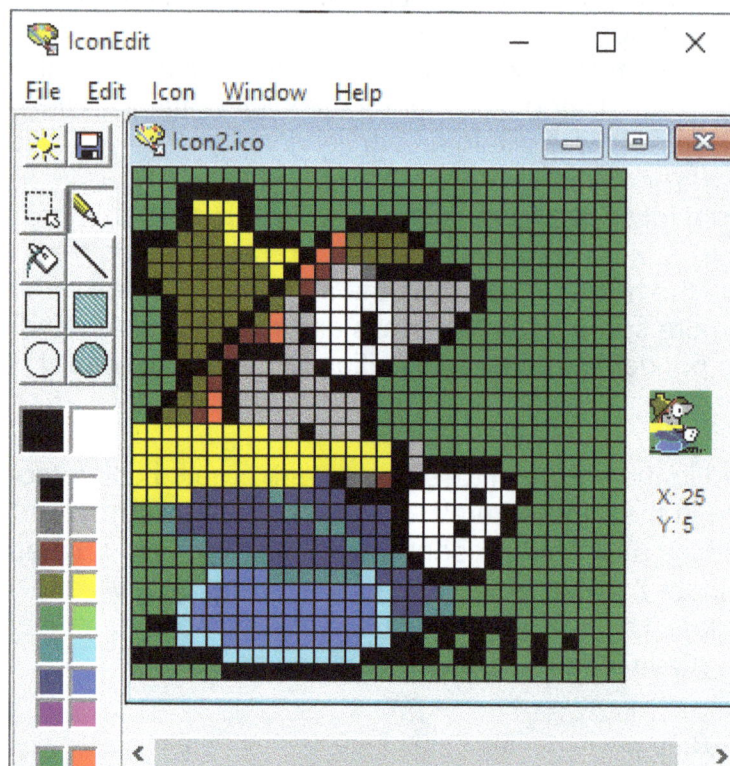

Notice you can get quite a lot of detail into a 32 x 32 space. I, personally, have no artistic talent. Someone drew all the graphics in this program for me.

Open the second player file if you like or look ahead at the graphics to represent snowmen and snowballs. Right now, let's look at how to display these little guys in the panel control on our form.

Displaying Icons with Java

The usual Java code to establish an **Image** object (**myImage**) is:

```
myImage = new ImageIcon(imageFile).getImage();
```

where **imageFile** is the file holding the image. We have one big problem – even though we have an object named **ImageIcon**, we cannot open a Windows icon file (**ico** file) using this code. Our we out of luck? Of course not.

A quick search of the Internet finds many sites offering Java code that opens an **ico** file as an **Image** object. We include one such offering with these notes (found from the **SourceForge** website). The zip file (current version is **aclibico-2.1.zip**) is in the **\HomeJava\HomeJava Projects** folder. Extract (unzip) the files to a directory on your computer (I used **c:\icofiles**). Many files will be written to your computer, including documentation and source files. The actual jar files needed (**aclibico-2.1.jar** and **log4j-1.2.8.jar**) will be in the **2.1** subfolder. The second jar file is needed for messaging by the icon reader.

You need to make your project aware you will be using these jar files. We'll give the steps using NetBeans. If you are using another IDE, consult its documentation to see how to add jar files to a project. Make sure **SnowballToss** is the active project.

In the menu, choose **Tools**, then **Libaries** to see:

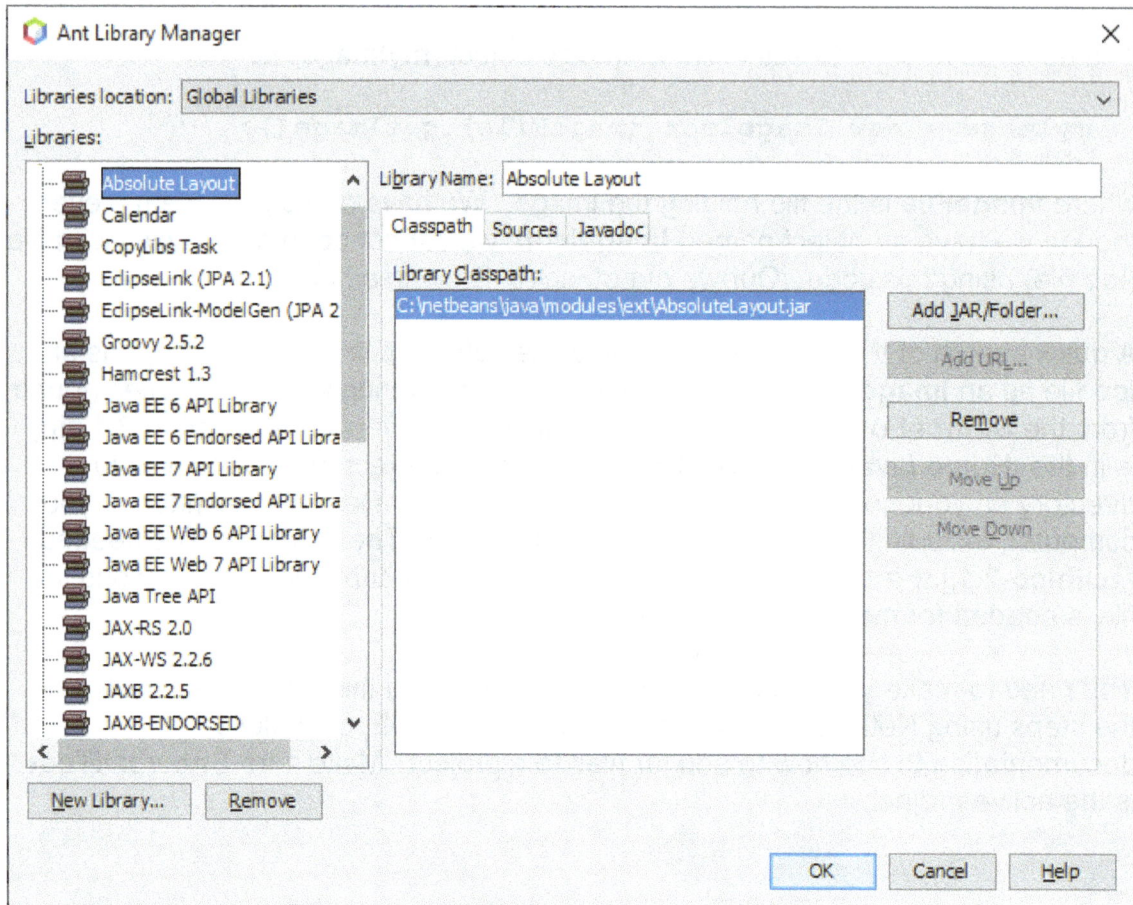

Click **New Library** and name it **IcoReader**:

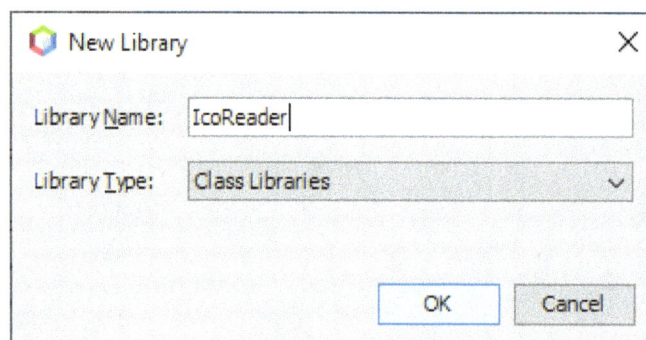

Click **OK** to accept name. In next window, click **Add JAR/Folder**. Navigate to jar location:

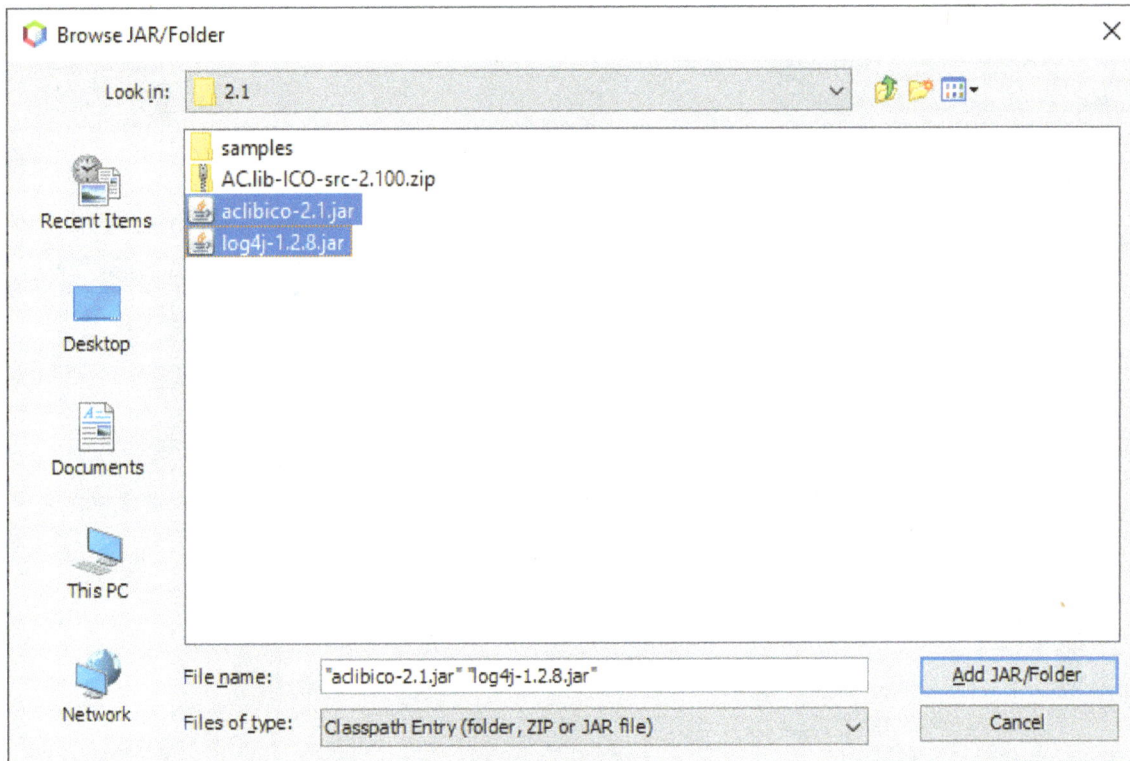

Select both jar files and click **Add JAR/Folder**.

Library is now there:

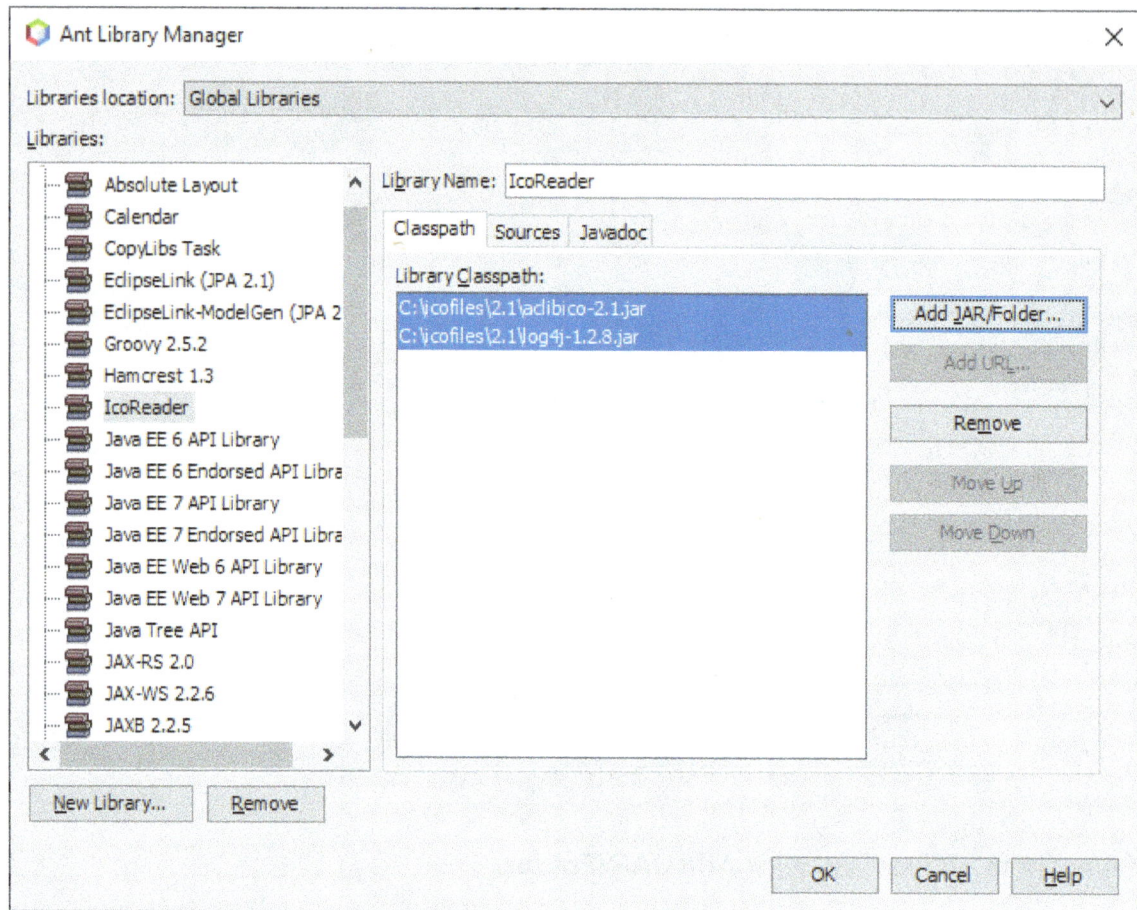

The **IcoReader** library can now be added to any project that needs it. Click **OK**.

To add this to your project, follow these steps:

In file view area, right-click the project name (**SnowballToss**) and click **Properties**. In the properties window, choose the **Libraries** category:

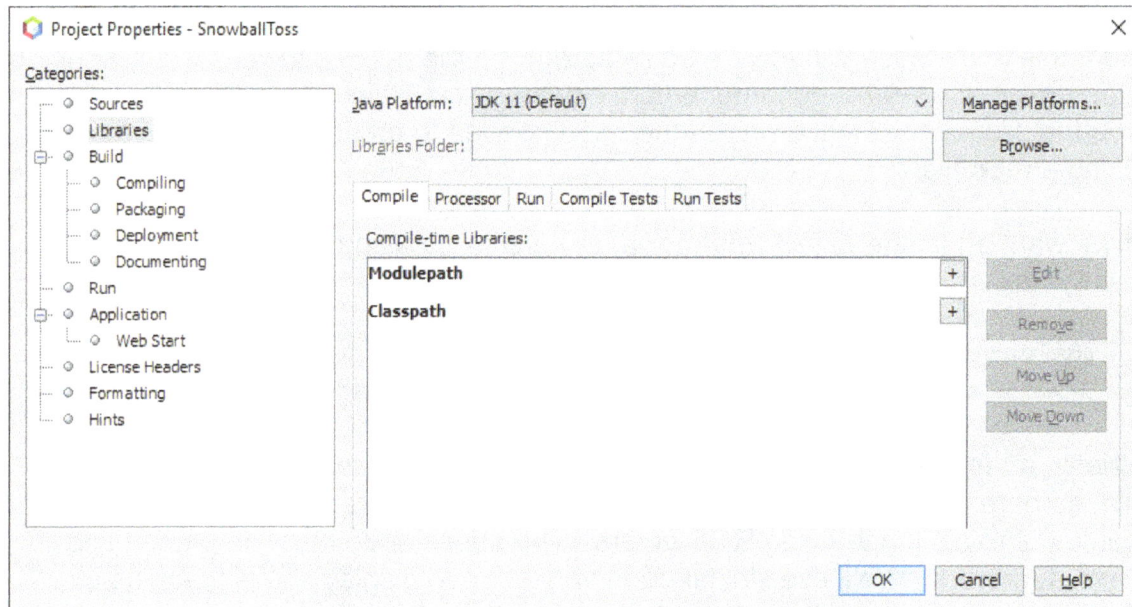

Click the **+** sign next to **Classpath** and choose **Add Library** to see

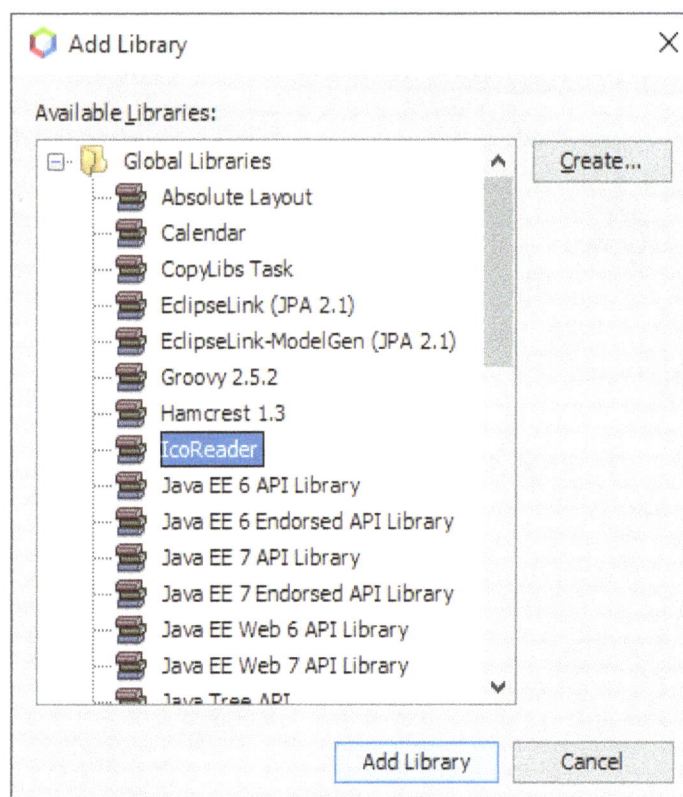

Choose **IcoReader**, then click **Add Library**. Click **OK** when returned to the **Properties** window. The file reading code can now be used in the snowball toss project with the addition of this **import** statement:

```
import com.ctreber.aclib.image.ico.ICOFile;
```

Add this to the code window. Also included with the download is a documentation file. Like many sets of documentation, however, it is difficult to read. We save you that trouble and just give you the code needed to create an **Image** object using an **ico** file.

If we want an Image object (**myImage**) to be created using an **ico** file (**icoFile**), the syntax is:

```
myImage = new
ICOFile(icoFile).getDescriptor(0).getImageRGB();
```

Briefly, an **ico** file may have more than one icon. We assume only one icon per file, so here we read the file, get the **descriptor** for the first icon (element 0) and convert it to an image using **RGB** colors. The above code must be placed in a **try/catch** block. We'll use similar code very soon to display some graphics.

Code Design – Sprite Class

We will have several images moving around in this project (players, snowballs, snowmen). This is a good place to try our object-oriented programming skills introduced in Chapter 9. We will build a class named **Sprite** to represent the two player objects.

Review the steps to add a class file to your Java project in Chapter 7. Name the added file **Sprite.java**. Delete the default code. Type these lines in the file:

```
package snowballtoss;
public class Sprite
{

}
```

We will be doing drawing with our class, so add these import statements:

```
import java.awt.geom.*;
import java.awt.*;
```

We will use three properties to describe a **Sprite** object – **image** (**Image** displayed), **rectangle** (**Rectangle2D.Double** describing size and location), and **isVisible** (**boolean** type saying whether object is visible). Add these declarations to the file, initializing **isVisible** to **false**: The file should look like this:

```
package snowballtoss;
import java.awt.geom.*;
import java.awt.*;

public class Sprite
{
  public Image image;
  public Rectangle2D.Double rectangle;
  public boolean isVisible = false;
}
```

We want to extend our class description by adding some **methods** to help with the animation task. Class methods allow objects to perform certain tasks. We will write two methods for our **Sprite** object, one that places it on a graphics object and one that moves it to a new location. These methods are added to the class description exactly like general methods are added to a frame's code file. To add a method to a class description, you select a name and a type of information the method will return (if there is any returned value). Also determine any needed arguments for the method.

The method **draw** positions a **Sprite** object into a graphics object named **g2D** (passed as an argument):

```
public void draw(Graphics2D g2D)
{
  g2D.drawImage(this.image, (int) this.rectangle.getX(),
(int) this.rectangle.getY(), null);
}
```

Note the use of the keyword **this** to refer to the current object. Once the object is placed on **g2D**.

The method **move** moves a **Sprite** object to a new location. The required arguments are **dx**, the change in **x** location and **dy**, the change in **y** location:

```
public void move(int dx, int dy)
{
  this.rectangle.setRect(this.rectangle.getX() + dx,
this.rectangle.getY() + dy, this.rectangle.getWidth(),
this.rectangle.getHeight());
}
```

This code updates the **Sprite** object location.

Add these methods (**draw**, **move**) to the **Sprite** class file to make the final version look like this:

```
package snowballtoss;
import java.awt.geom.*;
import java.awt.*;

public class Sprite
{
  public Image image;
  public Rectangle2D.Double rectangle;
  public boolean isVisible = false;

  public void draw(Graphics2D g2D)
  {
    g2D.drawImage(this.image, (int) this.rectangle.getX(),
(int) this.rectangle.getY(), null);
  }

  public void move(int dx, int dy)
  {
    this.rectangle.setRect(this.rectangle.getX() + dx,
this.rectangle.getY() + dy, this.rectangle.getWidth(),
this.rectangle.getHeight());
  }
}
```

With this class, a **Sprite** object is created with:

```
Sprite mySprite;
```

It is constructed with:

```
mySprite = new Sprite();
```

Once constructed, the **image** property can be set using the **ICOFile** method and the **rectangle** property equated to a **Rectangle2D** shape.

The **Sprite** object is drawn in a graphics object (**g2D**) using:

```
mySprite.draw(g2D);
```

It is moved using:

```
mySprite.move(dx, dy);
```

where **dx** is how much you want to move the object horizontally and **dy** how much you want to move the object vertically.

At long last, we have all the background needed to draw something on the panel control (**snowPanel**) where we play the snowball toss game.

Code Design – Start/Stop Game

We'll now write the code to start and stop the game. We first define some class level variables to play and control the game. Return to the **SnowballToss.java** file. Add these declarations to the project:

```
static Sprite player1, player2;
int player1Hits, player2Hits, player1Left, player2Left;
final int maximumBalls = 20;
```

Two **Sprite** objects (**player1** and **player2**) represent the two 'tossers'. We give them the **static** preface anticipating their need in the panel **paintComponent** method. **player1Hits** and **player2Hits** will keep track of how many successful snowball tosses each player has. **player1Left** and **player2Left** keep track of how many snowballs each player still has. A constant **maximumBalls** (you can change this if you want) sets the number of snowballs a player starts with.

We add some code to the end of the frame constructor to initialize each of these variables. The added code is:

```
player1Left = maximumBalls;
player2Left = maximumBalls;
player1LeftTextField.setText(String.valueOf(player1Left));
player2LeftTextField.setText(String.valueOf(player2Left));

// create sprites
player1 = new Sprite();
player2 = new Sprite();
// read in icon files and sounds
try
{
  player1.image = new
ICOFile("player1.ico").getDescriptor(0).getImageRGB();
  player2.image = new
ICOFile("player2.ico").getDescriptor(0).getImageRGB();
}
catch (Exception ex)
{
  // can print error message if desired
}
```

Note the code to create the two **Sprite** objects and initialize the **image** properties. Copy the **player1.ico** and **player2.ico** graphics files into your project folder or this code will not work. Also, make sure you have this import statement in your project to use the icon reading code:

```
import com.ctreber.aclib.image.ico.ICOFile;
```

At this point, the user can click **New Game** (**gameButton**) to start a game. The following preliminary steps should happen (more steps will be added later):

> ➢ Change **gameButton text** property to **Stop Game**.
> ➢ Disable **optionsButton**.
> ➢ Disable **exitButton**.
> ➢ Reset **player1Hits** and **player2Hits** to **0**.
> ➢ Reset **player1Left** and **player2Left** to **maximumBalls**.
> ➢ Place **player1** and **player2** objects in initial positions.
> ➢ Set **player1** and **player2** objects **isVisible** property to **true**.
> ➢ Repaint **snowPanel**.

The code behind these steps is straightforward. The **player1** object will be centered vertically in **snowPanel** near the left edge. The **player2** object will be centered vertically near the right edge.

This same button (**gameButton**) is used to stop a game. When a user clicks the button (when **Stop Game** is displayed), the following should happen:

> ➢ Set **player1** and **player2** objects **isVisible** property to **false**.
> ➢ Change **gameButton text** property to **Start Game**.
> ➢ Enable **optionsButton**.
> ➢ Enable **exitButton**.
> ➢ Write **Game Over** message.
> ➢ Repaint **snowPanel**.

The code for all these steps is placed in the **gameButtonActionPerformed** method. That code is:

```
private void gameButtonActionPerformed(ActionEvent e)
{
  if (gameButton.getText().equals("New Game"))
  {
    gameButton.setText("Stop Game");
    optionsButton.setEnabled(false);
    exitButton.setEnabled(false);
    player1Hits = 0;
    player2Hits = 0;
    player1HitsTextField.setText("0");
    player2HitsTextField.setText("0");
    player1Left = maximumBalls;
    player2Left = maximumBalls;

player1LeftTextField.setText(String.valueOf(player1Left));

player2LeftTextField.setText(String.valueOf(player2Left));
    player1.rectangle = new Rectangle2D.Double(5, 0.5 *
snowPanel.getHeight() - 0.5 *
player1.image.getHeight(null),
player1.image.getWidth(null),
player1.image.getHeight(null));
    player2.rectangle = new
Rectangle2D.Double(snowPanel.getWidth() -
player2.image.getWidth(null) - 5, 0.5 *
snowPanel.getHeight() - 0.5 *
player2.image.getHeight(null),
player2.image.getWidth(null),
player2.image.getHeight(null));
    player1.isVisible = true;
    player2.isVisible = true;
    snowPanel.repaint();
  }
  else
  {
    player1.isVisible = false;
    player2.isVisible = false;
    gameButton.setText("New Game");
    optionsButton.setEnabled(true);
    exitButton.setEnabled(true);
    snowPanel.repaint();
  }
}
```

Add this method to your project. Use of the Rectangle2D object necessitates addition of this import statement:

```
import java.awt.geom.*;
```

You may wonder where the code to actually draw the two players and the '**Game Over**' message is. That goes in the snow panel **paintComponent** method.

Currently, the **SnowPanel paintComponent** method has a single line, one to repaint **optionsPanel**:

```
class SnowPanel extends JPanel
{
  public void paintComponent(Graphics g)
  {
    Graphics2D g2D = (Graphics2D) g;
    super.paintComponent(g2D);

    SnowballToss.optionsPanel.repaint();

    g2D.dispose();
  }
}
```

We only want the options panel to be repainted when it is displayed. When the game is being played, we want graphics elements to be drawn and when the game is stopped, we want the 'Game Over' message to appear. We will use the state/status of the **gameButton** to tell us which of three modes we are in: game being played, game stopped, options being selected. So, a first step is to add a static preface to the declaration for that button:

```
static JButton gameButton = new JButton();
```

Now, here's the logic. If **gameButton** says '**Stop Game**', the game is being played and we want to draw graphics elements. If the **gameButton** says '**New Game**' and is enabled, we are stopped and want to display **Game Over**. If the **gameButton** says '**New Game**' and is disabled, we are selecting options. The code that implements this logic is (changes are shaded):

```
class SnowPanel extends JPanel
{
  public void paintComponent(Graphics g)
  {
    Graphics2D g2D = (Graphics2D) g;
    super.paintComponent(g2D);

    if (SnowballToss.gameButton.getText().equals("Stop
Game"))
    {
      SnowballToss.player1.draw(g2D);
      SnowballToss.player2.draw(g2D);
    }
    else
    {
      if (SnowballToss.gameButton.isEnabled())
      {
        g2D.setFont(new Font("Arial", Font.BOLD, 36));
        g2D.setPaint(Color.YELLOW);
        g2D.drawString("Game Over", 180, 180);
      }
      else
      {
        SnowballToss.optionsPanel.repaint();
      }
    }
    g2D.dispose();
  }
}
```

The positioning of the **Game Over** message was obtained with trial and error.

Save and run the project. You will see the **Game Over** message. At this point, you have the option to start a new game, change options or exit.

mmkmkkmmkk

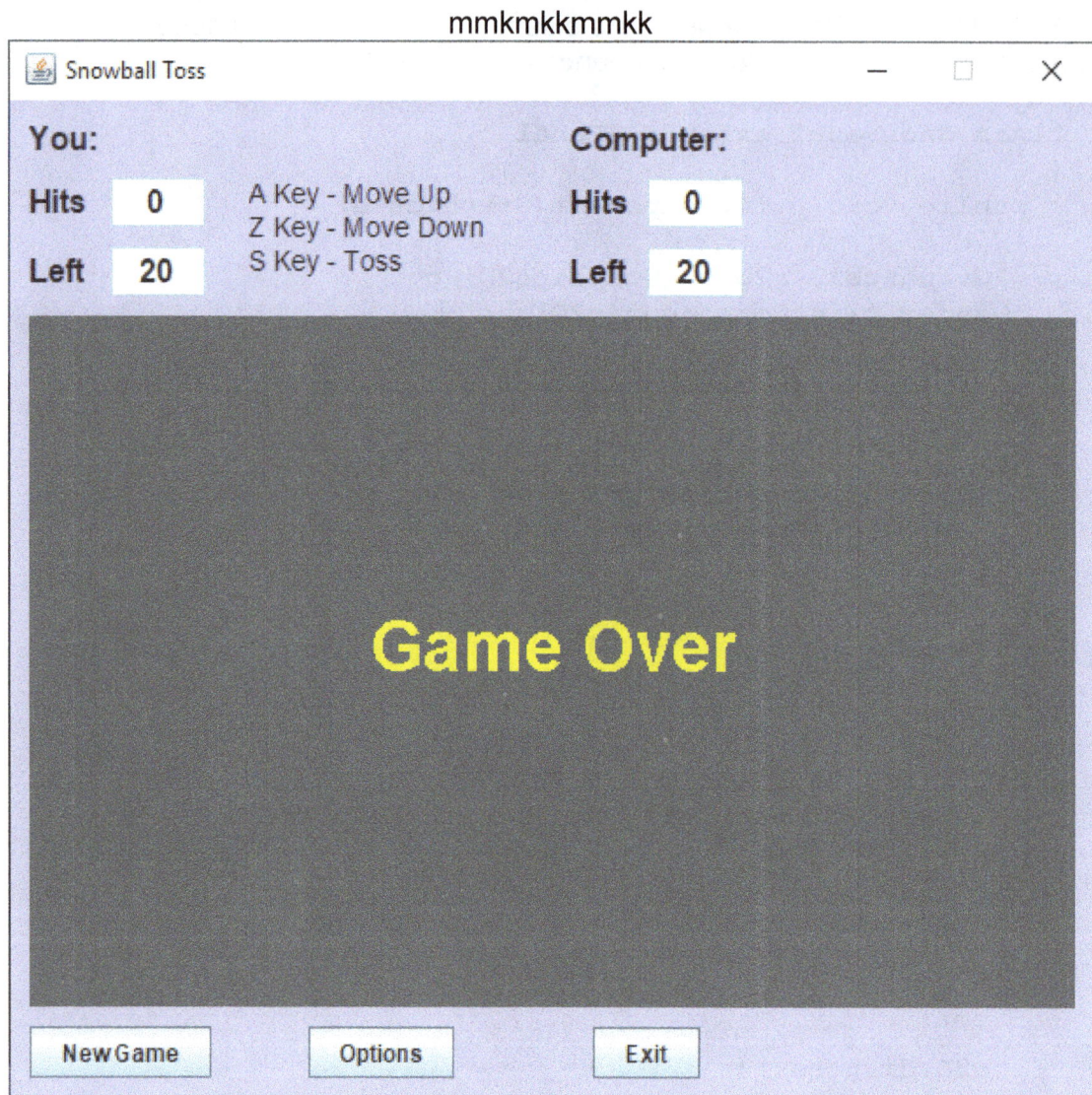

You may notice when you run the project that the icon reader code prints out a bunch of messages into your IDE's output window. There's probably a way to turn this off, but I didn't look into it.

Click **New Game** and the two guys should appear:

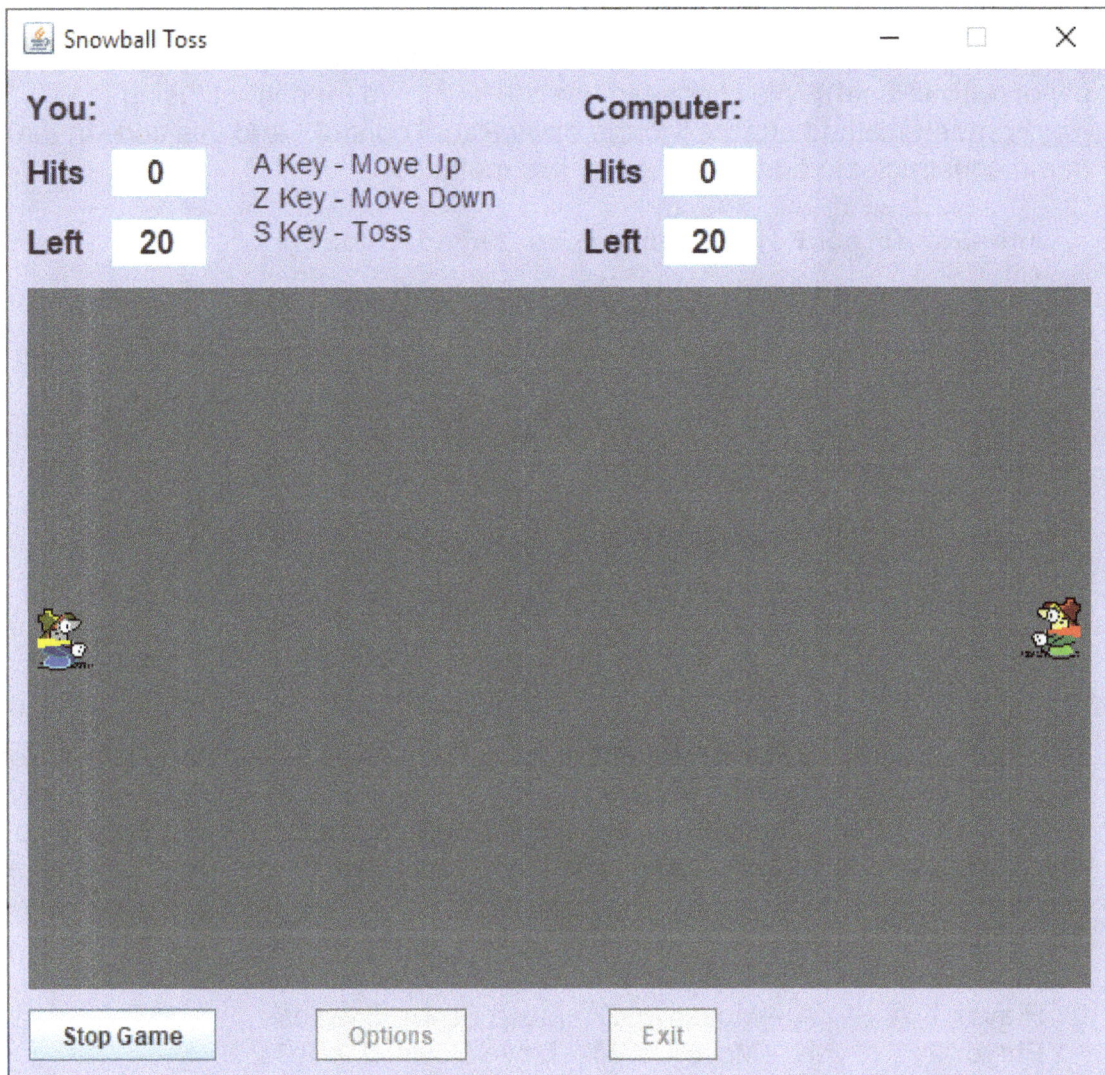

The game is ready to play – once we add the capability of moving the guys and throwing snowballs. It took a lot of work to get this far. We had a lot of new information to learn about animation. Things should progress a little faster from now on.

Before leaving, click **Stop Game** to make sure the stop method works and **Game Over** appears again. Click **Options** to make sure the options panel still displays properly.

Code Design – Moving the Tossers

We need the capability to move our snowball tossers up and down in the display panel (**snowPanel**). We choose to use the keyboard for control, using the **KeyPressed** method attached to the **snowPanel** control. Add this code in the frame constructor to add a listener for this method:

```
snowPanel.addKeyListener(new KeyAdapter()
{
  public void keyPressed(KeyEvent e)
  {
    snowPanelKeyPressed(e);
  }
});
```

Then add the empty method we will use to determine which key is pressed:

```
private void snowPanelKeyPressed(KeyEvent e)
{
}
```

In the above method, The **KeyEvent** argument **e** tells us which key was pressed by providing what is called a **key code**. There is a key code value for each key on the keyboard. By evaluating the **e.getKeyCode()** argument, we can determine which key was pressed. In the snowball toss game, we choose the following keys to control player motion and tossing of snowballs (selected based on location on the keyboard):

Player 1	**A** – Move Up, **Z** – Move Down, **S** – Toss
Player 2	**K** – Move Up, **M** – Move Down, **J** – Toss

You can change these if you'd like. Key codes for these keys are:

e.getKeyCode()	Description
e.VK_A	The letter A.
e.VK_Z	The letter Z.
e.VK_S	The letter S.
e.VK_K	The letter K.
e.VK_M	The letter M.
e.VK_J	The letter J.

Each time a movement key is pressed, we will move (using the **Sprite** class **move** method) the player an amount **playerIncrement** (a value you can adjust if needed) if going down and an amount **–playerIncrement** if going up. Add a class level constant declaration for this value:

```
final int playerIncrement = 5;
```

You might wonder how I came up with this value. I tried several values finding one that resulted in smooth motion that wasn't too small or too large. Any time you program a game, you will have several adjustable parameters. There is no real science to setting values – just some guessing, trying and refining. Feel free to change any of the "built-in" values in the snowball toss game.

The code to move the tossers (we'll add throwing logic later) is placed in the **snowPanelKeyPressed** method. That code is:

```
private void snowPanelKeyPressed(KeyEvent e)
{
  if (gameButton.getText().equals("New Game"))
     return;
  // get current location for possible update
  double newY1 = player1.rectangle.getY(), newY2 =
player2.rectangle.getY();
  if (e.getKeyCode() == e.VK_A)
  {
    newY1 -= playerIncrement;
    if (newY1 < 0)
      newY1 = 0;
  }
  else if (e.getKeyCode() == e.VK_Z)
  {
    newY1 += playerIncrement;
    if (newY1 > snowPanel.getHeight() -
player1.rectangle.getHeight())
       newY1 = snowPanel.getHeight() -
player1.rectangle.getHeight();
  }
  else if (e.getKeyCode() == e.VK_K)
  {
    newY2 -= playerIncrement;
    if (newY2 < 0)
      newY2 = 0;
  }
  else if (e.getKeyCode() == e.VK_M)
  {
    newY2 += playerIncrement;
```

```
      if (newY2 > snowPanel.getHeight() -
player2.rectangle.getHeight())
        newY2 = snowPanel.getHeight() -
player2.rectangle.getHeight();
    }
    player1.rectangle = new
Rectangle2D.Double(player1.rectangle.getX(), newY1,
player1.rectangle.getWidth(),
player1.rectangle.getHeight());
    player2.rectangle = new
Rectangle2D.Double(player2.rectangle.getX(), newY2,
player2.rectangle.getWidth(),
player2.rectangle.getHeight());
    snowPanel.repaint();
  }
```

Notice we don't allow any key down events if we haven't started a game (that is, if **gameButton** is displaying **New Game**). Also notice that most of code is involved with insuring a player never leaves the playing field. Add this method to your project.

We want to make sure the snow panel always has focus to intercept the movement keystrokes. To insure this, add this line:

```
snowPanel.requestFocus();
```

at the end of the **gameButton**ActionPerformed method code used to start a new game.

Save and run the project. Select the **Two Players** option so you can see if both players can move. Click **New Game**. Press the **A** and **Z** keys to move **Player 1** (the guy on the left) and press the **K** and **M** keys to move **Player 2** (the guy on the right). Make sure they can't move off the top or bottom of the panel control. Here I've moved one to the top and one to the bottom of the panel:

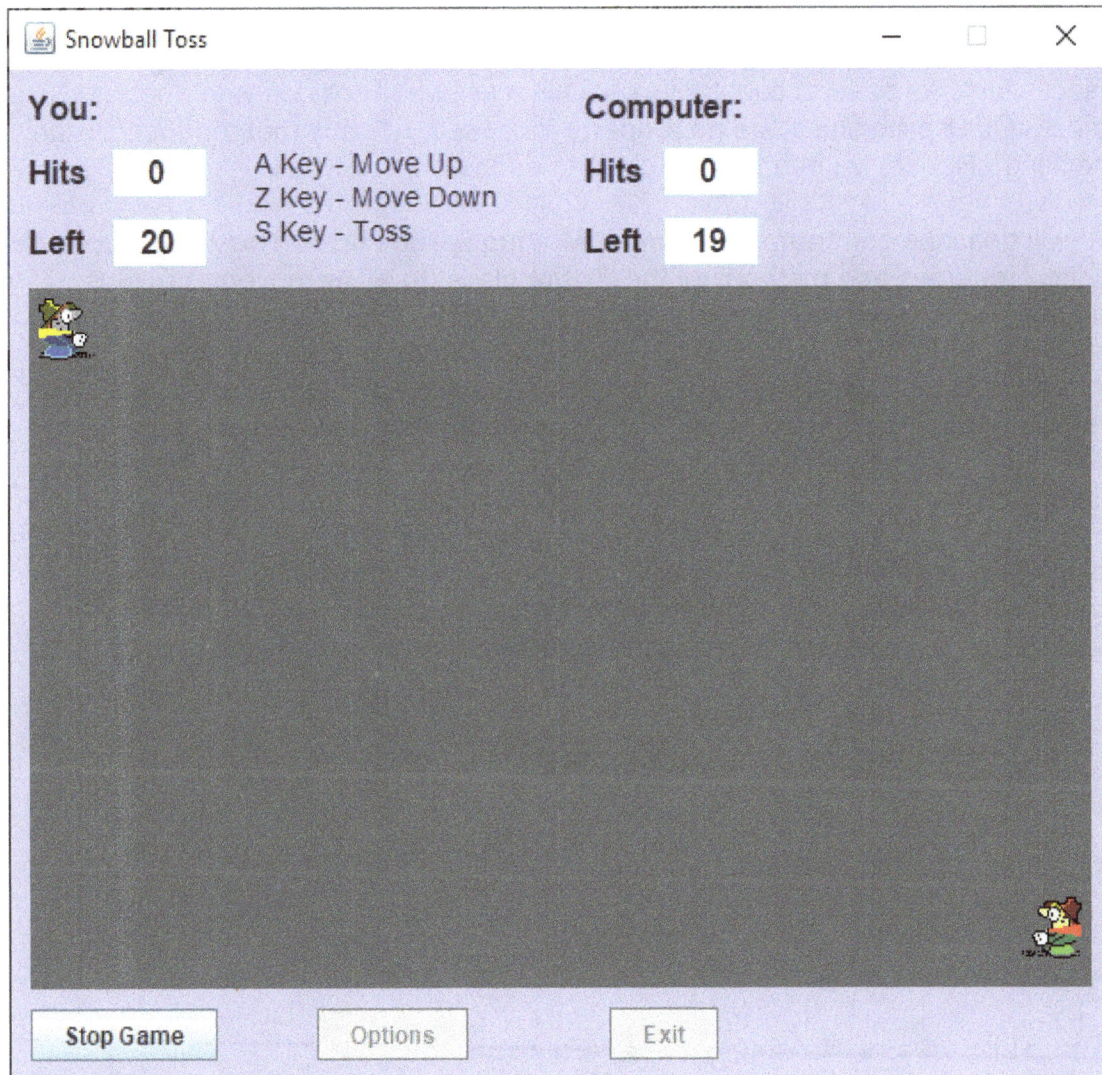

Now, let's start throwing some snowballs.

Code Design – MovingSprite Class

We want to give our player's the capability of throwing a snowball at each other. The snowballs will be represented by **Image** objects similar to our players, so you might be thinking they fit within the **Sprite** class we've already developed. The one difference here is that once a snowball is thrown, it moves without user interaction at some predetermined speed, its position being updated by a timer object. And, we need to constantly check if a snowball collides with another object. Our **Sprite** class has no property for speed, nor any method for collision checking. Hence, we need a new class to define our snowballs.

We will describe our snowballs using a **MovingSprite** class. This class will have all the properties and methods of the **Sprite** class (to allow movement), plus additional speed properties and a method to check for collisions. To build this class, we could start from scratch – with all new properties and all new methods. Or, we could take advantage of a very powerful concept in object-oriented programming, **inheritance**. Inheritance is the idea that you can base one class on an existing class, adding properties and/or methods as needed. This saves lots of work.

Let's see how inheritance works with our snowballs, considering the speed properties for now. We'll add the collision checking method later. Add another class file to the project, naming it **MovingSprite**. Use this code for the class:

```
package snowballtoss;
public class MovingSprite extends Sprite
{
  public int xSpeed;
  public int ySpeed;
}
```

The key line here is:

```
public class MovingSprite extends Sprite
```

The shaded addition makes all the properties and methods of the **Sprite** class available to our new class (**MovingSprite**). The remaining lines add the speed properties (**sSpeed**, speed in horizontal direction; **ySpeed**, speed in vertical direction). These speeds represent how much the **MovingSprite** will move in the corresponding direction with each update of position.

Code Design – Throwing Snowballs

We can use the **MovingSprite** class to add the capability of throwing snowballs to our project. We include two icon files to represent the snowballs (included in the **\HomeJava\HomeJava Projects\SnowballToss**\folder) named **player1ball.ico** and **player2ball.ico**. Move these files to your project folder. If you open **player1ball.ico** in the **IconEdit** program, you can see the detail:

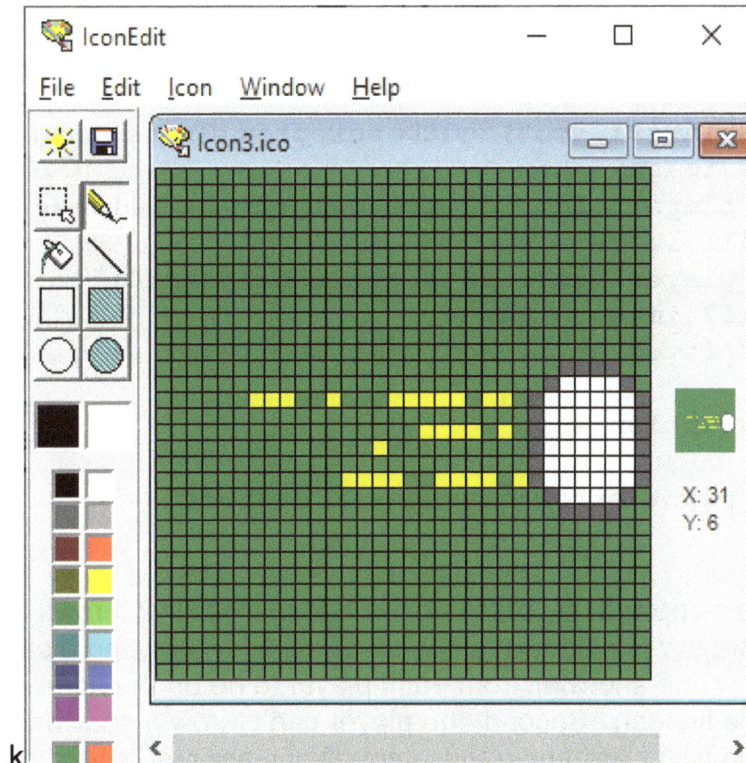

Snowballs are represented by two **MovingSprite** objects (**snowball1** is player 1's snowball, while **snowball2** is player 2's snowball). The horizontal speed is set by the constant **snowballSpeed**. The vertical speed is zero. Add these class level declarations to your project (**SnowballToss.java**):

```
static MovingSprite snowball1, snowball2;
final int snowballSpeed = 20;
```

Again, the sprites are declared as **static** to allow use in the graphics code. The speed is another parameter set by playing around with the program (again, a value you might like to change).

Snowballs are constructed in the frame constructor code. Add the shaded four lines to the code already there that establishes the player **Sprite** objects:

```
// create sprites
player1 = new Sprite();
player2 = new Sprite();
snowball1 = new MovingSprite();
snowball2 = new MovingSprite();
// read in icon files and sounds
try
{
  player1.image = new
ICOFile("player1.ico").getDescriptor(0).getImageRGB();
  player2.image = new
ICOFile("player2.ico").getDescriptor(0).getImageRGB();
  snowball1.image = new
ICOFile("player1ball.ico").getDescriptor(0).getImageRGB();
  snowball2.image = new
ICOFile("player2ball.ico").getDescriptor(0).getImageRGB();
}
catch (Exception ex)
{
  // can print error message if desired
}
```

Player 1 throws a snowball by pressing the **S** key. Player 2 throws a snowball by pressing the **J** key. We establish a couple of rules for throwing a snowball. First, we will only allow one snowball from each player to be on the screen at any one time (no multiple firings!). Second, the player can't throw a snowball if he is out of snowballs (obviously). Assuming these conditions are met, when a player makes a throw, the following steps occur:

> ➢ Decrement the number of snowballs left.
> ➢ Update display of snowballs left.
> ➢ Position snowball next to throwing player (just to right of Player 1, just to left of Player 2).
> ➢ Set snowball **isVisible** property to **true**.

This 'throwing' code goes in the existing form **snowPanelKeyPressed** method. The modified code is (changes are shaded):

```java
private void snowPanelKeyPressed(KeyEvent e)
{
  if (gameButton.getText().equals("New Game"))
      return;
  // get current location for possible update
  double newY1 = player1.rectangle.getY(), newY2 =
player2.rectangle.getY();
  if (e.getKeyCode() == e.VK_A)
  {
    newY1 -= playerIncrement;
    if (newY1 < 0)
      newY1 = 0;
  }
  else if (e.getKeyCode() == e.VK_Z)
  {
    newY1 += playerIncrement;
    if (newY1 > snowPanel.getHeight() -
player1.rectangle.getHeight())
        newY1 = snowPanel.getHeight() -
player1.rectangle.getHeight();
  }
  else if (e.getKeyCode() == e.VK_S)
  {
    if (!snowball1.isVisible && player1Left > 0)
    {
      player1Left--;

player1LeftTextField.setText(String.valueOf(player1Left));
      snowball1.rectangle = new
Rectangle2D.Double(player1.rectangle.getX() +
player1.rectangle.getWidth(), player1.rectangle.getY(),
snowball1.image.getWidth(null),
snowball1.image.getHeight(null));
      snowball1.isVisible = true;
    }
  }
  else if (e.getKeyCode() == e.VK_K)
  {
    newY2 -= playerIncrement;
    if (newY2 < 0)
      newY2 = 0;
  }
  else if (e.getKeyCode() == e.VK_M)
  {
```

```
      newY2 += playerIncrement;
      if (newY2 > snowPanel.getHeight() -
player2.rectangle.getHeight())
        newY2 = snowPanel.getHeight() -
player2.rectangle.getHeight();
  }
  else if (e.getKeyCode() == e.VK_J)
  {
    if (!snowball2.isVisible && player2Left > 0)
    {
      player2Left--;

player2LeftTextField.setText(String.valueOf(player2Left));
      snowball2.rectangle = new
Rectangle2D.Double(player2.rectangle.getX() -
snowball2.image.getWidth(null),  player2.rectangle.getY(),
snowball2.image.getWidth(null),
snowball2.image.getHeight(null));
      snowball2.isVisible = true;
    }
  }
  player1.rectangle = new
Rectangle2D.Double(player1.rectangle.getX(), newY1,
player1.rectangle.getWidth(),
player1.rectangle.getHeight());
  player2.rectangle = new
Rectangle2D.Double(player2.rectangle.getX(), newY2,
player2.rectangle.getWidth(),
player2.rectangle.getHeight());
  snowPanel.repaint();
}
```

Make the noted changes.

Make the shaded change to the **SnowPanel paintComponent** method to draw the snowballs (if visible):

```java
class SnowPanel extends JPanel
{
  public void paintComponent(Graphics g)
  {
    Graphics2D g2D = (Graphics2D) g;
    super.paintComponent(g2D);

    if (SnowballToss.gameButton.getText().equals("Stop
Game"))
    {
      SnowballToss.player1.draw(g2D);
      SnowballToss.player2.draw(g2D);
      if (SnowballToss.snowball1.isVisible)
        SnowballToss.snowball1.draw(g2D);
      if (SnowballToss.snowball2.isVisible)
        SnowballToss.snowball2.draw(g2D);
    }
    else
    {
      if (SnowballToss.gameButton.isEnabled())
      {
        g2D.setFont(new Font("Arial", Font.BOLD, 36));
        g2D.setPaint(Color.YELLOW);
        g2D.drawString("Game Over", 180, 180);
      }
      else
      {
        SnowballToss.optionsPanel.repaint();
      }
    }
    g2D.dispose();
  }
}
```

Save, run. Click **New Game**. Press the **S** key, then the **J** key. Two snowballs should appear:

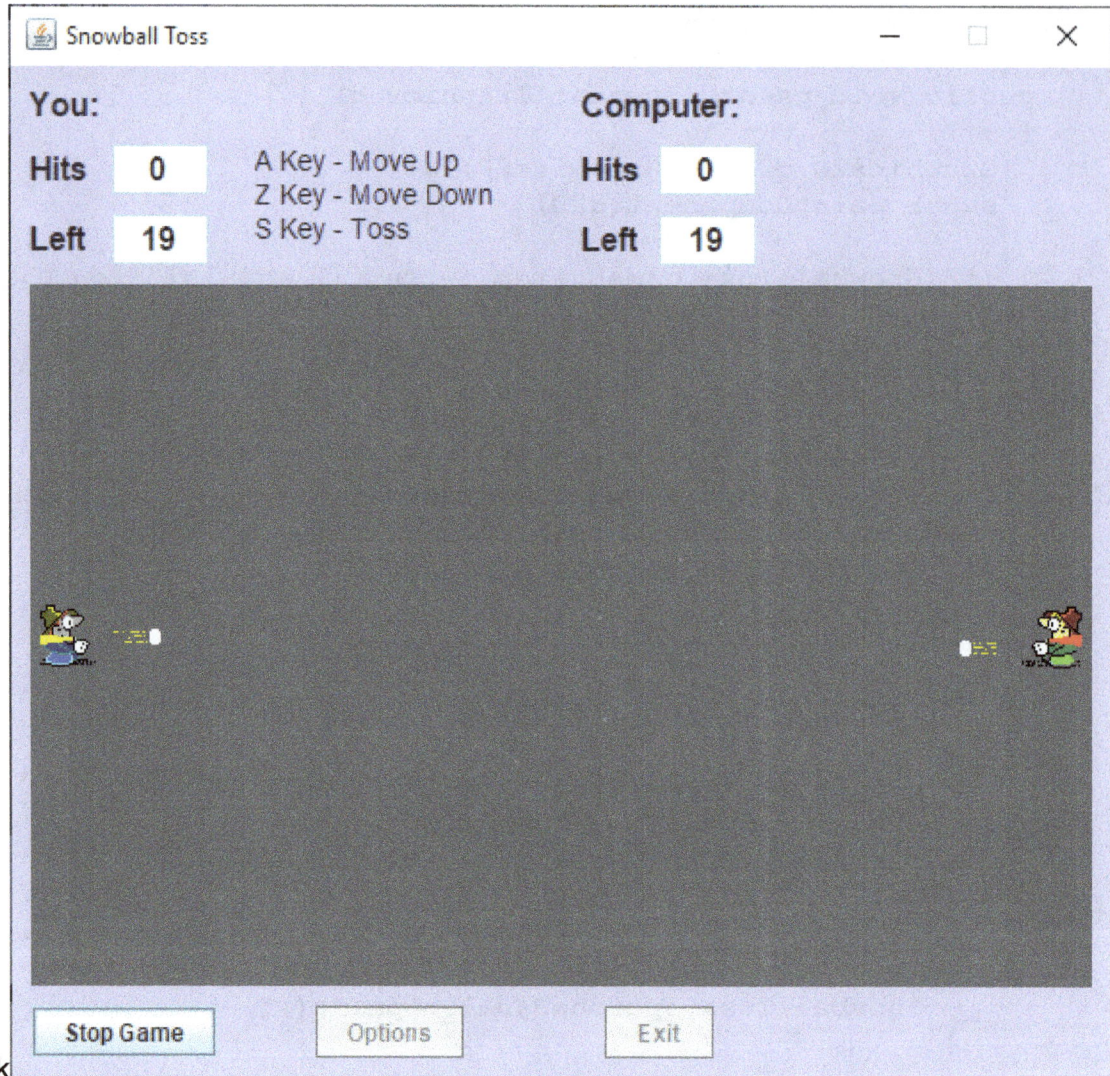

This code gets a snowball started. Let's look at the code to get a snowball moving.

Once thrown, motion of the snowball(s) is updated by a timer object (**gameTimer**) with a **delay** property of 50 milliseconds (again, determined by playing around with the game). Declare the timer using:

```
Timer gameTimer;
```

Add this code to the frame constructor:

```
gameTimer = new Timer(50, new ActionListener()
{
  public void actionPerformed(ActionEvent e)
  {
    gameTimerActionPerformed(e);
  }
});
```

And, add this empty **ActionPerformed** method:

```
private void gameTimerActionPerformed(ActionEvent e)
{
}
```

We need code in the **gameButtonActionPerformed** method to start that timer (when **New Game** is clicked) and to stop the timer (when **Stop Game** is clicked). We also remove the snowballs when **Stop Game** is clicked. The modified **gameButtonActionPerformed** method (changes are shaded, most unmodified code is not shown) is:

```java
private void gameButtonActionPerformed(ActionEvent e)
{
  if (gameButton.getText().equals("New Game"))
  {
    .
    .
    gameTimer.start();
    snowPanel.requestFocus();
  }
  else
  {
    gameTimer.stop();
    player1.isVisible = false;
    player2.isVisible = false;
    snowball1.isVisible = false;
    snowball2.isVisible = false;
    .
    .
  }
}
```

Add the new lines.

In the **gameTimerActionPerformed** method, we update the position of thrown snowballs using the horizontal speed value and the **move** method. We also check to see if a snowball goes off the edge of the panel control. If it does, we remove it from the panel to allow another throw. We also check for the end of the game (both players are out of snowballs and none are visible). If the game has ended, we 'click' **gameButton**. The code that does all this is:

```
private void gameTimerActionPerformed(ActionEvent e)
{
  // status of player 1 snowball
  if (snowball1.isVisible)
  {
    snowball1.move(snowballSpeed, 0);
    if (snowball1.rectangle.getX() > snowPanel.getWidth())
      snowball1.isVisible = false; // off screen
  }
  // status of player 2 snowball
  if (snowball2.isVisible)
  {
    snowball2.move(-snowballSpeed, 0);
    if (snowball2.rectangle.getX() < 0)
      snowball2.isVisible = false; // off screen
  }
  snowPanel.repaint();
  // check status of game
  if (!snowball1.isVisible && player1Left == 0 &&
!snowball2.isVisible && player2Left == 0)
    gameButton.doClick();
}
```

Add this method to your project.

Save and run the project. Make sure you are still using the two player option. Click **New Game**. Click **S** and **J** to throw snowballs. Make sure the labels reflect the proper number of remaining snowballs. Here is a run I made with one snowball flying:

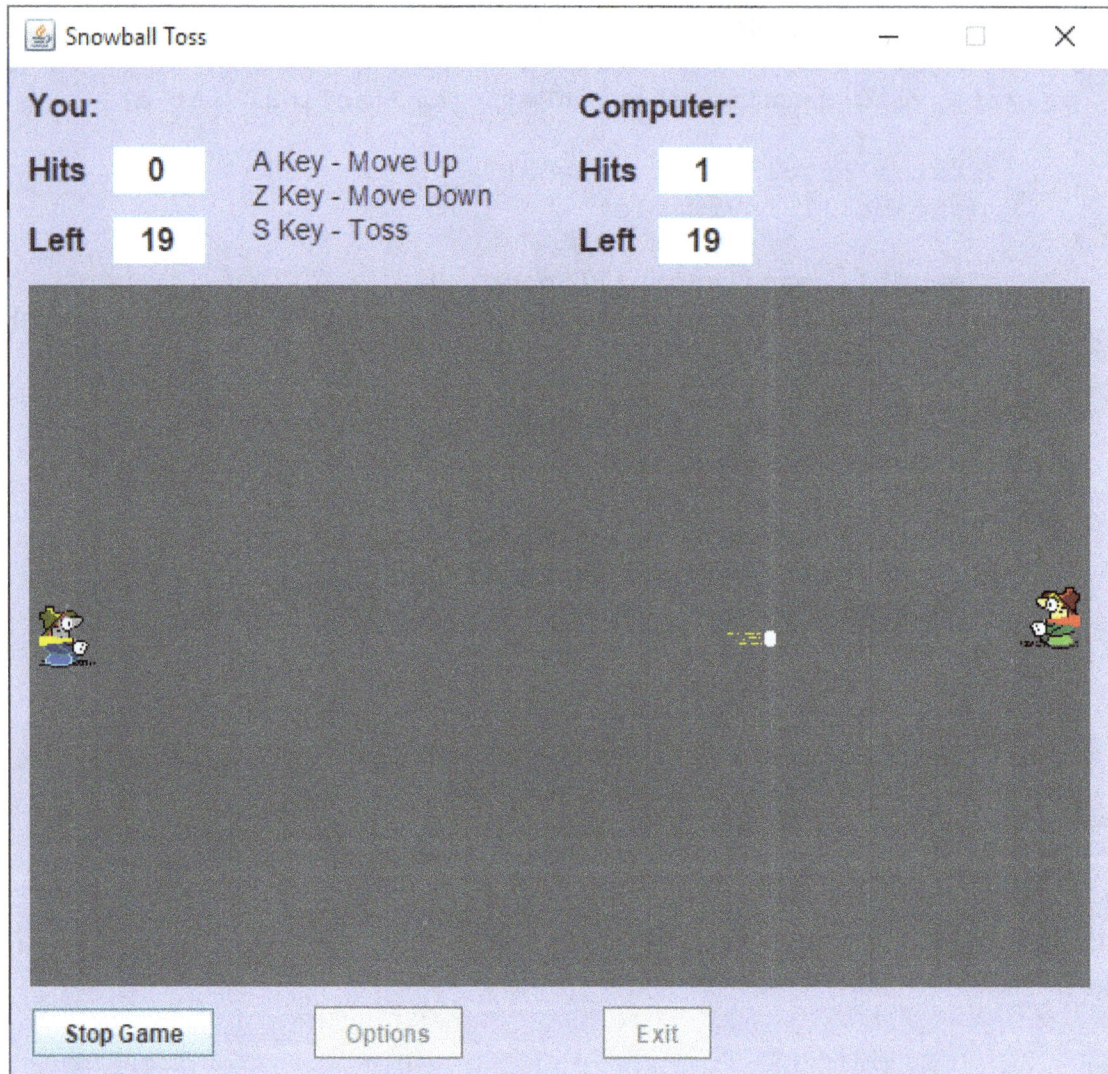

Stop the game when you want or throw snowballs until neither player has any remaining. Notice we don't have any scoring (counting hits). To do this, we need collision logic, which is discussed next.

Code Design - Collision Detection

If a thrown snowball hits a player, the other player gets a point (a **Hit**). We need some way to check for such a 'collision.' Since rectangular regions describe the moving objects here, we want to know if two rectangles intersect. In Java, this test can be accomplished using the **createIntersection** method of the **Rectangle2D** shape.

To use the **createIntersection** method, we need three **Rectangle2D** shapes. The first two (call them **rectangle1** and **rectangle2**) describe the rectangles being checked for intersection. The rectangle describing the intersection of these two rectangles (**collided**) is then defined by:

```
collided = rectangle1.createIntersection(rectangle2);
```

Once the intersection (or collision) rectangle is created using **createIntersection**, we check the intersection by examining the **isEmpty** Boolean property:

```
collided.isEmpty()
```

If this property is **true**, there is no intersection or collision. If **isEmpty** is **false**, there is intersection and properties (**x**, **y**, **width**, **height**) of the **collided** rectangle define that intersection region.

To use this in our project, we will add a **collided** method to our **MovingSprite** class. Open the **MovingSprite.java** file and make the shaded changes:

```
package snowballtoss;
import java.awt.geom.*;

public class MovingSprite extends Sprite
{
  public int xSpeed;
  public int ySpeed;

  public boolean collided(Rectangle2D.Double r)
  {
    return
(!this.rectangle.createIntersection(r).isEmpty());
  }
}
```

The method is passed the rectangle shape (**r**) to check for collision with the **MovingSprite** object. The import statement is needed because we use the **Rectangle2D** shape.

As an example of using this new method, say we want to check if **snowball1** has hit **player2**. The **boolean** value:

```
snowball1.collided(player2.rectangle)
```

will be **true** if a collision has occurred. If a collision occurs, we remove the snowball and update the successful tosser's score.

We check for collisions between snowballs and players in the **gameTimerActionPerformed** method. The modified code (shaded) checks for collisions and updates the score accordingly:

```
private void gameTimerActionPerformed(ActionEvent e)
{
   // status of player 1 snowball
  if (snowball1.isVisible)
  {
    snowball1.move(snowballSpeed, 0);
    if (snowball1.rectangle.getX() > snowPanel.getWidth())
      snowball1.isVisible = false; // off screen
    else if (snowball1.collided(player2.rectangle))
    {
      player1Hits++;

player1HitsTextField.setText(String.valueOf(player1Hits));
      snowball1.isVisible = false;
    }
  }
  // status of player 2 snowball
  if (snowball2.isVisible)
  {
    snowball2.move(-snowballSpeed, 0);
    if (snowball2.rectangle.getX() < 0)
      snowball2.isVisible = false; // off screen
    else if (snowball2.collided(player1.rectangle))
    {
      player2Hits++;

player2HitsTextField.setText(String.valueOf(player2Hits));
      snowball2.isVisible = false;
    }
  }
  snowPanel.repaint();
  // check status of game
  if (!snowball1.isVisible && player1Left == 0 &&
!snowball2.isVisible && player2Left == 0)
    gameButton.doClick();
}
```

Make the noted modifications.

Save and run the project. Now if you throw a snowball and hit the other player, the snowball should disappear, but not the player. Give it a try. Here's the middle of a game I played:

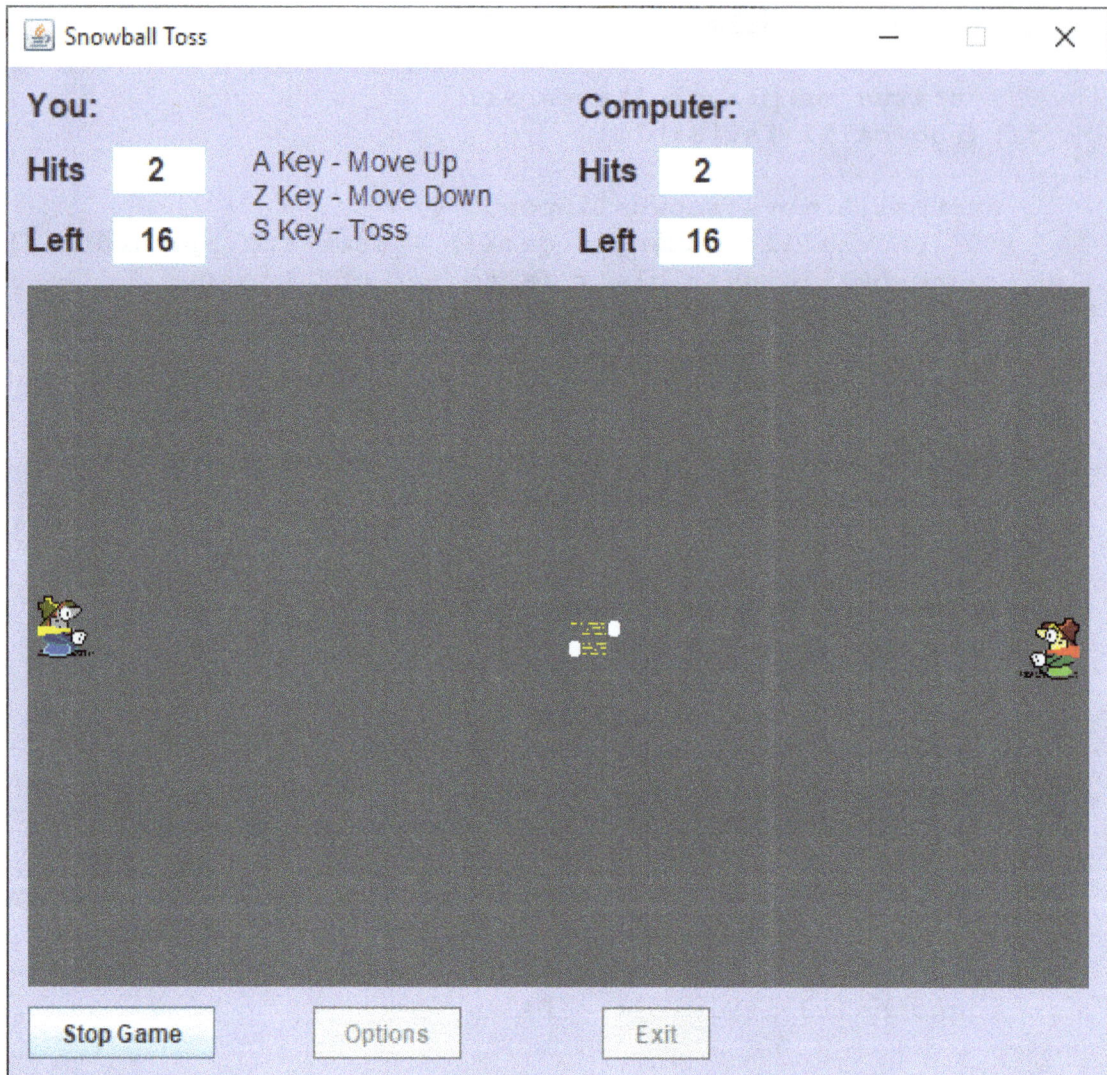

Make sure the score updates properly after each successful toss.

Code Design – Zombie Snowmen

As designed, the players have no protection from thrown snowballs other than their ability to move up and down. We'll change that now. We'll invent a tribe of "zombie" snowmen that roam up and down in the middle of the playing field. These snowmen will deflect (stop) any snowball that has been thrown.

The icon file **snowman.ico** (included in the **\HomeJava\HomeJava Projects\SnowballToss**folder) depicts a snowman. Move this file to your project folder. If you open **snowman.ico** in the **IconEdit** program, you can see the detail:

I know – he looks pretty happy for a zombie!

We will have two snowmen (you can choose more if you want). Snowmen are represented by **MovingSprite** objects (**snowman1** and **snowman2**). Their motion will be random, with some restrictions. Add these class level declarations to your project to declare the snowman objects (again use **static** preface) and the random number object.

```
static MovingSprite snowman1, snowman2;
Random myRandom = new Random();
```

You will need this import statement for the **Random** object:

```
import java.util.Random;
```

Our snowmen will move according to some predetermined rules. **snowman1** will move vertically just to the left of the center of playing field, while **snowman2** will move vertically just to the right of center. The horizontal speed for both will be zero. The vertical speed will be a random value between 1 and 4 (a value you might want to change). The snowmen can move either up or down. If moving up, they start at the bottom of the field. If moving down, they start at the top. How did I come up with all these rules for my zombies? I made them up. That's the nice thing about being a game programmer. You can make your characters do whatever you want them to. Come up with rules for your own set of zombie snowmen if you want.

Like the other sprites, the snowmen are constructed in the frame constructor method. Add these shaded lines to that section of code:

```
// create sprites
player1 = new Sprite();
player2 = new Sprite();
snowball1 = new MovingSprite();
snowball2 = new MovingSprite();
snowman1 = new MovingSprite();
snowman2 = new MovingSprite();
// read in icon files and sounds
try
{
  player1.image = new
ICOFile("player1.ico").getDescriptor(0).getImageRGB();
  player2.image = new
ICOFile("player2.ico").getDescriptor(0).getImageRGB();
  snowball1.image = new
ICOFile("player1ball.ico").getDescriptor(0).getImageRGB();
  snowball2.image = new
ICOFile("player2ball.ico").getDescriptor(0).getImageRGB();
  snowman1.image = new
ICOFile("snowman.ico").getDescriptor(0).getImageRGB();
  snowman2.image = new
ICOFile("snowman.ico").getDescriptor(0).getImageRGB();
}
catch (Exception ex)
{
  // can print error message if desired
}
```

The snowmen are initially placed in the field when **New Game** is clicked. When this occurs, they are randomly placed within the vertical constraints of the graphics object. And, they are assigned a random speed. The snowmen are removed when **Stop Game** is clicked. The modified **gameButtonActionPerformed** method that accomplishes these tasks (changes are shaded, with much unmodified code not shown) is:

```java
private void gameButtonActionPerformed(ActionEvent e)
{
  if (gameButton.getText().equals("New Game"))
  {
    .
    .
    snowman1.rectangle = new Rectangle2D.Double(0.5 *
snowPanel.getWidth() - snowman1.image.getWidth(null),
myRandom.nextInt(snowPanel.getHeight()),
snowman1.image.getWidth(null),
snowman1.image.getHeight(null));
    snowman2.rectangle = new Rectangle2D.Double(0.5 *
snowPanel.getWidth(),
myRandom.nextInt(snowPanel.getHeight()),
snowman2.image.getWidth(null),
snowman2.image.getHeight(null));
    snowman1.ySpeed = snowmanSpeed();
    snowman2.ySpeed = snowmanSpeed();
    snowman1.isVisible = true;
    snowman2.isVisible = true;
    snowPanel.repaint();
    gameTimer.start();
    snowPanel.requestFocus();
  }
  else
  {
    gameTimer.stop();
    player1.isVisible = false;
    player2.isVisible = false;
    snowball1.isVisible = false;
    snowball2.isVisible = false;
    snowman1.isVisible = false;
    snowman2.isVisible = false;
    .
    .
  }
}
```

snowman1 is just to the left of the middle of the panel control, while **snowman2** is just to the right. Notice how the snowmen are randomly positioned vertically.

The snowman speed is assigned using a general method **snowmanSpeed**. As mentioned, we choose this value to be random, between 1 and 4. The speed can be positive (for downward motion) or negative (for upward motion). This choice of sign is also random. The code that incorporates this speed assignment is:

```
private int snowmanSpeed()
{
  final int speedMin = 1;
  final int speedMax = 4;
  int speed;
  speed = myRandom.nextInt(speedMax - speedMin + 1) +
speedMin;
  if (myRandom.nextInt(2) == 0)
    speed = -speed;
  return(speed);
}
```

Computing the speed value is straightforward. To choose the sign, we do a computerized "coin flip". This flip is done by looking at the value of:

```
myRandom.nextInt(2)
```

This can return one of two values, 0 ("heads") or 1 ("tails").

Snowman motion is updated in the **gameTimerActionPerformed** method. At each update, for each snowman, we need to perform the following steps:

➢ Move the snowman using the current **ySpeed** property.
➢ Check to see if the snowman has moved off the playing field.
➢ If off field, do this:
    ○ Compute a new speed.
    ○ If speed is positive, position snowman off top of playing field so it can start moving down.
    ○ If speed is negative, position snowman off bottom of playing field so it can start moving up.
➢ After moving or repositioning snowman, check to see if a thrown snowball has collided with it. If there is a collision, remove the snowball from the field.

The modified **gameTimerActionPerformed** method that implements these steps is (changes are shaded):

```
private void gameTimerActionPerformed(ActionEvent e)
{
  // move snowmen
  snowman1.move(0, snowman1.ySpeed);
  if (snowman1.rectangle.getY() < -
snowman1.image.getHeight(null) ||
snowman1.rectangle.getY() > snowPanel.getHeight())
  {
    // recompute speed
    snowman1.ySpeed = snowmanSpeed();
    if (snowman1.ySpeed > 0)
      snowman1.rectangle = new
Rectangle2D.Double(snowman1.rectangle.getX(), -
snowman1.image.getHeight(null),
snowman1.rectangle.getWidth(),
snowman1.rectangle.getHeight());
    else
      snowman1.rectangle = new
Rectangle2D.Double(snowman1.rectangle.getX(),
snowPanel.getHeight(), snowman1.rectangle.getWidth(),
snowman1.rectangle.getHeight());
  }
  snowman2.move(0, snowman2.ySpeed);
  if (snowman2.rectangle.getY() < -
snowman2.image.getHeight(null) ||
snowman2.rectangle.getY() > snowPanel.getHeight())
  {
    // recompute speed
    snowman2.ySpeed = snowmanSpeed();
    if (snowman2.ySpeed > 0)
      snowman2.rectangle = new
Rectangle2D.Double(snowman2.rectangle.getX(), -
snowman2.image.getHeight(null),
snowman2.rectangle.getWidth(),
snowman2.rectangle.getHeight());
    else
      snowman2.rectangle = new
Rectangle2D.Double(snowman2.rectangle.getX(),
snowPanel.getHeight(), snowman2.rectangle.getWidth(),
snowman2.rectangle.getHeight());
  }
  // status of player 1 snowball
  if (snowball1.isVisible)
  {
```

```
    snowball1.move(snowballSpeed, 0);
    if (snowball1.rectangle.getX() > snowPanel.getWidth())
      snowball1.isVisible = false; // off screen
    else if (snowball1.collided(player2.rectangle))
    {
      player1Hits++;

player1HitsTextField.setText(String.valueOf(player1Hits));
      snowball1.isVisible = false;
    }
    else if (snowball1.collided(snowman1.rectangle) ||
snowball1.collided(snowman2.rectangle))
      snowball1.isVisible = false;
  }
  // status of player 2 snowball
  if (snowball2.isVisible)
  {
    snowball2.move(-snowballSpeed, 0);
    if (snowball2.rectangle.getX() < 0)
      snowball2.isVisible = false; // off screen
    else if (snowball2.collided(player1.rectangle))
    {
      player2Hits++;

player2HitsTextField.setText(String.valueOf(player2Hits));
      snowball2.isVisible = false;
    }
    else if (snowball2.collided(snowman1.rectangle) ||
snowball2.collided(snowman2.rectangle))
      snowball2.isVisible = false;
  }
  snowPanel.repaint();
  // check status of game
  if (!snowball1.isVisible && player1Left == 0 &&
!snowball2.isVisible && player2Left == 0)
    gameButton.doClick();
}
```

Make the noted changes. You should understand how all the zombie rules have been applied.

Lastly, make the shaded change to the **SnowPanel paintComponent** method to
draw the snowmen (always visible while the game is being played):

```
class SnowPanel extends JPanel
{
  public void paintComponent(Graphics g)
  {
    Graphics2D g2D = (Graphics2D) g;
    super.paintComponent(g2D);

    if (SnowballToss.gameButton.getText().equals("Stop
Game"))
      {
        SnowballToss.player1.draw(g2D);
        SnowballToss.player2.draw(g2D);
        if (SnowballToss.snowball1.isVisible)
          SnowballToss.snowball1.draw(g2D);
        if (SnowballToss.snowball2.isVisible)
          SnowballToss.snowball2.draw(g2D);
        SnowballToss.snowman1.draw(g2D);
        SnowballToss.snowman2.draw(g2D);
      }
    else
      {
        if (SnowballToss.gameButton.isEnabled())
        {
          g2D.setFont(new Font("Arial", Font.BOLD, 36));
          g2D.setPaint(Color.YELLOW);
          g2D.drawString("Game Over", 180, 180);
        }
        else
        {
          SnowballToss.optionsPanel.repaint();
        }
      }
    g2D.dispose();
  }
}
```

Save and run the project. The snowmen should be moving through the middle of the field deflecting any snowballs they might block. They should move both up and down at varying speeds. Watch them for a while. Here's a run I made:

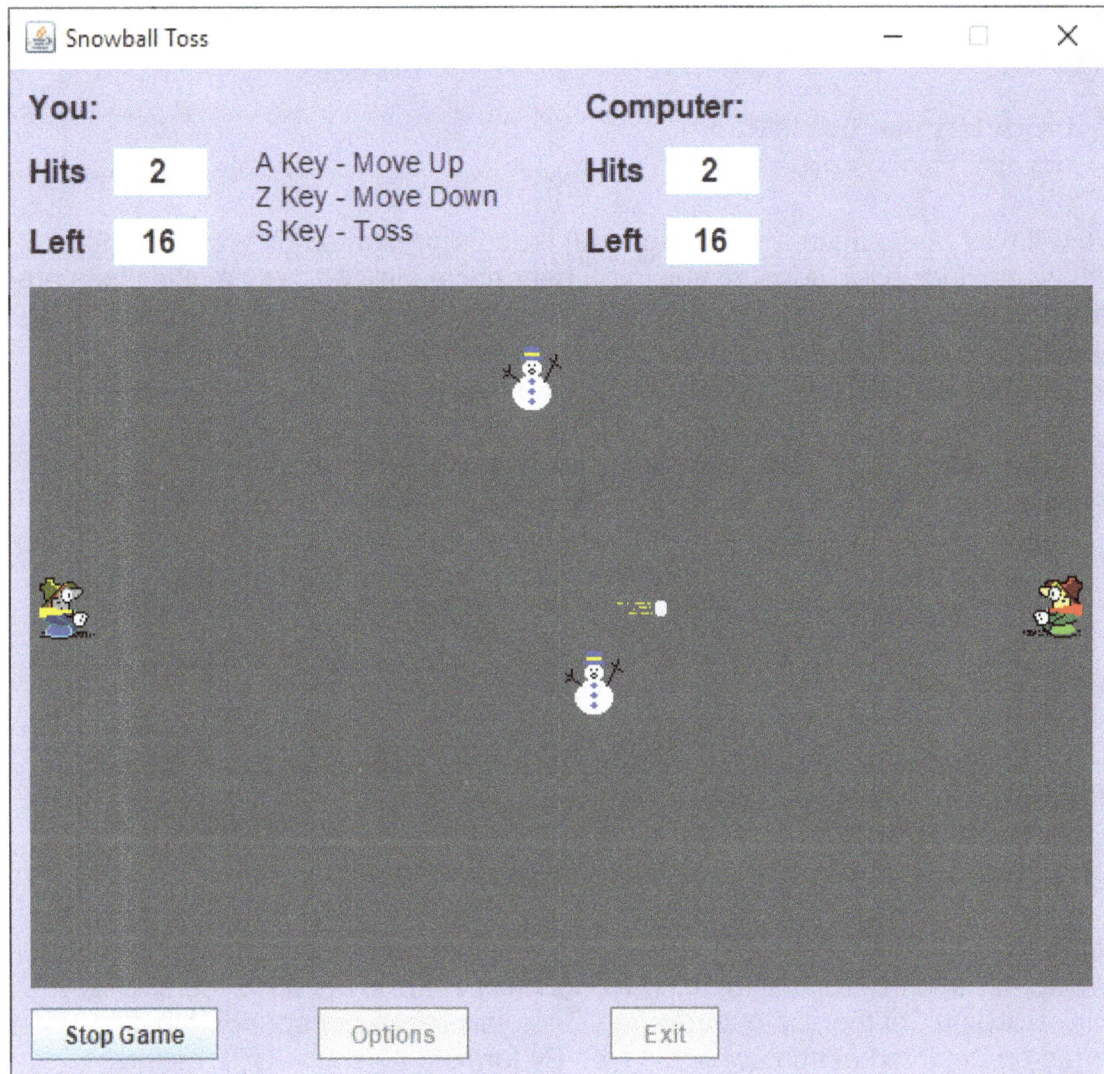

The two player version of the snowball toss game is essentially complete. All the animation steps are implemented – we can move the players, we can throw snowballs, the zombie snowmen can block snowballs and the score is properly kept. Next, we'll program the one player version, making the computer control Player 2.

Before doing the one player version, however, let's address one sorely lacking feature – sounds! Any good game has sound and we should have some in this game. Let's add a throwing sound, a splat sound when a snowman is hit and an "Ouch" sound when a player is hit. And, let's add a little tune when the game is over.

Code Design – Playing Sounds

Most games feature sounds that take advantage of stereo sound cards. By using the Java **Applet** class, we can add such sounds to our snowball toss game. This class requires these import statements:

```
import java.net.URL;
import java.applet.*;
```

We will play one particular type of sound, those represented by **wav** files (files with wav extensions). Most sounds you hear played in Windows applications are saved as **wav** files. These are the files formed when you record using one of the many sound recorder programs available. In the **\HomeJava\HomeJava Projects\SnowballToss**folder are four **wav** files for use in this program:

throw.wav	sound to play when a snowball is thrown
splat.wav	sound to play when a snowball hits a snowman
ouch.wav	sound to play when a snowball hits a player
gameover.wav	sound to play when game is over (both players are out of snowballs)

You can play each of these sounds in your computer's media player if you want.

A sound file is loaded using the **newAudioClip** method. If we name the sound **mySound**, the sound is loaded using:

```
mySound = Applet.newAudioClip(mySoundURL);
```

where **mySoundURL** is the "address" of the sound file. You may note that URL is an Internet address (universal resource locator) – this is because the sound utilities are part of the applet package. Does this mean our sounds must be stored on the Internet somewhere? No. By forming a special URL as the argument, we can load sound files from our project folder, just like we have loaded graphics files.

A URL for use in the **newAudioClip** method is formed using the Java **URL** method. If the sound file is **mySoundFile** (**String** type), the URL is formed with:

```
mySoundURL = new URL("file: " + mySoundFile);
```

The addition of the "**file:**" string tells Java the sound is loaded from a file rather than the Internet. This assumes the sound file is located in the project folder. If it is in another folder, you need to "prepend" the file name with the appropriate directory information.

The URL can only be formed within a **try/catch** loop to catch potential exceptions. Hence, the complete code segment to load a sound (**mySound**) from a file (**mySoundFile**) is:

```
try
{
  mySound = Applet.newAudioClip(new URL("file: " +
mySoundFile));
}
catch (Exception ex)
{
   [Error message]
}
```

Such code to create sounds is usually placed in at the end of your application's constructor with all sounds declared as class level variables.

Once we have created a sound clip, there are three methods used to play or stop the corresponding sound. To play **mySound** one time, use the **play** method:

```
mySound.play();
```

To play the sound in a continuous loop, use the **loop** method:

```
mySound.loop();
```

To stop the sound from playing, use the **stop** method:

```
mySound.stop();
```

It's that easy.

It is normal practice to include any sound files an application uses in the project folder. This makes them easily accessible. As such, when distributing your application to other users, you must remember to include the sound files in the package. Copy the four included sound files into your project's folder.

Let's modify the snowball toss game code to include the sounds. Add these import statements:

```
import java.net.URL;
import java.applet.*;
```

Add class level declarations for the variables used to represent the sounds:

```
AudioClip throwSound;
AudioClip splatSound;
AudioClip ouchSound;
AudioClip gameOverSound;
```

The code to construct the **AudioClip** objects (using the **wav** files) goes in the frame constructor method. Place the shaded lines in the same **try/catch** loop used to load the sprite image files:

```
// read in icon files and sounds
try
{
  player1.image = new
ICOFile("player1.ico").getDescriptor(0).getImageRGB();
  player2.image = new
ICOFile("player2.ico").getDescriptor(0).getImageRGB();
  snowball1.image = new
ICOFile("player1ball.ico").getDescriptor(0).getImageRGB();
  snowball2.image = new
ICOFile("player2ball.ico").getDescriptor(0).getImageRGB();
  snowman1.image = new
ICOFile("snowman.ico").getDescriptor(0).getImageRGB();
  snowman2.image = new
ICOFile("snowman.ico").getDescriptor(0).getImageRGB();
  throwSound = Applet.newAudioClip(new URL("file:" +
"throw.wav"));
  splatSound = Applet.newAudioClip(new URL("file:" +
"splat.wav"));
  ouchSound = Applet.newAudioClip(new URL("file:" +
"ouch.wav"));
  gameOverSound = Applet.newAudioClip(new URL("file:" +
"gameover.wav"));
}
catch (Exception ex)
{
  // can print error message if desired
}
```

throwSound will play when a snowball is thrown. This action occurs in the **snowPanelKeyPressed** method. The modified code (changes are shaded, most unmodified code is not shown) is:

```java
private void snowPanelKeyPressed(KeyEvent e)
{
  if (gameButton.getText().equals("New Game"))
      return;
  // get current location for possible update
  double newY1 = player1.rectangle.getY(), newY2 =
player2.rectangle.getY();
  if (e.getKeyCode() == e.VK_A)
  {
    .
    .
    .

  else if (e.getKeyCode() == e.VK_S)
  {
    if (!snowball1.isVisible && player1Left > 0)
    {
      throwSound.play();
      player1Left--;

player1LeftTextField.setText(String.valueOf(player1Left));
      snowball1.rectangle = new
Rectangle2D.Double(player1.rectangle.getX() +
player1.rectangle.getWidth(), player1.rectangle.getY(),
snowball1.image.getWidth(null),
snowball1.image.getHeight(null));
      snowball1.isVisible = true;
    }
    .
    .
    .

  else if (e.getKeyCode() == e.VK_J)
  {
    if (!snowball2.isVisible && player2Left > 0)
    {
      throwSound.play();
      player2Left--;

player2LeftTextField.setText(String.valueOf(player2Left));
      snowball2.rectangle = new
Rectangle2D.Double(player2.rectangle.getX() -
snowball2.image.getWidth(null),  player2.rectangle.getY(),
snowball2.image.getWidth(null),
snowball2.image.getHeight(null));
      snowball2.isVisible = true;
    }
```

.
.
```
        }
    player1.rectangle = new
Rectangle2D.Double(player1.rectangle.getX(), newY1,
player1.rectangle.getWidth(),
player1.rectangle.getHeight());
    player2.rectangle = new
Rectangle2D.Double(player2.rectangle.getX(), newY2,
player2.rectangle.getWidth(),
player2.rectangle.getHeight());
    snowPanel.repaint();
}
```

Make the two changes.

splatSound will play when a snowman is hit by a snowball, **ouchSound** will play when a player is hit by a snowball and **gameOverSound** will play when the players run out of snowballs. All of these actions occur in the **gameTimerActionPerformed** method. The modified code (changes are shaded) is:

```
private void gameTimerActionPerformed(ActionEvent e)
{
  // move snowmen
  snowman1.move(0, snowman1.ySpeed);
  if (snowman1.rectangle.getY() < -
snowman1.image.getHeight(null) ||
snowman1.rectangle.getY() > snowPanel.getHeight())
    {
      // recompute speed
      snowman1.ySpeed = snowmanSpeed();
      if (snowman1.ySpeed > 0)
        snowman1.rectangle = new
Rectangle2D.Double(snowman1.rectangle.getX(), -
snowman1.image.getHeight(null),
snowman1.rectangle.getWidth(),
snowman1.rectangle.getHeight());
      else
        snowman1.rectangle = new
Rectangle2D.Double(snowman1.rectangle.getX(),
snowPanel.getHeight(), snowman1.rectangle.getWidth(),
snowman1.rectangle.getHeight());
    }
  snowman2.move(0, snowman2.ySpeed);
```

```java
if (snowman2.rectangle.getY() < -
snowman2.image.getHeight(null) ||
snowman2.rectangle.getY() > snowPanel.getHeight())
  {
    // recompute speed
    snowman2.ySpeed = snowmanSpeed();
    if (snowman2.ySpeed > 0)
      snowman2.rectangle = new
Rectangle2D.Double(snowman2.rectangle.getX(), -
snowman2.image.getHeight(null),
snowman2.rectangle.getWidth(),
snowman2.rectangle.getHeight());
    else
      snowman2.rectangle = new
Rectangle2D.Double(snowman2.rectangle.getX(),
snowPanel.getHeight(), snowman2.rectangle.getWidth(),
snowman2.rectangle.getHeight());
  }
  // status of player 1 snowball
  if (snowball1.isVisible)
  {
    snowball1.move(snowballSpeed, 0);
    if (snowball1.rectangle.getX() > snowPanel.getWidth())
      snowball1.isVisible = false; // off screen
    else if (snowball1.collided(player2.rectangle))
    {
      ouchSound.play();
      player1Hits++;

player1HitsTextField.setText(String.valueOf(player1Hits));
      snowball1.isVisible = false;
    }
    else if (snowball1.collided(snowman1.rectangle) ||
snowball1.collided(snowman2.rectangle))
    {
      splatSound.play();
      snowball1.isVisible = false;
    }
  }
  // status of player 2 snowball
  if (snowball2.isVisible)
  {
    snowball2.move(-snowballSpeed, 0);
    if (snowball2.rectangle.getX() < 0)
      snowball2.isVisible = false; // off screen
    else if (snowball2.collided(player1.rectangle))
    {
```

```
        ouchSound.play();
        player2Hits++;

player2HitsTextField.setText(String.valueOf(player2Hits));
        snowball2.isVisible = false;
      }
      else if (snowball2.collided(snowman1.rectangle) ||
snowball2.collided(snowman2.rectangle))
      {
        splatSound.play();
        snowball2.isVisible = false;
      }
    }
    snowPanel.repaint();
    // check status of game
    if (!snowball1.isVisible && player1Left == 0 &&
!snowball2.isVisible && player2Left == 0)
    {
      gameOverSound.play();
      gameButton.doClick();
    }
}
```

Make the noted changes. This is the final version of this method.

Save and run the project. Play the two player game. Listen for the throw, splat and ouch sounds. And, play until all the snowballs are thrown to hear the cute little "game over" tune. Make these changes. I think you'll agree that the sounds make the game far more fun to play.

Code Design – One Player Game

You can't always find someone to play a game with. So why not let the computer be your opponent? In a one player snowball toss game, we will let the computer control Player 2.

For such computer control, we need to develop some rules for the computer to use. In the **Blackjack** card game built earlier in these notes, we played against the computer. The rules used there by the computer were predetermined by those used in most casinos. Here, in the snowball toss game, we have no such rules. We need to develop them ourselves. This is a fun part of programming – giving the computer some semblance of intelligence. The logic presented here are ideas that I just made up as I went along. They seem to work. Feel free to make changes you think are needed.

There are two approaches we could take in writing code for a computer competitor. We could use very simple logic, making it easy for a human to win. Or, we could write more detailed logic, emulating steps you, as a human, might take in playing the game. With more detailed logic, it would be harder for a human to win. In the snowball toss game, we take both approaches. We first develop a simple, random game playing logic, then a more detailed logic. Then, we use the level of difficulty selected with the **Options** button to determine how often we use the random logic versus how often we use the detailed logic. The values I chose to use are:

Difficulty Level	Random Logic (%)	Detailed Logic (%)
Easiest	100	0
Easy	75	25
Hard	50	50
Hardest	25	75

So, when the **Easiest** level is selected, we use the random logic 100 percent of the time. When the **Hardest** level is selected, we use the random logic 25 percent of the time (we don't want our computer to be too smart) and the detailed logic 75 percent of the time

Another value selected by the level of difficulty will be how often the computer makes a move. The computer moves will be controlled by a separate timer control (**computerTimer**). For easier games, we want a larger value for the **delay** property for this control. This slows down the computer's thought process. The **delay** values I chose are:

Difficulty Level	delay
Easiest	1000
Easy	750
Hard	500
Hardest	250

So with the **Hardest** difficulty, the computer makes moves 4 times as often as when the **Easiest** difficulty is selected.

Declare the timer using:

```
Timer computerTimer;
```

Add this code to the frame constructor (using the **Easiest delay** value):

```
computerTimer = new Timer(1000, new ActionListener()
{
  public void actionPerformed(ActionEvent e)
  {
    computerTimerActionPerformed(e);
  }
});
```

And, add this empty **ActionPerformed** method:

```
private void computerTimerActionPerformed(ActionEvent e)
{
}
```

We will use an **int** variable (**computerRandom**) to represent the percentage of time random logic is used and an **int** variable (**computerTime**) to represent the timer control **delay** property. Add these class level declarations to the project:

```
int computerRandom, computerTime;
```

Values for these two new variables are set in the **rdoDifficultyActionPerformed** method. The modified method is (changes are shaded):

```
private void
difficultyRadioButtonActionPerformed(ActionEvent e)
{
  String s = e.getActionCommand();
  if (s.equals("Easiest"))
  {
    difficulty = 1;
    computerRandom = 100;
    computerTime = 1000;
  }
  else if (s.equals("Easy"))
  {
    difficulty = 2;
    computerRandom = 75;
    computerTime = 750;
  }
  else if (s.equals("Hard"))
  {
    difficulty = 3;
    computerRandom = 50;
    computerTime = 500;
  }
  else if (s.equals("Hardest"))
  {
    difficulty = 4;
    computerRandom = 25;
    computerTime = 250;
  }
  computerTimer.setDelay(computerTime);
}
```

Make the noted modifications.

We need to start the computer's timer control (**computerTimer**) when playing the one player game. And, we need to stop it when done playing. This is done in the **gameButtonActionPerformed** method (new lines are shaded):

```
private void gameButtonActionPerformed(ActionEvent e)
{
  if (gameButton.getText().equals("New Game"))
  {
    gameButton.setText("Stop Game");
    optionsButton.setEnabled(false);
    exitButton.setEnabled(false);
    player1Hits = 0;
    player2Hits = 0;
    player1HitsTextField.setText("0");
    player2HitsTextField.setText("0");
    player1Left = maximumBalls;
    player2Left = maximumBalls;

player1LeftTextField.setText(String.valueOf(player1Left));

player2LeftTextField.setText(String.valueOf(player2Left));
    player1.rectangle = new Rectangle2D.Double(5, 0.5 *
snowPanel.getHeight() - 0.5 *
player1.image.getHeight(null),
player1.image.getWidth(null),
player1.image.getHeight(null));
    player2.rectangle = new
Rectangle2D.Double(snowPanel.getWidth() -
player2.image.getWidth(null) - 5, 0.5 *
snowPanel.getHeight() - 0.5 *
player2.image.getHeight(null),
player2.image.getWidth(null),
player2.image.getHeight(null));
    player1.isVisible = true;
    player2.isVisible = true;
    snowman1.rectangle = new Rectangle2D.Double(0.5 *
snowPanel.getWidth() - snowman1.image.getWidth(null),
myRandom.nextInt(snowPanel.getHeight()),
snowman1.image.getWidth(null),
snowman1.image.getHeight(null));
    snowman2.rectangle = new Rectangle2D.Double(0.5 *
snowPanel.getWidth(),
myRandom.nextInt(snowPanel.getHeight()),
snowman2.image.getWidth(null),
snowman2.image.getHeight(null));
    snowman1.ySpeed = snowmanSpeed();
    snowman2.ySpeed = snowmanSpeed();
```

```
        snowman1.isVisible = true;
        snowman2.isVisible = true;
        snowPanel.repaint();
        gameTimer.start();
        if (numberPlayers == 1)
          computerTimer.start();
        snowPanel.requestFocus();
      }
    else
      {
        gameTimer.stop();
        computerTimer.stop();
        player1.isVisible = false;
        player2.isVisible = false;
        snowball1.isVisible = false;
        snowball2.isVisible = false;
        snowman1.isVisible = false;
        snowman2.isVisible = false;
        gameButton.setText("New Game");
        optionsButton.setEnabled(true);
        exitButton.setEnabled(true);
        snowPanel.repaint();
      }
  }
```

Add the shaded lines. We have listed the entire **gameButtonActionPerformed** method – it is now complete.

Now, let's write the computer playing rules. We'll start with the simple, random rules. In these rules, the computer will just make random moves up and down the field, occasionally tossing a snowball. The only non-random element we add is that we only allow the computer to throw a snowball if it has at least as many snowballs left as the human player. This prevents the computer from tossing all its snowballs and becoming an easy target for the human. The rules I use are:

> ➢ Generate a random number from 0 to 4.
> ➢ If number is 0, toss snowball if computer has at least as many snowballs as player.
> ➢ If number is 1 or 2, move up.
> ➢ If number is 3 or 4, move down.

With these rules, a snowball is thrown 1 out of 5 times the computer makes a move, the computer's player moves up 2 of 5 times and moves down 2 of 5 times. There's no real intelligence involved – just random moves. Let's write some more intelligent rules.

In writing more detailed (smarter) playing rules, just think about how you would play the game. Smarter rules would be if the other player is "in range", take a toss. Otherwise, move away from the other player if he's tossed a snowball (defensive move) or move toward the other player to keep him range (offensive move). In our rules, we define "in range" to mean the difference between the two players' vertical position no more than 80 percent of a player's height. The rules I used are:

> - If "in range" and computer has at least as many snowballs as player, take toss.
> - If human player has tossed snowball or computer has no snowballs remaining, make defensive move:
>   - If human player is above computer player, move down.
>   - If human player is below computer player, move up.
> - Else, make offensive move:
>   - If human player is above computer player, move up.
>   - If human player is below computer player, move down.

Notice we still only toss a snowball when the computer has at least as many snowballs remaining as the player. We don't want the computer to run out of snowballs before the human player.

The code for both the simple and detailed computer logic is placed in the **computerTimerActionPerformed** method. Before writing this code, however, we need to address how we can make the computer player take a toss, move up or move down. With a human second player, pressing **J** would make Player 2 toss, pressing **K** would move Player 2 up and pressing **M** would move Player 2 down. It would be nice if there was a way we could make the computer player press these same keys for the desired action. And, we can. Java has something called a **Robot** object (cool name, huh?) that can be used to simulate a key press on the keyboard. To press the **J** key, the code is:

```
Robot robot = new Robot();
robot.keyPress(KeyEvent.VK_J);
```

where **KeyEvent.VK_J** is the integer key code for a **J**.

Java requires the **Robot** object and methods be in a **try/catch** block. We write a general method (**robotKeyPress**) to implement a robot key press. As an argument, this method requires the **int** key code. Add this method to your project:

```
private void robotKeyPress(int k)
{
  try
  {
    Robot robot = new Robot();
    robot.keyPress(k);
  }
  catch (Exception ex)
  {
  }
}
```

With this method, to press the J key requires this line of code:

```
robotKeyPress(KeyEvent.VK_J);
```

A word of warning ... if the **Snowball Toss** game is running and you switch to another program, like a word processor or text editor, the keystrokes generated by the robot will appear in your editor!! You could use this method to be a phantom typist!!

The **computerTimerActionPerformed** method that implements the computer player logic is (note where computer key presses are used):

```
private void computerTimerActionPerformed(ActionEvent e)
{
  int i;
  if (myRandom.nextInt(100) < computerRandom)
  {
    i = myRandom.nextInt(5); // random move
    if (i == 0)
    {
      if (player2Left >= player1Left)
        robotKeyPress(KeyEvent.VK_J); // take toss
    }
    else if (i <= 2)
      robotKeyPress(KeyEvent.VK_K); // move up
    else
      robotKeyPress(KeyEvent.VK_M); // move down
  }
  else
  {
    if (Math.abs(player1.rectangle.getY() -
player2.rectangle.getY()) < (int)(0.8 *
player1.image.getHeight(null)) && player2Left >=
player1Left)
        robotKeyPress(KeyEvent.VK_J); // take toss
    if (snowball1.isVisible || player2Left == 0)
    {
      if (player1.rectangle.getY() -
player2.rectangle.getY() < 0)
        robotKeyPress(KeyEvent.VK_M); // move down
      else
        robotKeyPress(KeyEvent.VK_K); // move up
    }
    else
    {
      if (player1.rectangle.getY() -
player2.rectangle.getY() < 0)
        robotKeyPress(KeyEvent.VK_K); // move up
      else
        robotKeyPress(KeyEvent.VK_M); // move down
    }
  }
}
```

Add this method to your project. You should be able to identify each step in the different computer player logics. Make sure you understand how the **computerRandom** value is used to determine whether randommmmk or detailed logic is used.

Save and run the project. Click **Options**, select a **One Player** game. Select a difficulty level. Click **OK**, then **New Game**. Then, watch out, the computer opponent will start tossing snowballs at you!

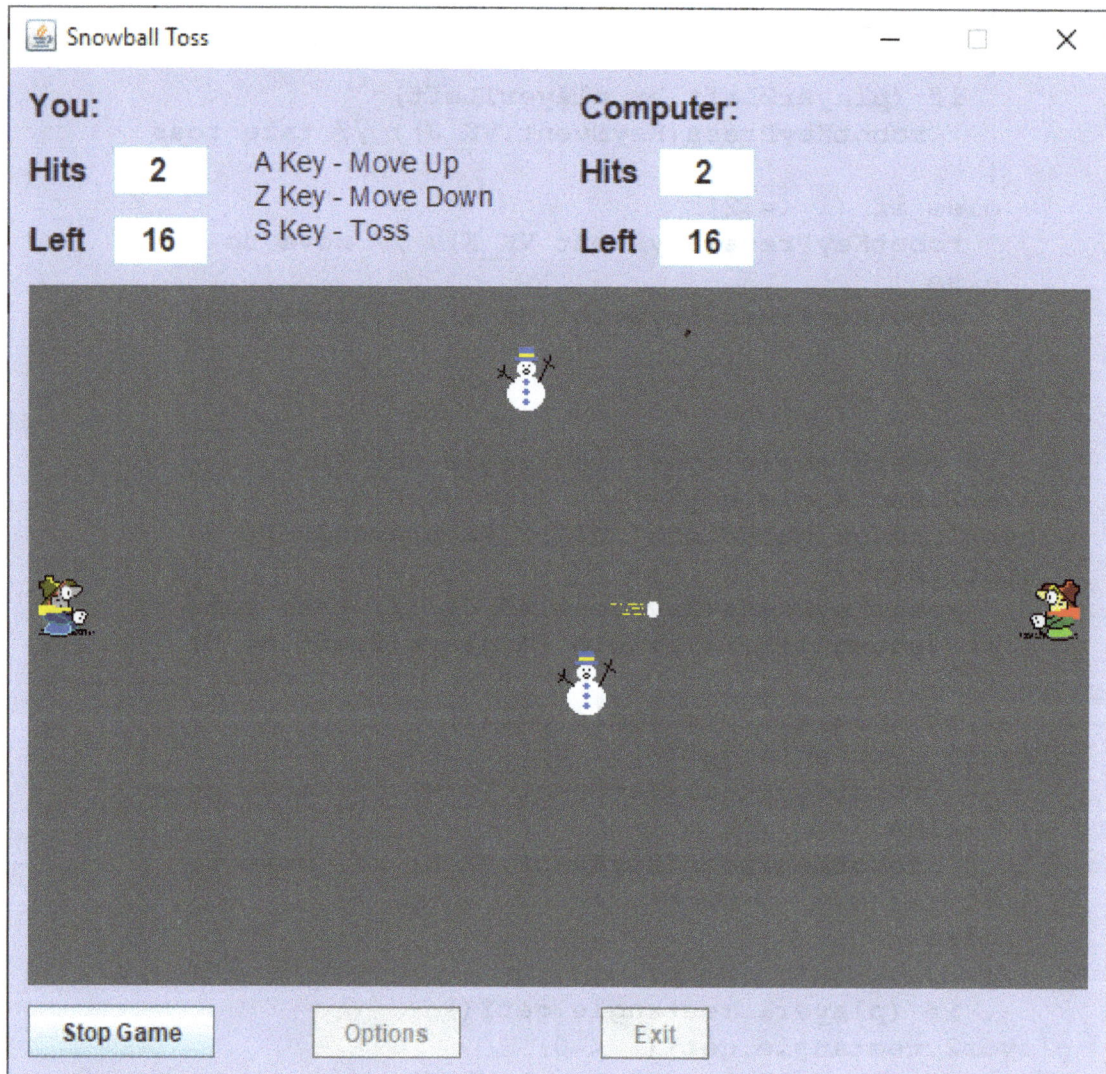

This completes the snowball toss game. As you play the game, against another player or against the computer, you'll find modifications you want to make. This is a fun part of game programming – tailoring themm game play to your desires and needs.

Snowball Toss Game Project Review

The **Snowball Toss Game Project** is now complete. Save and run the project and make sure it works as designed. Have fun playing the game against friends and family or against the computer. In the Appendix, we'll show you how you can share this game (or any other project) with other users.

If there are errors in your implementation, go back over the steps of frame and code design. Go over the developed code – make sure you understand how different parts of the project were coded. As mentioned in the beginning of this chapter, the completed project is saved as **SnowballToss** in the **\HomeJava\HomeJava Projects** project group.

While completing this project, new concepts and skills you should have gained include:

> ➢ Use of the **Rectangle2D** strshapeucture in graphics.
> ➢ How the **drawImage** graphics method are used.
> ➢ Using a tool like **IconEdit** to develop graphics files.
> ➢ How to add methods to classes.
> ➢ Using inheritance with classes.
> ➢ Using the keyboard for control of animated characters.
> ➢ Detecting collisions between **Rectangle2D** shapes.
> ➢ How to play sounds.
> ➢ How to develop game playing rules for the computer.

This is the last project in these notes. By now, you should be a fairly competent Java programmer. There's always more to learn though. Consult the Internet and bookstores for more books about skills you might want to gain.

Snowball Toss Game
Project Enhancements

Possible enhancements to the snowball toss game project include:

➤ Add another option to allow the user to select the number of snowballs to use. Look at the Swing **JSpinner** control to set such a value. Modify the configuration file so this value is saved.

➤ Players like to see their name "in lights." Add an option to have player's name placed on the frame instead of the generic titling information used now. You might want to save the names in the configuration file.

➤ Add some horizontal motion to the zombie snowmen.

➤ In the computer playing logic, no consideration is given to position of the zombie snowmen. Modify the logic so a toss is taken only when a snowman is not blocking the toss.

➤ If you play the game against a 'smart' computer, you will find it is possible to trap the computer player at the top or bottom of the playing field and fire away. Modify the code to have the computer player move away from such trapped situations.

➤ In the one player game, it is still possible to control the computer player manually using the J, K and M keys. Can you write code so this is not possible? It's not an easy task because of the **robotKeyPressed** method.

Snowball Toss Game Project
Java Code Listing

There are three files, **SnowballToss.java**, **Sprite.java** and **MovingSprite.java**.

<u>SnowballToss.java:</u>

```java
/*
 * SnowballToss.java
 */

package snowballtoss;
import javax.swing.*;
import java.awt.*;
import java.awt.event.*;
import java.io.*;
import java.awt.geom.*;
import java.util.Random;
import java.net.URL;
import java.applet.*;

import com.ctreber.aclib.image.ico.ICOFile;


public class SnowballToss extends JFrame
{

    JLabel player1Label = new JLabel();
    JLabel player1HitsLabel = new JLabel();
    JTextField player1HitsTextField = new JTextField();
    JLabel player1LeftLabel = new JLabel();
    JTextField player1LeftTextField = new JTextField();
    JTextArea player1TextArea = new JTextArea();
    JLabel player2Label = new JLabel();
    JLabel player2HitsLabel = new JLabel();
    JTextField player2HitsTextField = new JTextField();
    JLabel player2LeftLabel = new JLabel();
    JTextField player2LeftTextField = new JTextField();
    JTextArea player2TextArea = new JTextArea();
    SnowPanel snowPanel = new SnowPanel();
    static JPanel optionsPanel  = new JPanel();
    JPanel playersPanel  = new JPanel();
    ButtonGroup playersButtons = new ButtonGroup();
    JRadioButton onePlayerRadioButton = new JRadioButton();
    JRadioButton twoPlayersRadioButton = new JRadioButton();
```

```java
JPanel difficultyPanel  = new JPanel();
ButtonGroup difficultyButtons = new ButtonGroup();
JRadioButton easiestRadioButton = new JRadioButton();
JRadioButton easyRadioButton = new JRadioButton();
JRadioButton hardRadioButton = new JRadioButton();
JRadioButton hardestRadioButton = new JRadioButton();
JButton okButton = new JButton();
static JButton gameButton = new JButton();
JButton optionsButton = new JButton();
JButton exitButton = new JButton();

int numberPlayers, difficulty;
static Sprite player1, player2;
int player1Hits, player2Hits, player1Left, player2Left;
final int maximumBalls = 20;
final int playerIncrement = 5;
static MovingSprite snowball1, snowball2;
final int snowballSpeed = 20;
static MovingSprite snowman1, snowman2;
Random myRandom = new Random();
int computerRandom, computerTime;

Timer gameTimer;
Timer computerTimer;

AudioClip throwSound;
AudioClip splatSound;
AudioClip ouchSound;
AudioClip gameOverSound;

public static void main(String args[])
{
  // create frame
  new SnowballToss().setVisible(true);
}

public SnowballToss()
{
  // frame constructor
  setTitle("Snowball Toss");
  getContentPane().setBackground(new Color(192, 192, 255));
  setResizable(false);
  addWindowListener(new WindowAdapter()
  {
    public void windowClosing(WindowEvent evt)
    {
      exitForm(evt);
```

```
        }
    });

    getContentPane().setLayout(new GridBagLayout());
    GridBagConstraints gridConstraints;

    Font myFont = new Font("Arial", Font.BOLD, 16);

    player1Label.setText("You:");
    player1Label.setFont(myFont);
    gridConstraints = new GridBagConstraints();
    gridConstraints.gridx = 0;
    gridConstraints.gridy = 0;
    gridConstraints.gridwidth = 2;
    gridConstraints.insets = new Insets(10, 10, 0, 0);
    gridConstraints.anchor = GridBagConstraints.WEST;
    getContentPane().add(player1Label, gridConstraints);

    player1HitsLabel.setText("Hits");
    player1HitsLabel.setFont(myFont);
    gridConstraints = new GridBagConstraints();
    gridConstraints.gridx = 0;
    gridConstraints.gridy = 1;
    gridConstraints.insets = new Insets(10, 10, 0, 0);
    gridConstraints.anchor = GridBagConstraints.WEST;
    getContentPane().add(player1HitsLabel, gridConstraints);

    player1HitsTextField.setPreferredSize(new Dimension(50,
25));
    player1HitsTextField.setText("0");
    player1HitsTextField.setFont(myFont);
    player1HitsTextField.setEditable(false);
    player1HitsTextField.setBackground(Color.WHITE);

player1HitsTextField.setHorizontalAlignment(SwingConstants.CE
NTER);
    gridConstraints = new GridBagConstraints();
    gridConstraints.gridx = 1;
    gridConstraints.gridy = 1;
    gridConstraints.insets = new Insets(10, 10, 0, 0);
    getContentPane().add(player1HitsTextField,
gridConstraints);

    player1LeftLabel.setText("Left");
    player1LeftLabel.setFont(myFont);
    gridConstraints = new GridBagConstraints();
    gridConstraints.gridx = 0;
```

```
    gridConstraints.gridy = 2;
    gridConstraints.insets = new Insets(10, 10, 0, 0);
    gridConstraints.anchor = GridBagConstraints.WEST;
    getContentPane().add(player1LeftLabel, gridConstraints);

    player1LeftTextField.setPreferredSize(new Dimension(50,
25));
    player1LeftTextField.setText("20");
    player1LeftTextField.setFont(myFont);
    player1LeftTextField.setEditable(false);
    player1LeftTextField.setBackground(Color.WHITE);

player1LeftTextField.setHorizontalAlignment(SwingConstants.CE
NTER);
    gridConstraints = new GridBagConstraints();
    gridConstraints.gridx = 1;
    gridConstraints.gridy = 2;
    gridConstraints.insets = new Insets(10, 10, 0, 0);
    getContentPane().add(player1LeftTextField,
gridConstraints);

    player1TextArea.setPreferredSize(new Dimension(160, 60));
    player1TextArea.setText("A Key - Move Up\nZ Key - Move
Down\nS Key - Toss");
    player1TextArea.setFont(new Font("Arial", Font.PLAIN,
14));
    player1TextArea.setEditable(false);

player1TextArea.setBackground(getContentPane().getBackground(
));
    gridConstraints = new GridBagConstraints();
    gridConstraints.gridx = 2;
    gridConstraints.gridy = 1;
    gridConstraints.gridheight = 2;
    gridConstraints.insets = new Insets(10, 20, 0, 0);
    getContentPane().add(player1TextArea, gridConstraints);

    player2Label.setText("Computer:");
    player2Label.setFont(myFont);
    gridConstraints = new GridBagConstraints();
    gridConstraints.gridx = 3;
    gridConstraints.gridy = 0;
    gridConstraints.gridwidth = 2;
    gridConstraints.insets = new Insets(10, 10, 0, 0);
    gridConstraints.anchor = GridBagConstraints.WEST;
    getContentPane().add(player2Label, gridConstraints);
```

```
    player2HitsLabel.setText("Hits");
    player2HitsLabel.setFont(myFont);
    gridConstraints = new GridBagConstraints();
    gridConstraints.gridx = 3;
    gridConstraints.gridy = 1;
    gridConstraints.insets = new Insets(10, 10, 0, 0);
    gridConstraints.anchor = GridBagConstraints.WEST;
    getContentPane().add(player2HitsLabel, gridConstraints);

    player2HitsTextField.setPreferredSize(new Dimension(50,
25));
    player2HitsTextField.setText("0");
    player2HitsTextField.setFont(myFont);
    player2HitsTextField.setEditable(false);
    player2HitsTextField.setBackground(Color.WHITE);

player2HitsTextField.setHorizontalAlignment(SwingConstants.CE
NTER);
    gridConstraints = new GridBagConstraints();
    gridConstraints.gridx = 4;
    gridConstraints.gridy = 1;
    gridConstraints.insets = new Insets(10, 10, 0, 0);
    getContentPane().add(player2HitsTextField,
gridConstraints);

    player2LeftLabel.setText("Left");
    player2LeftLabel.setFont(myFont);
    gridConstraints = new GridBagConstraints();
    gridConstraints.gridx = 3;
    gridConstraints.gridy = 2;
    gridConstraints.insets = new Insets(10, 10, 0, 0);
    gridConstraints.anchor = GridBagConstraints.WEST;
    getContentPane().add(player2LeftLabel, gridConstraints);

    player2LeftTextField.setPreferredSize(new Dimension(50,
25));
    player2LeftTextField.setText("20");
    player2LeftTextField.setFont(myFont);
    player2LeftTextField.setEditable(false);
    player2LeftTextField.setBackground(Color.WHITE);

player2LeftTextField.setHorizontalAlignment(SwingConstants.CE
NTER);
    gridConstraints = new GridBagConstraints();
    gridConstraints.gridx = 4;
    gridConstraints.gridy = 2;
    gridConstraints.insets = new Insets(10, 10, 0, 0);
```

```
    getContentPane().add(player2LeftTextField,
gridConstraints);

    player2TextArea.setPreferredSize(new Dimension(140, 60));
    player2TextArea.setText("K Key - Move Up\nM Key - Move
Down\nJ Key - Toss");
    player2TextArea.setFont(new Font("Arial", Font.PLAIN,
14));
    player2TextArea.setEditable(false);

player2TextArea.setBackground(getContentPane().getBackground(
));
    gridConstraints = new GridBagConstraints();
    gridConstraints.gridx = 5;
    gridConstraints.gridy = 1;
    gridConstraints.gridheight = 2;
    gridConstraints.insets = new Insets(10, 20, 0, 0);
    getContentPane().add(player2TextArea, gridConstraints);

    snowPanel.setPreferredSize(new Dimension(550, 350));
    snowPanel.setBackground(Color.GRAY);
    snowPanel.setLayout(new GridBagLayout());
    gridConstraints = new GridBagConstraints();
    gridConstraints.gridx = 0;
    gridConstraints.gridy = 3;
    gridConstraints.gridwidth = 6;
    gridConstraints.insets = new Insets(10, 10, 10, 10);
    getContentPane().add(snowPanel, gridConstraints);
    snowPanel.addKeyListener(new KeyAdapter()
    {
      public void keyPressed(KeyEvent e)
      {
        snowPanelKeyPressed(e);
      }
    });

    optionsPanel.setPreferredSize(new Dimension(200, 280));
    optionsPanel.setBackground(new Color(255, 255, 192));
    optionsPanel.setVisible(false);
    optionsPanel.setLayout(new GridBagLayout());
    gridConstraints = new GridBagConstraints();
    gridConstraints.gridx = 0;
    gridConstraints.gridy = 0;
    snowPanel.add(optionsPanel, gridConstraints);

    playersPanel.setPreferredSize(new Dimension(140, 55));
```

```
playersPanel.setBorder(BorderFactory.createTitledBorder("Numb
er of Players"));
    playersPanel.setBackground(new Color(255, 255, 192));
    playersPanel.setLayout(new GridBagLayout());
    gridConstraints = new GridBagConstraints();
    gridConstraints.gridx = 0;
    gridConstraints.gridy = 0;
    optionsPanel.add(playersPanel, gridConstraints);

    onePlayerRadioButton.setText("One");
    onePlayerRadioButton.setBackground(new Color(255, 255,
192));
    onePlayerRadioButton.setSelected(true);
    onePlayerRadioButton.setLayout(new GridBagLayout());
    playersButtons.add(onePlayerRadioButton);
    gridConstraints = new GridBagConstraints();
    gridConstraints.gridx = 0;
    gridConstraints.gridy = 0;
    playersPanel.add(onePlayerRadioButton, gridConstraints);
    onePlayerRadioButton.addActionListener(new ActionListener
()
    {
      public void actionPerformed(ActionEvent e)
      {
        playersRadioButtonActionPerformed(e);
      }
    });

    twoPlayersRadioButton.setText("Two");
    twoPlayersRadioButton.setBackground(new Color(255, 255,
192));
    twoPlayersRadioButton.setLayout(new GridBagLayout());
    playersButtons.add(twoPlayersRadioButton);
    gridConstraints = new GridBagConstraints();
    gridConstraints.gridx = 1;
    gridConstraints.gridy = 0;
    playersPanel.add(twoPlayersRadioButton, gridConstraints);
    twoPlayersRadioButton.addActionListener(new
ActionListener ()
    {
      public void actionPerformed(ActionEvent e)
      {
        playersRadioButtonActionPerformed(e);
      }
    });
```

```
    difficultyPanel.setPreferredSize(new Dimension(140,
140));

difficultyPanel.setBorder(BorderFactory.createTitledBorder("D
ifficulty"));
    difficultyPanel.setBackground(new Color(255, 255, 192));
    difficultyPanel.setLayout(new GridBagLayout());
    gridConstraints = new GridBagConstraints();
    gridConstraints.gridx = 0;
    gridConstraints.gridy = 1;
    optionsPanel.add(difficultyPanel, gridConstraints);

    easiestRadioButton.setText("Easiest");
    easiestRadioButton.setBackground(new Color(255, 255,
192));
    easiestRadioButton.setSelected(true);
    easiestRadioButton.setLayout(new GridBagLayout());
    difficultyButtons.add(easiestRadioButton);
    gridConstraints = new GridBagConstraints();
    gridConstraints.gridx = 0;
    gridConstraints.gridy = 0;
    gridConstraints.anchor = GridBagConstraints.WEST;
    difficultyPanel.add(easiestRadioButton, gridConstraints);
    easiestRadioButton.addActionListener(new ActionListener
()
    {
      public void actionPerformed(ActionEvent e)
      {
        difficultyRadioButtonActionPerformed(e);
      }
    });

    easyRadioButton.setText("Easy");
    easyRadioButton.setBackground(new Color(255, 255, 192));
    easyRadioButton.setLayout(new GridBagLayout());
    difficultyButtons.add(easyRadioButton);
    gridConstraints = new GridBagConstraints();
    gridConstraints.gridx = 0;
    gridConstraints.gridy = 1;
    gridConstraints.anchor = GridBagConstraints.WEST;
    difficultyPanel.add(easyRadioButton, gridConstraints);
    easyRadioButton.addActionListener(new ActionListener ()
    {
      public void actionPerformed(ActionEvent e)
      {
        difficultyRadioButtonActionPerformed(e);
      }
```

```
});

hardRadioButton.setText("Hard");
hardRadioButton.setBackground(new Color(255, 255, 192));
hardRadioButton.setLayout(new GridBagLayout());
difficultyButtons.add(hardRadioButton);
gridConstraints = new GridBagConstraints();
gridConstraints.gridx = 0;
gridConstraints.gridy = 2;
gridConstraints.anchor = GridBagConstraints.WEST;
difficultyPanel.add(hardRadioButton, gridConstraints);
hardRadioButton.addActionListener(new ActionListener ()
{
  public void actionPerformed(ActionEvent e)
  {
    difficultyRadioButtonActionPerformed(e);
  }
});

hardestRadioButton.setText("Hardest");
hardestRadioButton.setBackground(new Color(255, 255,
192));
hardestRadioButton.setLayout(new GridBagLayout());
difficultyButtons.add(hardestRadioButton);
gridConstraints = new GridBagConstraints();
gridConstraints.gridx = 0;
gridConstraints.gridy = 3;
gridConstraints.anchor = GridBagConstraints.WEST;
difficultyPanel.add(hardestRadioButton, gridConstraints);
hardestRadioButton.addActionListener(new ActionListener
()
{
  public void actionPerformed(ActionEvent e)
  {
    difficultyRadioButtonActionPerformed(e);
  }
});

okButton.setText("OK");
gridConstraints = new GridBagConstraints();
gridConstraints.gridx = 0;
gridConstraints.gridy = 2;
gridConstraints.insets = new Insets(10, 0, 0, 0);
optionsPanel.add(okButton, gridConstraints);
okButton.addActionListener(new ActionListener ()
{
  public void actionPerformed(ActionEvent e)
```

```
      {
        okButtonActionPerformed(e);
      }
});

gameButton.setText("New Game");
gridConstraints = new GridBagConstraints();
gridConstraints.gridx = 0;
gridConstraints.gridy = 4;
gridConstraints.gridwidth = 2;
gridConstraints.insets = new Insets(0, 10, 10, 0);
getContentPane().add(gameButton, gridConstraints);
gameButton.addActionListener(new ActionListener ()
{
  public void actionPerformed(ActionEvent e)
  {
    gameButtonActionPerformed(e);
  }
});

optionsButton.setText("Options");
gridConstraints = new GridBagConstraints();
gridConstraints.gridx = 2;
gridConstraints.gridy = 4;
gridConstraints.insets = new Insets(0, 0, 10, 0);
getContentPane().add(optionsButton, gridConstraints);
optionsButton.addActionListener(new ActionListener ()
{
  public void actionPerformed(ActionEvent e)
  {
    optionsButtonActionPerformed(e);
  }
});

exitButton.setText("Exit");
gridConstraints = new GridBagConstraints();
gridConstraints.gridx = 3;
gridConstraints.gridy = 4;
gridConstraints.gridwidth = 2;
gridConstraints.insets = new Insets(0, 0, 10, 0);
getContentPane().add(exitButton, gridConstraints);
exitButton.addActionListener(new ActionListener ()
{
  public void actionPerformed(ActionEvent e)
  {
    exitButtonActionPerformed(e);
  }
```

```
    });

    gameTimer = new Timer(50, new ActionListener()
    {
      public void actionPerformed(ActionEvent e)
      {
        gameTimerActionPerformed(e);
      }
    });

    computerTimer = new Timer(1000, new ActionListener()
    {
      public void actionPerformed(ActionEvent e)
      {
        computerTimerActionPerformed(e);
      }
    });

    pack();
    Dimension screenSize =
Toolkit.getDefaultToolkit().getScreenSize();
    setBounds((int) (0.5 * (screenSize.width - getWidth())),
(int) (0.5 * (screenSize.height - getHeight())), getWidth(),
getHeight());

    try
    {
      BufferedReader inputFile = new BufferedReader(new
FileReader("snowball.ini"));
      numberPlayers =
Integer.valueOf(inputFile.readLine()).intValue();
      difficulty =
Integer.valueOf(inputFile.readLine()).intValue();
      inputFile.close();
    }
    catch (Exception ex)
    {
      numberPlayers = 1;
      difficulty = 1;
    }
    if (difficulty == 1)
      easiestRadioButton.doClick();
    else if (difficulty == 2)
      easyRadioButton.doClick();
    else if (difficulty == 3)
      hardRadioButton.doClick();
    else
```

```
      hardestRadioButton.doClick();
    if (numberPlayers == 1)
      onePlayerRadioButton.doClick();
    else
      twoPlayersRadioButton.doClick();

    player1Left = maximumBalls;
    player2Left = maximumBalls;

player1LeftTextField.setText(String.valueOf(player1Left));

player2LeftTextField.setText(String.valueOf(player2Left));

    // create sprites
    player1 = new Sprite();
    player2 = new Sprite();
    snowball1 = new MovingSprite();
    snowball2 = new MovingSprite();
    snowman1 = new MovingSprite();
    snowman2 = new MovingSprite();
    // read in icon files and sounds
    try
    {
      player1.image = new
ICOFile("player1.ico").getDescriptor(0).getImageRGB();
      player2.image = new
ICOFile("player2.ico").getDescriptor(0).getImageRGB();
      snowball1.image = new
ICOFile("player1ball.ico").getDescriptor(0).getImageRGB();
      snowball2.image = new
ICOFile("player2ball.ico").getDescriptor(0).getImageRGB();
      snowman1.image = new
ICOFile("snowman.ico").getDescriptor(0).getImageRGB();
      snowman2.image = new
ICOFile("snowman.ico").getDescriptor(0).getImageRGB();
      throwSound = Applet.newAudioClip(new URL("file:" +
"throw.wav"));
      splatSound = Applet.newAudioClip(new URL("file:" +
"splat.wav"));
      ouchSound = Applet.newAudioClip(new URL("file:" +
"ouch.wav"));
      gameOverSound = Applet.newAudioClip(new URL("file:" +
"gameover.wav"));
    }
    catch (Exception ex)
    {
      // can print error message if desired
```

```
    }

  }

  private void exitForm(WindowEvent evt)
  {
    try
    {
      PrintWriter outputFile = new PrintWriter(new
BufferedWriter(new FileWriter("snowball.ini")));
      outputFile.println(numberPlayers);
      outputFile.println(difficulty);
      outputFile.flush();
      outputFile.close();
    }
    catch (Exception ex)
    {
    }
    System.exit(0);
  }

  private void playersRadioButtonActionPerformed(ActionEvent
e)
  {
    if (e.getActionCommand().equals("One"))
    {
      numberPlayers = 1;
      player1Label.setText("You:");
      player2Label.setText("Computer:");
      player2TextArea.setVisible(false);
      difficultyPanel.setVisible(true);
    }
    else
    {
      numberPlayers = 2;
      player1Label.setText("Player 1:");
      player2Label.setText("Player 2:");
      player2TextArea.setVisible(true);
      difficultyPanel.setVisible(false);
    }
  }

  private void
difficultyRadioButtonActionPerformed(ActionEvent e)
  {
    String s = e.getActionCommand();
    if (s.equals("Easiest"))
```

```java
    {
      difficulty = 1;
      computerRandom = 100;
      computerTime = 1000;
    }
    else if (s.equals("Easy"))
    {
      difficulty = 2;
      computerRandom = 75;
      computerTime = 750;
    }
    else if (s.equals("Hard"))
    {
      difficulty = 3;
      computerRandom = 50;
      computerTime = 500;
    }
    else if (s.equals("Hardest"))
    {
      difficulty = 4;
      computerRandom = 25;
      computerTime = 250;
    }
    computerTimer.setDelay(computerTime);
  }

  private void okButtonActionPerformed(ActionEvent e)
  {
    gameButton.setEnabled(true);
    optionsButton.setEnabled(true);
    exitButton.setEnabled(true);
    optionsPanel.setVisible(false);
  }

  private void gameButtonActionPerformed(ActionEvent e)
  {
    if (gameButton.getText().equals("New Game"))
    {
      gameButton.setText("Stop Game");
      optionsButton.setEnabled(false);
      exitButton.setEnabled(false);
      player1Hits = 0;
      player2Hits = 0;
      player1HitsTextField.setText("0");
      player2HitsTextField.setText("0");
      player1Left = maximumBalls;
      player2Left = maximumBalls;
```

```
player1LeftTextField.setText(String.valueOf(player1Left));

player2LeftTextField.setText(String.valueOf(player2Left));
      player1.rectangle = new Rectangle2D.Double(5, 0.5 *
snowPanel.getHeight() - 0.5 * player1.image.getHeight(null),
player1.image.getWidth(null), player1.image.getHeight(null));
      player2.rectangle = new
Rectangle2D.Double(snowPanel.getWidth() -
player2.image.getWidth(null) - 5, 0.5 * snowPanel.getHeight()
- 0.5 * player2.image.getHeight(null),
player2.image.getWidth(null), player2.image.getHeight(null));
      player1.isVisible = true;
      player2.isVisible = true;
      snowman1.rectangle = new Rectangle2D.Double(0.5 *
snowPanel.getWidth() - snowman1.image.getWidth(null),
myRandom.nextInt(snowPanel.getHeight()),
snowman1.image.getWidth(null),
snowman1.image.getHeight(null));
      snowman2.rectangle = new Rectangle2D.Double(0.5 *
snowPanel.getWidth(),
myRandom.nextInt(snowPanel.getHeight()),
snowman2.image.getWidth(null),
snowman2.image.getHeight(null));
      snowman1.ySpeed = snowmanSpeed();
      snowman2.ySpeed = snowmanSpeed();
      snowman1.isVisible = true;
      snowman2.isVisible = true;
      snowPanel.repaint();
      gameTimer.start();
      if (numberPlayers == 1)
        computerTimer.start();
      snowPanel.requestFocus();
    }
    else
    {
      gameTimer.stop();
      computerTimer.stop();
      player1.isVisible = false;
      player2.isVisible = false;
      snowball1.isVisible = false;
      snowball2.isVisible = false;
      snowman1.isVisible = false;
      snowman2.isVisible = false;
      gameButton.setText("New Game");
      optionsButton.setEnabled(true);
      exitButton.setEnabled(true);
```

```java
      snowPanel.repaint();
    }
  }

  private void optionsButtonActionPerformed(ActionEvent e)
  {
    gameButton.setEnabled(false);
    optionsButton.setEnabled(false);
    exitButton.setEnabled(false);
    optionsPanel.setVisible(true);
  }

  private void exitButtonActionPerformed(ActionEvent e)
  {
    exitForm(null);
  }

  private void snowPanelKeyPressed(KeyEvent e)
  {
    if (gameButton.getText().equals("New Game"))
        return;
    // get current location for possible update
    double newY1 = player1.rectangle.getY(), newY2 =
player2.rectangle.getY();
    if (e.getKeyCode() == e.VK_A)
    {
      newY1 -= playerIncrement;
      if (newY1 < 0)
        newY1 = 0;
    }
    else if (e.getKeyCode() == e.VK_Z)
    {
      newY1 += playerIncrement;
      if (newY1 > snowPanel.getHeight() -
player1.rectangle.getHeight())
        newY1 = snowPanel.getHeight() -
player1.rectangle.getHeight();
    }
    else if (e.getKeyCode() == e.VK_S)
    {
      if (!snowball1.isVisible && player1Left > 0)
      {
        throwSound.play();
        player1Left--;

player1LeftTextField.setText(String.valueOf(player1Left));
```

```
        snowball1.rectangle = new
Rectangle2D.Double(player1.rectangle.getX() +
player1.rectangle.getWidth(), player1.rectangle.getY(),
snowball1.image.getWidth(null),
snowball1.image.getHeight(null));
        snowball1.isVisible = true;
      }
    }
    else if (e.getKeyCode() == e.VK_K)
    {
      newY2 -= playerIncrement;
      if (newY2 < 0)
        newY2 = 0;
    }
    else if (e.getKeyCode() == e.VK_M)
    {
      newY2 += playerIncrement;
      if (newY2 > snowPanel.getHeight() -
player2.rectangle.getHeight())
        newY2 = snowPanel.getHeight() -
player2.rectangle.getHeight();
    }
    else if (e.getKeyCode() == e.VK_J)
    {
      if (!snowball2.isVisible && player2Left > 0)
      {
        throwSound.play();
        player2Left--;

player2LeftTextField.setText(String.valueOf(player2Left));
        snowball2.rectangle = new
Rectangle2D.Double(player2.rectangle.getX() -
snowball2.image.getWidth(null), player2.rectangle.getY(),
snowball2.image.getWidth(null),
snowball2.image.getHeight(null));
        snowball2.isVisible = true;
      }
    }
    player1.rectangle = new
Rectangle2D.Double(player1.rectangle.getX(), newY1,
player1.rectangle.getWidth(), player1.rectangle.getHeight());
    player2.rectangle = new
Rectangle2D.Double(player2.rectangle.getX(), newY2,
player2.rectangle.getWidth(), player2.rectangle.getHeight());
    snowPanel.repaint();
  }
```

```
private void gameTimerActionPerformed(ActionEvent e)
{
  // move snowmen
  snowman1.move(0, snowman1.ySpeed);
  if (snowman1.rectangle.getY() < -
snowman1.image.getHeight(null) || snowman1.rectangle.getY() >
snowPanel.getHeight())
    {
      // recompute speed
      snowman1.ySpeed = snowmanSpeed();
      if (snowman1.ySpeed > 0)
        snowman1.rectangle = new
Rectangle2D.Double(snowman1.rectangle.getX(), -
snowman1.image.getHeight(null),
snowman1.rectangle.getWidth(),
snowman1.rectangle.getHeight());
      else
        snowman1.rectangle = new
Rectangle2D.Double(snowman1.rectangle.getX(),
snowPanel.getHeight(), snowman1.rectangle.getWidth(),
snowman1.rectangle.getHeight());
    }
  snowman2.move(0, snowman2.ySpeed);
  if (snowman2.rectangle.getY() < -
snowman2.image.getHeight(null) || snowman2.rectangle.getY() >
snowPanel.getHeight())
    {
      // recompute speed
      snowman2.ySpeed = snowmanSpeed();
      if (snowman2.ySpeed > 0)
        snowman2.rectangle = new
Rectangle2D.Double(snowman2.rectangle.getX(), -
snowman2.image.getHeight(null),
snowman2.rectangle.getWidth(),
snowman2.rectangle.getHeight());
      else
        snowman2.rectangle = new
Rectangle2D.Double(snowman2.rectangle.getX(),
snowPanel.getHeight(), snowman2.rectangle.getWidth(),
snowman2.rectangle.getHeight());
    }
  // status of player 1 snowball
  if (snowball1.isVisible)
    {
      snowball1.move(snowballSpeed, 0);
      if (snowball1.rectangle.getX() > snowPanel.getWidth())
        snowball1.isVisible = false; // off screen
```

```
      else if (snowball1.collided(player2.rectangle))
      {
        ouchSound.play();
        player1Hits++;

player1HitsTextField.setText(String.valueOf(player1Hits));
        snowball1.isVisible = false;
      }
      else if (snowball1.collided(snowman1.rectangle) ||
snowball1.collided(snowman2.rectangle))
      {
        splatSound.play();
        snowball1.isVisible = false;
      }
    }
    // status of player 2 snowball
    if (snowball2.isVisible)
    {
      snowball2.move(-snowballSpeed, 0);
      if (snowball2.rectangle.getX() < 0)
        snowball2.isVisible = false; // off screen
      else if (snowball2.collided(player1.rectangle))
      {
        ouchSound.play();
        player2Hits++;

player2HitsTextField.setText(String.valueOf(player2Hits));
        snowball2.isVisible = false;
      }
      else if (snowball2.collided(snowman1.rectangle) ||
snowball2.collided(snowman2.rectangle))
      {
        splatSound.play();
        snowball2.isVisible = false;
      }
    }
    snowPanel.repaint();
    // check status of game
    if (!snowball1.isVisible && player1Left == 0 &&
!snowball2.isVisible && player2Left == 0)
    {
      gameOverSound.play();
      gameButton.doClick();
    }
  }

  private void computerTimerActionPerformed(ActionEvent e)
```

```java
  {
    int i;
    if (myRandom.nextInt(100) < computerRandom)
    {
      i = myRandom.nextInt(5); // random move
      if (i == 0)
      {
        if (player2Left >= player1Left)
          robotKeyPress(KeyEvent.VK_J); // take toss
      }
      else if (i <= 2)
        robotKeyPress(KeyEvent.VK_K); // move up
      else
        robotKeyPress(KeyEvent.VK_M); // move down
    }
    else
    {
      if (Math.abs(player1.rectangle.getY() -
player2.rectangle.getY()) < (int)(0.8 *
player1.image.getHeight(null)) && player2Left >= player1Left)
        robotKeyPress(KeyEvent.VK_J); // take toss
      if (snowball1.isVisible || player2Left == 0)
      {
        if (player1.rectangle.getY() -
player2.rectangle.getY() < 0)
          robotKeyPress(KeyEvent.VK_M); // move down
        else
          robotKeyPress(KeyEvent.VK_K); // move up
      }
      else
      {
        if (player1.rectangle.getY() -
player2.rectangle.getY() < 0)
          robotKeyPress(KeyEvent.VK_K); // move up
        else
          robotKeyPress(KeyEvent.VK_M); // move down
      }
    }
  }

  private int snowmanSpeed()
  {
    final int speedMin = 1;
    final int speedMax = 4;
    int speed;
    speed = myRandom.nextInt(speedMax - speedMin + 1) +
speedMin;
```

```java
    if (myRandom.nextInt(2) == 0)
      speed = -speed;
    return(speed);
  }

  private void robotKeyPress(int k)
  {
    try
    {
      Robot robot = new Robot();
      robot.keyPress(k);
    }
    catch (Exception ex)
    {
    }
  }

}

class SnowPanel extends JPanel
{
  public void paintComponent(Graphics g)
  {
    Graphics2D g2D = (Graphics2D) g;
    super.paintComponent(g2D);

    if (SnowballToss.gameButton.getText().equals("Stop
Game"))
    {
      SnowballToss.player1.draw(g2D);
      SnowballToss.player2.draw(g2D);
      if (SnowballToss.snowball1.isVisible)
        SnowballToss.snowball1.draw(g2D);
      if (SnowballToss.snowball2.isVisible)
        SnowballToss.snowball2.draw(g2D);
      SnowballToss.snowman1.draw(g2D);
      SnowballToss.snowman2.draw(g2D);
    }
    else
    {
      if (SnowballToss.gameButton.isEnabled())
      {
        g2D.setFont(new Font("Arial", Font.BOLD, 36));
        g2D.setPaint(Color.YELLOW);
        g2D.drawString("Game Over", 180, 180);
      }
      else
```

```
            {
                SnowballToss.optionsPanel.repaint();
            }
        }
        g2D.dispose();
    }
}
```

Sprite.java:

```java
package snowballtoss;
import java.awt.geom.*;
import java.awt.*;


public class Sprite
{
  public Image image;
  public Rectangle2D.Double rectangle;
  public boolean isVisible = false;

  public void draw(Graphics2D g2D)
  {
    g2D.drawImage(this.image, (int) this.rectangle.getX(),
(int) this.rectangle.getY(), null);
  }

  public void move(int dx, int dy)
  {
    this.rectangle.setRect(this.rectangle.getX() + dx,
this.rectangle.getY() + dy, this.rectangle.getWidth(),
this.rectangle.getHeight());
  }
}
```

MovingSprite.java:

```java
package snowballtoss;
import java.awt.geom.*;

public class MovingSprite extends Sprite
{
  public int xSpeed;
  public int ySpeed;

  public boolean collided(Rectangle2D.Double r)
  {
    return (!this.rectangle.createIntersection(r).isEmpty());
  }
}
```

Appendix
Distributing a Java Project

Preview

I bet you're ready to show your friends and colleagues some of the projects you have built using Java. Just give them a copy of all your project files, ask them to download and install the Java SDK, download and install NetBeans and learn how to open and run a project. Then, have them open your project and run the application.

I think you'll agree this is asking a lot of your friends, colleagues, and, ultimately, your user base. Fortunately, there are other solutions. In this Appendix, we will look at two possibilities, one simple, one not so simple. We'll use the **Snowball Toss** game just built as an example. You can easily make needed modifications for other projects. The example is built using Windows. Similar steps can be taken using other operating systems (Linux, UNIX, MacOS).

Executable (jar) Files

A simple way to run a Java application outside of the IDE environment is with an executable version of the application, a so-called **jar** (java **ar**chive) file. With such a file, a user can simply double-click the file and the corresponding application will run. As mentioned, we will work with the **Snowball Toss** project in the **\HomeJava\HomeJava Projects** folder.

jar files are created using the Java **jar.exe** application. You can make your jar file runnable by telling **jar.exe** which class has main. To do that, you first need to create a **manifest** file. A manifest is a text file with a "Main-Class" directive and "Class-Path" directives for any external jar files needed.

Creating a Manifest File in NetBeans

Make the **Snowball Toss** project the main project. Then,

1. Right-click the project's name and choose **Properties**.
2. Select the **Run** category and **snowballtoss.SnowballToss** in the **Main Class** field.
3. Click **OK** to close the **Project Properties** dialog box.

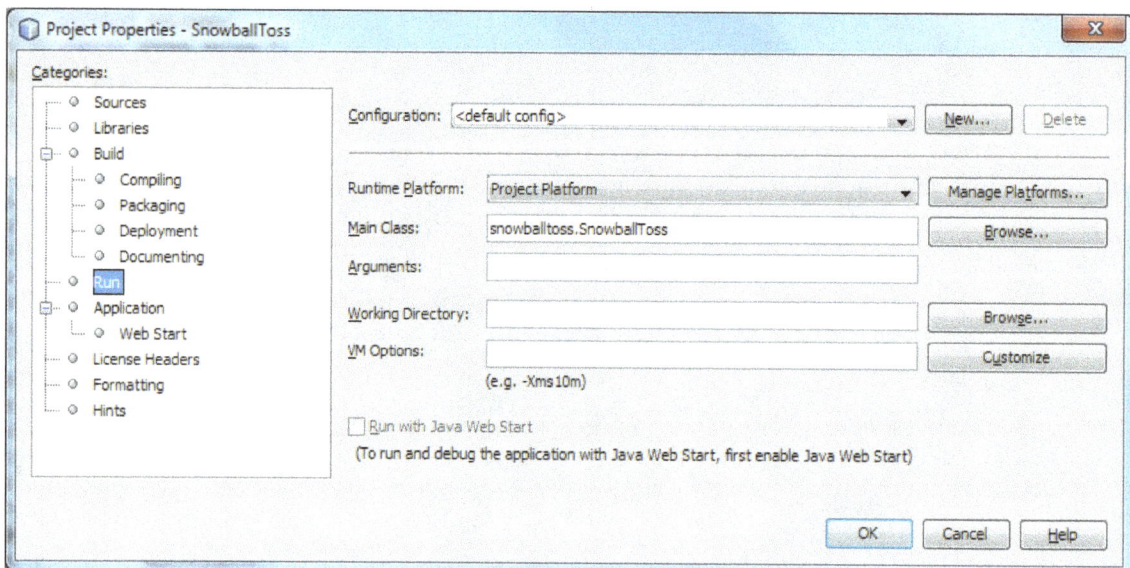

Creating a jar File in NetBeans

Now that you have your sources ready and your project configured, it is time to build your project. To build the project:

- Choose **Run** > **Build Project**
- Alternatively, right-click the project's name in the **Projects** window and choose **Build**.

When you build your project, a **jar** file containing your project is created inside the project's **/dist** folder.

With Windows Explorer, go to your project folder. Open the **dist** folder. The **SnowballToss.jar** file will be there (as will a **lib** folder, containing external jar files).

Copy that file and folder to your project folder (the folder with all the graphics and sound files). Double-click the **SnowballToss.jar** file and the **Snowball Toss** program will appear:

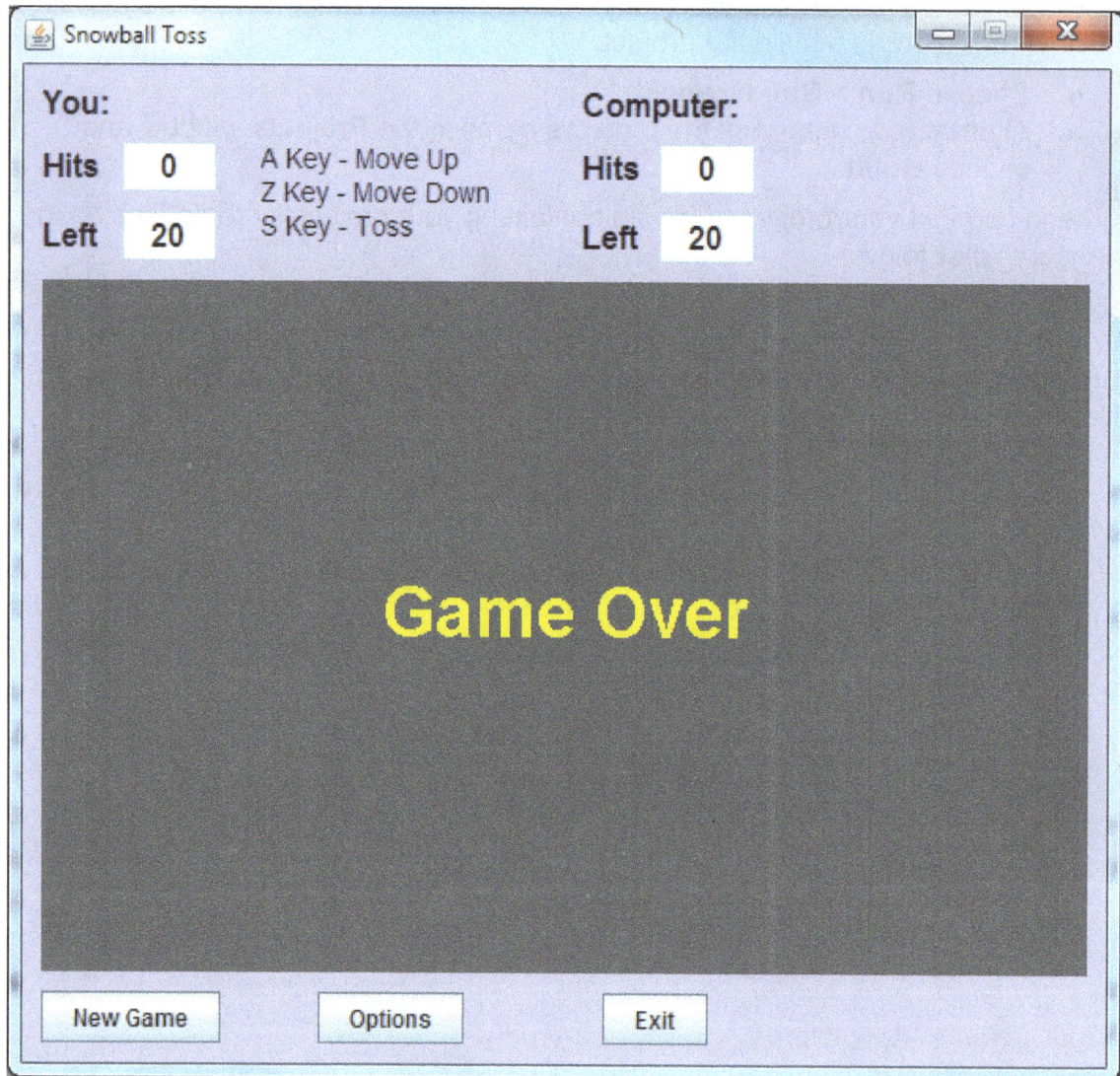

Notice the file has a "plain vanilla" Java frame icon in the title bar area – we will change that soon.

So, to distribute a Java project to other users, you need to give them a copy of the project's **jar** file and copies of any additional files the project needs to run (jar files, data files, graphics files, sound files). These files can be copied to a floppy disk or CD-ROM and transferred to other users. For the **Snowball Toss** game, the files to distribute are:

SnowballToss.jar
aclibico-2.1.jar, log4j-1.2.8.jar
snowball.ini
player1.ico, player1Ball.ico, player2.ico, player2Ball.ico, snowman.ico
gameover.wav, ouch.wav, splat.wav, throw.wav

For another user to run the project on his/her computer, they need to copy the files you give them to a folder they create. To run the project, they would then navigate to that folder and double-click the **jar** file (just like we did for the **Snowball Toss** game). Alternatively, the user could create a shortcut to the **jar** file and place it on their desktop or **Programs** file menu. We will see how to do this soon, but first let's "dress up" our application a bit.

One more thing before moving on. **Snowball Toss** runs on my computer (and will work on yours) because I have the **Java Run-Time Environment** (JRE) installed (it is installed when Java is installed). Every Java application needs the JRE to be installed on the hosting computer. Installing the JRE is similar to installing the Java SDK. Full details can be found at:

http://java.com/en/download/index.jsp

So, in addition to our application's files, we also need to point potential users to the JRE and ask them to download and install the environment on their computer.

Application Icons

Recall there is a plain Java icon that appears in the upper left hand corner of the frame. Icons are also used to represent programs in the **Programs** menu and to represent programs on the desktop. The default icons are ugly! We need the capability to change them. The icon associated with the frame is different from the icons used to represent the application in the Windows menu and desktop. We discuss both.

The icon associated with a frame is based on a graphics file. Changing this icon is simple. The idea is to assign a unique icon to indicate the frame's function. To assign an icon, use this line of code when the frame (**myFrame** in this example) is first created:

```
myFrame.setIconImage(new ImageIcon(icon).getImage());
```

where **icon** is some graphics file (usually a **gif** file). If the file is a **ico** file, we must use the **ICOFile** method:

```
myFrame.setIconImage(new
ICOFile(icon).getDescriptor(0).getImageRGB());
```

Open the **Snowball Toss** project in NetBeans. We will use the **snowman.ico** graphic for the icon. Add the shaded lines of code to the top of the frame constructor code:

```java
public SnowballToss()
{
  // frame constructor
  setTitle("Snowball Toss");
  getContentPane().setBackground(new Color(192, 192,
255));
  try
  {
    setIconImage(new
ICOFile("snowman.ico").getDescriptor(0).getImageRGB());
  }
  catch (Exception ex)
  {
  }
  setResizable(false);
  addWindowListener(new WindowAdapter()
  {
    public void windowClosing(WindowEvent evt)
    {
      exitForm(evt);
    }
  });

  getContentPane().setLayout(new GridBagLayout());
  GridBagConstraints gridConstraints;
    .
    .
```

Save, compile and run the project again. The cute little icon appears:

At this point, rebuild the jar file for the project so the icon is included.

Icons associated with the program menu and desktop are always Windows icon files (**ico** extension). They are special 32 x 32 graphics. The Internet and other sources offer a wealth of such icon files from which you can choose. But, it's also fun to design your own icon to add that personal touch.

Using IconEdit

Remember the **IconEdit** program we used in the snowball toss game. We can use that here to to design and save icons. Recall it is included with these notes in the folder **\HomeJava\HomeJava Projects\IconEdit**. To run **IconEdit**, click **Start** on the Windows task bar, then click **Run**. Find the **IconEdit** program (use **Browse** mode), then click **OK**. When the **IconEdit** program window appears, click the **File** menu heading, then choose **New** (we are creating a new icon). The following editor window will appear:

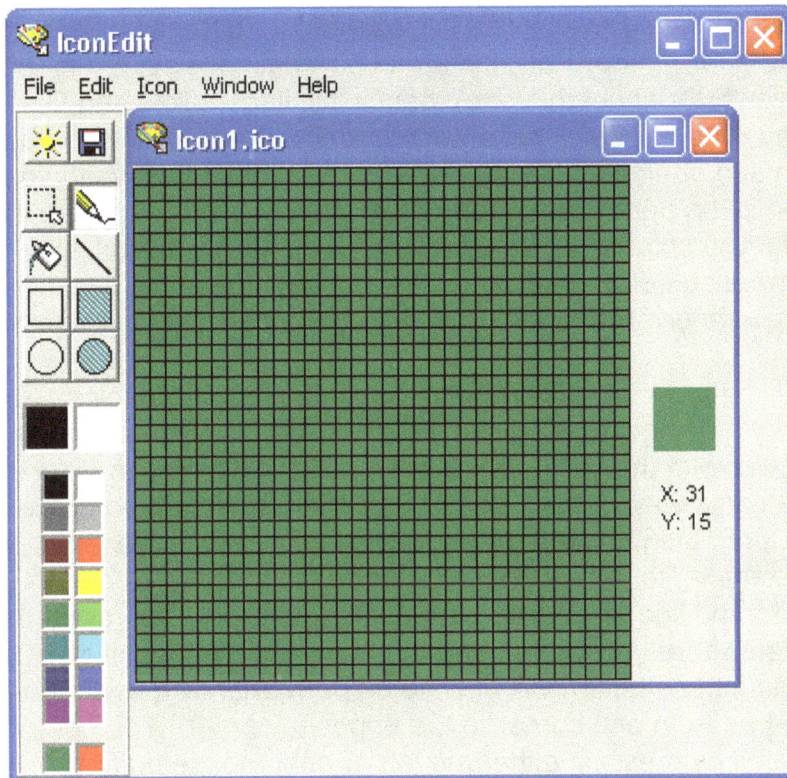

The editor window displays two representations of the icon: a large zoomed-in square (a 32 x 32 grid) that's eight times bigger than the actual icon, and a small square to its right that's actual size. The zoomed square is where the editing takes place. New icons appear as solid green with a black square surrounding each pixel representation. The **pixels** (small squares) are, of course, eight times actual size like the square itself for ease of editing. The green color is not actually the starting color of the icon, but instead represents the transparent "color" (whatever is behind this green color on the screen will be seen).

The basic idea of **IconEdit** is to draw an icon in the 32 x 32 grid displayed. You can draw single points, lines, open rectangles and ovals, and filled rectangles and ovals. Various colors are available. Once completed, the icon file can be saved for attaching to a form. **IconEdit** has a tool bar that consists of eight tools: capture (we won't talk about this one), pencil, fill, line, hollow and filled rectangle, and hollow and filled ellipse. These will be familiar to anyone who has used a paint program and on-line help is available. The default tool when you start editing an icon is the pencil, since this is the tool you'll probably use the most. The pencil let's you color one pixel at a time. To change a pixel, simply place the point of the pencil cursor over a pixel in the big editing square and click. You can pencil-draw several pixels at once by dragging the pencil over an area.

To change editing tools, simply click the tool button of your choice. The fill tool (represented by a paint can) will color the pixel you point to and all adjacent pixels of the same color with the color you've selected. The remaining five tools all operate in the same way. You click and hold the mouse button at the starting pixel position, drag the mouse to an ending position, and release the mouse button. For example, to draw a line, click and hold the mouse button on the starting point for the line and drag to the ending point. As you drag, the line will stretch between where you started and the current ending position. Only when you release the mouse button will the line be permanently drawn. For a rectangle or an ellipse, drag from one corner to the opposite corner. You control the color that the tool uses by pressing either the left or right mouse button.

The two large color squares right under the tools are the current colors for the left and right mouse buttons, respectively. When you start **IconEdit**, the left mouse button color is black and the right mouse button color is white. If you click with the left mouse button on a pixel with the pencil tool, for example, the pixel will turn black. Click with the right mouse button and the pixel will turn white. To change the default colors, click on one of the 16 colors in the palette just below the current color boxes with either the left or right mouse button. Clicking on a palette color with the left button will change the left button color and a right button click will change the right button color. You can pick the transparent "color" at the bottom of the editor if you want a pixel to be transparent.

Try drawing an icon using **IconEdit**. It's really pretty easy. Once you have finished your icon, save it. Click **File**, then **Save**. Icon files are special graphics files saved with an **ico** extension. The save window is just like the window you've used to save files in other Windows programs. Remember where you saved your icon (usually in your project folder).

With **IconEdit**, you can now customize your games with your own icons. And, another fun thing to do is load in other icon files you find (click **File**, then **Open**) and see how much artistic talent really goes into creating an icon. You can even modify these other icons and save them for your use.

I found an icon on the Internet to use with the **Snowball Toss** game – a snowflake!!. The file **snowflake.ico** is included in the **\HomeJava\HomeJava Projects\Snowball Toss Projects** folder. When you open this file in **IconEdit**, you can see the detail in the icon:

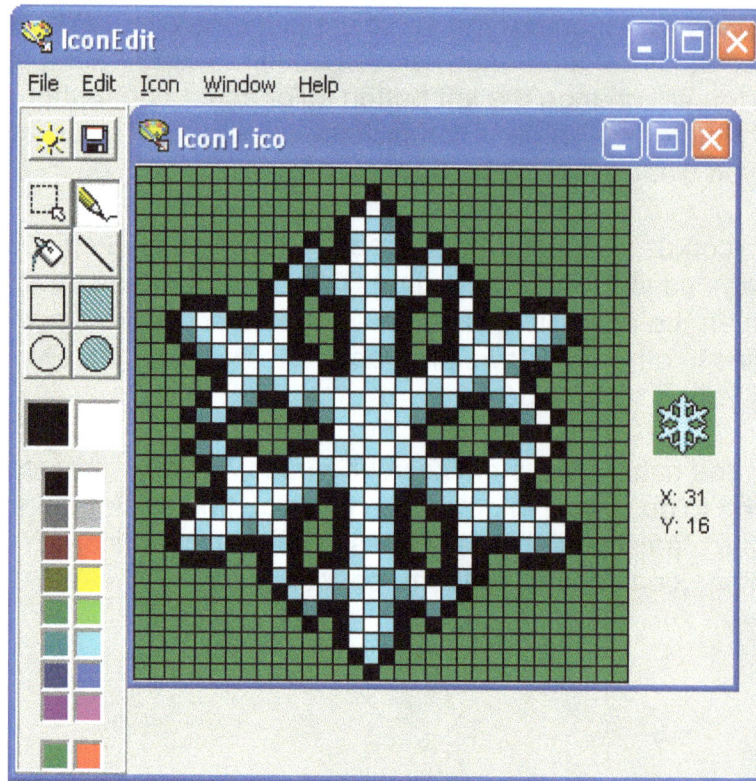

We'll now use this icon to help your user run the game.

Running a Project on Another Computer

As mentioned, users of your program need to copy the files you give them into a folder of their choice. Once done, they should do one or both of these steps to make it easier to run the project:

1. Add a shortcut to the computer desktop.
2. Add a shortcut to the **All Programs** item on the **Start** menu.

Let's see how to do both of these steps with our example. We do this for Windows 7. The steps are similar for other versions of Windows.

I copied all the needed files to a folder named **MySnowballToss** on my computer. Examining the files in that folder, I see:

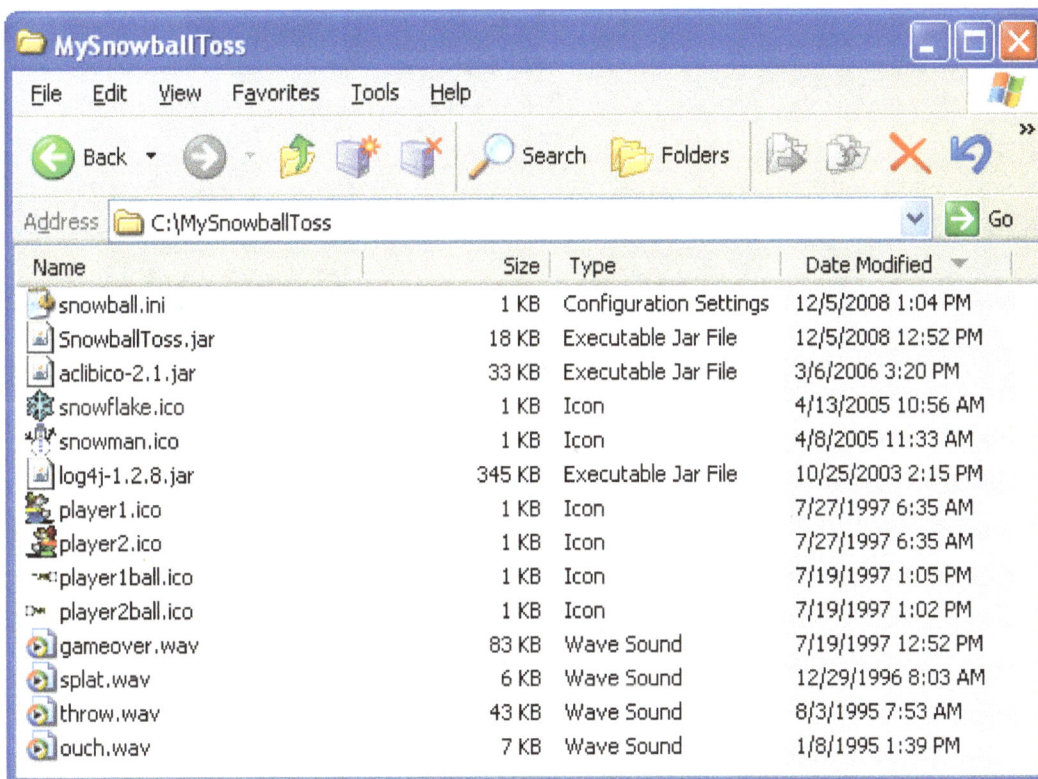

Name	Size	Type	Date Modified
snowball.ini	1 KB	Configuration Settings	12/5/2008 1:04 PM
SnowballToss.jar	18 KB	Executable Jar File	12/5/2008 12:52 PM
aclibico-2.1.jar	33 KB	Executable Jar File	3/6/2006 3:20 PM
snowflake.ico	1 KB	Icon	4/13/2005 10:56 AM
snowman.ico	1 KB	Icon	4/8/2005 11:33 AM
log4j-1.2.8.jar	345 KB	Executable Jar File	10/25/2003 2:15 PM
player1.ico	1 KB	Icon	7/27/1997 6:35 AM
player2.ico	1 KB	Icon	7/27/1997 6:35 AM
player1ball.ico	1 KB	Icon	7/19/1997 1:05 PM
player2ball.ico	1 KB	Icon	7/19/1997 1:02 PM
gameover.wav	83 KB	Wave Sound	7/19/1997 12:52 PM
splat.wav	6 KB	Wave Sound	12/29/1996 8:03 AM
throw.wav	43 KB	Wave Sound	8/3/1995 7:53 AM
ouch.wav	7 KB	Wave Sound	1/8/1995 1:39 PM

To create a shortcut to the executable file, right-click **SnowballToss.jar** and choose **Create Shortcut**. The shortcut will appear in the folder:

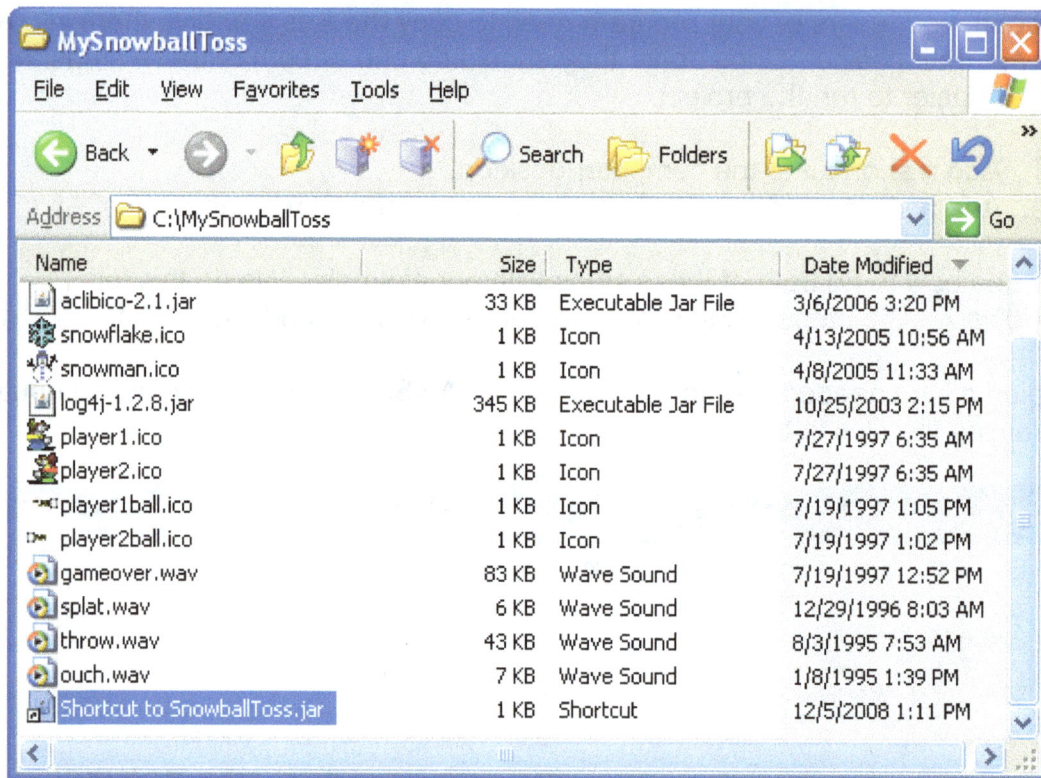

Give the shortcut an appropriate name (I used **Snowball Toss**).

To move the shortcut to the desktop, right-click the shortcut and choose **Copy**. Then, navigate to your computer's desktop. Right-click the desktop and choose **Paste**. The shortcut will appear on the desktop:

Let's change the icon. Right-click the shortcut and choose **Properties**. This window appears:

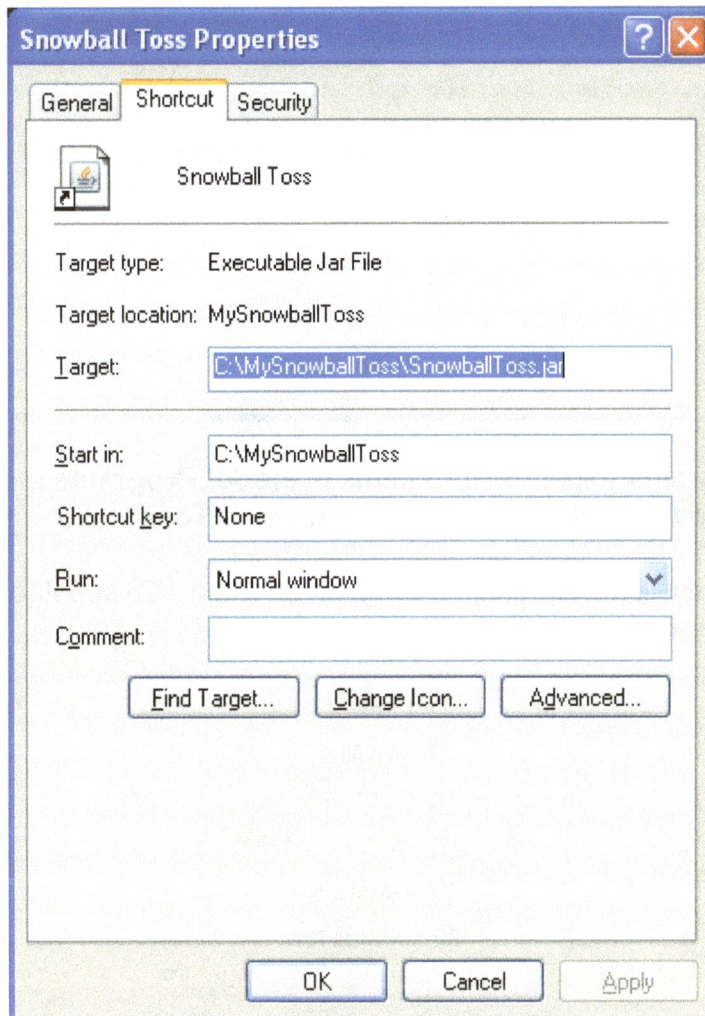

Click the **Change Icon** button. Navigate to your project folder and select the **snowflake.ico** file. Close out the properties window and the desktop shortcut should now appear as:

If you double-click this icon, the **Snowball Toss** game will begin.

To add the program shortcut to the **All Programs** item on the **Start** menu, Click **Start**, then select **All Programs**. Right-click **All Programs** and select **Open**.

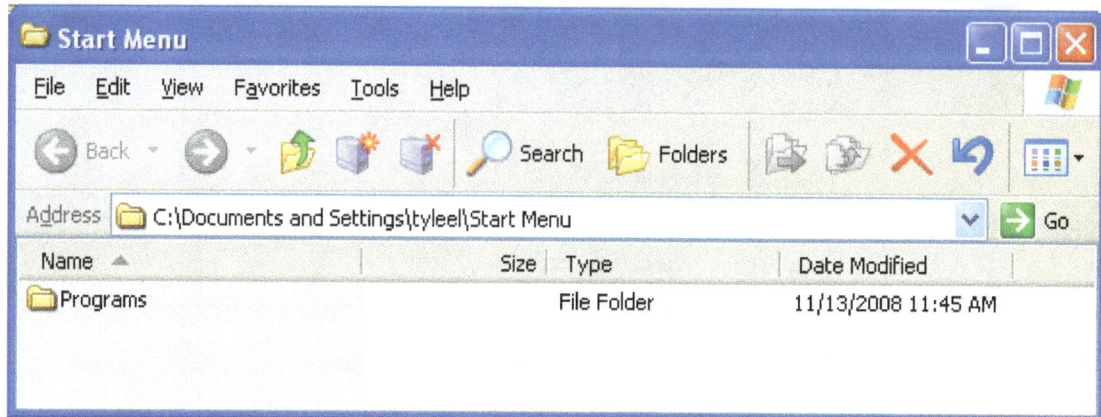

Open the **Programs** folder. All programs in the **All Programs** menu will be listed. Copy and paste the desktop shortcut to **Snowball Toss** into this folder.

The **Start** menu will now contain the project shortcut. To see it, click **Start**, then choose **All Programs**:

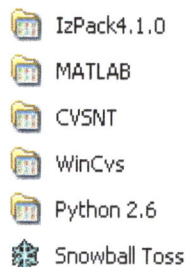

Click **Snowball Toss** and the game begins.

Your user now has two ways to run the project on their computer – via the desktop or via the **Programs** menu. If you ever modify your program, you will need to provide your user with a new copy of the **jar** file (and any additional files that may have changed).

Appendix - Installing Java and NetBeans

Downloading and Installing Java

To write and run programs using Java, you need the **Java Development Kit** (JDK) and the **NetBeans Integrated Development Environment** (IDE). These are free products that you can download from the Internet. This simply means we will copy a file onto our computer to allow installation of Java. Each product requires a separate download and installation process.

Java Development Kit

1. Start up your web browser (Internet Explorer, Chrome, Firefox, Safari or other browser) and go to Java web site:

https://www.oracle.com/technetwork/java/javase/downloads/jdk11-downloads-5066655.html

This web site has lots of useful Java information. As you become more proficient in your programming skills, you will go to this site often for answers to programming questions, interaction with other Java programmers, and lots of sample programs.

2. Once on the page with the JDK download links, accept the Licensing Agreement and choose the link corresponding to your computer's operating system.

For Microsoft Windows: select the Windows exe file

Java SE Development Kit 11.0.3

You must accept the Oracle Technology Network License Agreement for Oracle Java SE to download this software.
Thank you for accepting the Oracle Technology Network License Agreement for Oracle Java SE; you may now download this software.

Product / File Description	File Size	Download
Linux	147.31 MB	jdk-11.0.3_linux-x64_bin.deb
Linux	154.04 MB	jdk-11.0.3_linux-x64_bin.rpm
Linux	171.37 MB	jdk-11.0.3_linux-x64_bin.tar.gz
macOS	166.2 MB	jdk-11.0.3_osx-x64_bin.dmg
macOS	166.52 MB	jdk-11.0.3_osx-x64_bin.tar.gz
Solaris SPARC	186.85 MB	jdk-11.0.3_solaris-sparcv9_bin.tar.gz
Windows	150.98 MB	jdk-11.0.3_windows-x64_bin.exe
Windows	171 MB	jdk-11.0.3_windows-x64_bin.zip

Instructions for installing Java on other platforms such as Linux or Solaris can also be found on the website. My screenshots in these notes will be Microsoft Windows.

For Mac OS: click on the macOS dmg file

Java SE Development Kit 11.0.3

You must accept the Oracle Technology Network License Agreement for Oracle Java SE to download this software.
Thank you for accepting the Oracle Technology Network License Agreement for Oracle Java SE; you may now download this software.

Product / File Description	File Size	Download
Linux	147.31 MB	⬇jdk-11.0.3_linux-x64_bin.deb
Linux	154.04 MB	⬇jdk-11.0.3_linux-x64_bin.rpm
Linux	171.37 MB	⬇jdk-11.0.3_linux-x64_bin.tar.gz
macOS	166.2 MB	⬇jdk-11.0.3_osx-x64_bin.dmg
macOS	166.52 MB	⬇jdk-11.0.3_osx-x64_bin.tar.gz
Solaris SPARC	186.85 MB	⬇jdk-11.0.3_solaris-sparcv9_bin.tar.gz
Windows	150.98 MB	⬇jdk-11.0.3_windows-x64_bin.exe
Windows	171 MB	⬇jdk-11.0.3_windows-x64_bin.zip

For Linux OS: click on the Linux deb file

Java SE Development Kit 11.0.3

You must accept the Oracle Technology Network License Agreement for Oracle Java SE to download this software.
Thank you for accepting the Oracle Technology Network License Agreement for Oracle Java SE; you may now download this software.

Product / File Description	File Size	Download
Linux	147.31 MB	⬇jdk-11.0.3_linux-x64_bin.deb
Linux	154.04 MB	⬇jdk-11.0.3_linux-x64_bin.rpm
Linux	171.37 MB	⬇jdk-11.0.3_linux-x64_bin.tar.gz
macOS	166.2 MB	⬇jdk-11.0.3_osx-x64_bin.dmg
macOS	166.52 MB	⬇jdk-11.0.3_osx-x64_bin.tar.gz
Solaris SPARC	186.85 MB	⬇jdk-11.0.3_solaris-sparcv9_bin.tar.gz
Windows	150.98 MB	⬇jdk-11.0.3_windows-x64_bin.exe
Windows	171 MB	⬇jdk-11.0.3_windows-x64_bin.zip

Once you select a file, you may be asked to create an Oracle Account – follow the requested steps.

3. You will be asked what you want to do with the selected download file. Click **Run**. The installation begins.

4. The Java installer will unpack some files and an introductory window will appear:

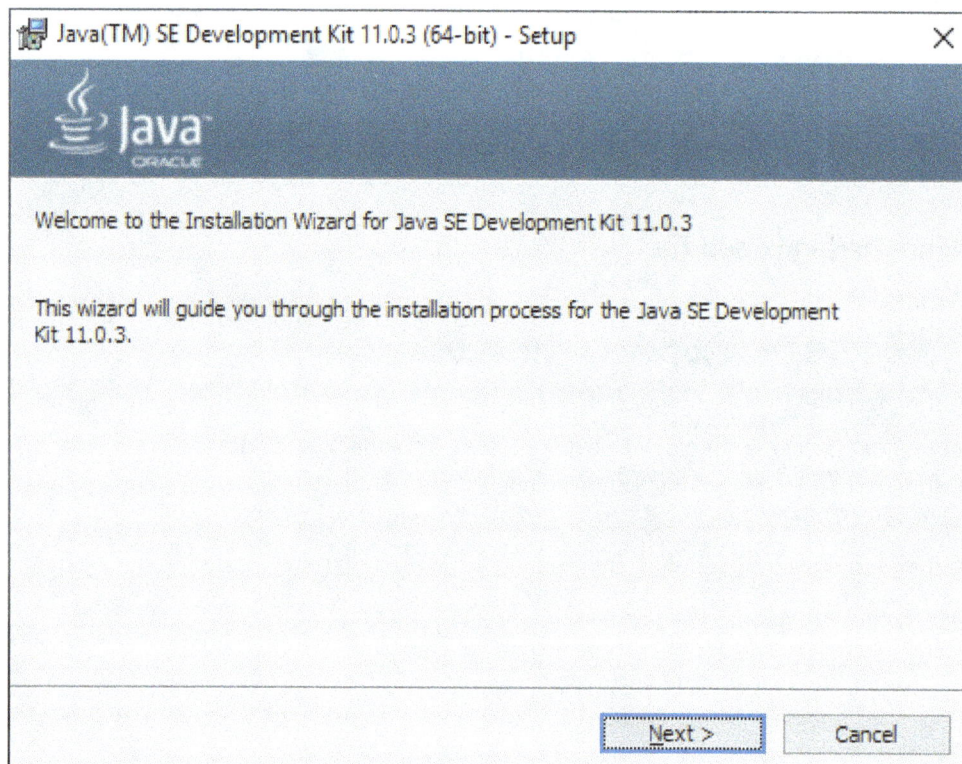

Click **Next** to start the installation. Several windows will appear in sequence. Accept the default choices by clicking **Next** at each window.

When complete (it will take a while), you will see this window:

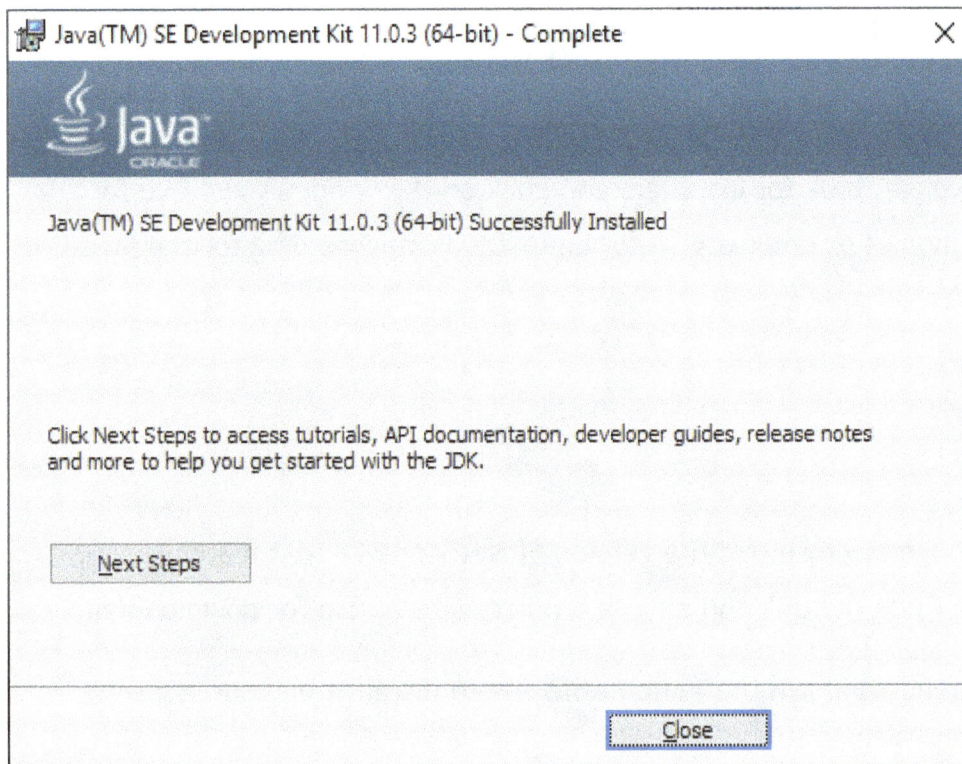

Click **Close** and the installation will complete. Next, let's install NetBeans.

NetBeans Integrated Development Environment

1. Go to this website:

2. https://netbeans.apache.org/download/nb111/nb111.html

3. On this web page, look for Installers and click on the windows-x64.exe for Microsoft Windows or linux-x64.sh for Linux OS or macosx.dmg for the MAC OS:

- Apache-NetBeans-11.1-bin-windows-x64.exe (SHA-512, PGP ASC)
- Apache-NetBeans-11.1-bin-linux-x64.sh (SHA-512, PGP ASC)
- Apache-NetBeans-11.1-bin-macosx.dmg (SHA-512, PGP ASC)

Click on the link above to download the version of NetBeans 11 that matches your Operating System. Click the link and choose a mirror site to use for downloading.

Once downloaded, click and run the **executable** file to install it on your system.

Running NetBeans

You now have Java and the **NetBeans** IDE installed on your computer. All of our programming work will be done using NetBeans. Let's make sure **NetBeans** installed correctly. To start using NetBeans under Microsoft Windows,

- Double-click the **NetBeans** shortcut on your computer's desktop

You can rename this shortcut if you choose. To start using NetBeans under the MAC OS,

- Click on the **Finder** and go to the **Applications Folder**.

The NetBeans program should start (several windows and menus will appear).

We will learn more about NetBeans in the notes. For now, we want to make some formatting changes. In Java programming, indentations in the code we write are used to delineate common blocks. The NetBeans IDE uses four spaces for indentations as a default. This author (and these notes) uses two spaces. To make this change, choose the **Tools** menu item and click **Options**. In the window that appears, choose the **Editor** option and the **Formatting** tab:

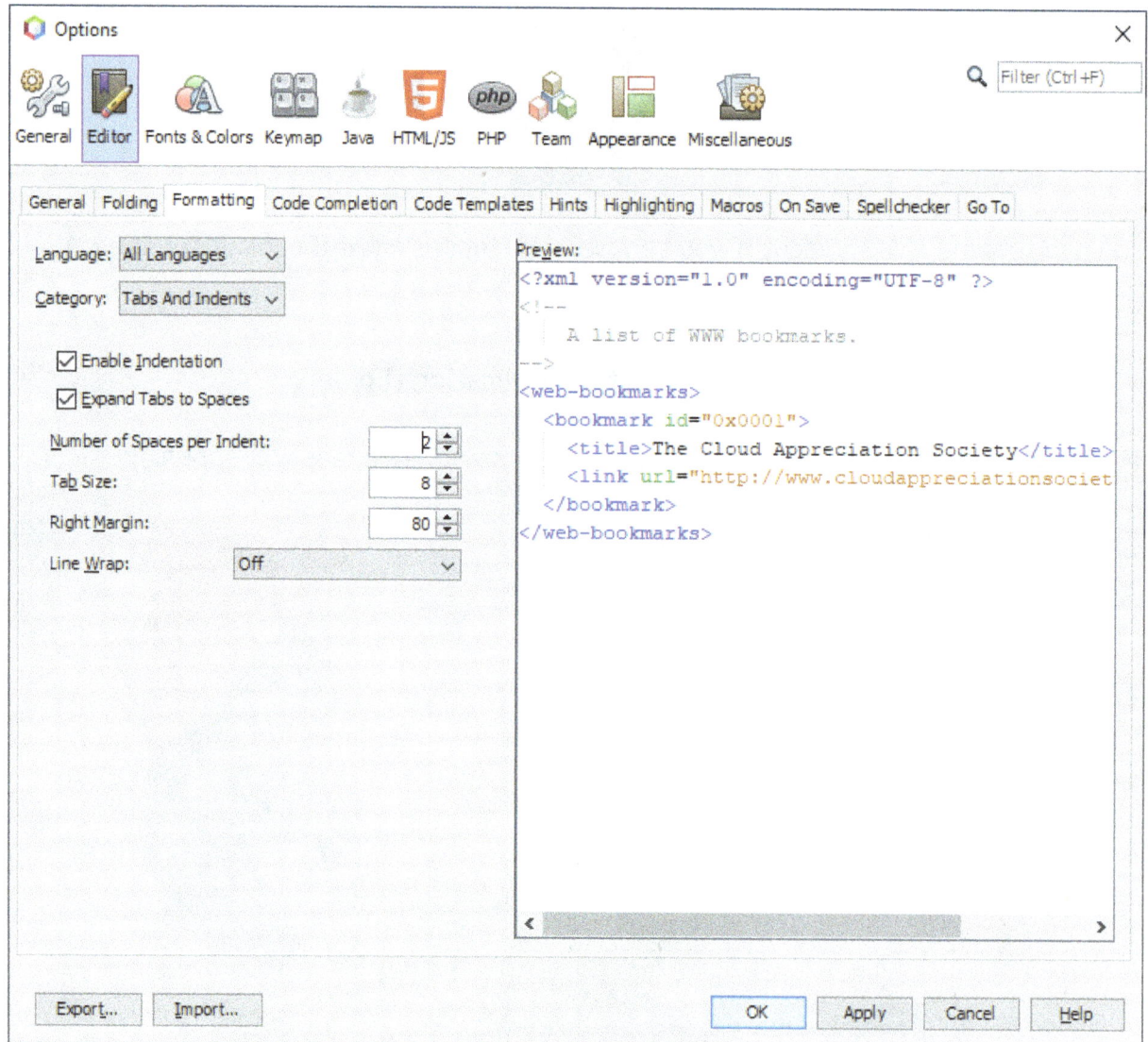

As shown, choose the **Tabs and Indents Category** and set the **Number of Spaces per Indent** to **2.**

Before leaving this window, we make another change. Braces (curly brackets) are used to start and stop blocks of code. We choose to have these brackets always be on a separate line – it makes checking code much easier.

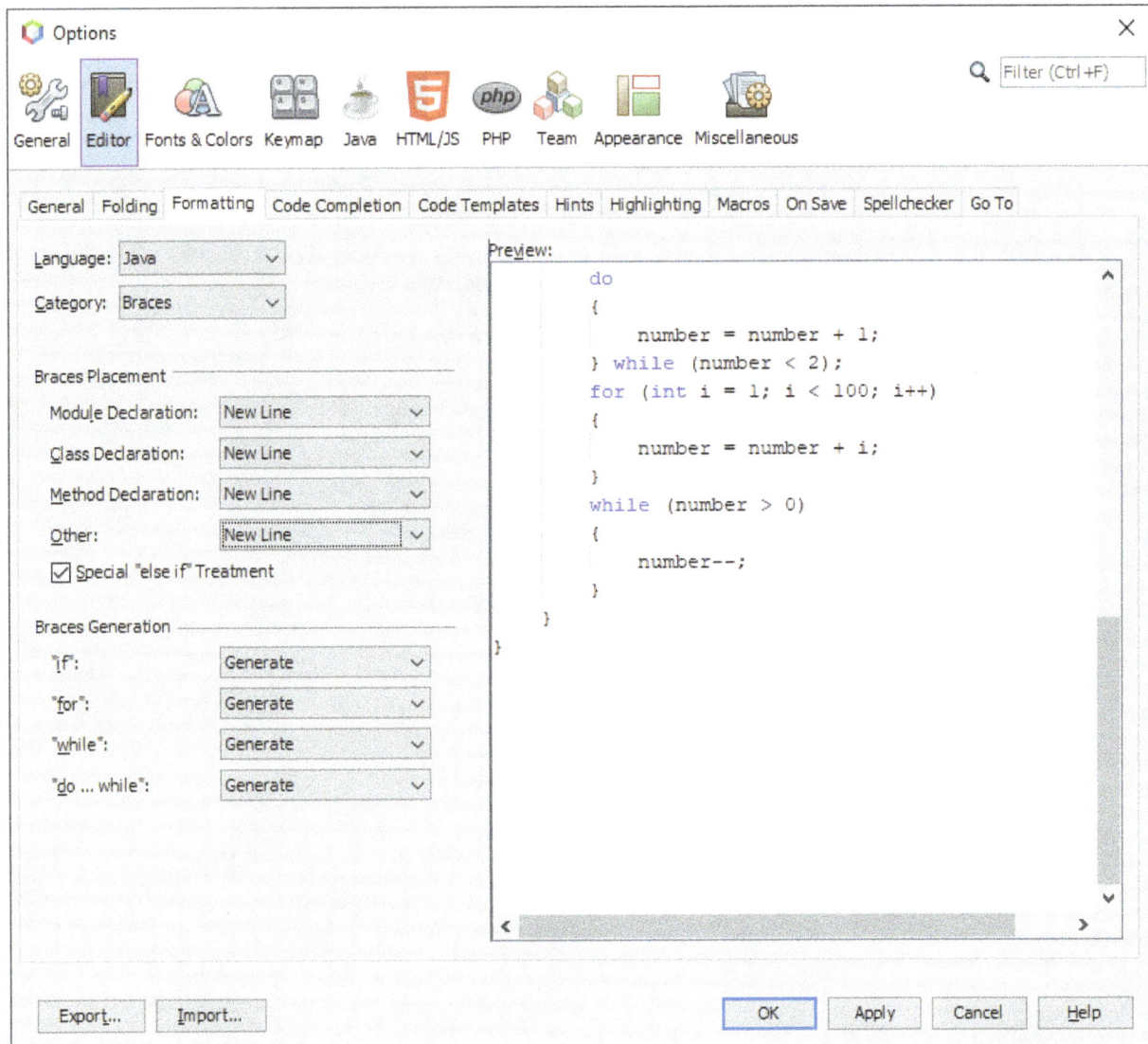

As shown, choose the **Braces Category** and under **Braces Placement**, set all choices to **New Line**. Click **Apply**, then **OK**. Stop **NetBeans** – you're ready to go!

More Self-Study or Instructor-Led Computer Programming Tutorials by Kidware Software

ORACLE JAVA PROGRAMMING TUTORIALS

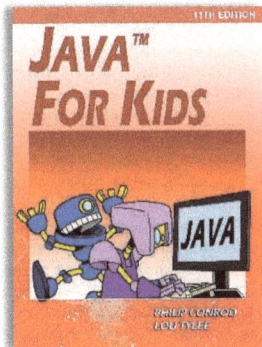

Java™ For Kids is a beginning programming tutorial consisting of 10 chapters explaining (in simple, easy-to-follow terms) how to build a Java application. Students learn about project design, object-oriented programming, console applications, graphics applications and many elements of the Java language. Numerous examples are used to demonstrate every step in the building process. The projects include a number guessing game, a card game, an allowance calculator, a state capitals game, Tic-Tac-Toe, a simple drawing program, and even a basic video game. Designed for kids ages 12 and up.

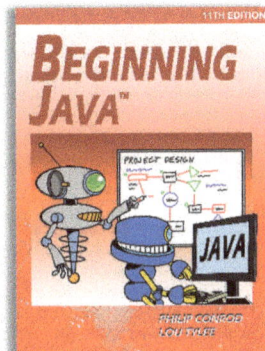

Beginning Java™ is a semester long "beginning" programming tutorial consisting of 10 chapters explaining (in simple, easy-to-follow terms) how to build a Java application. The tutorial includes several detailed computer projects for students to build and try. These projects include a number guessing game, card game, allowance calculator, drawing program, state capitals game, and a couple of video games like Pong. We also include several college prep bonus projects including a loan calculator, portfolio manager, and checkbook balancer. Designed for students age 15 and up.

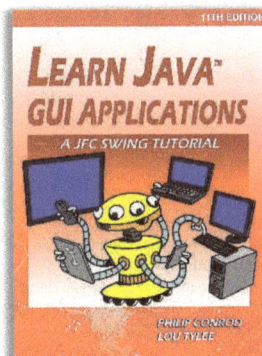

Learn Java™ GUI Applications is a 9 lesson Tutorial covering object-oriented programming concepts, using an integrated development environment to create and test Java projects, building and distributing GUI applications, understanding and using the Swing control library, exception handling, sequential file access, graphics, multimedia, advanced topics such as printing, and help system authoring. Our Beginning Java or Java For Kids tutorial is a pre-requisite for this tutorial

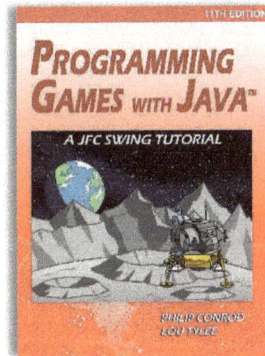

Programming Games with Java™ is a semester long "intermediate" programming tutorial consisting of 10 chapters explaining (in simple, easy-to-follow terms) how to build a Visual C# Video Games. The games built are non-violent, family-friendly and teach logical thinking skills. Students will learn how to program the following Visual C# video games: Safecracker, Tic Tac Toe, Match Game, Pizza Delivery, and Moon Landing. This intermediate level self-paced tutorial can be used at home or school. The tutorial is simple enough for kids yet engaging enough for beginning adults. Our Learn Java GUI Applications tutorial is a required pre-requisite for this tutorial.

Java™ Homework Projects is a Java GUI Swing tutorial covering object-oriented programming concepts. It explains (in simple, easy-to-follow terms) how to build Java GUI project to use around the home. Students learn about project design, the Java Swing controls, many elements of the Java language, and how to distribute finished projects. The projects built include a Dual-Mode Stopwatch, Flash Card Math Quiz, Multiple Choice Exam, Blackjack Card Game, Weight Monitor, Home Inventory Manager and a Snowball Toss Game. Our Learn Java GUI Applications tutorial is a pre-requisite for this tutorial

MICROSOFT SMALL BASIC PROGRAMMING TUTORIALS

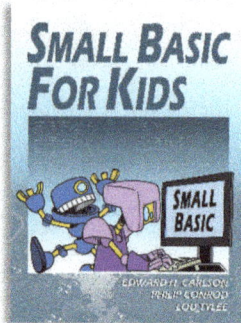

Small Basic For Kids is an illustrated introduction to computer programming that provides an interactive, self-paced tutorial to the new Small Basic programming environment. The book consists of 30 short lessons that explain how to create and run a Small Basic program. Elementary students learn about program design and many elements of the Small Basic language. Numerous examples are used to demonstrate every step in the building process. The tutorial also includes two complete games (Hangman and Pizza Zapper) for students to build and try. Designed for kids ages 8+.

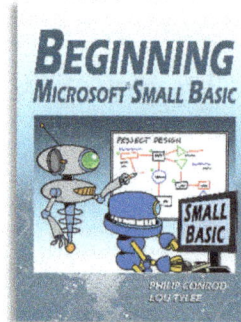

The Beginning Microsoft Small Basic Programming Tutorial is a self-study first semester "beginner" programming tutorial consisting of 11 chapters explaining (in simple, easy-to-follow terms) how to write Microsoft Small Basic programs. Numerous examples are used to demonstrate every step in the building process. The last chapter of this tutorial shows you how four different Small Basic games could port to Visual Basic, Visual C# and Java. This beginning level self-paced tutorial can be used at home or at school. The tutorial is simple enough for kids ages 10+ yet engaging enough for adults.

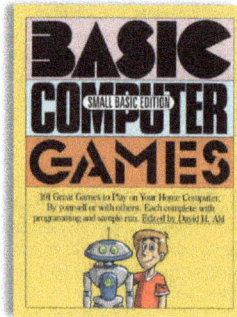

Basic Computer Games - Small Basic Edition is a re-make of the classic BASIC COMPUTER GAMES book originally edited by David H. Ahl. It contains 100 of the original text based BASIC games that inspired a whole generation of programmers. Now these classic BASIC games have been re-written in Microsoft Small Basic for a new generation to enjoy! The new Small Basic games look and act like the original text based games. The book includes all the original spaghetti code and GOTO commands!

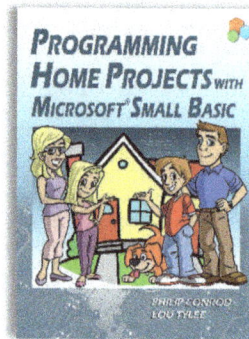

Programming Home Projects with Microsoft Small Basic is a self-paced programming tutorial explains (in simple, easy-to-follow terms) how to build Small Basic Windows applications. Students learn about program design, Small Basic objects, many elements of the Small Basic language, and how to debug and distribute finished programs. Sequential file input and output is also introduced. The projects built include a Dual-Mode Stopwatch, Flash Card Math Quiz, Multiple Choice Exam, Blackjack Card Game, Weight Monitor, Home Inventory Manager and a Snowball Toss Game.

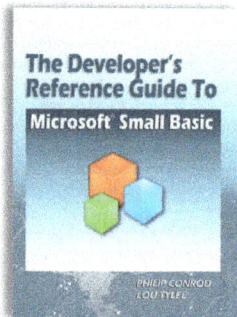

The Developer's Reference Guide to Microsoft Small Basic While developing all the different Microsoft Small Basic tutorials we found it necessary to write The Developer's Reference Guide to Microsoft Small Basic. The Developer's Reference Guide to Microsoft Small Basic is over 500 pages long and includes over 100 Small Basic programming examples for you to learn from and include in your own Microsoft Small Basic programs. It is a detailed reference guide for new developers.

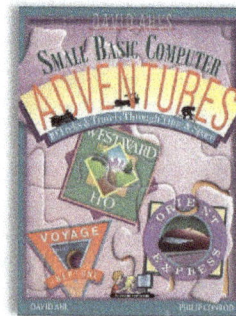

David Ahl's Small Basic Computer Adventures is a Microsoft Small Basic re-make of the classic *Basic Computer Games* programming *book* originally written by David H. Ahl. This new book includes the following classic adventure simulations; Marco Polo, Westward Ho!, The Longest Automobile Race, The Orient Express, Amelia Earhart: Around the World Flight, Tour de France, Subway Scavenger, Hong Kong Hustle, and Voyage to Neptune. Learn how to program these classic computer simulations in Microsoft Small Basic.

MICROSOFT VISUAL BASIC PROGRAMMING TUTORIALS

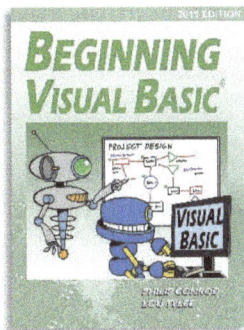

Beginning Visual Basic® is a semester long self-paced "beginner" programming tutorial consisting of 10 chapters explaining (in simple, easy-to-follow terms) how to build a Visual Basic Windows application. The tutorial includes several detailed computer projects for students to build and try. These projects include a number guessing game, card game, allowance calculator, drawing program, state capitals game, and a couple of video games like Pong. We also include several college prep bonus projects including a loan calculator, portfolio manager, and checkbook balancer. Designed for students age 15 and up.

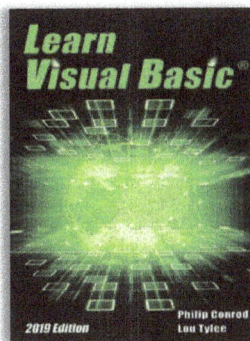

LEARN VISUAL BASIC is a comprehensive college level programming tutorial covering object-oriented programming, the Visual Basic integrated development environment, building and distributing Windows applications using the Windows Installer, exception handling, sequential file access, graphics, multimedia, advanced topics such as web access, printing, and HTML help system authoring. The tutorial also introduces database applications (using ADO .NET) and web applications (using ASP.NET).

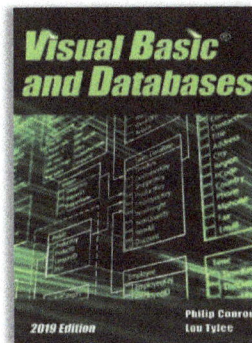

VISUAL BASIC AND DATABASES is a tutorial that provides a detailed introduction to using Visual Basic for accessing and maintaining databases for desktop applications. Topics covered include: database structure, database design, Visual Basic project building, ADO .NET data objects (connection, data adapter, command, data table), data bound controls, proper interface design, structured query language (SQL), creating databases using Access, SQL Server and ADOX, and database reports. Actual projects developed include a book tracking system, a sales invoicing program, a home inventory system and a daily weather monitor.

MICROSOFT VISUAL C# PROGRAMMING TUTORIALS

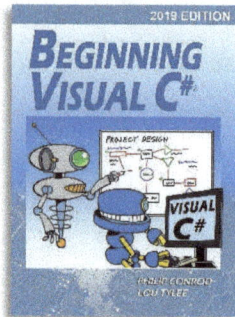

Beginning Visual C#® is a semester long "beginning" programming tutorial consisting of 10 chapters explaining (in simple, easy-to-follow terms) how to build a C# Windows application. The tutorial includes several detailed computer projects for students to build and try. These projects include a number guessing game, card game, allowance calculator, drawing program, state capitals game, and a couple of video games like Pong. We also include several college prep bonus projects including a loan calculator, portfolio manager, and checkbook balancer. Designed for students ages 15+.

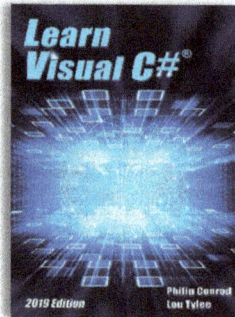

LEARN VISUAL C# is a comprehensive college level computer programming tutorial covering object-oriented programming, the Visual C# integrated development environment and toolbox, building and distributing Windows applications (using the Windows Installer), exception handling, sequential file input and output, graphics, multimedia effects (animation and sounds), advanced topics such as web access, printing, and HTML help system authoring. The tutorial also introduces database applications (using ADO .NET) and web applications (using ASP.NET).

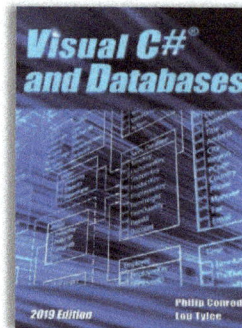

VISUAL C# AND DATABASES is a tutorial that provides a detailed introduction to using Visual C# for accessing and maintaining databases for desktop applications. Topics covered include: database structure, database design, Visual C# project building, ADO .NET data objects (connection, data adapter, command, data table), data bound controls, proper interface design, structured query language (SQL), creating databases using Access, SQL Server and ADOX, and database reports. Actual projects developed include a book tracking system, a sales invoicing program, a home inventory system and a daily weather monitor.